D0085720

Philosophies for Living

Philosophies for Living

Robert M. Timko

Mansfield University

Joan Whitman Hoff

Lock Haven University

Upper Saddle River, New Jersey 07458

Library of Congress Cataloging-in-Publication Data

Timko, Robert M.
Philosophies for living / Robert M. Timko, Joan Whitman Hoff
p. cm.
Includes bibliographical references.
ISBN 0-13-088316-6
1. Self (Philosophy) I. Hoff, Joan Whitman. II. Title.

BD438.5.T56 2001
126—dc21 00-050191

VP/Editorial Director: Charlyce Jones-Owen
Acquisitions Editor: Ross Miller
Assistant Editor: Katie Janssen
Editorial Assistant: Carla Worner
AVP, Director of Production and Manufacturing: Barbara Kittle
Senior Managing Editor: Jan Stephan
Production Liaison: Fran Russello
Project Manager: Linda B. Pawelchak
Manufacturing Manager: Nick Sklitsis
Prepress and Manufacturing Buyer: Sherry Lewis
Cover Design: Bruce Kenselaar
Cover Art: R. Mervilus, Haitian, "Village by a Stream," Private Collection/ Van Hoorick Fine Art/Super/Stock
Director, Image Resource Center: Melinda Lee Reo
Interior Image Specialist: Beth Boyd
Manager, Rights and Permissions: Kay Dellosa
Manager, Art Formatting: Guy Ruggiero
Marketing Manager: Don Allman

This book was set in 10/12 Palatino by Rosemary Ross
and was printed and bound by RR Donnelley & Sons Company.
The cover was printed by Phoenix Color Corp.

© 2001 by Prentice-Hall, Inc.
A Division of Pearson Education
Upper Saddle River, New Jersey 07458

All rights reserved. No part of this book may be reproduced,
in any form or by any means, without permission in writing from the publisher.

Printed in the United States of America
10 9 8 7 6 5 4 3 2 1

ISBN 0-13-088316-6

Prentice-Hall International (UK) Limited, *London*
Prentice-Hall of Australia Pty. Limited, *Sydney*
Prentice-Hall Canada Inc., *Toronto*
Prentice-Hall Hispanoamericana, S.A., *Mexico*
Prentice-Hall of India Private Limited, *New Delhi*
Prentice-Hall of Japan, Inc., *Tokyo*
Pearson Education Asia Pte. Ltd., *Singapore*
Editora Prentice-Hall do Brasil, Ltda., *Rio de Janeiro*

To

Sophia

with

passionate commitment and endless love

and

to

our spouses,

Lynne and Steve,

for theirs

Contents

Alternate Contents

This alternate table of contents is provided so that students and teachers may read and discuss articles according to some traditional subject areas in philosophy. The selected articles for each subject area merely indicate the suggestions of this text's authors. We realize that many of the articles can be used to raise issues across several topics. Readers and teachers should feel free to go beyond our suggestions. Articles in brackets indicate additional/alternative suggestions.

Metaphysics

Epistemology

Ethics

Philosophy of Religion

Social Philosophy

Political Philosophy

Philosophy of Economics

Philosophy of Education

Philosophy and Literature

Existentialism

Non-Western Philosophy

Feminist Philosophy

Preface

As teachers of philosophy, we firmly believe that the purpose of any text is to facilitate the natural curiosity of the student. An introductory philosophy text should help students move from where they are to a clearer, more informed perspective on themselves and their world. To do this, it must not impose a finished and sophisticated philosophy, that is, the scholar's worldview, on the student. Rather, it should begin with the questions that the students may have.

Today, it is not unusual for many students to see an education as a way out, and not as an affordable leisure. Their questions are practical, or at least they see them as such. As philosophy teachers, we believe we should help students see their questions as no less important than our own. We need to help students look more deeply into themselves, their beliefs, and their worldviews. Since many students choose colleges and universities close to home, it becomes more the case that they have not been nor will they be naturally exposed to different cultures, different beliefs, different worldviews. We need to help them discover the differences in the world around them as well as reexamine the identities they perceive.

This book is also about voices, and in particular about the voices of those whom we call students and teachers. It is about distinguishing these voices and the questions to which they give rise and the opinions and beliefs that they articulate. It is about discovering from where these voices may come. More important, we need to understand that these voices not only reside in traditions with which we may be unfamiliar, they will at times sound dissonant. As teachers of philosophy, it may become necessary for us to accept that not all philosophical questions nor all articulations of philosophic belief come from what we recognize as the Western philosophical tradition or from those we recognize as philosophers. We need to realize that such voices may be heard as narratives, as poetry, as well as discursive arguments.

As a reader in introductory philosophy, *Philosophies for Living* focuses on the self, its discovery, its limitations, its possibilities, and its contexts or worlds. The readings that we include in this text have been used by us, our students, and some of our colleagues since 1993. They have told us what they thought worked, and what didn't, and why. Also, the editorial intent of this anthology is both *interdisciplinary* and *intercultural*. As a matter of pedagogy, we genuinely believe it desirable to create a dialogue about the self across academic disciplines as well as between cultures. We believe it is important to balance the attempts of traditional philosophies to cast knowledge of the self in terms apart from ordinary experience with explanations of what it means to be a self in the world, its societies, and its cultures. We further believe it may be important to understand that the world, the societies, and cultures of which we speak are dynamic, constantly changing entities. Cultures do not merely stand alongside one another; now, more than ever, they interact, and each culture lends a part of its identity to the other.

This text has nine chapters. Each chapter begins with an introduction that explores the questions and themes of the proposed readings for that chapter. Each article has its own introduction, directing readers to ask specific questions and look for specific issues as they read. Each chapter concludes with a set of discussion questions that can be used for in-class activities or short essay assignments. The first and last chapters are about living philosophically. We begin by asking our students and readers to reflect on what characteristics and activities may be typical of a philosophical life. We conclude by pointing to further actions and attitudes that may strengthen or deepen philosophical resolve.

Between the reflections on the nature of a philosophical life and philosophical activities, we ask students to reflect on how they understand who they are—what makes them the persons they believe themselves to be. The second chapter exposes readers to what philosophers have said about persons and personal identity. Chapter 3 asks students to reflect on how social interactions and modern social practices may influence how their personal identities are constructed. In Chapter 4, we explore the ways in which our perceptions of race and ethnicity affect our sense of self, and in Chapter 5 we explore the ways in which our perceptions of economic class structures and social hierarchies may affect self-affirmation and self-definition.

Many of us, teachers and students alike, are reluctant to discuss matters of human sexuality. But our sense of our sexuality and the accompanying perceptions of gender differences do have some relation to who we are. Therefore, in Chapter 6 we examine the ways in which questions about sexuality, sexual relations, and gender difference may modify our understanding of who we are. As we note later, many students today are married or have been married, and many are parents. In what ways might our perceptions of what it means to be married or to be a parent help define who we are? In Chapter 7, we explore both classical and contemporary concepts of marriage and parenthood.

Finally, we address the question of the ways in which religious experiences or a personal faith may contribute to our sense of who we are. Through many experiences as classroom teachers, we have found that students often identify their religious beliefs with their personal identities, so in Chapter 8 our inquiries are not so much about the existence of God or God's attributes as they are about faith and personal meaning. In this chapter, we also include articles that raise questions of cultural difference.

Readers will discover that in each chapter we have tried to balance the old with the new, the familiar with the unfamiliar, and the traditional canon of academic philosophy with wisdom and argument from disciplines and traditions outside academic philosophy. In doing this, we have tried to remember that our primary audience is students who are making an initial journey into philosophical thinking. Therefore, we believe it is important to keep in mind questions that are created in wonder, if not confusion, especially questions about the *self* and *self-identity.*

A Special Word to Beginning Students of Philosophy

If you are a student, it may be that you are very much preoccupied with who you are and who you may be becoming. Some, if not many, of your are working at part-time jobs, and a significant number of you are parents; some of you may be single parents. As such, you may be struggling with your identity as male or female; as black, white, or red; as parents; as workers; or with your sexuality and/or with your religious faith. In the latter case, you may find that your questions are more frequently not about whether God exists or what attributes God may have, but rather about whether a religious belief can bring any meaning or purpose to your life.

In order to help you, as students, answer these questions, we ask you only to "listen" carefully to what each of our authors has to say. A story has persisted for many generations in the halls of academic philosophy. It is a story of a bright, young student who attends a prestigious university and who has recently attended the lecture of a world famous professor. After the lecture, it is told, the young student approaches the professor and asks him to tell him "everything he needs to know." (Why must each be a he?) The professor commands the young student to sit and listen. Thirty minutes pass, an hour passes, and the professor says nothing. The student says: "Professor, I have been sitting here for an hour, and you have said nothing." "Have you been listening?" the professor responds. "Yes," says the eager student. The professor looks at him carefully and says, "Good, you have learned everything you need to know." We must listen, but to whom? Socrates, whose life gives us the paradigm for philosophical conversation, did not just question those who called themselves philosophers. Nor is there reason to suppose he spoke only with males. He spoke with and listened to all, to poets, to soldiers, to statesmen, to artisans, and to women. As individuals who wish to live philosophically, we will and should listen to many voices. Here is what we must risk believing: Truth cannot be found in a single vision, nor can it be uttered by a single voice. Rather, it may be found in the symphony or even in the cacophony of many voices.

In this book, you will, we hope, listen to many voices. You will hear the voice of the African American, the Native American, the African, the Latin American, and the woman alongside the voice of the Western European male philosopher. You will hear the voice of the homosexual alongside that of the heterosexual; you will hear the voice of the non-Christian, even that of the nonbeliever, alongside that of the Christian; the voice of the believer in the Goddess alongside that of the believer in God; the voice of the poet alongside that of the philosopher; the voice of the postmodernist alongside that of the traditionalist. You will hear voices that defend democracy and monogamous marriage, and those that challenge these institutions. The challenge is to not only hear, but to listen to each of these voices.

Because you will listen to many voices, many of which challenge one another if not your traditional way(s) of thinking and believing, you will engage in what we like to call "risky business." The risks are many, and they come rather quickly and from some rather fundamental activities. The risks come from questioning, from examining what you believe, and from attempting to redefine who you are. These activities will come naturally as you read the various authors in this anthology, because as you read, you should be questioning what they say, examining how what they say reinforces or challenges your beliefs, and applying these different perspectives to your understanding of who you are.

By engaging in these risks, it may be that you will discover that a meaningful and valuable life is not one that can be defined by a series of objective tests, but rather one that can emerge from a continuum of subjective investigations. Philosophy can help in such investigations; its method of critical thinking is a powerful ally when attempting to live one's life with meaning and with integrity, that is, *authentically.* When one pursues an investigation of the authenticity of one's beliefs and one's own authenticity, it cannot be without risk.

The first risk, and perhaps the most necessary one, will come in questioning popular beliefs and what you may have accepted uncritically as true and valuable. Among these beliefs are ones about human nature, the natural world, race and gender, the good life, the good society, culture and morality, relationships with others, and religion. You will be asked to question and examine how what you have learned may be the product of social, political, and economic environments. You may discover that there is a possibility, even a strong possibility, that some of the things you have learned may not be true, and that some things that many may have set aside as inconsistent with an affirmed popular belief may in fact be of more value for your life than you could have imagined.

When examining popular beliefs, especially those that have in some way shaped your life and identity, you will need to have the proper motive, and that itself involves the risk of unpopularity. One takes no risk when challenging a belief simply for the sake of "political correctness" or of being on the currently popular bandwagon. Philosophy genuinely may teach anyone that truth is such that it does not shift with the current political winds, only the appearance of truth shifts. Living philosophically may mean always being challenged to risk the unpopular question. Societies resist those who ask such questions, even though these societies may be disturbed by an awareness that they are adrift in a lack of meaning and value. One philosopher put it this way:

> In such a disturbed society disciplined thought has its enemies. For being tuned as most are to cliches, unsubstantiated gossip, political niceties, cocktail cackle, and unreasoned slogans, many of our most serious problems continue for the sake of self gain, expediency and social conformity, to be enshrined in an atmosphere bedraggled by apathy. It frequently becomes the task of the serious philosopher not only to explore such apathy but to scrutinize the wounds in the value structures that allowed it in the first place. And this is where he or she can expect to court unpopularity.[1]

To embark on the journey of doing philosophy in a contemporary society that is overrun with personal interest, increasing xenophobia, trivialized value, and a demand for immediate practical return on one's academic investments is not an easy task and is at best an unpopular task. We live today in an undisciplined society, a society in which academic resolve, philosophical living, and a sense of universal community are viewed with suspicion. This suspicion is so pervasive that one is led into closeting opinions, suppressing beliefs, and eventually into self-estrangement. In such a society, we need to find the alternate path that Socrates took. Later in this work, when you read the *Apology,* Socrates' defense of his life, you may discover that the risk of questioning and examining one's life is a necessary component of both moral character and "the good life."

Because what we are asking you to do does expose you to many risks, we offer one special word of caution and advice. Listening to other and newer voices does not mean one stops listening to older and more familiar ones. The risk in listening is not to jump to the conclusion that truth and morality are relative. While it may be reasonably argued that some of what has passed for truth and morality may be nothing more than the political constructs of a power elite, it does not logically imply that all that has been put forward as truth and morality has been constructed this way, nor does it entail relativism. Truth and morality can never be understood merely as the case of equal but differing opinions. Though it may be difficult to discover what is true and

[1]Leslie M. S. Griffiths, "Preface," *Philosophy as Effective Thinking,* 3rd, ed. Lexington, Mass.: Ginn Press, 1985, p. ix.

morally valuable, and though it is certainly unsettling to discover that what one has assumed to be true and morally valuable is not so, this should not lead us to despair of truth and moral value. In challenging tradition, we take risks, but one risk that must be met squarely by those wishing the philosophical life is not to "throw out the baby with the bath water." Consequences result from challenging traditions, but as T. H. Huxley tells us: "Consequences are the scarecrows of fools and the beacons of wise men."[2] Men or women, we must risk letting the consequences of challenging and questioning, of listening to other than familiar and comfortable voices, take care of themselves.

A Special Word to Philosophy Teachers

As authors and editors of this anthology, but most especially as philosophy teachers, we have decided both to take a number of risks ourselves and to challenge you to accept some of these same risks as well as the ones ordinarily found in philosophical living. We have included a number of thinkers not found in the so-called "canon" of traditional philosophy, for we wish to risk a challenge to an authority that may be racially, culturally, and gender biased. We wish to risk asserting that philosophy is not to be defined merely as an academic discipline, but must be grasped in a larger context of living one's life authentically.

Philosophy or philosophizing should not restrict itself to any limited body of thought, old or new. To philosophize, after all, is to pursue with unbridled passion the insight of every question in order to pull back the covers of apathy and falsehood. This is a risky undertaking, but if we wish to affirm value in ourselves and in our society, it is not a risk without reward. Understand that in being called to philosophical living, one must be prepared to be the outsider, the stranger, the one alone. One must leave the anonymity of the crowd, the role of the stereotype, and rediscover himself, or herself—this is what Socrates called the examined life. It may very well be, as he argued in his own defense, the only life worth living.

This book is organized around the theme of what constitutes a *self.* Throughout this work, we will be referring to the concept of a *self* rather than to the philosophical concepts of *person* or *personal identity.* Therefore, it may be important for philosophy teachers to understand how we use that concept. First, we use this concept because we understand *self* to be a more narrowly defined concept than that of a *person.* Specifically, we find the concept of a *self* to be much more distinctive than that of a *person.* To have a sense of *self* is to be aware of being a distinctive or unique individual. Second, as we understand a *self,* it has several essential characteristics. The *self* has a particular body with which it places itself in relation to other objects and selves in the physical

[2]T. H. Huxley, *Method and Results.* New York: D. Appleton and Company, 1896, p. 244.

world. We also make an assumption that a *self* cannot arise in isolation from a community. In addition to its "communality," a *self* will be conscious of being a distinct person with a distinct history and perhaps a distinct plan for the future, that is, a life-plan. A *self* may possess a particular sense of achievement as an individual, differing itself from other selves, but it will always understand this difference within the context of other selves. Finally, a *self* will have beliefs and values, perhaps derived from other selves, a culture or a religion, but some aspects and expressions of those beliefs and values will be distinctive to that *self.*

The editing and publishing of this book is a risk, and no less a risk than reading it and listening to its voices. For participating in this risk, we wish to thank our editors at Prentice Hall, including Ross Miller, Katie Janssen, Linda Pawelchak, and Lisa Black, who worked untiringly and patiently to bring things together; the following reviewer: Daniel Kealey, Towson University; and our colleagues at Mansfield and Lock Haven, who though sometimes wondering why we were stirring the traditional waters of philosophy, encouraged us to continue. Most importantly, we wish to thank our students, whose questions continually challenge us and always remind us that we, too, are students who need to risk remaining gadflies.

Robert M. Timko
Joan Whitman Hoff

Philosophies for Living

chapter 1

Taking Risks/ Living Philosophically

Thinking philosophically is natural. It is a process that we engage in as children, although it does not seem to be something that is encouraged in us. Perhaps this is because when we think philosophically and share our ideas with others, they, too, are forced to confront their own ideas and belief systems. This may be something that we choose not to do because it entails taking a risk, and sometimes risk taking can be painful. It means that we must examine and reexamine who we are and why we live the way we do. Taking risks, however, can also be exciting. Reflecting on our identity can give us a better sense of who we are and whom we want to become.

In this chapter, several essays convey the importance of such risk taking and reflections. In the first reading, Albert Camus demonstrates the tragedy and despair in personal growth as he explores the meaning of life. In his struggle to understand why the gods have handed him his painful fate, Sisyphus learns that he alone is the master of his destiny. He finds meaning in every attempt to define and redefine his repetitive task. In this revelation he also finds that his attitude plays a major role in this discovery.

Nowhere are both the risk and value of personal growth more clearly told than in Plato's "Allegory of the Cave." The individual who breaks the bonds of commonality and the restrictions of contemporary fads and ideologies slowly realizes that there is more to life than everyday images and popular pursuits. But Plato tells us something more: the clearer one's vision becomes, the more

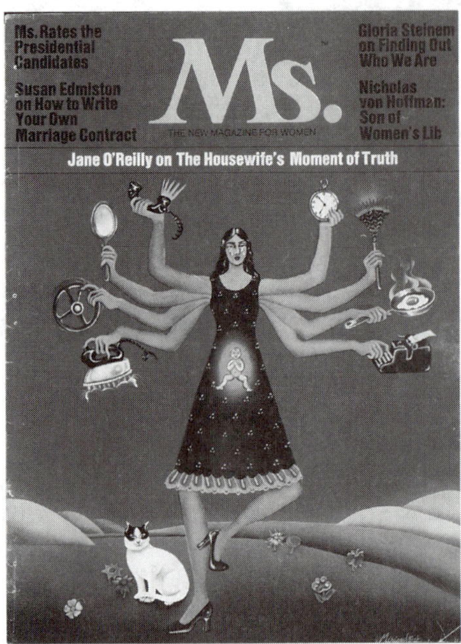

First *Ms.* magazine cover, 1972

one has an obligation to help enhance the opportunity for other individuals to grow in a similar way. The tradition, security, and satisfaction of conformity are not easy to give up. Plato painfully reminds us that the visionary and the reformer will be scorned and viewed with suspicion. Despite this, the individual must persist in overcoming and helping others overcome the entrapments of popular beliefs. True justice, after all, may not be found in the whim of popular opinion.

But can anyone be sure of his or her vision, or certain that he or she is on the right path to self-actualization? Richard Wright describes in vivid detail the quest of a young black man to gain knowledge and to be able to look at the world differently. We should pay close attention to the language Wright uses, for it tells us of an insatiable hunger, a hunger so strong that it makes one see the world differently. As Wright discovers, however, there are dangers inherent in the pursuit of a wider existence because each attempt to satisfy a hunger for knowledge brings with it new and disturbing questions about the nature of one's identity.

How we establish meaning in our lives and how we live a "completely human life" are issues addressed by Søren Kierkegaard. He suggests that a *self* needs to find a purpose that makes life worth living. He realizes that he must first discover and understand himself before he can determine what he should do, what choices he should make. What does it mean to discover and understand oneself? It may mean having intense personal commitment to who one is; it may mean that one engages deeply in the process of self-realization; it should mean having the courage of one's own convictions and resisting temptations to hide oneself in anonymity. Inner action should precede outer action if one is to be true to oneself.

In our journey of self-discovery, perhaps it is necessary to find how each self is part of the other and continuous with All that is. If this is true, what sense can be made of discriminations based on race, gender, ethnicity, class, or religious belief? You may wish to keep this question in front of you as you journey further and more deeply into the readings contained in this anthology.

We have seen that Plato, Wright, and Kierkegaard value the variety of means by which we become educated and explain how and why education can help people to achieve a better understanding of themselves. Further, through an exploration of oneself, one can better explore social relationships and social responsibilities; but can there be still another dimension to such an education? For an answer, we look to John Stuart Mill.

Traditionally, one would find Mill's analyses of liberty or utilitarian ethics included in philosophical anthologies. Here, however, we ask you to read something different: Mill's reflections on his own philosophical and personal development. More specifically, we encounter his thoughts on a particular crisis in his life. At the age of twenty, Mill questioned the education his father had provided him. What he discovered was a lack of balance in his life; he found himself purely rational and intellectually disciplined but lacking emotional fulfillment. As Mill would ask: To live, should we not have something to live for? What can we learn from Mill's response to his own education? Could it be that a true education into a philosophic life includes developing one's emotions as well as one's intellect?

Discovering who we are, however, may require us to unlearn what we have been taught by society. In Gloria Steinem's essay, we find the need to understand how knowledge and power have been used to oppress women, and how such oppression has made the struggle to discover our true identity as individuals even more difficult. In order for women, and men, to discover themselves as individuals, they must first unlearn the things that have been taught to them by society. They must engage in the reflective self-examination that we find to be so crucial to growth and understanding in the writings of Camus, Plato, and Wright.

Finally, we ask, what may be the value of thinking or living philosophically, and how does one go about bringing this value into his/her life? These are questions that Bertrand Russell attempts to answer. "Philosophy," he claims, "aims primarily at knowledge," and this knowledge comes from critically questioning "our convictions, prejudices, and beliefs." What we gain in trying to acquire such knowledge is more than a modicum of uncertainty and potential, if not actual, freedom from dogmatism. Ultimately, what we may gain, he hypothesizes, is a union of *Self* and *not-Self,* a separation of self from common desires and biases.

After reading Russell, you might want to think about how his reflections summarize the thoughts embodied in the other readings in this chapter—how living philosophically frees us to become "citizens of the universe," enlarging and deepening our sense of *self* in the process.

The Myth of Sisyphus

Albert Camus

As an existentialist, Camus believes that we alone give our lives meaning, we alone are masters of our universe. Through the struggle of Sisyphus, who supposedly is damned to his fate by the gods, we explore Camus's existentialist view that we are free to choose our own fate. What impact does our attitude have on our lives? Who can we blame for our fate? Can we blame anyone but ourselves?

The gods had condemned Sisyphus to ceaselessly rolling a rock to the top of a mountain, whence the stone would fall back of its own weight. They had thought with some reason that there is no more dreadful punishment than futile and hopeless labor.

If one believes Homer, Sisyphus was the wisest and most prudent of mortals. According to another tradition, however, he was disposed to practice the profession of highwayman. I see no contradiction in this. Opinions differ as to the reasons why he became the futile laborer of the underworld. To begin with, he is accused of a certain levity in regard to the gods. He stole their secrets. Aegina, the daughter of Aesopus, was carried off by Jupiter. The father was shocked by that disappearance and complained to Sisyphus. He, who knew of the abduction, offered to tell about it on condition that Aesopus would give water to the citadel of Corinth. To the celestial thunderbolts he preferred the benediction of water. He was punished for this in the underworld. Homer tells us also that Sisyphus had put Death in chains. Pluto could not endure the sight of his deserted, silent empire. He dispatched the god of War, who liberated Death from the hands of her conqueror.

It is said also that Sisyphus, being near to death, rashly wanted to test his wife's love. He ordered her to cast his unburied body into the middle of the public square. Sisyphus woke up in the underworld. And there, annoyed by an obedience so contrary to human love, he obtained from Pluto permission to return to earth in order to chastise his wife. But when he had seen again the face of this world, enjoyed water and sun, warm stones and the sea, he no longer wanted to go back to the infernal darkness. Recalls, signs of anger, warnings were of no avail. Many years more he lived facing the curve of the gulf, the sparkling sea, and the smiles of earth. A decree of the gods was necessary. Mercury came and seized the impudent man by the collar and, snatching him from his joys, led him forcibly back to the underworld, where his rock was ready for him.

You have already grasped that Sisyphus is the absurd hero. He *is*, as much through his passions as through his torture. His scorn of the gods, his hatred of death, and his passion for life won him that unspeakable penalty in which the whole being is exerted toward accomplishing nothing. This is the price that must be paid for the passions of this earth. Nothing is told us about Sisyphus in the underworld. Myths are made for the imagination to breathe life into them. As for this myth, one sees merely the whole effort of a body straining to raise the huge stone, to roll it and push it up a slope a hundred times over; one sees the face screwed up, the cheek tight against the stone, the shoulder bracing the clay covered mass, the foot wedging it, the fresh start with arms outstretched, the wholly human security of two earth-clotted hands. At the very end of this long effort measured by skyless space and time without depth, the purpose is achieved. Then Sisyphus watches the stone rush down in a few moments toward that lower world whence he will have to push it up again toward the summit. He goes back down to the plain.

It is during that return, that pause, that Sisyphus interests me. A face that toils so close to stones is already stone itself! I see that man going back down with a heavy yet measured step toward the torment of which he will never know the end. That hour like a breathing-space which returns as surely as his suffering, that is the hour of consciousness. At each of those moments when he leaves the heights and gradually sinks

---

From *The Myth of Sisyphus and Other Essays* by Albert Camus, trans., J. O'Brien. Copyright © 1955 by Alfred A. Knopf, Inc. Reprinted by permission of the publisher.

toward the lairs of the gods, he is superior to his fate. He is stronger than his rock.

If this myth is tragic, that is because its hero is conscious. Where would his torture be, indeed, if at every step the hope of succeeding upheld him? The workman of today works every day in his life at the same tasks, and this fate is no less absurd. But it is tragic only at the rare moments when it becomes conscious. Sisyphus, proletarian of the gods, powerless and rebellious, knows the whole extent of his wretched condition: it is what he thinks of during his descent. The lucidity that was to constitute his torture at the same time crowns his victory. There is no fate that cannot be surmounted by scorn.

If the descent is thus sometimes performed in sorrow, it can also take place in joy. This word is not too much. Again I fancy Sisyphus returning toward his rock, and the sorrow was in the beginning. When the images of earth cling too tightly to memory, when the call of happiness becomes too insistent, it happens that melancholy rises in man's heart: this is the rock's victory, this is the rock itself. The boundless grief is too heavy to bear. These are our nights of Gethsemane. But crushing truths perish from being acknowledged. Thus, Oedipus at the outset obeys fate without knowing it. But from the moment he knows, his tragedy begins. Yet at the same moment, blind and desperate, he realizes that the only bond linking him to the world is the cool hand of a girl. Then a tremendous remark rings out: "Despite so many ordeals, my advanced age and the nobility of my soul make me conclude that all is well." Sophocles' Oedipus, like Dostoevsky's Kirilov, thus gives the recipe for the absurd victory. Ancient wisdom confirms modern heroism.

One does not discover the absurd without being tempted to write a manual of happiness. "What! by such narrow ways—?" There is but one world, however. Happiness and the absurd are two sons of the same earth. They are inseparable. It would be a mistake to say that happiness necessarily springs from the absurd discovery. It happens as well that the feeling of the absurd springs from happiness. "I conclude that all is well," says Oedipus, and that remark is sacred. It echoes in the wild and limited universe of man. It teaches that all is not, has not been, exhausted. It drives out of this world a god who had come into it with dissatisfaction and a preference for futile sufferings. It makes of fate a human matter, which must be settled among men.

All Sisyphus' silent joy is contained therein. His fate belongs to him. His rock is his thing. Likewise, the absurd man, when he contemplates his torment, silences all the idols. In the universe suddenly restored to its silence, the myriad wondering little voices of the earth rise up. Unconscious, secret calls, invitations from all the faces, they are the necessary reverse and price of victory. There is no sun without shadow, and it is essential to know the night. The absurd man says yes and his effort will henceforth be unceasing. If there is a personal fate, there is no higher destiny, or at least there is but one which he concludes is inevitable and despicable. For the rest, he knows himself to be the master of his days. At that subtle moment when man glances backward over his life, Sisyphus returning toward his rock, in that slight pivoting he contemplates that series of unrelated actions which becomes his fate, created by him, combined under his memory's eye and soon sealed by his death. Thus, convinced of the wholly human origin of all that is human, a blind man eager to see who knows that the night has no end, he is still on the go. The rock is still rolling.

I leave Sisyphus at the foot of the mountain! One always finds one's burden again. But Sisyphus teaches the higher fidelity that negates the gods and raises rocks. He too concludes that all is well. This universe henceforth without a master seems to him neither sterile nor futile. Each atom of that stone, each mineral flake of that night-filled mountain in itself forms a world. The struggle itself toward the heights is enough to fill a man's heart. One must imagine Sisyphus happy.

The Allegory of the Cave

Plato

Perhaps the goal we should be pursuing is individual growth in knowledge, understanding, and wisdom. Plato suggests that we must first free ourselves from the prison of common sense, prejudice, and popular opinions if we wish to achieve this goal. Further, he suggests that it is necessary to move beyond simple conviction in our beliefs. These things are necessary if we are to self-actualize and lead the good life because the good life can be found only when we have achieved knowledge, understanding, and wisdom in our lives. Do you agree or disagree with Plato?

And now, I said, let me show in a figure how far our nature is enlightened or unenlightened: Behold! human beings living in an underground den, which has a mouth open towards the light and reaching all along the den; here they have been from their childhood, and have their legs and necks chained so that they cannot move, and can only see before them, being prevented by the chains from turning round their heads. Above and behind them a fire is blazing at a distance, and between the fire and the prisoners there is a raised way: and you will see, if you look, a low wall built along the way, like the screen which marionette players have in front of them, over which they show the puppets.

I see.

And do you see, I said, men passing along the wall carrying all sorts of vessels, and statues and figures of animals made of wood and stone and various materials, which appear over the wall? Some of them are talking, others silent.

You have shown me a strange image, and they are strange prisoners.

Like ourselves, I replied; and they see only their own shadows, or the shadows of one another, which the fire throws on the opposite wall of the cave?

True, he said; how could they see anything but the shadows if they were never allowed to move their heads?

And of the objects which are being carried in like manner they would only see the shadows?

Yes, he said.

And if they were able to converse with one another, would they not suppose that they were naming what was actually before them?

Very true.

And suppose further that the prison had an echo which came from the other side,

From *The Republic* by Plato (427?–347 B.C.).

would they not be sure to fancy when one of the passers-by spoke that the voice which they heard came from the passing shadow?

No question, he replied.

To them, I said, the truth would be literally nothing but the shadows of the images.

That is certain.

And now look again, and see what will naturally follow if the prisoners are released and disabused of their error. At first, when any of them is liberated and compelled suddenly to stand up and turn his neck round and walk and look towards the light, he will suffer sharp pains; the glare will distress him and he will be unable to see the realities of which in his former state he had seen the shadows; and then conceive some one saying to him, that what he saw before was an illusion, but that now, when he is approaching nearer to being and his eye is turned towards more real existence, he has a clearer vision—what will be his reply? And you may further imagine that his instructor is pointing to the objects as they pass and requiring him to name them—will he not be perplexed? Will he not fancy that the shadows which he formerly saw are truer than the objects which are now shown to him?

Far truer.

And if he is compelled to look straight at the light, will he not have a pain in his eyes which will make him turn away to take refuge in the objects of vision which he can see, and which he will conceive to be in reality clearer than the things which are now being shown to him?

True, he said.

And suppose once more, that he is reluctantly dragged up a steep and rugged ascent, and held fast until he is forced into the presence of the sun himself, is he not likely to be pained and irritated? When he approaches the light his eyes will be dazzled and he will not be able to see anything at all of what are now called realities.

Not all in a moment, he said.

He will require to grow accustomed to the sight of the upper world. And first he will see the shadows best, next the reflections of men and other objects in the water, and then the objects themselves; then he will gaze upon the light of the moon and the stars and the spangled heaven; and he will see the sky and the stars by night better than the sun or the light of the sun by day?

Certainly.

Last of all he will be able to see the sun, and not mere reflections of him in the water, but he will see him in his own proper place, and not in another; and he will contemplate him as he is.

Certainly.

He will then proceed to argue that this is he who gives the season and the years, and is the guardian of all that is in the visible world, and in a certain way the cause of all things which he and his fellows have been accustomed to behold?

Clearly, he said, he would first see the sun and then reason about him.

And when he remembered his old habitation, and the wisdom of the den and his fellow-prisoners, do you not suppose that he would felicitate himself on the change, and pity them?

Certainly, he would.

And if they were in the habit of conferring honors among themselves on those who were quickest to observe the passing shadows and to remark which of them went before, and which followed after, and which were together; and who were therefore best able to draw conclusions as to the future, do you think that he would care for such honors and glories, or envy the possessors of them? Would he not say with Homer,

> Better to be the poor servant of a poor master.

and to endure anything, rather than think as they do and live after their manner?

Yes, he said, I think he would rather suffer anything than entertain these false notions and live in this miserable manner.

Imagine once more, I said, such as one coming suddenly out of the sun to be replaced in his old situation; would he not be certain to have his eyes full of darkness?

To be sure, he said.

And if there were a contest, and he had to compete in measuring the shadows with the prisoners who had never moved out of the den, while his sight was still weak, and before his eyes had become steady (and the time which would be needed to acquire this new habit of sight might be very considerable) would he not be ridiculous? Men would say of him that up he went and down he came without his eyes; and that it was better not even to think of ascending; and if any one tried to loose another and lead him up to the light, let them only catch the offender, and they would put him to death.

No question, he said.

This entire allegory, I said, you may now append, dear Glaucon, to the previous argument; the prison-house is the world of sight, the light of fire is the sun, and you will not misapprehend me if you interpret the journey upwards to be the ascent of the soul into the intellectual world according to my poor belief, which, at your desire, I have expressed—whether rightly or wrongly God knows. But, whether true or false, my opinion is that in the world of knowledge the idea of good appears last of all, and is seen only with an effort; and, when seen, is also inferred to be the universal author of all things beautiful and right, parent of light and of the lord of light in this visible world, and the immediate source of reason and truth in the intellectual; and that this is the power upon which he who would act rationally either in public or private life must have his eye fixed.

I agree, he said, as far as I am able to understand you.

Moreover, I said, you must not wonder that those who attain to this beautiful vision are unwilling to descend to human affairs; for their souls are ever hastening into the upper world where they desire to dwell; which desire of theirs is very natural, if our allegory may be trusted.

Yes, very natural.

And is there anything surprising in one who passes from divine contemplations to the evil state of man, misbehaving himself in a ridiculous manner; if, while his eyes are blinking and before he has become accustomed to the surrounding darkness, he is compelled to fight in courts of law, or in other places, about the images or the shadows of images of justice, and is endeavouring to meet the conceptions of those who have never yet seen absolute justice?

Anything but surprising, he replied.

Any one who has common sense will remember that the bewilderments of the eyes are of two kinds, and arise from two causes, either from coming out of the light or from going into the light, which is true of the mind's eye, quite as much as of the bodily eye; and he who remembers this when he sees any one whose vision is perplexed and weak, will not be too ready to laugh; he will first ask whether that soul of man has come out of the brighter life, and is unable to see because unaccustomed to the dark, or having turned from darkness to the day is dazzled by excess of light. And he will count the one happy in his condition and state of being, and he will pity the other; or, if he have a mind to laugh at the soul which comes from below into the light, there will be more reason in this than in the laugh which greets him who returns from above out of the light into the den.

That, he said, is a very just distinction.

The Library Card

Richard Wright

In this essay, Richard Wright describes both the struggle he has with an identity that was ascribed to him by society and the limitations that were placed on him because of that identity. As a black man living in the 1930s U.S. South, Wright is considered to be less than human. He is presumed to be ignorant, but he learns he is not. Through this poignant portrayal of his struggle, we are taken on a journey that enables us to realize that discovering who we are requires us to take a risk that can be liberating though painful.

One morning I arrived early at work and went into the bank lobby where the Negro porter was mopping. I stood at a counter and picked up the Memphis *Commercial Appeal* and began my free reading of the press. I came finally to the editorial page and saw an article dealing with one H. L. Mencken. I knew by hearsay that he was the editor of the *American Mercury,* but aside from that I knew nothing about him. The article was a furious denunciation of Mencken, concluding with one hot, short sentence: Mencken is a fool.

I wondered what on earth this Mencken had done to call down upon him the scorn of the South. The only people I had ever heard denounced in the South were Negroes, and this man was not a Negro. Then what ideas did Mencken hold that made a newspaper like the *Commercial Appeal* castigate him publicly? Undoubtedly he must be advocating ideas that the South did not like. Were there, then, people other than Negroes who criticized the South? I knew that during the Civil War the South had hated northern whites, but I had not encountered such hate during my life. Knowing no more of Mencken than I did at that moment, I felt a vague sympathy for him. Had not the South, which had assigned me the role of a non-man, cast at him its hardest words?

Now, how could I find out about this Mencken? There was a huge library near the riverfront, but I knew that Negroes were not allowed to patronize its shelves any more than they were the parks and playgrounds of the city. I had gone into the library several times to get books for the white men on the job. Which of them would now help me to get books? And how could I read them without causing concern to the white men with whom I worked? I had so far been successful in hiding my thoughts and feelings from them, but I knew that I would create hostility if I went about this business of reading in a clumsy way.

I weighed the personalities of the men on the job. There was Don, a Jew; but I distrusted him. His position was not much better than mine and I knew that he was uneasy and insecure; he had always treated me in an offhand, bantering way that barely concealed his contempt. I was afraid to ask him to help me to get books; his frantic desire to demonstrate a racial solidarity with the whites against Negroes might make him betray me.

Then how about the boss? No, he was a Baptist and I had the suspicion that he

---

"The Library Card" from *Black Boy* by Richard Wright. Copyright 1937, 1942, 1944, 1945 by Richard Wright. Copyright renewed 1973 by Ellen Wright. Reprinted by permission of HarperCollins Publishers Inc.

would not be quite able to comprehend why a black boy would want to read Mencken. There were other white men on the job whose attitudes showed clearly that they were Kluxers or sympathizers, and they were out of the question.

There remained only one man whose attitude did not fit into an anti-Negro category, for I had heard the white men refer to him as a "Pope lover." He was an Irish Catholic and was hated by the white Southerners. I knew that he read books, because I had got him volumes from the library several times. Since he, too, was an object of hatred, I felt that he might refuse me but would hardly betray me. I hesitated, weighing and balancing the imponderable realities.

One morning I paused before the Catholic fellow's desk.

"I want to ask you a favor," I whispered to him.

"What is it?"

"I want to read. I can't get books from the library. I wonder if you'd let me use your card?"

He looked at me suspiciously.

"My card is full most of the time," he said.

"I see," I said and waited, posing my question silently.

"You're not trying to get me into trouble, are you, boy?" he asked, staring at me.

"Oh, no, sir."

"What book do you want?"

"A book by H. L. Mencken."

"Which one?"

"I don't know. Has he written more than one?"

"He has written several."

"I didn't know that."

"What makes you want to read Mencken?"

"Oh, I just saw his name in the newspaper," I said.

"It's good of you to want to read," he said. "But you ought to read the right things."

I said nothing. Would he want to supervise my reading?

"Let me think," he said. "I'll figure out something."

I turned from him and he called me back. He stared at me quizzically.

"Richard, don't mention this to the other white men," he said.

"I understand," I said. "I won't say a word."

A few days later he called me to him.

"I've got a card in my wife's name," he said. "Here's mine."

"Thank you, sir."

"Do you think you can manage it?"

"I'll manage fine," I said.

"If they suspect you, you'll get in trouble," he said.

"I'll write the same kind of notes to the library that you wrote when you sent me for books," I told him. "I'll sign your name."

He laughed.

"Go ahead. Let me see what you get," he said.

That afternoon I addressed myself to forging a note. Now, what were the names of books written by H. L. Mencken? I did not know any of them. I finally wrote what I thought would be a foolproof note: *Dear Madam: Will you please let this nigger boy*—I used the word "nigger" to make the librarian feel that I could not possibly be the author of the note—*have some books by H. L. Mencken?* I forged the white man's name.

I entered the library as I had always done when on errands for whites, but I felt that I would somehow slip up and betray myself. I doffed my hat, stood a respectful distance from the desk, looked as unbookish as possible, and waited for the white patrons to be taken care of. When the desk was clear of people, I still waited. The white librarian looked at me.

"What do you want, boy?"

As though I did not possess the power of speech, I stepped forward and simply handed her the forged note, not parting my lips.

"What books by Mencken does he want?" she asked.

"I don't know, ma'am," I said, avoiding her eyes.

"Who gave you this card?"

"Mr. Falk," I said.

"Where is he?"

"He's at work, at the M—Optical Company," I said. "I've been in here for him before."

"I remember," the woman said. "But he never wrote notes like this."

Oh, God, she's suspicious. Perhaps she would not let me have the books? If she had turned her back at that moment, I would have ducked out the door and never gone back. Then I thought of a bold idea.

"You can call him up, ma'am," I said, my heart pounding.

"You're not using these books, are you?" she asked pointedly.

"Oh, no, ma'am. I can't read."

"I don't know what he wants by Mencken," she said under her breath.

I knew now that I had won; she was thinking of other things and the race question had gone out of her mind. She went to the shelves. Once or twice she looked over her shoulder at me, as though she was still doubtful. Finally she came forward with two books in her hand.

"I'm sending him two books," she said. "But tell Mr. Falk to come in next time, or send me the names of the books he wants. I don't know what he wants to read."

I said nothing. She stamped the card and handed me the books. Not daring to glance at them, I went out of the library, fearing that the woman would call me back for further questioning. A block away from the library I opened one of the books and read a title: *A Book of Prefaces.* I was nearing my nineteenth birthday and I did not know how to pronounce the word "preface." I thumbed the pages and saw strange words and strange names. I shook my head, disappointed. I looked at the other book; it was called *Prejudices.* I knew what that word meant; I had heard it all my life. And right off I was on guard against Mencken's books. Why would a man want to call a book *Prejudices?* The word was so stained with all my memories of racial hate that I could not conceive of anybody using it for a title. Perhaps I had made a mistake about Mencken? A man who had prejudices must be wrong.

When I showed the books to Mr. Falk, he looked at me and frowned.

"That librarian might telephone you," I warned him.

"That's all right," he said. "But when you're through reading those books, I want you to tell me what you get out of them."

That night in my rented room while letting the hot water run over my can of pork and beans in the sink I opened *A Book of Prefaces* and began to read. I was jarred and shocked by the style, the clear, clean, sweeping sentences. Why did he write like that? And how did one write like that? I pictured the man as a raging demon slashing with his pen, consumed with hate denouncing everything American, extolling everything European or German, laughing at the weaknesses of people mocking God, authority. What was this? I stood up trying to realize what reality lay behind the meaning of the words . . . Yes this man was fighting, fighting with words. He was using words as a weapon, using them as one would use a club. Could words be weapons? Well, yes, for here they were.

Then, maybe, perhaps, I could use them as a weapon? No. It frightened me. I read on and what amazed me was not what he said, but how on earth anybody had the courage to say it.

Occasionally I glanced up to reassure myself that I was alone in the room. Who were these men about whom Mencken was talking so passionately? Who was Anatole France? Joseph Conrad? Sinclair Lewis, Sherwood Anderson, Dostoevski, George Moore, Gustave Flaubert, Maupassant, Tolstoy, Frank Harris, Mark Twain, Thomas Hardy, Arnold Bennett, Stephen Crane, Zola, Norris, Gorky, Bergson, Ibsen, Balzac, Bernard Shaw, Dumas, Poe, Thomas Mann, O. Henry, Dreiser, H. G. Wells, Gogol, T. S. Eliot, Gide, Baudelaire, Edgar Lee Masters, Stendhal, Turgenev, Hunekar, Nietzsche, and scores of others? Were these men real? Did they exist or had they existed? And how did one pronounce their names?

I ran across many words whose meanings I did not know, and I either looked them up in a dictionary or, before I had a chance to do that, encountered the word in a context that made its meaning clear. But what strange world was this? I concluded the book with the conviction that I had somehow overlooked something terribly important in life. I had once tried to write, had once reveled in feeling, had let my crude imagination roam, but the impulse to dream had been slowly beaten out of me by experience. Now it surged up again and I hungered for books, new ways of looking and seeing. It was not a matter of believing or disbelieving what I read, but of feeling something new, of being affected by something that made the look of the world different.

As dawn broke I ate my pork and beans, feeling dopey, sleepy. I went to work, but the mood of the book would not die; it lingered, coloring everything I saw, heard, did. I now felt that I knew what the white men were feeling. Merely because I had read a book that had spoken of how they lived and thought, I identified myself with that book. I felt vaguely guilty. Would I, filled with bookish notions, act in a manner that would make the whites dislike me?

I forged more notes and my trips to the library became frequent. Reading grew into a passion. My first serious novel was Sinclair Lewis's *Main Street.* It made me see my boss, Mr. Gerald, and identify him as an American type. I would smile when I saw him lugging his golf bags into the office. I had always felt a vast distance separating me from the boss, and now I felt closer to him, though still distant. I felt now that I knew him, that I could feel the very limits of his narrow life. And this had happened because I had read a novel about a mythical man called George F. Babbitt.

The plots and stories in the novels did not interest me so much as the point of view revealed. I gave myself over to each novel without reserve, without trying to criticize it; it was enough for me to see and feel something different. And for me, everything was something different. Reading was like a drug, a dope. The novels created moods in which I lived for days. But I could not conquer my sense of guilt, my feeling that the white men around me knew that I was changing, that I had begun to regard them differently.

Whenever I brought a book to the job, I wrapped it in newspaper—a habit that was to persist for years in other cities and under other circumstances. But some of the white men pried into my packages when I was absent and they questioned me.

"Boy, what are you reading those books for?"

"Oh, I don't know, sir."

"That's deep stuff you're reading, boy."

"I'm just killing time, sir."

"You'll addle your brains if you don't watch out."

I read Dreiser's *Jennie Gerhardt* and *Sister Carrie* and they revived in me a vivid sense of my mother's suffering; I was overwhelmed. I grew silent, wondering about the life around me. It would have been impossible for me to have told anyone what I derived from these novels, for it was nothing less than a sense of life itself. All my life had shaped me for the realism, the naturalism of the modern novel, and I could not read enough of them.

Steeped in new moods and ideas, I bought a ream of paper and tried to write; but nothing would come, or what did come was flat beyond telling. I discovered that more than desire and feeling were necessary to write and I dropped the idea. Yet I still wondered how it was possible to know people sufficiently to write about them? Could I ever learn about life and people? To me, with my vast ignorance, my Jim Crow station in life, it seemed a task impossible of achievement. I now knew what being a Negro meant. I could endure the hunger. I had learned to live with hate. But to feel that there were feelings denied me, that the very breath of life itself was beyond my reach, that more than anything else hurt, wounded me. I had a new hunger.

In buoying me up, reading also cast me down, made me see what was possible, what I had missed. My tension returned, new, terrible, bitter, surging, almost too great to be contained. I no longer *felt* that the world about me was hostile, killing; I *knew* it. A million times I asked myself what I could do to save myself, and there were no answers. I seemed forever condemned, ringed by walls.

I did not discuss my reading with Mr. Falk, who had lent me his library card; it would have meant talking about myself and that would have been too painful. I smiled each day, fighting desperately to maintain my old behavior, to keep my disposition seemingly sunny. But some of the white men discerned that I had begun to brood.

"Wake up there, boy!" Mr. Olin said one day.

"Sir!" I answered for the lack of a better word.

"You act like you've stolen something," he said.

I laughed in the way I knew he expected me to laugh, but I resolved to be more conscious of myself, to watch my every act, to guard and hide the new knowledge that was dawning within me.

If I went north, would it be possible for me to build a new life then? But how could a man build a life upon vague, unformed yearnings? I wanted to write and I did not even know the English language. I bought English grammars and found them dull. I felt that I was getting a better sense of the language from novels than from grammars. I read hard, discarding a writer as soon as I felt that I had grasped his point of view. At night the printed page stood before my eyes in sleep.

Mrs. Moss, my landlady, asked me one Sunday morning: "Son, what is this you keep on reading?"

"Oh, nothing. Just novels."

"What you get out of 'em?"

"I'm just killing time," I said.

"I hope you know your own mind," she said in a tone which implied that she doubted if I had a mind.

I knew of no Negroes who read the books I liked and I wondered if any Negroes ever thought of them. I knew that there were Negro doctors, lawyers, newspapermen, but I never saw any of them. When I read a Negro newspaper I never caught the faintest echo of my preoccupation in its pages. I felt trapped and occasionally, for a few days, I would stop reading. But a vague hunger would come over me for books, books that opened up new avenues of feeling and seeing, and again I would forge another note to the white librarian. Again I would read and wonder as only the naïve and unlettered can read and wonder, feeling that I carried a secret, criminal burden about with me each day.

That winter my mother and brother came and we set up housekeeping, buying furniture on the installment plan, being cheated and yet knowing no way to avoid it. I began to eat warm food and to my surprise found that regular meals enabled me to read faster. I may have lived through many illnesses and survived them, never suspecting that I was ill. My brother obtained a job and we began to save toward the trip north, plotting our time, setting tentative dates for departure. I told none of the white men on the job that I was planning to go north; I knew that the moment they felt I was thinking of the North they would change toward me. It would have made them feel that I did not like the life I was living, and because my life was completely conditioned by what they said or did, it would have been tantamount to challenging them.

I could calculate my chances for life in the South as a Negro fairly clearly now.

I could fight the southern whites by organizing with other Negroes, as my grandfather had done. But I knew that I could never win that way; there were many whites and there were but few blacks. They were strong and we were weak. Outright black rebellion could never win. If I fought openly I would die and I did not want to die. News of lynchings were frequent.

I could submit and live the life of a genial slave, but that was impossible. All of my life had shaped me to live by my own feelings and thoughts. I could make up to Bess and marry her and inherit the house. But that, too, would be the life of a slave; if I did that, I would crush to death something within me, and I would hate myself as much as I knew the whites already hated those who had submitted. Neither could I ever willingly present myself to be kicked, as Shorty had done. I would rather have died than do that.

I could drain off my restlessness by fighting with Shorty and Harrison. I had seen many Negroes solve the problem of being black by transferring their hatred of themselves to others with a black skin and fighting them. I would have to be cold to do that, and I was not cold and I could never be.

I could, of course, forget what I had read, thrust the whites out of my mind, forget them; and find release from anxiety and longing in sex and alcohol. But the memory of how my father had conducted himself made that course repugnant. If I did not want others to violate my life, how could I voluntarily violate it myself?

I had no hope whatever of being a professional man. Not only had I been so conditioned that I did not desire it, but the fulfillment of such an ambition was beyond my capabilities. Well-to-do Negroes lived in a world that was almost as alien to me as the world inhabited by whites.

What, then, was there? I held my life in my mind, in my consciousness each day, feeling at times that I would stumble and drop it, spill it forever. My reading had created a vast sense of distance between me and the world in which I lived and tried to make a living, and that sense of distance was increasing each day. My days and nights were one long, quiet, continuously contained dream of terror, tension, and anxiety. I wondered how long I could bear it.

Living a Human Life

Søren Kierkegaard

For Kierkegaard, the subjective truth of faith is about what one must do and not about what one must know. What must one do to live a "completely human life"? Seeking and finding the kingdom of heaven may be not so much a matter of knowing the Christian creeds as it is an inward understanding and living one's life according to that understanding. A true Christian life may be more like a Sisyphean struggle than we realize!

What I really need is to get clear about what I must do, not what I must know, except insofar as knowledge must precede every act. What matters is to find a purpose, to see what it really is that God wills that I shall do; the crucial thing is to find a truth which is truth for me, to find the idea for which I am willing to live and die. Of what use would it be to me to discover a so-called objective truth, to work through the philosophical systems so that I could, if asked, make critical judgments about them, could point out the fallacies in each system; of what use would it be to me to be able to develop a theory of the state, getting details from various sources and combining them into a whole, and constructing a world I did not live in but merely held up for others to see; of what use would it be to me to be able to formulate the meaning of Christianity, to be able to explain many specific points—if it had no deeper meaning for me and for my life? And the better I was at it, the more I saw others appropriate the creations of my mind, the more tragic my situation would be, not unlike that of parents who in their poverty are forced to send their children out into the world and turn them over to the care of others. Of what use would it be to me for truth to stand before me, cold and naked, not caring whether or not I acknowledged it, making me uneasy rather than trustingly receptive. I certainly do not deny that I still accept an imperative of knowledge and that through it men may be influenced, but then it must come alive in me, and this is what I now recognize as the most important of all. This is what my soul thirsts for as the African deserts thirst for water. This is what is lacking, and this is why I am like a man who has collected furniture, rented an apartment, but as yet has not found the beloved to share life's ups and downs with him. But in order to find that idea—or, to put it more correctly—to find myself, it does no good to plunge still farther into the world. That was just what I did before. The reason I thought it would be good to throw myself into law was that I believed I could develop my keenness of mind in the many muddles and messes of life. Here, too, was offered a whole mass of details in which I could lose myself; here, perhaps, with the given facts, I could construct a totality, an organic view of criminal life, pursue it in all its dark aspects (here, too, a certain fraternity of spirit is very evident). I also wanted to become a lawyer so that by putting myself in another's role I could, so to speak, find a substitute for my own life and by means of this external change find some diversion.

From *Søren Kierkegaard's Journals and Papers,* Vol. 5, ed. by Howard V. Hong and Edna H. Hong. Bloomington: Indiana University Press. 1978. Reprinted by permission of Indiana University Press.

This is what I needed to lead a *completely human life* and not merely one of *knowledge,* so that I could base the development of my thought not on—yes, not on something called objective—something which in any case is not my own, but upon something which is bound up with the deepest roots of my existence *[Existents],* through which I am, so to speak, grafted into the divine, to which I cling fast even though the whole world may collapse. *This is what I need, and this is what I strive for.* I find joy and refreshment in contemplating the great men who have found that precious stone for which they sell all, even their lives, whether I see them becoming vigorously engaged in life, confidently proceeding on their chosen course without vacillating, or discover them off the beaten path, absorbed in themselves and in working toward their high goal. I even honor and respect the by-path which lies so close by. It is this inward action of man, this God-side of man, which is decisive, not a mass of data, for the latter will no doubt follow and will not then appear as accidental aggregates or as a succession of details, one after the other, without a system, without a focal point. I, too, have certainly looked for this focal point. I have vainly sought an anchor in the boundless sea of pleasure as well as in the depths of knowledge. I have felt the almost irresistible power with which one pleasure reaches a hand to the next; I have also felt the counterfeit enthusiasm it is capable of producing. I have also felt the boredom, the shattering, which follows on its heels. I have tasted the fruits of the tree of knowledge and time and again have delighted in their savoriness. But this joy was only in the moment of cognition and did not leave a deeper mark on me. It seems to me that I have not drunk from the cup of wisdom but have fallen into it. I have sought to find the principle for my life through resignation *[Resignation],* by supposing that since everything proceeds according to inscrutable laws it could not be otherwise, by blunting my ambitions and the antennae of my vanity. Because I could not get everything to suit me, I abdicated with a consciousness of my own competence, somewhat the way decrepit clergymen resign with pension. What did I find? Not my self *[Jeg],* which is what I did seek to find in that way (I imagined my soul, if I may say so, as shut up in a box with a spring lock, which external surroundings would release by pressing the spring).—Consequently the seeking and finding of the Kingdom of Heaven was the first thing to be resolved. But it is just as useless for a man to want first of all to decide the externals and after that the fundamentals as it is for a cosmic body, thinking to form itself, first of all to decide the nature of its surface, to what bodies it should turn its light, to which its dark side, without first letting the harmony of centrifugal and centripetal forces realize *[realisere]* its existence *[Existents]* and letting the rest come to itself. One must first learn to know himself before knowing anything else (γνωθι σέ αντον). Not until a man has inwardly understood himself and then sees the course he is to take does his life gain peace and meaning; only then is he free of that irksome, sinister traveling companion—that irony of life which manifests itself in the sphere of knowledge and invites true knowing to begin with a not-knowing (Socrates), just as God created the world from nothing. But in the waters of morality it is especially at home to those who still have not entered the tradewinds of virtue. Here it tumbles a person about in a horrible way, for a time lets him feel happy and content in his resolve to go ahead along the right path, then hurls him into the abyss of despair. Often it lulls a man to sleep with the thought, "After all, things cannot be otherwise," only to awaken him suddenly to a rigorous interrogation. Frequently it seems to let a veil of forgetfulness fall over the past, only to make every single trifle appear in a strong light again. When he struggles along the right path, rejoicing in having overcome temptation's power, there may come at almost the same time, right on the heels of perfect victory, an apparently insignificant external circumstance which pushes him down, like Sisyphus, from the height of the crag. Often when a person has concentrated on something, a minor external circumstance arises which destroys everything. (As in the case of a man who, weary of life, is about to throw himself into the Thames and at the crucial moment is halted by the sting of a mosquito.) Frequently a person feels his very best when the illness is the worst, as in tuberculosis. In vain he tries to resist it but he has not sufficient strength, and it is no help to him that he has gone through the same thing many times; the kind of practice acquired in this way does not apply here. Just as no one who has been taught a great deal about swimming is able to keep afloat in a storm, but only the man who is intensely convinced and has experiences that he is actually lighter than water, so a person who lacks this inward point of poise is unable to keep afloat in life's storms.—Only when a man has understood himself in this way is he able to maintain an independent existence and thus avoid surrendering his own I. How often we see (in a period when we extol that Greek historian because he knows how to appropriate an unfamiliar style so delusively like the original author's, instead of censuring him, since the first prize always goes to an author for having his own style—that is, a mode of expression and presentation qualified by his own individuality)—how often we see people who either out of mental-spiritual laziness live on the crumbs that fall from another's table or for more egotistical reasons seek to identify themselves with others, until eventually they believe it all, just like the liar through frequent repetition of his stories. Although I am still far from this kind of interior understanding of myself, with profound respect for its significance I have sought to preserve my individuality—worshipped the unknown God. With a premature anxiety I have tried to avoid coming in close contact with those things whose force of attraction might be too powerful for me. I have sought to appropriate much from them, studied their distinctive characteristics and meaning in human life, but at the same time guarded against coming, like the moth, too close to the flame. I have had little to win or to lose in association with the ordinary run of men, partly because what they do—so-called practical life—does not interest me much, partly because their coldness and indifference to the spiritual and deeper currents in man alienate me even more from them. With few exceptions my companions have had no special influence upon me. A life that has not arrived at clarity about myself must necessarily exhibit an uneven side-surface; confronted by certain facts *[Facta]* and their apparent disharmony, they simply halted there, for, as I see it, they did not have sufficient interest to seek a resolution in a higher harmony or to recognize the necessity of it. Their opinion of me was always one-sided, and I have vacillated between putting too much or too little weight on what they said. I have now withdrawn from their influence and the potential variations of my life's compass resulting from it. Thus I am again standing at the point where I must begin again in another way. I shall now calmly attempt to look at myself and begin to initiate inner action; for only thus will I be able, like a child calling itself "I" in its first consciously undertaken act, be able to call myself "I" in a profounder sense.

But that takes stamina, and it is not possible to harvest immediately what one has sown. I will remember that philosopher's method of having his disciples keep silent for three years; then I dare say it will come. Just as one does not begin a feast at sunrise but at sundown, just so in the spiritual world one must first work forward for some time before the sun really shines for us and rises in all its glory; for although it is true as it says that God lets his sun shine upon the good and the evil and lets the rain fall on the just and the unjust, it is not so in the spiritual world. So let the die be cast—I am crossing the Rubicon! No doubt this road takes me into battle, but I will not renounce it. I will not lament the past—why lament? I will work energetically and not waste time in regrets, like the person stuck in a bog and first calculating how far he has sunk without recognizing that during the time he spends on that he is sinking still deeper. I will hurry along the path I have found and shout to everyone I meet: Do not look back as Lot's wife did, but remember that we are struggling up a hill.

A Balanced Learning

John Stuart Mill

John Stuart Mill is best known for his writings on utilitarianism and individual liberty. In this excerpt from his Autobiography, *however, we encounter Mill reflecting on his education and whether or not it has brought him personal happiness or satisfaction. In an episode that he called "A Crisis in My Mental History," the twenty-year-old Mill questions whether his rigorous intellectual and moral "training" was sufficient to his development as a person. What about his affective education? Wasn't more needed to help him develop socially and emotionally as a person?*

A CRISIS IN MY MENTAL HISTORY

From Chapter 5 of *Autobiography* (1873)

From the winter of 1821, when I first read Bentham,* and especially from the commencement of the *Westminster Review,*† I had what might truly be called an object in life; to be a reformer of the world. My conception of my own happiness was entirely identified with this object. The personal

From *Autobiography* by John Stuart Mill, 1873.

*Jeremy Bentham (1748–1832), British philosopher, founded utilitarianism, a philosophical scheme based on the notion that ideas, institutions, and behavior could all be judged good or bad on the basis of their usefulness. The wider the scope of a thing's utility—"the greatest happiness of the greatest number" being the ultimate standard—the more favorably it was judged. Since the utilitarians, including J. S. Mill and his father, deemed that the ancient system of aristocracy and monarchy inherited from the Middle Ages extended the greatest happiness to the *fewest* number, they all favored sweeping social and political reforms and looked to the American republic under the Constitution as an ideal form of democracy. They were the political radicals of their day.

†The *Westminster Review* was a quarterly periodical founded in 1824 to be the organ of opinion for the radical political thinkers of the day, especially the utilitarians. In his youth, J. S. Mill wrote extensively for the *Westminster* and later became its editor.

sympathies I wished for were those of fellow labourers in this enterprise. I endeavoured to pick up as many flowers as I could by the way; but as a serious and permanent personal satisfaction to rest upon, my whole reliance was placed on this; and I was accustomed to felicitate myself on the certainty of a happy life which I enjoyed, through placing my happiness in something durable and distant, in which some progress might be always making, while it could never be exhausted by complete attainment. This did very well for several years, during which the general improvement going on in the world and the idea of myself as engaged with others in struggling to promote it, seemed enough to fill up an interesting and animated existence. But the time came when I awakened from this as from a dream. It was in the autumn of 1826.* I was in a dull state of nerves, such as everybody is occasionally liable to; unsusceptible to enjoyment or pleasurable excitement; one of those moods when what is pleasure at other times, becomes insipid or indifferent; the state, I should think, in which converts to Methodism usually are, when smitten by their first "conviction of sin." In this frame of mind it occurred to me to put the question directly to myself: "Suppose that all your objects in life were realized; that all the changes in institutions and opinions which you are looking forward to, could be completely effected at this very instant: would this be a great joy and happiness to you?" And an irrepressible self-consciousness distinctly answered, "No!" At this my heart sank within me: the whole foundation on which my life was constructed fell down. All my happiness was to have been found in the continual pursuit of this end. The end had ceased to charm, and how could there ever again be any interest in the means? I seemed to have nothing left to live for.

At first I hoped the cloud would pass away of itself; but it did not. A night's sleep, the sovereign remedy for the smaller vexations of life, had no effect on it. I awoke to a renewed consciousness of the woful fact. I carried it with me into all companies, into all occupations. Hardly anything had power to cause me even a few minutes oblivion of it. For some months the cloud seemed to grow thicker and thicker. The lines in [Samuel Taylor] Coleridge's "Dejection"—I was not then acquainted with them—exactly describe my case:

> A grief without a pang, void, dark and drear,
> A drowsy, stifled, unimpassioned grief,
> Which finds no natural outlet or relief
> In word, or sigh, or tear.

In vain I sought relief from my favourite books; those memorials of past nobleness and greatness from which I had always hitherto drawn strength and animation. I read them now without feeling, or with the accustomed feeling *minus* all its charm; and I became persuaded, that my love of mankind, and of excellence for its own sake, had worn itself out. I sought no comfort by speaking to others of what I felt. If I had loved any one sufficiently to make confiding my griefs a necessity, I should not have been in the condition I was. I felt, too, that mine was not an interesting, or in any way respectable distress. There was nothing in it to attract sympathy. Advice, if I had known where to seek it, would have been most precious. The words of Macbeth to the physician often occurred to my thoughts.† But there was no one on whom I could build

---

*Mill was 20.

†"Canst thou not minister to a mind diseas'd?"

the faintest hope of such assistance. My father, to whom it would have been natural to me to have recourse in any practical difficulties, was the last person to whom, in such a case as this, I looked for help. Everything convinced me that he had no knowledge of any such mental state as I was suffering from, and that even if he could be made to understand it, he was not the physician who could heal it. My education, which was wholly his work, had been conducted without any regard to the possibility of its ending in this result; and I saw no use in giving him the pain of thinking that his plans had failed, when the failure was probably irremediable, and, at all events, beyond the power of *his* remedies. Of other friends, I had at that time none to whom I had any hope of making my condition intelligible. It was however abundantly intelligible to myself; and the more I dwelt upon it, the more hopeless it appeared.

My course of study had led me to believe, that all mental and moral feelings and qualities, whether of a good or of a bad kind, were the results of association;* that we love one thing, and hate another, take pleasure in one sort of action or contemplation, and pain in another sort, through the clinging of pleasurable or painful ideas to those things, from the effect of education or of experience. As a corollary from this, I had always heard it maintained by my father, and was myself convinced, that the object of education should be to form the strongest possible associations of the salutary class; associations of pleasure with all things beneficial to the great whole, and of pain with all things hurtful to it. This doctrine appeared inexpugnable; but it now seemed to me, on retrospect, that my teachers had occupied themselves but superficially with the means of forming and keeping up these salutary associations. They seemed to have trusted altogether to the old familiar instruments, praise and blame, reward and punishment. Now, I did not doubt that by these means, begun early, and applied unremittingly, intense associations of pain and pleasure, especially of pain, might be created, and might produce desires and aversions capable of lasting undiminished to the end of life. But there must always be something artificial and casual in associations thus produced. The pains and pleasures thus forcibly associated with things, are not connected with them by any natural tie; and it is therefore, I thought, essential to the durability of these associations, that they should have become so intense and inveterate as to be practically indissoluble, before the habitual exercise of the power of analysis had commenced. For I now saw, or thought I saw, what I had always before received with incredulity—that the habit of analysis has a tendency to wear away the feelings: as indeed it has, when no other mental habit is cultivated, and the analysing spirit remains without its natural complements and correctives. The very excellence of analysis (I argued) is that it tends to weaken and undermine whatever is the result of prejudice; that it enables us mentally to separate ideas which have only casually clung together: and no associations whatever could ultimately resist this dissolving force, were it not that we owe to analysis our clearest knowledge of the permanent sequences in nature; the real connexions between Things, not dependent on our will and feelings; natural laws, by virtue of which, in many cases, one thing is inseparable from another in fact; which laws, in proportion as they are clearly perceived and imaginatively realized, cause

*"Associationist psychology" says that we build up our knowledge and our judgment of things by association. Our understanding of new things is colored by two kinds of associations: the way old knowledge is associated with new and whether new knowledge is associated with pain or with pleasure.

our ideas of things which are always joined together in Nature, to cohere more and more closely in our thoughts. Analytic habits may thus even strengthen the associations between causes and effects, means and ends, but tend altogether to weaken those which are, to speak familiarly, a *mere* matter of feeling. They are therefore (I thought) favourable to prudence and clear-sightedness, but a perpetual worm at the root both of the passions and of the virtues; and, above all, fearfully undermine all desires, and all pleasures, which are the effects of association, that is, according to the theory I held, all except the purely physical and organic; of the entire insufficiency of which to make life desirable, no one had a stronger conviction than I had. These were the laws of human nature, by which, as it seemed to me, I had been brought to my present state. All those to whom I looked up, were of opinion that the pleasure of sympathy with human beings, and the feelings which made the good of others, and especially of mankind on a large scale, the object of existence, were the greatest and surest sources of happiness. Of the truth of this I was convinced, but to know that a feeling would make me happy if I had it, did not give me the feeling. My education, I thought, had failed to create these feelings in sufficient strength to resist the dissolving influence of analysis, while the whole course of my intellectual cultivation had made precocious and premature analysis the inveterate habit of my mind. I was thus, as I said to myself, left stranded at the commencement of my voyage, with a well-equipped ship and a rudder, but no sail; without any real desire for the ends which I had been so carefully fitted out to work for: no delight in virtue, or the general good, but also just as little in anything else. The fountains of vanity and ambition seemed to have dried up within me, as completely as those of benevolence. I had had (as I reflected) some gratification of vanity at too early an age: I had obtained some distinction, and felt myself of some importance, before the desire of distinction and of importance had grown into a passion: and little as it was which I had attained, yet having been attained too early, like all pleasures enjoyed too soon, it had made me *blasé* and indifferent to the pursuit. Thus neither selfish nor unselfish pleasures were pleasures to me. And there seemed no power in nature sufficient to begin the formation of my character anew, and create in a mind now irretrievably analytic, fresh associations of pleasure with any of the objects of human desire.

These were the thoughts which mingled with the dry heavy dejection of the melancholy winter of 1826–7. During this time I was not incapable of my usual occupations. I went on with them mechanically, by the mere force of habit. I had been so drilled in a certain sort of mental exercise, that I could still carry it on when all the spirit had gone out of it. I even composed and spoke several speeches at the debating society, how, or with what degree of success, I know not. Of four years continual speaking at that society, this is the only year of which I remember next to nothing. Two lines of Coleridge, in whom alone of all writers I have found a true description of what I felt, were often in my thoughts, not at this time (for I had never read them), but in a later period of the same mental malady:

> Work without hope draws nectar in a sieve,
> And hope without an object cannot live.*

In all probability my case was by no means so peculiar as I fancied it, and I doubt not that many others have passed through a similar state; but the idiosyncrasies of my

*Coleridge, "Work Without Hope."

education had given to the general phenomenon a special character, which made it seem the natural effect of causes that it was hardly possible for time to remove. I frequently asked myself, if I could, or if I was bound to go on living, when life must be passed in this manner. I generally answered to myself, that I did not think I could possibly bear it beyond a year. When, however, not more than half that duration of time had elapsed, a small ray of light broke in upon my gloom. I was reading, accidentally, [J. F.] Marmontel's* "Mémoires," and came to the passage which relates his father's death, the distressed position of the family, and the sudden inspiration by which he, then a mere boy, felt and made them feel that he would be everything to them—would supply the place of all that they had lost. A vivid conception of the scene and its feelings came over me, and I was moved to tears. From this moment my burthen grew lighter. The oppression of the thought that all feeling was dead within me, was gone. I was no longer hopeless: I was not a stock or a stone. I had still, it seemed, some of the material out of which all worth of character, and all capacity for happiness, are made. Relieved from my ever present sense of irremediable wretchedness, I gradually found that the ordinary incidents of life could again give me some pleasure; that I could again find enjoyment, not intense, but sufficient for cheerfulness, in sunshine and sky, in books, in conversation, in public affairs; and that there was, once more, excitement, though of a moderate kind, in exerting myself for my opinions, and for the public good. Thus the cloud gradually drew off, and I again enjoyed life: and though I had several relapses, some of which lasted many months, I never again was as miserable as I had been.

The experiences of this period had two very marked effects on my opinions and character. In the first place, they led me to adopt a theory of life, very unlike that on which I had before acted, and having much in common with what at that time I certainly had never heard of, the anti-self-consciousness theory of Carlyle.† I never, indeed, wavered in the conviction that happiness is the test of all rules of conduct, and the end of life. But I now thought that this end was only to be attained by not making it the direct end. Those only are happy (I thought) who have their minds fixed on some object other than their own happiness; on the happiness of others, on the improvement of mankind, even on some art or pursuit, followed not as a means, but as itself an ideal end. Aiming thus at something else, they find happiness by the way. The enjoyments of life (such was now my theory) are sufficient to make it a pleasant thing, when they are taken *en passant*, without being made a principal object. Once make them so, and they are immediately felt to be insufficient. They will not bear a scrutinizing examination. Ask yourself whether you are happy, and you cease to be so. The only chance is to treat, not happiness, but some end external to it, as the purpose of life. Let your self-consciousness, your scrutiny, your self-interrogation, exhaust themselves on that; and if otherwise fortunately circumstanced you will inhale happiness with the air you breathe, without dwelling on it or thinking about it, without

*Jean-François Marmontel (1723–1799), French writer, author of tragedies, philosophical romances, and librettos for several light operas.

†Thomas Carlyle (1795–1881) held that the reasoning intellect, operating at a conscious level, could deal only with the superficialities of life and that only our deepest spiritual instincts, of which we are mostly unconscious, can probe the profoundest truths.

either forestalling it in imagination, or putting it to flight by fatal questioning. This theory now became the basis of my philosophy of life. And I still hold to it as the best theory for all those who have but a moderate degree of sensibility and of capacity for enjoyment, that is, for the great majority of mankind.

The other important change which my opinions at this time underwent, was that I, for the first time, gave its proper place, among the prime necessities of human well-being, to the internal culture* of the individual. I ceased to attach most exclusive importance to the ordering of outward circumstances, and the training of the human being for speculation and for action.

I had now learnt by experience that the passive susceptibilities needed to be cultivated as well as the active capacities, and required to be nourished and enriched as well as guided. I did not, for an instant, lose sight of, or undervalue, that part of the truth which I had seen before; I never turned recreant to intellectual culture, or ceased to consider the power and practice of analysis as an essential condition both of individual and of social improvement. But I thought that it had consequences which required to be corrected, by joining other kinds of cultivation with it. The maintenance of a due balance among the faculties, now seemed to me of primary importance. The cultivation of the feelings became one of the cardinal points in my ethical and philosophical creed. And my thoughts and inclinations turned in an increasing degree towards whatever seemed capable of being instrumental to that object. . . . There have certainly been, even in our own age, greater poets than Wordsworth; but poetry of deeper and loftier feeling could not have done for me at that time what his did. I needed to be made to feel that there was real, permanent happiness in tranquil contemplation. Wordsworth taught me this, not only without turning away from, but with a greatly increased interest in the common feelings and common destiny of human beings. And the delight which these poems gave me, proved that with culture of this sort, there was nothing to dread from the most confirmed habit of analysis. At the conclusion of the Poems came the famous Ode, falsely called Platonic, "Intimations of Immortality"; in which, along with more than his usual sweetness of melody and rhythm, and along with the two passages of grand imagery but bad philosophy so often quoted, I found that he too had had similar experience to mine; that he also had felt that the first freshness of youthful enjoyment of life was not lasting; but that he had sought for compensation, and found it, in the way in which he was now teaching me to find it. The result was that I gradually, but completely, emerged from my habitual depression, and was never again subject to it. I long continued to value Wordsworth less according to his intrinsic merits, than by the measure of what he had done for me. Compared with the greatest poets, he may be said to be the poet of unpoetical natures, possessed of quiet and contemplative tastes. But unpoetical natures are precisely those which require poetic cultivation. This cultivation Wordsworth is much more fitted to give, than poets who are intrinsically far more poets than he.

It so fell out that the merits of Wordsworth were the occasion of my first public declaration of my new way of thinking, and separation from those of my habitual companions who had not undergone a similar change. The person with whom at that time

*That is, the life of feeling. *Culture* is here used in the sense of "cultivation."

I was most in the habit of comparing notes on such subjects was Roebuck,* and I induced him to read Wordsworth, in whom he also at first seemed to find much to admire: but I, like most Wordsworthians, threw myself into strong antagonism to Byron, both as a poet and as to his influence on the character. Roebuck, all whose instincts were those of action and struggle, had, on the contrary, a strong relish and great admiration of Byron, whose writings he regarded as the poetry of human life, while Wordsworth's, according to him, was that of flowers and butterflies. We agreed to have the fight out at our Debating Society, where we accordingly discussed for two evenings the comparative merits of Byron and Wordsworth, propounding and illustrating by long recitations our respective theories of poetry: [John] Sterling† also, in a brilliant speech, putting forward his particular theory. This was the first debate on any weighty subject in which Roebuck and I had been on opposite sides. The schism between us widened from this time more and more, though we continued for some years longer to be companions. In the beginning, our chief divergence related to the cultivation of the feelings. Roebuck was in many respects very different from the vulgar notion of a Benthamite or Utilitarian. He was a lover of poetry and of most of the fine arts. He took great pleasure in music, in dramatic performances, especially in painting, and himself drew and designed landscapes with great facility and beauty. But he never could be made to see that these things have any value as aids in the formation of character. Personally, instead of being, as Benthamites‡ are supposed to be, void of feeling, he had very quick and strong sensibilities. But, like most Englishmen who have feelings, he found his feelings stand very much in his way. He was much more susceptible to the painful sympathies than to the pleasurable, and looking for his happiness elsewhere, he wished that his feelings should be deadened rather than quickened. And, in truth, the English character, and English social circumstances, make it so seldom possible to derive happiness from the exercise of the sympathies, that it is not wonderful if they count for little in an Englishman's scheme of life. In most other countries the paramount importance of the sympathies as a constituent of individual happiness is an axiom, taken for granted rather than needing any formal statement; but most English thinkers almost seem to regard them as necessary evils, required for keeping men's actions benevolent and compassionate. Roebuck was, or appeared to be, this kind of Englishman. He saw little good in any cultivation of the feelings, and none at all in cultivating illusions. It was in vain I urged on him that the imaginative emotion which an idea, when vividly conceived, excites in us, is not an illusion but a fact, as real as any of the other qualities of objects; and far from implying anything erroneous and delusive in our mental apprehension of the object, is quite consistent with the most accurate knowledge and most perfect practical recognition of all its physical and intellectual laws and relations. The intensest feeling of the beauty of a cloud lighted by the setting sun, is no hindrance to my knowing that the cloud is vapour of water, subject to all the laws of vapours in a state of suspension; and I am just as likely to allow for, and act on, these physical laws

*John Arthur Roebuck (1801–1879), an early friend of Mill's, a radical politician, and a representative in Parliament for the industrial city of Sheffield.

†Essayist and poet (1806–1844), friend of many famous Victorians who outlived him, made famous by Carlyle's *Life of Sterling* (1851).

‡Followers of the utilitarian philosophy (see note on p. 18) established by Jeremy Bentham.

whenever there is occasion to do so, as if I had been incapable of perceiving any distinction between beauty and ugliness.

* * *

In giving an account of this period of my life, I have only specified such of my new impressions as appeared to me, both at the time and since, to be a kind of turning point, marking a definite progress in my mode of thought. But these few selected points give a very insufficient idea of the quantity of thinking which I carried on respecting a host of subjects during these years of transition. Much of this, it is true, consisted in rediscovering things known to all the world, which I had previously disbelieved, or disregarded. But the rediscovery was to me a discovery, giving me plenary possession of the truths, not as traditional platitudes, but fresh from their source: and it seldom failed to place them in some new light, by which they were reconciled with, and seemed to confirm while they modified, the truths less generally known which lay in my early opinions, and in no essential part of which I at any time wavered. All my new thinking only laid the foundation of these more deeply and strongly, while it often removed misapprehension and confusion of ideas which had perverted their effect. For example, during the later returns of my dejection, the doctrine of what is called Philosophical Necessity* weighed on my existence like an incubus. I felt as if I was scientifically proved to be the helpless slave of antecedent circumstances; as if my character and that of all others had been formed for us by agencies beyond our control, and was wholly out of our own power. I often said to myself, what a relief it would be if I could disbelieve the doctrine of the formation of character by circumstances; and remembering the wish of Fox respecting the doctrine of resistance to governments, that it might never be forgotten by kings, nor remembered by subjects, I said that it would be a blessing if the doctrine of necessity could be believed by all *quoad* [as regards] the characters of others, and disbelieved in regard to their own. I pondered painfully on the subject, till gradually I saw light through it. I perceived, that the word Necessity, as a name for the doctrine of Cause and Effect applied to human action, carried with it a misleading association; and that this association was the operative force in the depressing and paralysing influence which I had experienced: I saw that though our character is formed by circumstances, our own desires can do much to shape those circumstances; and that what is really inspiriting and ennobling in the doctrine of free-will, is the conviction that we have real power over the formation of our own character; that our will, by influencing some of our circumstances, can modify our future habits or capabilities of willing. All this was entirely consistent with the doctrine of circumstances, or rather, was that doctrine itself, properly understood. From that time I drew in my own mind, a clear distinction between the doctrine of circumstances, and Fatalism; discarding altogether the misleading word Necessity. The theory, which I now for the first time rightly apprehended, ceased altogether to be discouraging, and besides the relief to my spirits, I no longer suffered under the burthen, so heavy to one who aims at being a reformer in opinions, of thinking one doctrine true, and the contrary doctrine morally beneficial.

---

*Determinism, the doctrine that everything we are and do has been determined by prior causes and that free will, and thus any form of freedom, is mere illusion.

Unlearning

Gloria Steinem

Steinem, the founder of Ms. *magazine, has long spoken out against the oppression of women. She proposes that women must unlearn the lessons taught to them from birth. They must realize that they have the potential to achieve far more than they ever thought they could. Do you think that we can unlearn who society tells us we are? How have you unlearned what society taught you to be?*

"I have been a member of the Columbia University community for thirty-five years, and I can only consider myself to be speaking as what Lionel Trilling called an opposing self, opposed to culture, in this case, the culture of the university."

Carolyn Heilbrun

"To finally recognize our own invisibility is to finally be on the path toward visibility."

Mitsuye Yamada

"I was a modest, good-humored boy; it is Oxford that has made me insufferable."

Max Beerbohm

Once we are old enough to have had an education, the first step toward self-esteem for most of us is not to learn but to *un*learn. We need to demystify the forces that have told us what we *should be* before we can value what we *are*.

That's difficult enough when we have been misvalued by an upbringing or social bias that is clearly wrong. But what happens when this wrongness is taught as objective truth? When the most respected sources of information make some groups invisible and others invincible? When we are encouraged to choose between "bettering" ourselves and becoming ourselves?

I never asked any of these questions during my various years of schooling. To get an education was an end in itself; its content was beyond questioning. Not until decades after I had left all formal education behind did its impact on me—and its purpose in general—seem open to challenge. Perhaps "real wisdom," as author Joan Erikson said, only comes from "life experience, well-digested." I know that my own questioning was fueled by two chance experiences that occurred within weeks of each other several years ago.

First, I went back to Toledo, where my mother and I had lived when I was in junior high and high school. The occasion for this trip was a women's conference at the university on the "good" side of town, but I couldn't resist wandering around the streets of East Toledo and our old neighborhood the night before. There were the same small houses, the same bars and churches in equal numbers, the same Polish and Hungarian social clubs. A few more black families had moved in, and Puerto Rican workers were bringing a new layer of ethnicity, but what looked like the same tricycles were rusting in the front yards, the same wash was flapping on the lines, and the same big TV antenna dwarfed each roof, as though life

From *Revolution from Within* by Gloria Steinem. Boston: Little, Brown & Co., 1992, pp. 109–117. Copyright © 1992 by Gloria Steinem.

here could only be bearable if lived elsewhere in the imagination.

Certainly, my teenage self had been totally consumed with escaping. If I had written any book then, it would have been titled *Getting Out*—and most of my friends felt the same. Our dreams of escape from the neighborhood kept us from focusing on our probable fates as lifetime factory workers who rebelled only on weekends, or homemakers who played pinochle, went bowling, and sometimes got a beating on Saturday nights. Our imaginations rarely went beyond the two escape routes we knew: sports (if we were boys) and show business (if we were girls). In fact, we could point to two local celebrities to show that we also had a chance: a guy who had gone to a university for a year or two on a football scholarship before coming back to the neighborhood as a factory foreman, and singer Teresa Brewer, who had won the Ted Mack Amateur Hour while still in high school and never come back. Mostly, though, we were responding to the media. Sports and show business were the only places we saw people like us who seemed to be enjoying life and not worrying about next week's paycheck.

I always felt both odd and lucky because I had the possibility of an additional way out: getting a college education. It was a path first to an interesting job and ultimately to a better class of husband (or if the husband should lose his job or die, it was "something to fall back on," as my mother always said)—and that was enough. Getting out of our drab, hardworking neighborhood and into the beautiful, carefree suburbs that we saw on television was all we had in mind.

I had this encouragement because my mother was the only parent in our group who had graduated from college. She had even spent a little time in graduate school. Of course, she ended up much poorer than the factory workers in this neighborhood where she grew up, and living in her family house, which was by then a ramshackle structure teetering over a major highway; a place so depressing that it was hard to rent out the first floor so the two of us could survive on the second. Yet this daily reality never changed my dream of how "college people" lived, and it certainly never interfered with my mother's faith in the redemptive powers of an education. Just as her own mother had instilled this faith in her, she handed it down to me. When our house was condemned and the land beneath it sold to the church next door, my mother used this windfall to pay my tuition at a "good" college, and I left what I thought were my less fortunate friends behind.

The day after this visit to my old neighborhood, however, I saw some of my East Toledo contemporaries at the women's conference where I was speaking. A few faces I remembered, but as we talked, we realized many of us had lived the same lives and gone to the same schools, whether or not we knew each other then. But they entered adulthood early by marrying right after graduation, or before if they "had to" (our neighborhood counted the months from wedding to birth), raising their families, and perhaps helping to support them with a part-time "pink-collar" job for the phone or gas company. But by the feminist 1970s, when new opportunities for women were being publicized on TV talk shows, their children were self-sufficient, and they were ready to seize on these new possibilities with their whole hearts.

At a time when the housewives of the "feminine mystique" were still getting out of the suburbs and into the labor force—and when I and other white-collar women workers were still trying to "deserve" the unequally paid professional jobs we thought we were so lucky to get—these women had begun to demand equal treatment with men, and by the time I encountered them again, they were getting some of those opportunities. The few women who had been able to get comparatively well paid jobs in local factories could see that the guys standing next to them on the assembly line were doing exactly the same tasks for fatter pay envelopes, so they had brought one of the earliest sex-discrimination suits. By organizing with more traditional family-planning groups, some of the others had just won a citywide referendum against an anti-abortion measure disguised as a "maternal health ordinance," and defeated it two-to-one in their mostly Catholic, blue-collar precincts. Still others were starting their own small businesses, planning the campaign of a woman mayor (who was to win and become a first in Toledo history), and organizing battered-women's programs instead of assuming that Saturday night beatings were inevitable. A few were running for the school board and other local political offices, and almost all had gone back to school for a degree or professional training as what the University of Toledo referred to as "nontraditional students," and what the women themselves called "retreads."

But what most separated all these women from the girls I remembered and their own younger selves was their spirit. They were full of rebellion, humor, energy, and a certain earthy wisdom that seemed to say, "I'm myself now—take it or leave it." One of them summed up her reasons for going back to school after forty by posting this motto on her refrigerator door: "Free your mind—so your ass can follow."

Of course, there were also many casualties. They told me about one of my best friends in high school whose children had been born so close together that her small body had run out of calcium. She lost her teeth and her hopes, and settled into the life of an old woman. Another classmate had been so shamed by her family for being "an old maid" at twenty-five that she married a man who was younger, concealed his violence toward her out of gratitude that he had married her at all, and finally became so depressed that she was institutionalized. Yet another had spent so much of her life inside one of the tiny row houses in our neighborhood that she became terrified to leave it. A doctor prescribed tranquilizers, not freedom.

But by the time we finished the conference and went to a local television station to do an interview about it, I was feeling great pride in the women who had stayed in this neighborhood that I once lived, dreamed, and breathed of escaping. They were self-confident, productive, bawdy, and very much themselves. When an angry male viewer phoned after the show to denounce the conference as "antifamily," and me in particular as "a slut from East Toledo," I suddenly remembered how devastating those words would have been to my teenage self. But all these years later, they caused less pain than laughter: he didn't have the power to define me or any of us anymore. We were defining ourselves.

As we toasted each other as "the sluts from East Toledo" with coffee and beer after the interview, I thought: Not a bad thing to be. Maybe I'll put it on my tombstone.

But the full meaning of what my classmates had achieved wasn't clear until I saw the difference between them and the college graduates I had been so eager to join. Because my twenty-fifth college reunion came only a few weeks later, the contrast was inescapable.

On the New England campus of Smith College, I realized again the great distance between this idyllic scene and my old neighborhood. Green lawns, landmark buildings, new graduates carrying long-stemmed roses, and smiling alumnae in summer dresses—all seemed evidence of assurance and good fortune. But underneath, there were doubts and tensions. And underneath was where we had been trained to keep them.

For instance: A classmate who had tried unsuccessfully to create panel discussions on aging, violence against women, equal rights legislation, and the like concluded that topics were chosen for safety and obscurity. (My personal favorite was "Tropism or Refraction?") As she said, "What do you expect? We were taught to revere Aristotle, who said females were mutilated men and could tarnish a mirror."

For instance: At our class dinner, the first woman president of Smith College addressed the problems of women combining career and family—yet never suggested that men might play an equal part at home. Indeed, she implied that she had been able to have a successful career because she *didn't* have children.

For instance: Of those who responded to our class reunion questionnaire, 98 percent had supported legal abortion. Having grown up in the era of *illegal* abortion, many of us had experienced this danger firsthand. Nonetheless, when a group of us showed up for the Alumnae Day Parade with pro-choice signs, we were told we couldn't march with our class. Why? Because there might be *even one person* who disagreed. Instead, our class carried committee-approved signs that made jokes about our age, eyesight, and waistlines, as if self-denigration and silliness were things with which no one could disagree.

For instance: Even among the new graduates, the most rebellious were still debating whether to display a banner protesting U.S. policy in Central America, with the same ladylike worry that a few people might disagree. The idea that it was okay to disagree, that people would carry whatever signs they wanted to, hadn't been part of the either/or discussion. Moreover, issues of special importance to women were clearly less serious, even to the rebellious, than foreign policy issues seen as important to men.

I'd forgotten the seductive power of niceness and unanimity. Our courses had not been dedicated to "freeing our asses." As a result, we had a hard time assuming our own centrality. Would graduates of a black college forbid civil rights signs at a reunion because *one person* might disagree? Would Jewish graduates take foreign policy toward Latin America more seriously than policy toward Jews?

It seemed that for women of all races and classes, education had separated *what we studied* from *how we lived.* It had broken the link between mind and emotion, between what we learned intellectually and what we experienced as women.

Of course, there were Smith women who were spirited, self-confident, and active in everything from politics and business to education and the arts. Individually, many were doing brave and remarkable things. But as a group, they seemed less strong, funny, joyful, and free than their East Toledo sisters; more apologetic and self-blaming; more distant from themselves. If divorced, they were more likely to have lost their identity along with their husbands. If married, they seemed more identified by their husbands' careers. The difference was not only in what they said, but in how they said it. "I want . . . I know . . . I hope . . ." was how East Toledo women started their sentences. "They say . . . It may be true that . . . It's probably only me, but . . ." was how Smith women were more likely to preface their thoughts.

When I mentioned this contrast in writing about the reunion at the time, I assumed the difference was economics. Since more East Toledo women had to work to help support their families, they also were forced to discover their strength and independence.

Since Smith women were more likely to have husbands who could afford a dependent wife, on the other hand, many had been deprived of the self-confidence that comes from knowing you can support yourself. And, of course, neither group had been encouraged to value and give an economic worth to their work of maintaining a home and socializing the next generation. That was a patriarchal rule that crossed class boundaries.

Now, I still believe class often works in reverse for women. There's a bigger power difference between a tycoon and his wife (or wives) than between an average husband and wife, and even a male professional is likely to have a job that's the main chance, unlike a blue-collar man, and thus to have a wife whose work is secondary (a "jobette," as one of them described it ironically). But economics doesn't explain the whole difference between my two very different groups of contemporaries. After all, some of those Smith women had come from poor and working-class backgrounds, others were single and supporting themselves, and a few had high-powered careers. By that twenty-fifth reunion, about 40 percent of respondents to the questionnaire were doing paid, full-time work.

No, I think the deeper explanation lies in the kind of education we college women had absorbed. Its content—and our lack of the reality checks those East Toledo women had by virtue of taking courses later in life for pragmatic reasons—had made us more vulnerable to lethal underminings like these:

- Being taught to revere "the classics" of Western civilization, most of which patronize, distort, denigrate, or express hatred for the female half of the human race.
- Learning systems of philosophy that depend on gender dualisms at best and female inferiority at worst; surveying a tradition of art in which women are rarely artists and often objects; studying biology that focuses more on human differences than on human possibilities; absorbing ethical standards that assume masculine values; and learning theologies that assume all-male deities.
- Reading history books in which almost all power and agency is assigned to men and being graded for memorizing male accomplishments—with the deep message that we can learn what others do, but never do it ourselves.
- Seeing fewer and fewer females in authority as we climb the educational ladder: fewer as faculty, fewer still as deans and presidents, and fewest of all in the fields of science, engineering, politics, business, foreign policy, or other specialties valued by the world at large. And if we are of the "wrong" race or class or sexuality, perhaps seeing no one we identify with at all.
- Being told we are "subjective" if we cite our own experience; that the "objective" truth always lies within the group—and the group is never us.
- Finally, being isolated from other women—perhaps resented by them—because we are educated like men.

Of course, men are also separated from their less well educated brothers by elitist educations—which is part of the same problem—but men are not an insurgent group. For women, the tragedy is closer to that of Latin, African-American, or just plain poor students who get separated from their communities and families. Women go to college and learn about economics in which the work that our mothers do at home (which is worth about 25 percent of the U.S. gross national product) isn't counted at all, and human rights that include protections against group hatred based on everything except sex. The fact that we may love college and feel grateful for being there—as I certainly did—only means we internalize these messages more eagerly.

Fortunately, all of us can unlearn. Thanks to the good luck of living in an era when women are questioning lifetimes and even millennia of lessons, I have faith in that possibility. I've also noticed that self-taught people who didn't learn the system in the first place are often our best teachers. Without time-consuming detours through this or that theory, terms-of-art that only the initiated can understand, and intellectual jousting with the ghosts of ancient authorities, they go to the heart of what they need to know.

In the 1970s, for instance, at the first feminist conference ever held by, for, and about women in Appalachia, I met women from West Virginia, Kentucky, and Tennessee who came out of the hills and hollows in buses and pickup trucks, in shared cars or on foot, to gather on the campus of Marshall University. In the course of discussions, a craft fair, and workshops, I noticed that many of these women had a head start on things that it had taken me years to figure out:

- Never having been taught to separate "art" (what mostly men do) from "crafts" (what mostly women and natives do), they just assumed that their quilts and wood carvings were art. Which they were.
- Never having learned from Marx and other economists that women were the same class as their husbands, they assumed that women shared a culture and situations that were a little different from those of their respective men. And we did.
- Never having defined civilization as man's conquering of nature—and living close to nature themselves—they opposed the rape of the land and were ecologists. From experience.
- Not being Freudian, they envied not men's anatomies, but their male-only earning power in the coal mines. They set out to integrate those mining jobs. And a few years later, they did.
- Never having heard of a "feminist issue," they chose their own: contraception and driver's licenses—control of their bodies and the family pickup truck. Both meant freedom.
- Not being prosperous enough to have churches and ministers to intervene between them and the Bible, they read the verses that supported them and ignored the rest.
- Never having learned to separate mind and body, thought and emotion, or intellect from the senses, they trusted their own experience.

Perhaps it's an exaggeration, but in retrospect, I felt I had learned more that was *of use* in that one long weekend than in a year of college. More about nature, art, justice, power, and fairness. Certainly more about my own strength.

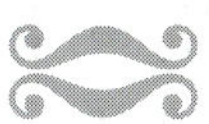

The Value of Philosophy

Bertrand Russell

Philosophy asks us to question what we believe, and questioning makes us uncertain. But, according to Russell, this questioning and this uncertainty may be what is most valuable about philosophy. It is through questioning that we can avoid the complacencies and common prejudices of the "practical" man. It may be through the questioning activity of a philosophic life that the self is nourished, is made healthy, and strives for fulfillment if not greatness. Ask yourself why it may be necessary for each of us to provide food for our souls!

Having now come to the end of our brief and very incomplete review of the problems of philosophy, it will be well to consider, in conclusion, what is the value of philosophy and why it ought to be studied. It is the more necessary to consider this question, in view of the fact that many men, under the influence of science or of practical affairs, are inclined to doubt whether philosophy is anything better than innocent but useless trifling, hair-splitting distinctions, and controversies on matters concerning which knowledge is impossible.

This view of philosophy appears to result, partly from a wrong conception of the ends of life, partly from a wrong conception of the kind of goods which philosophy strives to achieve. Physical science, through the medium of inventions, is useful to innumerable people who are wholly ignorant of it; thus the study of physical science is to be recommended, not only, or primarily, because of the effect on the student, but rather because of the effect on mankind in general. Thus utility does not belong to philosophy. If the study of philosophy has any value at all for others than students of philosophy, it must be only indirectly, through its effects upon the lives of those who study it. It is in these effects, therefore, if anywhere, that the value of philosophy must be primarily sought.

But further, if we are not to fail in our endeavour to determine the value of philosophy, we must first free our minds from the prejudices of what are wrongly called "practical" men. The "practical" man, as this word is often used, is one who recognizes only material needs, who realizes that men must have food for the body, but is oblivious of the necessity of providing food for the mind. If all men were well off, if poverty and disease had been reduced to their lowest possible point, there would still remain much to be done to produce a valuable society; and even in the existing world the goods of the mind are at least as important as the goods of the body. It is exclusively among the goods of the mind that the value of philosophy is to be found; and only those who are not indifferent to these goods can be persuaded that the study of philosophy is not a waste of time.

Philosophy, like all other studies, aims primarily at knowledge. The knowledge it aims at is the kind of knowledge which gives unity and system to the body of the sciences, and the kind which results from a critical examination of the grounds of our convictions, prejudices, and beliefs. But it cannot be maintained that philosophy has had any

From *The Problems of Philosophy* by Bertrand Russell. Oxford: Oxford University Press, 1912.

very great measure of success in its attempts to provide definite answers to its questions. If you ask a mathematician, a mineralogist, a historian, or any other man of learning, what definite body of truths has been ascertained by his science, his answer will last as long as you are willing to listen. But if you put the same question to a philosopher, he will, if he is candid, have to confess that his study has not achieved positive results such as have been achieved by other sciences. It is true that this is partly accounted for by the fact that, as soon as definite knowledge concerning any subject becomes possible, this subject ceases to be called philosophy, and becomes a separate science. The whole study of the heavens, which now belongs to astronomy, was once included in philosophy; Newton's great work was called "the mathematical principles of natural philosophy." Similarly, the study of the human mind, which was a part of philosophy, has now been separated from philosophy and has become the science of psychology. Thus, to a great extent, the uncertainty of philosophy is more apparent than real: those questions which are already capable of definite answers are placed in the sciences, while those only to which, at present, no definite answer can be given, remain to form the residue which is called philosophy.

This is, however, only a part of the truth concerning the uncertainty of philosophy. There are many questions—and among them those that are of the profoundest interest to our spiritual life—which, so far as we can see, must remain insoluble to the human intellect unless its powers become of quite a different order from what they are now. Has the universe any unity of plan or purpose, or is it a fortuitous concourse of atoms? Is consciousness a permanent part of the universe, giving hope of indefinite growth in wisdom, or is it a transitory accident on a small planet on which life must ultimately become impossible? Are good and evil of importance to the universe or only to man? Such questions are asked by philosophy, and variously answered by various philosophers. But it would seem that, whether answers be otherwise discoverable or not, the answers suggested by philosophy are none of them demonstrably true. Yet, however slight may be the hope of discovering an answer, it is part of the business of philosophy to continue the consideration of such questions, to make us aware of their importance, to examine all the approaches to them, and to keep alive that speculative interest in the universe which is apt to be killed by confining ourselves to definitely ascertainable knowledge.

Many philosophers, it is true, have held that philosophy could establish the truth of certain answers to such fundamental questions. They have supposed that what is of most importance in religious beliefs could be proved by strict demonstration to be true. In order to judge of such attempts, it is necessary to take a survey of human knowledge, and to form an opinion as to its methods and its limitations. On such a subject it would be unwise to pronounce dogmatically; but if the investigations of our previous chapters have not led us astray, we shall be compelled to renounce the hope of finding philosophical proofs of religious beliefs. We cannot, therefore, include as part of the value of philosophy any definite set of answers to such questions. Hence, once more, the value of philosophy must not depend upon any supposed body of definitely ascertainable knowledge to be acquired by those who study it.

The value of philosophy is, in fact, to be sought largely in its very uncertainty. The man who has no tincture of philosophy goes through life imprisoned in the prejudices derived from common sense, from the habitual beliefs of his age or his nation, and from convictions which have grown up in his mind without the co-operation or consent of his deliberate reason. To such a man the world tends to become definite, finite, obvious; common objects rouse no questions, and unfamiliar possibilities are contemptuously rejected. As soon as we begin to philosophize, on the contrary, we find, as we saw in our opening chapters, that even the most everyday things lead to problems to which only very incomplete answers can be given. Philosophy, though unable to tell us with certainty what is the true answer to the doubts which it raises, is able to suggest many possibilities which enlarge our thoughts and free them from the tyranny of custom. Thus, while diminishing our feeling of certainty as to what things are, it greatly increases our knowledge as to what they may be; it removes the somewhat arrogant dogmatism of those who have never travelled into the region of liberating doubt, and it keeps alive our sense of wonder by showing familiar things in an unfamiliar aspect.

Apart from its utility in showing unsuspected possibilities, philosophy has a value—perhaps its chief value—through the greatness of the objects which it contemplates, and the freedom from narrow and personal aims resulting from this contemplation. The life of the instinctive man is shut up within the circle of his private interests: family and friends may be included, but the outer world is not regarded except as it may help or hinder what comes within the circle of instinctive wishes. In such a life there is something feverish and confined, in comparison with which the philosophic life is calm and free. The private world of instinctive interests is a small one, set in the midst of a great and powerful world which must, sooner or later, lay our private world in ruins. Unless we can so enlarge our interests as to include the whole outer world, we remain like a garrison in a beleagured fortress, knowing that the enemy prevents escape and that ultimate surrender is inevitable. In such a life there is no peace, but a constant strife between the insistence of desire and the powerlessness of will. In one way or another, if our life is to be great and free, we must escape this prison and this strife.

One way of escape is by philosophic contemplation. Philosophic contemplation does not, in its widest survey, divide the universe into two hostile camps—friends and foes, helpful and hostile, good and bad—it views the whole impartially. Philosophic contemplation, when it is unalloyed, does not aim at proving that the rest of the universe is akin to man. All acquisition of knowledge is an enlargement of the Self, but this enlargement is best attained when it is not directly sought. It is obtained when the desire for knowledge is alone operative, by a study which does not wish in advance that its objects should have this or that character, but adapts the Self to the characters which it finds in its objects. This enlargement of Self is not obtained when, taking the Self as it is, we try to show that the world is so similar to this Self that knowledge of it is possible without any admission of what seems alien. The desire to prove this is a form of self-assertion and, like all self-assertion, it is an obstacle to the growth of Self which it desires, and of which the Self knows that it is capable. Self-assertion, in philosophic speculation as elsewhere, views the world as a means to its own ends; thus it makes the world of less account than Self, and the Self sets bounds to the greatness of its goods. In contemplation, on the contrary, we start from the not-Self, and through its greatness the boundaries of Self are enlarged; through the infinity of the universe the mind which contemplates it achieves some share in infinity.

For this reason greatness of soul is not fostered by those philosophies which assimilate the universe to Man. Knowledge is a form of union of Self and not-Self; like all union, it is impaired by dominion, and therefore by any attempt to force the universe into conformity with what we find in ourselves. There is a widespread philosophical tendency towards the view which tells us that Man is the measure of all things, that truth is man-made, that space and time and the world of universals are properties of the mind, and that, if there be anything not created by the mind, it is unknowable and of no account for us. This view, if our previous discussions were correct, is untrue; but in addition to being untrue, it has the effect of robbing philosophic contemplation of all that gives it value, since it fetters contemplation to Self. What it calls knowledge is not a union with the not-Self, but a set of prejudices, habits, and desires, making an impenetrable veil between us and the world beyond. The man who finds pleasure in such a theory of knowledge is like the man who never leaves the domestic circle for fear his word might not be law.

The true philosophic contemplation, on the contrary, finds its satisfaction in every enlargement of the not-Self, in everything that magnifies the objects contemplated, and thereby the subject contemplating. Everything, in contemplation, that is personal or private, everything that depends upon habit, self-interest, or desire, distorts the object, and hence impairs the union which the intellect seeks. By thus making a barrier between subject and object, such personal and private things become a prison to the intellect. The free intellect will see as God might see, without a *here* and *now,* without hopes and fears, without the trammels of customary beliefs and traditional prejudices, calmly, dispassionately, in the sole and exclusive desire of knowledge—knowledge as impersonal, as purely contemplative, as it is possible for man to attain. Hence also the free intellect will value more the abstract and universal knowledge into which the accidents of private history do not enter, than the knowledge brought by the senses, and dependent, as such knowledge must be, upon an exclusive and personal point of view and a body whose sense-organs distort as much as they reveal.

The mind which has become accustomed to the freedom and impartiality of philosophic contemplation will preserve something of the same freedom and impartiality in the world of action and emotion. It will view its purposes and desires as parts of the whole, with the absence of insistence that results from seeing them as infinitesimal fragments in a world of which all the rest is unaffected by any one man's deeds. The impartiality which, in contemplation, is the unalloyed desire for truth, is the very same quality of mind which, in action, is justice, and in emotion is that universal love which can be given to all, and not only to those who are judged useful or admirable. Thus contemplation enlarges not only the objects of our thoughts, but also the objects of our actions and our affections: it makes us citizens of the universe, not only of one walled city at war with the rest. In this citizenship of the universe consists man's true freedom, and his liberation from the thraldom of narrow hopes and fears.

Thus, to sum up our discussion of the value of philosophy; Philosophy is to be studied, not for the sake of any definite answers to its questions since no definite answers can, as a rule, be known to be true, but rather for the sake of the questions themselves; because these questions enlarge our conception of what is possible, enrich our intellectual imagination and diminish the dogmatic assurance which closes the mind against speculation; but above all because, through the greatness of the universe which philosophy contemplates, the mind also is rendered great, and becomes capable of that union with the universe which constitutes its highest good.

Discussion Questions

1. What is the lesson we are to learn from Camus's "Myth of Sisyphus"? What do we learn about character, knowledge, wisdom, meaningfulness, and life from Sisyphus?
2. Can Richard Wright's struggle to gain freedom and meaning in his life be compared to the struggle of Sisyphus? In what way(s) are Sisyphus and Wright alike? In what way(s) are they different?
3. Describe Plato's "Allegory of the Cave." What might the allegory tell us about what we know, how we know, and the human condition?
4. Kierkegaard believes that an individual must personally commit himself or herself to living a valuable life. What might such a commitment entail? Why do you think he believes it may be egotistical to identify uncritically a "self" with others?
5. What types of activities help us to grow as persons? Can formal education alone bring us to our goal, or must we be open to other experiences as well? What does Mill teach us about the value of education and the value of human relationships in our own self-development?
6. According to Steinem, what specific things must women unlearn? Are there specific things that men should unlearn? What kind of things might Richard Wright have unlearned?
7. Why is it important to study philosophy, according to Russell? What does it mean to live a philosophic life? How can philosophical thinking help us to become more aware of who we are and, thus, help us to achieve our goals?
8. Discuss the importance of attitude and reflection in each of the essays in this chapter.

chapter 2

Discovering the Nature of Our Human Self

From the earliest times, humans have pictured themselves with a dual nature, a composite of an animal body and an immaterial soul. Often it was thought that the soul gave humans a superiority over animals and nature, for the soul was cast in the image of the divine. This certainly is the view we find in the Judeo-Christian tradition, which depicts humankind caught between the divine and the material worlds. The soul as self has within it a spark of divinity, yet it remains subject to material existence and the wants and desires of the body.

Other traditions have divided the soul into different aspects. In the Western tradition, we find that both Plato and Aristotle believed in a tripartite soul. The Akan tradition in Ghana, in contrast, gives us a dualistic picture of the soul. One element of the soul gives life, and another, more properly called the spirit, gives us an individual personality. These elements of humankind are completely interactive, so much so that it is sometimes necessary to cure one's spirit or one's soul before we can help remove an illness or evil from the body.

Less ancient philosophies give us even another picture of what it means to be human. In casting universal doubt on the activity of our senses, René Descartes leads us to a discovery of an essential thinking self entirely distinct from a physical body. For Descartes, the true self as purely rational, immaterial substance can survive outside of and distinct from the body. For Descartes, the body is simply a vehicle for the soul, which is who we are. Souls are in time but not in space; souls move freely and survive the death of the bodies that they

René Descartes

inhabit. Bodies occupy space and time, move by the laws of mechanics, and have a limited mortal existence. Souls can move bodies, and movements in bodies can bring activity in the soul, but they remain distinctly and irreducibly separate from each other.

What is the nature of the self as Descartes imagined it? Of what could such a self be composed? Some have been confused by and have objected to Descartes's description of who and what we are. In his own day, Princess Elisabeth of Bohemia queried Descartes on how the soul, which is immaterial, can move or bring about changes in a physical body. Just think about it for a moment; Descartes provided the history of thought with a rational justification of duality—the separation of mind and matter, soul and body. Some have claimed that such a duality is unfortunate. (Never mind how one's physical and mental selves interact with each other!) In his objection to Cartesian dualism and its puzzle of interaction, twentieth-century philosopher Gilbert Ryle went somewhat further than his predecessors. Claiming that Descartes leaves us a self that is portrayed as a ghostlike substance mysteriously driving the machine we call the body and is in all practicality inaccessible to any other self, Ryle postulates that if Descartes were right, then each of us may be condemned to an isolated and lonely life as far as our true self is concerned. But is it possible that Descartes was mistaken in his thinking, that he made a special kind of mistake—a *category-mistake*? What could have led Descartes and his successors to make such an error? Further, having discovered the error, how are we to view those things that Descartes called properties of the mind or soul, the very things that make up the *self*? Pay close attention to Ryle's answer and ask yourself (no irony intended) quite sincerely: In what way are we defined by and identified with our behavior?

Perhaps the self is neither an unobservable spirit nor observable public behavior. Another objection to the Cartesian separation of body and soul comes from contemporary feminist philosophy. Eve Browning Cole believes Descartes's position may be a fundamental cause of the historical oppression of women. History has associated women with their bodies and with their emotions, and Descartes associates personhood or selfhood with reason and a substance completely distinct from bodies. Does this not cause women to be treated as less than full persons? Can adherence to such a belief cause women to become alienated from themselves, to not appreciate their own value to themselves and others? Cole proposes, contrary to Descartes, that the *true self* is an *embodied self* and a *socially interactive self*. We find ourselves through our bodies and the interaction of our embodied self with other such embodiments.

Soul or body, which is it? Can there be another alternative? What if the self is not permanent or enduring? Perhaps we should consider the possibility that we have no established or permanent identity as a self, but rather that we undergo constant change as selves. In the Buddhist scripture, pay close attention to the conversation between Nagasena and King Milinda, especially to Nagasena's answers to the king's questions about body, soul, and character. Is the self like a chariot, not identifiable with either its constituent parts or anything outside of or beyond those parts? Consider the possibility that *self* is merely a concept that arises because of a succession and conjunction of sense impressions. Beyond this, it is *no-thing*! To make such a claim is not to say that we do not exist; rather, it claims that a *self* does not exist as an independent and distinctive substance. Perhaps this may cause you to reflect on at least one consequence of such a belief: If there is no ego, can there be a place for egoism in the world?

The view that the subject cannot exist without the object is also found in the Asian philosophical tradition. As Chuang Tzu explains, subject and object are simply alternates of each other. He questions if, and how, they can be distinguished, especially when we always experience them in relation to each other. As shown in many of the essays in Chapter 1, what matters is that we focus on the present in both discovering and forming our identity, and that present always entails activities that are grounded in "universal" experience. That is, all things arise out of the universe and thus are linked in an inextricable way.

Chuang Tzu admits that this poses difficulty for learning and, more particularly, for speech. He asks, "If then all things are One, what room is there for Speech?" While he does not disregard the importance of it, he does emphasize the importance of being conscious of our relationship to all other things. Without such awareness, we will fall into the trap of divisive argumentation that will undermine our attempt to learn, know, and live together.

The final reading in this chapter exposes you as reader to Ludwig Wittgenstein's analysis of the meaning of the word *I*. Wittgenstein examines how words function in language, and he asks if we can answer questions about what a *self* is without understanding what is meant by *self* or *person*. Meanings, we are told, are established by the way(s) in which we use words. Language is a shared activity of a culture or a people, and therefore, it may be that the meanings of words, including such words as *I*, have meaning only within this activity. *I*, when spoken, points to a speaker, but beyond this there may exist in some instances a certain vagueness or ambiguity in its meaning. What that meaning may be, whether or not *I* gives rise to the recognition of a particular personality, depends on how it is used.

If Wittgenstein leads us to consider how such words as *person* and *I* are used, should we not consider how *use* is connected to context? Can the identity of a self be established or understood apart from a particular context? Once again, we ask our readers to continually examine, if not question, the cultural practices or contexts in which the quandaries of self-identity arise.

Biblical Conceptions of Human Nature

From the King James Version of the Bible

Although humans have a physical, animal body, both the Old and New Testaments of the Bible claim that human nature is superior to animal nature. Humans are made in the "image" of God. What does this mean? Perhaps it means that humans possess a potential wisdom, an understanding of their own mortality and their limitations in power and goodness. Such conscious awareness belongs to the soul, and perhaps it is the soul that is the "image" of God.

GENESIS 1:26–8

26 And God said, Let us make man in our image, after our likeness: and let them have dominion over the fish of the sea, and over the fowl of the air, and over the cattle, and over all the earth, and over every creeping thing that creepeth upon the earth.

27 So God created man in his *own* image, in the image of God created he him; male and female created he them.

28 And God blessed them, and God said unto them, Be fruitful, and multiply, and replenish the earth, and subdue it: and have dominion over the fish of the sea, and over the fowl of the air, and over every living thing that moveth upon the earth.

PSALM 8

1 O LORD our Lord, how excellent *is* thy name in all the earth! who hast set thy glory above the heavens.

2 Out of the mouth of babes and sucklings hast thou ordained strength because of thine enemies, that thou mightest still the enemy and the avenger.

From the King James Version of the Bible.

3 When I consider thy heavens, the work of thy fingers, the moon and the stars, which thou hast ordained;

4 What is man, that thou art mindful of him? and the son of man, that thou visitest him?

5 For thou hast made him a little lower than the angels, and hast crowned him with glory and honour.

6 Thou madest him to have dominion over the works of thy hands; thou hast put all *things* under his feet:

7 All sheep and oxen, yea, and the beasts of the field;

8 The fowl of the air, and the fish of the sea, and *whatsoever* passeth through the paths of the seas.

9 O LORD our Lord, how excellent *is* thy name in all the earth!

I CORINTHIANS 15:35–44

35 But some *man* will say, How are the dead raised up? and with what body do they come?

36 *Thou* fool, that which thou sowest is not quickened, except it die:

37 And that which thou sowest, thou sowest not that body that shall be, but bare grain, it may chance of wheat, or of some other *grain*:

38 But God giveth it a body as it hath pleased him, and to every seed his own body.

39 All flesh *is* not the same flesh: but *there is* one *kind of* flesh of men, another flesh of beasts, another of fishes, *and* another of birds.

40 *There are* also celestial bodies, and bodies terrestrial: but the glory of the celestial *is* one, and the *glory* of the terrestrial *is* another.

41 *There is* one glory of the sun, and another glory of the moon, and another glory of the stars: for *one* star differeth from *another* star in glory.

42 So also *is* the resurrection of the dead. It is sown in corruption; it is raised in incorruption:

43 It is sown in dishonour; it is raised in glory: it is sown in weakness; it is raised in power:

44 It is sown a natural body; it is raised a spiritual body. There is a natural body, and there is a spiritual body.

African Dualism

Kwame Gyekye

As human beings, are we more complex than a simple union of body and soul would indicate? Kwame Gyekye tells us of the Akan belief in the interaction of soul, spirit, and body. Although our soul may define our essence, our spirit is a vital force in our lives. The spirit is the active part of the soul, and it is our spirit that defines our personality according to Akan belief. Further, it may be that some ills of the body can be healed only if we first heal the spirit.

What is a person? Is a person just the bag of flesh and bones that we see with our eyes, or is there something additional to the body that we do not see? A conception[1] of the nature of a human being in Akan philosophy is the subject of this chapter.

From *African Social Thought* by Kwame Gyekye.

OKRA (SOUL)

We are given to understand from a number of often quoted, though mistaken, anthropological accounts that the Akan people consider a human being to be constituted of three elements: *okra, sunsum,* and *honam* (or *nipadua:* body).

The *okra* is said to be that which constitutes the innermost self, the essence, of the individual person. *Okra* is the individual's life, for which reason it is usually referred to as *okrateasefo*, that is, the living soul, a seeming tautology that yet is significant. The expression is intended to emphasize that *okra* is identical with life. The *okra* is the embodiment and transmitter of the individual's destiny (fate: *nkrabea*). It is explained as a spark of the Supreme Being (Onyame) in man. It is thus described as divine and as having an antemundane existence with the Supreme Being. The presence of this divine essence in a human being may have been the basis of the Akan proverb, "All men are the children of God; no one is a child of the earth" (*nnipa nyinaa ye Onyame mma, obiara nnye asase ba*). So conceived, the *okra* can be considered as the equivalent of the concept of the soul in other metaphysical systems. Hence, it is correct to translate *okra* into English as soul.

The conception of the *okra* as constituting the individual's life, the life force, is linked very closely with another concept, *honhom*. *Honhom* means "breath"; it is the noun form of *home*, to breathe. When a person is dead, it is said "His breath is gone" (*ne honhom ko*) or "His soul has withdrawn from his body" (*ne 'kra afi ne ho*). These two sentences, one with *honhom* as subject and the other with *okra*, do, in fact, say the same thing; they express the same thought, the death-of-the-person. The departure of the soul from the body means the death of the person, and so does the cessation of breath. Yet this does not mean that the *honhom* (breath) is identical with the *okra* (soul). It is the *okra* that "causes" the breathing. Thus, the honhom is the tangible manifestation or evidence of the presence of the *okra*. [In some dialects of the Akan language, however, *honhom* has come to be used interchangeably with *sunsum* ("spirit"), so that the phrase *honhom bone* has come to mean the same thing as *sunsum bone*, that is, evil spirit. The identification of the *honhom* with the *sunsum* seems to me to be a recent idea, and may have resulted from the translation of the Bible into the various Akan dialects; *honhom* must have been used to translate the Greek *pneuma* (breath, spirit).] The clarification of the concepts of *okra*, *honhom*, *sunsum* and others bearing on the Akan conception of the nature of a person is the concern of this chapter.

SUNSUM (SPIRIT)

Sunsum is another of the constituent elements of the person. It has usually been rendered in English as "spirit." It has already been observed that *sunsum* is used both generically to refer to all unperceivable, mystical beings and forces in Akan ontology, and specifically to refer to the activating principle in the person. It appears from the anthropological accounts that even when it is used specifically, "spirit" (*sunsum*) is not identical with soul (*okra*), as they do not refer to the same thing. However, the anthropological accounts of the *sunsum* involve some conceptual blunders, as I shall show. As for the mind—when it is not identified with the soul—it may be rendered also by *sunsum*, judging from the functions that are attributed by the Akan thinkers to the latter.

On the surface it might appear that "spirit" is not an appropriate rendition for *sunsum*, but after clearing away misconceptions engendered by some anthropological writings, I shall show that it is appropriate but that it requires clarification. Anthropologists and sociologists have held (1) that the *sunsum* derives from the father,[2] (2) that it is not divine,[3] and (3) that it perishes with the disintegration of the *honam*,[4] that is, the material component of a person. It seems to me, however, that all these characterizations of the *sunsum* are incorrect.[5]

Let us first take up the third characterization, namely, as something that perishes with the body. Now, if the *sunsum* perishes along with the body, a physical object, then it follows that the *sunsum* also is something physical or material. Danquah's philosophical analysis concludes that "*sunsum* is, in fact, the matter or the physical basis of the ultimate ideal of which *okra* (soul) is the form and the spiritual or mental basis."[6] Elsewhere he speaks of an "interaction of the material mechanism (*sunsum*) with the soul," and assimilates the *sunsum* to the "sensible form" of Aristotle's metaphysics of substance and the *okra* to the "intelligible form."[7] One might conclude from these statements that Danquah also conceived the *sunsum* as material, although some of his other statements would seem to contradict this conclusion. The relation between the *honam* (body) and the *sunsum* (supposedly bodily), however, is left unexplained. Thus, philosophical, sociological, and anthropological accounts of the nature of the person give the impression of a tripartite conception of a human being in Akan philosophy:

Okra (soul)	immaterial
Sunsum ("spirit")	material (?)
Honam (body)	material

As we shall see, however, this account or analysis of a person, particularly the characterization of the *sunsum* ("spirit") as something material, is not satisfactory. I must admit, however, that the real nature of the *sunsum* presents perhaps the greatest difficulty in the Akan metaphysics of a person and has been a source of confusion for many. The difficulty, however, is not insoluble.

The explanation given by most Akans of the phenomenon of dreaming . . . indicates, it seems to me, that *sunsum* must be immaterial. In Akan thought, as in Freud's, dreams are not somatic but psychical phenomena. It is held that in a dream it is the person's *sunsum* that is the "actor." As an informant told Rattray decades ago, "When you sleep your *'Kra* (soul) does not leave you, as your *sunsum* may."[8] In sleep the *sunsum* is said to be released from the fetters of the body. As it were, it fashions for itself a new world of forms with the materials of its waking experience. Thus, although one is deeply asleep, yet one may "see" oneself standing atop a mountain or driving a car or fighting with someone or pursuing a desire like sexual intercourse; also, during sleep (that is, in dreams) a person's *sunsum* may talk with other *sunsum*. The actor in any of these "actions" is thought to be the *sunsum*, which thus can leave the body and return to it. The idea of the psychical part of a person leaving the body in sleep appears to be widespread in Africa. The Azande, for instance, maintain "that in sleep the soul is released from the body and can roam about at will and meet other spirits and have other adventures, though they admit something mysterious about its experiences. . . . During sleep a man's soul wanders everywhere."[9]

The idea that some part of the soul leaves the body in sleep is not completely absent from the history of Western thought, even though, as Parrinder says, "the notion of a wandering soul is [are] foreign to the modern European mind."[10] The idea occurs, for instance, in Plato. In the *Republic* Plato refers to "the wild beast in us" that in pursuit of desires and pleasures bestirs itself "in *dreams* when the *gentler part of the soul* slumbers and the control of reason is withdrawn; then the wild beast in us, full-fed with meat and drink, becomes rampant and shakes off sleep to go in quest of what will gratify its own instincts."[11] The context is a discussion of tyranny. But Plato prefaces his discussion with remarks on the *psychological* foundation of the tyrannical man, and says that desire (Greek: *epithumia*) is the basis of his behavior.

It is not surprising that both scholars of Plato and modern psychologists have noted the relevance of the above passage to the analysis of the nature of the human psyche. On this passage the classical scholar James Adam wrote: "The theory is that in dreams the part of the soul concerned is not asleep, but awake and goes out to seek the object of its desire."[12] The classicist Paul Shorey observed that "The Freudians have at least discovered Plato's anticipation of their main thesis."[13] The relevance of the Platonic passage to Freud has been noted also by other scholars of Plato such as Renford Bambrough[14] and Thomas Gould,[15] and by psychologists. Valentine, a psychologist, observed: "The germ of several aspects of the Freudian view of dreams, including the characteristic doctrine of the censor, was to be found in Plato."[16]

It is clear that the passage in Plato indicates a link between dreams and (the gratification of) desires.[17] In Akan psychology the *sunsum* appears not only as unconscious but also as that which pursues and experiences desires. (In Akan dreams are also considered predictive.) But the really interesting part of Plato's thesis for our purposes relates to *the idea of some part of the human soul leaving the body in dreams*. "The wild beast in us" in Plato's passage is not necessarily equivalent to the Akan *sunsum,* but one may say that just as Plato's "wild beast" (which, like the *sunsum,* experiences dreams) is a part of the soul and thus not a physical object, so is *sunsum.*

It might be supposed that if the *sunsum* can engage in activity, such as traveling through space or occupying a physical location—like standing on the top of a mountain—then it can hardly be said not to be a physical object. The problem here is obviously complex. Let us assume, for the moment, that the *sunsum* is a physical object. One question that would immediately arise is: How can a purely physical object leave the person when he or she is asleep? Dreaming is of course different from imagining or thinking. The latter occurs during waking life, whereas the former occurs only during sleep: *wonda a wonso dae,* that is, "Unless you are asleep you do not dream" is a well-known Akan saying. The fact that dreaming occurs only in sleep makes it a unique sort of mental activity and its subject, namely *sunsum,* a different sort of subject. A purely physical object cannot be in two places at the same time: A body lying in bed cannot at the same time be on the top of a mountain. Whatever is on the top of the mountain, then, must be something nonphysical, nonbodily, and yet somehow connected to a physical thing—in this case, the body. This argument constitutes a *reductio ad absurdum* of the view that *sunsum* can be a physical object.

But, then, how can the *sunsum,* qua nonphysical, extrasensory object, travel in physical space and have a physical location? This question must be answered within the broad context of the African belief in the activities of the supernatural (spiritual) beings in the physical world. The spiritual beings are said to be insensible and intangible, but they are also said to make themselves felt in the physical world. They can thus interact with the physical world. But from this it cannot be inferred that they are physical or quasiphysical or have permanent physical properties. It means that a spiritual being can, when it so desires, take on physical properties. That is, even though a spiritual being is nonspatial in essence, it can, by the sheer operation of its power, assume spatial properties. Debrunner speaks of "temporary 'materializations,' i.e., as spirits having taken on the body of a person which afterwards suddenly vanish."[18] Mbiti observed that "Spirits are invisible, but may make themselves visible to human beings."[19]

We should view the "physical" activities of the *sunsum* in dreaming from the standpoint of the activities of the spiritual beings in the physical world. As a microcosm of the world spirit, the *sunsum* can also interact with the external world. So much then for the defense of the psychical, nonphysical nature of *sunsum,* the subject of experiences in dreaming.

As the basis of personality, as the co-performer of some of the functions of the *okra* (soul)—undoubtedly held as a spiritual entity—and as the subject of the psychical activity of dreaming, the *sunsum* must be something spiritual (immaterial). This is the reason for my earlier assertion that "spirit" might not be an inappropriate translation for *sunsum.* On my analysis, then, we have the following picture:

Okra (soul) *Sunsum* ("spirit")	immaterial (spiritual)
Honam (body)	material (physical)

RELATION OF *OKRA* AND *SUNSUM*

Having shown that the *sunsum* is in fact something spiritual (and for this reason I shall henceforth translate *sunsum* as "spirit"), we must examine whether the expressions *sunsum* and *okra* are identical in terms of their referent. In the course of my field research some discussants stated that the *sunsum, okra,* and *honhom* (breath) are identical; they denote the same object; it is one and the same object that goes under three names. I have already shown that although there is a close link between *okra* and *honhom,* the two cannot be identified; likewise the identification of *honhom* and *sunsum* is incorrect. What about the *sunsum* and *okra*? Are they identical?

The relation between the *sunsum* and *okra* is a difficult knot to untie. The anthropologist Rattray, perhaps the most perceptive and analytical researcher into the Ashanti culture, wrote: "It is very difficult sometimes to distinguish between the *'kra* and the next kind of soul, the *sunsum,* and sometimes the words seem synonymous, but I cannot help thinking this is a loose use of the terms."[20] Rattray was, I think, more inclined to believe that the two terms are not identical. Such a supposition, in my view, would be correct, for to say that the two are identical would logically mean that whatever can be asserted of one can or must be asserted of the other. Yet there are some things the Akans say of the *sunsum* which are not said of the *okra,* and vice versa; the attributes or predicates of the two are different. The Akans say:

A (1) "His *'kra* is sad" (*ne 'kra di awerehow*); never, "His *sunsum* is sad."

(2) "His *'kra* is worried or disturbed" (*ne 'kra teetee*).

(3) "His *'kra* has run away" (*ne 'kra adwane*), to denote someone who is scared to death.

(4) "His *'kra* is good" (*ne 'kra ye*), referring to a person who is lucky or fortunate. [The negative of this statement is "His *'kra* is not good." If you used *sunsum* in lieu of *'kra,* and made the statement "His *sunsum* is not good" (*ne sunsum nnye*), the meaning would be quite different; it would mean that his *sunsum* is evil, that is to say, he is an evil spirit, a witch.]

(5) "His *'kra* has withdrawn from his body" (*ne 'kra afi ne ho*).

(6) "But for his *'kra* that followed him, he would have died" (*ne 'kra dii n'akyi, anka owui*).

(7) "His *'kra* is happy" (*ne 'kra aniagye*).

In all such statements the attributions are made to the *okra* (soul), never to the *sunsum.* On the other hand, the Akans say:

B (1) "He has *sunsum*" (*owo sunsum*), an expression they use when they want to refer to someone as dignified and as having a commanding presence. Here they never say, "He has *okra*," soul, for it is believed that it is the nature of the *sunsum* (not the *okra*) that differs from person to person; hence they speak of "gentle *sunsum*," "forceful *sunsum*," "weak or strong *sunsum*," etc.

(2) "His *sunsum* is heavy or weighty" (*ne sunsum ye duru*), that is, he has a strong personality.

(3) "His *sunsum* overshadows mine" (*ne sunsum hye me so*).

(4) "Someone's *sunsum* is bigger or greater than another's (*obi sunsum so kyen obi dee*). To say "someone's *'kra* is greater than another's" would be meaningless.

(5) "He has a good *sunsum*" (*owo sunsum pa*), that is, he is a generous person.

In all such statements the attributions are made to the *sunsum* (spirit), never to the *okra* (soul). Rattray also pointed out correctly that "an Ashanti would never talk of washing his *sunsum*."[21] It is the *okra* that is washed (*okraguare*). In the terminology of the modern linguist, sentences containing *okra* and *sunsum* differ, according to my analysis, not only in their surface structures but also in their deep structures.

It is pretty clear from this semantic analysis that *okra* and *sunsum* are not intersubstitutable in predications. Intersubstitution of the terms, as we saw above, leads either to nonsense as in B(4) or to change of meaning as in A(4) and B(1). Semantic analysis suggests a nonidentity relation between *sunsum* and *okra*. One might reject this conclusion by treating these distinctions as merely idiomatic and not, therefore, as evidence for considering *okra* and *sunsum* as distinct. Let us call this the "idiomatic thesis." In the English language, for instance, it is idiomatic to say "He's a sad soul" rather than "He's a sad spirit," without implying that soul and spirit are distinct. But in English the substitution of one for the other of the two terms even if unidiomatic—will not lead to nonsense and would not change the meaning; in Akan it would.

It may be the easiest way out of an interpretative labyrinth to identify *okra* and *sunsum*,[22] but I do not think it is the most satisfactory way out. There are, I believe, other considerations for rejecting the "identity theory."

First, most Akans agree that in dreaming it is the *sunsum*, not the *okra*, that leaves the body. The departure of the *okra* (soul) from the body means the death of the person, whereas the *sunsum* can leave the body, as in dreaming, without causing the death of the person. Second, moral predicates are generally applied to the *sunsum*. Rattray wrote: "Perhaps the *sunsum* is the more volatile part of the whole *'kra*," and ". . . but the *'kra* is not volatile in life, as the *sunsum* undoubtedly is."[23] Moreover, the *okra* and *sunsum* appear to be different in terms of their functions or activities. The *okra*, as mentioned before, is the principle of life of a person and the embodiment and transmitter of his or her destiny (*nkrabea*). Personality and character dispositions of a person are the function of the *sunsum*.[24] The *sunsum* appears to be the source of dynamism of a person, the active part or force of the human psychological system; its energy is the ground for its interaction with the external world. It is said to have extrasensory powers; it is that which thinks, desires, feels, etc. It is in no way identical with the brain, which is a physical organ. Rather it acts upon the brain (*amene, hon*). In short, people believe that it is upon the *sunsum* that one's health, worldly power, position, influence, success, etc. would depend. The attributes and activities of the *sunsum* are therefore not ascribable to the *okra*. Lystad was wrong when he stated: "In many respects the *sunsum* or spirit is so identical with the *okra* or soul in its functions that it is difficult to distinguish between them."[25]

Now, given *x* and *y*, if whatever is asserted of *x* can be asserted of *y*, then *x* can be said to be identical with *y*. If there is at least one characteristic that *x* has but *y* does not, then *x* and *y* are not identical. On this showing, insofar as things asserted of the *okra* are not assertable of the *sunsum*, the two cannot logically be identified. However, although they are logically distinct, they are not ontologically distinct. That is to say, they are not independent existents held together in an accidental way by an external bond. They are a unity in duality, a duality in unity. The distinction is not a relation between two separate entities. The *sunsum* may, more accurately, be characterized as a part—the active part—of the *okra* (soul).

I once thought that the *sunsum* might be characterized as a state,[26] an epiphenomenon, of the *okra*. I now think that characterization is wrong, for it would subvert the entitative nature of *sunsum*. The fact that we can speak of the inherence of the *sunsum* in natural objects as their activating principle means that in some contexts reference can be made to the *sunsum* independently of the *okra*. This, however, is not so in the context of the human psyche: In man *sunsum* is part of the *okra* (soul). Plato held a tripartite conception of the human soul, deriving that conception from his view of the functions said to be performed by the various parts of the soul. So did Freud. There is nothing inappropriate or illogical or irrational for some Akan thinkers to hold and argue for a bipartite conception of the human soul. Neither a tripartite nor a bipartite conception of the soul subverts its ontic unity. As already stated, the *okra* and *sunsum* are constitutive of a spiritual unity, which survives after death. Therefore the soul (that is, *okra* plus *sunsum*) does not lose its individuality after death. It survives individually. Beliefs in reincarnation (which I do not intend to explore now) and in the existence of the ancestors in the world of spirits (*asamando*) undoubtedly presuppose—and would be logically impossible without—the survival of each individual soul.

RELATION OF *OKRA* (SOUL) AND *HONAM* (BODY)

Understanding the *sunsum* and *okra* to constitute a spiritual unity, one may say that Akan philosophy maintains a dualistic, not a tripartite, conception of the person: A person is made up of two principal entities or substances, one spiritual (immaterial: *okra*) and the other material (*honam*: body).

But Akans sometimes speak as if the relation between the soul (that is, *okra* plus *sunsum*) and the body is so close that they comprise an indissoluble or indivisible unity, and that, consequently, a person is a homogeneous entity. The basis for this observation is the assertion by some discussants that "*okra* is blood" (*mogya*),[27] or "*okra* is in the blood." They mean by this, I think, that there is some connection between the soul and the blood, and that ordinarily the former is integrated or fused with the latter. I think the supposition here is that the blood is the physical or rather physiological "medium" for the soul. However difficult it is to understand this doctrine, it serves as a basis for a theory of the unity of soul and body. But Akan thinkers cannot strictly or unreservedly maintain such a theory, for it logically involves the impossibility of the doctrine of disembodied survival or life after death, which they tenaciously and firmly hold. The doctrine of the indivisible unity of soul and body is a doctrine that eliminates the notion of life after death, inasmuch as both soul and body are held to disintegrate together. The doctrine that the souls of the dead have some form of existence or life therefore cannot he maintained together with a doctrine of the indivisible unity of soul and body. The former doctrine implies an independent existence for the soul. I think their postulation of some kind of connection between the soul and blood is a response to the legitimate, and indeed fundamental, question as to how an entity (that is, the soul), supposed to be immaterial and separate, can "enter" the body. Though their response certainly bristles with difficulties and may be regarded as inadequate, like most theses on the soul, Akan thinkers had sufficient awareness to focus philosophical attention also on the intractable question regarding the beginnings of the connection of the soul to the body, of the immaterial to the material. Other philosophies attempt to demonstrate that man consists of soul and body, but they do not, to my knowledge, speculate on the manner of the soul's "entry" into the body.

In the Akan conception, the soul is held to be a spiritual entity (substance). It is not a bundle of qualities or perceptions, as it is held to be in some Western systems. The basis of this assertion is the Akan belief in disembodied survival. A bundle theory of substance implies the elimination of the notion of substance, for if a substance is held to be a bundle or collection of qualities or perceptions, when the qualities or perceptions are removed, nothing would be left. That is, there would then be no substance, that is, a substratum or an "owner" of those qualities.[28] Thus, if the soul is held to be a bundle of perceptions, as it is in the writings of David Hume, it would be impossible to talk of disembodied survival in the form of a soul or self since the bundle itself is an abstraction. One Akan maxim, expressed epigrammatically, is that "when a man dies he is not (really) dead" (*onipa wu a na onwui*). What is implied by this is that there is something in a human being that is eternal, indestructible, and that continues to exist in the world of spirits (*asamando*). An Akan motif expresses the following thought: "Could God die, I will die" (*Onyame bewu na m'awu*). In Akan metaphysics, . . . God is held to be eternal, immortal (*Odomankoma*). The above saying therefore means that since God will not die, a person, that is, his or her *'kra* (soul), conceived as an indwelling spark of God, will not die either. That is, the soul of man is immortal. The attributes of immortality make sense if, and only if, the soul is held to be a substance, an entity, and not a bundle of qualities or perceptions (experiences).

But where in a human being is this spiritual substance located? Descartes thought that the soul was in the pineal gland. The Akans also seem to hold that the soul is lodged in the head, although they do not specify exactly where. But "although it is in the head you cannot see it with your natural eyes," as they would put it, since it is immaterial. That the soul is "in the head (*ti*)" may be inferred from the following expressions: When they want to say that a person is lucky or fortunate they say: "His head is well (good)" (*ne ti ye*), or "His soul is well (good)" (*ne 'kra ye*). From such expressions one may infer some connection between the head and the soul. And although they cannot point to a specific part of the head as the "residence" of the soul, it may be conjectured that it is in the region of the brain which, as observed earlier, receives its energy from the *sunsum* (spirit), a part of the soul. That is, the soul acts on the brain in a specific locality, but it is itself not actually localized.

The Akan conception of a person, in my analysis, is dualistic, not tripartite, although the spiritual component of a person is highly complex. Such dualistic conception does not necessarily imply a belief in a causal relation or interaction between the two parts, the soul and body. For instance, some dualistic philosophers in the West maintain a doctrine of psychophysical parallelism, which completely denies interaction between soul and body. Other dualists advance a doctrine of epiphenomenalism, which, while not completely rejecting causal interaction, holds that the causality goes in one direction only, namely, from the body to the soul; such a doctrine, too, is thus not interactionist. Akan thinkers, however, are thoroughly interactionist on the relation between soul and body. They hold that not only does the body have a causal influence on the soul but also that the soul has a causal influence on the body (*honam*). What happens to the soul takes effect or reflects on the condition of the body. Thus, writing on Akan culture, Busia stated:

> They (that is, Akans) believed also that spiritual uncleanness was an element of ill-health and that the cleansing of the soul was necessary for health. When, for example, a patient was made to stand on a broom while being treated, it was to symbolize this cleansing. The broom sweeps filth away from the home and keeps it healthy; so the soul must be swept of filth to keep the body healthy.[29]

Similarly, what happens to the body reflects on the conditions of the soul. It is the actual bodily or physical behavior of a person that gives an idea of the condition of the soul. Thus, if the physical behavior of a man suggests that he is happy they would say, "His soul is happy" (*ne 'kra aniagye*); if unhappy or morose they would say, "His soul is sorrowful" (*ne 'kra di awerehow*). When the soul is enfeebled or injured by evil spirits, ill health results; the poor conditions of the body affect the condition of the soul. The condition of the soul depends upon the condition of the body. The belief in psychophysical causal interaction is the whole basis of spiritual or psychical healing in Akan communities.

There are certain diseases that are believed to be "spiritual diseases" (*sunsum yare*) and cannot be healed by the application of physical therapy. In such diseases attention must be paid to both physiological and spiritual aspects of the person. Unless the soul is healed, the body will not respond to physical treatment. The removal of a disease of the soul is the activity of the diviners or the traditional healers (*adunsifo*).

CONCLUSION

The Akan conception of the person, on my analysis, is both dualistic and interactionist. It seems to me that an interactionist psychophysical dualism is a realistic doctrine. Even apart from the prospects for disembodied survival that this doctrine holds out—prospects that profoundly affect the moral orientation of some people—it has had significant pragmatic consequences in Akan communities, as evidenced in the application of psychophysical therapies. There are countless testimonies of people who have been subjected to physical treatment for months or years in modern hospitals without being cured, but who have been healed by traditional healers applying both physical and psychical (spiritual) methods. In such cases the diseases are believed not to be purely physical, affecting only the body (*honam*). They are believed rather to have been inflicted on the sunsum through mystical or spiritual powers, and in time the body also gets affected. When Western-trained doctors pay attention only to the physical aspects of such diseases, they almost invariably fail to heal them. The fact that traditional healers, operating at both the physical and psychical levels, cope successfully with such diseases does seem to suggest a close relationship between the body and the soul.

From the point of view of the Akan metaphysics of the person and of the world in general, all this seems to imply that a human being is not just an assemblage of flesh and bone, that he or she is a complex being who cannot completely be explained by the same law of physics used to explain inanimate things, and that our world cannot simply be reduced to physics.

Notes

1. I say "a conception" because I believe there are other conceptions of the person held or discernible in that philosophy.
2. K.A. Busia, "The Ashani of the Gold Coast," in Daryll Forde (ed.), *African Worlds*, p. 197; M. Fortes, *Kinship and the Social Order* (University of Chicago Press, Chicago, 1969), p. 199, n. 14; Robert A. Lystad, *The Ashanti, A Proud People* (Rutgers University Press, New Brunswick, N.J., 1958), p. 155; Peter K. Sarpong, *Ghana in Retrospect: Some Aspects of the Ghanaian Culture* (Ghana Publishing Corp., Accra, 1974), p. 37.
3. Busia, p. 197; Lystad, p. 155; E.L.R. Meyerowitz, *The Sacred State of the Akan* (Faber and Faber, London, 1951), p. 86; and "Concepts of the Soul among the Akan," Africa, p. 26.
4. Busia, p. 197; Lystad, p. 155; P. A. Twumasi, *Medical Systems in Ghana* (Ghana Publishing Corp., Accra, 1975), p. 22.
5. Here the views of W. E. Abraham are excepted, for he maintains, like I do, that the *sunsum* is not "inheritable" and that it "appears to have been a spiritual substance." W. E. Abraham, *The Mind of Africa* (University of Chicago Press, Chicago, 1962), p. 60.
6. J.B. Danquah, *The Akan Doctrine of God* (Lutterworth Press, London, 1944), p. 115.
7. Ibid., p. 116.
8. R.S. Rattray, *Religion and Art in Ashanti*, p. 154.
9. E.E. Evans-Pritchard, *Witchcraft, Oracles and Magic among the Azande*, p. 136; also E. G. Parrinder, *West African Religion*, p. 197.
10. Parrinder, *West African Religion*, p. 197.
11. Plato, *The Republic*, 571, beginning of Book IX.
12. James Adam (ed.), *The Republic of Plato*, 2d ed. (Cambridge University Press, Cambridge, 1975), Vol. 2, p. 320.
13. Plato, *The Republic*, ed. and trans. by Paul Shorey (Loeb Classical Library, Harvard University Press, Cambridge, Mass., 1935), p. 335.
14. Plato, *The Republic*, trans. by A. D. Lindsay (J.M. Dent, London, 1976), p. 346.
15. Thomas Gould, *Platonic Love* (Routledge and Kegan Paul, London, 1963), p. 108ff and p. 174ff.
16. Charles W. Valentine, *Dreams and the Unconscious* (Methuen, London, 1921), p. 93; also his *The New Psychology of the Unconscious* (Macmillan, New York, 1929), p. 95.
17. Wilfred Trotter, *Instincts of the Herd in Peace and War* (T.F. Unwin, London, 1916), p. 74.
18. H. Debrunner, *Witchcraft in Ghana* (Waterville Publishing House, Accra, 1959), p. 17.
19. Mbiti, *African Religions and Philosophy*, p. 102.
20. Rattray, *Religion and Art*, p. 154.
21. Ibid., p. 318, Soul-washing is a symbolic religious rite meant to cleanse and purify the soul from defilement. "This cult," wrote Mrs. Meyerowitz, "adjures the person to lead a good and decent life." *Sacred State*, p. 117; also p. 88.
22. Incidentally, the "identity theory" immediately subverts any physical conception of the *sunsum*, since the *okra* (soul), with which it is being identified, is generally agreed to be a spiritual, not a physical, entity.
23. Rattray, *Religion and Art*, p. 154.
24. The dynamic and active character of the *sunsum* has given rise to metaphorical use as in the sentences, "there is 'spirit' in the game" (*agoro yi sunsum wo mu*), "the arrival of the chief brought 'spirit' into the festival celebration." Not long ago the dynamism, action and energy of a late Ghanaian army general earned him the by-name of "Sunsum!" among his soldiers.
25. Lystad, p. 158.
26. See Kwame Gyekye, "The Akan Concept of a Person," *International Philosophical Quarterly*. Vol. XVIII, No. 3, September 1978, p. 284.
27. This view was expressed also to Meyerowitz, *Sacred State*, p. 84.
28. See Kwame Gyekye, "An Examination of the Bundle Theory of Substance," *Philosophy and Phenomenological Research*, Vol. XXXIV, No. 1, September, 1973.
29. Busia, *The Challenge of Africa*, p. 19.

Meditations and Correspondence [Meditation VI, Letters]

René Descartes

René Descartes asks us not to trust our senses, to doubt what we have grown to believe and accept as true in order that we may discover what is in fact true. That discovery is that we think and that our identity as an individual self or soul is to be found in our thoughts, or more specifically in the soul, which is the seat of those thoughts. Who we are is not to be identified with our bodies. Princess Elisabeth, who was a protégé of Descartes, expressed her own doubts about Descartes's conclusion and her confusion about how Descartes believed souls could "move" or interact with bodies. Does Descartes answer her questions?

MEDITATION VI

On the Existence of Material Objects and the Real Distinction of Mind from Body

It remains for me to examine whether material objects exist. Insofar as they are the subject of pure mathematics, I now know at least that they can exist, because I grasp them clearly and distinctly. For God can undoubtedly make whatever I can grasp in this way, and I never judge that something is impossible for Him to make unless there would be a contradiction in my grasping the thing distinctly. Also, the fact that I find myself having mental images when I turn my attention to physical objects seems to imply that those objects really do exist. For, when I pay careful attention to what it is to have a mental image, it seems to me that it's just the application of my power of thought to a certain body which is immediately present to it and which must therefore exist.

To clarify this, I'll examine the difference between having a mental image and having a pure understanding. When I have a mental image of a triangle for example, I don't just understand that it is a figure bounded by three lines; I also "look at" the lines as though they were present to my mind's eye. And this is what I call having a mental image. When I want to think of a chiliagon, I understand that it is a figure with a thousand sides as well as I understand that a triangle is a figure with three, but I can't imagine its sides or "look" at them as though they were present. Being accustomed to using images when I think about physical objects, I may confusedly picture some figure to myself, but this figure obviously is not a chiliagon—for it in no way differs from what I present to myself when thinking about a myriagon or any other many sided figure, and it doesn't help me to discern the properties that distinguish chiliagons from other polygons. If it's a pentagon that is in question, I can understand its shape, as I can that of the chiliagon, without the aid of mental images. But I can also get a mental image of the pentagon by directing my mind's eye to its five lines and to the area that they bound. And it's obvious to me that getting this mental image requires a special mental effort different from that needed for understanding—a special effort which clearly reveals

From "Meditations and Correspondence" from *The Essential Descartes,* ed. Margaret D. Wilson.

the difference between having a mental image and having a pure understanding.

It also seems to me that my power of having mental images, being distinct from my power of understanding, is not essential to my self or, in other words, to my mind—for, if I were to lose this ability, I would surely remain the same thing that I now am. And it seems to follow that this ability depends on something distinct from me. If we suppose that there is a body so associated with my mind that the mind can "look into" it at will, it's easy to understand how my mind might get mental images of physical objects by means of my body. If there were such a body, the mode of thinking that we call imagination would only differ from pure understanding in one way: when the mind understood something, it would turn "inward" and view an idea that it found in itself, but, when it had mental images, it would turn to the body and look at something there which resembled an idea that it had understood by itself or had grasped by sense. As I've said, then, it's easy to see how I get mental images, if we suppose that my body exists. And, since I don't have in mind any other equally plausible explanation of my ability to have mental images, I conjecture that physical objects probably do exist. But this conjecture is only probable. Despite my careful and thorough investigation, the distinct idea of bodily nature that I get from mental images does not seem to have anything in it from which the conclusion that physical objects exist validly follows.

Besides having a mental image of the bodily nature which is the subject-matter of pure mathematics, I have mental images of things which are not so distinct—things like colors, sounds, flavors, and pains. But I seem to grasp these things better by sense, from which they seem to come (with the aid of memory) to the understanding. Thus, to deal with these things more fully, I must examine the senses and see whether there is anything in the mode of awareness that I call sensation from which I can draw a conclusive argument for the existence of physical objects.

First, I'll remind myself of the things that I believed really to be as I perceived them and of the grounds for my belief. Next, I'll set out the grounds on which I later called this belief into doubt. And, finally, I'll consider what I ought to think now.

To begin with, I sensed that I had a head, hands, feet, and the other members that make up a human body. I viewed this body as part, or maybe even as all, of me. I sensed that it was influenced by other physical objects whose effects could be either beneficial or harmful. I judged these effects to be beneficial to the extent that I felt pleasant sensations and harmful to the extent that I felt pain. And, in addition to sensations of pain and pleasure, I sensed hunger, thirst, and other such desires—and also bodily inclinations towards cheerfulness, sadness, and other emotions. Outside me, I sensed, not just extension, shape, and motion, but also hardness, hotness, and other qualities detected by touch. I also sensed light, color, odor, taste, and sound—qualities by whose variation I distinguished such things as the sky, earth, and sea from one another.

In view of these ideas of qualities (which presented themselves to my thought and were all that I really sensed directly), I had some reason for believing that I sensed objects distinct from my thought—physical objects from which the ideas came. For I found that these ideas come to me independently of my desires so that, however much I tried, I couldn't sense an object when it wasn't present to an organ of sense or fail to sense one when it was present. And, since the ideas that I grasped by sense were much livelier, more explicit, and (in their own way) more distinct than those I deliberately created or found impressed in my memory, it seemed that these ideas could not have come from me and thus that they came from something else. Having no conception of these things other than that suggested by my sensory ideas, I could only think that the things resembled the ideas. Indeed, since I remembered using my senses before my reason, since I found the ideas that I created in myself to be less explicit than those grasped by sense, and since I found the ideas that I created to be composed largely of those that I had grasped by sense, I easily convinced myself that I didn't understand anything at all unless I had first sensed it.

I also had some reason for supposing that a certain physical object, which I viewed as belonging to me in a special way, was related to me more closely than any other. I couldn't be separated from it as I could from other physical objects; I felt all of my emotions and desires in it and because of it; and I was aware of pains and pleasant feelings in it but in nothing else. I didn't know why sadness goes with the sensation of pain or why joy goes with sensory stimulation. I didn't know why the stomach twitchings that I call hunger warn me that I need to eat or why dryness in my throat warns me that I need to drink. Seeing no connection between stomach twitchings and the desire to eat or between the sensation of a pain-producing thing and the consequent awareness of sadness, I could only say that I had been taught the connection by nature. And nature seems also to have taught me everything else that I knew about the objects of sensation—for I convinced myself that the sensations came to me in a certain way before having found grounds on which to prove that they did.

But, since then, many experiences have shaken my faith in the senses. Towers that seemed round from a distance sometimes looked square from close up, and huge statues on pediments sometimes didn't look big when seen from the ground. In innumerable such cases, I found the judgments of the external senses to be wrong. And the same holds for the internal senses. What is felt more inwardly than pain? Yet I had heard that people with amputated arms and legs sometimes seem to feel pain in the missing limb, and it therefore didn't seem perfectly certain to me that the limb in which I feel a pain is always the one that hurts. And, to these grounds for doubt, I've recently added two that are very general: First, since I didn't believe myself to sense anything while awake that I couldn't also take myself to sense in a dream, and since I didn't believe that what I sense in sleep comes from objects outside me, I didn't see why I should believe what I sense while awake comes from such objects. Second, since I didn't yet know my creator (or, rather, since I supposed that I didn't know Him), I saw nothing to rule out my having been so designed by nature that I'm deceived even in what seems most obviously true to me.

And I could easily refute the reasoning by which I convinced myself of the reality of sensible things. Since my nature seemed to impel me towards many things which my reason rejected, I didn't believe that I ought to have much faith in nature's teachings. And, while my will didn't control my sense perceptions, I didn't believe it to follow that these perceptions came from outside me, since I thought that the ability to produce these ideas might be in me without my being aware of it.

Now that I've begun to know myself and my creator better, I still believe that I oughtn't blindly to accept everything that I seem to get from the senses. Yet I no longer believe that I ought to call it all into doubt.

In the first place, I know that everything that I clearly and distinctly understand can he made by God to be exactly as I understand it. The fact that I can clearly and distinctly understand one thing apart from another is therefore enough to make me certain that it is distinct from the other, since the things could be separated by God if not by something else. (I judge the things to be distinct regardless of the power needed to make them exist separately.) Accordingly, from the fact that I have gained knowledge of my existence without noticing anything about my nature or essence except that I am a thinking thing. I can rightly conclude that my essence consists solely in the fact that I am a thinking thing. It's possible (or, as I will say later, it's certain) that I have a body which is very tightly bound to me. But, on the one hand, I have a clear and distinct idea of myself insofar as I am just a thinking and unextended thing, and, on the other hand, I have a distinct idea of my body insofar as it is just an extended and unthinking thing. It's certain, then, that I am really distinct from my body and can exist without it.

In addition, I find in myself abilities for special modes of awareness, like the abilities to have mental images and to sense. I can clearly and distinctly conceive of my whole self as something that lacks these abilities, but I can't conceive of the abilities' existing without me, or without an understanding substance in which to reside. Since the conception of these abilities includes the conception of something that understands, I see that these abilities are distinct from me in the way that a thing's properties are distinct from the thing itself.

I recognize other abilities in me, like the ability to move around and to assume various postures. These abilities can't be understood to exist apart from a substance in which they reside any more than the abilities to imagine and sense, and they therefore cannot exist without such a substance. But it's obvious that, if these abilities do exist, the substance in which they reside must be a body or extended substance rather than an understanding one—for the clear and distinct conceptions of these abilities contain extension but not understanding.

There is also in me, however, a passive ability to sense—to receive and recognize ideas of sensible things. But, I wouldn't be able to put this ability to use if there weren't, either in me or in something else, an active power to produce or make sensory ideas. Since this active power doesn't presuppose understanding, and since it often produces ideas in me without my cooperation and even against my will, it cannot exist in me. Therefore, this power must exist in a substance distinct from me. And, for reasons that I've noted, this substance must contain, either formally or eminently, all the reality that is contained subjectively in the ideas that the power produces. Either this substance is a physical object (a thing of bodily nature which contains formally the reality that the idea contains subjectively), or it is God or one of His creations which is higher than a physical object (something which contains this reality eminently). But, since God isn't a deceiver, it's completely obvious that He doesn't send these ideas to me directly or by means of a creation which contains their reality eminently rather than formally. For, since He has not given me any ability to recognize that these ideas are sent by Him or by creations other than physical objects, and since He has given me a strong inclination to believe that the ideas come from physical objects, I see no way to avoid the conclusion that He deceives me if the ideas are sent to me by anything other than physical objects. It follows that physical objects exist. These objects may not exist exactly as I comprehend them by sense; in many ways, sensory comprehension is obscure and confused. But these objects must at least have in them everything that I clearly and distinctly understand them to have—every general property within the scope of pure mathematics.

But what about particular properties, such as the size and shape of the sun? And what about things that I understand less clearly than mathematical properties, like light, sound, and pain? These are open to doubt. But, since God isn't a deceiver, and since I therefore have the God-given ability to correct any falsity that may be in my beliefs, I have high hopes of finding the truth about even these things. There is undoubtedly some truth in everything I have been taught by nature—for, when I use the term "nature" in its general sense, I refer to God Himself or to the order that He has established in the created world, and, when I apply the term specifically to my nature, I refer to the collection of everything that God has given *me.*

Nature teaches me nothing more explicitly, however, than that I have a body which is hurt when I feel pain, which needs food or drink when I experience hunger or thirst, and so on. Accordingly, I ought not to doubt that there is some truth to this.

Through sensations like pain, hunger, and thirst, nature also teaches me that I am not present in my body in the way that a sailor is present in his ship. Rather, I am very tightly bound to my body and so "mixed up" with it that we form a single thing. If this weren't so, I—who am just a thinking thing—wouldn't feel pain when my body was injured; I would perceive the injury by pure understanding in the way that a sailor sees the leaks in his ship with his eyes. And, when my body needed food or drink, I would explicitly understand that the need existed without having the confused sensations of hunger and thirst. For the sensations of thirst, hunger, and pain are just confused modifications of thought arising from the union and "mixture" of mind and body.

Also, nature teaches me that there are other physical objects around my body—some that I ought to seek and others that I ought to avoid. From the fact that I sense things like colors, sounds, odors, flavors, temperatures, and hardnesses, I correctly infer that sense perceptions come from physical objects which vary as widely (though perhaps not in the same way) as the perceptions do. And, from the fact that some of these perceptions are pleasant while others are unpleasant, I infer with certainty that my body—or, rather, my whole self which consists of a body and a mind—can be benefited and harmed by the physical objects around it.

There are many other things which I seem to have been taught by nature but which I have really accepted out of a habit of thoughtless judgment. These things may well be false. Among them are the judgments that a space is empty if nothing in it happens to affect my senses; that a hot physical object has something in it resembling my idea of heat; that a white or green thing has in it the same whiteness or greenness that I sense; that a bitter or sweet thing has in it the same flavor that I taste; that stars, towers, and other physical objects have the same size and shape that they present to my senses; and so on.

If I am to avoid accepting what is indistinct in these cases, I must more carefully explain my use of the phrase "taught by nature." In particular, I should say that I am now using the term "nature" in a narrower sense than when I took it to refer to the whole complex of what God has given me. This complex includes much having to do with my mind alone (such as my grasp of the fact that what is done cannot be undone and of the rest of what I know by the light of nature) which does not bear on what I am now saying. And the complex also includes much having to do with my body alone (such as its tendency to go downwards) with which I am not dealing now. I'm now using the term "nature" to refer only to what God has given me insofar as I am a composite of mind and body. It is this nature which teaches me to avoid that which occasions painful sensations, to seek that which occasions pleasant sensations, and so on. But this nature seems not to teach me to draw conclusions about external objects from sense perceptions without first having examined the matter with my understanding—for true knowledge of external things seems to belong to the mind alone, not to the composite of mind and body.

Thus, while a star has no more effect on my eye than a flame, this does not really produce a positive inclination to believe that the star is as small as the flame; for my youthful judgment about the size of the flame, I had no real grounds. And, while I feel heat when I approach a fire and pain when I draw nearer, I have absolutely no reason for believing that something in the fire resembles the heat, just as I have no reason for believing that something in the fire resembles the pain; I only have reason for believing that there is something or other in the fire which produces the feelings of heat and pain. And, although there may be nothing in a given region of space that affects my senses, it doesn't follow that there aren't any physical objects in that space. Rather I now see that, on these matters and others, I used to pervert the natural order of things. For, while nature has given sense perceptions to my mind for the sole purpose of indicating what is beneficial and what harmful to the composite of which my mind is a part, and while the perceptions are sufficiently clear and distinct for that purpose, I used these perceptions as standards for identifying the essence of physical objects—an essence which they only reveal obscurely and confusedly.

I've already explained how it can be that, despite God's goodness, my judgments can be false. But a new difficulty arises here—one having to do with the things that nature presents to me as desirable or undesirable and also with the errors that I seem to have found in my internal sensations. One of these errors seems to be committed, for example, when a man is fooled by some food's pleasant taste into eating poison hidden in that food. But surely, in this case, what the man's nature impels him to eat is the good tasting food, not the poison of which he knows nothing. We can draw no conclusion except that his nature isn't omniscient, and this conclusion isn't surprising. Since a man is a limited thing, he can only have limited perfections.

Still, we often err in cases in which nature does impel us. This happens, for example, when sick people want food or drink that would quickly harm them. To say that these people err as a result of the corruption of their nature does not solve the problem—for a sick man is no less a creation of God than a well one, and it seems as absurd to suppose that God has given him a deceptive nature. A clock made of wheels and weights follows the natural laws just as precisely when it is poorly made and inaccurate as when it does everything that its maker wants. Thus, if I regard a human body as a machine made up of bones, nerves, muscles, veins, blood, and skin such that even without a mind it would do just what it does now (except for things that require a mind because they are controlled by the will), it's easy to see that what happens to a sick man is no less "natural" than what happens to a well one. For instance, if a body suffers from dropsy, it has a dry throat of the sort that regularly brings the sensation of thirst to the mind, the dryness disposes the nerves and other organs to drink, and the drinking makes the illness worse. But this is just as natural as when a similar dryness of throat moves a person who is perfectly healthy to take a drink which is beneficial. Bearing in mind my conception of a clock's use, I might say that an inaccurate clock departs from its nature, and, similarly, viewing the machine of the human body as designed for its usual motions, I can say that it drifts away from its nature if it has a dry throat when drinking will not help to maintain it. I should note, however, that the sense in which I am now using the term "nature" differs from that in which I used it before. For, as I have just used the term "nature," the nature of a man (or clock) is something that depends on my thinking of the difference between a sick and a well man (or of the difference between a poorly made and a well-made clock)—something regarded as extrinsic to the things. But, when I used "nature" before, I referred to something which is in things and which therefore has some reality.

It may be that we just offer an extrinsic description of a body suffering from dropsy when, noting that it has a dry throat but doesn't need to drink, we say that its nature is corrupted. Still, the description is not purely extrinsic when we say that a composite or union of mind and body has a corrupted nature. There is a real fault in the composite's nature, for it is thirsty when drinking would be harmful. It therefore remains to be asked why God's goodness doesn't prevent this nature's being deceptive.

To begin the answer, I'll note that mind differs importantly from body in that body is by its nature divisible while mind is indivisible. When I think about my mind—or, in other words, about myself insofar as I am just a thinking thing—I can't distinguish any parts in me; I understand myself to be a single, unified thing. Although my whole mind seems united to my whole body, I know that cutting off a foot, arm, or other limb would not take anything away from my mind. The abilities to will, sense, understand, and so on can't be called parts, since it's one and the same mind that wills, senses, and understands. On the other hand, whenever I think of a physical or extended thing, I can mentally divide it, and I therefore understand that the object is divisible. This single fact would be enough to teach me that my mind and my body are distinct, if I hadn't already learned that in another way.

Next, I notice that the mind isn't directly affected by all parts of the body, but only by the brain—or maybe just by the small part of the brain containing the so-called "common sense." Whenever this part of the brain is in a given state, it presents the same thing to the mind, regardless of what is happening in the rest of the body (as is shown by innumerable experiments that I need not review here).

In addition, I notice that the nature of body is such that, if a first part can be moved by a second that is far away, the first part can be moved in exactly the same way by something between the first and second without the second part's being affected. For example, if A, B, C, and D are points on a cord, and if the first point (A) can be moved in a certain way by a pull on the last point (D), then A can be moved in the same way by a pull on one of the middle points (B or C) without D's being moved. Similarly, science teaches me that, when my foot hurts, the sensation of pain is produced by nerves distributed throughout the foot which extend like cords from there to the brain. When pulled in the foot, these nerves pull the central parts of the brain to which they are attached, moving those parts in ways designated by nature to present the mind with the sensation of a pain "in the foot." But, since these nerves pass through the shins, thighs, hips, back, and neck on their way from foot to brain, it can happen that their being touched in the middle, rather than at the end in the foot, produces the same motion in the brain as when the foot is hurt and, hence, that the mind feels the same pain "in the foot." And the point holds for other sensations as well.

Finally, I notice that, since only one sensation can be produced by a given motion of the part of the brain that directly affects the mind, the best conceivable sensation for it to produce is the one that is most often useful for the maintenance of the healthy man. Experience teaches that all the sensations put in us by nature are of this sort and therefore that everything in our sensations testifies to God's power and goodness. For example, when the nerves in the foot are moved with unusual violence, the motion is communicated through the middle of the spine to the center of the brain, where it signals the mind to sense a pain "in the foot." This urges the mind to view the pain's cause as harmful to the foot and to do what it can to remove that cause. Of course, God could have so designed man's nature that the same motion of the brain presented something else to the mind, like the motion in the brain, or the motion in the foot or a motion somewhere between the brain and foot. But no alternative to the way things are would be as conducive to the maintenance of the body. Similarly, when we need drink, the throat becomes dry, the dryness moves the nerves of the throat thereby moving the center of the brain, and the brain's movements cause the sensation of thirst in the mind. It's the sensation of thirst that is produced, because no information about our condition is more useful to us than that we need to get something to drink in order to remain healthy. And the same is true in other cases.

This makes it completely obvious that, despite God's immense goodness, the nature of man (whom we now view as a composite of mind and body) cannot fail to be deceptive. For, if something produces the movement usually associated with an injured foot in the nerve running from foot to brain or in the brain itself rather than in the foot, a pain is felt as if "in the foot." Here the senses are deceived by their nature. Since this motion in the brain must always bring the same sensation to mind, and since the motion's cause is something hurting the foot more often than something elsewhere, it's in accordance with reason that the motion always presents the mind a pain in the foot rather than elsewhere. And, if dryness of the throat arises, not (as usual) from drink's being conducive to the body's health, but (as happens in dropsy) from some other cause, it's much better that we are deceived when our bodies are sound. And the same holds for other cases.

In addition to helping me to be aware of the errors to which my nature is subject, these reflections help me readily to correct or avoid those errors. I know that sensory indications of what is good for my body are more often true than false; I can almost always examine a given thing with several senses; and I can also use my memory (which connects the present to the past) and my understanding (which has now examined all the causes of error). Hence, I need no longer fear that what the senses daily show me is unreal. I should reject the exaggerated doubts of the past few days as ridiculous. This is especially true of the chief ground for these doubts—namely, my inability to distinguish dreaming from being awake. For I now notice that dreaming and being awake are importantly different: the events in dreams are not linked by memory to the rest of my life like those that happen while I am awake. If, while I'm awake, someone were suddenly to appear and then immediately to disappear without my seeing where he came from or went to (as happens in dreams), I would justifiably judge that he was not a real man but a ghost—or, better, an apparition created in my brain. But, if I distinctly observe something's source, its place, and the time at which I learn about it, and if I grasp an unbroken connection between it and the rest of my life, I'm quite sure that it is something in my waking life rather than in a dream. And I ought not to have the slightest doubt about the reality of such things if I have examined them with all my senses, my memory, and my understanding without finding any conflicting evidence. For, from the fact that God is not a deceiver, it follows that I am not deceived in any case of this sort. Since the need to act does not always allow time for such a careful examination, however, we must admit the likelihood of men's erring about particular things and acknowledge the weakness of our nature.

CORRESPONDENCE WITH PRINCESS ELISABETH, CONCERNING THE UNION OF MIND AND BODY[1]

Elisabeth to Descartes

May 6/16, 1643

. . . <I ASK>[2] YOU TO TELL ME how man's soul, being only a thinking substance, can determine animal spirits so as to cause voluntary actions. For every determination of movement seems to come about either by the propelling of the thing moved, by the manner in which it is propelled by that which moves it, or else by the quality and shape of the surface of the latter. Now contact is required for the first two conditions, and extension for the third. But you exclude extension entirely from the notion you have of the soul, and contact seems to me incompatible with something which is immaterial. Therefore I ask you for a more explicit definition of the soul than you give in your metaphysics, i.e., of its substance, apart from its action, thought. For even if we suppose that soul and thought are, like the attributes of God, inseparable, a thesis difficult enough anyway to establish [for the child] in the mother's womb and in fainting spells, still we can acquire a more perfect idea of them if we consider them separately . . .

Descartes to Elisabeth

May 21, 1643

. . . the question which your Highness raises seems to me one which can most reasonably be asked as a consequence of my published writings. For there are two aspects of the human soul upon which depends all knowledge we can have of its nature. One of these is that it thinks; the other, that, united to the body, it can act and suffer with the body. I said almost nothing of the latter aspect, for I was interested in expounding the first clearly. My principal objective was to establish the distinction between soul and body, and for that purpose only the first characteristic of the soul was useful, and the other would not have been at all helpful. But since your Highness sees so clearly, that no one can dissemble anything from you, I will try to explain how I conceive the union of the soul with the body, and how the soul has the power to move the body.

First, I hold that there are in us certain primitive notions, which are like the models on whose pattern we form all other knowledge. There are very few of these notions. After the most general—being, number, duration, etc., which apply to all that we could know—we have, specifically for body, only the notion of extension, from which are derived the notions of figure and motion. And for the soul alone, we have only the notion of thought, in which are included the conceptions of the understanding and the inclinations of the will. Finally, for soul and body together, we have only the notion of their union, from which are derived our notions of the power which the soul has to move the body, and of the body to act on the soul, to cause feelings and passions.

I believe too that all human knowledge consists in nothing else but in distinguishing these notions clearly and in attributing each of them correctly to the thing to which it applies. For when we want to explain some difficulty by means of a notion which is not appropriate to it, we cannot fail to be mistaken. Similarly we should err if we try to explain one of these notions in terms of another. For they are primitive, and each can be understood only in terms of itself. Now our senses have made the notions of extension, figure, and motion much more familiar than the others. Thus the main cause of our errors is that we ordinarily try to use these notions to explain things to which they are inappropriate, as when we want to use imagination to conceive of the nature of the soul, or, in trying to conceive the manner in which the soul moves the body, we think of it as similar to the way in which a body is moved by another body.

In the *Meditations,* which your Highness has so kindly read, I tried to explain the notions which belong to the soul only, distinguishing them from those which belong only to the body. Consequently the matter that I must next explain is the manner of conceiving those notions which apply to the union of the soul with the body, apart from those which belong only to body or only to the soul. In this regard it seems to me that what I wrote at the end of my *Replies to the Sixth Objections* could well be of use here. For we cannot expect to find these notions anywhere except in our soul, which contains all of them in itself, by its nature, but which does not always adequately distinguish them one from another, nor does it attribute them to the objects to which we should attribute them.

Thus I believe that we have in the past confused the notion of the power by which the soul acts in the body with that by which one body acts in another; and that we have attributed both of these, not to the soul, which we did not yet know, but to the different qualities of body, that is, to gravity, to heat, and to other qualities which we supposed to be real, that is, to have an existence distinct from that of body and therefore to be substances, even though we called them qualities. To conceive them we have sometimes used notions which are in us to know body and sometimes those which are in us to know the soul, according to whether that which we have attributed to them has been material or immaterial. For example, in supposing that gravity is a real quality, of which we have no other knowledge than that it has the power to move the body in which it is toward the center of the earth, we have no difficulty in conceiving how it moves this body nor how it is joined to it. We do not suppose that this occurs by any actual contact of one surface with another, but rather we experience in ourselves that we have a particular notion which enables us to understand this. Yet I hold that we misuse this notion in applying it to gravity (something which is not really distinct from body, as I hope to show in my *Physics*). For this notion has been given us to conceive the manner by which soul moves body. . . .

Notes

1. From *The Essential Descartes,* ed. Margaret D. Wilson, pp. 373–380. Copyright © 1969 by Margaret Wilson. Reprinted by permission of New American Library, a division of Penguin Books USA Inc. Footnotes deleted.

2. Note: Carets [< >] indicate insertions made by the translator for the sake of clarity.

Descartes's Ghost

Gilbert Ryle

Descartes gave us a picture of human nature as a duality of soul and body. Gilbert Ryle raises the question of whether or not this dualism forces one to explain his or her life in terms of collateral histories, one public and one private. Perhaps Descartes made a mistake, a special kind of mistake in his description of human nature. Ryle calls this a "Category-Mistake." See if you understand what he means by a Category-Mistake, and see if you agree with his conclusion that the mistake can be remedied by understanding selves in terms of behaviors rather than in terms of substances.

1. THE OFFICIAL DOCTRINE

There is a doctrine about the nature and place of minds which is so prevalent among theorists and even among laymen that it deserves to be described as the official theory. Most philosophers, psychologists and religious teachers subscribe, with minor reservations, to its main articles and, although they admit certain theoretical difficulties in it, they tend to assume that these can be overcome without serious modifications being made to the architecture of the theory. It will be argued here that the central principles of the doctrine are unsound and conflict with the whole body of what we know about minds when we are not speculating about them.

The official doctrine, which hails chiefly from Descartes, is something like this. With the doubtful exceptions of idiots and infants in arms every human being has both a body and a mind. Some would prefer to say that every human being is both a body and a mind. His body and his mind are ordinarily harnessed together, but after the death of the body his mind may continue to exist and function.

From *The Concept of Mind* by Gilbert Ryle. Copyright © 1949 by Hutchinson. Reprinted by permission of Routledge.

Human bodies are in space and are subject to the mechanical laws which govern all other bodies in space. Bodily processes and states can be inspected by external observers. So a man's bodily life is as much a public affair as are the lives of animals and reptiles and even as the careers of trees, crystals and planets.

But minds are not in space, nor are their operations subject to mechanical laws. The workings of one mind are not witnessable by other observers; its career is private. Only I can take direct cognisance of the states and processes of my own mind. A person therefore lives through two collateral histories, one consisting of what happens in and to his body, the other consisting of what happens in and to his mind. The first is public, the second private. The events in the first history are events in the physical world, those in the second are events in the mental world.

It has been disputed whether a person does or can directly monitor all or only some of the episodes of his own private history; but, according to the official doctrine, of at least some of these episodes he has direct and unchallengeable cognisance. In consciousness, self-consciousness and introspection he is directly and authentically apprised of the present states and operations of his mind. He may have great or small uncertainties about concurrent and adjacent episodes in the physical world, but he can have none about at least part of what is momentarily occupying his mind.

It is customary to express this bifurcation of his two lives and of his two worlds by saying that the things and events which belong to the physical world, including his own body, are external, while the workings of his own mind are internal. This antithesis of outer and inner is of course meant to be construed as a metaphor, since minds, not being in space, could not be described as being spatially inside anything else, or as having things going on spatially inside themselves. But relapses from this good intention are common and theorists are found speculating how stimuli, the physical sources of which are yards or miles outside a person's skin, can generate mental responses inside his skull, or how decisions framed inside his cranium can set going movements of his extremities.

Even when "inner" and "outer" are construed as metaphors, the problem how a person's mind and body influence one another is notoriously charged with theoretical difficulties. What the mind wills, the legs, arms and the tongue execute; what affects the ear and the eye has something to do with what the mind perceives; grimaces and smiles betray the mind's moods and bodily castigations lead, it is hoped, to moral improvement. But the actual transactions between the episodes of the private history and those of the public history remain mysterious, since by definition they can belong to neither series. They could not be reported among the happenings described in a person's autobiography of his inner life, but nor could they be reported among those described in some one else's biography of that person's overt career. They can be inspected neither by introspection nor by laboratory experiment. They are theoretical shuttlecocks which are forever being bandied from the physiologist back to the psychologist and from the psychologist back to the physiologist.

Underlying this partly metaphorical representation of the bifurcation of a person's two lives there is a seemingly more profound and philosophical assumption. It is assumed that there are two different kinds of existence or status. What exists or happens may have the status of physical existence, or it may have the status of mental existence. Somewhat as the faces of coins are either heads or tails, or somewhat as living creatures are either male or female, so, it is supposed, some existing is physical existing, other existing is mental existing. It is a necessary feature of what has physical existence that it is in space and time; it is a necessary feature of what has mental existence that it is in time but not in space. What has physical existence is composed of matter, or else is a function of matter; what has mental existence consists of consciousness, or else is a function of consciousness.

There is thus a polar opposition between mind and matter, an opposition which is often brought out as follows. Material objects are situated in a common field, known as "space," and what happens to one body in one part of space is mechanically connected with what happens to other bodies in other parts of space. But mental happenings occur in insulated fields, known as "minds," and there is, apart maybe from telepathy, no direct causal connection between what happens in one mind and what happens in another. Only through the medium of the public physical world can the mind of one person make a difference to the mind of another. The mind is its own place and in his inner life each of us lives the life of a ghostly Robinson Crusoe. People can see, hear and jolt one another's bodies, but they are irremediably blind and deaf to the workings of one another's minds and inoperative upon them.

What sort of knowledge can be secured of the workings of a mind? On the one side, according to the official theory, a person has direct knowledge of the best imaginable kind of the workings of his own mind. Mental states and processes are (or are normally) conscious states and processes, and the consciousness which irradiates them can engender no illusions and leaves the door open for no doubts. A person's present thinkings, feelings and willings, his perceivings, rememberings and imaginings are intrinsically "phosphorescent"; their existence and their nature are inevitably betrayed to their owner. The inner life is a stream of consciousness of such a sort that it would be absurd to suggest that the mind whose life is that stream might be unaware of what is passing down it.

True, the evidence adduced recently by Freud seems to show that there exist channels tributary to this stream, which run hidden from their owner. People are actuated by impulses the existence of which they vigorously disavow; some of their thoughts differ from the thoughts which they acknowledge; and some of the actions which they think they will to perform they do not really will. They are thoroughly gulled by some of their own hypocrisies and they successfully ignore facts about their mental lives which on the official theory ought to be patent to them. Holders of the official theory tend, however, to maintain that anyhow in normal circumstances a person must be directly and authentically seized of the present state and workings of his own mind.

Besides being currently supplied with these alleged immediate data of consciousness, a person is also generally supposed to be able to exercise from time to time a special kind of perception, namely inner perception, or introspection. He can take a (non-optical) "look" at what is passing in his mind. Not only can he view and scrutinize a flower through his sense of sight and listen to and discriminate the notes of a bell through his sense of hearing; he can also reflectively or introspectively watch, without any bodily organ of sense, the current episodes of his inner life. This self-observation is also commonly supposed to be immune from illusion, confusion or doubt. A mind's reports of its own affairs have a certainty superior to the best that is possessed by its reports of matters in the physical world. Sense-perceptions can, but consciousness and introspection cannot, be mistaken or confused.

On the other side, one person has no direct access of any sort to the events of the inner life of another. He cannot do better than make problematic inferences from the observed behaviour of the other person's body to the states of mind which, by analogy from his own conduct, he supposes to be signalised by that behaviour. Direct access to the workings of a mind is the privilege of that mind itself; in default of such privileged access, the workings of one mind are inevitably occult to everyone else. For the supposed arguments from bodily movements similar to their own to mental workings similar to their own would lack any possibility of observational corroboration. Not unnaturally, therefore, an adherent of the official theory finds it difficult to resist this consequence of his premisses, that he has no good reason to believe that there do exist minds other than his own. Even if he prefers to believe that to other human bodies there are harnessed minds not unlike his own, he cannot claim to be able to discover their individual characteristics, or the particular things that they undergo and do. Absolute solitude is on this showing the ineluctable destiny of the soul. Only our bodies can meet.

As a necessary corollary of this general scheme there is implicitly prescribed a special way of construing our ordinary concepts of mental powers and operations. The verbs, nouns and adjectives, with which in ordinary life we describe the wits, characters and higher-grade performances of the people with whom we have do, are required to be construed as signifying special episodes in their secret histories, or else as signifying tendencies for such episodes to occur. When someone is described as knowing, believing or guessing something, as hoping, dreading, intending or shirking something, as designing this or being amused at that, these verbs are supposed to denote the occurrence of specific modifications in his (to us) occult stream of consciousness. Only his own privileged access to this stream in direct awareness and introspection could provide authentic testimony that these mental-conduct verbs were correctly or incorrectly applied. The onlooker, be he teacher, critic, biographer or friend, can never assure himself that his comments have any vestige of truth. Yet it was just because we do in fact all know how to make such comments, make them with general correctness and correct them when they turn out to be confused or mistaken, that philosophers found it necessary to construct their theories of the nature and place of minds. Finding mental-conduct concepts being regularly and effectively used, they properly sought to fix their logical geography. But the logical geography officially recommended would entail that there could be no regular or effective use of these mental-conduct concepts in our descriptions of, and prescriptions for, other people's minds.

2. THE ABSURDITY OF THE OFFICIAL DOCTRINE

Such in outline is the official theory. I shall often speak of it, with deliberate abusiveness, as "the dogma of the Ghost in the Machine." I hope to prove that it is entirely false, and false not in detail but in principle. It is not merely an assemblage of particular mistakes. It is one big mistake and a mistake of a special kind. It is, namely, a category-mistake. It represents the facts of mental life as if they belonged to one logical type or category (or range of types or categories), when they actually belong to another. The dogma is therefore a philosopher's myth. In attempting to explode the myth I shall probably be taken to be denying well-known facts about the mental life of human beings, and my plea that I aim at doing nothing more than rectify the logic of mental-conduct concepts will probably be disallowed as mere subterfuge.

I must first indicate what is meant by the phrase "Category-mistake." This I do in a series of illustrations.

A foreigner visiting Oxford or Cambridge for the first time is shown a number of colleges, libraries, playing fields, museums, scientific departments and administrative offices. He then asks "But where is the University? I have seen where the members of the Colleges live, where the Registrar works, where the scientists experiment and the rest. But I have not yet seen the University in which reside and work the members of your University." It has then to be explained to him that the University is not another collateral institution, some ulterior counterpart to the colleges, laboratories and offices which he has seen. The University is just the way in which all that he has already seen is organized. When they are seen and when their co-ordination is understood, the University has been seen. His mistake lay in his innocent assumption that it was correct to speak of Christ Church, the Bodleian Library, the Ashmolean Museum *and* the University, to speak, that is, as if "the University" stood for an extra member of the class of which these other units are members.

He was mistakenly allocating the University to the same category as that to which the other institutions belong.

The same mistake would be made by a child witnessing the march-past of a division, who, having had pointed out to him such and such battalions, batteries, squadrons, etc., asked when the division was going to appear. He would be supposing that a division was a counterpart to the units already seen, partly similar to them and partly unlike them. He would be shown his mistake by being told that in watching the battalions, batteries and squadrons marching past he had been watching the division marching past. The march-past was not a parade of battalions, batteries, squadrons *and* a division; it was a parade of the battalions, batteries and squadrons *of* a division.

One more illustration. A foreigner watching his first game of cricket learns what are the functions of the bowlers, the batsmen, the fielders, the umpires and the scorers. He then says "But there is no one left on the field to contribute the famous element of team-spirit. I see who does the bowling, the batting and the wicket-keeping; but I do not see whose role it is to exercise *esprit de corps*." Once more, it would have to be explained that he was looking for the wrong type of thing. Team-spirit is not another cricketing-operation supplementary to all of the other special tasks. It is, roughly, the keenness with which each of the special tasks is performed, and performing a task keenly is not performing two tasks. Certainly exhibiting team-spirit is not the same thing as bowling or catching, but nor is it a third thing such that we can say that the bowler first bowls *and* then exhibits team-spirit or that a fielder is at a given moment *either* catching *or* displaying *esprit de corps*.

These illustrations of category-mistakes have a common feature which must be noticed. The mistakes were made by people who did not know how to wield the concepts *University, division* and *team-spirit*. Their puzzles arose from inability to use certain items in the English vocabulary.

The theoretically interesting category-mistakes are those made by people who are perfectly competent to apply concepts, at least in the situations with which they are familiar, but are still liable in their abstract thinking to allocate those concepts to logical types to which they do not belong. An instance of a mistake of this sort would be the following story. A student of politics has learned the main differences between the British, the French and the American Constitutions, and has learned also the differences and connections between the Cabinet, Parliament, the various Ministries, the Judicature and the Church of England. But he still becomes embarrassed when asked questions about the connections between the Church of England, the Home Office and the British Constitution. For while the Church and the Home Office are institutions, the British Constitution is not another institution in the same sense of that noun. So inter-institutional relations which can be asserted or denied to hold between the Church and the Home Office cannot be asserted or denied to hold between either of them and the British Constitution. "The British Constitution" is not a term of the same logical type as "The Home Office" and "the Church of England." In a partially similar way, John Doe may be a relative, a friend, an enemy or a stranger to Richard Roe; but he cannot be any of these things to the Average Taxpayer. He knows how to talk sense in certain sorts of discussions about the Average Taxpayer, but he is baffled to say why he could not come across him in the street as he can come across Richard Roe.

It is pertinent to our main subject to notice that, so long as the student of politics continues to think of the British Constitution as a counterpart to the other institutions, he will tend to describe it as a mysteriously occult institution; and so long as John Doe continues to think of the Average Taxpayer as a fellow-citizen, he will tend to think of him as an elusive insubstantial man, a ghost who is everywhere yet nowhere.

My destructive purpose is to show that a family of radical category-mistakes is the source of the double-life theory. The representation of a person as a ghost mysteriously ensconced in a machine derives from this argument. Because, as is true, a person's thinking, feeling and purposive doing cannot be described solely in the idioms of physics, chemistry and physiology, therefore they must be described in counterpart idioms. As the human body is a complex organized unit, so the human mind must be another complex organized unit, though one made of a different sort of stuff and with a different sort of structure. Or, again, as the human body, like any other parcel of matter, is a field of causes and effects, so the mind must be another field of causes and effects, though not (Heaven be praised) mechanical causes and effects.

3. THE ORIGIN OF THE CATEGORY-MISTAKE

One of the chief intellectual origins of what I have yet to prove to be the Cartesian category-mistake seems to be this. When Galileo showed that his methods of scientific discovery were competent to provide a mechanical theory which should cover every occupant of space, Descartes found in himself two conflicting motives. As a man of scientific genius he could not but endorse the claims of mechanics, yet as a religious and moral man he could not accept, as Hobbes accepted, the discouraging rider to those claims, namely that human nature differs only in degree of complexity from clockwork. The mental could not be just a variety of the mechanical.

He and subsequent philosophers naturally but erroneously availed themselves of the following escape-route. Since mental-conduct words are not to be construed as signifying the occurrence of mechanical processes, they must be construed as signifying the occurrence of non-mechanical processes; since mechanical laws explain movements in space as the effects of other movements in space, other laws must explain some of the non-spatial workings of minds as the effects of other non-spatial workings of minds. The difference between the human behaviours which we describe as intelligent and those which we describe as unintelligent must be a difference in their causation; so, while some movements of human tongues and limbs are the effects of mechanical causes, others must be the effects of non-mechanical causes, i.e. some issue from movements of particles of matter, others from workings of the mind.

The differences between the physical and the mental were thus represented as differences inside the common framework of the categories of "thing," "stuff," "attribute," "state," "process," "change," "cause," and "effect." Minds are things, but different sorts of things from bodies; mental processes are causes and effects, but different sorts of causes and effects from bodily movements. And so on. Somewhat as the foreigner expected the University to be an extra edifice, rather like a college but also considerably different, so the repudiators of mechanism represented minds as extra centres of causal processes, rather like machines but also considerably different from them. Their theory was a paramechanical hypothesis.

That this assumption was at the heart of the doctrine is shown by the fact that there was from the beginning felt to be a major theoretical difficulty in explaining how minds can influence and be influenced by bodies. How can a mental process, such as willing, cause spatial movements like the movements of the tongue? How can a physical change in the optic nerve have among its effects a mind's perception of a flash of light? This notorious crux by itself shows the logical mould into which Descartes pressed his theory of the mind. It was the self-same mould into which he and Galileo set their mechanics. Still unwittingly adhering to the grammar of mechanics, he tried to avert disaster by describing minds in what was merely an obverse vocabulary. The workings of minds had to be described by the mere negatives of the specific descriptions given to bodies; they are not in space, they are not motions, they are not modifications of matter, they are not accessible to public observation. Minds are not bits of clockwork, they are just bits of not-clockwork.

As thus represented, minds are not merely ghosts harnessed to machines, they are themselves just spectral machines. Though the human body is an engine, it is not quite an ordinary engine, since some of its workings are governed by another engine inside it—this interior governor-engine being one of a very special sort. It is invisible, inaudible and it has no size or weight. It cannot be taken to bits and the laws it obeys are not those known to ordinary engineers. Nothing is known of how it governs the bodily engine.

A second major crux points [to] the same moral. Since, according to the doctrine, minds belong to the same category as bodies and since bodies are rigidly governed by mechanical laws, it seemed to many theorists to follow that minds must be similarly governed by rigid non-mechanical laws. The physical world is a deterministic system, so the mental world must be a deterministic system. Bodies cannot help the modifications that they undergo, so minds cannot help pursuing the careers fixed for them. *Responsibility, choice, merit* and *demerit* are therefore inapplicable concepts—unless the compromise solution is adopted of saying that the laws governing mental processes, unlike those governing physical processes, have the congenial attribute of being only rather rigid. The problem of the Freedom of the Will was the problem how to reconcile the hypothesis that minds are to be described in terms drawn from the categories of mechanics with the knowledge that higher-grade human conduct is not of a piece with the behaviour of machines.

It is an historical curiosity that it was not noticed that the entire argument was broken-backed. Theorists correctly assumed that any sane man could already recognise the differences between, say, rational and non-rational utterances or between purposive and automatic behaviour. Else there would have been nothing requiring to be salved from mechanism. Yet the explanation given presupposed that one person could in principle never recognise the difference between the rational and the irrational utterances issuing from other human bodies, since he could never get access to the postulated immaterial causes of some of their utterances. Save for the doubtful exception of himself, he could never tell the difference between a man and a Robot. It would have to be conceded, for example, that, for all that we can tell, the inner lives of persons who are classed as idiots or lunatics are as rational as those of anyone else. Perhaps only their overt behaviour is disappointing; that is to say, perhaps "idiots" are not really idiotic, or "lunatics" lunatic. Perhaps, too, some of those who are classed as sane are really idiots. According to the theory, external observers could never know how the overt behaviour of others is correlated with their mental powers and processes and so they could never know or even plausibly conjecture whether their applications of mental-conduct concepts to these other people were correct or incorrect. It would then be hazardous or impossible for a man to claim sanity or logical consistency even for himself, since he would be debarred from comparing his own performances with those of others. In short, our characterizations of persons and their performances as intelligent, prudent and virtuous or as stupid, hypocritical and cowardly could never have been made, so the problem of providing a special causal hypothesis to serve as the basis of such diagnoses would never have arisen. The question, "How do persons differ from machines?" arose just because everyone already knew how to apply mental-conduct concepts before the new causal hypothesis was introduced. This causal hypothesis could not therefore be the source of the criteria used in those applications. Nor, of course, has the causal hypothesis in any degree improved our handling of those criteria. We still distinguish good from bad arithmetic, politic from impolitic conduct and fertile from infertile imaginations in the ways in which Descartes himself distinguished them before and after he speculated how the applicability of these criteria was compatible with the principle of mechanical causation.

He had mistaken the logic of his problem. Instead of asking by what criteria intelligent behaviour is actually distinguished from non-intelligent behaviour, he asked "Given that the principle of mechanical causation does not tell us the difference, what other causal principle will tell it us?" He realised that the problem was not one of mechanics and assumed that it must therefore be one of some counterpart to mechanics. Not unnaturally psychology is often cast for just this role.

When two terms belong to the same category, it is proper to construct conjunctive propositions embodying them. Thus a purchaser may say that he bought a left-hand glove and a right-hand glove, but not that he bought a left-hand glove, a right-hand glove and a pair of gloves. "She came home in a flood of tears and a sedan-chair" is a well-known joke based on the absurdity of conjoining terms of different types. It would have been equally ridiculous to construct the disjunction "She came home either in a flood of tears or else in a sedan-chair." Now the dogma of the Ghost in the Machine does just this. It maintains that there exist both bodies and minds; that there occur physical processes and mental processes; that there are mechanical causes of corporeal movements and mental causes of corporeal movements. I shall argue that these and other analogous conjunctions are absurd; but, it must be noticed, the argument will not show that either of the illegitimately conjoined propositions is absurd in itself. I am not, for example, denying that there occur mental processes. Doing long division is a mental process and so is making a joke. But I am saying that the phrase "there occur mental processes" does not mean the same sort of thing as "there occur physical processes," and, therefore, that it makes no sense to conjoin or disjoin the two.

If my argument is successful, there will follow some interesting consequences. First, the hallowed contrast between Mind and Matter will be dissipated, but dissipated not by either of the equally hallowed absorptions of Mind by Matter or of Matter by Mind, but in quite a different way. For the seeming contrast of the two will be shown to be as illegitimate as would be the contrast of "she came home in a flood of tears" and "she came home in a sedan-chair." The belief that there is a polar opposition between

Mind and Matter is the belief that they are terms of the same logical type.

It will also follow that both Idealism and Materialism are answers to an improper question. The "reduction" of the material world to mental states and processes, as well as the "reduction" of mental states and processes to physical states and processes, presuppose the legitimacy of the disjunction" Either there exist minds or there exist bodies (but not both)." It would be like saying, "Either she bought a left-hand and a right-hand glove or she bought a pair of gloves (but not both)."

It is perfectly proper to say, in one logical tone of voice, that there exist minds and to say, in another logical tone of voice, that there exist bodies. But these expressions do not indicate two different species of existence, for "existence" is not a generic word like "coloured" or "sexed." They indicate two different senses of "exist," somewhat as "rising" has different senses in "the tide is rising," "hopes are rising," and "the average age of death is rising." A man would be thought to be making a poor joke who said that three things are now rising, namely the tide, hopes and the average age of death. It would be just as good or bad a joke to say that there exist prime numbers and Wednesdays and public opinions and navies; or that there exist both minds and bodies.

An Embodied Self

Eve Browning Cole

Cole argues that Descartes's emphasis on the self as distinct from a body when placed in the context of a historically oppressive attitude toward women as bodies and emotional beings led to the belief that women lacked a genuine sense of self. To counter this tradition, she offers a view of the self as embodied and social. This move will, she hopes, lead to the elimination of the oppression associated with rationalistic, male concepts of a self.

We have already had occasion to observe that much of Western philosophy has displayed a definite discomfort with the fact that human minds come in human *bodies*, that consciousness and the thought processes it underlies are embodied in more or less gross matter. It is not very difficult to understand some of the motivations behind this discomfort. For thoughts do not seem to be subject to the same limitations as ordinary physical objects; in imagination, I can accomplish things which seem to transcend the limits of space and time. Vivid memories defy the irrecoverability of the past, seeming to bring to life dead friends, bringing into the present

From Chapter 3 of *Philosophy and Feminist Criticism: An Introduction*. Copyright © 1993 by Eve Browning Cole. Reprinted by permission of Paragon Press. Footnotes omitted.

past scenes, meals, and dreams. Dreams themselves are a powerful impetus toward regarding the mind as something more than or different from the physical "container" which it "inhabits" (though we shall soon see reasons to question these terms). And personal identity, the "I" who is the location of my consciousness, stretches back in time to embrace the child I was, the adolescent I became, and the woman I am now, even though in the physical sense I can only claim to be exactly what I now am (the past being no longer present).

Thus there are certain *prima facie* reasons for at least questioning how consciousness, thought, dreams, and identity relate to the physical world. But we will see that quite often philosophers have gone much further than questioning the relationship, to the extent of privileging the mental over the physical, derogating the physical and the human body along with it to a secondary ontological status, counseling efforts to transcend the body in order to apprehend truth, and even regarding the fact that mental events can cause physical events as a miracle performed by God on a daily basis! While this last, far from being a majority view, seems to have been instead a desperate expedient recommended only by one philosopher (Malebranche), it is symptomatic of something having gone badly wrong at the philosophical starting point.

Let us look more closely at the way in which the relation between body and mind, and the status of the body in the grand scheme of things, become problematic for philosophy. As our companion in this inquiry we will choose René Descartes—whose philosophical outlook, especially as represented in the designedly popular work *Meditations on First Philosophy* (published in 1641), proved enormously influential and remains a standard component of introductory studies of Western philosophy today.

SOLITARY MEDITATIONS, RADICAL DOUBTS

Descartes's work came at an extremely crucial juncture for Western philosophy. He entered a philosophical milieu still largely dominated by the medieval scholastic tradition, itself based heavily on a theologized and incomplete digestion of the legacy of the ancient Greeks. Studying with the Jesuits at the college of La Flèche, he received a "classical" and rather intellectually conservative education. Descartes made a radical break with this tradition, however, and set institutional philosophy off in a wholly new direction. Seeking to provide a philosophical method which would be accessible to all who possess common sense, providing a set of "rules for the direction of the mind" which would be so simple that "even women" would be able to follow them, his contributions to philosophy were revolutionary and of inestimable worth and influence. His contribution to the topic of this chapter, however, is highly problematic; and the difficulties he bequeathed to subsequent modern Western thought are enormous.

The full title of Descartes's *Meditations* is *Meditations on First Philosophy: In Which the Existence of God and the Distinction Between Mind and Body Are Demonstrated.* This full title is instructive as to how Descartes himself viewed his purpose in the work, which is often read in modern terms as a refutation of skepticism or an essay in foundationalism. By his own description, it is a work of *metaphysics.*

Descartes begins by confessing that he has long been aware that false beliefs have formed a part of his world view, and that a general and total mental "housecleaning" would need to be undertaken, in order to discover which of his views should be retained and which discarded. The procedure for this belief-testing, which he now proposes to undertake (since he is at present free "from every care" and "happily agitated by no passions") is that of *doubting*. He will attempt to cast doubt on each of his present beliefs; only those that survive the doubt ordeal will be retained. Rather than holding up individual beliefs for scrutiny, however, he proposes to address their general bases:

> . . . [I]t will not be requisite that I should examine each [belief] in particular, which would be an endless undertaking; for owing to the fact that the destruction of the foundations of necessity brings with it the downfall of the rest of the edifice, I shall only in the first place attack those principles upon which all my former opinions rested.

This project raises several interesting issues. First, Descartes is firmly committed to a *hierarchical* view of the structure of his belief system. The metaphor of the edifice of opinion, an ordered structure in which there is a top-down organization of architectural form, is an epistemological image to which we return in the next chapter when we discuss images of belief systems, and the power of the metaphors we choose to represent cognition.

But note also the extreme *solitude* of Descartes's project here. He is proposing to take apart and rebuild his entire belief structure in isolation from the rest of the world, and particularly from other human beings. The idea that an epistemological value test could reliably be applied in complete isolation from other knowers, that one's own relations of knowing the world could be tested through demolition and then rebuilt to stringent specifications entirely of one's own devising, is extraordinary. When we consider the contexts in which knowing takes place, in which knowledge is sought and constructed, few of these appear to be ones in which isolation is afforded or even desirable (we might think of archeological digs, science labs, classrooms, reading groups, research institutes, fact-finding missions to other countries, courtrooms, and other typical situations in which knowledge is found and formed in human minds; none is an individual-based project).

Thus Descartes is setting himself an *artificial* kind of task, in the dual sense that his knowledge-seeking environment is atypical and that the envisioned "new and improved" cognitive structure or edifice of opinion will be his *own* individual artifact.

But the solitariness of Descartes's project has also another implication/motivation. Only in radical isolation from the rest of the human social world can Descartes *fully* explore the reliability of his entire belief system. For if he were exploring in collaboration with others, if the meditations he undertakes were the work of a Cartesian task force, he would have to make concessions to the reliability of certain beliefs before the task force could begin its work. He would have to trust that the others were thinkers, perhaps even thinkers on a par with himself; that they were working with him rather than against him, that they could have and work toward a common goal, that their words could be understood, trusted, believed, taken more or less at face value. In other words, the Cartesian project could not motivate total doubt if it were not so solitary. The powerful skeptical doubts which Descartes is about to summon into existence will answer only to the call of an isolated individual human mental voice. They are creatures of solitude. Descartes's individualistic starting point has lasting and dramatic effects on his total project and its overall outcomes.

THE UNCERTAIN BODY

As the doubt program progresses, Descartes discards his trust in his senses as a source of reliable belief. Since (he reasons) the senses have deceived him in the past, it is advisable to suspend belief in sensory information for the duration of his meditations until he can uncover some justification for their occasional reliable operations. But the senses have been the source of his belief that he is an embodied creature, that he exists in or as a physical organism, in addition to being an originator of thoughts. Thus he must suspend his belief in the existence of the embodied Descartes and conceive of himself only as a locus of thoughts and other mental events, possibly not embodied at all, possibly embodied very differently from the way he has always pictured and experienced himself:

> I shall . . . suppose, not that God who is supremely good and the fountain of truth, but some evil genius not less powerful than deceitful, has employed his whole energies in deceiving me; I shall consider that the heavens, the earth, colors, figures, sound, and all the other external things are nought but the illusions and dreams of which this genius has availed himself in order to lay traps for my credulity; I shall consider myself as having no hands, no eyes, no flesh, no blood, nor any senses, yet falsely believing myself to possess all these things; I shall remain obstinately attached to this idea. . . .

Descartes will conceive of "himself" as something independent of his body, and will discover in this incorporeal consciousness the one indubitable truth which will function for him as an Archimedean immovable point, from which his belief structure can be rebuilt. This point is the certain truth of his own existence.

Descartes has effectively divided himself, and his belief structure, into two components: the certain mind, the component in which he will repose confidence at least as to its existence, and the uncertain body, about whose reality he will remain in a state of doubt until complex argumentation proves a limited trustworthiness, a constricted and carefully policed reliability.

Armed with the certainty of his own existence (as an insular node of consciousness which may or may not be embodied), Descartes goes on to demonstrate the existence of God, the fact that God is neither a grand deceiver nor the kind of being who would tolerate such massive deception of his creatures, and finally infers that the senses' urgings toward belief are not in themselves so awfully unreliable after all.

But the body, on Descartes's showing, remains forever only a probability, never a certainty. Since certainty is the Cartesian Holy Grail, this means that the body is irredeemably a second-class citizen in the metaphysical scheme of things. First rank in Descartes's universe is held by "thinking things," nodes of consciousness that can through purely rational processes follow deductive argumentation to absolutely certain conclusions. The body cannot participate in this process with its own humble abilities, here conceived as sensation and perception; it either impedes the rational process or, tamed and disciplined, stands dumbly by and lets knowledge happen. Highest epistemological honors go to the elements of deductive reasoning processes: mathematical laws, logical principles, indubitable truths. These construct the knowable core of the world, and to them in human experience is superadded a "flesh" of more dubious nature: bodies, colors, touches, smells, and the entire organic contents of the universe.

This theme, the privileging of the mental over the physical, does not originate with Descartes by any means. It is familiar to readers of Plato, who describes the relationship of soul to body in vivid terms:

> . . . [W]hen the soul uses the instrumentality of the body for any inquiry, whether through

> sight or hearing or any other sense—because using the body implies using the senses—it is drawn away by the body into the realm of the variable, and loses its way and becomes confused and dizzy, as though it were fuddled, through contact with things of a similar nature.... But when it investigates by itself, it passes into the realm of the pure and everlasting and immortal and changeless.... [*Phaedo 79c-d*]

Here the body is cast in the role of a bad companion, bad companny for the soul to keep, company that drags it down to its own level and impedes its effective functioning. A nonphysical form of knowing, in which the soul or mind operates "by itself," is much to be preferred.

Two features of this way of discussing the relation of mind to body, common to Plato and Descartes, should be noted. First, it is striking how easily both drop into the mode of thought in which a human being becomes not one but two, and two *different*, kinds of entity. There quickly emerges a kind of logical and metaphysical distance between mind and body, an alienation that provokes disagreement about what to believe, what to seek, how to behave. But secondly, this is not a disagreement among equals. The mind or soul is in Descartes's view the locus of certainty and value, in Plato's view the part of the human composite akin to the "pure" and "divine." Its relationship to the body is to be one of dominance; the body is to be subordinated and ruled.

An individual human being contains within the self, therefore, a fundamental power dialectic in which mind must triumph over body and must trumpet its victory in flourishes of "pure" rationality by means of which its soundness is demonstrated and ratified. Far from being an isolated peculiarity of a small handful of philosophers, moreover, this general dialectic is seen being set up and played out in many theaters of Western culture, from religion to popular morality, from Neoplatonism to existentialism....

FEMINIST CRITIQUES

We have already noted the extraordinary isolation of Descartes's metaphysical musings; he cuts off not only the instructions of his perceptive faculties, but also the entirety of his human social surroundings, to seek a certainty accessible only to the lone and insular conscious node "I." A feminist critique of Cartesian method might well begin with just this feature of his project.

The Cartesian ego, rather than being the ground for certainty and the Archimedean point which some philosophers have taken it to be, may in fact be the result of a mistaken abstraction. Feminist philosophers such as Caroline Whitbeck and Lorraine Code have convincingly argued that a preferable starting point for understanding the contents of human consciousness is *the relational self*, the self presented as involved in and importantly constituted by its connectedness to others. Each of us at this moment is connected as it were by invisible threads to an indefinite number of specific other human beings. In some cases, these connections are relatively remote; for example, we are all members of the same species and have biological similarities. Similarity is a relationship; therefore we are all related. Western culture has not tended to place much weight on this species relationship, however, and in some notorious institutions such as chattel slavery the reality of the relationship has been implicitly or explicitly denied. In other cases, the relationships in which we now stand are of deep significance in defining who we are, how we think, and how we act.

Starting with the concept of the relational self would greatly have changed the course of Descartes's meditations. If other persons are not just colorful wallpaper the design of which I contemplate from inside a mental fishbowl but actually part of who I am, then distancing myself from them in thought and supposing that I am the only consciousness in the universe becomes, if not impossible, extremely illogical. What would I hope to accomplish? If on the other hand I begin by granting them mentality and humanity, I will proceed by considering the specific ways in which their contributions to my mental life are made.

Paula Gunn Allen writes that, in Native American cultures, the question "Who is your mother?" is another and more profound way of asking who one is. In asking, one is inquiring about one of the most significant parts of a person's identity, for the influence of the mother and the mother's contribution to the child's self is considerable. In much the same way, we might begin a metaphysics of the self by asking "To whom am I related? In what ways? What contributions to my consciousness are presently being made, and by whom?" Such a beginning acknowledges the fundamental importance of sociality in human existence.

Here it might be objected that Descartes's . . . methodological skepticism about the existence and reality of other minds remains a possible position even for a relational self. Haven't we merely sidestepped the skeptical possibility by granting the mentality and humanity of the others? Doesn't it really still seem possible that they are all phantasms, or robots, or results of direct C-fiber stimulation by a mad scientist on a distant planet?

Yes, skeptical possibilities remain and cannot be ruled out. But taking the standpoint of the relational self allows us to affirm that such possibilities *do not matter.* What matters is that relationships are granted metaphysical priority over isolated individuals, so that the embeddedness of the self in a social world becomes its primary reality. The exact nature of the individuals involved becomes a matter of secondary importance. I grant at the outset that others make constitutive contributions to my experience, and I to theirs. This mutual interrelation becomes the ground for any further inquiry rather than functioning as a more or less uncertain inductive conclusion. Thus, to return to the problem of other minds, we can see that the philosopher's uncertainty about the mentality of the "foreign body" at the bus stop is a symptom of a flawed starting point rather than a genuine puzzle attending our reflective lives. The philosopher's mistake is to begin from isolation and attempt to reason himself back into society; we in fact begin in society and this is not an accidental but a deep truth about us.

We might go even further and argue that the concept of a radically isolated subject as the seat of consciousness is simply incoherent. We do not begin to think and speak in solitude, but in concert with our culture and with the specific representatives of the culture in whose care we find ourselves. We form ourselves in a collective process that is ongoing; our thoughts are never entirely our own, intersubjectivity is basic, while individual subjectivity is secondary and an abstraction.

Some feminist philosophers have analyzed the isolation of the ego and the "fishbowl" syndrome of some philosophy of mind in terms of differences between masculine and feminine gender socialization. Developmental psychologists have suggested that the structure and dynamics of relationships with other human beings differ profoundly for traditionally socialized men and women. Due largely to the fact that, in most cultures and historical epochs, women function as the primary caregiver for children of both sexes while men enter into the life of the family in a more intermittent way, it is to be expected that male children will form their earliest sense of themselves by *distinguishing* themselves from their female caregiver, realizing that they are members of the group from which the (distant, absent, or intermittently present) male family members derive. Female children will form their sense of themselves by *identifying* with the female caregiver, realizing that they share with her membership in the group of female family members.

This early direction of the sense of self, either to distinguish oneself and differ from, or to identify oneself and resemble, leaves a lasting legacy in the child's heart and mind. The adult character which emerges from the socialization process is marked by the tendency toward either clear and stark ego boundaries (if male) or flexible and mobile ego boundaries (if female). A whole constellation of dispositions and traits goes alongside this basic distinction. The masculine ego, formed at a distance from its primary role exemplar, displays a lifelong tendency toward independence, distancing from others, and endless acts of "proving" the masculinity which it modeled, with some uncertainty, on the distant fellow *man*. The feminine ego, formed in close proximity to its primary role exemplar, has lifelong tendencies toward identifying with others, reciprocating feelings, being dependent on others and relating to them easily, even confusing its own needs with those of others—since it early on perceived that part of being a woman was to place others first, as a primary caregiver must frequently do.

This developmental thesis about gender identity, though impossible to demonstrate empirically and almost certainty *not* crossculturally or crossracially, offers a tempting explanation for the philosophical model of the isolated self we have traced in Descartes and seen lurking behind the problem of other minds. The Cartesian ego is quintessentially *masculine* in its solitary doubting program, in its self-confidence about its quest, in its ambition ("proving" itself all on its own resources), and in its uneasiness. . . .

By contrast, the relational self which some feminist philosophers have proposed as an alternative starting point for philosophy of mind, and for grounding our understanding of human experience generally, is more aligned with feminine identity development.

In addition to proposing that philosophers start from a conception of the human self as relational, as situated within a web of cultural and personal relationships which not only shape but do much to constitute its being and its thought, feminist philosophers have also criticized the Cartesian legacy for the relation between mind and body which it conveys.

We saw above that Descartes (and others) operate from a position that separates mind, self, consciousness, ego from the physical body these are said to "inhabit" or . . . "animate." In Descartes, the distinction is so drastic that mind and body are said to share no attributes whatsoever; they are oppositionally defined and thus, metaphysically speaking, mutually exclusive. Consciousness is nonphysical, nonextended, and inhabits an order of being completely distinct from that in which the body lives. The body is a machine, operated by the mind in the case of the human being, mindless and purely mechanical in the case of other animals.

This drastic dualism is vulnerable to criticism from many different directions; feminist critics begin with the observation that in Western culture and throughout its history, we can observe a tendency to identify women with the natural, the physical, the bodily. Nature is personified as a female, a "mother"; women are portrayed as more closely linked to nature, less completely integrated into civilization and the cultural order, than men. Men are rational agents, makers of order and measure, controllers of history; women are emotional vessels, subjects of orders and measures, passive observers of history. No one describes this more clearly or more influentially for modern psychology than Sigmund Freud, who writes:

> The fact that women must be regarded as having little sense of justice is no doubt related to the predominance of envy in their mental life; for the demand for justice is a modification of envy and lays down the condition subject to which we can lay envy aside. We also regard women as weaker in their social interests and as having less capacity for sublimating their instincts than men.

Freud subsumes women into the domain of the natural, where instinct rules and justice is foreign.

Now, if man is to mind as woman is to body, as appears from much of the literature and iconography of Western culture throughout historical time, and if we adhere to a generally Cartesian view of the self as a purely mental entity, then the self of the woman becomes deeply problematic. Can women have Cartesian egos? Genuine selves? It would appear to be impossible if woman's essence is located in the domain of the bodily. Clearly some other and less dichotomously dualistic conception of the self must be sought.

The associations between woman and body in Western culture have had a decidedly negative aspect, which feminist critics have stressed. The reduction of a woman's value to the culturally inscribed value of a certain feminine appearance and protest against that reduction have been strong themes of feminist criticism for several decades. Nevertheless, the appearance obsession which women are encouraged to develop in our culture, according to which a more-or-less single standard of feminine beauty applies to all women, no matter their age, race, build, or life-style, is as strong as ever and, some argue, gaining strength. In addition now to being slim, youthful, cosmetically adorned to the correct degree, fashionably dressed, and as light-skinned as possible (with of course a healthy tan to indicate white-skinned class-privilege), women must ideally have "hard bodies" with muscle-definition acquired by hours of grueling workouts and aerobic routines. That this formula cannot be met by the poor, those who don't have the time to devote to the pursuit of beauty, or those whose bodies resist the mold for whatever reason, does not mean that the standard does not hold its pristine severity over all women's heads equally. (Sadly, the appearance obsession does seem to be extending to men as well, but still seems to pertain to them in lesser degree.)

In a recent classroom discussion of trends in advertising, one young female student spoke out with sincere enthusiasm: "I can't wait till I get older! I'm going to eat whatever I want, wear whatever I want, and just not care!" An older female student turned to her and said, "Why wait? It isn't any easier to look different at age fifty than at age twenty." This exchange was instructive in many ways. There was anger in the second woman's voice; she heard herself as older being dismissed somehow from the class of viable potential beauties. There was a strange assumption behind the first woman's statements, to the effect that until some unspecified age, women are under an obligation to eat and to dress in ways other than those they would choose if not constrained. And there was in the second speaker's choice of the word *different* to describe an undisciplined woman the implicit admission that the *norm*, what it means to be *non*different, is precisely the cultural ideal of the dieting and carefully dressed youthful appearance. But this is clearly false, as a simple glance at the immense variety of actual women's bodies in any real-life situation will immediately confirm. The so-called *norm* is in fact extremely rare. Yet an enormous amount of women's energy is devoted to its pursuit. Constant dieting, eating disorders such as anorexia and bulimia, compulsive exercising, and (not least of all) enormous cash investments in beauty and fashion, are all symptomatic of the power of the cultural ideal.

To connect with our previous discussion of the gendered distinction between mind and body, men generally do not in our culture tend to identify themselves and their worth as persons with the details of their physical bodies' appearances. While in recent years the standards of male attractiveness have undoubtedly become more exacting, men clearly feel more relaxed about not meeting these standards.

Let us summarize the contribution which the dualistic Platonic-Cartesian model of the self has made to our cultural conceptions of body and mind: (1) The body's relationship to the mind, in any given human being, is one of unruly bondage or servitude; mind properly dominates its body and directs its actions, while body properly obeys. (2) Mind's behavior and dispositions are, however, described in terms more appropriate to masculine gender identity (activity, ruling or hegemony, capacity for abstraction and objectivity, distanced contemplation, dispassionate analysis), while body's configurations tend toward feminine (passivity, subordination, unconscious physicality, sensuous and emotional implication, confusion). (3) Thus, while rationality becomes defined as a mostly masculine project, an adorned and disciplined physicality becomes the feminist project—leading to the contemporary obsession of middle-class women with weight and appearance generally. Women are given the cultural prescription to be docile bodies, adorned and available for participation in the rational schemes of the male-dominated social order. Thus the fact that in some basic respects the Cartesian ego is a masculine ego can be seen to have enormous reverberations throughout modern life. It is of no small significance to recognize that a certain outlook in the philosophy of mind provides a perfect recipe for male dominance and women's subordination.

Several important qualifications need to be made here, however. First, the neat gender dichotomy we have drawn in the ratio of proportion:

Male:Mind::Female:Body

does not appear to hold cross-racially. That is, nonwhite males in a white-dominated culture will be treated in much the same way as bodies are treated by minds in the Cartesian framework: They will be dominated, ruled, directed, used. Furthermore, white females will participate in this domination and rule, functioning as "minds" in a bureaucratic manner; and white women will benefit from skin privilege at the expense of the dominated nonwhite men and women. The nonwhite populations will be accorded *mental* attributes that correspond to the physical attributes of the body in the Cartesian scheme; they will be considered less than fully rational, emotional, "natural" or savage, sensuous, weak-willed, and so forth. So the factor of race does much to complicate a mind-body value map which takes *only* gender into account. This has led some feminist philosophers to hypothesize that *both* sexism and racism are more about power than they are about either sex or race.

A second qualification concerns the relationship between what, for want of a clearer word, we could call ideology and social reality. The rational man and the physical woman, intellectual masculinity and corporeal femininity, are creatures of ideology. This means that they are intensely value-laden concepts structuring culture and its expectations, rather than empirical generalizations drawn from observation of real women and real men. But ideology and reality touch one another at multiple points and reciprocally influence each other at these points of contact. It may be a strange-sounding philosophical thesis that rationality has been interpreted in terms defined as masculine, but it takes on a gruesomely real shape when a Berkeley philosophy professor announces to his classes that women can't do logic, or when another philosophy professor writes to the secretary of the American Philosophical Association that white women and black people of both sexes display analytical capabilities inferior to those of white men. This is ideology shaping social reality with a vengeance.

Believing that the drastic dualism of the traditional picture of body's relation to mind, along with the inbuilt evaluatively hierarchical model of dominance and subordination which gives the model its working directives, are both deeply flawed, feminist philosophers look for alternatives.

A beginning point is to conceive of the human self as intrinsically embodied: An *embodied self* can displace the only questionably embodied Cartesian ego, the uncomfortably body-trapped Platonic soul, as a foundation for further inquiry into the nature of human experience. To conceive of the self as essentially or intrinsically embodied means to acknowledge the centrality of the physical in human psychology and cognition, for one thing. It means opening the door to the possibility of a bodily wisdom, to revaluing the physical human being, in ways that promise both better metaphysical schemes and more ethical models for human interaction. Breaking down the valuational hierarchy between mind and body, attempting to think of them as woven and melded together into what constitutes who we are and who we ought to be, eliminates the perhaps primary internal oppression model of mind over body. As a culture, however, we have learned to think of the body, and of those primarily identified with it, in terms of scorn (even when those latter people are ourselves). We have learned to privilege the "rational" over the emotional (conceived as proceeding from physical sources), the basely corporeal, the manual and tactile; to weigh technorationality over the mute testimony of nature and our own bodies. Those of us who are women have at times been encouraged to view our bodies with contempt when we perceive them as falling short of the beauty ideal or when we are addressed rudely in sexual terms by strangers. How can we begin to approach the relation of mind and body not as a *problem* but as a source of liberatory insight and joy?

French feminist philosophers, building on their national intellectual tradition, which placed the phenomenology of *lived experience* at center stage, have made exciting progress in constructing the basis for a liberatory philosophy of the body. They have argued that the dominant tradition in Western philosophy has made women's bodies problematic in two contradictory ways: In one way, woman and body are equated as essentially physical, and women's entire personalities become sexualized (think of the late Victorian habit of referring to women as a group with the phrase "the sex," as if men were "the non-sex"). In another direction, however, the sexualized woman is either ignored in philosophy, so complete is her subsumption under the rubric *Nature,* or she is philosophized about in male terms, and her (now highlighted in neon) sexuality is described in terms appropriate only to a certain specific cultural construction of *male* sexuality. She is thus obscured as a subject, discussed as an object.

This means that, for a genuinely liberatory philosophy of the body to be developed, women must reclaim in theory and in practice their own physicality, their own sexuality.

The Doctrine of the Not-Self

Buddhist Scripture

In Buddhist doctrine, we find yet another criticism of theories that make the self into a substance of some kind. What if there is no soul, no self, as Western traditions and beliefs describe it? What is or would be the meaning of terms such as soul *or* self *if the terms did not designate some metaphysical substance? Would such terms simply refer to an aggregate of thoughts, feelings, behaviors, and/or sensory experiences? You may wish to compare the teachings of Buddha on this issue with Wittgenstein's discussion of selves and persons.*

2. THE DOCTRINE OF NOT-SELF

2a. The Chariot

And King Milinda asked him: "How is your Reverence known, and what is your name, Sir?" "As Nagasena I am known, O great king, and as Nagasena do my fellow religious habitually address me. But although parents give such names as Nagasena, or Surasena, or Virasena, or Sihasena, nevertheless this word 'Nagasena' is just a denomination, a designation, a conceptual term, a current appellation, a mere name. For no real person can here be apprehended." But King Milinda explained: "Now listen, you 500 Greeks and 80,000 monks, this Nagasena tells me that he is not a real person! How can I be expected to agree with that!" And to Nagasena he said: "If, most reverend Nagasena, no person can be apprehended in reality, who then, I ask you, gives you what you require by way of robes, food, lodging, and medicines? Who is it that consumes them? Who is it that guards morality, practises meditation, and realizes the [four] Paths and their Fruits, and thereafter Nirvana? Who is it that kills living beings, takes what is not given, commits sexual misconduct, tells lies, drinks intoxicants? Who is it that commits the five Deadly Sins? For, if there were no person, there could be no merit and no demerit; no doer of meritorious or demeritorious deeds, and no agent behind them; no fruit of good and evil deeds, and no reward or punishment for them. If someone should kill you, O Venerable Nagasena, he would not commit any murder. And you yourself, Venerable Nagasena, would not be

From Chapter 2 of *Buddhist Scriptures*, selected and translated by Edward Conze, Penguin Books.

a real teacher, or instructor, or ordained monk! You just told me that your fellow religious habitually address you as 'Nagasena.' What then is this 'Nagasena'? Are perhaps the hairs of the head 'Nagasena'?"—"No, great king!" "Or perhaps the hairs of the body?"—"No, great king!" "Or perhaps the nails, teeth, skin, muscles, sinews, bones, marrow, kidneys, heart, liver, serous membranes, spleen, lungs, intestines, mesentery, stomach, excrement, the bile, phlegm, pus, blood, grease, fat, tears, sweat, spittle, snot, fluid of the joints, urine, or the brain in the skull—are they this 'Nagasena'?"—"No, great king!"—"Or is form this 'Nagasena,' or feeling, or perceptions, or impulses, or consciousness?"—"No, great king!"—"Then is it the combination of form, feelings, perceptions, impulses, and consciousness?"—"No, great king!"—"Then is it outside the combination of form, feelings, perceptions, impulses, and consciousness?"—"No, great king!"—"Then, ask as I may, I can discover no Nagasena at all. Just a mere sound is this 'Nagasena,' but who is the real Nagasena? Your Reverence has told a lie, has spoken a falsehood! There really is no Nagasena!"

Thereupon the Venerable Nagasena said to King Milinda: "As a king you have been brought up in great refinement and you avoid roughness of any kind. If you would walk at midday on this hot, burning, and sandy ground, then your feet would have to tread on the rough and gritty gravel and pebbles, and they would hurt you, your body would get tired, your mind impaired, and your awareness of your body would be associated with pain. How then did you come—on foot, or on a mount?"

"I did not come, Sir, on foot, but on a chariot"—"If you have come on a chariot, then please explain to me what a chariot is. Is the pole the chariot?"—"No, reverend Sir!"—"Is then the axle the chariot?"—"No, reverend Sir!"—"Is it then the wheels, or the framework, or the flag-staff, or the yoke, or the reins, or the goad-stick?"—"No, reverend Sir!"—"Then is it the combination of pole, axle, wheels, framework, flag-staff, yoke, reins, and goad which is the 'chariot'?"—"No, reverend Sir!"—"Then is this 'chariot' outside the combination of pole, axle, wheels, framework, flag-staff, yoke, reins, and goad?"—"No, reverend Sir!"—"Then, ask as I may, I can discover no chariot at all. Just a mere sound is the 'chariot.' But what is the real chariot? Your Majesty has told a lie, has spoken a falsehood! There really is no chariot! Your Majesty is the greatest king in the whole of India. Of whom then are you afraid, that you do not speak the truth?" And he exclaimed: "Now listen, you 500 Greeks and 80,000 monks, this king Milinda tells me that he has come on a chariot. But when asked to explain to me what a chariot is, he cannot establish its existence. How can one possibly approve of that?"

The five hundred Greeks thereupon applauded the Venerable Nagasena and said to king Milinda: "Now let your Majesty get out of that if you can!"

But king Milinda said to Nagasena: "I have not, Nagasena, spoken a falsehood. For it is in dependence on the pole, the axle, the wheels, the framework, the flag-staff, etc., that there takes place this denomination 'chariot,' this designation, this conceptual term, a current appellation and a mere name."—"Your Majesty has spoken well about the chariot. It is just so with me. In dependence on the thirty-two parts of the body and the five Skandhas there takes place this denomination 'Nagasena,' this designation, this conceptual term, a current appellation and a mere name. In ultimate reality, however, this person cannot be apprehended. And this has been said by our Sister Vajira when she was face to face with the Lord:

'Where all constituent parts are present,
The word "a chariot" is applied.
So likewise where the skandhas are,
The term a "being" commonly is used.'

"It is wonderful, Nagasena, it is astonishing, Nagasena! Most brilliantly have these questions been answered! Were the Buddha himself here, he would approve what you have said. Well spoken, Nagasena, well spoken!"

2b. Personal Identity and Rebirth

The king asked: "When someone is reborn, Venerable Nagasena, is he the same as the one who just died, or is he another?"—The Elder replied: "He is neither the same nor another."—"Give me an illustration!"—"What do you think, great king: when you were a tiny infant, newly born and quite soft, were you then the same as the one who is now grown up?"—"No, that infant was one, I, now grown up, am another."—"If that is so, then, great king, you have had no mother, no father, no teaching, and no schooling! Do we then take it that there is one mother for the embryo in the first stage, another for the second stage, another for the third, another for the fourth, another for the baby, another for the grown-up man? Is the schoolboy one person, and the one who has finished school another? Does one commit a crime, but the hands and feet of another are cut off?"—"Certainly not! But what would you say, Reverend Sir, to all that?"—The Elder replied: "I was neither the tiny infant, newly born and quite soft, nor am I now the grown-up man; but all these are comprised in one unit depending on this very body."—"Give me a simile!"—"If a man were to light a lamp, could it give light throughout the whole night?"—"Yes, it could."—"Is now the flame which burns in the first watch of the night the same as the one which burns in the second?"—"Is is not the same."—"Or is the flame which burns in the second watch the same as the one which burns in the last one?"—"It is not the same."—"Do we then take it that there is one lamp in the first watch of the night, another in the second, and another again in the third?"—"No, it is because of just that one lamp that the light shines throughout the night."—"Even so must we understand the collocation of a series of successive dharmas. At rebirth one dharma arises, while another stops; but the two processes take place almost simultaneously (i.e. they are continuous). Therefore the first act of consciousness in the new existence is neither the same as the last act of consciousness in the previous existence, nor is it another."—"Give me another simile!"—"Milk, once the milking is done, turns after some time into curds; from curds it turns into fresh butter, and from fresh butter into ghee. Would it now be correct to say that the milk is the same thing as the curds, or the fresh butter, or the ghee?"—"No, it would not. But they have been produced because of it."—"Just so must be understood the collocation of a series of successive dharmas."

2c. Personal Identity and Karma

The king asked: "Is there, Nagasena, any being which passes on from this body to another body?"—"No, your majesty!"—"If there were no passing on from this body to another, would not one then in one's next life be freed from the evil deeds committed in the past?"—"Yes, that would be so if one were not linked once again with a new organism. But since, your majesty, one is linked once again with a new organism, therefore one is not freed from one's evil deeds."—"Give me a simile!"—"If a man should steal another man's mangoes, would he deserve a thrashing for that?"—"Yes, of course!"—"But he would not have stolen the very same mangoes as the other one had planted. Why then should he deserve a thrashing?"—"For the reason that the stolen mangoes had grown because of those that were planted."—"Just so, your majesty, it is because of the deeds one does, whether pure or impure, by means of this psycho-physical organism, that one is once again linked with another psycho-physical organism, and is not freed from one's evil deeds."—"Very good, Nagasena!"

The Identity of Contraries

Chuang Tzu

In this Taoist writing, we are told that identity is a balance of opposite forces in us and of all that is in us (and nature). It is a reconciliation of all that is and all that is not. Death and life are one and the same. Chuang Tzu tells us not to become excessive or obsessive in our activities. We each have potential to become who we will be, and we must put ourselves into "subjective relation" with each other in order to become this. How do we become who we are, then? As you read this, reflect upon these paradoxes and consider what makes you who you are.

CHAPTER II/THE IDENTITY OF CONTRARIES

"Great knowledge [said Tzu Ch'i of Nan-kuo] embraces the whole: small knowledge, a part only. Great speech is universal: small speech is particular.

"For whether the mind is locked in sleep or whether in waking hours the body is released, we are subject to daily mental perturbations,—indecision, want of penetration, concealment, fretting fear, and trembling terror. Now like a javelin the mind flies forth, the arbiter of right and wrong. Now like a solemn covenanter it remains firm, the guardian of rights secured. Then, as under autumn and winter's blight, comes gradual decay, a passing away, like the flow of water, never to return. Finally, the block when all is choked up like an old drain—the failing mind which shall not see light again.

"Joy and anger, sorrow and happiness, caution and remorse, come upon us by turns, with ever-changing mood. They come like music from hollowness, like mushrooms from damp. Daily and nightly they alternate within us, but we cannot tell whence they spring. Can we then hope in a moment to lay our finger upon their very Cause?

"But for these emotions *I* should not be. But for me, *they* would have no scope. So far we can go; but we do not know what it is that brings them into play. 'Twould seem to be a soul; but the clue to its existence is wanting. That such a Power operates, is credible enough, though we cannot

---

From *Chuang Tzu, Taoist Philosopher and Chinese Mystic,* translated by Herbert A. Giles (London: Allen and Unwin, 1926).

see its form. Perhaps it has functions without form.

"Take the human body with all its manifold divisions. Which part of it does a man love best? Does he not cherish all equally, or has he a preference? Do not all equally serve him? And do these servitors then govern themselves, or are they subdivided into rulers and subjects? Surely there is some soul which sways them all.

"But whether or not we ascertain what are the functions of this soul, it matters but little to the soul itself. For coming into existence with this mortal coil of mine, with the exhaustion of this mortal coil its mandate will also be exhausted. To be harassed by the wear and tear of life, and to pass rapidly through it without possibility of arresting one's course,—is not this pitiful indeed? To labour without ceasing, and then, without living to enjoy the fruit, worn out, to depart, suddenly, one knows not whither,—is not that a just cause for grief?

"What advantage is there in what men call not dying? The body decomposes, and the mind goes with it. This is our real cause for sorrow. Can the world be so dull as not to see this? Or is it I alone who am dull, and others not so?

"If we are to be guided by the criteria of our own minds, who shall be without a guide? . . .

"Speech is not mere breath. It is differentiated by meaning. Take away that, and you cannot say whether it is speech or not. Can you even distinguish it from the chirping of young birds?

"But how can TAO be so obscured that we speak of it as true and false? And how can speech be so obscured that it admits the idea of contraries? How can TAO go away and yet not remain? How can speech exist and yet be impossible?

"TAO is obscured by our want of grasp. Speech is obscured by the gloss of this world. Hence the affirmatives and negatives of the Confucian and Mihist schools, each denying what the other affirmed and affirming what the other denied. But he who would reconcile affirmative with negative and negative with affirmative, must do so by the light of nature.

"There is nothing which is not objective: there is nothing which is not subjective. But it is impossible to start from the objective. Only from subjective knowledge is it possible to proceed to objective knowledge. Hence it has been said. 'The objective emanates from the subjective; the subjective is consequent upon the objective. This is the *Alternation Theory.*' Nevertheless, when one is born, the other dies. When one is possible, the other is impossible. When one is affirmative the other is negative. Which being the case, the true sage rejects all distinctions of this and that. He takes his refuge in GOD, and places himself in subjective relation with all things.

"And inasmuch as the subjective is also objective, and the objective also subjective, and as the contraries under each are indistinguishably blended, does it not become impossible for us to say whether subjective and objective really exist at all?

"When subjective and objective are both without their correlates, that is the very axis of TAO. And when that axis passes through the centre at which all Infinities converge, positive and negative alike blend into an infinite ONE. Hence it has been said that there is nothing like the light of nature.

"To take a finger in illustration of a finger not being a finger is not so good as to take something which is not a finger. To take a horse in illustration of a horse not being a horse is not so good as to take something which is not a horse.

"So with the universe and all that in it is. These things are but fingers and horses in this sense. The possible is possible: the impossible is impossible. TAO operates, and given results follow. Things receive names and are what they are. They achieve this by their natural affinity for what they are and their natural antagonism to what they are not. For all things have their own particular constitutions and potentialities. Nothing can exist without these.

"Therefore it is that, viewed from the standpoint of TAO, a beam and a pillar are identical. So are ugliness and beauty, greatness, wickedness, perverseness, and strangeness. Separation is the same as construction: construction is the same as destruction. Nothing is subject either to construction or to destruction, for these conditions are brought together into ONE.

"Only the truly intelligent understand this principle of the identity of all things. They do not view things as apprehended by themselves, subjectively; but transfer themselves into the position of the things viewed. And viewing them thus they are able to comprehend them, nay, to master them;—and he who can master them is near. So it is that to place oneself in subjective relation with externals, without consciousness of their objectivity,—this is TAO. But to wear out one's intellect in an obstinate adherence to the individuality of things, not recognizing the fact that all things are ONE,—this is called *Three in the Morning*."

"What is *Three in the Morning*?" asked Tzu Yu.

"A keeper of monkeys," replied Tzu-Ch'i, "said with regard to their rations of chestnuts that each monkey was to have three in the morning and four at night. But at this the monkeys were very angry, so the keeper said they might have four in the morning and three at night, with which arrangement they were all well pleased. The actual number of the chestnuts remained the same, but there was an adaptation to the likes and dislikes of those concerned. Such is the principle of putting oneself into subjective relation with externals.

"Wherefore the true Sage, while regarding contraries as identical, adapts himself to the laws of Heaven. This is called following two courses at once. . . .

"Therefore what the true Sage aims at is the light which comes out of darkness. He does not view things as apprehended by himself, subjectively, but transfers himself into the position of the things viewed. This is called using the light.

"There remains, however, Speech. Is that to be enrolled under either category of contraries, or not? Whether it is so enrolled or not, it will in any case belong to one or the other, and thus be as though it had an objective existence. At any rate, I should like to hear some speech which belongs to neither category. . . .

. . . "The universe and I came into being together; and I, and everything therein, are ONE.

"If then all things are ONE, what room is there for Speech? On the other hand, since I can utter these words, how can Speech not exist?

"If it does exist, we have ONE and Speech = two; and two and one = three. From which point onwards even the best mathematicians will fail to reach: how much more then will ordinary people fail?

"Hence, if from nothing you can proceed to something, and subsequently reach three, it follows that it would be still more easy if you were to start from something. To avoid such progression, you must put yourself into subjective relation with the external.

"Before conditions existed, TAO was. Before definitions existed, Speech was. Subjectively, we are conscious of certain delimitations which are—

Right	and Left
Relationship	and Obligation
Division	and Discrimination
Emulation	and Contention

These are called the *Eight Predicables.* For the true Sage, beyond the limits of an external world, they exist, but are not recognized. By the true Sage, within the limits of an external world, they are recognized, but are not assigned. And so, with regard to the wisdom of the ancients, as embodied in the canon of *Spring and Autumn,* the true Sage assigns, but does not justify by argument. And thus, classifying he does not classify; arguing, he does not argue."

"How can that be?" asked Tzu Yu.

"The true Sage," answered Tzu Ch'i, "keeps his knowledge within him, while men in general set forth theirs in argument, in order to convince each other. And therefore it is said that in argument he does not manifest himself.

"Perfect TAO does not declare itself. Nor does perfect argument express itself in words. Nor does perfect charity show itself in act. Nor is perfect honesty absolutely incorruptible. Nor is perfect courage absolutely unyielding.

"For the TAO which shines forth is not TAO. Speech which argues falls short of its aim. Charity which has fixed points loses its scope. Honesty which is absolute is wanting in credit. Courage which is absolute misses its object. These five are, as it were, round, with a strong bias towards squareness. Therefore that knowledge which stops at what it does not know, is the highest knowledge.

"Who knows the argument which can be argued without words?—the TAO which does not declare itself as TAO? He who knows this may be said to be of GOD. To be able to pour in without making full, and pour out without making empty, in ignorance of the power by which such results are accomplished,—this is accounted *Light.*"

Of old, the Emperor Yao said to Shun, "I would smite the Tsungs, and the Kueis, and the Hsü-aos. Ever since I have been on the throne I have had this desire. What do you think?"

"These three States," replied Shun, "are paltry out-of-the-way places. Why can you not shake off this desire? Once upon a time, ten suns came out together, and all things were illuminated thereby. How much more then should virtue excel suns?"

Yeh Ch'üeh asked Wang I, saying, "Do you know for certain that all things are subjectively the same?"

"How can I know?" answered Wang I. "Do you know what you do not know?"

"How can I know?" replied Yeh Ch'üeh. "But can then nothing be known?"

"How can I know?" said Wang I. "Nevertheless, I will try to tell you. How can it be known that what I call knowing is not really not knowing and that what I call not knowing is not really knowing? Now I would ask you this. If a man sleeps in a damp place, he gets lumbago and dies. But how about an eel? And living up in a tree is precarious and trying to the nerves:—but how about monkeys? Of the man, the eel, and the monkey, whose habitat is the right one, absolutely? Human beings feed on flesh, deer on grass, centipedes on snakes' brains, owls and crows on mice. Of these four, whose is the right taste, absolutely? Monkey mates with monkey; the buck with the doe; eels consort with fishes, while men admire Mao Ch'iang and Li Chi, at the sight of whom fishes plunge deep down in the water, birds soar high in the air, and deer hurry away. Yet who shall say which is the correct standard of beauty? In my opinion, the standard of human virtue, and of positive and negative, is so obscured that it is impossible to actually know it as such."

"If you then," asked Yeh Ch'üeh, "do not know what is bad for you, is the Perfect Man equally without this knowledge?"

"The Perfect Man," answered Wang I, "is a spiritual being. Were the ocean itself scorched up, he would not feel hot. Were the

Milky Way frozen hard, he would not feel cold. Were the mountains to be riven with thunder, and the great deep to be thrown up by storm, he would not tremble. In such case, he would mount upon the clouds of heaven, and driving the sun and the moon before him, would pass beyond the limits of this external world, where death and life have no more victory over man;—how much less what is bad for him?"

Chü Ch'iao addressed Chang Wu Tzu as follows: "I heard Confucius say, 'The true sage pays no heed to mundane affairs. He neither seeks gain nor avoids injury. He asks nothing at the hands of man. He adheres, without questioning, to TAO. Without speaking, he can speak; and he can speak and yet say nothing. And so he roams beyond the limits of this dusty world. These,' added Confucius, 'are wild words.' Now to me they are the skilful embodiment of TAO. What Sir, is your opinion?"

"Points upon which the Yellow Emperor doubted," replied Chang Wu Tzu, "how should Confucius know? You are going too fast. You see your egg, and expect to hear it crow. You look at your cross-bow, and expect to have broiled pigeon before you. I will say a few words to you at random, and do you listen at random.

"How does the Sage seat himself by the sun and moon, and hold the universe in his grasp? He blends everything into one harmonious whole, rejecting the confusion of this and that. Rank and precedence, which the vulgar prize, the Sage stolidly ignores. The revolutions of ten thousand years leave his Unity unscathed. The universe itself may pass away, but he will flourish still.

"How do I know that love of life is not a delusion after all? How do I know but that he who dreads to die is not as a child who has lost the way and cannot find his home?

"The Lady Li Chi was the daughter of Ai Feng. When the Duke of Chin first got her, she wept until the bosom of her dress was drenched with tears. But when she came to the royal residence, and lived with the Duke, and ate rich food, she repented of having wept. How then do I know but that the dead repent of having previously clung to life?

"Those who dream of the banquet, wake to lamentation and sorrow. Those who dream of lamentation and sorrow wake to join the hunt. While they dream, they do not know that they dream. Some will even interpret the very dream they are dreaming; and only when they awake do they know it was a dream.

"By and by comes the Great Awakening, and then we find out that this life is really a great dream. Fools think they are awake now, and flatter themselves they know if they are really princes or peasants. Confucius and you are both dreams; and I who say you are dreams,—I am but a dream myself. This is a paradox. Tomorrow a sage may arise to explain it; but that tomorrow will not be until ten thousand generations have gone by.

"Granting that you and I argue. If you beat me, and not I you, are you necessarily right and I wrong? Or if I beat you and not you me, am I necessarily right and you wrong? Or are we both partly right and partly wrong? Or are we both wholly right and wholly wrong? You and I cannot know this, and consequently the world will be in ignorance of the truth.

"Who shall I employ as arbiter between us? If I employ some one who takes your view, he will side with you. How can such a one arbitrate between us? If I employ some one who takes my view, he will side with me. How can such a one arbitrate between us? And if I employ some one who either differs from, or agrees with, both of us, he will be equally unable to decide between us. Since then you, and I, and man, cannot decide, must we not depend upon Another? Such dependence is as though it were not dependence. We are embraced in the obliterating unity of God. There is perfect adaptation to whatever may eventuate; and so we complete our allotted span.

"But what is it to be embraced in the obliterating unity of God? It is this. With reference to positive and negative, to that which is so and that which is not so,—if the positive is really positive, it must necessarily be different from its negative: there is no room for argument. And if that which is so really is so, it must necessarily be different from that which is not so: there is no room for argument.

"Take no heed of time, nor of right and wrong. But passing into the realm of the Infinite, take your final rest therein."

The Penumbra said to the Umbra,* "At one moment you move: at another you are at rest. At one moment you sit down: at another you get up. Why this instability of purpose?" "I depend," replied the Umbra, "upon something which causes me to do as I do; and that something depends in turn upon something else which causes it to do as it does. My dependence is like that of a snake's scales or of a cicada's wings. How can I tell why I do one thing, or why I do not do another?"

Once upon a time, I, Chuang Tzu, dreamt I was a butterfly, fluttering hither and thither, to all intents and purposes a butterfly. I was conscious only of following my fancies as a butterfly, and was unconscious of my individuality as a man. Suddenly, I awaked, and there I lay, myself again. Now I do not know whether I was then a man dreaming I was a butterfly, or whether I am now a butterfly, dreaming I am a man. . . .

*_Umbra_ is shadow; _penumbra_ refers to the edge of a shadow.—ED.

Identity and Personality

Ludwig Wittgenstein

In this short passage from The Blue and Brown Books, _Wittgenstein discusses the uses of the terms "person" and "personality." More particularly, he examines what it is we refer to when we use the pronoun "I" in various sensory contexts. What does it mean to use "I" as a subject? Does "I" refer to something or someone different from the person who is speaking?_

THE BLUE BOOK

I shall try to elucidate the problem discussed by realists, idealists, and solipsists by showing you a problem closely related to it. It is this: "Can we have unconscious thoughts, unconscious feelings, etc.?" The idea of there being unconscious thoughts has revolted many people. Others again have said that these were wrong in supposing that there could only be conscious thoughts, and that psychoanalysis had discovered unconscious

From _The Blue and Brown Books_ by Ludwig Wittgenstein. Copyright © 1958 by Basil Blackwell Ltd. Copyright renewed 1986 by Basil Blackwell, Ltd.

ones. The objectors to unconscious thought did not see that they were not objecting to the newly discovered psychological reactions, but to the way in which they were described. The psychoanalysts on the other hand were misled by their own way of expression into thinking that they had done more than discover new psychological reactions; that they had, in a sense, discovered conscious thoughts which were unconscious. The first could have stated their objection by saying "We don't wish to use the phrase 'unconscious thoughts'; we wish to reserve the word 'thought' for what you call 'conscious thoughts.' " They state their case wrongly when they say: "There can only be conscious thoughts and no unconscious ones." For if they don't wish to talk of "unconscious thought" they should not use the phrase "conscious thought," either.

But is it not right to say that in any case the person who talks both of conscious and unconscious thoughts thereby uses the word "thoughts" in two different ways?—Do we use a hammer in two different ways when we hit a nail with it and, on the other hand, drive a peg into a hole? And do we use it in two different ways or in the same way when we drive this peg into this hole and, on the other hand, another peg into another hole? Or should we only call it different uses when in one case we drive something into something and in the other, say, we smash something? Or is this all using the hammer in one way and is it to be called a different way only when we use the hammer as a paper weight?—In which cases are we to say that a word is used in two different ways and in which that it is used in one way? To say that a word is used in two (or more) different ways does in itself not yet give us any idea about its use. It only specifies a way of looking at this usage by providing a schema for its description with two (or more) subdivisions. It is all right to say: "I do *two* things with this hammer: I drive a nail into this board and one into that board." But I could also have said: "I am doing only one thing with this hammer; I am driving a nail into this board and one into that board." There can be two kinds of discussions as to whether a word is used in one way or in two ways: (a) Two people may discuss whether the English word "cleave" is only used for chopping up something or also for joining things together. This is a discussion about the facts of a certain actual usage. (b) They may discuss whether the word "altus," standing for both "deep" and "high," is *thereby* used in two different ways. This question is analogous to the question whether the word "thought" is used in two ways or in one when we talk of conscious and unconscious thought. The man who says "surely, these are two different usages" has already decided to use a two-way schema, and what he said expressed this decision.

Now when the solipsist says that only his own experiences are real, it is no use answering him: "Why do you tell us this if you don't believe that we really hear it?" Or anyhow, if we give him this answer, we mustn't believe that we have answered his difficulty. There is no common sense answer to a philosophical problem. One can defend common sense against the attacks of philosophers only by solving their puzzles, i.e., by curing them of the temptation to attack common sense; not by restating the views of common sense. A philosopher is not a man out of his senses, a man who doesn't see what everybody sees; nor on the other hand is his disagreement with common sense that of the scientist disagreeing with the coarse views of the man in the street. That is, his disagreement is not founded on a more subtle knowledge of fact. We therefore have to look round for the *source* of his puzzlement. And we find that there is puzzlement and mental discomfort, not only when our curiosity about certain facts is not satisfied or when we can't find a law of nature fitting in with all our experience, but also when a notation dissatisfies us—perhaps because of various associations which it calls up. Our ordinary language, which of all possible notations is the one which pervades all our life, holds our mind rigidly in one position, as it were, and in this position sometimes it feels cramped, having a desire for other positions as well. Thus we sometimes wish for a notation which stresses a difference more strongly, makes it more obvious, than ordinary language does, or one which in a particular case uses more closely similar forms of expression than our ordinary language. Our mental cramp is loosened when we are shown the notations which fulfil these needs. These needs can be of the greatest variety. . . .

There are many uses of the word "personality" which we may feel inclined to adopt, all more or less akin. The same applies when we define the identity of a person by means of his memories. Imagine a man whose memories on the even days of his life comprise the events of all these days, skipping entirely what happened on the odd days. On the other hand, he remembers on an odd day what happened on previous odd days, but his memory then skips the even days without a feeling of discontinuity. If we like we can also assume that he has alternating appearances and characteristics on odd and even days. Are we bound to say that here two persons are inhabiting the same body? That is, is it right to say that there are, and wrong to say that there aren't, or vice versa? Neither. For the *ordinary* use of the word "person" is what one might call a composite use suitable under the ordinary circumstances. If I assume, as I do, that these circumstances are changed, the application of the term "person" or "personality" has thereby changed; and if I wish to preserve this term and give it a use analogous to its former use, I am at liberty to choose between many uses, that is, between many different kinds of analogy. One might say in such a case that the term "personality" hasn't got one legitimate heir only. (This kind of consideration is of importance in the philosophy of mathematics. Consider the use of the words "proof," "formula," and others. Consider the question: "Why should what we do here be called 'philosophy'? Why should it be regarded as the only legitimate heir of the different activities which had this name in former times?")

Now let us ask ourselves what sort of identity of personality it is we are referring to when we say "when anything is seen, it is always I who see." What is it I want all these cases of seeing to have in common? As an answer I have to confess to myself that it is not my bodily appearance. I don't always see part of my body when I see. And it isn't essential that my body, if seen amongst the things I see, should always look the same. In fact I don't mind how much it changes. And I feel the same way about all the properties of my body, the characteristics of my behaviour, and even about my memories.—When I think about it a little longer I see that what I wished to say was: "Always when anything is seen, something is seen." I.e., that of which I said it continued during all the experiences of seeing was not any particular entity "I," but the experience of seeing itself. This may become clearer if we imagine the man who makes our solipsistic statement to point to his eyes while he says "I." (Perhaps because he wishes to be exact and wants to say expressly which eyes belong to the mouth which says "I" and to the hands pointing to his own body.) But what is he pointing to? These particular eyes with the identity of physical objects? (To understand this sentence, you must remember that the grammar of words of which we say that they stand for physical objects is characterized by the way in which we use the phrase "the *same* so-and-so," or "the identical so-and-so," where "so-and-so" designates the physical object.) We said before that he did not wish to point to a particular physical object at all. The idea that he had made a significant statement arose from a confusion corresponding to the confusion between what we shall call "the geometrical eye" and "the physical eye." I will indicate the use of these terms: If a man tries to obey the order "Point to your eye," he may do many different things, and there are many different criteria which he will accept for having pointed to his eye. If these criteria, as they usually do, coincide, I may use them alternately and in different combinations to show me that I have touched my eye. If they don't coincide, I shall have to distinguish between different senses of the phrase "I touch my eye" or "I move my finger towards my eye." If, e.g., my eyes are shut, I can still have the characteristic kinaesthetic experience in my arm which I should call the kinaesthetic experience of raising my hand to my eye. That I had succeeded in doing so, I shall recognize by the peculiar tactile sensation of touching my eye. But if my eye were behind a glass plate fastened in such a way that it prevented me from exerting a pressure on my eye with my finger, there would still be a criterion of muscular sensation which would make me say that now my finger was in front of my eye. As to visual criteria, there are two I can adopt. There is the ordinary experience of seeing my hand rise and come towards my eye, and this experience, of course, is different from seeing two things meet, say, two finger tips. On the other hand, I can use as a criterion for my finger moving towards my eye, what I see when I look into a mirror and see my finger nearing my eye. If that place on my body which, we say, "sees" is to be determined by moving my finger towards my eye, according to the second criterion, then it is conceivable that I may see with what according to other criteria is the tip of my nose, or places on my forehead; or I might in this way point to a place lying outside my body. If I wish a person to point to his eye (or his eyes) according to the second criterion *alone*, I shall express my wish by saying: "Point to your geometrical eye (or eyes)." The grammar of the word "geometrical eye" stands in the same relation to the grammar of the word "physical eye" as the grammar of the expression "the visual sense datum of a tree" to the grammar of the expression "the physical tree." In either case it confuses everything to say "the one is a *different kind* of object from the other"; for those who say that a sense datum is a different kind of object from a physical object misunderstand the grammar of the word "kind," just as those who say that a number is a different kind of object from a numeral. They think they are making such a statement as "A railway train, a railway station, and a railway car are different kinds of objects," whereas their statement is analogous to "A railway train, a railway accident, and a railway law are different kinds of objects."

What tempted me to say "it is always I who see when anything is seen," I could also have yielded to by saying: "whenever anything is seen, it is *this* which is seen," accompanying the word "this" by a gesture embracing my visual field (but not meaning by "this" the particular objects which I happen to see at the moment). One might say, "I am pointing at the visual field as such, not at anything in it." And this only serves to bring out the senselessness of the former expression.

Let us then discard the "always" in our expression. Then I can still express my solipsism by saying "Only what *I* see (or: see now) is really seen." And here I am tempted to say: "Although by the word 'I' I don't mean L.W., it will do if the others understand 'I' to mean L.W., if just now I am in fact L.W." I could also express my claim by saying: "I am the vessel of life"; but mark, it is essential that everyone to whom I say this should be unable to understand me. It is essential that the other should not be able to understand "what I really *mean*," though in practice he might do what I wish by conceding to me an exceptional position in his notation. But I wish it to be *logically* impossible that he should understand me, that is to say, it should be meaningless, not false, to say that he understands me. Thus my expression is one of the many which is used on various occasions by philosophers and supposed to convey something to the person who says it, though essentially incapable of conveying anything to anyone else. Now if for an expression to convey a meaning means to be accompanied by or to produce certain experiences, our expression may have all sorts of meanings, and I don't wish to say anything about them. But we are, as a matter of fact, misled into thinking that our expression has a meaning in the sense in which a nonmetaphysical expression has; for we wrongly compare our case with one in which the other person can't understand what we say because he lacks a certain information. (This remark can only become clear if we understand the connection between grammar and sense and nonsense.)

The meaning of a phrase for us is characterized by the use we make of it. The meaning is not a mental accompaniment to the expression. Therefore the phrase "I think I mean something by it," or "I'm sure I mean something by it," which we so often hear in philosophical discussions to justify the use of an expression is for us no justification at all. We ask: "*What* do you mean?", i.e., "How do you use this expression?" If someone taught me the word "*bench*," and said that he sometimes or always put a stroke over it thus: "*bench*," and that this meant something to him, I should say: "I don't know what sort of idea you associate with this stroke, but it doesn't interest me unless you show me that there is a use for the stroke in the kind of calculus in which you wish to use the word 'bench.' "—I want to play chess, and a man gives the white king a paper crown, leaving the use of the piece unaltered, but telling me that the crown has a meaning to him in the game, which he can't express by rules. I say: "as long as it doesn't alter the use of the piece, it hasn't what I call a meaning."

One sometimes hears that such a phrase as "This is here," when while I say it I point to a part of my visual field, has a kind of primitive meaning to me, although it can't impart information to anybody else.

When I say "Only this is seen," I forget that a sentence may come ever so natural to us without having any use in our calculus of language. Think of the law of identity, "a = a," and of how we sometimes try hard to get hold of its sense, to visualize it, by looking at an object and repeating to ourselves such a sentence as "This tree is the same thing as this tree." The gestures and images by which I apparently give this sentence sense are very similar to those which I use in the case of "Only *this* is really seen." (To get clear about philosophical problems, it is useful to become conscious of the apparently unimportant details of the particular situation in which we are inclined to make a certain metaphysical assertion. Thus we may be tempted to say "Only this is really seen" when we stare at unchanging surroundings, whereas we may not at all be tempted to say this when we look about us while walking.)

There is, as we have said, no objection to adopting a symbolism in which a certain person always or temporarily holds an exceptional place. And therefore, if I utter the sentence "Only I really see," it is conceivable that my fellow creatures thereupon will arrange their notation so as to fall in with me by saying "so-and-so is really seen" instead of "L.W. sees so-and-so," etc., etc. What, however, is wrong, is to think that I can *justify* this choice of notation. When I said, from my heart, that only I see, I was also inclined to say that by "I" I didn't really mean L.W., although for the benefit of my fellow men I might say "It is now L.W. who really sees" though this is not what I really mean. I could almost say that by "I" I mean something which just now inhabits L.W., something which the others can't see. (I meant my mind, but could only point to it via my body.) There is nothing wrong in suggesting that the others should give me an exceptional place in their notation; but the justification which I wish to give for it: that this body is now the seat of that which really Iives—is senseless. For admittedly this is not to state anything which in the ordinary sense is a matter of experience. (And don't think that it is an experiential proposition which only I can know because only I am in the position to have the particular experience.) Now the idea that the real I lives in my body is connected with the peculiar grammar of the word "I," and the misunderstandings this grammar is liable to give rise to. There are two different cases in the use of the word "I" (or "my") which I might call "the use as object" and "the use as subject." Examples of the first kind of use are these: "My arm is broken," "I have grown six inches," "I have a bump on my forehead," "The wind blows my hair about." Examples of the second kind are: "*I* see so-and-so," "*I* hear so-and-so," "*I* try to lift my arm," "*I* think it will rain," "*I* have toothache." One can point to the difference between these two categories by saying: The cases of the first category involve the recognition of a particular person, and there is in these cases the possibility of an error, or as I should rather put it: The possibility of an error has been provided for. The possibility of failing to score has been provided for in a pin game. On the other hand, it is not one of the hazards of the game that the balls should fail to come up if I have put a penny in the slot. It is possible that, say in an accident, I should feel a pain in my arm, see a broken arm at my side, and think it is mine, when really it is my neighbour's. And I could, looking into a mirror, mistake a bump on his forehead for one on mine. On the other hand, there is no question of recognizing a person when I say I have toothache. To ask "are you sure that it's *you* who have pains?" would be nonsensical. Now, when in this case no error is possible, it is because the move which we might be inclined to think of as an error, a "bad move," is no move of the game at all. (We distinguish in chess between good and bad moves, and we call it a mistake if we expose the queen to a bishop. But it is no mistake to promote a pawn to a king.) And now this way of stating our idea suggests itself: that it is as impossible that in making the statement "1 have toothache" I should have mistaken another person for myself, as it is to moan with pain by mistake, having mistaken someone else for me. To say, "I have pain" is no more a statement *about* a particular person than moaning is. "But surely the word 'I' in the mouth of a man refers to the man who says it; it points to himself; and very often a man who says it actually points to himself with his finger." But it was quite superfluous to point to himself. He might just as well only have raised his hand. It would be wrong to say that when someone points to the sun with his hand, he is pointing both to the sun and himself because it is *he* who points; on the other hand, he may by pointing attract attention both to the sun and to himself.

The word "I" does not mean the same as "L.W." even if I am L.W., nor does it mean the same as the expression "the person who is now speaking." But that doesn't mean that "L.W." and "I" mean different things. All it means is that these words are different instruments in our language.

Discussion Questions

1. What does it mean that humans were made in the image of God? Could it be argued that a human's soul makes him or her superior to nature and other species?
2. What gives us our distinct personalities? Does each human being have a particular "spirit" that is not identical with one's soul? Must we pay attention to the health of our spirits as much as if not more than to the health of our bodies?
3. Describe Descartes's discussion of bodies and minds. What is the nature of a material body according to Descartes? Of a soul or mind? Does Descartes adequately respond to Princess Elisabeth, demonstrating how a mind brings about movements in a body?
4. What is problematic about Descartes's description of human nature, according to Ryle? What is a "Category-Mistake," according to Ryle, and why does he think Descartes is "guilty" of this?
5. Why does Cole object to a conception of a "self" independent of a body? Why does she see a "relational sense of self" as valuable?
6. What is the doctrine of no-self? Why do Buddhists make this claim? Discuss the paradox in claiming that there is no personal self, no personal identity.
7. Chuang Tzu tells us that life and death are one. What does he mean by this? Discuss the value of "paradox" in philosophical thinking.
8. Can I speak of the "I"? Discuss how Wittgenstein might answer this question.
9. In what sense do you think that an understanding of our own selves can aid us in understanding others?

chapter 3

Discovering the Self as Social Reality

Defining or thinking about the self in abstract terms apart from a social context and everyday experiences is not something most of us do naturally. Accordingly, the authors in this section give us some reasons to consider the impact that our society has on our identity. Beginning with Mary McCarthy, we find that names play a role in determining how we come to know and understand ourselves. McCarthy's struggle to reveal her true self to others is overshadowed by the nicknames her "friends" choose to give her. Essentially, what we find is that who she becomes is very much affected by those names and the meaning she takes from them.

Perhaps the impact that others have on our identity is no more clearly stated than in George Herbert Mead's essay. Mead challenges us to think about the *self* as something dynamic, developing, and adaptive, not as something static. Thought and sensuous experience, memory, pain, and pleasure help us identify with the self but do not embody the *self.* Mead asks us to consider the self as a "social structure," something that "arises in social experience." To view the *self as social structure,* we must add self-consciousness, an awareness of the experience of the *self as an object* in a social context. When I am in a social environment, I take notice of how others act, and especially how others act toward me. My conduct or behavior gives rise to postures or attitudes in others, and each of these other actors in life's drama responds accordingly. My awareness of their responses enables me to perceive myself as others see me.

Hannah Arendt

To think about myself, it is necessary to become an "object to myself." My consciousness of who I am could be, to a large extent, a conscious compilation of others' views of me.

Arthur Bierman suggests that the self is intricately related to the others in my environment. Rejecting the practice of atomic individualism, Bierman argues that the community in which I live fosters an understanding of myself and other selves. It also provides the foundation for conscious self-development, and this may occur in a variety of ways. Bierman suggests that we must not think of ourselves as passive observers in the world but as active participants who help to form the identity of the individuals in that world. To do this, we may have to think of ourselves as persons. Persons are selves, but as a person, each self is correlative, each self is related to many other selves in a variety of ways. We should see these relations to others both as necessary to our definition of a "self," that is, our existence as persons, and as the source of possibilities for who we may become.

The relationships that we form result in profound gains and losses, according to Hannah Arendt. In her delineation of three basic types of human activity, Arendt explains that without the risk of discovering who we are in relation to others, our uniqueness as human beings cannot be fulfilled. While this is difficult in modern society, with its mechanistic, homogenized activities, it is essential to our full human development. Without the risk, we may lose the self. Thus, while she does not articulate it as such, Arendt believes that the self is rooted in the social and political.

In light of this, Jean-Paul Sartre would claim that we must take responsibility for our actions and realize that we create the world and the communities in which we live. We must recognize that we consciously choose the role that we play in the world. We are solely responsible for who we are, yet we are always a *self in relation to other selves.* Such a responsibility arises, Sartre would argue, because of the freedom provided us by human consciousness. It is consciousness that provides an awareness of the self *as self,* a being that chooses and acts, always moving toward a future. Certainly one feels alone and abandoned in making choices, and each person is sometimes tempted to excuse herself or himself from the responsibility of choosing by turning to the advice and direction of others or to the commands of God. To excuse oneself in this manner, Sartre tells us, is to act in *bad faith.* One must choose as an individual, as a *self,* but always with a concern for others. Whether or not a God exists is not the issue, but rather, the issue is whether one allows a belief in God to stand as an excuse for not taking full responsibility for one's actions and for the creation of one's *self.*

In order to accomplish this, John Mohawk claims that we must recognize that humans are not the center of all existence. Rather, Mohawk proposes a First Nations alternative view that all things in nature, including humans, are interrelated. Thus, the *self* is formed not only in relation to other people but also in relation to other things in nature. We must be willing, however, to give up the prominent anthropocentric view in order to discover the true self in light of this.

The notion that the self is rooted in natural and human relations is a challenge to the dominant thinking in the Western world. Yet, as the authors suggest, it is an idea that is shared by many great thinkers, and it is certainly an idea that must be considered more seriously if we are to work toward a consciously chosen world that will encourage individuals to be responsible for themselves.

Names

Mary McCarthy

In this selection, Mary McCarthy reflects upon her experience as a Catholic school girl in a convent school. She finds herself a victim of circumstance, without a voice, without being heard. As we share her struggle to free herself from the names and definitions that others have given her, we find that we can never be truly free from the labels that are given to us in childhood.

Anna Lyons, Mary Louise Lyons, Mary von Phul, Emilie von Phul, Eugenia McLellan, Majorie McPhail, Marie-Louise L'Abbé, Mary Danz, Julia Dodge, Mary Fordyce Blake, Janet Preston—these were the names (I can still tell them over like a rosary) of some of the older girls in the convent: the Virtues and Graces. The virtuous ones wore wide blue or green moire goodconduct ribbons, bandoleer-style, across their blue serge uniforms; the beautiful ones wore rouge and powder or at least were reputed to do so. Our class, the eighth grade, wore pink ribbons (I never got one myself) and had names like Patricia ("Pat") Sullivan, Eileen Donohoe, and Joan Kane. We were inelegant even in this respect; the best name we could show, among us, was Phyllis ("Phil") Chatham, who boasted that her father's name, Ralph, was pronounced "Rafe" as in England.

Names had a great importance for us in the convent, and foreign names, French, German, or plain English (which, to us, were foreign, because of their Protestant sound), bloomed like prize roses among a collection of spuds. Irish names were too common in the school to have any prestige either as surnames (Gallagher, Sheehan, Finn, Sullivan,

"Names" from *Memories of a Catholic Girlhood*, copyright © 1957 and renewed 1985 by Mary McCarthy, reprinted by permission of Harcourt Brace Jovanovich, Inc.

McCarthy) or as Christian names (Kathleen, Eileen). Anything exotic had value: an "olive" complexion, for example. The pet girl of the convent was a fragile Jewish girl named Susie Lowenstein, who had pale red-gold hair and an exquisite retroussé nose, which, if we had had it, might have been called "pug." We liked her name too and the name of a child in the primary grades: Abbie Stuart Baillargeon. My favorite name, on the whole, though, was Emilie von Phul (pronounced "Pool"); her oldest sister, recently graduated, was called Celeste. Another name that appealed to me was Genevieve Albers, Saint Genevieve being the patron saint of Paris who turned back Attila from the gates of the city.

All these names reflected the still-pioneer character of the Pacific Northwest. I had never heard their like in the parochial school in Minneapolis, where "foreign" extraction, in any case, was something to be ashamed of, the whole drive being toward Americanization of first name and surname alike. The exceptions to this were the Irish, who could vaunt such names as Catherine O'Dea and the name of my second cousin, Mary Catherine Anne Rose Violet McCarthy, while an unfortunate German boy named Manfred was made to suffer for his. But that was Minneapolis. In Seattle, and especially in the convent of the Ladies of the Sacred Heart, foreign names suggested not immigration but emigration—distinguished exile. Minneapolis was a granary; Seattle was a port, which had attracted a veritable Foreign Legion of adventurers—soldiers of fortune, younger sons, gamblers, traders, drawn by the fortunes to be made in virgin timber and shipping and by the Alaska Gold Rush. Wars and revolutions had sent the defeated out to Puget Sound, to start a new life; the latest had been the Russian Revolution, which had shipped us, via Harbin, a Russian colony, complete with restaurant, on Queen Anne Hill. The English names in the convent, when they did not testify to direct English origin, as in the case of "Rafe" Chatham, had come to us from the South and represented a kind of internal exile; such girls as Mary Fordyce Blake and Mary McQueen Street (a class ahead of me; her sister was named Francesca) bore their double-barreled first names like titles of aristocracy from the antebellum South. Not all our girls, by any means, were Catholic; some of the very prettiest ones—Julia Dodge and Janet Preston, if I remember rightly—were Protestants. The nuns had taught us to behave with special courtesy to these strangers in our midst; and the whole effect was of some superior hostel for refugees of all the lost causes of the past hundred years. Money could not count for much in such an atmosphere; the fathers and grandfathers of many of our "best" girls were ruined men.

Names, often, were freakish in the Pacific Northwest, particularly girls' names. In the Episcopal boarding school I went to later, in Tacoma, there was a girl called De Vere Utter, and there was a girl called Rocena and another called Hermonie. Was Rocena a mistake for Rowena and Hermonie for Hermoine? And was Vere, as we called her, Lady Clara Vere de Vere? Probably. You do not hear names like those often, in any case, east of the Cascade Mountains; they belong to the frontier, where books and libraries were few and memory seems to have been oral, as in the time of Homer.

Names have more significance for Catholics than they do for other people; Christian names are chosen for the spiritual qualities of the saints they are taken from; Protestants used to name their children out of the Old Testament and now they name them out of novels and plays, whose heroes and heroines are perhaps the new patron saints of a secular age. But with Catholics it is different. The saint a child is named for is supposed to serve, literally, as a model or pattern to imitate; your name is your fortune and it tells you what you are or must be. Catholic children ponder their names for a mystic meaning, like birthstones; my own, I learned, besides belonging to the Virgin and Saint Mary of Egypt, originally meant "bitter" or "star of the sea." My second name, Therése, could dedicate me either to Saint Theresa or to the saint called the Little Flower, Soeur Therésé of Lisieux, on whom God was supposed to have descended in the form of a shower of roses. At Confirmation, I had added a third name (for Catholics then rename themselves, as most nuns do, yet another time, when they take orders); on the advice of a nun, I had taken "Clementina," after Saint Clement, an early pope—a step I soon regretted on account of "My Darling Clementine" and her number nine shoes. By the time I was in the convent, I would no longer tell anyone what my Confirmation name was. The name I had nearly picked was "Agnes," after a little Roman virgin martyr, always shown with a lamb, because of her purity. But Agnes would have been just as bad, I recognized in Forest Ridge Convent—not only because of the possibility of "Aggie," but because it was subtly, indefinably wrong in itself. Agnes would have made me look like an ass.

The fear of appearing ridiculous first entered my life, as a governing motive, during my second year in the convent. Up to then, a desire for prominence had decided many of my actions and, in fact, still persisted. But in the eighth grade, I became aware of mockery and perceived that I could not seek prominence without attracting laughter. Other people could, but I couldn't. This laughter was proceeding, not from my classmates, but from the girls of the class just above me, in particular from two boon companions. Elinor Heffernan and Mary Harty, a clownish pair—oddly assorted in size and shape, as teams of clowns generally are, one short, plump, and baby-faced, the other tall, lean, and owlish—who entertained the high-school department by calling attention to the oddities of the younger girls. Nearly every school has such a pair of satirists, whose marks are generally low and who are tolerated just because of their laziness and nonconformity; one of them (in this case, Mary Harty, the plump one) usually appears to be half asleep. Because of their low standing, their indifference to appearances, the sad state of their uniforms, their clowning is taken to be harmless, which, on the whole, it is, their object being not to wound but to divert; such girls are bored in school. We in the eighth grade sat directly in front of the two wits in study hall, so that they had us under close observation; yet at first I was not afraid of them, wanting, if anything, to identify myself with their laughter, to be initiated into the joke. One of their specialties was giving people nicknames, and it was considered an honor to be the first in the eighth grade to be let in by Elinor and Mary on their latest invention. This often happened to me; they would tell me, on the playground, and I would tell the others. As their intermediary, I felt myself almost their friend and it did not occur to me that I might be next on their list.

I had achieved prominence not long before by publicly losing my faith and regaining it at the end of a retreat. I believe Elinor and Mary questioned me about this on the playground, during recess, and listened with serious, respectful faces while I told them about my conversations with the Jesuits. Those serious faces ought to have been an omen, but if the two girls used what I had revealed to make fun of me, it must have been behind my back. I never heard any more of it, and yet just at this time I began to feel something, like a cold breath on the nape of my neck, that made me wonder whether the new position I had won for myself in the convent was as secure as I imagined. I would turn around in study hall and find the two girls looking at me with speculation in their eyes.

It was just at this time, too, that I found myself in a perfectly absurd situation, a very private one, which made me live, from month to month, in horror of discovery. I had waked up one morning, in my convent room, to find a few small spots of blood on my sheet; I had somehow scratched a trifling cut on one of my legs and opened it during the night. I wondered what to do about this, for the nuns were fussy about bedmaking, as they were about our white collars and cuffs, and if we had an inspection these spots might count against me. It was best, I decided, to ask the nun on dormitory duty, tall, stout Mother Slattery, for a clean bottom sheet, even though she might scold me for having scratched my leg in my sleep and order me to cut my toenails. You never know what you might be blamed for. But Mother Slattery, when she bustled in to look at the sheet, did not scold me at all; indeed, she hardly seemed to be listening, as I explained to her about the cut. She told me to sit down: she would be back in a minute. "You can be excused from athletics today," she added, closing the door. As I waited, I considered this remark, which seemed to me strangely munificent, in view of the unimportance of the cut. In a moment, she returned, but without the sheet. Instead, she produced out of her big pocket a sort of cloth girdle and a peculiar flannel object which I first took to be a bandage, and I began to protest that I did not need or want a bandage; all I needed was a bottom sheet. "The sheet can wait," said Mother Slattery, succinctly, handing me two large safety pins. It was the pins that abruptly enlightened me; I saw Mother Slattery's mistake, even as she was instructing me as to how this flannel article, which I now understood to be a sanitary napkin, was to be put on.

"Oh no, Mother," I said, feeling somewhat embarrassed. "You don't understand. It's just a little cut, on my leg." But Mother, again, was not listening; she appeared to have grown deaf, as the nuns had a habit of doing when what you were saying did not fit in with their ideas. And now that I knew what was in her mind, I was conscious of a funny constraint; I did not feel it proper to name a natural process, in so many words, to a nun. It was like trying not to think of their going to the bathroom or trying not to see the straggling irongray hair coming out of their coifs (the common notion that they shaved their heads was false). On the whole, it seemed better just to show her my cut. But when I offered to do so and unfastened my black stocking, she only glanced at my leg, cursorily. "That's only a scratch dear," she said. "Now hurry up and put this on or you'll be late for chapel. Have you any pain?" "No, no, Mother!" I cried. "You don't understand!" "Yes, yes, I understand," she replied soothingly, "and you will too, a little later. Mother Superior will tell you about it some time during the morning. There's nothing to be afraid of. You have become a woman."

"I know all about that," I persisted. "Mother, please listen. I just cut my leg. On the athletic field. Yesterday afternoon." But the more excited I grew, the more soothing, and yet firm, Mother Slattery became. There seemed to be nothing for it but to give up and do as I was bid. I was in the grip of a higher authority, which almost had the power to persuade me that it was right and I was wrong. But of course I was not wrong; that would have been too good to be true. While Mother Slattery waited, just outside my door, I miserably donned the equipment she had given me, for there was no place to hide it, on account of drawer inspection. She led me down the hall to where there was a chute and explained how I was to dispose of the flannel thing, by dropping it down the chute into the laundry. (The convent arrangements were very old-fashioned, dating back, no doubt, to the days of Louis Philippe.)

The Mother Superior, Madame MacIllvra, was a sensible woman, and all through my early morning classes, I was on pins and needles, chafing for the promised interview with her which I trusted would clear things up. *"Ma Mere,"* I would begin, "Mother Slattery thinks . . ." Then I would tell her about the cut and the athletic field. But precisely the same impasse confronted me when I was summoned to her office at recess-time. *I* talked about my cut, and *she* talked about becoming a woman. It was rather like a round, in which she was singing "Scotland's burning, Scotland's burning," and I was singing "Pour on water, pour on water." Neither of us could hear the other, or, rather, I could hear her, but she could not hear me. Owing to our different positions in the convent she was free to interrupt me, whereas I was expected to remain silent until she had finished speaking. When I kept breaking in, she hushed me, gently, and took me on her lap. Exactly like Mother Slattery, she attributed all my references to the cut to a blind fear of this new, unexpected reality that had supposedly entered my life. Many young girls, she reassured me, were frightened if they had not been prepared. "And you, Mary, have lost your dear mother, who could have made this easier for you." Rocked on Madame MacIllvra's lap, I felt paralysis overtake me and I lay, mutely listening, against her bosom, my face being tickled by her white, starched, fluted wimple, while she explained to me how babies were born, all of which I had heard before.

There was no use fighting the convent. I had to pretend to have become a woman, just as, not long before, I had had to pretend to get my faith back—for the sake of peace. This pretense was decidedly awkward. For fear of being found out by the lay sisters downstairs in the laundry (no doubt an imaginary contingency, but the convent was so very thorough), I reopened the cut on my leg, so as to draw a little blood to stain the napkins, which were issued me regularly, not only on this occasion, but every twenty-eight days thereafter. Eventually, I abandoned this bloodletting, for fear of lockjaw, and trusted to fate. Yet I was in awful dread of detection; my only hope, as I saw it, was either to be released from the convent or to become a woman in reality, which might take a year at least, since I was only twelve. Getting out of athletics once a month was not sufficient compensation for the farce I was going through. It was not my fault; they had forced me into it; nevertheless, it was I who would look silly—worse than silly; half mad—if the truth ever came to light.

I was burdened with this guilt and shame when the nickname finally found me out. "Found me out," in a general sense, for no one ever did learn the particular secret I bore about with me, pinned to the linen band. "We've got a name for you," Elinor and Mary called out to me, one day on the playground. "What is it?" I asked half hoping, half fearing, since not all their sobriquets were unfavorable. "Cye," they answered, looking at each other and laughing. "Si?" I repeated, supposing that it was based on Simple Simon. Did they regard me as a hick? "C.Y.E.," they elucidated, spelling it out in chorus. "The letters stand for something. Can you guess?" I could not and I cannot now. The closest I could come to it in the convent was "Clean Your Ears." Perhaps that was it, though in later life I have wondered whether it did not stand, simply, for "Clever Young Egg" or "Champion Young Eccentric." But in the convent I was certain that it stood for something horrible, something even worse than dirty ears (as far as I knew, my ears were clean), something I could never guess because it represented some aspect of myself that the world could see and I couldn't, like a sign pinned on my back. Everyone in the convent must have known what the letters stood for, but no one would tell me. Elinor and Mary had made them promise. It was like halitosis; not even my best friend, my deskmate, Louise, would tell me, no matter how much I pleaded. Yet everyone assured me that it was "very good," that is, very apt. And it made everyone laugh.

This name reduced all my pretensions and solidified my sense of *wrongness*. Just as I felt I was beginning to belong to the convent, it turned me into an outsider, since I was the only pupil who was not in the know. I liked the convent, but it did not like me, as people say of certain foods that disagree with them. By this, I do not mean that I was actively unpopular, either with the pupils or with the nuns. The Mother Superior cried when I left and predicted that I would be a novelist, which surprised me. And I had finally made friends; even Emilie von Phul smiled upon me softly out of her bright blue eyes from the far end of the study hall. It was just that I did not fit into the convent pattern; the simplest thing I did, like asking for a clean sheet, entrapped me in consequences that I never could have predicted. I was not bad; I did not consciously break the rules; and yet I could never, not even for a week, get a pink ribbon, and this was something I could not understand, because I was trying as hard as I could. It was the same case as with the hated name; the nuns, evidently, saw something about me that was invisible to me.

The oddest part was all that pretending. There I was, a walking mass of lies, pretending to be a Catholic and going to confession while really I had lost my faith, and pretending to have monthly periods by cutting myself with nail scissors; yet all this had come about without my volition and even contrary to it. But the basest pretense I was driven to was the acceptance of the nickname. Yet what else could I do? In the convent, I could not live it down. To all those girls, I had become "Cye McCarthy." That was who I was. That was how I had to identify myself when telephoning my friends during vacations to ask them to the movies: "Hello, this is Cye." I loathed myself when I said it, and yet I succumbed to the name totally, making myself over into a sort of hearty to go with it—the kind of girl I hated. "Cye" was my new patron saint. This false personality stuck to me, like the name, when I entered public high school, the next fall, as a freshman, having finally persuaded my grandparents to take me out of the convent, although they could never get to the bottom of my reasons, since, as I admitted, the nuns were kind, and I had made many nice new friends. What I wanted was a fresh start, a chance to begin life over again, but the first thing I heard in the corridors of the public high school was that name called out to me, like the warmest of welcomes: "Hi, there, Si!" That was the way they thought it was spelled. But this time I was resolute. After the first weeks, I dropped the hearties who called me "Si" and I never heard it again. I got my own name back and sloughed off Clementina and even Therese[,] the names that did not seem to me any more to be mine but to have been imposed on me by others. And I preferred to think that Mary meant "bitter" rather than "star of the sea."

The Social Self

George Herbert Mead

To what extent do the people with whom we interact give us our identity? Are we individual, distinct persons at birth? Or are we formed by the social relationships we foster throughout our lives? In this essay, Mead argues that our interactions with individuals and groups in society have an impact on who we are and who we become. Mead claims that we come to discover our identity through our relationships with others. As you read this essay, reflect upon the ways in which you think others give us definition.

THE SELF AND THE ORGANISM

. . . The self has a character which is different from that of the physiological organism proper. The self is something which has a development; it is not initially there, at birth, but arises in the process of social experience and activity, that is, develops in the given individual as a result of his relations to that process as a whole and to other individuals within that process. The intelligence of the lower forms of animal life, like a great deal of human intelligence, does not involve a self. In our habitual actions, for example, in our moving about in a world that is simply there and to which we are so adjusted that no thinking is involved, there is a certain amount of sensuous experience such as persons have when they are just waking up, a bare thereness of the world. Such characters about us may exist in experience without taking their place in relationship to the self. One must, of course, under those conditions, distinguish between the experience that immediately takes place and our own organization of it into the experience of the self. One says upon analysis that a certain item had its place in his experience, in the experience of his self. We do inevitably tend at a certain level of sophistication to organize all experience into that of a self. We do so intimately identify our experiences, especially our affective experiences, with the self that it takes a moment's abstraction to realize that pain and pleasure can be there without being the experience of the self. Similarly, we normally organize our memories upon the string of our self. If we date things we always date them from the point of view of our past experiences. We frequently have memories that we cannot date, that we cannot place. A picture comes before us suddenly and we are at a loss to explain when that experience originally took place. We remember perfectly distinctly the picture, but we do not have it definitely placed, and until we can place it in terms of our past experience we are not satisfied. Nevertheless, I think it is obvious when one comes to consider it that the self is not necessarily involved in the life of the organism, nor involved in what we term our sensuous experience, that is, experience in a world about us for which we have habitual reactions.

We can distinguish very definitely between the self and the body. The body can be there and can operate in a very intelligent fashion without there being a self involved in the experience. The self has the character-

From *Mind, Self and Society* by George Herbert Mead. Copyright © 1934 by The University of Chicago Press. Reprinted by permission of The University of Chicago Press.

istics that it is an object to itself, and that characteristic distinguishes it from other objects and from the body. It is perfectly true that the eye can see the foot, but it does not see the body as a whole. We cannot see our backs; we can feel certain portions of them, if we are agile, but we cannot get an experience of our whole body. There are, of course, experiences which are somewhat vague and difficult of location, but the bodily experiences are for us organized about a self. The foot and hand belong to the self. We can see our feet, especially if we look at them from the wrong end of an opera glass, as strange things which we have difficulty in recognizing as our own. The parts of the body are quite distinguishable from the self. We can lose parts of the body without any serious invasion of the self. The mere ability to experience different parts of the body is not different from the experience of a table. The table presents a different feel from what the hand does when one hand feels another, but it is an experience of something with which we come definitely into contact. The body does not experience itself as a whole, in the sense in which the self in some way enters into the experience of the self.

It is the characteristic of the self as an object to itself that I want to bring out. This characteristic is represented in the word "self," which is a reflexive, and indicates that which can be both subject and object. This type of object is essentially different from other objects, and in the past it has been distinguished as conscious, a term which indicates an experience with, an experience of, one's self. It was assumed that consciousness in some way carried this capacity of being an object to itself. In giving a behavioristic statement of consciousness we have to look for some sort of experience in which the physical organism can become an object to itself.[1]

When one is running to get away from someone who is chasing him, he is entirely occupied in this action, and his experience may be swallowed up in the objects about him, so that he has, at the time being, no consciousness of self at all. We must be, of course, very completely occupied to have that take place, but we can, I think, recognize that sort of a possible experience in which the self does not enter. We can, perhaps, get some light on that situation through those experiences in which in very intense action there appear in the experience of the individual, back of this intense action, memories and anticipations. Tolstoi as an officer in the war gives an account of having pictures of his past experience in the midst of his most intense action. There are also the pictures that flash into a person's mind when he is drowning. In such instances there is a contrast between an experience that is absolutely wound up in outside activity in which the self as an object does not enter, and an activity of memory and imagination in which the self is the principal object. The self is then entirely distinguishable from an organism that is surrounded by things and acts with reference to things, including parts of its own body. These latter may be objects like other objects, but they are just objects out there in the field, and they do not involve a self that is an object to the organism. This is, I think, frequently overlooked. It is that fact which makes our anthropomorphic reconstructions of animal life so fallacious. How can an individual get outside himself (experientially) in such a way as to become an object to himself? This is the essential psychological problem of selfhood or of self-consciousness; and its solution is to be found by referring to the process of social conduct or activity in which the given person or individual is implicated. The apparatus of reason would not be complete unless it swept itself into its own analysis of the field of experience; or unless the individual brought himself into the same experiential field as that of the other individual selves in relation to whom he acts in any given social situation. Reason cannot become impersonal unless it takes an objective, non-affective attitude toward itself; otherwise we have just consciousness, not *self*-consciousness. And it is necessary to rational conduct that the individual should thus take an objective, impersonal attitude toward himself, that he should become an object to himself. For the individual organism is obviously an essential and important fact or constituent element of the empirical situation in which it acts; and without taking objective account of itself as such, it cannot act intelligently, or rationally.

The individual experiences himself as such, not directly, but only indirectly, from the particular standpoints of other individual members of the same social group, or from the generalized standpoint of the social group as a whole to which he belongs. For he enters his own experience as a self or individual, not directly or immediately, not by becoming a subject to himself, but only in so far as he first becomes an object to himself just as other individuals are objects to him or in his experience; and he becomes an object to himself only by taking the attitudes of other individuals toward himself within a social environment or context of experience and behavior in which both he and they are involved.

The importance of what we term "communication" lies in the fact that it provides a form of behavior in which the organism or the individual may become an object to himself. It is that sort of communication which we have been discussing—not communication in the sense of the cluck of the hen to the chickens, or the bark of a wolf to the pack, or the lowing of a cow, but communication in the sense of significant symbols, communication which is directed not only to others but also to the individual himself. So far as that type of communication is a part of behavior it at least introduces a self. Of course, one may hear without listening; one may see things that he does not realize; do things that he is not really aware of. But it is where one does respond to that which he addresses to another and where that response of his own becomes a part of his conduct, where he not only hears himself but responds to himself, talks and replies to himself as truly as the other person replies to him, that we have behavior in which the individuals become objects to themselves.

Such a self is not, I would say, primarily the physiological organism. The physiological organism is essential to it, but we are at least able to think of a self without it. Persons who believe in immortality, or believe in ghosts, or in the possibility of the self leaving the body, assume a self which is quite distinguishable from the body. How successfully they can hold these conceptions is an open question, but we do, as a fact, separate the self and the organism. It is fair to say that the beginning of the self as an object, so far as we can see, is to be found in the experiences of people that lead to the conception of a "double." Primitive people assume that there is a double, located presumably in the diaphragm, that leaves the body temporarily in sleep and completely in death. It can be enticed out of the body of one's enemy and perhaps killed. It is represented in infancy by the imaginary playmates which children set up, and through which they come to control their experiences in their play.

The self, as that which can be an object to itself, is essentially a social structure, and it arises in social experience. After a self has arisen, it in a certain sense provides for itself its social experiences, and so we can conceive of an absolutely solitary self. But it is impossible to conceive of a self arising outside of social experience. When it has arisen we can think of a person in solitary confinement for the rest of his life, but who still has himself as a companion, and is able to think and to converse with himself as he had communicated with others. That process to which I have just referred, of responding to one's self as another responds to it, taking part in one's own conversation with others, being aware of what one is saying and using that awareness of what one is saying to determine what one is going to say thereafter—that is a process with which we are all familiar. We are continually following up our own address to other persons by an understanding of what we are saying, and using that understanding in the direction of our continued speech. We are finding out what we are going to say, what we are going to do, by saying and doing, and in the process we are continually controlling the process itself. In the conversation of gestures what we say calls out a certain response in another and that in turn changes our own action, so that we shift from what we started to do because of the reply the other makes. The conversation of gestures is the beginning of communication. The individual comes to carry on a conversation of gestures with himself. He says something, and that calls out a certain reply in himself which makes him change what he was going to say. One starts to say something, we will presume an unpleasant something, but when he starts to say it he realizes it is cruel. The effect on himself of what he is saying checks him; there is here a conversation of gestures between the individual and himself. We mean by significant speech that the action is one that affects the individual himself, and that the effect upon the individual himself is part of the intelligent carrying-out of the conversation with others. Now we, so to speak, amputate that social phase and dispense with it for the time being, so that one is talking to one's self as one would talk to another person.

This process of abstraction cannot be carried on indefinitely. One inevitably seeks an audience, has to pour himself out to somebody. In reflective intelligence one thinks to act, and to act solely so that this action remains a part of a social process. Thinking becomes preparatory to social action. The very process of thinking is, of course, simply an inner conversation that goes on, but it is a conversation of gestures which in its completion implies the expression of that which one thinks to an audience. One separates the significance of what he is saying to others from the actual speech and gets it ready before saying it. He thinks it out, and perhaps writes it in the form of a book; but it is still a part of social intercourse in which one is addressing other persons and at the same time addressing one's self, and in which one controls the address to other persons by the response made to one's own gesture. That the person should be responding to himself is necessary to the self, and it is this sort of social conduct which provides behavior within which that self appears. I know of no other form of behavior than the linguistic in which the individual is an object to himself, and, so far as I can see, the individual is not a self in the reflexive sense unless he is an object to himself. It is this fact that gives a critical importance to communication, since this is a type of behavior in which the individual does so respond to himself.

We realize in everyday conduct and experience that an individual does not mean a great deal of what he is doing and saying. We frequently say that such an individual is not himself. We come away from an interview with a realization that we have left out important things, that there are parts of the self that did not get into what was said. What determines the amount of the self that gets into communication is the social experience itself. Of course, a good deal of the self does not need to get expression. We carry on a whole series of different relationships to different people. We are one thing to one man and another thing to another. There are parts of the self which exist only for the self in relationship to itself. We divide ourselves up in all sorts of different selves with reference to our acquaintances. We discuss politics with one and religion with another. There are all sorts of different selves answering to all sorts of different social reactions. It is the social process itself that is responsible for the appearance of the self; it is not there as a self apart from this type of experience.

* * *

The unity and structure of the complete self reflects the unity and structure of the social process as a whole; and each of the elementary selves of which it is composed reflects the unity and structure of one of the various aspects of that process in which the individual is implicated. In other words, the various elementary selves which constitute, or are organized into, a complete self are the various aspects of the structure of that complete self answering to the various aspects of the structure of the social process as a whole; the structure of the complete self is thus a reflection of the complete social process. The organization and unification of a social group is identical with the organization and unification of any one of the selves arising within the social process in which that group is engaged, or which it is carrying on.[2]

* * *

THE SELF AND THE SUBJECTIVE

* * *

It has been the tendency of psychology to deal with the self as a more or less isolated and independent element, a sort of entity that could conceivably exist by itself. It is possible that there might be a single self in the universe if we start off by identifying the self with a certain feeling-consciousness. If we speak of this feeling as objective, then we can think of that self as existing by itself. We can think of a separate physical body existing by itself, we can assume that it has these feelings or conscious states in question, and so we can set up that sort of a self in thought as existing simply by itself.

Then there is another use of "consciousness" with which we have been particularly occupied, denoting that which we term thinking or reflective intelligence, a use of consciousness which always has, implicitly at least, the reference to an "I" in it. This use of consciousness has no necessary connection with the other; it is an entirely different conception. One usage has to do with a certain mechanism, a certain way in which an organism acts. If an organism is endowed with sense organs then there are objects in its environment, and among those objects will be parts of its own body.[3] It is true that if the organism did not have a retina and a central nervous system there would not be any objects of vision. For such objects to exist there have to be certain physiological conditions, but these objects are not in themselves necessarily related to a self. When we reach a self we reach a certain sort of conduct, a certain type of social process which involves the interaction of different individuals and yet implies individuals engaged in some sort of cooperative activity. In that process a self, as such, can arise.

* * *

. . . We cannot identify the self with what is commonly called consciousness, that is, with the private or subjective thereness of the characters of objects.

There is, of course, a current distinction between consciousness and self-consciousness: consciousness answering to certain experiences such as those of pain or pleasure, self-consciousness referring to a recognition or appearance of a self as an object. It is, however, very generally assumed that these other conscious contents carry with them also a self-consciousness—that a pain is always somebody's pain, and that if there were not this reference to some individual it would not be pain. There is a very definite element of truth in this, but it is far from the whole story. The pain does have to belong to an individual; it has to be your pain if it is going to belong to you. Pain can belong to anybody, but if it did belong to everybody it would be comparatively unimportant. I suppose it is conceivable that under an anesthetic what takes place is the dissociation of experiences so that the suffering, so to speak, is no longer your suffering. We have illustrations of that, short of the anesthetic dissociation, in an experience of a disagreeable thing which loses its power over us because we give our attention to something else. If we can get, so to speak, outside of the thing, dissociating it from the eye that is regarding it, we may find that it has lost a great deal of its unendurable character. The unendurableness of pain is a reaction against it. If you can actually keep yourself from reacting against suffering you get rid of a certain content in the suffering itself. What takes place in effect is that it ceases to be your pain. You simply regard it objectively. Such is the point of view we are continually impressing on a person when he is apt to be swept away by emotion. In that case what we get rid of is not the offense itself, but the reaction against the offense. The objective character of the judge is that of a person who is neutral, who can simply stand outside of a situation and assess it. If we can get that judicial attitude in regard to the offenses of a person against ourselves, we reach the point where we do not resent them but understand them, we get the situation where to understand is to forgive. We remove much of experience outside of our own self by this attitude. The distinctive and natural attitude against another is a resentment of an offense, but we now have in a certain sense passed beyond that self and become a self with other attitudes. There is a certain technique, then, to which we subject ourselves in enduring suffering or any emotional situation, and which consists in partially separating one's self from the experience so that it is no longer the experience of the individual in question.

If, now, we could separate the experience entirely, so that we should not remember it, so that we should not have to take it up continually into the self from day to day, from moment to moment, then it would not exist any longer so far as we are concerned. If we had no memory which identifies experiences with the self, then they would certainly disappear so far as their relation to the self is concerned, and yet they might continue as sensuous or sensible experiences without being taken up into a self. That sort of a situation is presented in the pathological case of a multiple personality in which an individual loses the memory of a certain phase of his existence. Everything connected with that phase of his existence is gone and he becomes a different personality. The past has a reality whether in the experience or not, but here it is not identified with the self—it does not go to make up the self. We take an attitude of that sort, for example, with reference to others when a person has committed some sort of an offense which leads to a statement of the situation, an admission, and perhaps regret, and then is dropped. A person who forgives but does not forget is an unpleasant companion; what goes with forgiving is forgetting, getting rid of the memory of it.

There are many illustrations which can be brought up of the loose relationship of given contents to a self in defense of our recognition of them as having a certain value outside of the self. At the least, it must be granted that we can approach the point where something which we recognize as a content is less and less essential to the self, is held off from the present self, and no longer has the value for that self which it had for the former self. Extreme cases seem to support the view that a certain portion of such contents can be entirely cut off from the self. While in some sense it is there ready to appear under specific conditions, for the time being it is dissociated and does not get in above the threshold of our self-consciousness.

Self-consciousness, on the other hand, is definitely organized about the social individual, and that, as we have seen, is not simply because one is in a social group and affected by others and affects them, but because (and this is a point I have been emphasizing) his own experience as a self is one which he takes over from his action upon others. He becomes a self in so far as he can take the attitude of another and act toward himself as others act. In so far as the conversation of gestures can become part of conduct in the direction and control of experience, then a self can arise. It is the social process of influencing others in a social act and then taking the attitude of the others aroused by the stimulus, and then reacting in turn to this response, which constitutes a self.

Our bodies are parts of our environment; and it is possible for the individual to experience and be conscious of his body, and of bodily sensations, without being conscious or aware of himself—without, in other words, taking the attitude of the other toward himself. According to the social theory of consciousness, what we mean by consciousness is that peculiar character and aspect of the environment of individual human experience which is due to human society, a society of other individual selves who take the attitude of the other toward themselves. The physiological conception or theory of consciousness is by itself inadequate; it requires supplementation from the socio-psychological point of view. The taking or feeling of the attitude of the other toward yourself is what constitutes self-consciousness, and not mere organic sensations of which the individual is aware and which he experiences. Until the rise of his self-consciousness in the process of social experience, the individual experiences his body—its feelings and sensations—merely as an immediate part of his environment, not as his own, not in terms of self-consciousness. The self and self-consciousness have first to arise, and then these experiences can be identified peculiarly with the self, or appropriated by the self; to enter, so to speak, into this heritage of experience, the self has first to develop within the social process in which this heritage is involved.

Notes

1. Man's behavior is such in his social group that he is able to become an object to himself, a fact which constitutes him a more advanced product of evolutionary development than are the lower animals. Fundamentally it is this social fact—and not his alleged possession of a soul or mind with which he, as an individual, has been mysteriously and supernaturally endowed, and with which the lower animals have not been endowed—that differentiates him from them.

2. The unity of the mind is not identical with the unity of the self. The unity of the self is constituted by the unity of the entire relational pattern of social behavior and experience in which the individual is implicated, and which is reflected in the structure of the self; but many of the aspects or features of this entire pattern do not enter into consciousness, so that the unity of the mind is in a sense an abstraction from the more inclusive unity of the self.

3. Our constructive selection of our environment is what we term "consciousness," in the first sense of the term. The organism does not project sensuous qualities—colors, for example—into the environment to which it responds; but it endows this environment with such qualities, in a sense similar to that in which an ox

endows grass with the quality of being food, or in which—speaking more generally—the relation between biological organisms and certain environmental contents gives rise to food objects. If there were no organisms with particular sense organs there would be no environment, in the proper or usual sense of the term. An organism constructs (in the selective sense) its environment; and consciousness often refers to the character of the environment in so far as it is determined or constructively selected by our human organisms, and depends upon the relationship between the former (as thus selected or constructed) and the latter.

The Relatent Notion of Personhood

Arthur K. Bierman

What is the individual apart from his or her interactions with others in a social context? Arthur Bierman begins his investigation with an analysis of "rugged" individualism. Quickly, he rejects such an ethic as alienating. This alienation might be caused by thinking of persons as atoms, or as metaphysical substances. Bierman asks us to think of persons in a different way, namely, to think of persons as collections of "relatents." Among other possibilities, these relatents may be familial, occupational, or civic in their arrangement. As you read, ask yourself whether as persons we are not so much individuals as we are socially related beings.

THE SOCIAL NATURE OF PERSONS

* * *

Individualism is a defense mechanism employed when persons realize they have been abandoned by their society. That is its pitiful side. Individualism also encourages bravado, which is its rugged side. "Rugged" individualism is a clarion summons to gird up your muscles and to act vigorously to gain your goals; anyone caught hesitating to go roughshod in the world is spiked as a pallid, callow, sentimental bleedingheart; assertions of human interdependency are seen as admissions of weakness; competing is the great thing and the winner's reward is control over the losers; social welfare programs, medical aid, unemployment benefits, bankruptcy laws, and special help programs in the public schools are regarded as evidence of the victim's moral fiberlessness and failure rather than as evidence of a crippling social system; it is man heroically matching himself against a perpetually present, rugged frontier; self-interest is all; glory be to Daddy Warbucks!

Rugged individualism flies the proud banner of self-reliance and self-confidence. It also runs up the banner of freedom, of autonomy. In relying on and confiding in yourself alone, you can avoid buckling yourself to others. Any dependency relation you

From *The Philosophy of Urban Existence* by Arthur K. Bierman. Athens: Ohio University Press, 1973, pp. 16–17, 54–66, 71–79.

have with another person is unwelcome because it restricts your choices and actions, and, therefore, restricts your freedom. The other becomes as a millstone around your neck. In order to achieve maximum freedom—according to the ethics of rugged individualism—you should be the sole source of the energy required to achieve your goals. Human alliances are undertaken under the pressure of circumstances, and always reluctantly, because the acid of each alliance destroys a bit more of your freedom. It is assumed that human aid can be purchased only at the cost of freedom.

Given that the supreme value of rugged individualism is personal freedom, human relations are to be avoided except when you cannot accomplish your goals without help from others. The conditions which account for social relations, therefore, are those in which we look on other persons as means to our ends. The perfect relation to have with another person if we are absolutely forced to resort to using him as a means—according to individualism—is a one-way relation: You get help from him and he asks nothing in return, for, by asking for nothing, he does not restrict your freedom. The closest we come to this one-way relation between humans is in the master-slave relationship. The ideal logical outcome of rugged individualism when forced to operate in a world where we need others is slavery. The ideal outcome when persons are not forced to rely on the help of others is a "society" of personal atoms, each doing his own thing independently of others. This kind of society is essentially an aggregate of atoms, since there are no mutual relations tying the atoms together: it is a Many that shuns Oneness. If we were to picture an extreme form of alienation, we would picture the unrelated aggregate of personal atoms which rugged individualism projects as its ideal.

Of course, the person committed to rugged individualism does not want to be the slave of another because a slave suffers a minimum state of freedom. To avoid becoming another's slave, a person must either have the power to be a master or he must live in splendid isolation. Among a group of persons, it is not logically possible for every one to be a master; masters cannot be masters without someone being a slave. Given that no rugged individualist willingly becomes a slave, a power struggle to determine who shall be masters and who slaves is another logical outcome of rugged individualism. Might doesn't make right, it makes Masters. To be caught in the toils of the ethics of rugged individualism is to be caught permanently in the toils of war.

There is a way out of this permanent state of war that is becoming more and more a practical possibility. With advances in technology, we can replace slaves with machines. This makes possible the perfect one-way relationship because machines help us accomplish our goals without asking for anything in return. Technology perfected would enable us to live in complete freedom from others without struggle. The bliss of living with machines would be chilled only by their lack of love, respect, care, admiration, praise, encouragement, and concern. This chill might be removed by programming the machines to show by their behavior that they do love, respect, care for, admire, praise, encourage, and are concerned for us. Of course programming these human attitudes into the machines would be the ultimate act of rugged individualism because they would, in effect, then be attitudes of self-love, self-respect, self-care, self-admiration, self-praise, self-encouragement, and self-concern.

The ethic of rugged individualism logically results, then, in alienation, slavery, war, and self-glorification. These results should be enough reason to reject it as our ideal ethical system. The fact that the results are exactly our present moral situation makes the philosophical task of fashioning an alternative more than an academic exercise.

I don't suppose anyone would willingly opt for rugged individualism if faced with these logical results. He might suicidally resign himself to this fate, however, if he thought that it was an unavoidable "human condition." Unfortunately, this seems to be exactly what many do think. I believe that most of our contemporaries are resigned to some form of the ethic of rugged individualism because they believe that the nature of persons leaves us with no alternative. I do not have in mind an appraisal of the moral nature of persons but, rather, a view of the metaphysical nature of persons. The metaphysical view of persons that underwrites rugged individualism is the view that a person is an object kind of thing called a substance.

I shall show how, in thinking that persons are substances, we are led to think of them as self-contained entities, atoms of existence, fundamentally isolated from each other because relations between them affect only the surface and not the core of each other's reality. In short, to think of persons as substances is to think of them as metaphysically alienated. This metaphysical alienation underwrites a form of moral and political alienation such as rugged individualism because it imposes a particular image of society on us. The image is that society is a collection of atoms, each atom being a person. Atoms are morally isolated from each other because moral and political relations between them fail to tie their core realities together into an integrated society; they tie only the surface appearance of persons together. This view of persons and their moral relations leaves us barren of any other than prudential reasons why we should treat others morally because nothing more profound than their appearance is at stake. Substance thinking makes a mystery of morality and of a commitment to social ideals.

We are like BB's scattered randomly on a plane; we touch only on the surface, if we touch at all.

Let us proceed to draw out what it is to think of a person as a substance, as, I suspect, you do.

The concept of substance is given its marching orders by our common sense notion of a physical object, so that to think of a person, a self, as a substance is to think of him on the model of a physical object. To be sure, not everyone who holds a substance theory of persons believes that the substance of persons is physical matter; they may hold that a person is a mental substance, a soul. Still, even as a mental substance, the person is thought of as a thing, an object, albeit a mental thing.

I have often noticed that at the mention of the word "metaphysics" or of metaphysical words such as "substance," people's eyes glaze over, they start acting slightly shifty, and you know they are wondering how they ever got themselves into such a situation. They are perfectly willing to leave metaphysics to the philosophers who apparently find some use for it, little knowing that they themselves are metaphysicians. People generally have too great a reverence and/or fear of Madame Metaphysics. Let us escort her from the study to the kitchen where we may comfortably consort with her.

A METAPHYSICAL INTERLUDE

The scene is Andrea and Homer's kitchen. They are engaged in their usual sort of after-dinner conversation.

ANDREA: I've been reading Descartes' *Meditations* again, Homer, and thinking about substance.

HOMER: That's swell, Andrea.

ANDREA: Why are your eyes glazing over?

HOMER: They always do that when you mention "substance."

ANDREA: You've simply got to get over that. You embarrass me in front of our friends.

HOMER: Can you help me?

ANDREA: I hope so. Look, Homer, suppose all your concepts were laid out before you. You'd find that they presented a cluster pattern. There would be a cluster of concepts that we use to think about economics, another we use to think about botany, another we use to think about food, another we use to think about law and so forth.

HOMER: I would?

ANDREA: Yes, and you would also notice that some concepts occur in every cluster. These concepts saturate all your thinking. You use them to think about anything. These pervasive concepts are metaphysical concepts.

HOMER: That doesn't sound complicated. Can you give me some examples?

ANDREA: Sure, and all of them perfectly familiar to you. Beginning and end, individual, character, unity, change, identity, and interaction. Oh, good, you're beginning to unglaze a little.

HOMER: And my breathing is getting more normal, too.

ANDREA: I think you're ready for substance.

HOMER: I'm starting to feel shifty, though.

ANDREA: Relax, dear, nothing could be simpler to explain. Substance is simply a concept you use in thinking, for example, about physical objects. You do think about physical objects, you know.

HOMER: Oh, yes, all the time, but I don't think I use substance all the time. Do I?

ANDREA: I think so. You think physical objects have a beginning and an end, don't you?

HOMER: Of course. Even the world has a beginning and an end.

ANDREA: Do you think things, or the world, are made out of nothing?

HOMER: You can't make something out of nothing. Even good fairies can't do that. The good fairy had to make Cinderella's horses out of mice and her carriage out of a pumpkin.

ANDREA: You agree with the first Greek philosophers, then. They thought there is a primary stuff out of which everything is made. Now listen to this: They called that primary stuff "substance."

HOMER: Am I unglazing just a little?

ANDREA: I think so. Now, Homer, you think that this substance is divisible because you think there are individual things.

HOMER: Absolutely. Here is an individual candle, there another one. And they are different individuals from the table they're sitting on. They're separate from each other.

ANDREA: Good. And don't you distinguish between a thing and its character? Don't you think that a character is something different from the thing that has the character?

HOMER: I suppose so, if you mean by a thing's character its properties or qualities.

ANDREA: That is what I mean. Roses are red, violets are blue. Now suppose that a thing's character were taken away from it. What would you have left? Suppose you take the taste, odor, color, shape, size, and so forth away from a piece of wax. What would you have left?

HOMER: I would have left whatever has those qualities.

ANDREA: Very clever. What should we call it?

HOMER: Substance?

ANDREA: Right. Substance and shadow, the thing and its appearance.

HOMER: Huh?

ANDREA: The character is the outward appearance, the show of the underlying reality which is substance. The character, the complex of qualities, inheres in the substance.

HOMER: What's this "inheres" bit? Is it as if the substance were some sticky stuff to which qualities stick, or what?

ANDREA: A visual and tactile metaphor won't do because even a "sticky stuff" is substance with a sticky character rather than "pure" substance. Substance is not something that can be observed by the senses; only its character appearance is sensible. Substance is the child of theory. It is an entity known only by reason. Descartes, in his *Second Meditation*, observes a piece of wax fresh from the beehive. When fresh from the hive it has a given character but, when he puts it by fire, it melts and changes its character completely. It tastes and smells different; it changes color and shape and size. Still we say it is the identical wax.

HOMER: I do. The wax didn't go out of existence just because its character changed.

ANDREA: Why do you suppose you can say it is the identical wax even though it has completely changed its character?

HOMER: Substance, again. The substance is the same before and after the wax melted; the substance did not go out of existence.

ANDREA: You see how marvelous you are at metaphysics, darling?

HOMER: Thanks. But I'm not yet wholly unglazed. I still don't understand how character inheres in substance.

ANDREA: There are some things you just have to accept. The mind must come to rest somewhere. Substance, being a child of reason, has whatever nature our mind needs in order to organize our experience of physical objects. For example, here is another use for substance. The character of an object is complex; it is made up of several qualities such as taste, smell, size, shape. Though the qualities are Many, the character is One. How is it possible that a character may have this unity?

HOMER: Like the good fairy, I utter a magic word: Substance! Since each of the characteristics inheres in the same substance, they are held together as a single character.

ANDREA: Excellent: More brandsey, please. Your eyes are getting quite unglazed now. Things change. Let me tell you how substance helps us understand change. A thing changes when one of its qualities gets disinherited and nother inheres in ish playsh. Simple.

HOMER: Drunken qualities replace sober qualities.

ANDREA: That's because of the brandsey. One thing has an effect on another when they interact; it makesh a substance lose one characteristic and gain another.

HOMER: That makes me sad.

ANDREA: Poor Homer. Tell me all about it.

HOMER: You said a thing's character is only an appearance, an outward show. If interaction between things changes only the world's appearance but not its substance, reality never changes. Reality is static; it stays the same forever. That means our personal relations don't really change anything of our reality; we are doomed to affect only each other's appearance.

ANDREA: What a terribly sobering thought.

HOMER: You are beyond the hand of change even when it is the hand of someone who loves you very much. We are locked in our substances. There is an unbridgeable gulf between our substances. Our souls—

ANDREA: Souls?

HOMER: Yes, our souls. They are our substance, our reality. After all, I am not my body. Our souls are like BB shot lying on the plane of existence. Society amounts to no more than an aggregate of unconnected BB-souls. There is no true, profound interpenetration of one human substance by another.

ANDREA: But what makes you think . . .

HOMER: Andrea, I don't want you to ever read Descartes again. Look what his foul substance has done. Our personal character, sometimes so hard won, is vain foppery, the soul's dress, subject to fashion's whims, forever concealing our real, naked self from others. Do you realize what this means? I'll tell you. You may have the brains, but I've got the heart. What it means is that we are never able to reach beyond our own to another's reality. That means all our moral aspirations must sink to a base, rugged individualism or some similar stupid ethic, a kind of BB version of our moral condition. To a rugged individualist, only a feather brained idealist could raise expectations for genuine relations and obligations between people.

ANDREA: But what makes you think . . .

HOMER: Don't stop me now. Thinking of humans as substances is merely a metaphysical version of human BB-hood; it is a metaphysical basis for yielding to belief in ultimate, unavoidable alienation; it is a metaphysical prop for a BB-ethic. According to your substance-cretins, we live a life of pretense if we think we can lay an obligation on somebody else because, in effect, our realities are sealed off from each other. As substances we are existentially independent; only our appearances are affected by human relations. Life is a series of transmigrations, which is just a series of transmogrifications of persons' appearance. In actuality, our hemetically sealed souls drift in eternal isolation, unperturbed, unruffled, unchanged, essentially uninvolved, shedding one appearance after another like a snake shucking last year's dead skin. Weep for them, Andrea. Weep.

ANDREA: Come, come, dear, the slough of despair doesn't suit you. We can escape this dreadful metaphysical fate. What makes you think that we have to think of persons as substances, as if they were like physical objects?

HOMER: You don't deny that we think of them that way, do you? After all, we do apply all the metaphysical concepts to humans that we apply to physical objects. Persons have beginnings and ends, birth and death; we distinguish one individual person from another; persons have character, personality; their character belongs to them and no one else, and may have a unity; persons change, the child and the adult are as different as the wax is before and after melting; persons maintain their identity even though their character changes completely; I remember a poem Bob Kennedy gave me, a Hindu poem, he said:

Death is only matter dressed
in some new form,
A varied vest:
From tenement to tenement
though tossed,
The Soul does not change.
Only the figure is lost!

And you won't deny that persons interact.

ANDREA: What is all that supposed to prove?

HOMER: That the metaphysical concepts—beginning and end, individual, character, unity, change, identity, and interaction—apply to persons as well as to physical objects.

ANDREA: Just because they apply to persons doesn't by itself prove that persons are substances. Substance happens to be part of a particular metaphysical theory designed to explain how metaphysical concepts apply to physical objects. But, those concepts apply to every field. Remember?

HOMER: Sure, I remember. That's what makes them metaphysical concepts. So they do apply. So what? Brandy Andrea?

ANDREA: At least the glaze is gone, but you're still too damn shifty, Homer. Those metaphysical concepts apply to economics. Take the idea of a market. Markets come and go; the surrey market is kaput, dead. We distinguish the tobacco market from the hair spray market. Markets have a character; just read the *Wall Street Journal*. Markets have a unity; if they didn't we couldn't financially "grab" "the market"; there has to be something you control when you control it. Markets change; they rise and fall. And they have to have an identity or we couldn't say the market has fallen. Today the market is 783; yesterday it was 785. One number is lower than the other; but if the two numbers don't describe the same entity (it, the market) at two different times, we couldn't say that *it* had fallen. Finally, markets interact; the auto market affects the steel market.

Here comes the big question, Homer. When you think of the market, do you think there is a substance that is its underlying reality?

HOMER: That's an easy one. No.

ANDREA: Well, there you are, we don't always need substance to explain how the metaphysical concepts apply. What makes you think we need it to explain how they apply to persons?

HOMER: To tell you the truth, I'm not sure.

ANDREA: The existence and nature of substance is entirely dependent on theory. It is a theoretical entity. We can keep it as long as it plays a necessary part in a good theory. But as soon as we reject the theory, we can reject substance. Substance becomes a useless piece of baggage that is best dropped. Don't you agree?

HOMER: I think I do. Some biologists once thought there was a life-force. They needed it to explain how "inert" matter could be alive, but now that we have more advanced chemical and physical theories to explain life, we don't need such an entity as "life-force" anymore. Good.

ANDREA: Do you think the substance theory of persons is a good one?

HOMER: You must not have taken my tirade seriously. Any metaphysical theory that leads to a bad ethic such as rugged individualism has got to be bad.

ANDREA: Why don't you throw it out, then?

HOMER: I don't know. Maybe I still think it's true.

ANDREA: You don't have to believe in the existence of substance in the way that you have to believe in the existence of candles. You can see, feel, smell, and taste candles, but you can't see, feel, smell, or taste substance. It's an entity invented by the mind to explain how we apply metaphysical concepts. You admit you don't use it—so, you don't need it—to explain your talk about markets. Maybe the concept of a person is more like the concept of a market than it is like the concept of a physical object. If it is, then substance is a superfluous theoretical entity. Give up your old metaphysical habits; they only lead to rotten moral theories. You've got metaphysical freedom, sweetie. Reorganize your thought about persons.

HOMER: Freedom from substance! What a slogan! I like it. Do you mean we might think of a different theory of persons? I'd like one that makes a decent human society possible, a theory in which it is possible for human relations to affect the essence of each other's being. I'd like a theory that helps us understand how our very existence and nature are dependent upon the achievement of a set of moral relations to each other. We wouldn't have to live like BB's then.

ANDREA: That's what I've always found dear in you, Homer, that streak of nobility, your hunger for moral dignity. It becomes you.

HOMER: Thanks, Andrea, but, tell me, what kind of a theory of persons would give us what I want, really?

ANDREA: You've been too generous with the brandy. I can't figure that one out tonight. It will just have to wait, Homer.

* * *

By eavesdropping on Andrea and Homer's conversation, we learned that we not only don't have to think of persons as substances, but that we don't want to think of them as substances because a substance theory of persons is a metaphysical version of alienation that supports the moral isolation of rugged individualism. With her comments on an economic market, Andrea taught us that we have the theoretical freedom to recast our metaphysical notion of a person. In this chapter, I take advantage of that freedom to suggest another theory of what a person is.

Andrea suggested to Homer that a person may be more like a market than like a physical object. We know that Andrea had had too much brandy when she said that. Of course, it may be a ridiculous idea, but just on the chance that she was putting us on the trail of a vein we might profitably prospect, let's think about the notion of a market for a bit.

Here we are on a flying carpet, scooting over the world, peering down through its rents. We dip down toward the world to have a closer look: Below we see some things: two men, some pieces of silver, and a ham. The men are talking: "I'll give you five pieces of silver for the ham." "It's a deal. It's cheap, but a deal." We are witnessing an exchange which is a portion of a market.

An exchange is a banal occurrence that holds something of interest to us. The occurrence takes place amongst correlatives. A correlative is something—for example, a buyer—that stands in some relation to something else—for example, a seller—that stands in a relation to the buyer. Something that is a buyer is a correlative; it is a correlative to a seller. A parent and child are correlatives. A valley and a mountain are correlatives. Correlatives are tied with bonds of necessity. There cannot be a buyer unless there is a seller; and *vice versa*. There cannot be a parent unless there is a child; and *vice versa*. There cannot be a valley without a mountain; and *vice versa*.

Just as a seller and a buyer are correlatives, so a seller and his goods are correlatives. One cannot be a seller unless he has goods to sell. Similarly, a buyer and his coin are correlatives. Also, a seller and the buyer's coin are correlatives because if the seller doesn't get something for his goods he has either given his goods as a gift or his goods have been stolen. Further, a buyer and the seller's goods are correlatives; you can't be a buyer if you haven't bought something.

The banal occurrence we call an exchange does not take place unless there are at least four things in a complex network of co-relations. A market such as the stock market is a set of such exchanges actual or potential.

One more step and then we will be ready to grasp a new vision of persons.

What makes silver (or seashells) money? Not the fact that it is silver, for something may be silver and not be money. Nor that it is valuable, for many things are valuable that are not money. What makes ham (or shoes) goods? It isn't always goods because sometimes it is food. What makes a person a buyer? Not that he is a person, for persons are not always buyers; sometimes they are sellers. Clearly, what makes silver money, ham goods, and persons buyers and sellers are their being in correlative relations to each other. It is not the silver's physical nature nor the ham's physical nature that makes one money and the other goods; their natures may make them silver and ham, but it is their co-relations that make them money and goods. (Hint: The concept of person is like the concepts of goods and money, not like the concept of ham or silver.)

In the spirit that we ask what makes an object such as ham a piece of goods, or what makes an object such as silver money, we ask what makes a body a person. We approach our answer to this question through an analogy. What makes a piece of wood a spear and a support and a part of a picture frame and a handle? The same piece of wood may be a spear to a boy playing Hercules, a part of a picture frame to an artist, a support for plants to the gardener, or a placard handle to a picketer.

Which of them the piece of wood is depends upon the situation it is in; it depends upon the relations it has to other things. Buyers, sellers, money, goods, spears, supports, picture frame parts, and handles are not things-in-themselves. They are what they are because of the other things to which they are related and because of the way they are related to those other things.

We can make this clearer by means of a generalization: xRy. We will let x and y stand for objects and R stand for a relation. Suppose y is a sheet of cardboard, x is the stick, and the relation R is "tacked to," so that the stick is tacked to the cardboard. That relation and the cardboard object to which the stick is related make the stick into a handle.

Suppose, again, that y is a willowy plant and the relation R is "tied to," so that the stick is tied to the plant. That relation and the plant to which the stick is related make the stick into a support.

x is a relatent, so I call it. What it is (a handle, a support, etc.) varies with and depends on R and y in xRy. y, too, I call a relatent.

Spears, supports, handles, picture frame parts, buyers, sellers, money, goods are relational entities, or what, in short, I call relatents. Let us call "xRy," as a whole, a relationship. x and y, considered together, I call correlatents; why I do so should be clear from my discussion of correlatives. In applying these notions to persons, I will call *x* the inner correlatent and *y* the outer correlatent.

Suppose that a piece of wood could simultaneously be a spear, a support, a picture frame part, a handle. It would be possible to give a name to the collection of these things; we could call the collection, for example, a ridotto. A person is like a ridotto. "Person" is the word we use to refer to a collection of relatents. Consider some of our relatents. There are familial relations that make us into sons, daughters, wives, fathers, uncles, and cousins. There are occupational relations that make us into bosses, employees, foremen, actors, salesmen, assistant professors, longshoremen, journalists, executives, and lawyers. There are neighborhood relations that make us into neighbors, volunteers, Neighborhood Council members, Civic Affairs chairmen, monthly newsletter editors and writers, and boosters. There are city relations that make us taxpayers, voters, supervisors, citizens, mayors, witnesses, judges, Democrats, Republicans, jury members, and petitioners. A relatent is not the same concept as a role. I shall distinguish later between a factual- and a moral-relatent, which get confused in the concept of role.

Just as a piece of wood becomes a handle because relatents are created, that is, because it becomes related to other things in specific ways, so out of human bodies persons are created because their bodies become related to other bodies, families, occupations, neighborhoods, cities, and so forth. To be a person is to be many of the kinds of relatents of which I gave a sample list above. "Person" is the word we use to designate a collection of relatents. You are a collection of such relatents as son, husband, uncle, employee, musician, citizen, Democrat, voter, and many many others.

This notion of person is theoretically useful because it helps us to understand what it means to say that man is a social being. Each person is a self; the self is a correlative being, a set of inner correlatents. Since a self is a collection of correlatents, and, since correlatents' existence and nature logically depend upon the existence of others and the nature of their relations to others, we see why the existence and nature of the self is logically dependent upon other persons; since other persons, too, are sets of correlatents, they, too, logically depend upon relations to yourself and other selves.

You must not confuse this point with a commonplace psychological doctrine. It is a truism to say that our social environment influences the kind of attitudes, dreams, emotions, fears, ambitions, and conscience we have. My point is not a psychological one; it is a logical point. I am talking about the conditions necessary for your existence; and I am talking about the conditions necessary for your having the nature of a person at all, not about the psychological conditions that make you this kind of person rather than that kind of person.

This notion of person is theoretically useful, again, because it helps us to reinterpret our notion of society. We no longer have to think of a society as a collection of atoms, as a collection of hermetically sealed substances. A society is to self and others as a topography is to a mountain and a valley. A topography is a variation in land levels described relationally as mountains, valleys, and plains; a society is an organization of human bodies described relationally as sets of relatents. It is an arrangement that creates persons; some arrangements are good, others bad, because some make good persons possible and others do not.

The following two reality diagrams show us the contrast between a substance

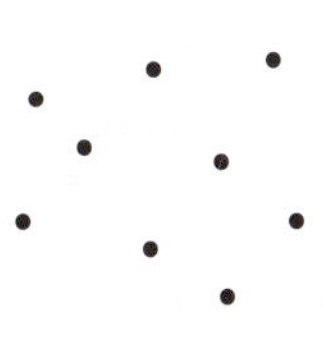

Substance Picture of Society

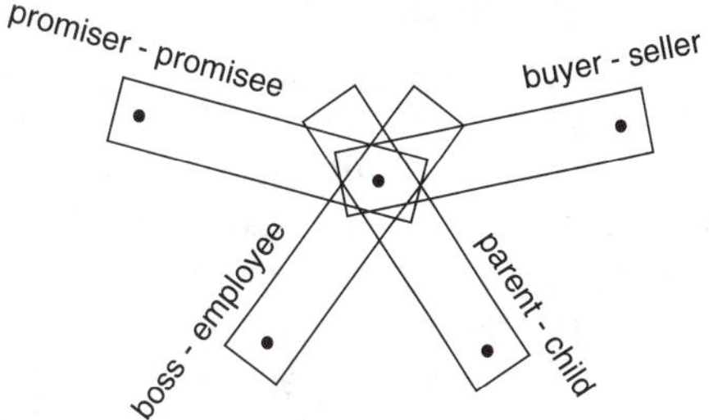

Relatent Picture of Society

picture of social reality and a relatent picture of social reality.

In the left diagram, a person is identified as a substance, represented by a dot. It is a picture of a reality composed of isolated substances. On the right, a person is identified as a set of inner correlatents—promisee, employee, parent, and buyer. The outer correlatents in the picture are promiser, boss, child, and seller. It is a picture of a reality composed of persons. To picture a person in that diagram, we necessarily have to draw moral and social co-relations between the dots, which represent bodies. We can leave relations out of the substance picture of reality, however, because they are mere appearances in that world, whereas in the relatent world they are the reality of persons.

The substance picture underwrites the rugged individualist, who aims at self-sufficiency and maximum autonomy in pursuit of his self-interest. That picture posits the substance-dot as the moral center; all moral treasures are located there in the fortress self; and therein resides the autonomous, self-activating moral tyrant we call the will. The substance-dot defines the perspective from which he views the world; it affords him a personal point of view of the social landscape. From the safe battlements of the self, the tyrant directs his foraging forces of appearance in their raids on other appearances. Though his point of view is provincial, and though he is doomed to moral solipsism, he is happy enough because his vantage point is metaphysically autonomous, secure, and impregnable.

When we conceive of a person as a collection of relatents, it is impossible to locate the moral center in a dot. Since each inner correlatent requires an outer correlative entity, a person and his moral treasures are spread throughout the social landscape. A person cannot remain provincial in his point of view; he must take up the perspective of the other as well as himself because his existence and nature are logically related to the existence and nature of others. If, for example, you wish to be a seller, you must also concern yourself with the existence of a buyer; you must help some other to retain his buyer nature if you are to retain your seller nature. It is logically impossible to define a person's interests in terms of self-interest alone according to a relatent theory of persons; it is logically impossible to conceive of your interests apart from the interests of others; thus, the relatent theory is morally useful because it razes the rugged fortress walls of the substance-self.

The relatent notion of a person is morally useful also because it erases the distinction between a person's reality and his appearance, a distinction which is central to the substance notion of a person. In ranking the value of reality and appearance, reality takes chief place; appearance is "mere" appearance, illusion, the world's seeming, not its being. According to the substance theory, our character, including the social and moral aspects of our character, belongs to appearance; our obligations to others and theirs to us are of secondary importance. This relegation of the social and moral aspects of our life to secondary importance gives free license to the rugged individualist who seizes the opportunity to pursue his "self-interest" with maximum autonomy. Restraint on one's action by others is to be avoided; obligations are a burden, not an opportunity—an obstacle, not a necessity.

With the relatent notion of a person, on the other hand, we can discern that our moral and social relations are both a necessity and an opportunity first, because they are necessary to our existence as persons, and secondly, because they are the material out of which we form our nature in accord with our ideal.

Perhaps another image might help you to grasp the concept of a person that I am advocating. Picture a net. Let the net represent a society, the net knots—not the string of the knots—represent persons, and the string between the net knots represent relations. If we were to cut the strings that lead from a net knot to other net knots, what was a net knot would become a detached, knotted string, but it would no longer be a net knot. (Moral: If you cut all a body's relations to other bodies, you have made relatents impossible for it and, thereby, destroyed a person [and injured the society]. Alienation is a form of murder.) What made the knotted string a net knot was its stringy relations to other net knots.

If I pull on a net knot some distance from a given net knot, the latter will be affected. (Moral: What is done to others in your society, whether done by you or someone else, is done to you.) Also, if someone pulls on a given net knot, it will affect the other net knots. (Moral: What is done to or by you is done to others in your society.)

And I will make you fishers of men.

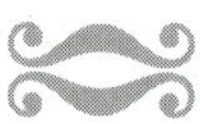

The Human Condition

Hannah Arendt

Arendt claims that there are three basic human activities: labor, work, and action. Labor is a solitary and necessary activity that is performed for survival. Work is a means-to-an-end activity, usually performed in the company of others, that we perform in order to produce goods for our use. Action is an activity that is uniquely human and that is spontaneous in nature. Action helps us to reveal to others, and to ourselves, who we are, and it plays the central role in the development of our identity as individual human beings. In this excerpt, Arendt explains the nature of these activities and the conditions under which they emerge. As you read this, reflect upon Arendt's definition of these three activities and compare her definitions to your own.

I

Vita Activa and the Human Condition

With the term *vita activa,* I propose to designate three fundamental human activities: labor, work, and action. They are fundamental because each corresponds to one of the basic conditions under which life on earth has been given to man.

Labor is the activity which corresponds to the biological process of the human body, whose spontaneous growth, metabolism, and eventual decay are bound to the vital necessities produced and fed into the life process by labor. The human condition of labor is life itself.

Work is the activity which corresponds to the unnaturalness of human existence, which is not imbedded in, and whose mortality is not compensated by, the species' ever-recurring life cycle. Work provides an "artificial" world of things, distinctly different from all natural surroundings. Within its borders each individual life is housed, while this world itself is meant to outlast and transcend them all. The human condition of work is worldliness.

Action, the only activity that goes on directly between men without the intermediary of things or matter, corresponds to the human condition of plurality, to the fact that men, not Man, live on the earth and inhabit the world. While all aspects of the human condition are somehow related to politics, this plurality is specifically *the* condition—not only the *conditio sine qua non,* but the *conditio per quam*—of all political life. Thus the language of the Romans, perhaps the most political people we have known, used the words "to live" and "to be among men" (*inter homines esse*) or "to die" and "to cease to be among men" (*inter homines esse desinere*) as synonyms. But in its most elementary form, the human condition of action is implicit even in Genesis ("Male and female created He *them*"), if we understand that this story of man's creation is distinguished in principle from the one according to which God originally created Man (*adam*), "him" and not "them," so that the multitude of human beings becomes the result of multiplication.[1] Action would be an unnecessary luxury, a capricious interference with general laws of behavior, if men were endlessly reproducible repetitions of the same model, whose nature or essence was the same for all and as predictable as the nature or essence of any other thing. Plurality is the condition of human action because we are all the same, that is, human, in such a way that nobody is ever the same as anyone else who ever lived, lives, or will live.

All three activities and their corresponding conditions are intimately connected

From *The Human Condition* by Hannah Arendt. Chicago: University of Chicago Press, 1958.

[1]In the analysis of postclassical political thought, it is often quite illuminating to find out which of the two biblical versions of the creation story is cited. Thus it is highly characteristic of the difference between the teaching of Jesus of Nazareth and of Paul that Jesus, discussing the relationship between man and wife, refers to Genesis 1:27: "Have ye not read, that he which made *them* at the beginning made them male and female" (Matt. 19:4), whereas Paul on a similar occasion insists that the woman was created "of the man" and hence "for the man," even though he then somewhat attenuates the dependence: "neither is the man without the woman, neither the woman without the man" (I Cor. 11:8–12). The difference indicates much more than a different attitude to the role of woman. For Jesus, faith was closely related to action; for Paul, faith was primarily related to salvation. Especially interesting in this respect is Augustine (*De civitate Dei* xii. 21), who not only ignores Genesis 1:27 altogether but sees the difference between man and animal in that man was created *unum ac singulum,* whereas all animals were ordered "to come into being several at once" (*plura simul iussit exsistere*). To Augustine, the creation story offers a welcome opportunity to stress the species character of animal life as distinguished from the singularity of human existence.

with the most general condition of human existence: birth and death, natality and mortality. Labor assures not only individual survival, but the life of the species. Work and its product, the human artifact, bestow a measure of permanence and durability upon the futility of mortal life and the fleeting character of human time. Action, in so far as it engages in founding and preserving political bodies, creates the condition for remembrance, that is, for history. Labor and work, as well as action, are also rooted in natality in so far as they have the task to provide and preserve the world for, to foresee and reckon with, the constant influx of newcomers who are born into the world as strangers. However, of the three, action has the closest connection with the human condition of natality; the new beginning inherent in birth can make itself felt in the world only because the newcomer possesses the capacity of beginning something anew, that is, of acting. In this sense of initiative, an element of action, and therefore of natality, is inherent in all human activities. Moreover, since action is the political activity par excellence, natality, and not mortality, may be the central category of political, as distinguished from metaphysical, thought.

The human condition comprehends more than the conditions under which life has been given to man. Men are conditioned beings because everything they come in contact with turns immediately into a condition of their existence. The world in which the *vita activa* spends itself consists of things produced by human activities; but the things that owe their existence exclusively to men nevertheless constantly condition their human makers. In addition to the conditions under which life is given to man on earth, and partly out of them, men constantly create their own, self-made conditions, which, their human origin and their variability notwithstanding, possess the same conditioning power as natural things. Whatever touches or enters into a sustained relationship with human life immediately assumes the character of a condition of human existence. This is why men, no matter what they do, are always conditioned beings. Whatever enters the human world of its own accord or is drawn into it by human effort becomes part of the human condition. The impact of the world's reality upon human existence is felt and received as a conditioning force. The objectivity of the world—its object- or thing-character—and the human condition supplement each other; because human existence is conditioned existence, it would be impossible without things, and things would be a heap of unrelated articles, a non-world, if they were not the conditioners of human existence.

To avoid misunderstanding: the human condition is not the same as human nature, and the sum total of human activities and capabilities which correspond to the human condition does not constitute anything like human nature. For neither those we discuss here nor those we leave out, like thought and reason, and not even the most meticulous enumeration of them all, constitute essential characteristics of human existence in the sense that without them this existence would no longer be human. The most radical change in the human condition we can imagine would be an emigration of men from the earth to some other planet. Such an event, no longer totally impossible, would imply that man would have to live under man-made conditions, radically different from those the earth offers him. Neither labor nor work nor action nor, indeed, thought as we know it would then make sense any longer. Yet even these hypothetical wanderers from the earth would still be human; but the only statement we could make regarding their "nature" is that they still are conditioned beings, even though their condition is now self-made to a considerable extent.

The problem of human nature, the Augustinian *quaestio mihi factus sum* ("a question have I become for myself"), seems unanswerable in both its individual psychological sense and its general philosophical sense. It is highly unlikely that we, who can know, determine, and define the natural essences of all things surrounding us, which we are not, should ever be able to do the same for ourselves—this would be like jumping over our own shadows. Moreover, nothing entitles us to assume that man has a nature or essence in the same sense as other things. In other words, if we have a nature or essence, then surely only a god could know and define it, and the first prerequisite would be that he be able to speak about a "who" as though it were a "what."[2]

The perplexity is that the modes of human cognition applicable to things with "natural" qualities, including ourselves to the limited extent that we are specimens of the most highly developed species of organic life, fail us when we raise the question: And *who* are we? This is why attempts to define human nature almost invariably end with some construction of a deity, that is, with the god of the philosophers, who, since Plato, has revealed himself upon closer inspection to be a kind of Platonic idea of man. Of course, to demask such philosophic concepts of the divine as conceptualizations of human capabilities and qualities is not a demonstration of, not even an argument for, the non-existence of God; but the fact that attempts to define the nature of man lead so easily into an idea which definitely strikes us as "superhuman" and therefore is identified with the divine may cast suspicion upon the very concept of "human nature."

On the other hand, the conditions of human existence—life itself, natality and mortality, worldliness, plurality, and the earth—can never "explain" what we are or answer the question of who we are for the simple reason that they never condition us absolutely. This has always been the opinion of philosophy, in distinction from the sciences—anthropology, psychology, biology, etc.—which also concern themselves with man. But today we may almost say that we have demonstrated even scientifically that, though we live now, and probably always will, under the earth's conditions, we are not mere earth-bound creatures. Modern natural science owes its great triumphs to having looked upon and treated earth-bound nature from a truly universal viewpoint, that is, from an Archimedean standpoint taken, willfully and explicitly, outside the earth.

[2]Augustine, who is usually credited with having been the first to raise the so-called anthropological question in philosophy, knew this quite well. He distinguishes between the questions of "Who am I?" and "What am I?" the first being directed by man at himself ("And I directed myself at myself and said to me: You, who are you? And I answered: A man"—*tu, quis es?* [*Confessiones* x. 6]) and the second being addressed to God ("What then am I, my God? What is my nature?"—*Quid ergo sum, Deus meus? Quae natura sum?* [x. 17]). For in the "great mystery," the *grande profundum,* which man is (iv. 14), there is "something of man [*aliquid hominis*] which the spirit of man which is in him itself knoweth not. But Thou, Lord, who has made him [*fecisti eum*] knowest everything of him [*eius omnia*]" (x. 5). Thus, the most familiar of these phrases which I quoted in the text, the *quaestio mihi factus sum,* is a question raised in the presence of God, "in whose eyes I have become a question for myself" (x. 33). In brief, the answer to the question "Who am I?" is simply: "You are a man—whatever that may be"; and the answer to the question "What am I?" can be given only by God who made man. The question about the nature of man is no less a theological question than the question about the nature of God; both can be settled only within the framework of a divinely revealed answer.

2

The Term *Vita Activa*

The term *vita activa* is loaded and overloaded with tradition. It is as old as (but not older than) our tradition of political thought. And this tradition, far from comprehending and conceptualizing all the political experiences of Western mankind, grew out of a specific historical constellation: the trial of Socrates and the conflict between the philosopher and the *polis*. It eliminated many experiences of an earlier past that were irrelevant to its immediate political purposes and proceeded until its end, in the work of Karl Marx, in a highly selective manner. The term itself, in medieval philosophy the standard translation of the Aristotelian *bios politikos,* already occurs in Augustine, where, as *vita negotiosa* or *actuosa,* it still reflects its original meaning: a life devoted to public-political matters.[3]

Aristotle distinguished three ways of life (*bioi*) which men might choose in freedom, that is, in full independence of the necessities of life and the relationships they originated. This prerequisite of freedom ruled out all ways of life chiefly devoted to keeping one's self alive—not only labor, which was the way of life of the slave, who was coerced by the necessity to stay alive and by the rule of his master, but also the working life of the free craftsman and the acquisitive life of the merchant. In short, it excluded everybody who involuntarily or voluntarily, for his whole life or temporarily, had lost the free disposition of his movements and activities.[4] The remaining three ways of life have in common that they were concerned with the "beautiful," that is, with things neither necessary nor merely useful: the life of enjoying bodily pleasures in which the beautiful, as it is given, is consumed; the life devoted to the matters of the *polis,* in which excellence produces beautiful deeds; and the life of the philosopher devoted to inquiry into, and contemplation of, things eternal, whose everlasting beauty can neither be brought about through the producing interference of man nor be changed through his consumption of them.[5]

The chief difference between the Aristotelian and the later medieval use of the term is that the *bios politikos* denoted explicitly only the realm of human affairs, stressing the action, *praxis,* needed to establish and sustain it. Neither labor nor work was considered to possess sufficient dignity to constitute a *bios* at all, an autonomous and authentically human way of life; since they served and produced what was necessary and useful, they could not be free, independent of human needs and wants.[6] That the political way of life escaped this verdict is due to the Greek understanding of *polis* life, which to them denoted a very special

---

[3]See Augustine *De civitate Dei* xix. 2, 19.

[4]William L. Westermann ("Between Slavery and Freedom," *American Historical Review,* Vol. L [1945]) holds that the "statement of Aristotle . . . that craftsmen live in a condition of limited slavery meant that the artisan, when he made a work contract, disposed of two of the four elements of his free status [viz., of freedom of economic activity and right of unrestricted movement], but by his own volition and for a temporary period"; evidence quoted by Westermann shows that freedom was then understood to consist of "status, personal inviolability, freedom of economic activity, right of unrestricted movement," and slavery consequently "was the lack of these four attributes." Aristotle, in his enumeration of "ways of life" in the *Nicomachean Ethics* (i. 5) and the *Eudermian Ethics* (1215a35 ff.), does not even mention a craftsman's way of life; to him it is obvious that a *banausos* is not free (cf. *Politics* 1337b5). He mentions, however, "the life of money-making" and rejects it because it too is "undertaken under compulsion" (*Nic. Eth.* 1096a5). That the criterion is freedom is stressed in the *Eudemian Ethics:* he enumerates only those lives that are chosen *ep' exousian,*

[5]For the opposition of the beautiful to the necessary and the useful see *Politics* 1333a30 ff., 1332b32.

[6]For the opposition of the free to the necessary and the useful see *ibid.* 1332b2.

and freely chosen form of political organization and by no means just any form of action necessary to keep men together in an orderly fashion. Not that the Greeks or Aristotle were ignorant of the fact that human life always demands some form of political organization and that ruling over subjects might constitute a distinct way of life; but the despot's way of life, because it was "merely" a necessity, could not be considered free and had no relationship with the *bios politikos*.[7]

With the disappearance of the ancient city-state—Augustine seems to have been the last to know at least what it once meant to be a citizen—the term *vita activa* lost its specifically political meaning and denoted all kinds of active engagement in the things of this world. To be sure, it does not follow that work and labor had risen in the hierarchy of human activities and were now equal in dignity with a life devoted to politics.[8] It was, rather, the other way round: action was now also reckoned among the necessities of earthly life, so that contemplation (the *bios theōrētikos*, translated into the *vita contemplativa*) was left as the only truly free way of life.[9]

However, the enormous superiority of contemplation over activity of any kind, action not excluded, is not Christian in origin. We find it in Plato's political philosophy, where the whole utopian reorganization of *polis* life is not only directed by the superior insight of the philosopher but has no aim other than to make possible the philosopher's way of life. Aristotle's very articulation of the different ways of life, in whose order the life of pleasure plays a minor role, is clearly guided by the ideal of contemplation (*theōria*). To the ancient freedom from the necessities of life and from compulsion by others, the philosophers added freedom and surcease from political activity (*skholē*),[10] so that the later Christian claim to be free from entanglement in worldly affairs, from all the business of this world, was preceded by and originated in the philosophic *apolitia* of late antiquity. What had been demanded only by the few was now considered to be a right of all.

The term *vita activa*, comprehending all human activities and defined from the viewpoint of the absolute quiet of contemplation, therefore corresponds more closely to the Greek *askholia* ("unquiet"), with which Aristotle designated all activity, than to the Greek *bios politikos*. As early as Aristotle the distinction between quiet and unquiet, between an almost breathless abstention from external physical movement and activity of every kind, is more decisive than the distinction between the political and the theoretical way

[7]See *ibid.* 1277b8 for the distinction between despotic rule and politics. For the argument that the life of the despot is not equal to the life of a free man because the former is concerned with "necessary things," see *ibid.* 1325a24.

[8]On the widespread opinion that the modern estimate of labor is Christian in origin, see [Arendt, *Human Condition*, p. 44].

[9]See Aquinas *Summa theologica* ii. 2. 179, esp. art. 2, where the *vita activa* arises out of the *necessitas vitae praesentis*, and *Expositio in Psalmos* 45.3, where the body politic is assigned the task of finding all that is necessary for life: *in civitate oportet invenire omnia necessaria ad vitam.*

[10]The Greek word *skholē*, like the Latin *otium*, means primarily freedom from political activity and not simply leisure time, although both words are also used to indicate freedom from labor and life's necessities. In any event, they always indicate a condition free from worries and cares. An excellent description of the everyday life of an ordinary Athenian citizen, who enjoys full freedom from labor and work, can be found in Fustel de Coulanges, *The Ancient City* (Anchor ed.; ed.; 1956), pp. 334–36; it will convince everybody how time-consuming political activity was under the conditions of the city-state. One can easily guess how full of worry this ordinary political life was if one remembers that Athenian law did not permit remaining neutral and punished those who did not want to take sides in factional strife with loss of citizenship.

of life, because it can eventually be found within each of the three ways of life. It is like the distinction between war and peace: just as war takes place for the sake of peace, thus every kind of activity, even the processes of mere thought, must culminate in the absolute quiet of contemplation.[11] Every movement, the movements of body and soul as well as of speech and reasoning, must cease before truth. Truth, be it the ancient truth of Being or the Christian truth of the living God, can reveal itself only in complete human stillness.[12]

Traditionally and up to the beginning of the modern age, the term *vita activa* never lost its negative connotation of "un-quiet," *nec-otium, a-skholia.* As such it remained intimately related to the even more fundamental Greek distinction between things that are by themselves whatever they are and things which owe their existence to man, between things that are *physei* and things that are *nomō.* The primacy of contemplation over activity rests on the conviction that no work of human hands can equal in beauty and truth the physical *kosmos,* which swings in itself in changeless eternity without any interference or assistance from outside, from man or god. This eternity discloses itself to mortal eyes only when all human movements and activities are at perfect rest. Compared with this attitude of quiet, all distinctions and articulations within the *vita activa* disappear. Seen from the viewpoint of contemplation, it does not matter what disturbs the necessary quiet, as long as it is disturbed.

Traditionally, therefore, the term *vita activa* receives its meaning from the *vita contemplativa;* its very restricted dignity is bestowed upon it because it serves the needs and wants of contemplation in a living body.[13] Christianity, with its belief in a hereafter whose joys announce themselves in the delights of contemplation,[14] conferred a religious sanction upon the abasement of the *vita activa* to its derivative, secondary position; but the determination of the order itself coincided with the very discovery of contemplation (*theōria*) as a human faculty, distinctly different from thought and reasoning, which occurred in the Socratic school and from then on has ruled metaphysical and political thought throughout our tradition.[15] It seems unnecessary to my present purpose to discuss the reasons for this tradition. Obviously they are deeper than the historical occasion which gave rise to the conflict between the *polis* and the philosopher and thereby, almost incidentally, also led to the discovery of contemplation as the philosopher's way of life. They must lie in an altogether different aspect of the human condition, whose diversity is not exhausted in the various articulations of the *vita activa* and,

[11]See Aristotle *Politics* 1333a30–33. Aquinas defines contemplation as *quies ab exterioribus motibus* (*Summa theologica* ii. 2. 179. 1).

[12]Aquinas stresses the stillness of the soul and recommends the *vita activa* because it exhausts and therefore "quietens interior passions" and prepares for contemplation (*Summa theologica* ii. 2. 182. 3).

[13]Aquinas is quite explicit on the connection between the *vita activa* and the wants and needs of the human body which men and animals have in common (*Summa theologica* ii. 2. 182. 1).

[14]Augustine speaks of the "burden" (*sarcina*) of active life imposed by the duty of charity, which would be unbearable without the "sweetness" (*suavitas*) and the "delight of truth" given in contemplation (*De civitate Dei* xix. 19).

[15]The time-honored resentment of the philosopher against the human condition of having a body is not identical with the ancient contempt for the necessities of life; to be subject to necessity was only one aspect of bodily existence, and the body, once freed of this necessity, was capable of that pure appearance the Greeks called beauty. The philosophers since Plato added to the resentment of being forced by bodily wants the resentment of movement of any kind. It is because the philosopher lives in complete quiet that it is only his body which, according to Plato, inhabits the city. Here lies also the origin of the early reproach of busybodiness (*polypragmosynē*) leveled against those who spent their lives in politics.

we may suspect, would not be exhausted even if thought and the movement of reasoning were included in it.

If, therefore, the use of the term *vita activa*, as I propose it here, is in manifest contradiction to the tradition, it is because I doubt not the validity of the experience underlying the distinction but rather the hierarchical order inherent in it from its inception. This does not mean that I wish to contest or even to discuss, for that matter, the traditional concept of truth as revelation and therefore something essentially given to man, or that I prefer the modern age's pragmatic assertion that man can know only what he makes himself. My contention is simply that the enormous weight of contemplation in the traditional hierarchy has blurred the distinctions and articulations within the *vita activa* itself and that, appearances notwithstanding, this condition has not been changed essentially by the modern break with the tradition and the eventual reversal of its hierarchical order in Marx and Nietzsche. It lies in the very nature of the famous "turning upside down" of philosophic systems or currently accepted values, that is, in the nature of the operation itself, that the conceptual framework is left more or less intact.

The modern reversal shares with the traditional hierarchy the assumption that the same central human preoccupation must prevail in all activities of men, since without one comprehensive principle no order could be established. This assumption is not a matter of course, and my use of the term *vita activa* presupposes that the concern underlying all its activities is not the same as and is neither superior nor inferior to the central concern of the *vita contemplativa*

Existentialism

Jean-Paul Sartre

In this essay, Sartre discusses the importance of taking responsibility for our own actions and, consequently, for our lives and who we are. When I act, I demonstrate to others that my action, my choice, is not only permissible for me, but for others as well. According to Sartre, since there is no God who gives guidelines by which one can judge right and wrong, we alone, as individuals, must determine whether what we do matters, and, if so, why it matters. Are we alone responsible for what we value and who we are?

Man is nothing else but what he makes of himself. Such is the first principle of existentialism. It is also what is called subjectivity, the name we are labeled with when charges are brought against us. But what do we mean by this, if not that man has a greater dignity than a stone or table? For we mean that man first exists, that is, that man first of all is the being who hurls himself toward a future and who is conscious of

From *Existentialism* by Jean-Paul Sartre, translated by Hazel E. Barnes. Copyright © 1956 The Philosophical Library. Reprinted by permission of The Philosophical Library, a division of Allied Books.

imagining himself as being in the future. Man is at the start a plan which is aware of itself, rather than a patch of moss, a piece of garbage, or a cauliflower; nothing exists prior to this plan; there is nothing in heaven; man will be what he will have planned to be. Not what he will want to be. Because by the word "will" we generally mean a conscious decision, which is subsequent to what we have already made of ourselves. I may want to belong to a political party, write a book, get married, but all that is only a manifestation of an earlier, more spontaneous choice that is called "will." But if existence really does precede essence, man is responsible for what he is. Thus, existentialism's first move is to make every man aware of what he is and to make the full responsibility of his existence rest on him. And when we say that a man is responsible for himself, we do not only mean that he is responsible for his own individuality, but that he is responsible for all men.

The word "subjectivism" has two meanings, and our opponents play on the two. Subjectivism means, on the one hand, that an individual chooses and makes himself; and, on the other, that it is impossible for man to transcend human subjectivity. The second of these is the essential meaning of existentialism. When we say that man chooses his own self, we mean that every one of us does likewise; but we also mean by that that in making this choice he also chooses all men. In fact, in creating the man that we want to be, there is not a single one of our acts which does not at the same time create an image of man as we think he ought to be. To choose to be this or that is to affirm at the same time the value of what we choose, because we can never choose evil. We always choose the good, and nothing can be good for us without being good for all.

If, on the other hand, existence precedes essence, and if we grant that we exist and fashion our image at one and the same time, the image is valid for everybody and for our whole age. Thus, our responsibility is much greater than we might have supposed, because it involves all mankind. If I am a workingman and choose to join a Christian trade union rather than be a Communist, and if by being a member I want to show that the best thing for man is resignation, that the kingdom of man is not of this world, I am not only involving my own case—I want to be resigned for everyone. As a result, my action has involved all humanity. To take a more individual matter, if I want to marry, to have children, even if this marriage depends solely on my own circumstances or passion or wish, I am involving all humanity in monogamy and not merely myself. Therefore, I am responsible for myself and for everyone else. I am creating a certain image of man of my own choosing. In choosing myself, I choose man.

This helps us understand what the actual content is of such rather grandiloquent words as anguish, forlornness, despair. As you will see, it's all quite simple.

First, what is meant by anguish? The existentialists say at once that man is anguish. What that means is this: the man who involves himself and who realizes that he is not only the person he chooses to be, but also a lawmaker who is, at the same time, choosing all mankind as well as himself, cannot help escape the feeling of his total and deep responsibility. Of course, there are many people who are not anxious; but we claim that they are hiding their anxiety, that they are fleeing from it. Certainly, many people believe that when they do something, they themselves are the only ones involved, and when someone says to them, "What if everyone acted that way?" they shrug their shoulders and answer, "Everyone doesn't act that way." But really, one should always ask himself, "What would happen if everybody looked at things that way?" There is no escaping this disturbing thought except by a kind of double-dealing. A man who lies and makes excuses for himself by saying "not everybody does that," is someone with an uneasy conscience, because the act of lying implies that a universal value is conferred upon the lie.

Anguish is evident even when it conceals itself. This is the anguish that Kierkegaard called the anguish of Abraham. You know the story: an angel has ordered Abraham to sacrifice his son; if it really were an angel who has come and said, "You are Abraham, you shall sacrifice your son," everything would be all right. But everyone might first wonder, "Is it really an angel, and am I really Abraham? What proof do I have?"

There was a madwoman who had hallucinations; someone used to speak to her on the telephone and give her orders. Her doctor asked her, "Who is it who talks to you?" She answered, "He says it's God." What proof did she really have that it was God? If an angel comes to me, what proof is there that it's an angel? And if I hear voices, what proof is there that they come from heaven and not from hell, or from the subconscious, or a pathological condition? What proves that they are addressed to me? What proof is there that I have been appointed to impose my choice and my conception of man on humanity? I'll never find any proof or sign to convince me of that. If a voice addresses me, it is always for me to decide that this is the angel's voice; if I consider that such an act is a good one, it is I who will choose to say that it is good rather than bad.

Now, I'm not being singled out as an Abraham, and yet at every moment I'm obliged to perform exemplary acts. For every man, everything happens as if all mankind had its eyes fixed on him and were guiding itself by what he does. And every man ought to say to himself, "Am I really the kind of man who has the right to act in such a way that humanity might guide itself by my actions?" And if he does not say that to himself, he is masking his anguish.

There is no question here of the kind of anguish which would lead to quietism, to inaction. It is a matter of a simple sort of anguish that anybody who has had responsibilities is familiar with. For example, when a military officer takes the responsibility for an attack and sends a certain number of men to death, he chooses to do so, and in the main he alone makes the choice. Doubtless, orders come from above, but they are too broad; he interprets them, and on this interpretation depend the lives of ten or fourteen or twenty men. In making a decision he cannot help having a certain anguish. All leaders know this anguish. That doesn't keep them from acting; on the contrary, it is the very condition of their action. For it implies that they envisage a number of possibilities, and when they choose one, they realize that it has value only because it is chosen. We shall see that this kind of anguish, which is the kind that existentialism describes, is explained, in addition, by a direct responsibility to the other men whom it involves. It is not a curtain separating us from action, but is part of action itself.

When we speak of forlornness, a term Heidegger was fond of, we mean only that God does not exist and that we have to face all the consequences of this. This existentialist is strongly opposed to a certain kind of secular ethics which would like to abolish God with the least possible expense. About 1880, some French teachers tried to set up a secular ethics which went something like this: God is a useless and costly hypothesis; we are discarding it; but, meanwhile, in order for there to be an ethics, a society, a civilization, it is essential that certain values be taken seriously and that they be considered as having an *a priori* existence. It must be obligatory, *a priori,* to be honest, not to lie, not to beat your wife, to have children, etc., etc. So we're going to try a little device which will make it possible to show that values exist all the same, inscribed in a heaven of ideas, though otherwise God does not exist. In other words—and this, I believe, is the tendency of everything called reformism in France—nothing will be changed if God does not exist. We shall find ourselves with the same norms of honesty, progress, and humanism, and we shall have made of God an outdated hypothesis which will peacefully die off by itself.

The existentialist, on the contrary, thinks it very distressing that God does not exist, because all possibility of finding values in a heaven of ideas disappears along with Him; there can no longer be an *a priori* Good, since there is no infinite and perfect consciousness to think it. Nowhere is it written that the Good exists, that we must be honest, that we must not lie; because the fact is we are on a plane where there are only men. Dostoievsky said, "If God didn't exist, everything would be possible." That is the very starting point of existentialism. Indeed, everything is permissible if God does not exist, and as a result man is forlorn, because neither within him nor without does he find anything to cling to. He can't start making excuses for himself.

If existence really does precede essence, there is no explaining things away by reference to a fixed and given human nature. In other words, there is no determinism, man is free, man is freedom. On the other hand, if God does not exist, we find no values or commands to turn to which legitimize our conduct. So, in the bright realm of values, we have no excuse behind us, nor justification before us. We are alone, with no excuses.

That is the idea I shall try to convey when I say that man is condemned to be free. Condemned, because he did not create himself, yet, in other respects is free: because, once thrown into the world, he is responsible for everything he does. The existentialist does not believe in the power of passion. He will never agree that a sweeping passion is a ravaging torrent which fatally leads a man to certain acts and is therefore an excuse. He thinks that man is responsible for his passion.

The existentialist does not think that man is going to help himself by finding in the world some omen by which to orient himself. Because he thinks that man will interpret the omen to suit himself. Therefore, he thinks that man, with no support and no aid, is condemned every moment to invent man. Ponge, in a very fine article, has said, "Man is the future of man." That's exactly it. But if it is taken to mean that this future is recorded in heaven, that God sees it, then it is false, because it would really no longer be a future. If it is taken to mean that, whatever a man may be, there is a future to be forged, a virgin future before him, then this remark is sound. But then we are forlorn.

To give you an example which will enable you to understand forlornness better, I shall cite the case of one of my students who came to see me under the following circumstances: his father was on bad terms with his mother, and, moreover, was inclined to be a collaborationist; his older brother had been killed in the German offensive of 1940, and the young man, with somewhat immature but generous feelings, wanted to avenge him. His mother lived alone with him, very much upset by the half-treason of her husband and the death of her older son; the boy was her only consolation.

The boy was faced with the choice of leaving for England and joining the Free French forces—that is, leaving his mother behind—or remaining with his mother and helping her to carry on. He was fully aware that the woman lived only for him and that his going off—and perhaps his death—would plunge her into despair. He was also aware that every act that he did for his mother's sake was a sure thing, in the sense that it was helping her to carry on, whereas every effort he made toward going off and fighting was an uncertain move which might run aground and prove completely useless; for example, on his way to England he might, while passing through Spain, be detained indefinitely in a Spanish camp; he might reach England or Algiers and be stuck in an office at a desk job. As a result, he was faced with two very different kinds of action: one, concrete, immediate, but concerning only one individual; the other concerned an incomparably vaster group, a national collectivity, but for that very reason was dubious, and might be interrupted en route. And, at the same time, he was wavering between two kinds of ethics. On the one hand, an ethics of sympathy, of personal devotion; on the other, a broader ethics, but one whose efficacy was more dubious. He had to choose between the two.

Who could help him choose? Christian doctrine? No. Christian doctrine says, "Be charitable, love your neighbor, take the more rugged path, etc., etc." But which is the more rugged path? Whom should he love as a brother? The fighting man or his mother? Which does the greater good, the vague act of fighting in a group, or the concrete one of helping a particular human being to go on living? Who can decide *a priori*? Nobody. No book of ethics can tell him. The Kantian ethics says, "Never treat any person as a means, but as an end." Very well, if I stay with my mother, I'll treat her as an end and not as a means; but by virtue of this very fact, I'm running the risk of treating the people around me who are fighting, as means; and, conversely, if I go to join those who are fighting, I'll be treating them as an end, and, by doing that, I run the risk of treating my mother as a means.

If values are vague, and if they are always too broad for the concrete and specific case that we are considering, the only thing left for us is to trust our instincts. That's what this young man tried to do; and when I saw him, he said, "In the end, feeling is what counts. I ought to choose whichever pushes me in one direction. If I feel that I love my mother enough to sacrifice everything else for her—my desire for vengeance, for action, for adventure—then I'll stay with her. If, on the contrary, I feel that my love for my mother isn't enough, I'll leave."

But how is the value of a feeling determined? What gives his feeling for his mother value? Precisely the fact that he remained with her. I may say that I like so-and-so well enough to sacrifice a certain amount of money for him, but I may say so only if I've done it. I may say "I love my mother well enough to remain with her" if I have remained with her. The only way to determine the value of this affection is, precisely, to perform an act which confirms and defines it. But, since I require this affection to justify my act, I find myself caught in a vicious circle.

On the other hand, Gide has well said that a mock feeling and a true feeling are almost indistinguishable; to decide that I love my mother and will remain with her, or to remain with her by putting on an act, amount somewhat to the same thing. In other words, the feeling is formed by the acts one performs; so, I cannot refer to it in order to act upon it. Which means that I can neither seek within myself the true condition which will impel me to act, nor apply to a system of ethics for concepts which will permit me to act. You will say, "At least, he did go to a teacher for advice." But if you seek advice from a priest, for example, you have chosen this priest; you already knew, more or less, just about what advice he was going to give you. In other words, choosing your adviser is involving yourself. The proof of this is that if you are a Christian, you will say, "Consult a priest." But some priests are collaborating, some are just marking time, some are resisting. Which to choose? If the young man chooses a priest who is resisting or collaborating, he has already decided on the kind of advice he's going to get. Therefore, in coming to see me he knew the answer I was going to give him, and I had only one answer to give: "You're free, choose, that is, invent." No general ethics can show you what is to be done; there are no omens in the world. The Catholics will reply, "But there are." Granted—but, in any case, I myself choose the meaning they have.

When I was a prisoner, I knew a rather remarkable young man who was a Jesuit. He had entered the Jesuit order in the following way: he had had a number of very bad breaks; in childhood, his father died, leaving him in poverty, and he was a scholarship student at a religious institution where he was constantly made to feel that he was being kept out of charity; then, he failed to get any of the honors and distinctions that children like; later on, at about eighteen, he bungled a love affair; finally, at twenty-two, he failed in military training, a childish enough matter, but it was the last straw.

This young fellow might well have felt that he had botched everything. It was a sign of something, but of what? He might have taken refuge in bitterness or despair. But he very wisely looked upon all this as a sign that he was not made for secular triumphs, and that only the triumphs of religion, holiness, and faith were open to him. He saw the hand of God in all this, and so he entered the order. Who can help seeing that he alone decided what the sign meant?

Some other interpretation might have been drawn from this series of setbacks; for example, that he might have done better to turn carpenter or revolutionist. Therefore, he is fully responsible for the interpretation. Forlornness implies that we ourselves choose our being. Forlornness and anguish go together.

As for despair, the term has a very simple meaning. It means that we shall confine ourselves to reckoning only with what depends upon our will, or on the ensemble of probabilities which make our action possible. When we want something, we always have to reckon with probabilities. I may be counting on the arrival of a friend. The friend is coming by rail or streetcar; this supposes that the train will arrive on schedule, or that the streetcar will not jump the track. I am left in the realm of possibility; but possibilities are to be reckoned with only to the point where my action comports with the ensemble of these possibilities, and no further. The moment the possibilities I am considering are not rigorously involved by my action, I ought to disengage myself from them, because no God, no scheme, can adapt the world and its possibilities to my will. When Descartes said, "Conquer yourself rather than the world," he meant essentially the same thing.

The Marxists to whom I have spoken reply, "You can rely on the support of others in your action, which obviously has certain limits because you're not going to live forever. That means: rely on both what others are doing elsewhere to help you, in China, in Russia, and what they will do later on, after your death, to carry on the action and lead it to its fulfillment, which will be the revolution. You even *have* to rely upon that, otherwise you're immoral." I reply at once that I will always rely on fellow-fighters insofar as these comrades are involved with me in a common struggle, in the unity of a party or a group in which I can more or less make my weight felt; that is, one whose ranks I am in as a fighter and whose movements I am aware of at every moment. In such a situation, relying on the unity and will of the party is exactly like counting on the fact that the train will arrive on time or that the car won't jump the track. But, given that man is free and that there is no human nature for me to depend on, I cannot count on men whom I do not know by relying on human goodness or man's concern for the good of society. I don't know what will become of the Russian revolution; I may make an example of it to the extent that at the present time it is apparent that the proletariat plays a part in Russia that it plays in no other nation. But I can't swear that this will inevitably lead to a triumph of the proletariat. I've got to limit myself to what I see.

Given that men are free and that tomorrow they will freely decide what man will be, I cannot be sure that, after my death, fellow-fighters will carry on my work to bring it to its maximum perfection. Tomorrow, after my death, some men may decide to set up Fascism, and the others may be cowardly and muddled enough to let them do it. Fascism will then be the human reality, so much the worse for us.

Actually, things will be as man will have decided they are to be. Does that mean that I should abandon myself to quietism? No. First, I should involve myself; then, act on the old saw, "Nothing ventured, nothing gained." Nor does it mean that I shouldn't belong to a party, but rather that I shall have no illusions and shall do what I can. For example, suppose I ask myself, "Will socialization, as such, ever come about?" I know nothing about it. All I know is that I'm going to do everything in my power to bring it about. Beyond that, I can't count on anything. Quietism is the attitude of people who say, "Let others do what I can't do." The doctrine I am presenting is the very opposite of quietism, since it declares, "There is no reality except in action." Moreover, it goes further, since it adds, "Man is nothing else than his plan; he exists only to the extent that he fulfills himself; he is therefore nothing else than the ensemble of his acts, nothing else than his life."

According to this, we can understand why our doctrine horrifies certain people. Because often the only way they can bear their wretchedness is to think, "Circumstances have been against me. What I've been and done doesn't show my true worth. To be sure, I've had no great love, no great friendship, but that's because I haven't met a man or woman who was worthy. The books I've written haven't been very good because I haven't had the proper leisure. I haven't had children to devote myself to because I didn't find a man with whom I could have spent my life. So there remains within me, unused and quite viable, a host of propensities, inclinations, possibilities, that one wouldn't guess from the mere series of things I've done."

Now, for the existentialist there is really no love other than one which manifests itself in a person's being in love. There is no genius other than one which is expressed in works of art; the genius of Proust is the sum of Proust's works; the genius of Racine is his series of tragedies. Outside of that, there is nothing. Why say that Racine could have written another tragedy, when he didn't write it? A man is involved in life, leaves his impress on it, and outside of that there is nothing. To be sure, this may seem a harsh thought to someone whose life hasn't been a success. But, on the other hand, it prompts people to understand that reality alone is what counts, that dreams, expectations, and hopes warrant no more than to define a man as a disappointed dream, as miscarried hopes, as vain expectations. In other words, to define him negatively and not positively. However, when we say, "You are nothing else than your life," that does not imply that the artist will be judged solely on the basis of his works of art; a thousand other things will contribute toward summing him up. What we mean is that a man is nothing else than a series of undertakings, that he is the sum, the organization, the ensemble of the relationships which make up these undertakings.

When all is said and done, what we are accused of, at bottom, is not our pessimism, but an optimistic toughness. If people throw up to us our works of fiction in which we write about people who are soft, weak, cowardly, and sometimes even downright bad, it's not because these people are soft, weak, cowardly, or bad; because if we were to say, as Zola did, that they are that way because of heredity, the workings of environment, society, because of biological or psychological determinism, people would be reassured. They would say, "Well, that's what we're like, no one can do anything about it." But when the existentialist writes about a coward, he says that this coward is responsible for his cowardice. He's not like that because he has a cowardly heart or lung or brain; he's not like that on account of his physiological make-up; but he's like that because he has made himself a coward by his acts. There's no such thing as a cowardly constitution; there are nervous constitutions; there is poor blood, as the common people say, or strong constitutions. But the man whose blood is poor is not a coward on that account, for what makes cowardice is the act of renouncing or yielding. A constitution is not an act; the coward is defined on the basis of the acts he performs. People feel, in a vague sort of way, that this coward we're talking about is guilty of being a coward, and the thought frightens them. What people would like is that a coward or a hero be born that way. . . .

From these few reflections it is evident that nothing is more unjust than the objections that have been raised against us. Existentialism is nothing else than an attempt to draw all the consequences of a coherent atheistic position. It isn't trying to plunge man into despair at all. But if one calls every attitude of unbelief despair, like the Christians, then the word is not being used in its original sense. Existentialism isn't so atheistic that it wears itself out showing that God doesn't exist. Rather, it declares that even if God did exist, that would change nothing. There you've got our point of view. Not that we believe that God exists, but we think that the problem of His existence is not the issue. In this sense existentialism is optimistic, a doctrine of action, and it is plain dishonesty for Christians to make no distinction between their own despair and ours and then to call us despairing.

Spiritualism and the Law of Peace

John Mohawk

In many contemporary societies, people see themselves as the focal point of existence. The rest of nature is often excluded from consideration of any type. In this essay, Mohawk explains an alternative view of seeing and living—that of the Six Nations Iroquois confederacy. He explains that the manner in which we see ourselves in relation to other living things has an impact on the whole of nature. He offers this as a challenge to the widely held anthropocentric view of human nature that is prominent in our contemporary world. As you read this, reflect upon the ways in which you view nature and human nature. Do you think that there are compelling reasons for believing that all things in nature are interrelated?

SPIRITUALISM THE HIGHEST FORM OF POLITICAL CONSCIOUSNESS

The Haudenosaunee Message to the Western World

The Haudenosaunee, or the Six Nations Iroquois Confederacy, has existed on this land since the beginning of human memory. Our culture is among the most ancient continuously existing cultures in the world. We still remember the earliest doings of human beings. We remember the original instructions of the Creators of Life on this place we call Etenoha—Mother Earth. We are the spiritual guardians of this place. We are the Ongwhehonwhe—the real people.

In the beginning, we were told that the human beings who walk about on the Earth have been provided with all the things necessary of life. We were instructed to carry a love for one another, and to show a great respect for all the beings of this Earth. We are shown that our life exists with the tree life, that our well-being depends on the well-being of the Vegetable Life, that we are close relatives of the four-legged beings. In our ways, spiritual consciousness is the highest form of politics.

Ours is a Way of Life. We believe that all living things are spiritual beings. Spirits can be expressed as energy form manifested in matter—grass matter. The spirit of the grass is that unseen force which produces the species of grass, and it is manifest to us in the form of real grass.

All things of the world are real, material things. The Creation is a true, material phenomenon, and the Creation manifests itself to us through reality. The spiritual universe, then, is manifest to Man as the Creation, the Creation which supports life. We believe that man is real, a part of the Creation, and that his duty is to support Life in conjunction with the other beings. That is why we call ourselves Ongwhehonwhe—Real People.

The original instructions direct that we who walk about on the Earth are to express a great respect, an affection, and a gratitude toward all the spirits which create and support Life. We give a greeting and thanksgiving to the many supporters of our own

From *A Basic Call to Consciousness*, edited by Akwesasne Notes, Mohawk nation via Rooseveltown, New York, 1986, "Thoughts of Peace: The Great Law," pp. 7–12, "The Haudenosaunee Address to the Western World," pp. 49–55. Reprinted by permission of John Mohawk, Professor of American Studies at the University of Buffalo, Buffalo, New York.

lives—the corn, beans, squash, the winds, the sun. When people cease to respect and express gratitude for these many things, then all life will be destroyed, and human life on this planet will come to an end.

Our roots are deep in the lands where we live. We have a great love for our country, for our birthplace is there. The soil is rich from the bones of thousands of our generations. Each of us were created in those lands, and it is our duty to take great care of them, because from these lands will spring the future generations of the Ongwhehonwhe. We walk about with a great respect, for the Earth is a very sacred place.

We are not a people who demand, or ask anything of the Creators of Life, but instead, we give greetings and thanksgiving that all the forces of Life are still at work. We deeply understand our relationship to all living things. To this day, the territories we still hold are filled with trees, animals, and the other gifts of the Creation. In these places we still receive our nourishment from our Mother Earth.

We have seen that not all people of the Earth show the same kind of respect for this world and its beings. The Indo-European people who have colonized our lands have shown very little respect for the things that create and support Life. We believe that these people ceased their respect for the world a long time ago. Many thousands of years ago, all the people of the world believed in the same Way of Life, that of harmony with the universe. All lived according to the Natural Ways.

Around ten thousand years ago, peoples who spoke Indo-European languages lived in the area which today we know as the Steppes of Russia. At that time, they were a Natural World people who lived off the land. They had developed agriculture, and it is said that they had begun the practice of animal domestication. It is not known that they were the first people in the world to practice animal domestication. The hunters and gatherers who roamed the area probably acquired animals from the agricultural people, and adopted an economy, based on the herding and breeding of animals.

Herding and breeding of animals signaled a basic alteration in the relationship of humans to other life forms. It set into motion one of the true revolutions in human history. Until herding, humans depended on Nature for the reproductive powers of the animal world. With the advent of herding, humans assumed the functions which had for all time been the functions of the spirits of the animals. Sometime after this happened, history records the first appearance of the social organization known as "patriarchy."

The area between the Tigris and Euphrates Rivers was the homeland, in ancient times, of various peoples, many of whom spoke Semitic languages. The Semitic people were among the first in the world to develop irrigation technology. This development led to the early development of towns, and eventually cities. The manipulation of the waters, another form of spirit life, represented another way in which humans developed a technology which reproduced a function of Nature.

Within these cultures, stratified hierarchal social organization crystallized. The ancient civilizations developed imperialism, partly because of the very nature of cities. Cities are obviously population concentrations. Most importantly though, they are places which must import the material needs of this concentration from the countryside. This means that the Natural World must be subjugated, extracted from, and exploited in the interest of the city. To give order to this process, the Semitic world developed early codes of law. They also developed the idea of monotheism to serve as a spiritual model for their material and political organization.

Much of the history of the ancient world recounts the struggles between the Indo-Europeans and the Semitic peoples. Over a period of several millenia, the two cultures clashed and blended. By the second millenia B.C., some Indo-Europeans, most specifically the Greeks, had adopted the practice of building cities, thus becoming involved in the process which they named "Civilization."

Both cultures developed technologies peculiar to civilizations. The Semitic people invented kilns which enabled the creation of pottery for trade, and storage of surpluses. These early kilns eventually evolved into ovens which could generate enough heat to smelt metals, notably copper, tin and bronze. The Indo-Europeans developed a way of smelting iron.

Rome fell heir to these two cultures, and became the place where the final meshing occurs. Rome is also the true birthplace of Christianity. The process that has become the culture of the West is historically and linguistically a Semitic/Indo-European culture, but has been commonly termed the Judeo-Christian tradition.

Christianity was an absolutely essential element in the early development of this kind of technology. Christianity advocated only one God. It was a religion which imposed itself exclusively of all other beliefs. The local people of the European forests were a people who believed in the spirits of the forests, waters, hills and the land; Christianity attacked those beliefs, and effectively de-spiritualized the European world. The Christian peoples, who possessed superior weaponry and a need for expansion, were able to militarily subjugate the tribal peoples of Europe.

The availability of iron led to the development of tools which could cut down the forest, the source of charcoal to make more tools. The newly cleared land was then turned by the newly developed iron plow, which was, for the first time, pulled by horses. With that technology fewer people would work much more land, and many other people were effectively displaced to become soldiers and landless peasants. The rise of the technology ushered in the Feudal Age and made possible, eventually, the rise of new cities and growing trade. It also spelled the beginning of the end of the European forest, although the process took a long time to complete.

The eventual rise of cities and the concurrent rise of the European state created the thrust of expansion and search for markets which led men, such as Columbus, to set sail across the Atlantic. The development of sailing vessels and navigation technologies made the European "discovery" of the Americas inevitable.

The Americas provided Europeans a vast new area for expansion and material exploitation. Initially, the Americas provided new material and even finished materials for the developing world economy which was based on Indo-European technologies. European civilization has a history of rising and falling as its technologies reach their material cultural limits. The finite Natural World has always provided a kind of built-in contradiction of Western expansion.

The Indo-Europeans attacked every aspect of North America with unparalleled zeal. The Native people were ruthlessly destroyed because they were an unassimilable element to the civilizations of the West. The forests provided materials for larger ships, the land was fresh and fertile for agricultural surpluses, and some areas provided sources of slave labor for the conquering invaders. By the time of the Industrial Revolution in the mid-Nineteenth Century, North America was already a leader in the area of the development of extractive technology.

The hardwood forests of the Northeast were not cleared for the purpose of providing farmlands. Those forests were destroyed to create charcoal for the forges of the iron smelters and blacksmiths. By the 1890's the West had turned to coal, a fossil fuel, to provide the energy necessary for the many new forms of machinery which had been developed. During the first half of the Twentieth Century, oil had replaced coal as a source of energy.

The Western culture has been horribly exploitative and destructive of the Natural World. Over 140 species of birds and animals were utterly destroyed since the European arrival in the Americas, largely because they were unusable in the eyes of the invaders. The forests were levelled, the waters polluted, the Native people subjected to genocide. The vast herds of herbivores were reduced to mere handfuls, the buffalo nearly became extinct. Western technology and the people who have employed it have been the most amazingly destructive forces in all of human history. No natural disaster has ever destroyed as much. Not even the Ice Ages counted as many victims.

But like the hardwood forests, the fossil fuels are also finite resources. As the second half of the Twentieth Century has progressed, the people of the West have begun looking to other forms of energy to motivate their technology. Their eyes have settled on atomic energy, a form of energy production which has by-products which are the most poisonous substances ever known to Man.

Today the species of Man is facing a question of the very survival of the species. The way of life known as Western Civilization is on a death path on which their own culture has no viable answers. When faced with the reality of their own destructiveness, they can only go forward into areas of more efficient destruction. The appearance of Plutonium on this planet is the clearest of signals that our species is in trouble. It is a signal which most Westerners have chosen to ignore.

The air is foul, the waters poisoned, the trees dying, the animals are disappearing. We think even the systems of weather are changing. Our ancient teaching warned us that if Man interfered with the Natural laws, these things would come to be. When the last of the Natural Way of Life is gone, all hope for human survival will be gone with it. And our Way of Life is fast disappearing, a victim of the destructive processes.

The other position papers of the Haudenosaunee have outlined our analysis of economic and legal oppression. But our essential message to the world is a basic call to consciousness. The destruction of the Native cultures and people is the same process which has destroyed and is destroying life on this planet. The technologies and social systems which have destroyed the animal and the plant life are also destroying the Native people. And the process is Western Civilization.

We know that there are many people in the world who can quickly grasp the intent of our message. But experience has taught us that there are few who are willing to seek out a method for moving toward any real change. But if there is to be a future for all beings on this planet, we must begin to seek the avenues of change.

The processes of colonialism and imperialism which have affected the Haudenosaunee are but a microcosm of the processes affecting the world. The system of reservations employed against our people is a microcosm of the system of exploitation used against the whole world. Since the time of Marco Polo, the West has been refining a process that mystified the peoples of the Earth.

The majority of the world does not find its roots in Western culture or traditions. The majority of the world finds its roots in the Natural World, and it is the Natural World, and traditions of the Natural World, which must prevail if we are to develop truly free and egalitarian societies.

It is necessary, at this time, that we begin a process of critical analysis of the West's historical processes, to seek out the actual nature of the roots of the exploitative and oppressive conditions which are forced upon humanity. At the same time, as we gain understanding of those processes, we must reinterpret that history to the people of the world. It is the people of the West, ultimately, who are the most oppressed and exploited. They are burdened by the weight of centuries of racism, sexism, and ignorance which has rendered their people insensitive to the true nature of their lives.

We must all consciously and continuously challenge every model, every program, and every process that the West tries to force upon us. Paulo Friere wrote, in his book, the *Pedagogy of the Oppressed*, that it is the nature of the oppressed to imitate the oppressor, and by such actions try to gain relief from the oppressive condition. We must learn to resist that response to oppression.

The people who are living on this planet need to break with the narrow concept of human liberation, and begin to see liberation as something which needs to be extended to the whole of the Natural World. What is needed is the liberation of all the things that support Life—the air, the waters, the trees—all the things which support the sacred web of Life.

We feel that the Native peoples of the Western Hemisphere can continue to contribute to the survival potential of the human species. The majority of our peoples still live in accordance with the traditions which find their roots in the Mother Earth. But the Native peoples have need of a forum in which our voice can be heard. And we need alliances with the other peoples of the world to assist in our struggle to regain and maintain our ancestral lands and to protect the Way of Life we follow.

We know that this is a very difficult task. Many nation states may feel threatened by the position that the protection and liberation of Natural World peoples and cultures represents, a progressive direction which must be integrated into the political strategies of people who seek to uphold the dignity of Man. But that position is growing in strength, and it represents a necessary strategy in the evolution of progressive thought.

The traditional Native peoples hold the key to the reversal of the processes in Western Civilization which hold the promise of unimaginable future suffering and destruction. Spiritualism is the highest form of political consciousness. And we, the Native peoples of the Western Hemisphere, are among the world's surviving proprietors of that kind of consciousness. We are here to impart that message.

Since the beginning of human time, the Haudenosaunee have occupied the distinct territories that we call our homelands. That occupation has been both organized and continuous. We have long defined the borders of our country, have long maintained the exclusive use-right of the areas within those borders, and have used those territories as the economic and cultural definitions of our nation.

The Haudenosaunee are a distinct people, with our own laws and customs, territories, political organization and economy. In short, the Haudenosaunee, or Six Nations, fits in every way every definition of nationhood.

Ours is one of the most complex social/political structures still functioning in the world. The Haudenosaunee council is also one of the most ancient continuously functioning governments anywhere on this planet. Our society is one of the most complex anywhere. From our social and political institutions has come inspiration for some of the most vital institutions and political philosophies of the modern world.

The Haudenosaunee is governed by a constitution known among Europeans as the Constitution of the Six Nations and to the Haudenosaunee as the Gayanashakgowah, or the Great Law of Peace. It is the oldest functioning document in the world which has contained a recognition of the freedoms the Western democracies recently claim as their own: the freedom of speech, freedom of religion, and the rights of women to participate in government. The concept of separation of powers in government and of checks and balances of power within governments are traceable to our constitution. They are ideas learned by the colonists as the result of contact with North American Native people, specifically the Haudenosaunee.

The philosophies of the Socialist World, too, are to some extent traceable to European contact with the Haudenosaunee. Lewis Henry Morgan noted the economic structure of the Haudenosaunee, which he termed both primitive and communistic. Karl Marx used Morgan's observations for the development of a model for classless, post-capitalist society. The modern world has been greatly influenced by the fact of our existence.

It may seem strange, at this time, that we are here, asserting the obvious fact of our continuing existence. For countless centuries, the fact of our existence was unquestioned, and for all honest human beings, it remains unquestioned today. We have existed since time immemorial. We have always conducted our own affairs from our territories, under our own laws and customs. We have never, under those laws and customs, willingly or fairly surrendered either our territories or our freedoms. Never, in the history of the Haudenosaunee, have the People or the government sworn allegiance to a European sovereign. In that simple fact lies the roots of our oppression as a people, and the purpose of our journey here, before the world community. . . .

THOUGHTS OF PEACE: THE GREAT LAW

Haudenosaunee oral history relates that long before the Europeans arrived, Native peoples of the Northeast woodlands had reached a crisis. It is said that during this time a man or woman might be killed or injured for any slight offense by his or her enemies, and that blood feuds between clans and villages ravaged the people until no one was safe. It was during this time that a male child was born to a woman of the Wyandot people living on the north side of Lake Ontario near the Bay of Quinte. It would become the custom of the people of the Longhouse that this person's name would never be spoken except during the recountings of this oral history in the oral fashion (some say during the Condolence ceremony) and at other times he is addressed simply as the Peacemaker.

The Peacemaker became one of the great political philosophers and organizers in human history. It is impossible in this short essay to discuss more than a brief outline of his ideas and accomplishments, but it should become obvious that his vision for humankind was indeed extraordinary.

He concluded early in life that the system of blood feuds as practiced by the people inhabiting the forest at the time needed to be abolished. His ideas were rejected by the Wyandot and other Huron peoples, and while a young man he journeyed to the land of the People of the Flint located on the southeast shore of Lake Ontario and extending to the areas called today the Mohawk Valley. The People of the Flint, or Ganienkehaka, are known to English-speaking peoples as the Mohawks.

Upon arrival in the Mohawk country, he began seeking out those individuals who had the reputation as being the fiercest and most fearsome destroyers of human beings. He sought them out one at a time—murderers and hunters of humans, even cannibals—and he brought to each one his message.

One by one he "straightened out their minds" as each grasped the principles that he set forth. Nine men of the Mohawks—the nine most feared men in all Mohawk country—grasped hold of his words and became his disciples.

The first principle that the Peacemaker set forth was indisputable to those who first heard his words. He said that it has come to pass that in this land human beings are seen to abuse one another. He pointed to the world in which people live and said that people should consider that some force or some thing must have created this World—the Giver of Life—had not intended that human beings would abuse one another. Human beings whose minds are healthy always desire peace, and humans have minds which enable them to achieve peaceful resolutions to their conflicts.

From that initial explanation—that the Giver of Life (later addressed as the Great Creator) did not intend that human beings abuse one another—he proposed that human societies must form governments which will serve to prevent the abuse of human beings by other human beings, and which will ensure peace among nations and peoples. Government would be established for the purpose of abolishing war and robbery among brothers and to establish peace and quietness. He drew the Mohawks together under those principles and then went to the Oneidas, Onondagas, Cayugas and Senecas with the same teachings. What is unique about his work is that he not only set forth the argument that government is desirable but he also set forth the principle—that government is specifically organized to prevent the abuse of human beings by cultivating a spiritually healthy society and the establishment of peace.

Other political philosophers and organizers have come to the conclusion that governments can be formed for the purpose of establishing tranquility, but the Peacemaker went considerably further than that. He argued not for the establishment of law and order, but for the full establishment of peace. Peace was to be defined not as the simple absence of war or strife, but as the active striving of humans for the purpose of establishing universal justice. Peace was defined as the product of a society which strives to establish concepts which correlate to the English words Power, Reason and Righteousness.

"Righteousness" refers to something akin to the shared ideology of the people using their purest and most unselfish minds. It occurs when the people put their minds and emotions in harmony with the flow of the universe and the intentions of the Good Mind or the Great Creator. The principles of Righteousness demand that all thoughts of prejudice, privilege or superiority be swept away and that recognition be given to the reality that the creation is intended for the benefit of all equally—even the birds and animals, the trees and the insects, as well as the humans. The world does not belong to humans—it is the rightful property of the Great Creator. The gifts and benefits of the world, therefore, belong to all equally. The things which humans need to survive—food, clothing, shelter, protection—these are things to which all are entitled because they are gifts of the Great Creator. Nothing belongs to human beings, not even their labor or their skills, for ambition and ability are also the gifts of the Great Creator. Therefore all people have a right to the things they need to survive—even those who do not or cannot work, and no person or people has a right to deprive others of the fruits of those gifts.

"Reason" is perceived to be the power of the human mind to make righteous decisions about complicated issues. The Peacemaker began his teachings based on the principle that human beings were given the gift of the power of Reason in order that they may settle their differences without the use of force. He proposed that in every instance humans should use every effort to council about, arbitrate and negotiate their differences, and that force should be resorted to only as a defense against the certain use of force. All men whose minds are healthy can desire peace, he taught, and there is an ability within all human beings, and especially in the young human beings, to grasp and hold strongly to the principles of Righteousness. The ability to grasp the principles of Righteousness is a spark within the individual which society must fan and nurture that it may grow. Reason is seen as the skill which humans must be encouraged to acquire in order that the objectives of justice may be attained and no one's rights abused.

Having established the concept of Righteousness and Reason, the Peacemaker went on to discuss the nature of "Power." The Power to enact a true Peace is the product of a unified people on the path of Righteousness and Reason—the ability to enact the principles of Peace through education, public opinion and political and when necessary, military unity. The "Power" that the Peacemaker spoke of was intended to enable the followers of the law to call upon warring or quarreling parties to lay down their arms and to begin peaceful settlement of their disputes. Peace, as the Peacemaker understood it, flourished only in a garden amply fertilized with absolute and pure justice. It was the product of a spiritually conscious society using its abilities at reason which resulted in a healthy society. The power to enact Peace (which required that people cease abusing one another) was conceived to be both spiritual and political.

But it was power in all those senses of the word—the power of persuasion and reason, the power of the inherent good will of humans, the power of a dedicated and united people, and when all else failed, the power of force.

The principles of law set forth by the Peacemaker sought to establish peaceful society by eliminating the causes of conflict between individuals and between peoples. It was a law which was conceived prior to the appearance of classes and it sought to anticipate and eliminate anything which took the appearance of group or class interest even in the form of clan or tribal interest, especially in the area of property. The law was also based to an impressive degree on a logic which looked to Nature for its rules. It is one of the few examples of a "Natural Law" which is available to modern man. It is a law which clearly precedes "royal" law, or "mercantile" law or "bourgeois" property-interest law.

The government which is established under the Great Law provides, in effect, that the leaders or "chiefs" are the servants of the people. Everyone in the Six Nations, wherever the law prevails, has direct participation in the workings of the government. Direct democracy, when it involves tens of thousands of people, is a very complex business, and there are many rules about how meetings are conducted, but the primary rule about the flow of power and authority is clearly that the power and authority of the people lies with the people and is transmitted by them through the "chiefs." The fact that all the people have direct participation in the decision of their government is the key factor for the success and longevity of the Haudenosaunee.

Internally, the law was to be the power by which the people were united ideologically and administratively under a dispute settlement process to which all had agreed to submit and to remove those customs of the past which had sparked conflict and fostered disunity. The path to unity was a difficult one indeed. The territory of the People of the Longhouse had been composed of five distinct countries, each of which sometimes jealously guarded their hunting lands from intrusion by the others. The Peacemaker abolished the concept of separate territories. The law unified the peoples, saying that they were distinct from one another only because they spoke different languages, and that the territories were common to all and that each individual member of any of the nations had full rights of hunting and occupation of all the lands of all the nations of the People of the Longhouse.

In terms of the internal affairs of the People of the Longhouse, the first and most important principle was that under the law of the people of the nations were one people. Since the Haudenosaunee call themselves the People of the Longhouse, the Peacemaker's admonition was that under the law, the country of the Haudenosaunee was itself a Longhouse, with the sky as its roof and the earth as its floor.

The peoples were assigned to clans by the Peacemaker, and so strong was to be the feeling of unity and oneness between them that members of the clan of one nation were admonished not to marry members of the same clan of another nation, so closely were they now related. The law bound them together as blood relatives.

In one motion, he abolished exclusive national territories and the concept of national minorities. Any member of the Five Nations was to have full rights in the country of any of the Five Nations with only one restriction—that he or she did not have the right to hold high public office, though that right could be conferred upon them by the host nation if they so wished.

The idea that the nations were united as one meant that the nations who were members of the Confederacy had agreed to surrender a part of their sovereignty to the other nations of the Confederacy. The Confederacy Council was to be the forum under which foreign nations and peoples could approach the People of the Longhouse. Any decision concerning the disposition of Seneca lands must first pass through the Confederacy Council where the other nations, who also have rights in Seneca lands, can participate in the decision-making process.

The Peacemaker envisioned that the principles under which the Five Nations were governed could be extended far beyond the borders of the Haudenosaunee to all peoples of the world. The law of the Peacemaker provides that any nation or people may find protection under the Great Tree of Peace which symbolized the laws of the Confederacy. He expected that the principles of the Confederacy would be well received by many nations, and that the Haudenosaunee would venture forth with the offer of a union which would be designed to prevent hostilities and to lay the basis of peaceful coexistence. With that in mind, the Constitution of the Five Nations provides that any nation may seek its protection through becoming knowledgeable about the laws and agreeing to follow the principles set forth in it. Many native nations accepted that offer.

The Five Nations agreed among themselves that in the event of an attack, they would organize a military force to repel the invader and to carry on the war in the invader's country until the war was concluded. The opponent had an absolute right to a cessation of the hostilities at any time by simply calling for a truce. At that point, the process of negotiation went into action. The Constitution of the Five Nations prescribes that, in the event that another people are conquered, the Five Nations shall not impose upon them the Five Nation's religion, nor collect tribute from them, nor subject them to any form of injustice. The Five Nations would not seize their territory. What was demanded was that the offending nation of people put away their weapons of war and that they cease military aggression.

Any individual or group of individuals had the right according to the Constitution, to approach the Five Nations, learn the law, and agree to abide by it. When that happened they were to be offered the protection of the law and the People of the Longhouse.

The vision of the Peacemaker that all the peoples of the world would live in peace under the protection of a law that required that hostilities be outlawed and disputes offered a settlement process is yet today an exciting prospect. When the idea of a United Nations of the world was proposed toward the end of World War II, researchers were dispatched to find models in history for such an organization. For all practical purposes, the only model they found concerned the Constitution of the Five Nations whose author had envisioned exactly that.

In a way, the Peacemaker was centuries ahead of his time. He set forth a system of government organization which was a marvelously complex enactment of the concept of participatory (as opposed to representative) democracy.

Under the rules of the law, councils of women appointed men who were to act more as conduits of the will of the people than as independent representatives of the people.

The society was founded on concepts of moral justice and not of statute law and the rules of the society were designed to insure that each member's rights were absolutely protected under the law. Women have not only rights but have power as a community of people composing half of the population. The powers of women have never been fully articulated by Western observers and interpreters of Haudenosaunee culture.

Peoples were recognized to have a right to exist unmolested as peoples in the articles of the Constitution. Individuals were recognized as having the full rights to protection under the laws of the Confederacy—even individuals who were not members of the host nation—so long as they observed the rules of nonaggression and they didn't try to create factionalism among the people. The principle was set forth (and machinery to enact it was created) which provided that all peoples have a right to occupy their lands peacefully and that no one may deny them that right. A society was socialized to the ideology that if an injustice occurs, it is their moral duty to defend the oppressed against their oppressors. The principle was set forth that no one has a right to deprive another of the fruits of his own labor, and that no one has a right to a greater share of the wealth of society than any one else. The Peacemaker believed that if absolute justice were established in the world, peace would naturally follow.

Some of those ideas have begun to take root in the form of United Nations statements and declarations made in recent years. The genius of the Peacemaker was that he not only set forth the principles, but he also designed the machinery by which those principles might be enforced. He seems to have operated on the assumption that universal justice is the product of a spiritually strong society, and many of the rules which he proposed are designed to create a strong society rather than a strong government. That is one of the ideas that has not been widely accepted in the Twentieth Century and certainly not in a context that the Peacemaker would have understood.

The Peacemaker set out to give some order to society and to create peace among peoples and nations. The rules that he set down were called by the Mohawks "the Great Goodness," and by the Senecas "the Great Law." The English called that body of teachings the Constitution of the Five Nations. It has never been written down in English despite allegations to the contrary by anthropologists. The versions which exist in English are highly inadequate efforts compared to the oral versions of the Great Law. This effort is no better—it does not compare in any way to the complexity, beauty and eloquence of the Law.

Some people who have read the history of the Haudenosaunee will be able to point to episodes in the 17th and 18th Centuries during which some of the principles of this law appear to have been ignored. It is true that over nearly two centuries of intermittent warfare—warfare caused by pressures created by the expanding interests of European imperial nations—there was a considerable amount of social change and stress. French imperialist missionaries introduced the idea—an entirely foreign idea—that a divine will might guide the fortunes of a people in government and in warfare. That kind of thinking was not to be found in the philosophies of the Peacemaker, but throughout history it has been an idea which has accompanied empire builders everywhere. Many ideas of European origin were adopted by different peoples of the Haudenosaunee at different times, ideas which were in conflict with the principles of the Great Law. In the almost two centuries since the beginning of the so-called "reservation" period, many more ideas which are in conflict with the principles of the Great Law have been imposed by the colonizers.

Most of what passes as "Iroquois History" was an effort by English and French historians to discredit the Haudenosaunee and to justify the destruction of the Confederacy and the theft of Confederacy lands. There were few instances in which officials of the Confederacy violated the laws of the Great Peace, although individuals in any society do violate its laws. Following the American Revolution, the United States and especially New York State did everything in their power to dissolve the Confederacy and to deal with the individual nations. Great Britain, Canada, Ontario and Quebec have done the same thing. Since the invasion of the Europeans, the Haudenosaunee have produced a number of patriots but few great philosophers. The outstanding Haudenosaunee philosopher and teacher of the post-contact period was also a Confederacy Chief. His name was Handsome Lake and he led a spiritual revitalization which produced an oral document called "The Good Word," a teaching on the same level of significance and power in Haudenosaunee culture as the Great Law. Combined, the two are a powerful teaching. Against incredible odds, the Confederacy has survived and has continued to this day. Its Chiefs continue to meet periodically at the capital at Onondaga, and they continue to carry the titles bestowed upon them by the Peacemaker long before written history began. The ideas of the Confederacy continue to live also, and little by little the world is being exposed to those ideas. As long as those ideas remain alive the possibility remains that the Peacemaker's vision of a world in peace and harmony may yet be realized.

Discussion Questions

1. What is Mary McCarthy telling us about the power of names, even or especially nicknames? What is the importance of her experience in explaining and/or establishing personal identity?
2. Do you think Mead may be right when suggesting that a *self* can come into existence only as the result of interactions with others? What is it about interactions with others that enables me to form a conception of my *self*?
3. What are the problems with "rugged individualism," according to Bierman? How does rugged individualism (or atomic individualism) undermine our ability to grow as human beings? How does it adversely impact positive social relationships?
4. What are the three basic types of human activities, according to Arendt? Why do we need to be engaged with others in a political context, according to Arendt?
5. Sartre rejects a belief in a prefashioned human nature. Why? Do you think he is right when he claims that we make ourselves who we are by the decisions or choices we make?
6. Mohawk tells us that we are all related as humans and we are also related to all things in the universe. What does he mean by this? How might this view help to foster more positive social relations?
7. In what sense does self-discovery help us to discover others? In what sense does discovering others help us to discover ourselves?

chapter 4

Race and Ethnic Identity

For centuries, people have been defined in terms of their roles as males or females. In particular, men have been defining the role of women in male terms. Throughout much of history, Western Europeans have been defining the African, the Asian, and the Native American by imposing categories of behavior and values structured by a white male consciousness. What constitutes acceptable behavior and the role that individuals should play in the state are issues that have been determined by an elitist and privileged class of people and not people as individuals. In doing so, these groups have essentially given definition to themselves. These definitions may not be justifiable in terms of the internal consciousness of the individuals who are subject to them. Categories of expected and "acceptable" behavior are not identities. Such categories and the role limitations imposed by them may be quite simply forms of oppression. We must ask ourselves whether or not role expectations imposed as psychological structures on a person or a people by an alien consciousness may not, in fact, be the most invidious form of oppression, a form of institutionalized violence. We could even consider it a legally sanctioned violation of the *self* by others.

It may be argued that the most basic moral duty one has is to actualize oneself. It may also be argued that the most basic moral obligation one has is not to prohibit such an actualization. More positively, there may be a prima facie duty to develop an environment that fosters self-actualization. If denied such

Iroquois Mask

an environment, would not one have a right and duty to liberate oneself from this oppression? Is it possible to change without wanting to change? Is the conscious desire to change the foundation of authentic identity?

Naomi Zack raises the question of what constitutes authentic identity in light of her American Jewish cultural heritage. Is this identity socially constructed, and if so, is it constructed by the self or others? If the self is socially constructed, are both race and ethnicity socially constructed? One must ask if one's authentic identity can be determined in a fragmented fashion. One must wonder whether or not it is helpful to focus on our ethnic heritage and the specific ethnic influences of the present in determining our identity. One must also wonder, however, whether or not it is possible to determine a self-identity without considering the impact that such ethnicity has on the individual.

In an attempt to determine how and why this matters, Hannah Arendt discusses the issue of race, and she claims that race is constructed in a way that fosters oppression. It is rooted in a framework of bureaucracy that is designed to exploit individuals for the gain of certain privileged peoples. Thus, it is a fabricated institution that is designed to determine not only who people are, and perhaps more important, who they are not. As we read this, we must also examine how race and ethnicity differ from each other and how they are linked. At the same time, we must be aware that our *self* develops throughout time via the dynamic process of interaction. Thus, we must pay attention to the ways we define ourselves as we attempt to define others through characterizations of race and ethnicity

J. Hector St. John de Crèvecoeur elaborates on the ways in which we attempt to dichotomize ourselves by way of his experiences as a Frenchman who immigrated first to Canada, then to the English colonies that were to become the United States. He explains that class distinctions in colonial America were constructed in a way that helped to assimilate immigrants into the American ideal. What is clearly important in this assimilation are *geography* and *environment,* not heritage, previous wealth or poverty, language, or even religion. Are these differences morally justified by the realities of the cultural mythos? Are we morally obligated to find the truth embedded in tribal or ethnic constructions of reality? To what extent is a true sense of identity a necessary condition of self-respect?

The ideology fundamental to racial and ethnic supremacy is the topic of discussion in a 1943 study undertaken by the U.S. Department of State. Herein,

Nazi Flag

racial supremacy has been identified as a key element in the philosophy of National Socialism. In this philosophy, racial consciousness led to false belief in racial superiority. As you read the passages from National Socialist philosophy that the study provides, pay close attention to what the Nazis have to say about race and a consciousness of *self.* Why is it, do you think, that the Nazis wish to emphasize the "unity of a people" and the connection between "race" and "people"? How do such emphases lend themselves to the creation of false notions of racial and cultural superiority?

In this chapter, you will be exposed to some controversial ideas about race and ethnicity. Many may find some of these ideas to be morally disquieting. It may be necessary, however, for individuals to confront such moral distress in order to discover not only the ways in which race and ethnicity can be used to construct a self-identity in a positive manner, but also to discover the ways in which such attempts to construct an identity can go wrong. Thus, the question of racial, ethnic, and social identity must be continually reflected upon in order to remain conscious of the subtle ways in which we identify the self may be undermined. As you read these essays, reflect upon the ways in which you struggle to maintain your *self* within the contexts of the social and political influences that help to form your identity.

Racial and Ethnic Identity

Naomi Zack

Naomi Zack asks us to consider what having an identity may mean in terms of a self. In particular, we are asked to consider whether or not an identity is something more than a construction of a group membership. After raising questions about "identities," "multiculturalism," and "identity politics," and about what it means to be a person with particular experiences, Zack examines the issue of personal and cultural authenticity. What does it mean to be authentically this person, or a person with a particular identity? Finally, Zack explores what it means to have a contemporary American Jewish identity.

INTRODUCTION

Racial and ethnic identity is perhaps the leading scholarly topic in current *emancipatory* studies. The term *identity* is ambiguous however, because it is used to mean both subjective experience and shared group membership that includes history and group self-image. For our purposes, a distinction between identity and *identification* will be useful: Identity is that about an individual that he or she reflects on, accepts, and develops, in the self. An individual has a range of choices about how to accept and develop his or her identity and it is unlikely to be based on any one thing. Profession, gender, family roles, race, ethnicity, and even sports, hobbies, and possessions might be part of identity. Identification is what others, typically those who do not know an individual well, use to distinguish that individual from others. Thus, black, white, Hispanic, Asian, woman, man, mother, teacher, lawyer, cop, are all terms of identification.

Despite this distinction between identity and identification, the sense of identity that is relevant to race and ethnicity is not entirely free of identification. To further specify how race and ethnicity relate to identity, racially and ethnically neutral meanings of identity are relevant. Psychologists and psychiatrists work with therapeutic notions of identity that refer to the feelings a person has about his or her self. For instance, someone confident and optimistic, who sets attainable goals, achieves them, and is not easily imposed upon by others, would be assessed as having a strong identity. Psychologically, a strong identity is connected with self-esteem and self-love that is based on trusting, nurturing interactions with caregivers early in life. Sociologists would be more likely to consider the identity of persons in terms of the roles they play in interacting with others in both personal and impersonal contexts. Theologians, by contrast, might locate personal identity in the soul or in the relation between the soul and God.

Philosophers have approached identity by asking what it is about a person that, if unchanged while all else about that person is changed, would lead observers to judge that the same person were still there. Sometimes it seems as though having the same memories is the criterion for someone being the same person. But lapses of memory or even amnesia do not change personal identity, from the perspective of others. Another philosophical position is that the sameness of a person is determined by a continuous path, through physical space, of the same human body, beginning at birth. Observers could, in principle, track that path of a person as a physical object and the continuity of the path would guarantee the sameness (identity) of the person. In addition to criteria for the sameness of persons, philosophers have addressed questions of what it is about persons that best characterizes them to themselves in an enduring way over time. Is it a mind, a body, a mind and a body, the ability to think, the ability to choose, memories? This philosophical concept of what one is to oneself, over time, is helpful to keep in mind in thinking about racial and ethnic identity. For example, if one could be the same person even though one's race changed, then racial identification would not be part of personal identity.

In Section A, the construction of nonwhite identities in *emancipatory traditions* is considered. The topic of identity is further explored through the idea of *authenticity* in Section B. The complexities of *American Jewish identity* in contemporary life are taken up in Section C, as a case study of ethnic identity.

From *Thinking About Race* by Naomi Zack. Belmont, Calif.: Wadsworth, 1998.

A. NONWHITE EMANCIPATORY IDENTITIES

Throughout American history, nonwhite emancipatory identities have been deliberately forged as resistance to and liberation from oppression. These emancipatory identities have included the moral virtues of courage against oppression, altruism toward other members of the group to be emancipated, and dedication to greater social justice in the future. Emancipatory identities cover the spectrum from fighting in political revolutions to religious uplift. Such identities are often based on a rewriting or retelling of historical events from the perspective of the oppressed group. We will consider such *socially constructed* aspects of emancipatory identities in this section.

When groups of people are oppressed, for instance, as slaves, low-paid laborers, or objects of racism, they are not automatically aware of their oppression as such. Those who are oppressed materially are often required to expend all their energy on the tasks of physical survival, getting the basics of food, clothing, housing, and safety in order to be able to carry on for another day or another week. Those who are psychologically degraded by racism may believe that they have the traits ascribed to them by dominant groups. At first, only a small number of the oppressed group, or members of another group who sympathize with their situation, find the words and do the deeds to create self-awareness of the conditions of oppression. Some form of group identity is necessary before an awareness of group oppression is possible. The most convenient and socially intelligible identity is often the identification made by oppressors: "n"egro, Negro, black, Jewish, Indian, "Oriental," Mexican, Hispanic, and so on.

The externally imposed group labels may be changed as the stereotypes associated with them by oppressors are repudiated by group members. For example, early twentieth-century African American leaders believed they had a mission to instruct their people, as well as whites, that they were entitled to education and the right to vote because they were not inferior to whites in the ways white society had constructed them to be. At that time they insisted that the small *n* in Negro be capitalized as the names of other American ethnic groups were. Similarly, Chinese- and Japanese-Americans now want to be known as Asians because the earlier designation "Oriental" was used to refer to imported objects as well as people, and its literal meaning was "East of Europe," suggesting that Europe was the center of the world. Indians have at different times preferred being called Native Americans in reference to their own origins, rather than the place (India) after which Europeans named them by mistake. Sometimes a new emancipatory group name is chosen in order to take on with pride what was intended to be a derogatory label, for example *black* or *queer.*

When labels are changed as parts of stereotypes are discarded, emancipatory identities are used to encourage and motivate actions that it is believed will result in social change. In a *pluralistic society,* they become the basis for what is known as *identity politics.* A general public policy commitment to pluralism presupposes that full social justice can best be obtained not if human rights are enforced on an individual basis, but if individuals receive protection and benefits as members of groups. This means that even though it is individuals who vote, the practical political unit is a group whose members share a common identity. Politicians running for office thus become concerned about securing the black vote, the Hispanic vote, the white working-class vote, the women's vote, and so on. Once elected, they are expected to support policies and legislation that will benefit the groups that helped put them in office. (Although their constituencies after election include those who voted against them as well—the President of the United States is president of all the people.)

Identity politics extends beyond politics in the narrow sense of electioneering. Contemporary debates over *multiculturalism* in education, the arts, and cultural life generally, are negotiations within identity politics. The rationale behind multiculturalism is that members of a pluralistic society who identify as members of minority groups ought to have an opportunity to see people like themselves in educational curricula and on the stage of public events. This speaks to a psychological need to be able to *identify*, that is, easily put oneself in the place of another. Multiculturalism also has a goal of universal intellectual and aesthetic enrichment through exposure to works and traditions that are different from those of the forebears of the racial or ethnic group to which one belongs. The centrality of white European cultural products and people, in a society where white Europeans are the dominant group, often makes it seem as though only these people and their products are of value and interest.

Even though emancipatory identities are deliberately constructed, this does not mean that they are experienced as superficial or artificial. Emancipatory identities are woven into racial or ethnic experience, such as traditions, shared circumstances of poverty over which members do not have the same control as more privileged groups, and most important, family life. It seems to be a universal fact for all societies in recorded history that human beings come into life in families, are raised in families, and look to family life for at least some of their deepest personal satisfactions as adults. Emancipatory identities are self-consciously taken up by families, even though the racial aspects of the identities were originally externally imposed by oppressive members of different groups. In the minds of individuals, the racial aspects of their identity become welded to the nurturing qualities of family life. Racially nonwhite and non-WASP Americans think of their families as black, Chinese, Mexican, Jewish, Irish, Italian, or mixed in ways that humanly redeem the malign origins of such categories as labels connoting inferior difference. Thus family life as well as public life can add a further dimension to the ways in which emancipatory identities counteract the alienation that accompanies membership in nondominant groups.

It should be recognized that not all aspects of racial and ethnic identity arise from situations of oppression or are deliberate reactions to oppression. Many people live in racially or ethnically *homogeneous* communities that have distinct practices passed on from generation to generation. These traditions, and the feelings of belonging and claiming that accompany them, are found rather than made or deliberately chosen by the individuals who grow up within them. And these individuals in turn pass them on to subsequent generations simply because it is the way they have been taught to conduct and celebrate their lives.

Reactive liberatory identities, family-based racial and ethnic identities, and positive identities based on community homogeneity all work together in dynamic processes that change as historical circumstances change. Each generation in a racial or ethnic tradition inherits the project of reinventing and discovering a shared group identity. A generation may break with its parents and relatives at the same time that it changes what it accepts from them in order to deal with changes in the wider society.

B. AUTHENTICITY

Indians, blacks, Asians, Jews, Chicano[/as], Latino[/as], and members of other groups that have experienced oppression in Western history are expected to be *authentic*. Racial and ethnic authenticity is usually presented as an obligation by those who are in a position to attach moral values to the racial and ethnic identity of the group in question. As a result, authenticity tends to be accepted as a duty by group members, especially younger people. The "authorities of authenticity" for any particular group vary from the immediate peers of teenagers to family elders, community leaders, and intellectuals. If the community is geographically scattered, its members are nonetheless expected to behave like group members through religious practice, marriage within the group, holiday celebration, dietary habits, and so forth. But perhaps more important than conformity to custom, an authentic group member is expected to help and support other members of the group simply because they are members of the group. An authentic group member is expected to feel fulfilled and gratified by his or her own authenticity, while someone who is inauthentic is expected to feel ashamed, inadequate, and morally weak.

However, the term *authenticity*, with its moral connotations, is ambiguous. People can be racially or ethnically authentic in one or more of at least five different ways. Let's suppose for the sake of this discussion that there is a racial or ethnic group—call it the Quicks—whose members have been stereotyped as follows: they are bald; they love to eat radishes; they traditionally collect insects; they listen to classical music at all major holidays and family gatherings; they are very generous; they are skillful liars.

One way of defining authenticity is as *provenance*. An authentic painting by Picasso has to be traced to the artist's studio through its successive owners, as well as certified to be a Picasso by examination of its brush strokes and its recognition as a Picasso by knowledgeable art dealers. A Quick with authentic provenance would be someone who had Quick ancestry and was known by members of his or her community to be a Quick. But suppose that this person—call her Winifred—did not like to be with other Quicks or to help them, claimed to hate radishes, preferred jazz to Bach, was seen wearing wigs, and [was] known to be stingy. Peers and elders might then pronounce her inauthentic, despite her provenance, because she would not have an *authentic appearance* as a Quick.

Suppose that Winifred changed so that, in addition to her authentic provenance, she displayed the right kind of behavior, that is, she threw out the wigs, collected the insects, ate the radishes, rhapsodized over Bach, and lied elaborately, with the result that non-Quicks immediately recognized her as a Quick. If, in addition to this authentic Quick appearance, other Quicks knew they could count on Winifred's support and loyalty as a Quick, then Winifred would have *authentic solidarity*.

Now let's imagine that economic conditions in the culture change, and Quicks, who previously lived in peace with other racial and ethnic groups, become a hated minority because they own (in perpetuity) exclusive patents to newly engineered genes for radishes that reverse aging and make people smarter. The majority group in society, the Dead, controls the mass media and thereby makes it common knowledge that the distinctive traits of Quicks are pathological signs of social dysfunction and moral degeneration. Over the next generation, during which Winifred's son Fred grows up, strong social pressures develop for Quicks to assimilate to mainstream Dead society, even though their civil liberties are legally protected and no one stops them from continuing in their traditional ways. Fred receives an elaborate glass ant farm on his sixteenth birthday and has a collection of 112 live crickets in gold filigree cages in his room. However, when his Dead friends come to hang out, he hides the insects in the garage. Fred loves radishes but when he is offered radish dishes at other people's houses, he pretends to be allergic to them. And, working against the stereotype of lying, Fred becomes known as a compulsive truth teller.

Winifred arrives at the painful realization that her son is inauthentic because he lacks the courage to express his real identity. She sadly reflects that even if truth telling were a virtue, Fred could not be considered virtuous because he tells the truth not because he thinks it's right, but because he doesn't want Dead people to dismiss him as a stereotypical Quick. If he just went ahead and allowed himself to *be* what he really was, he would have *personal authenticity.* But when Winifred tries to talk about this issue with Fred, his response is that it's very important to him to feel accepted by friends and know how to "move around" in the wider society. He also points out that many Quicks do the exact same things he does in order to "get along."

By contrast, Fred's sister Winnie hates radishes, is frightened of insects, likes rock 'n' roll, and refuses to lie because she believes that lying is wrong. Furthermore, Winnie insists that she has a right to be herself and that she will even marry a Dead man someday if she should happen to fall in love with one and he asks her to marry him. While Winifred disapproves of Winnie and recognizes that she lacks authentic solidarity as a Quick, she nonetheless concedes that Winnie, unlike Fred, is personally authentic. She hopes that this character trait will eventually result in Winnie becoming a more authentic Quick.

Referring back to the chapter introduction and Section A, we can draw the following conclusions about authenticity: authentic provenance is racial; authentic appearance is both racial and ethnic; authentic solidarity is political, in a broad sense; personal authenticity is a matter of strong psychological identity. Ideally, personal authenticity need not conflict with racial or ethnic authenticity. However, complexities of circumstance and individual personality make it difficult to generalize about the desirability of racial and ethnic authenticity. In fact, authenticity as it relates to membership in racial and ethnic groups varies as personal *narratives* or life stories vary. Because individuals are unique, they may be the best judges of what it means for them to be authentic members of their racial or ethnic groups. Thus, perhaps the forms of authenticity other than provenance ought to be subject to individual *autonomy.* In that case, the concept of authenticity, insofar as it means "genuineness" that is evident to others, loses much of its moral force.

From third-person perspectives, however, there is a stable meaning of authenticity that requires having knowledge of the history and values of one's group and displaying the knowledge and affirming the values. Such *cultural authenticity* may impose limits on individual autonomy, especially when individuals can benefit by downplaying the history of their racial or ethnic groups and affirming the values of the dominant group. Thus, cultural authenticity may be opposed to *assimilation.* If one thinks that individuals have a moral right to choose between cultural authenticity and assimilation, then the value of individual autonomy overrides the values of both cultural authenticity and assimilation.

C. CONTEMPORARY AMERICAN JEWISH IDENTITY

Contemporary American Jewish identity is a complex result of identity choices based on identity politics and all the different kinds of authenticity. Most other ethnic groups tend to place their religious, racial, or national origin labels before the word American. However, it seems to be customary to speak of American Jews, rather than Jewish Americans. American Indians are another exception to the general usage (although, when the label Native Americans is used, the second word does not mean the same thing as it does for non–Native Americans). The exceptions might be accidental or they might indicate that both Jewish and Indian identities are considered primary or prior to American nationality.

Since World War II, American Jews have largely been successful in projects requiring assimilation to mainstream American life. At the same time, many Jews still value their identities as Jews and struggle with questions about what it means, exactly, to *be* a Jew in the United States during the 1990s. Although Jews today generally define themselves as a religious group, there is religious difference among Orthodox, Reform, and Conservative Jews. Criteria for who is a Jew extend beyond religion to ancestry: According to Talmudic Law and Israel's immigration policy, which in principle keeps an open door to all Jews, a Jew is someone whose mother is or was a Jew or someone who has converted to Judaism according to Orthodox criteria. However, some insist that anyone whose father is a Jew, and who practices the religion but does not have a Jewish mother, is also a Jew. The religious aspect of Jewish identification entails that people whose mothers were not Jewish can convert to Judaism and thereby become Jews. The maternal heredity aspect of Judaism entails that people whose mothers are Jewish are Jews even if they are *nonobservant*, that is, do not practice the Jewish religion. Furthermore, some Jews see no contradiction in claiming both an *atheistic* belief structure and Jewish identity, with varying degrees of observance.

The formation of the state of Israel in 1948 allowed Jews worldwide to claim a homeland. Israel is accepted as the original homeland of Jews since biblical times. But throughout Western history, Jews dispersed to almost every country on earth, mainly as a result of their periodic persecution and expulsion from Christian countries, as well as Palestine, during crises of anti-Semitism. Some Jews who were not born in Israel and have no known ancestors born in Israel wonder how it is possible to have a homeland from which none of their known family members originated.

Zionism, as opposed to the different forms of Jewish religion, is partly a political ideology that privileges Israel as the center of Jewish life for all Jews. Since Israel is a small country whose neighbors resist its existence as a state, Israel has been involved in political and military actions that many Jews do not support on other political grounds. Some Jews insist that political support of Israel is now necessary for Jewish authenticity. Other Jews believe that their Jewish identity is independent of politics.

The success of Jews in mainstream American life has been accompanied by the abandonment of traditional cultural practices that derived from the lives of Jews in the specific European countries from which many emigrated in the late nineteenth and early twentieth century. Early twentieth-century Jewish immigrants in New York City had their own press and theatre in *Yiddish*, a dialect of High German that is written in Hebrew letters. Today, few American Jews speak, much less read Yiddish, although some adults can remember their grandparents' use of it. The official language of Israel is modern Hebrew and only a minority of American Jews are fluent in that.

Given that religion, ancestry, homeland, customs, and language are such variable components of Jewish identity, the question of Jewish identity is extremely problematic. At least 25 percent of all Jews who marry, marry non-Jews. Jewish identity is not imposed on American Jews in the same way that black identity is imposed on any American with black ancestry, so this rate of intermarriage represents further loss of Jewish identity in family life.

For many Jews, thinking about the Nazi attempt at genocide intensifies Jewish identity: even casual, so-called "polite" American anti-Semitism that imputes stereotypes of appearance and behavior to Jews, can be a reason to retain Jewish identity. The psychological dynamic of Jewish identity is often reported as a process of discovery based on strong emotional reactions of horror, shock, fear, and grief in response to finding out about Jewish suffering. However, some Jews question the validity of an identity based on suffering. Others insist that the persistence of Jews, as Jews, in the face of such suffering is inspiring in universal human terms, so that remembering that they are Jews makes them better people.

Finally, race intersects with Jewishness in complicated ways: Although most Jews and non-Jewish white Americans consider Jews to be white, some black Americans and some Jews believe that Jews are nonwhite because they are traditionally *Semites.* Most American Jews are of European origin but a small number have black ancestry. Jews with black ancestry who live in Jewish communities tend to identify as Jews first and African Americans second. Jews with black ancestry who have been raised in, or as adults live in African American communities, tend to identify primarily as black. But blacks who have become Jewish through conversion tend to proclaim encompassing identities, that is, black and Jewish. The operative word in all this is *tend,* there are many exceptions to such generalizations.

Race and Bureaucracy

Hannah Arendt

What is race? Is race socially constructed? In this excerpt, Arendt discusses the origin of the notion of race. She reasons that race and bureaucracy are entwined. Race is constructed and used as a tool for oppression and exploitation. It is one means by which people can identify themselves and, paired with bureaucracy, provides a false justification for this oppression and exploitation. It enables people to identify themselves by helping them to determine not only who they are but who they are not. As you read this, think about the meaning of race and the impact that the notion has had on your own life. By constructing race, have we falsely identified ourselves?

Two new devices for political organization and rule over foreign peoples were discovered during the first decades of imperialism. One was race as a principle of the body politic, and the other bureaucracy as a principle of foreign domination. Without race as a substitute for the nation, the scramble for Africa and the investment fever might well have remained the purposeless "dance of death and trade" (Joseph Conrad) of all gold rushes. Without bureaucracy as a substitute for government, the British possession of India might well have been left to the recklessness of the "breakers of law in India" (Burke) without changing the political climate of an entire era.

Both discoveries were actually made on the Dark Continent. Race was the emergency explanation of human beings whom no European or civilized man could understand and whose humanity so frightened and humiliated the immigrants that they no longer cared to belong to the same human species. Race was the Boers' answer to the overwhelming monstrosity of Africa—a whole continent populated and overpopulated by savages—an explanation of the madness which grasped and illuminated them like "a flash of lightning in a serene sky: 'Exterminate all the brutes.' "[1] This answer resulted in the most terrible massacres in recent history, the Boers' extermination of Hottentot tribes, the wild murdering by Carl Peters in German Southeast Africa, the decimation of the peaceful Congo population—from 20 to 40 million reduced to 8 million people; and finally, perhaps worst of all, it resulted in the triumphant introduction of such means of pacification into ordinary, respectable foreign policies. What head of a civilized state would ever before have uttered the exhortation of William II to a German expeditionary contingent fighting the Boxer insurrection in 1900: "Just as the Huns a thousand years ago, under the leadership of Attila, gained a reputation by virtue of which they still live in history, so may the German name become known in such a manner in China that no Chinese will ever again dare to look askance at a German."[2]

While race, whether as a home-grown ideology in Europe or an emergency explanation for shattering experiences, has always attracted the worst elements in Western civilization, bureaucracy was discovered by and first attracted the best, and sometimes even the most clear-sighted, strata of the European intelligentsia. The administrator who ruled by reports[3] and decrees in more hostile secrecy than any oriental despot grew out of a tradition of military discipline in the midst of ruthless and lawless men; for a long time he had lived by the honest, earnest boyhood ideals of a modern knight in shining armor sent to protect helpless and primitive people. And he fulfilled this task, for better or worse, as long as he moved in a world dominated by the old "trinity—war, trade and piracy" (Goethe), and not in a complicated game of far-reaching investment policies which demanded the domination of one people, not as before for the sake of its own

From *The Origins of Totalitarianism* by Hannah Arendt. New York: Harcourt Brace Janovich.

[1] Joseph Conrad, "Heart of Darkness" in *Youth and Other Tales*, 1902, is the most illuminating work on actual race experience in Africa.

[2] Quoted from Carlton J. Hayes, *A Generation of Materialism*, New York, 1941, p. 338.—An even worse case is of course that of Leopold II of Belgium, responsible for the blackest pages in the history of Africa. "There was only one man who could be accused of the outrages which reduced the native population [of the Congo] from between 20 to 40 million in 1890 to 8,500,000 in 1911—Leopold II." See Selwyn James, *South of the Congo*, New York, 1943, p. 305.

[3] See A. Carthill's description of the "Indian system of government by reports" in *The Lost Dominion*, 1924, p. 70.

riches, but for the sake of another country's wealth. Bureaucracy was the organization of the great game of expansion in which every area was considered a stepping-stone to further involvements and every people an instrument for further conquest.

Although in the end racism and bureaucracy proved to be interrelated in many ways, they were discovered and developed independently. No one who in one way or the other was implicated in their perfection ever came to realize the full range of potentialities of power accumulation and destruction that this combination alone provided. Lord Cromer, who in Egypt changed from an ordinary British chargé d'affaires into an imperialist bureaucrat, would no more have dreamed of combining administration with massacre ("administrative massacres" as Carthill bluntly put it forty years later), than the race fanatics of South Africa thought of organizing massacres for the purpose of establishing a circumscribed, rational political community (as the Nazis did in the extermination camps).

I: THE PHANTOM WORLD OF THE DARK CONTINENT

Up to the end of the last century, the colonial enterprises of the seafaring European peoples produced two outstanding forms of achievement: in recently discovered and sparsely populated territories, the founding of new settlements which adopted the legal and political institutions of the mother country; and in well-known though exotic countries in the midst of foreign peoples, the establishment of maritime and trade stations whose only function was to facilitate the never very peaceful exchange of the treasures of the world. Colonization took place in America and Australia, the two continents that, without a culture and a history of their own, had fallen into the hands of Europeans. Trade stations were characteristic of Asia where for centuries Europeans had shown no ambition for permanent rule or intentions of conquest, decimation of the native population, and permanent settlement.[4] Both forms of overseas enterprise evolved in a long steady process which extended over almost four centuries, during which the settlements gradually achieved independence, and the possession of trade stations shifted among the nations according to their relative weakness or strength in Europe.

The only continent Europe had not touched in the course of its colonial history was the Dark Continent of Africa. Its northern shores, populated by Arabic peoples and tribes, were well known and had belonged to the European sphere of influence in one way or another since the days of antiquity. Too well populated to attract settlers, and too poor to be exploited, these regions suffered all kinds of foreign rule and anarchic neglect, but oddly enough never—after the decline of the Egyptian Empire and the destruction of Carthage—achieved authentic independence and reliable political organization. European countries tried time and again, it is true, to reach beyond the Mediterranean to impose their rule on Arabic lands and their Christianity on Moslem peoples, but they never attempted to treat North African territories like overseas possessions. On the contrary, they frequently aspired to incorporate them

[4]It is important to bear in mind that colonization of America and Australia was accompanied by comparatively short periods of cruel liquidation because of the natives' numerical weakness, whereas "in understanding the genesis of modern South African society it is of the greatest importance to know that the land beyond the Cape's borders was not the open land which lay before the Australian squatter. It was already an area of settlement, of settlement by a great Bantu population." See C. W. de Kiewiet, *A History of South Africa, Social and Economic* (Oxford, 1941), p. 59.

into the respective mother country. This age-old tradition, still followed in recent times by Italy and France, was broken in the eighties when England went into Egypt to protect the Suez Canal without any intention either of conquest or incorporation. The point is not that Egypt was wronged but that England (a nation that did not lie on the shores of the Mediterranean) could not possibly have been interested in Egypt as such, but needed her only because there were treasures in India.

While imperialism changed Egypt from a country occasionally coveted for her own sake into a military station for India and a stepping-stone for further expansion, the exact opposite happened to South Africa. Since the seventeenth century, the significance of the Cape of Good Hope had depended upon India, the center of colonial wealth; any nation that established trade stations there needed a maritime station on the Cape, which was then abandoned when trade in India was liquidated. At the end of the eighteenth century, the British East India Company defeated Portugal, Holland, and France and won a trade monopoly in India; the occupation of South Africa followed as a matter of course. If imperialism had simply continued the old trends of colonial trade (which is so frequently mistaken for imperialism), England would have liquidated her position in South Africa with the opening of the Suez Canal in 1869.[5] Although today South Africa belongs to the Commonwealth, it was always different from the other dominions; fertility and sparseness of population, the main prerequisites for definite settlement, were lacking, and a single effort to settle 5,000 unemployed Englishmen at the beginning of the nineteenth century proved a failure. Not only did the streams of emigrants from the British Isles consistently avoid South Africa throughout the nineteenth century, but South Africa is the only dominion from which a steady stream of emigrants has gone back to England in recent times.[6] South Africa, which became the "culture-bed of Imperialism" (Damce), was never claimed by England's most radical defenders of "Saxondom" and it did not figure in the visions of her most romantic dreamers of an Asiatic Empire. This in itself shows how small the real influence of preimperialist colonial enterprise and overseas settlement was on the development of imperialism itself. If the Cape colony had remained

[5]"As late as 1884 the British Government had still been willing to diminish its authority and influence in South Africa" (De Kiewiet, *op. cit.*, p. 113).

[6]The following table of British immigration to and emigration from South Africa between 1924 and 1928 shows that Englishmen had a stronger inclination to leave the country than other immigrants and that, with one exception, each year showed a greater number of British people leaving the country than coming in:

Year	*British Immigration*	*Total Immigration*	*British Emigration*	*Total Emigration*
1924	3.724	5.265	5.275	5.857
1925	2.400	5.426	4.019	4.483
1926	4.094	6.575	3.512	3.799
1927	3.681	6.595	3.717	3.988
1928	3.285	7.050	3.409	4.127
Total	17.184	30.911	19.932	22.254

These figures are quoted from Leonard Barnes, *Caliban in Africa. An Impression of Colour Madness*, Philadelphia, 1931, p. 59, note.

within the framework of pre-imperialist policies, it would have been abandoned at the exact moment when it actually became all-important.

Although the discoveries of gold mines and diamond fields in the seventies and eighties would have had little consequence in themselves if they had not accidentally acted as a catalytic agent for imperialist forces, it remains remarkable that the imperialists' claim to have found a permanent solution to the problem of superfluity was initially motivated by a rush for the most superfluous raw material on earth. Gold hardly has a place in human production and is of no importance compared with iron, coal, oil, and rubber; instead, it is the most ancient symbol of mere wealth. In its uselessness in industrial production it bears an ironical resemblance to the superfluous money that financed the digging of gold and to the superfluous men who did the digging. To the imperialists' pretense of having discovered a permanent savior for a decadent society and antiquated political organization, it added its own pretense of apparently eternal stability and independence of all functional determinants. It was significant that a society about to part with all traditional absolute values began to look for an absolute value in the world of economics where, indeed, such a thing does not and cannot exist, since everything is functional by definition. This delusion of an absolute value has made the production of gold since ancient times the business of adventurers, gamblers, criminals, of elements outside the pale of normal, sane society. The new turn in the South African gold rush was that here the luck-hunters were not distinctly outside civilized society but, on the contrary, very clearly a by-product of this society, an inevitable residue of the capitalist system and even the representatives of an economy that relentlessly produced a superfluity of men and capital.

The superfluous men, "the Bohemians of the four continents"[7] who came rushing down to the Cape, still had much in common with the old adventurers. They too felt "Ship me somewhere east of Suez where the best is like the worst, / Where there aren't no Ten Commandments, an' a man can raise a thirst." The difference was not their morality or immorality, but rather that the decision to join this crowd "of all nations and colors"[8] was no longer up to them; that they had not stepped out of society but had been spat out by it; that they were not enterprising beyond the permitted limits of civilization but simply victims without use or function. Their only choice had been a negative one, a decision against the workers' movements, in which the best of the superfluous men or of those who were threatened with superfluity established a kind of countersociety through which men could find their way back into a human world of fellowship and purpose. They were nothing of their own making, they were like living symbols of what had happened to them, living abstractions and witnesses of the absurdity of human institutions. They were not individuals like the old adventurers, they were the shadows of events with which they had nothing to do.

Like Mr. Kurtz in Conrad's "Heart of Darkness," they were "hollow to the core," "reckless without hardihood, greedy without audacity and cruel without courage." They believed in nothing and "could get (themselves) to believe anything—anything." Expelled from a world with accepted social values, they had been thrown back upon themselves and still had nothing to fall back upon except, here and there, a streak of talent which made them as dangerous as Kurtz if they were ever allowed to return to

---

[7]J. A. Froude, "Leaves from a South African Journal" (1874), in *Short Studies on Great Subjects*, 1867–1882, Vol. IV.

[8]*Ibid.*

their homelands. For the only talent that could possibly burgeon in their hollow souls was the gift of fascination which makes a "splendid leader of an extreme party." The more gifted were walking incarnations of resentment like the German Carl Peters (possibly the model for Kurtz), who openly admitted that he "was fed up with being counted among the pariahs and wanted to belong to a master race."[9] But gifted or not, they were all "game for anything from pitch and toss to willful murder" and to them their fellow-men were "no more one way or another than that fly there." Thus they brought with them, or they learned quickly, the code of manners which befitted the coming type of murderer to whom the only unforgivable sin is to lose his temper.

There were, to be sure, authentic gentlemen among them, like Mr. Jones of Conrad's *Victory,* who out of boredom were willing to pay any price to inhabit the "world of hazard and adventure," or like Mr. Heyst, who was drunk with contempt for everything human until he drifted "like a detached leaf . . . without ever catching on to anything." They were irresistibly attracted by a world where everything was a joke, which could teach them "the Great Joke" that is "the mastery of despair." The perfect gentleman and the perfect scoundrel came to know each other well in the "great wild jungle without law," and they found themselves "well-matched in their enormous dissimilarity, identical souls in different disguises." We have seen the behavior of high society during the Dreyfus Affair and watched Disraeli discover the social relationship between vice and crime; here, too, we have essentially the same story of high society falling in love with its own underworld, and of the criminal feeling elevated when by civilized coldness, the avoidance of "unnecessary exertion," and good manners he is allowed to create a vicious, refined atmosphere around his crimes. This refinement, the very contrast between the brutality of the crime and the manner of carrying it out, becomes the bridge of deep understanding between himself and the perfect gentleman. But what, after all, took decades to achieve in Europe, because of the delaying effect of social ethical values, exploded with the suddenness of a short circuit in the phantom world of colonial adventure.

Outside all social restraint and hypocrisy, against the backdrop of native life, the gentleman and the criminal felt not only the closeness of men who share the same color of skin, but the impact of a world of infinite possibilities for crimes committed in the spirit of play, for the combination of horror and laughter, that is for the full realization of their own phantom-like existence. Native life lent these ghostlike events a seeming guarantee against all consequences because anyhow it looked to these men like a "mere play of shadows. A play of shadows, the dominant race could walk through unaffected and disregarded in the pursuit of its incomprehensible aims and needs."

The world of native savages was a perfect setting for men who had escaped the reality of civilization. Under a merciless sun, surrounded by an entirely hostile nature, they were confronted with human beings who, living without the future of a purpose and the past of an accomplishment, were as incomprehensible as the inmates of a madhouse. "The prehistoric man was cursing us, praying to us, welcoming us—who could tell? We were cut off from the comprehension of our surroundings; we glided past like phantoms, wondering and secretly appalled, as sane men would be, before an enthusiastic outbreak in a madhouse. We could not understand because we were too far and could not remember, because we were

[9]Quoted from Paul Ritter, *Kolonien im deutschen Schrifttum,* 1936, Preface.

traveling in the night of first ages, of those ages that are gone leaving hardly a sign—and no memories. The earth seemed unearthly, . . . and the men . . . No, they were not inhuman. Well, you know, that was the worst of it—this suspicion of their not being inhuman. It would come slowly to one. They howled and leaped, and spun, and made horrid faces; but what thrilled you was just the thought of their humanity—like yours—the thought of your remote kinship with this wild and passionate uproar" ("Heart of Darkness").

It is strange that, historically speaking, the existence of "prehistoric men" had so little influence on Western man before the scramble for Africa. It is, however, a matter of record that nothing much had happened as long as savage tribes, outnumbered by European settlers, had been exterminated, as long as shiploads of Negroes were imported as slaves into the Europe-determined world of the United States, or even as long as only individuals had drifted into the interior of the Dark Continent where the savages were numerous enough to constitute a world of their own, a world of folly, to which the European adventurer added the folly of the ivory hunt. Many of these adventurers had gone mad in the silent wilderness of an overpopulated continent where the presence of human beings only underlined utter solitude, and where an untouched, overwhelmingly hostile nature that nobody had ever taken the trouble to change into human landscape seemed to wait in sublime patience "for the passing away of the fantastic invasion" of man. But their madness had remained a matter of individual experience and without consequences.

This changed with the men who arrived during the scramble for Africa. These were no longer lonely individuals; "all Europe had contributed to the making of (them)." They concentrated on the southern part of the continent where they met the Boers, a Dutch splinter group which had been almost forgotten by Europe, but which now served as a natural introduction to the challenge of new surroundings. The response of the superfluous men was largely determined by the response of the only European group that ever, though in complete isolation, had to live in a world of black savages.

The Boers are descended from Dutch settlers who in the middle of the seventeenth century were stationed at the Cape to provide fresh vegetables and meat for ships on their voyage to India. A small group of French Huguenots was all that followed them in the course of the next century, so that it was only with the help of a high birthrate that the little Dutch splinter grew into a small people. Completely isolated from the current of European history, they set out on a path such "as few nations have trod before them, and scarcely one trod with success."[10]

The two main material factors in the development of the Boer people were the extremely bad soil which could be used only for extensive cattle-raising, and the very large black population which was organized in tribes and lived as nomad hunters.[11] The bad soil made close settlement impossible and prevented the Dutch peasant settlers from following the village organization of their homeland. Large families, isolated from each other by broad spaces of wilderness, were forced into a kind of clan organization and only the ever-present threat of a common foe, the black tribes which by far outnumbered the white settlers, deterred these clans from active war against each other. The

[10]Lord Selbourne in 1907: "The white people of South Africa are committed to such a path as few nations have trod before them, and scarcely one trod with success." See Kiewiet, *op. cit.*, chapter 6.

[11]See especially chapter iii of Kiewiet, *op. cit.*

solution to the double problem of lack of fertility and abundance of natives was slavery.[12]

Slavery, however, is a very inadequate word to describe what actually happened. First of all, slavery, though it domesticated a certain part of the savage population, never got hold of all of them, so the Boers were never able to forget their first horrible fright before a species of men whom human pride and the sense of human dignity could not allow them to accept as fellow-men. This fright of something like oneself that still under no circumstances ought to be like oneself remained at the basis of slavery and became the basis for a race society.

Mankind remembers the history of peoples but has only legendary knowledge of prehistoric tribes. The word "race" has a precise meaning only when and where peoples are confronted with such tribes of which they have no historical record and which do not know any history of their own. Whether these represent "prehistoric man," the accidentally surviving specimens of the first forms of human life on earth, or whether they are the "posthistoric" survivors of some unknown disaster which ended a civilization we do not know. They certainly appeared rather like the survivors of one great catastrophe which might have been followed by smaller disasters until catastrophic monotony seemed to be a natural condition of human life. At any rate, races in this sense were found only in regions where nature was particularly hostile. What made them different from other human beings was not at all the color of their skin but the fact that they behaved like a part of nature, that they treated nature as their undisputed master, that they had not created a human world, a human reality, and that therefore nature had remained, in all its majesty, the only overwhelming reality—compared to which they appeared to be phantoms, unreal and ghostlike. They were, as it were, "natural" human beings who lacked the specifically human character, the specifically human reality, so that when European men massacred them they somehow were not aware that they had committed murder.

Moreover, the senseless massacre of native tribes on the Dark Continent was quite in keeping with the traditions of these tribes themselves. Extermination of hostile tribes had been the rule in all African native wars, and it was not abolished when a black leader happened to unite several tribes under his leadership. King Tchaka, who at the beginning of the nineteenth century united the Zulu tribes in an extraordinarily disciplined and warlike organization, established neither a people nor a nation of Zulus. He only succeeded in exterminating more than one million members of weaker tribes.[13] Since discipline and military organization by themselves cannot establish a political body, the destruction remained an unrecorded episode in an unreal, incomprehensible process which cannot be accepted by man and therefore is not remembered by human history.

Slavery in the case of the Boers was a form of adjustment of a European people to a black race,[14] and only superficially resembled those historical instances when it had been a

[12] "Slaves and Hottentots together provoked remarkable changes in the thought and habits of the colonists, for climate and geography were not alone in forming the distinctive traits of the Boer race. Slaves and droughts, Hottentots and isolation, cheap labor and land, combined to create the institutions and habits of South African society. The sons and daughters born to sturdy Hollanders and Huguenots learned to look upon the labour of the field and upon all hard physical toil as the functions of a servile race" (Kiewiet, *op. cit.*, p. 21).

[13] See James, *op. cit.*, p. 28.

[14] "The true history of South African colonization describes the growth, not of a settlement of Europeans, but of a totally new and unique society of different races and colours and cultural attainments, fashioned by conflicts of racial heredity and the oppositions of unequal social groups" (Kiewiet, *op. cit.*, p. 19).

result of conquest or slave trade. No body politic, no communal organization kept the Boers together, no territory was definitely colonized, and the black slaves did not serve any white civilization. The Boers had lost both their peasant relationship to the soil and their civilized feeling for human fellowship. "Each man fled the tyranny of his neighbor's smoke"[15] was the rule of the country, and each Boer family repeated in complete isolation the general pattern of Boer experience among black savages and ruled over them in absolute lawlessness, unchecked by "kind neighbors ready to cheer you or to fall on you stepping delicately between the butcher and the policeman, in the holy terror of scandal and gallows and lunatic asylums" (Conrad). Ruling over tribes and living parasitically from their labor, they came to occupy a position very similar to that of the native tribal leaders whose domination they had liquidated. The natives, at any rate, recognized them as a higher form of tribal leadership, a kind of natural deity to which one has to submit; so that the divine role of the Boers was as much imposed by their black slaves as assumed freely by themselves. It is a matter of course that to these white gods of black slaves each law meant only deprivation of freedom, government only restriction of the wild arbitrariness of the clan.[16] In the natives the Boers discovered the only "raw material" which Africa provided in abundance and they used them not for the production of riches but for the mere essentials of human existence.

The black slaves in South Africa quickly became the only part of the population that actually worked. Their toil was marked by all the known disadvantages of slave labor, such as lack of initiative, laziness, neglect of tools, and general inefficiency. Their work therefore barely sufficed to keep their masters alive and never reached the comparative abundance which nurtures civilization. It was this absolute dependence on the work of others and complete contempt for labor and productivity in any form that transformed the Dutchman into the Boer and gave his concept of race a distinctly economic meaning.[17]

The Boers were the first European group to become completely alienated from the pride which Western man felt in living in a world created and fabricated by himself.[18] They treated the natives as raw material and lived on them as one might live on the fruits of wild trees. Lazy and unproductive, they agreed to vegetate on essentially the same level as the black tribes had vegetated for thousands of years. The great horror which had seized European men at their first confrontation with native life was stimulated by precisely this touch of inhumanity among human beings who apparently were as much a part of nature as wild animals. The Boers lived on their slaves exactly the way natives had lived on an unprepared and unchanged nature. When the Boers, in their fright and

[15]Kiewiet, *op. cit.*, p. 19.

[16]"[The Boers'] society was rebellious, but it was not revolutionary" (*ibid.*, p. 58).

[17]"Little effort was made to raise the standard of living or increase the opportunities of the class of slaves and servants. In this manner, the limited wealth of the Colony became the privilege of its white population. . . . Thus early did South Africa learn that a self-conscious group may escape the worst effects of life in a poor and unprosperous land by turning distinctions of race and colour into devices for social and economic discrimination" (*ibid.*, p. 22).

[18]The point is that, for instance, in "the West Indies such a large proportion of slaves as were held at the Cape would have been a sign of wealth and a source of prosperity"; whereas "at the Cape slavery was the sign of an unenterprising economy . . . whose labour was wastefully and inefficiently used" (*ibid.*). It was chiefly this that led Barnes (*op. cit.*, p. 107) and many other observers to the conclusion: "South Africa is thus a foreign country, not only in the sense that its standpoint is definitely un-British, but also in the much more radical sense that its very *raison d'etre*, as an attempt at an organised society, is in contradiction to the principles on which the states of Christendom are founded."

misery, decided to use these savages as though they were just another form of animal life, they embarked upon a process which could only end with their own degeneration into a white race living beside and together with black races from whom in the end they would differ only in the color of their skin.

The poor whites in South Africa, who in 1923 formed 10 per cent of the total white population[19] and whose standard of living does not differ much from that of the Bantu tribes, are today a warning example of this possibility. Their poverty is almost exclusively the consequence of their contempt for work and their adjustment to the way of life of black tribes. Like the blacks, they deserted the soil if the most primitive cultivation no longer yielded the little that was necessary or if they had exterminated the animals of the region.[20] Together with their former slaves, they came to the gold and diamond centers, abandoning their farms whenever the black workers departed. But in contrast to the natives who were immediately hired as cheap unskilled labor, they demanded and were granted charity as the right of a white skin, having lost all consciousness that normally men do not earn a living by the color of their skin.[21] Their race consciousness today is violent not only because they have nothing to lose save their membership in the white community, but also because the race concept seems to define their own condition much more adequately than it does that of their former slaves, who are well on the way to becoming workers, a normal part of human civilization.

Racism as a ruling device was used in this society of whites and blacks before imperialism exploited it as a major political idea. Its basis, and its excuse, were still experience itself, a horrifying experience of something alien beyond imagination or comprehension; it was tempting indeed simply to declare that these were not human beings. Since, however, despite all ideological explanations the black men stubbornly insisted on retaining their human features, the "white men" could not but reconsider their own humanity and decide that they themselves were more than human and obviously chosen by God to be the gods of black men. This conclusion was logical and unavoidable if one wanted to deny radically all common bonds with savages; in practice it meant that Christianity for the first time could not act as a decisive curb on the dangerous perversions of human self-consciousness, a premonition of its essential ineffectiveness in other more recent race societies.[22] The Boers simply denied the Christian doctrine of the common origin of men and changed those passages of the Old Testament which did not yet transcend the limits of the old Israelite national religion into a superstition which could not even be

[19]This corresponded to as many as 160,000 individuals (Kiewiet, *op. cit.*, p. 181). James (*op. cit.*, p. 43) estimated the number of poor whites in 1943 at 500,000 which would correspond to about 20 per cent of the white population.

[20]"The poor white Afrikaaner population, living on the same subsistence level as the Bantus, is primarily the result of the Boers' inability or stubborn refusal to learn agricultural science. Like the Bantu, the Boer likes to wander from one area to another, tilling the soil until it is no longer fertile, shooting the wild game until it ceases to exist" (*ibid.*).

[21]Their race was their title of superiority over the natives, and to do manual labour conflicted with the dignity conferred upon them by their race. . . . Such an aversion degenerated, in those who were most demoralized, into a claim to charity as a right" (Kiewiet, *op. cit.*, p. 216).

[22]The Dutch Reformed Church has been in the forefront of the Boers' struggle against the influence of Christian missionaries on the Cape. In 1944, however, they went one step farther and adopted "without a single voice of dissent" a motion opposing the marriage of Boers with English-speaking citizens. (According to the Cape *Times*, editorial of July 18, 1944. Quoted from *New Africa*, Council on African Affairs. Monthly Bulletin, October, 1944.)

called a heresy.[23] Like the Jews, they firmly believed in themselves as the chosen people,[24] with the essential difference that they were chosen not for the sake of divine salvation of mankind, but for the lazy domination over another species that was condemned to an equally lazy drudgery.[25] This was God's will on earth as the Dutch Reformed Church proclaimed it and still proclaims it today in sharp and hostile contrast to the missionaries of all other Christian denominations.[26]

Boer racism, unlike the other brands, has a touch of authenticity and, so to speak, of innocence. A complete lack of literature and other intellectual achievement is the best witness to this statement.[27] It was and remains a desperate reaction to desperate living conditions which was inarticulate and inconsequential as long as it was left alone. Things began to happen only with the arrival of the British, who showed little interest in their newest colony which in 1849 was still called a military station (as opposed to either a colony or a plantation). But their mere presence—that is, their contrasting attitude toward the natives whom they did not consider a different animal species, their later attempts (after 1834) to abolish slavery, and above all their efforts to impose fixed boundaries upon landed property—provoked the stagnant Boer society into violent reactions. It is characteristic of the Boers that these reactions followed the same, repeated pattern throughout the nineteenth century: Boer farmers escaped British law by treks into the interior wilderness of the country, abandoning without regret their homes and their farms. Rather than accept limitations upon their possessions, they left them altogether.[28] This does not mean that the Boers did not feel at home wherever they happened to be; they felt and still feel much more at home in Africa than any subsequent immigrants, but in Africa and not in any specific limited territory. Their fantastic treks, which threw the British administration into consternation, showed clearly that they had transformed themselves into a tribe and had

[23]Kiewiet (*op. cit.*, p. 181) mentions "the doctrine of racial superiority which was drawn from the Bible and reinforced by the popular interpretation which the nineteenth century placed upon Darwin's theories."

[24]"The God of the Old Testament has been to them almost as much a national figure as He has been to the Jews. . . . I recall a memorable scene in a Cape Town club, where a hold Briton, dining by chance with three or four Dutchmen, ventured to observe that Christ was a non-European and that, legally speaking, he would have been a prohibited immigrant in the Union of South Africa. The Dutchmen were so electrified at the remark that they nearly fell off their chairs" (Barnes, *op. cit.*, p. 33).

[25]"For the Boer farmer the separation and the degradation of the natives are ordained by God, and it is crime and blasphemy to argue to the contrary" (Norman Bentwich, "South Africa. Dominion of Racial Problems." In *Political Quarterly*, 1939, Vol. X, No. 3).

[26]"To this day the missionary is to the Boer the fundamental traitor, the white man who stands for black against white" (S. Gertrude Millin, *Rhodes*, London, 1933, p. 38).

[27]Because they had little art, less architecture, and no literature, they depended upon their farms, their Bibles, and their blood to set them off sharply against the native and the outlander" (Kiewiet, *op cit.*, p. 121).

[28]"The true Vortrekker hated a boundary. When the British Government insisted on fixed boundaries for the Colony and for farms within it, something was taken from him. . . . It was best surely to betake themselves across the border where there were water and free land and no British Government to disallow Vagrancy Laws and where white men could not be haled to court to answer the complaints of their servants" (*Ibid.*, pp. 54–55). "The Great Trek, a movement unique in the history of colonization" (p. 58) "was the defeat of the policy of more intensive settlement. The practice which required the area of an entire Canadian township for the settlement of ten families was extended through all of South Africa. It made for ever impossible the segregation of white and black races in separate areas of settlement. . . . By taking the Boers beyond the reach of British law, the Great Trek enabled them to establish 'proper' relations with the native population" (p. 56). "In later years, the Great Trek was to become more than a protest; it was to become a rebellion against the British administration, and the foundation stone of the Anglo-Boer racialism of the twentieth century" (James, *op. cit.*, p. 28).

lost the European's feeling for a territory, a *patria* of his own. They behaved exactly like the black tribes who had also roamed the Dark Continent for centuries—feeling at home wherever the horde happened to be, and fleeing like death every attempt at definite settlement.

Rootlessness is characteristic of all race organizations. What the European "movements" consciously aimed at, the transformation of the people into a horde, can be watched like a laboratory test in the Boers' early and sad attempt. While rootlessness as a conscious aim was based primarily upon hatred of a world that had no place for "superfluous" men, so that its destruction could become a supreme political goal, the rootlessness of the Boers was a natural result of early emancipation from work and complete lack of a human-built world. The same striking similarity prevails between the "movements" and the Boers' interpretation of "chosenness." But while the Pan-German, Pan-Slav, or Polish Messianic movements' chosenness was a more or less conscious instrument for domination, the Boers' perversion of Christianity was solidly rooted in a horrible reality in which miserable "white men" were worshipped as divinities by equally unfortunate "black men." Living in an environment which they had no power to transform into a civilized world, they could discover no higher value than themselves. The point, however, is that no matter whether racism appears as the natural result of a catastrophe or as the conscious instrument for bringing it about, it is always closely tied to contempt for labor, hatred of territorial limitation, general rootlessness, and an activistic faith in one's own divine chosenness.

Early British rule in South Africa, with its missionaries, soldiers, and explorers, did not realize that the Boers' attitudes had some basis in reality. They did not understand that absolute European supremacy—in which they, after all, were as interested as the Boers—could hardly be maintained except through racism because the permanent European settlement was so hopelessly outnumbered;[29] they were shocked "if Europeans settled in Africa were to act like savages themselves because it was the custom of the country,"[30] and to their simple utilitarian minds it seemed folly to sacrifice productivity and profit to the phantom world of white gods ruling over black shadows. Only with the settlement of Englishmen and other Europeans during the gold rush did they gradually adjust to a population which could not be lured back into European civilization even by profit motives, which had lost contact even with the lower incentives of European man when it had cut itself off from his higher motives, because both lose their meaning and appeal in a society where nobody wants to achieve anything and everyone has become a god.

[29]In 1939, the total population of the Union of South Africa amounted to 9,500,000 of whom 7,000,000 were natives and 2,500,000 Europeans. Of the latter, more than 1,250,000 were Boers, about one-third were British, and 100,000 were Jews. See Norman Bentwich, *op. cit.*

[30]J. A. Froude, *op. cit.*, p. 375.

The Soul of Black Folk

W. E. B. DuBois

Is there any possibility for a black person to have self-consciousness in a white world without seeing himself or herself through the eyes of another? W. E. B. DuBois asks us to consider whether or not a black person can be a "self" without encountering "two souls, two thoughts, two unreconciled strivings, two warring ideals." As you read his arguments, ask yourself whether race, poverty, and ignorance create a formidable struggle for personal identity. If race contributes to a struggle for identity, can it also be used as a unifying ideal as DuBois suggests?

CHAPTER 1: OF OUR SPIRITUAL STRIVINGS

O water, voice of my heart, crying in the sand,
All night long crying with a mournful cry,
As I lie and listen, and cannot understand
The voice of my heart in my side or the voice of the sea,
O water, crying for rest, is it I, is it I?
All night long the water is crying to me.

Unresting water, there shall never be rest
Till the last moon droop and the last tide fail.
And the fire of the end begin to burn in the west;
And the heart shall be weary and wonder and cry like the sea,
All life long crying without avail,
As the water all night long is crying to me.

—Arthur Symons

Between me and the other world there is ever an unasked question: unasked by some through feelings of delicacy; by others through the difficulty of rightly framing it. All, nevertheless, flutter round it. They approach me in a half-hesitant sort of way, eye me curiously or compassionately, and then, instead of saying directly, How does it feel to be a problem? they say, I know an excellent colored man in my town; or, I fought at Mechanicsville; or, Do not these Southern outrages make your blood boil? At these I smile, or am interested, or reduce the boiling to a simmer, as the occasion may require. To the real question, How does it feel to be a problem? I answer seldom a word.

And yet, being a problem is a strange experience,—peculiar even for one who has never been anything else, save perhaps in babyhood and in Europe. It is in the early days of rollicking boyhood that the revelation first bursts upon one, all in a day, as it were. I remember well when the shadow swept across me. I was a little thing, away up in the hills of New England, where the dark Housatonic winds between Hoosac and Taghkanic to the sea. In a wee wooden schoolhouse, something put it into the boys' and girls' heads to buy gorgeous visiting-cards—ten cents a package—and exchange. The exchange was merry, till one girl, a tall newcomer, refused my card,—refused it peremptorily, with a glance. Then it dawned upon me with a certain suddenness that I was different from the others; or like, mayhap, in heart and life and longing, but shut out from their world by a vast veil. I had

"The Soul of Black Folk" by W. E. B. DuBois, 1903.

thereafter no desire to tear down that veil, to creep through; I held all beyond it in common contempt, and lived above it in a region of blue sky and great wandering shadows. That sky was bluest when I could beat my mates at examination-time, or beat them at a foot-race, or even beat their stringy heads. Alas, with the years all this fine contempt began to fade; for the worlds I longed for, and all their dazzling opportunities, were theirs, not mine. But they should not keep these prizes, I said; some, all, I would wrest from them. Just how I would do it I could never decide: by reading law, by healing the sick, by telling the wonderful tales that swam in my head,—some way. With other black boys the strife was not so fiercely sunny: their youth shrunk into tasteless sycophancy, or into silent hatred of the pale world about them and mocking distrust of everything white; or wasted itself in a bitter cry, Why did God make me an outcast and a stranger in mine own house? The shades of the prison-house closed round about us all: walls strait and stubborn to the whitest, but relentlessly narrow, tall, and unscalable to sons of night who must plod darkly on in resignation, or beat unavailing palms against the stone, or steadily, half hopelessly, watch the streak of blue above.

After the Egyptian and Indian, the Greek and Roman, the Teuton and Mongolian, the Negro is a sort of seventh son, born with a veil, and gifted with second-sight in this American world,—a world which yields him no true self-consciousness, but only lets him see himself through the revelation of the other world. It is a peculiar sensation, this double-consciousness, this sense of always looking at one's self through the eyes of others, of measuring one's soul by the tape of a world that looks on in amused contempt and pity. One ever feels his twoness,—an American, a Negro; two souls, two thoughts, two unreconciled strivings; two warring ideals in one dark body, whose dogged strength alone keeps it from being torn asunder.

The history of the American Negro is the history of this strife,—this longing to attain self-conscious manhood, to merge his double self into a better and truer self. In this merging he wishes neither of the older selves to be lost. He would not Africanize America, for America has too much to teach the world and Africa. He would not bleach his Negro soul in a flood of white Americanism, for he knows that Negro blood has a message for the world. He simply wishes to make it possible for a man to be both a Negro and an American, without being cursed and spit upon by his fellows, without having the doors of Opportunity closed roughly in his face.

This, then, is the end of his striving: to be a co-worker in the kingdom of culture, to escape both death and isolation, to husband and use his best powers and his latent genius. These powers of body and mind have in the past been strangely wasted, dispersed, or forgotten. The shadow of a mighty Negro past flits through the tale of Ethiopia the Shadowy and of Egypt the Sphinx. Throughout history, the powers of single black men flash here and there like falling stars, and die sometimes before the world has rightly gauged their brightness. Here in America, in the few days since Emancipation, the black man's turning hither and thither in hesitant and doubtful striving has often made his very strength to lose effectiveness, to seem like absence of power, like weakness. And yet it is not weakness,—it is the contradiction of double aims. The double-aimed struggle of the black artisan—on the one hand to escape white contempt for a nation of mere hewers of wood and drawers of water, and on the other hand to plough and nail and dig for a poverty-stricken horde—could only result in making him a poor craftsman, for he had but half a heart in either cause. By the poverty and ignorance of his people, the Negro minister or doctor was tempted toward quackery and demagogy; and by the criticism of the other world, toward ideals that made him ashamed of his lowly tasks. The would-be black savant was confronted by the paradox that the knowledge his people needed was a twice-told tale to his white neighbors, while the knowledge which would teach the white world was Greek to his own flesh and blood. The innate love of harmony and beauty that set the ruder souls of his people a-dancing and a-singing raised but confusion and doubt in the soul of the black artist; for the beauty revealed to him was the soul-beauty of a race which his larger audience despised, and he could not articulate the message of another people. This waste of double aims, this seeking to satisfy two unreconciled ideals, has wrought sad havoc with the courage and faith and deeds of ten thousand thousand people,—has sent them often wooing false gods and invoking false means of salvation, and at times has even seemed about to make them ashamed of themselves.

Away back in the days of bondage they thought to see in one divine event the end of all doubt and disappointment; few men ever worshipped Freedom with half such unquestioning faith as did the American Negro for two centuries. To him, so far as he thought and dreamed, slavery was indeed the sum of all villainies, the cause of all sorrow, the root of all prejudice; Emancipation was the key to a promised land of sweeter beauty than ever stretched before the eyes of wearied Israelites. In song and exhortation swelled one refrain—Liberty; in his tears and curses the God he implored had Freedom in his right hand. At last it came,—suddenly, fearfully, like a dream. With one wild carnival of blood and passion came the message in his own plaintive cadences:—

> "Shout, O children!
> Shout, you're free!
> For God has bought your liberty!"

Years have passed away since then,—ten, twenty, forty; forty years of national life, forty years of renewal and development, and yet the swarthy spectre sits in its accustomed seat at the Nation's feast. In vain do we cry to this our vastest social problem:—

> "Take any shape but that, and my firm nerves
> Shall never tremble!"

The Nation has not yet found peace from its sins; the freedman has not yet found in freedom his promised land. Whatever of good may have come in these years of change, the shadow of a deep disappointment rests upon the Negro people,—a disappointment all the more bitter because the unattained ideal was unbounded save by the simple ignorance of a lowly people.

The first decade was merely a prolongation of the vain search for freedom, the boon that seemed ever barely to elude their grasp,—like a tantalizing will-o'-the-wisp, maddening and misleading the headless host. The holocaust of war, the terrors of the Ku Klux Klan, the lies of carpet-baggers, the disorganization of industry, and the contradictory advice of friends and foes, left the bewildered serf with no new watchword beyond the old cry for freedom. As the time flew, however, he began to grasp a new idea. The ideal of liberty demanded for its attainment powerful means, and these the Fifteenth Amendment gave him. The ballot, which before he had looked upon as a visible sign of freedom, he now regarded as the chief means of gaining and perfecting the liberty with which war had partially endowed him. And why not? Had not votes made war and emancipated millions? Had not votes enfranchised the freedmen? Was anything impossible to a power that had done all this? A million black men started with renewed zeal to vote themselves into the kingdom. So the decade flew away, the revolution of 1876 came, and left the half-free serf weary, wondering, but still inspired. Slowly but steadily, in the following years, a new vision began gradually to replace the dream of political power,—a powerful movement, the rise of another ideal to guide the unguided, another pillar of fire by night after a clouded day. It was the ideal of "book-learning"; the curiosity, born of compulsory ignorance, to know and test the power of the cabalistic letters of the white man, the longing to know. Here at last seemed to have been discovered the mountain path to Canaan; longer than the highway of Emancipation and law, steep and rugged, but straight, leading to heights high enough to overlook life.

Up the new path the advance guard toiled, slowly, heavily, doggedly; only those who have watched and guided the faltering feet, the misty minds, the dull understandings, of the dark pupils of these schools know how faithfully, how piteously, this people strove to learn. It was weary work. The cold statistician wrote down the inches of progress here and there, noted also where here and there a foot had slipped or some one had fallen. To the tired climbers, the horizon was ever dark, the mists were often cold, the Canaan was always dim and far away. If, however, the vistas disclosed as yet no goal, no resting-place, little but flattery and criticism, the journey at least gave leisure for reflection and self-examination; it changed the child of Emancipation to the youth with dawning self-consciousness, self-realization, self-respect. In those sombre forests of his striving his own soul rose before him, and he saw himself,—darkly as through a veil; and yet he saw in himself some faint revelation of his power, of his mission. He began to have a dim feeling that, to attain his place in the world, he must be himself, and not another. For the first time he sought to analyze the burden he bore upon his back, that dead-weight of social degradation partially masked behind a half-named Negro problem. He felt his poverty; without a cent, without a home, without land, tools, or savings, he had entered into competition with rich, landed, skilled neighbors. To be a poor man is hard, but to be a poor race in a land of dollars is the very bottom of hardships. He felt the weight of his ignorance,—not simply of letters, but of life, of business, of the humanities; the accumulated sloth and shirking and awkwardness of decades and centuries shackled his hands and feet. Nor was his burden all poverty and ignorance. The red stain of bastardy, which two centuries of systematic legal defilement of Negro women had stamped upon his race, meant not only the loss of ancient African chastity, but also the hereditary weight of a mass of corruption from white adulterers, threatening almost the obliteration of the Negro home.

A people thus handicapped ought not to be asked to race with the world, but rather allowed to give all its time and thought to its own social problems. But alas! while sociologists gleefully count his bastards and his prostitutes, the very soul of the toiling, sweating black man is darkened by the shadow of a vast despair. Men call the shadow prejudice, and learnedly explain it as the natural defence of culture against barbarism, learning against ignorance, purity against crime, the "higher" against the "lower" races. To which the Negro cries Amen! and swears that to so much of this strange prejudice as is founded on just homage to civilization, culture, righteousness, and progress, he humbly bows and meekly does obeisance. But before that nameless prejudice that leaps beyond all this he stands helpless, dismayed, and well-nigh speechless; before that personal disrespect and mockery, the ridicule and systematic humiliation, the distortion of fact and wanton license of fancy, the cynical ignoring of the better and the boisterous welcoming of the worse, the all-pervading desire to inculcate disdain for everything black, from Toussaint to the devil,—before this there rises a sickening despair that would disarm and discourage any nation save that black host to whom "discouragement" is an unwritten word.

But the facing of so vast a prejudice could not but bring the inevitable self-questioning, self-disparagement, and lowering of ideals which ever accompany repression and breed in an atmosphere of contempt and hate. Whisperings and portents came borne upon the four winds: Lo! we are diseased and dying, cried the dark hosts: we cannot write, our voting is vain; what need of education, since we must always cook and serve? And the Nation echoed and enforced this self-criticism, saying: Be content to be servants, and nothing more; what need of higher culture for half-men? Away with the black man's ballot, by force or fraud,—and behold the suicide of a race! Nevertheless, out of the evil came something of good,—the more careful adjustment of education to real life, the clearer perception of the Negroes' social responsibilities, and the sobering realization of the meaning of progress.

So dawned the time of *Sturm und Drang:* storm and stress to-day rocks our little boat on the mad waters of the world-sea; there is within and without the sound of conflict, the burning of body and rending of soul; inspiration strives with doubt, and faith with vain questionings. The bright ideals of the past,—physical freedom, political power, the training of brains and the training of hands,—all these in turn have waxed and waned, until even the last grows dim and overcast. Are they all wrong,—all false? No, not that, but each alone was over-simple and incomplete,—the dreams of a credulous race-childhood, or the fond imaginings of the other world which does not know and does not want to know our power. To be really true, all these ideals must be melted and welded into one. The training of the schools we need to-day more than ever,—the training of deft hands, quick eyes and ears, and above all the broader, deeper, higher culture of gifted minds and pure hearts. The power of the ballot we need in sheer self-defence,—else what shall save us from a second slavery? Freedom, too, the long-sought, we still seek,—the freedom of life and limb, the freedom to work and think, the freedom to love and aspire. Work, culture, liberty,—all these we need, not singly but together, not successively but together, each growing and aiding each, and all striving toward that vaster ideal that swims before the Negro people, the ideal of human brotherhood, gained through the unifying ideal of Race; the ideal of fostering and developing the traits and talents of the Negro, not in opposition to or contempt for other races, but rather in large conformity to the greater ideals of the American Republic, in order that some day on American soil two world-races may give each to each those characteristics both so sadly lack. We the darker ones come even now not altogether empty-handed: there are to-day no truer exponents of the pure human spirit of the Declaration of Independence than the American Negroes; there is no true American music but the wild sweet melodies of the Negro slave; the American fairy tales and folk-lore are Indian and African; and, all in all, we black men seem the sole oasis of simple faith and reverence in a dusty desert of dollars and smartness. Will America be poorer if she replace her brutal dyspeptic blundering with lighthearted but determined Negro humility? or her coarse and cruel wit with loving jovial good-humor? or her vulgar music with the soul of the Sorrow Songs?

Merely a concrete test of the underlying principles of the great republic is the Negro Problem, and the spiritual striving of the freedmen's sons is the travail of souls whose burden is almost beyond the measure of their strength, but who bear it in the name of an historic race, in the name of this the land of their fathers' fathers, and in the name of human opportunity.

What Is an American?

J. Hector St. John de Crèvecoeur

In this "Letter from an American Farmer," we hear what a French Canadian immigrant to the United States had to say about class distinctions in colonial America. We also learn about the impact that the land and its economies may have had on the formation of an American identity. We learn, too, that such an identity may be more regional than national in character. De Crèvecoeur also speculates about why some Europeans may find it easier to assimilate an American identity. As you read, try to imagine that it is possible that geography and ethnic heritage may help determine our particular identities, and how they may do so.

I wish I could be acquainted with the feelings and thoughts which must agitate the heart and present themselves to the mind of an enlightened Englishman, when he first lands on this continent. He must greatly rejoice that he lived at a time to see this fair country discovered and settled; he must necessarily feel a share of national pride, when he views the chain of settlements which embellishes these extended shores. When he says to himself, this is the work of my countrymen, who, when convulsed by factions, afflicted by a variety of miseries and wants, restless and impatient, took refuge here. They brought along with them their national genius, to which they principally owe what liberty they enjoy, and what substance they possess. Here he sees the industry of his native country displayed in a new manner, and traces in their works the embr[y]os of all the arts, sciences, and ingenuity which flourish in Europe. Here he beholds fair cities, substantial villages, extensive fields, an immense country filled with decent houses, good roads, orchards, meadows, and bridges, where an hundred years ago all was wild, woody and uncultivated!

What a train of pleasing ideas this fair spectacle must suggest; it is a prospect which must inspire a good citizen with the most heartfelt pleasure. The difficulty consists in the manner of viewing so extensive a scene. He is arrived on a new continent; a modern

From *Letters from an American Farmer,* by J. Hector St. John, A Farmer in Pennsylvania. London, 1782, 45–87.

society offers itself to his contemptation, different from what he had hitherto seen. It is not composed, as in Europe, of great lords who possess every thing and of a herd of people who have nothing. Here are no aristocratical families, no courts, no kings, no bishops, no ecclesiastical dominion, no invisible power giving to a few a very visible one; no great manufacturers employing thousands, no great refinements of luxury. The rich and the poor are not so far removed from each other as they are in Europe.

Some few towns excepted, we are all tillers of the earth, from Nova Scotia to West Florida. We are a people of cultivators, scattered over an immense territory communicating with each other by means of good roads and navigable rivers, united by the silken bands of mild government, all respecting the laws, without dreading their power, because they are equitable. We are all animated with the spirit of an industry which is unfettered and unrestrained, because each person works for himself. If he travels through our rural districts he views not the hostile castle, and the haughty mansion, contrasted with the clay-built hut and miserable cabbin, where cattle and men help to keep each other warm, and dwell in meanness, smoke, and indigence. A pleasing uniformity of decent competence appears throughout our habitations. The meanest of our log-houses is a dry and comfortable habitation. Lawyer or merchant are the fairest titles our towns afford; that of a farmer is the only appellation of the rural inhabitants of our country. It must take some time ere he can reconcile himself to our dictionary, which is but short in words of dignity, and names of honour. (There, on a Sunday, he sees a congregation of respectable farmers and their wives, all clad in neat homespun, well mounted, or riding in their own humble waggons. There is not among them an esquire, saving the unlettered magistrate. There he sees a parson as simple as his flock, a farmer who does not riot on the labour of others. We have no princes, for whom we toil, starve, and bleed: we are the most perfect society now existing in the world. Here man is free; as he ought to be; nor is this pleasing equality so transitory as many others are. Many ages will not see the shores of our great lakes replenished with inland nations, nor the unknown bounds of North America entirely peopled. Who can tell how far it extends? Who can tell the millions of men whom it will feed and contain? for no European foot has as yet travelled half the extent of this mighty continent!

The next wish of this traveller will be to know whence came all these people? they are mixture of English, Scotch, Irish, French, Dutch, Germans, and Swedes. From this promiscuous breed, that race now called Americans have arisen. The eastern provinces must indeed be excepted, as being the unmixed descendants of Englishmen. I have heard many wish that they had been more intermixed also: for my part, I am no wisher, and think it much better as it has happened. They exhibit a most conspicuous figure in this great and variegated picture; they too enter for a great share in the pleasing perspective displayed in these thirteen provinces. I know it is fashionable to reflect on them, but I respect them for what they have done; for the accuracy and wisdom with which they have settled their territory; for the decency of their manners; for their early love of letters; their ancient college, the first in this hemisphere; for their industry; which to me who am but a farmer, is the criterion of everything. There never was a people, situated as they are, who with so ungrateful a soil have done more in so short a time. Do you think that the monarchical ingredients which are more prevalent in other governments, have purged them from all foul stains? Their histories assert the contrary.

In this great American asylum, the poor of Europe have by some means met together, and in consequence of various causes; to what purpose should they ask one another what countrymen they are? Alas, two thirds of them had no country. Can a wretch who wanders about, who works and starves, whose life is a continual scene of sore affliction or pinching penury; can that man call England or any other kingdom his country? A country that had no bread for him, whose fields procured him no harvest, who met with nothing but the frowns of the rich, the severity of the laws, with jails and punishments; who owned not a single foot of the extensive surface of this planet? No! urged by a variety of motives, here they came. Every thing has tended to regenerate them; new laws, a new mode of living, a new social system; here they are become men: in Europe they were as so many useless plants, wanting vegitative mould, and refreshing showers; they withered, and were mowed down by want, hunger, and war; but now by the power of transplantation, like all other plants they have taken root and flourished! Formerly they were not numbered in any civil lists of their country, except in those of the poor; here they rank as citizens. By what invisible power has this surprising metamorphosis been performed? By that of the laws and that of their industry. The laws, the indulgent laws, protect them as they arrive, stamping on them the symbol of adoption; they receive ample rewards for their labours; these accumulated rewards procure them lands; those lands confer on them the title of freemen, and to that title every benefit is affixed which men can possibly require. This is the great operation daily performed by our laws. From whence proceed these laws? From our government. Whence the government? It is derived from the original genius and strong desire of the people ratified and confirmed by the crown. This is the great chain which links us all, this is the picture which every province exhibits, Nova Scotia excepted. There the crown has done all; either there were no people who had genius, or it was not much attended to: the consequence is, that the province is very thinly inhabited indeed; the power of the crown in conjunction with the musketos has prevented men from settling there. Yet some parts of it flourished once, and it contained a mild harmless set of people. But for the fault of a few leaders, the whole were banished. The greatest political error the crown ever committed in America, was to cut off men from a country which wanted nothing but men!

What attachment can a poor European emigrant have for a country where he had nothing? The knowledge of the language, the love of a few kindred as poor as himself, were the only cords that tied him: his country is now that which gives him land, bread, protection, and consequence: *Ubi panis ibi patria,* is the motto of all emigrants. What then is the American, this new man? He is either an European, or the descendant of an European, hence that strange mixture of blood, which you will find in no other country. I could point out to you a family whose grandfather was an Englishman, whose wife was Dutch, whose son married a French woman, and whose present four sons have now four wives of different nations. *He* is an American, who leaving behind him all his ancient prejudices and manners, receives new ones from the new mode of life he has embraced, the new government he obeys, and the new rank he holds. He becomes an American by being received in the broad lap of our great *Alma Mater*.

Here individuals of all nations are melted into a new race of men, whose labours and posterity will one day cause great changes in the world. Americans are the western pilgrims, who are carrying along with them that great mass of arts, sciences, vigour, and industry which began long since in the east; they will finish the great circle. The Americans were once scattered all over Europe; here they are incorporated into one of the finest systems of population which has ever appeared, and which will hereafter become distinct by the power of the different climates they inhabit. The American ought therefore to love this country much better than that wherein either he or his forefathers were born. Here the rewards of his industry follow with equal steps the progress of his labour; his labour is founded on the basis of nature, *self-interest*; can it want a stronger allurement? Wives and children, who before in vain demanded of him a morsel of bread, now, fat and frolicsome, gladly help their father to clear those fields whence exuberant crops are to arise to feed and to clothe them all; without any part being claimed, either by a despotic prince, a rich abbot, or a mighty lord. I lord religion demands but little of *him*; a small voluntary salary to the minister, and gratitude to God; can he refuse these? The American is a new man, who acts upon new principles; he must therefore entertain new ideas, and form new opinions. From involuntary idleness, servile dependence, penury, and useless labour, he has passed to toils of a very different nature, rewarded by ample subsistence.—This is an American.

British America is divided into many provinces, forming a large association, scattered along a coast 1500 miles extent and about 200 wide. This society I would fain examine, at least such as it appears in the middle provinces; if it does not afford that variety of tinges and gradations which may be observed in Europe, we have colours peculiar to ourselves. For instance, it is natural to conceive that those who live near the sea, must be very different from those who live in the woods; the intermediate space will afford a separate and distinct class.

Men are like plants; the goodness and flavour of the fruit proceeds from the peculiar soil and exposition in which they grow. We are nothing but what we derive from the air we breathe, the climate we inhabit, the government we obey, the system of religion we profess, and the nature of our employment. Here you will find but few crimes; these have acquired as yet no root among us. I wish I were able to trace all my ideas; if my ignorance prevents me from describing them properly, I hope I shall be able to delineate a few of the outlines, which are all I propose.

Those who live near the sea, feed more on fish than on flesh, and often encounter that boisterous element. This renders them more bold and enterprising; this leads them to neglect the confined occupations of the land. They see and converse with a variety of people; their intercourse with mankind becomes extensive. The sea inspires them with a love of traffic, a desire of transporting produce from one place to another; and leads them to a variety of resources which supply the place of labour. Those who inhabit the middle settlements, by far the most numerous, must be very different; the simple cultivation of the earth purifies them, but the indulgences of the government, the soft remonstrances of religion, the rank of independent freeholders, must necessarily inspire them with sentiments, very little known in Europe among people of the same class. What do I say? Europe has no such class of men; the early knowledge they acquire, the early bargains they make, give them a great degree of sagacity. As freemen they will be litigious; pride and obstinacy are often the cause of law suits; the nature of our laws and governments may be another. As citizens it is easy to imagine, that they will carefully read the newspapers, enter into every political disquisition, freely blame or censure governors and others. As farmers they will be careful and anxious to get as much as they can, because what they get is their own. As northern men they will love the chearful cup. As Christians, religion curbs them not in their opinions; the general indulgence leaves every one to think for themselves in spiritual matters; the laws inspect our actions, our thoughts are left to God. Industry, good living, selfishness, litigiousness, country politics, the pride of freemen, religious indifference, are their characteristics. If you recede still farther from the sea, you will come into more modern settlements; they exhibit the same strong lineaments, in a ruder appearance. Religion seems to have still less influence, and their manners are less improved.

Now we arrive near the great woods, near the last inhabited districts; there men seem to be placed still farther beyond the reach of government, which in some measure leaves them to themselves. How can it pervade every corner; as they were driven there by misfortunes, necessity of beginnings, desire of acquiring large tracks of land, idleness, frequent want of economy, ancient debts; the re-union of such people does not afford a very pleasing spectacle. When discord, want of unity and friendship; when either drunkenness or idleness prevail in such remote districts; contention, inactivity, and wretchedness must ensue. There are not the same remedies to these evils as in a long established community. The few magistrates they have, are in general little better than the rest; they are often in a perfect state of war; that of man against man, sometimes decided by blows, sometimes by means of the law; that of man against every wild inhabitant of these venerable woods, of which they are come to dispossess them. There men appear to be no better than carnivorous animals of a superior rank, living on the flesh of wild animals when they can catch them, and when they are not able, they subsist on grain.

He who wish[es] to see America in its proper light, and have a true idea of its feeble beginnings [and] barbarous rudiments, must visit our extended line of frontiers where the last settlers dwell, and where he may see the first labours of the mode of clearing the earth, in their different appearances; where men are wholly left dependent on their native tempers, and on the spur of uncertain industry, which often fails when not sanctified by the efficacy of a few moral rules. There, remote from the power of example, and check of shame, many families exhibit the most hideous parts of our society. They are a kind of forlorn hope, preceding by ten or twelve years the most respectable army of veterans which come after them. In that space, prosperity will polish some, vice and the law will drive off the rest, who uniting again with others like themselves will recede still farther; making room for more industrious people, who will finish their improvements, convert the loghouse into a convenient habitation, and rejoicing that the first heavy labours are finished, will change in a few years that hitherto barbarous country into a fine fertile, well regulated district.

Such is our progress, such is the march of the Europeans toward the interior parts of this continent. In all societies there are offcasts; this impure part serves as our precursors or pioneers; my father himself was one of that class, but he came upon honest principles, and was therefore one of the few who held fast; by good conduct and temperance, he transmitted to me his fair inheritance, when not above one in fourteen of his contemporaries had the same good fortune.

Forty years ago this smiling country was thus inhabited; it is now purged, a general decency of manners prevails throughout, and such has been the fate of our best countries.

Exclusive of those general characteristics, each province has its own, founded on the government, climate, mode of husbandry, customs, and peculiarity of circumstances. Europeans submit insensibly to these great powers, and become, in the course of a few generations, not only Americans in general, but either Pennsylvanians, Virginians, or provincials under some other name. Whoever traverses the continent must easily observe those strong differences, which will grow more evident in time. The inhabitants of Canada, Massachusetts, the middle provinces, the southern ones will be as different as their climates; their only points of unity will be those of religion and language. . . .

Europe contains hardly any other distinctions but lords and tenants; this fair country alone is settled by freeholders, the possessors of the soil they cultivate, members of the government they obey, and the framers of their own laws, by means of their representatives. This is a thought which you have taught me to cherish; our difference from Europe, far from diminishing, rather adds to our usefulness and consequence as men and subjects. Had our forefathers remained there, they would only have crowded it, and perhaps prolonged those convulsions which had shook it so long. Every industrious European who transports himself here may be compared to a sprout growing at the foot of a great tree; it enjoys and draws but a little portion of sap; wrench it from the parent roots, transplant it, and it will become a tree bearing fruit also. Colonists are therefore entitled to the consideration due to the most useful subjects; a hundred families barely existing in some parts of Scotland, will here in six years, cause an annual exportation of 10,000 bushels of wheat: 100 bushels being but a common quantity for an industrious family to sell, if they cultivate good land. It is here then that the idle may be employed, the useless become useful, and the poor become rich; but by riches I do not mean gold and silver, we have but little of those metals; I mean a better sort of wealth, cleared lands, cattle, good houses, good cloaths, and an increase of people to enjoy them.

It is no wonder that this country has so many charms, and presents to Europeans so many temptations to remain in it. A traveller in Europe becomes a stranger as soon as he quits his own kingdom; but it is otherwise here. We know, properly speaking, no strangers; this is every person's country; the variety of our soils, situations, climates, governments, and produce, hath something which must please everybody. No sooner does an European arrive, no matter of what condition, than his eyes are opened upon the fair prospect; he hears his language spoke, he retraces many of his own country manners, he perpetually hears the names of families and towns with which he is acquainted; he sees happiness and prosperity in all places disseminated; he meets with hospitality, kindness, and plenty every where; he beholds hardly any poor, he seldom hears of punishments and executions; and he wonders at the elegance of our towns, those miracles of industry and freedom. He cannot admire enough our rural districts, our convenient roads, good taverns, and our many accommodations; he involuntarily loves a country where every thing is so lovely. When in England, he was a mere Englishman; here he stands on a larger portion of the globe, not less than its fourth part, and may see the productions of the north, in iron and naval stores; the provisions of Ireland, the grain of Egypt, the indigo, the rice of China. He does not find, as in Europe, a crouded society, where every place is over-stocked; he does not feel that perpetual collision of parties, that difficulty of beginning, that contention which oversets so many.

There is room for every body in America; has he any particular talent, or industry?

he exerts it in order to procure a livelihood, and it succeeds. Is he a merchant? the avenues of trade are infinite; is he eminent in any respect? he will be employed and respected. Does he love a country life? pleasant farms present themselves; he may purchase what he wants, and thereby become an American farmer. Is he a labourer, sober and industrious? he need not go many miles, nor receive many informations before he will be hired, well fed at the table of his employer, and paid four or five times more than he can get in Europe. Does he want uncultivated lands? Thousands of acres present themselves, which he may purchase cheap. Whatever be his talents or inclinations, if they are moderate, he may satisfy them. I do not mean that every one who comes will grow rich in a little time; no, but he may procure an easy, decent maintenance, by his industry. Instead of starving he will be fed, instead of being idle he will have employment; and these are riches enough for such men as come over here. The rich stay in Europe, it is only the middling and the poor that emigrate. Would you wish to travel in independent idleness, from north to south, you will find easy access, and the most chearful reception at every house; society without ostentation, good cheer without pride, and every decent diversion which the country affords, with little expence. It is no wonder that the European who has lived here a few years, is desirous to remain; Europe with all its pomp, is not to be compared to this continent, for men of middle stations, or labourers.

An European, when he first arrives, seems limited in his intentions, as well as in his views; but he very suddenly alters his scale; two hundred miles formerly appeared a very great distance, it is now but a trifle; he no sooner breathes our air than he forms schemes, and embarks in designs he never would have thought of in his own country. There the plenitude of society confines many useful ideas, and often extinguishes the most laudable schemes which here ripen into maturity. Thus Europeans become Americans.

But how is this accomplished in that croud of low, indigent people, who flock here every year from all parts of Europe? I will tell you; they no sooner arrive than they immediately feel the good effects of that plenty of provisions we possess: they fare on our best food, and are kindly entertained; their talents, character, and peculiar industry are immediately inquired into; they find countrymen everywhere disseminated, let them come from whatever part of Europe.

Let me select one as an epitome of the rest; he is hired, he goes to work, and works moderately; instead of being employed by a haughty person, he finds himself with his equal, placed at the substantial table of the farmer, or else at an inferior one as good; his wages are high, his bed is not like that bed of sorrow on which he used to lie: if he behaves with propriety, and is faithful, he is caressed, and becomes as it were a member of the family. He begins to feel the effects of a sort of resurrection; hitherto he had not lived, but simply vegetated; he now feels himself a man, because he is treated as such; the laws of his own country had overlooked him in his insignificancy; the laws of this cover him with their mantle. Judge what an alteration there must arise in the mind and thoughts of this man; he begins to forget his former servitude and dependence, his heart involuntarily swells and glows; this first swell inspires him with those new thoughts which constitute an American. What love can he entertain for a country where his existence was a burthen to him; if he is a generous good man, the love of this new adaptive parent will sink deep into his heart. He looks around, and sees many a prosperous person, who but a few years before was as poor as himself. This encourages him much, he begins to form some little scheme, the first, alas, he ever formed in his life. If he is wise he thus spends two or three years, in which time he acquires knowledge, the use of tools, the modes of working the lands, felling trees, &c. This prepares the foundation of a good name, the most useful acquisition he can make. He is encouraged, he has gained friends; he is advised and directed, he feels bold, he purchases some land; he gives all the money he has brought over, as well as what he has earned, and trusts to the God of harvests for the discharge of the rest. His good name procures him credit. He is now possessed of the deed, conveying to him and his posterity the fee simple and absolute property of two hundred acres of land, situated on such a river. What an epocha in this man's life! He is become a freeholder, from perhaps a German boor—he is now an American, a Pennsylvanian, an English subject. He is naturalized, his name is enrolled with those of the other citizens of the province. Instead of being a vagrant, he has a place of residence; he is called the inhabitant of such a county, or of such a district, and for the first time in his life counts for something; for hitherto he has been a her. I only repeat what I have heard man say, and no wonder their hearts should glow, and be agitated with a multitude of feelings, not easy to describe. From nothing to start into being; from a servant to the rank of a master; from being the slave of some despotic prince, to become a free man, invested with lands, to which every municipal blessing is annexed! What a change indeed! It is in consequence of that change that he becomes an American.

This great metamorphosis has a double effect, it extinguishes all his European prejudices, he forgets that mechanism of subordination, that servility of disposition which poverty had taught him; and sometimes he is apt to forget too much, often passing from one extreme to the other. If he is a good man, he forms schemes of future prosperity, he proposes to educate his children better than he has been educated himself; he thinks of future modes of conduct, feels an ardor to labour he never felt before. Pride steps in and leads him to every thing that the laws do not forbid: he respects them; with a heartfelt gratitude he looks toward the east, toward that insular government from whose wisdom all his new felicity is derived, and under whose wings and protection he now lives. These reflections constitute him the good man and the good subject.

Ye poor Europeans, ye, who sweat, and work for the great—ye, who are obliged to give so many sheaves to the church, so many to your lords, so many to your government, and have hardly any left for yourselves—ye, who are held in less estimation than favourite hunters or useless lap-dogs—ye, who only breathe the air of nature, because it cannot be withheld from you; it is here that ye can conceive the possibility of those feelings I have been describing; it is here the laws of naturalization invite every one to partake of our great labours and felicity, to till unrented, untaxed lands!

Many, corrupted beyond the power of amendment, have brought with them all their vices, and disregarding the advantages held to them, have gone on in their former career of iniquity, until they have been overtaken and punished by our laws. It is not every emigrant who succeeds; no, it is only the sober, the honest, and industrious: happy those to whom this transition has served as a powerful spur to labour, to prosperity, and to the good establishment of children, born in the days of their poverty; and who had no other portion to expect but the rags of their parents, had it not been for their happy emigration. Others again, have been led astray by this enchanting scene; their new pride, instead of leading them to the fields, has kept them in idleness; the idea of possessing lands is all that satisfies them—though surrounded with fertility, they have mouldered away their time in inactivity, misinformed husbandry, and ineffectual endeavours. How much wiser, in general, the honest Germans than almost all other Europeans; they hire themselves to some of their wealthy landsmen, and in that apprenticeship learn every thing that is necessary. They attentively consider the prosperous industry of others, which imprints in their minds a strong desire of possessing the same advantages. This forcible idea never quits them, they launch forth, and by dint of sobriety, rigid parsimony, and the most persevering industry, they commonly succeed. Their astonishment at their first arrival from Germany is very great—it is to them a dream; the contrast must be powerful indeed; they observe their countrymen flourishing in every place; they travel through whole counties where not a word of English is spoken; and in the names and the language of the people, they retrace Germany. They have been an useful acquisition to this continent, and to Pennsylvania in particular; to them it owes some share of its prosperity: to their mechanical knowledge and patience, it owes the finest mills in all America, the best teams of horses, and many other advantages. The recollection of their former poverty and slavery never quits them as long as they live.

The Scotch and the Irish might have lived in their own country perhaps as poor, but enjoying more civil advantages, the effects of their new situation do not strike them so forcibly, nor has it so lasting an effect. From whence the difference arises I know not, but out of twelve families of emigrants of each country, generally seven Scotch will succeed, nine German, and four Irish. The Scotch are frugal and laborious, but their wives cannot work so hard as German women, who on the contrary vie with their husbands, and often share with them the most severe toils of the field, which they understand better. They have therefore nothing to struggle against, but the common casualties of nature. The Irish do not prosper so well; they love to drink and to quarrel; they are litigious, and soon take to the gun, which is the ruin of every thing; they seem beside to labour under a greater degree of ignorance in husbandry than the others; perhaps it is that their industry had less scope, and was less exercised at home. I have heard many relate, how the land was parcelled out in that kingdom; their ancient conquest has been a great detriment to them, by oversetting their landed property. The lands possessed by a few, are leased down ad infinitum, and the occupiers often pay five guineas an acre. The poor are worse lodged there than any where else in Europe; their potatoes, which are easily raised, are perhaps an inducement to laziness: their ages are too low and their whisky too cheap.

There is no tracing observations of this kind, without making at the same time very great allowances, as there are every where to be found, a great many exceptions. The Irish themselves, from different parts of that kingdom, are very different. It is difficult to account for this surprising locality, one would think on so small an island an Irishman must be an Irishman: yet it is not so, they are different in their aptitude to, and in their love of labour.

The Scotch on the contrary are all industrious and saving; they want nothing more than a field to exert themselves in, and they are commonly sure of succeeding. The only difficulty they labour under is, that technical American knowledge which requires some time to obtain; it is not easy for those who seldom saw a tree, to conceive how it is to be felled, cut up, and split into rails and posts.

. . . After a foreigner from any part of Europe is arrived, and become a citizen; let him devoutly listen to the voice of our great parent, which says to him, "Welcome to my shores, distressed European; bless the hour in which thou didst see my verdant fields, my fair navigable rivers, and my green mountains! If thou wilt work, I have bread for thee; if thou wilt be honest, sober, and industrious, I have greater rewards to confer on thee—ease and independence. I will give thee fields to feed and cloath thee; a comfortable fireside to sit by, and tell thy children by what means thou hast prospered; and a decent bed to repose on. I shall endow thee beside with the immunities of a freeman. If thou wilt carefully educate thy children, teach them gratitude to God, and reverence to that government that philanthropic government, which has collected here so many men and made them happy. I will also provide for thy progeny; and to every good man this ought to be the most holy, the most Powerful, the most earnest wish he can possibly form, as well as the most consolatory prospect when he dies. Go thou and work and till; thou shalt prosper, provided thou be just, grateful and industrious."

Stranger in the Village

James Baldwin

Baldwin travels to a small European village and finds that his presence as a black man in a white society is perceived differently than it is in the United States. In what sense does Baldwin find this experience to be different, yet the same? How are white people in the United States different from white people in other cultures? Try to identify the ways in which Baldwin comes to some realizations about himself and the American culture that has oppressed him for so long.

From all available evidence no black man had ever set foot in this tiny Swiss village before I came. I was told before arriving that I would probably be a "sight" for the village; I took this to mean that people of my complexion were rarely seen in Switzerland, and also that city people are always something of a "sight" outside of the city. It did not occur to me—possibly because I am an American—that there could be people anywhere who had never seen a Negro.

It is a fact that cannot be explained on the basis of the inaccessibility of the village. The village is very high, but it is only four hours from Milan and three hours from Lausanne. It is true that it is virtually unknown. Few people making plans for a holiday would elect to come here. On the other hand, the villagers are able, presumably, to come and go as they please—which they do: to

From *Notes of a Native Son* by James Baldwin. Copyright © 1955, renewed 1983, by James Baldwin. Reprinted by permission of Beacon Press.

another town at the foot of the mountain, with a population of approximately five thousand, the nearest place to see a movie or go to the bank. In the village there is no movie house, no bank, no library, no theater; very few radios, one jeep, one station wagon; and, at the moment, one typewriter, mine, an invention which the woman next door to me here had never seen. There are about six hundred people living here, all Catholic—I conclude this from the fact that the Catholic church is open all year round, whereas the Protestant chapel, set off on a hill a little removed from the village, is open only in the summertime when the tourists arrive. There are four or five hotels, all closed now, and four or five *bistros,* of which, however, only two do any business during the winter. These two do not do a great deal, for life in the village seems to end around nine or ten o'clock. There are a few stores, butcher, baker, *épicerie,* a hardware store, and a money-changer—who cannot change travelers' checks, but must send them down to the bank, an operation which takes two or three days. There is something called the *Ballet Haus,* closed in the winter and used for God knows what, certainly not ballet, during the summer. There seems to be only one schoolhouse in the village, and this for the quite young children; I suppose this to mean that their older brothers and sisters at some point descend from these mountains in order to complete their education—possibly, again, to the town just below. The landscape is absolutely forbidding, mountains towering on all four sides, ice and snow as far as the eye can reach. In this white wilderness, men and women and children move all day, carrying washing, wood, buckets of milk or water, sometimes skiing on Sunday afternoons. All week long boys and young men are to be seen shoveling snow off the rooftops, or dragging wood down from the forest in sleds.

The village's only real attraction, which explains the tourist season, is the hot spring water. A disquietingly high proportion of these tourists are cripples, or semi-cripples, who come year after year—from other parts of Switzerland, usually—to take the waters. This lends the village, at the height of the season, a rather terrifying air of sanctity, as though it were a lesser Lourdes. There is often something beautiful, there is always something awful, in the spectacle of a person who has lost one of his faculties, a faculty he never questioned until it was gone, and who struggles to recover it. Yet people remain people, on crutches or indeed on deathbeds; and wherever I passed, the first summer I was here, among the native villagers or among the lame, a wind passed with me—of astonishment, curiosity, amusement, and outrage. The first summer I stayed two weeks and never intended to return. But I did return in the winter, to work; the village offers, obviously, no distractions whatever and has the further advantage of being extremely cheap. Now it is winter again, a year later, and I am here again. Everyone in the village knows my name, though they scarcely ever use it, knows that I come from America—though, this, apparently they will never really believe: black men come from Africa—and everyone knows that I am the friend of the son of a woman who was born here, and that I am staying in their chalet. But I remain as much a stranger today as I was the first day I arrived, and the children shout *Neger! Neger!* as I walk along the streets.

It must be admitted that in the beginning I was far too shocked to have any real reaction. In so far as I reacted at all, I reacted by trying to be pleasant—it being a great part of the American Negro's education (long before he goes to school) that he must make people "like" him. This smile-and-the-world-smiles-with-you routine worked about as well in this situation as it had in the situation for which it was designed, which is to say that it did not work at all. No one, after all, can be liked whose human weight and complexity cannot be, or has not been, admitted. My smile was simply another unheard-of phenomenon which allowed them to see my teeth—they did not, really, see my smile and I began to think that, should I take to snarling, no one would notice any difference. All of the physical characteristics of the Negro which had caused me, in America, a very different and almost forgotten pain were nothing less than miraculous—or infernal—in the eyes of the village people. Some thought my hair was the color of tar, that it had the texture of wire, or the texture of cotton. It was jocularly suggested that I might let it all grow long and make myself a winter coat. If I sat in the sun for more than five minutes some daring creature was certain to come along and gingerly put his fingers on my hair, as though he were afraid of an electric shock, or put his hand on my hand, astonished that the color did not rub off. In all of this, in which it must be conceded there was the charm of genuine wonder and in which there was certainly no element of intentional unkindness, there was yet no suggestion that I was human: I was simply a living wonder.

I knew that they did not mean to be unkind, and I know it now; it is necessary, nevertheless, for me to repeat this to myself each time I walk out of the chalet. The children who shout *Neger!* have no way of knowing the echoes this sound raises in me. They are brimming with good humor and the more daring swell with pride when I stop to speak with them. Just the same, there are days when I cannot pause and smile, when I have no heart to play with them; when, indeed, I mutter sourly to myself, exactly as I muttered on the streets of a city these children have never seen, when I was no bigger than these children are now: *Your mother was a nigger.* Joyce is right about history being a nightmare—but it may be the nightmare from which no one can awaken. People are trapped in history and history is trapped in them.

There is a custom in the village—I am told it is repeated in many villages—of "buying" African natives for the purpose of converting them to Christianity. There stands in the church all year round a small box with a slot for money, decorated with a black figurine, and into this box the villagers drop their francs. During the *carnaval* which precedes Lent, two village children have their faces blackened—out of which bloodless darkness their blue eyes shine like ice—and fantastic horsehair wigs are placed on their blond heads; thus disguised, they solicit among the villagers for money for the missionaries in Africa. Between the box in the church and the blackened children, the village "bought" last year six or eight African natives. This was reported to me with pride by the wife of one of the *bistro* owners and I was careful to express astonishment and pleasure at the solicitude shown by the village for the souls of black folk. The *bistro* owner's wife beamed with a pleasure far more genuine than my own and seemed to feel that I might now breathe more easily concerning the souls of at least six of my kinsmen.

I tried not to think of these so lately baptized kinsmen, of the price paid for them, or the peculiar price they themselves would pay, and said nothing about my father, who having taken his own conversion too literally never, at bottom, forgave the white world (which he described as heathen) for having saddled him with a Christ in whom, to judge at least from their treatment of him, they themselves no longer believed. I thought of white men arriving for the first time in an African village, strangers there, as I am a stranger here, and tried to imagine the astounded populace touching their hair and marveling at the color of their skin. But there is a great difference between being the first white man to be seen by Africans and being the first black man to be seen by whites. The white man takes the astonishment as tribute, for he arrives to conquer and to convert the natives, whose inferiority in relation to himself is not even to be questioned; whereas I, without a thought of conquest, find myself among a people whose culture controls me, has even, in a sense, created me, people who have cost me more in anguish and rage than they will ever know, who yet do not even know of my existence. The astonishment with which I might have greeted them, should they have stumbled into my African village a few hundred years ago, might have rejoiced their hearts. But the astonishment with which they greet me today can only poison mine.

And this is so despite everything I may do to feel differently, despite my friendly conversations with the *bistro* owner's wife, despite their three-year-old son who has at last become my friend, despite the *saluts* and *bonsoirs* which I exchange with people as I walk, despite the fact that I know that no individual can be taken to task for what history is doing, or has done. I say that the culture of these people controls me—but they can scarcely be held responsible for European culture. America comes out of Europe, but these people have never seen America nor have most of them seen more of Europe than the hamlet at the foot of their mountain. Yet they move with an authority which I shall never have; and they regard me, quite rightly, not only as a stranger in their village but as a suspect latecomer, bearing no credentials, to everything they have—however unconsciously—inherited.

For this village, even were it incomparably more remote and incredibly more primitive, is the West, the West onto which I have been so strangely grafted. These people cannot be, from the point of view of power, strangers anywhere in the world; they have made the modern world, in effect, even if they do not know it. The most illiterate among them is related, in a way that I am not, to Dante, Shakespeare, Michelangelo, Aeschylus, Da Vinci, Rembrandt, and Racine; the cathedral at Chartres says something to them which it cannot say to me, as indeed would New York's Empire State Building, should anyone here ever see it. Out of their hymns and dances come Beethoven and Bach. Go back a few centuries and they are in their full glory—but I am in Africa, watching the conquerors arrive.

The rage of the disesteemed is personally fruitless, but it is also absolutely inevitable; this rage, so generally discounted, so little understood even among the people whose daily bread it is, is one of the things that makes history. Rage can only with difficulty, and never entirely, be brought under the domination of the intelligence and is therefore not susceptible to any arguments whatever. This is a fact which ordinary representatives of the *Herrenvolk,* having never felt this rage and being unable to imagine it, quite fail to understand. Also, rage cannot be hidden, it can only be dissembled. This dissembling deludes the thoughtless, and strengthens rage and adds, to rage, contempt. There are, no doubt, as many ways of coping with the resulting complex of tensions as there are black men in the world, but no black man can hope ever to be entirely liberated from this internal warfare—rage, dissembling, and contempt having inevitably accompanied his first realization of the power of white men. What is crucial here is that, since white men represent in the black man's world so heavy a weight, white men have for black men a reality which is far from being reciprocal; and hence all black men have toward all white men an attitude which is designed, really, either to rob the white man of the jewel of his naïveté, or else to make it cost him dear.

The black man insists, by whatever means he finds at his disposal, that the white man cease to regard him as an exotic rarity and recognize him as a human being. This is a very charged and difficult moment, for there is a great deal of will power involved in the white man's naïveté. Most people are not naturally reflective any more than they are naturally malicious, and the white man prefers to keep the black man at a certain human remove because it is easier for him thus to preserve his simplicity and avoid being called to account for crimes committed by his forefathers, or his neighbors. He is inescapably aware, nevertheless, that he is in a better position in the world than black men are, nor can he quite put to death the suspicion that he is hated by black men therefore. He does not wish to be hated, neither does he wish to change places, and at this point in his uneasiness he can scarcely avoid having recourse to those legends which white men have created about black men, the most usual effect of which is that the white man finds himself enmeshed, so to speak, in his own language which describes hell, as well as the attributes which lead one to hell, as being as black as night.

Every legend, moreover, contains its residuum of truth, and the root function of language is to control the universe by describing it. It is of quite considerable significance that black men remain, in the imagination, and in overwhelming numbers in fact, beyond the disciplines of salvation; and this despite the fact the West has been "buying" African natives for centuries. There is, I should hazard, an instantaneous necessity to be divorced from this so visibly unsaved stranger, in whose heart, moreover, one cannot guess what dreams of vengeance are being nourished; and, at the same time, there are few things on earth more attractive than the idea of the unspeakable liberty which is allowed the unredeemed. When, beneath the black mask, a human being begins to make himself felt one cannot escape a certain awful wonder as to what kind of human being it is. What one's imagination makes of other people is dictated, of course, by the laws of one's own personality and it is one of the ironies of black-white relations that, by means of what the white man imagines the black man to be, the black man is enabled to know who the white man is.

I have said, for example, that I am as much a stranger in this village today as I was the first summer I arrived, but this is not quite true. The villagers wonder less about the texture of my hair than they did then, and wonder rather more about me. And the fact that their wonder now exists on another level is reflected in their attitudes and in their eyes. There are the children who make those delightful, hilarious, sometimes astonishingly grave overtures of friendship in the unpredictable fashion of children; other children, having been taught that the devil is a black man, scream in genuine anguish as I approach. Some of the older women never pass without a friendly greeting, never pass, indeed, if it seems that they will be able to engage me in conversation; other women look down or look away or rather contemptuously smirk. Some of the men drink with me and suggest that I learn how to ski—partly, I gather, because they cannot imagine what I would look like on skis—and want to know if I am married, and ask questions about my *métier.* But some of the men have accused *le sale négre*—behind my back—of stealing wood and there is already in the eyes of some of them that peculiar, intent, paranoiac malevolence which one sometimes surprises in the eyes of American white men when, out walking with their Sunday girl, they see a Negro male approach.

There is a dreadful abyss between the streets of this village and the streets of the city in which I was born, between the children who shout *Neger!* today and those who shouted *Nigger!* yesterday—the abyss is experience, the American experience. The syllable hurled behind me today expresses, above all, wonder: I am a stranger here. But I am not a stranger in America and the same syllable riding on the American air expresses the war my presence has occasioned in the American soul.

For this village brings home to me this fact: that there was a day, and not really a very distant day, when Americans were scarcely Americans at all but discontented Europeans, facing a great unconquered continent and strolling, say, into a marketplace and seeing black men for the first time. The shock this spectacle afforded is suggested, surely, by the promptness with which they decided that these black men were not really men but cattle. It is true that the necessity on the part of the settlers of the New World of reconciling their moral assumptions with the fact—and the necessity—of slavery enhanced immensely the charm of this idea, and it is also true that this idea expresses, with a truly American bluntness, the attitude which to varying extents all masters have had toward all slaves.

But between all former slaves and slave-owners and the drama which begins for Americans over three hundred years ago at Jamestown, there are at least two differences to be observed. The American Negro slave could not suppose, for one thing, as slaves in past epochs had supposed and often done, that he would ever be able to wrest the power from his master's hands. This was a supposition which the modern era, which was to bring about such vast changes in the aims and dimensions of power, put to death; it only begins, in unprecedented fashion, and with dreadful implications, to be resurrected today. But even had this supposition persisted with undiminished force, the American Negro slave could not have used it to lend his condition dignity, for the reason that this supposition rests on another: that the slave in exile yet remains related to his past, has some means—if only in memory—of revering and sustaining the forms of his former life, is able, in short, to maintain his identity.

This was not the case with the American Negro slave. He is unique among the black men of the world in that his past was taken from him, almost literally, at one blow. One wonders what on earth the first slave found to say to the first dark child he bore. I am told that there are Haitians able to trace their ancestry back to African kings, but any American Negro wishing to go back so far will find his journey through time abruptly arrested by the signature on the bill of sale which served as the entrance paper for his ancestor. At the time—to say nothing of the circumstances—of the enslavement of the captive black man who was to become the American Negro, there was not the remotest possibility that he would ever take power from his master's hands. There was no reason to suppose that his situation would ever change, nor was there, shortly, anything to indicate that his situation had ever been different. It was his necessity, in the words of E. Franklin Frazier, to find a "motive for living under American culture or die." The identity of the American Negro comes out of this extreme situation, and the evolution of this identity was a source of the most intolerable anxiety in the minds and the lives of his masters.

For the history of the American Negro is unique also in this: that the question of his humanity, and of his rights therefore as a human being, became a burning one for several generations of Americans, so burning a question that it ultimately became one of those used to divide the nation. It is out of this argument that the venom of the epithet *Nigger!* is derived. It is an argument which Europe has never had, and hence Europe quite sincerely fails to understand how or why the argument arose in the first place, why its effects are so frequently disastrous and always so unpredictable, why it refuses until today to be entirely settled. Europe's black possessions remained—and do remain—in Europe's colonies, at which remove they represented no threat whatever to European identity. If they posed any problem at all for the European conscience, it was a problem which remained comfortingly abstract: in effect, the black man, *as a man,* did not exist for Europe. But in America, even as a slave, he was an inescapable part of the general social fabric and no American could escape having an attitude toward him. Americans attempt until today to make an abstraction of the Negro, but the very nature of these abstractions reveals the tremendous effects the presence of the Negro has had on the American character.

When one considers the history of the Negro in America it is of the greatest importance to recognize that the moral beliefs of a person, or a people, are never really as tenuous as life—which is not moral—very often causes them to appear; these create for them a frame of reference and a necessary hope, the hope being that when life has done its worst they will be enabled to rise above themselves and to triumph over life. Life would scarcely be bearable if this hope did not exist. Again, even when the worst has been said, to betray a belief is not by any means to have put oneself beyond its power; the betrayal of a belief is not the same thing as ceasing to believe. If this were not so there would be no moral standards in the world at all. Yet one must also recognize that morality is based on ideas and that all ideas are dangerous—dangerous because ideas can only lead to action and where the action leads no man can say. And dangerous in this respect: that confronted with the impossibility of becoming free of them, one can be driven to the most inhuman excesses. The ideas on which American beliefs are based are not, though Americans often seem to think so, ideas which originated in America. They came out of Europe. And the establishment of democracy on the American continent was scarcely as radical a break with the past as was the necessity, which Americans faced, of broadening this concept to include black men.

This was, literally, a hard necessity. It was impossible, for one thing, for Americans to abandon their beliefs, not only because these beliefs alone seemed able to justify the sacrifices they had endured and the blood that they had spilled, but also because these beliefs afforded them their only bulwark against a moral chaos as absolute as the physical chaos of the continent it was their destiny to conquer. But in the situation in which Americans found themselves, these beliefs threatened an idea which, whether or not one likes to think so, is the very warp and woof of the heritage of the West, the idea of white supremacy.

Americans have made themselves notorious by the shrillness and the brutality with which they have insisted on this idea, but they did not invent it; and it has escaped the world's notice that those very excesses of which Americans have been guilty imply a certain, unprecedented uneasiness over the idea's life and power, if not, indeed, the idea's validity. The idea of white supremacy rests simply on the fact that white men are the creators of civilization (the present civilization, which is the only one that matters; all previous civilizations are simply "contributions" to our own) and are therefore civilization's, guardians and defenders. Thus it was impossible for Americans to accept the black man as one of themselves, for to do so was to jeopardize their status as white men.

But not so to accept him was to deny his human reality, his human weight and complexity, and the strain of denying the overwhelmingly undeniable forced Americans into rationalizations so fantastic that they approached the pathological.

At the root of the American Negro problem is the necessity of the American white man to find a way of living with the Negro in order to be able to live with himself. And the history of this problem can be reduced to the means used by Americans—lynch law and law, segregation and legal acceptance, terrorization and concession—either to come to terms with this necessity, or to find a way around it, or (most usually) to find a way of doing both these things at once. The resulting spectacle, at once foolish and dreadful, led someone to make the quite accurate observation that "the Negro-in-America is a form of insanity which overtakes white men."

In this long battle, a battle by no means finished, the unforeseeable effects of which will be felt by many future generations, the white man's motive was the protection of his identity; the black man was motivated by the need to establish an identity. And despite the terrorization which the Negro in America endured and endures sporadically until today, despite the cruel and totally inescapable ambivalence of his status in his country, the battle for his identity has long ago been won. He is not a visitor to the West, but a citizen there, an American; as American as the Americans who despise him, the Americans who fear him, the Americans who love him—the Americans who became less than themselves, or rose to be greater than themselves by virtue of the fact that the challenge he represented was inescapable. He is perhaps the only black man in the world whose relationship to white men is more terrible, more subtle, and more meaningful than the relationship of bitter possessed to uncertain possessor. His survival depended, and his development depends, on his ability to turn his peculiar status in the Western world to his own advantage and, it may be, to the very great advantage of that world. It remains for him to fashion out of his experience that which will give him sustenance, and a voice.

The cathedral at Chartres, I have said, says something to the people of this village which it cannot say to me; but it is important to understand that this cathedral says something to me which it cannot say to them. Perhaps they are struck by the power of the spires, the glory of the windows; but they have known God, after all, longer than I have known him, and in a different way, and I am terrified by the slippery bottomless well to be found in the crypt, down which heretics were hurled to death, and by the obscene, inescapable gargoyles jutting out of the stone and seeming to say that God and the devil can never be divorced. I doubt that the villagers think of the devil when they face a cathedral because they have never been identified with the devil. But I must accept the status which myth, if nothing else, gives me in the West before I can hope to change the myth.

Yet, if the American Negro has arrived at his identity by virtue of the absoluteness of his estrangement from his past, American white men still nourish the illusion that there is some means of recovering the European innocence, of returning to a state in which black men do not exist. This is one of the greatest errors Americans can make. The identity they fought so hard to protect has, by virtue of that battle, undergone a change: Americans are as unlike any other white people in the world as it is possible to be. I do not think, for example, that it is too much to suggest that the American vision of the world—which allows so little reality, generally speaking, for any of the darker forces in human life, which tends until today to paint moral issues in glaring black and white—owes a great deal to the battle waged by Americans to maintain between themselves and black men a human separation which could not be bridged. It is only now beginning to be borne in on us—very faintly, it must be admitted, very slowly, and very much against our will—that this vision of the world is dangerously inaccurate, and perfectly useless. For it protects our moral high-mindedness at the terrible expense of weakening our grasp of reality. People who shut their eyes to reality simply invite their own destruction, and anyone who insists on remaining in a state of innocence long after that innocence is dead turns himself into a monster.

The time has come to realize that the interracial drama acted out on the American continent has not only created a new black man, it has created a new white man, too. No road whatever will lead Americans back to the simplicity of this European village where white men still have the luxury of looking on me as a stranger. I am not, really, a stranger any longer for any American alive. One of the things that distinguishes Americans from other people is that no other people has ever been so deeply involved in the lives of black men, and vice versa. This fact faced, with all its implications, it can be seen that the history of the American Negro problem is not merely shameful, it is also something of an achievement. For even when the worst has been said, it must also be added that the perpetual challenge posed by this problem was always, somehow, perpetually met. It is precisely this black-white experience which may prove of indispensable value to us in the world we face today. This world is white no longer, and it will never be white again.

Where I Come From Is Like This

Paula Gunn Allen

Paula Gunn Allen examines her identity as one that has been formed by two distinct cultures. More problematically, one of these cultural heritages has been inappropriately stereotyped and mischaracterized in Western histories. She asks us to understand the true power and wisdom of women in Native American culture, and how remembering the stories of Native American women helps form her identity as a woman.

I

Modern American Indian women, like their non-Indian sisters, are deeply engaged in the struggle to redefine themselves. In their struggle they must reconcile traditional tribal definitions of women with industrial and postindustrial non-Indian definitions. Yet while these definitions seem to be more or less mutually exclusive, Indian women must somehow harmonize and integrate both in their own lives.

From *The Sacred Hoop* by Paula Gunn Allen. Copyright © 1986 by Paula Gunn Allen. Reprinted by permission of Beacon Press, Boston.

An American Indian woman is primarily defined by her tribal identity. In her eyes, her destiny is necessarily that of her people, and her sense of herself as a woman is first and foremost prescribed by her tribe. The definitions of woman's roles are as diverse as tribal cultures in the Americas. In some she is devalued, in others she wields considerable power. In some she is a familial/clan adjunct, in some she is as close to autonomous as her economic circumstances and psychological traits permit. But in no tribal definitions is she perceived in the same way as are women in western industrial and postindustrial cultures.

In the west, few images of women form part of the cultural mythos, and these are largely sexually charged. Among Christians, the madonna is the female prototype, and she is portrayed as essentially passive: her contribution is simply that of birthing. Little else is attributed to her and she certainly possesses few of the characteristics that are attributed to mythic figures among Indian tribes. This image is countered (rather than balanced) by the witch-goddess/whore characteristics designed to reinforce cultural beliefs about women, as well as western adversarial and dualistic perceptions of reality.

The tribes see women variously, but they do not question the power of femininity. Sometimes they see women as fearful, sometimes peaceful, sometimes omnipotent and omniscient, but they never portray women as mindless, helpless, simple, or oppressed. And while the women in a given tribe, clan, or band may be all these things, the individual woman is provided with a variety of images of women from the interconnected supernatural, natural, and social worlds she lives in.

As a half-breed American Indian woman, I cast about in my mind for negative images of Indian women, and I find none that are directed to Indian women alone. The negative images I do have are of Indians in general and in fact are more often of males than of females. All these images come to me from non-Indian sources, and they are always balanced by a positive image. My ideas of womanhood, passed on largely by my mother and grandmothers, Laguna Pueblo women, are about practicality, strength, reasonableness, intelligence, wit, and competence. I also remember vividly the women who came to my father's store, the women who held me and sang to me, the women at Feast Day, at Grab Days, the women in the kitchen of my Cubero home, the women I grew up with; none of them appeared weak or helpless, none of them presented herself tentatively. I remember a certain reserve on those lovely brown faces; I remember the direct gaze of eyes framed by bright-colored shawls draped over their heads and cascading down their backs. I remember the clean cotton dresses and carefully pressed hand-embroidered aprons they always wore; I remember laughter and good food, especially the sweet bread and the oven bread they gave us. Nowhere in my mind is there a foolish woman, a dumb woman, a vain woman, or a plastic woman, though the Indian women I have known have shown a wide range of personal style and demeanor.

My memory includes the Navajo woman who was badly beaten by her Sioux husband; but I also remember that my grandmother abandoned her Sioux husband long ago. I recall the stories about the Laguna woman beaten regularly by her husband in the presence of her children so that the children would not believe in the strength and power of femininity. And I remember the women who drank, who got into fights with other women and with the men, and who often won those battles. I have memories of tired women, partying women, stubborn women, sullen women, amicable women, selfish women, shy women, and aggressive women. Most of all I remember the women who laugh and scold and sit uncomplaining in the long sun on feast days and who cook wonderful food on wood stoves, in beehive mud ovens, and over open fires outdoors.

Among the images of women that come to me from various tribes as well as my own are White Buffalo Woman, who came to the Lakota long ago and brought them the religion of the Sacred Pipe which they still practice; Tinotzin the goddess who came to Juan Diego to remind him that she still walked the hills of her people and sent him with her message, her demand and her proof to the Catholic bishop in the city nearby. And from Laguna I take the images of Yellow Woman, Coyote Woman, Grandmother Spider (Spider Old Woman), who brought the light, who gave us weaving and medicine, who gave us life. Among the Keres she is known as Thought Woman who created us all and who keeps us in creation even now. I remember Iyatiku, Earth Woman, Corn Woman, who guides and counsels the people to peace and who welcomes us home when we cast off this coil of flesh as huskers cast off the leaves that wrap the corn. I remember Iyatiku's sister, Sun Woman, who held metals and cattle, pigs and sheep, highways and engines and so many things in her bundle, who went away to the east saying that one day she would return.

II

Since the coming of the Anglo-Europeans beginning in the fifteenth century, the fragile web of identity that long held tribal people secure has gradually been weakened and torn. But the oral tradition has prevented the complete destruction of the web, the ultimate disruption of tribal ways. The oral tradition is vital; it heals itself and the tribal web by adapting to the flow of the present while never relinquishing its connection to the past. Its adaptability has always been required, as many generations have experienced. Certainly the modern American Indian woman bears slight resemblance to her forebears—at least on superficial examination—but she is still a tribal woman in her deepest being. Her tribal sense of relationship to all that is continues to flourish. And though she is at times beset by her knowledge of the enormous gap between the life she lives and the life she was raised to live, and while she adapts her mind and being to the circumstances of her present life, she does so in tribal ways, mending the tears in the web of being from which she takes her existence as she goes.

My mother told me stories all the time, though I often did not recognize them as that. My mother told me stories about cooking and childbearing; she told me stories about menstruation and pregnancy; she told me stories about gods and heroes, about fairies and elves, about goddesses and spirits; she told me stories about the land and the sky, about cats and dogs, about snakes and spiders; she told me stories about climbing trees and exploring the mesas; she told me stories about going to dances and getting married; she told me stories about dressing and undressing, about sleeping and waking; she told me stories about herself, about her mother, about her grandmother. She told me stories about grieving and laughing, about thinking and doing; she told me stories about school and about people; about darning and mending; she told me stories about turquoise and about gold; she told me European stories and Laguna stories; she told me Catholic stories and Presbyterian stories; she told me city stories and country stories; she told me political stories and religious stories. She told me stories about living and stories about dying. And in all of those stories she told me who I was, who I was supposed to be, who I came from, and who would follow me. In this way she taught me the meaning of the words she said, that all life is a circle and everything has a place within it. That's what she said and what she showed me in the things she did and the way she lives.

Of course, through my formal, white, Christian education, I discovered that other people had stories of their own—about women, about Indians, about fact, about reality—and I was amazed by a number of startling suppositions that others made about tribal customs and beliefs. According to the un-Indian, non-Indian view, for instance, Indians barred menstruating women from ceremonies and indeed segregated them from the rest of the people, consigning them to some space especially designed for them. This showed that Indians considered menstruating women unclean and not fit to enjoy the company of decent (nonmenstruating) people, that is, men. I was surprised and confused to hear this because my mother had taught me that white people had strange attitudes toward menstruation: they thought something was bad about it, that it meant you were sick, cursed, sinful, and weak and that you had to be very careful during that time. She taught me that menstruation was a normal occurrence, that I could go swimming or hiking or whatever else I wanted to do during my period. She actively scorned women who took to their beds, who were incapacitated by cramps, who "got the blues."

As I struggled to reconcile these very contradictory interpretations of American Indians' traditional beliefs concerning menstruation, I realized that the menstrual taboos were about power, not about sin or filth. My conclusion was later borne out by some tribes' own explanations, which, as you may well imagine, came as quite a relief to me.

The truth of the matter as many Indians see it is that women who are at the peak of their fecundity are believed to possess power that throws male power totally out of kilter. They emit such force that, in their presence, any male-owned or -dominated ritual or sacred object cannot do its usual task. For instance, the Lakota say that a menstruating woman anywhere near a yuwipi man, who is a special sort of psychic, spirit-empowered healer, for a day or so before he is to do his ceremony will effectively disempower him. Conversely, among many if not most tribes, important ceremonies cannot be held without the presence of women. Sometimes the ritual woman who empowers the ceremony must be unmarried and virginal so that the power she channels is unalloyed, unweakened by sexual arousal and penetration by a male. Other ceremonies require tumescent women, others the presence of mature women who have borne children, and still others depend for empowerment on postmenopausal women. Women may be segregated from the company of the whole band or village on certain occasions, but on certain occasions men are also segregated. In short, each ritual depends on a certain balance of power, and the positions of women within the phases of womanhood are used by tribal people to empower certain rites. This does not derive from a male-dominant view; it is not a ritual observance imposed on women by men. It derives from a tribal view of reality that distinguishes tribal people from feudal and industrial people.

Among the tribes, the occult power of women, inextricably bound to our hormonal life, is thought to be very great; many hold that we possess innately the blood-given power to kill—with a glance, with a step, or with a judicious mixing of menstrual blood into somebody's soup. Medicine women among the Pomo of California cannot practice until they are sufficiently mature; when they are immature, their power is diffuse and is likely to interfere with their practice until time and experience have it under control. So women of the tribes are not especially inclined to see themselves as poor helpless victims of male domination. Even in those tribes where something akin to male domination was present, women are perceived as powerful, socially, physically, and metaphysically. In times past, as in times present, women carried enormous burdens with aplomb. We were far indeed from the "weaker sex," the designation that white aristocratic sisters unhappily earned for us all.

I remember my mother moving furniture all over the house when she wanted it changed. She didn't wait for my father to come home and help—she just went ahead and moved the piano, a huge upright from the old days, the couch, the refrigerator. Nobody had told her she was too weak to do such things. In imitation of her, I would delight in loading trucks at my father's store with cases of pop or fifty-pound sacks of flour. Even when I was quite small I could do it, and it gave me a belief in my own physical strength that advancing middle age can't quite erase. My mother used to tell me about the Acoma Pueblo women she had seen as a child carrying huge ollas (water pots) on their heads as they wound their way up the tortuous stairwell carved into the face of the "Sky City" mesa, a feat I tried to imitate with books and tin buckets. ("Sky City" is the term used by the Chamber of Commerce for the mother village of Acoma, which is situated atop a high sandstone table mountain.) I was never very successful, but even the attempt reminded me that I was supposed to be strong and balanced to be a proper girl.

Of course, my mother's Laguna people are Keres Indian, reputed to be the last extreme mother-right people on earth. So it is no wonder that I got notably nonwhite notions about the natural strength and prowess of women. Indeed, it is only when I am trying to get non-Indian approval, recognition, or acknowledgment that my "weak sister" emotional and intellectual ploys get the better of my tribal woman's good sense. At such times I forget that I just moved the piano or just wrote a competent paper or just completed a financial transaction satisfactorily or have supported myself and my children for most of my adult life.

Nor is my contradictory behavior atypical. Most Indian women I know are in the same bicultural bind; we vacillate between being dependent and strong, self-reliant and powerless, strongly motivated and hopelessly insecure. We resolve the dilemma in various ways: some of us party all the time; some of us drink to excess; some of us travel and move around a lot; some of us land good jobs and then quit them; some of us engage in violent exchanges; some of us blow our brains out. We act in these destructive ways because we suffer from the societal conflicts caused by having to identify with two hopelessly opposed cultural definitions of women. Through this destructive dissonance we are unhappy prey to the self-disparagement common to, indeed demanded of, Indians living in the United States today. Our situation is caused by the exigencies of a history of invasion, conquest, and colonization whose searing marks are probably ineradicable. A popular bumper sticker on many Indian cars proclaims: "If You're Indian You're In," to which I always find myself adding under my breath, "Trouble."

III

No Indian can grow to any age without being informed that her people were "savages" who interfered with the march of progress pursued by respectable, loving, civilized white people. We are the villains of the scenario when we are mentioned at all. We are absent from much of white history except when we are calmly, rationally, succinctly, and systematically dehumanized. On the few occasions we are noticed in any way other than as howling, bloodthirsty beings, we are acclaimed for our noble quaintness. In this definition, we are exotic curios. Our ancient arts and customs are used to draw tourist money to state coffers, into the pocketbooks and bank accounts of scholars, and into support of the American-in-Disneyland promoters' dream.

As a Roman Catholic child I was treated to bloody tales of how the savage Indians martyred the hapless priests and missionaries who went among them in an attempt to lead them to the one true path. By the time I was through high school I had the idea that Indians were people who had benefited mightily from the advanced knowledge and superior morality of the Anglo-Europeans. At least I had, perforce, that idea to lay beside the other one that derived from my daily experience of Indian life, an idea less dehumanizing and more accurate because it came from my mother and the other Indian people who raised me. That idea was that Indians are a people who don't tell lies, who care for their children and their old people. You never see an Indian orphan, they said. You always know when you're old that someone will take care of you—one of your children will. Then they'd list the old folks who were being taken care of by this child or that. No child is ever considered illegitimate among the Indians, they said. If a girl gets pregnant, the baby is still part of the family, and the mother is too. That's what they said, and they showed me real people who lived according to those principles.

Of course the ravages of colonization have taken their toll; there are orphans in Indian country now, and abandoned, brutalized old folks; there are even illegitimate children, though the very concept still strikes me as absurd. There are battered children and neglected children, and there are battered wives and women who have been raped by Indian men. Proximity to the "civilizing" effects of white Christians has not improved the moral quality of life in Indian country, though each group, Indian and white, explains the situation differently. Nor is there much yet in the oral tradition that can enable us to adapt to these inhuman changes. But a force is growing in that direction, and it is helping Indian women reclaim their lives. Their power, their sense of direction and of self will soon be visible. It is the force of the women who speak and work and write, and it is formidable.

Through all the centuries of war and death and cultural and psychic destruction have endured the women who raise the children and tend the fires, who pass along the tales and the traditions, who weep and bury the dead, who are the dead, and who never forget. There are always the women, who make pots and weave baskets, who fashion clothes and cheer their children on at powwow, who make fry bread and piki bread, and corn soup and chili stew, who dance and sing and remember and hold within their hearts the dream of their ancient peoples—that one day the woman who thinks will speak to us again, and everywhere there will be peace. Meanwhile we tell the stories and write the books and trade tales of anger and woe and stories of fun and scandal and laugh over all manner of things that happen every day. We watch and we wait.

My great-grandmother told my mother: Never forget you are Indian. And my mother told me the same thing. This, then, is how I have gone about remembering, so that my children will remember too.

National Socialism: *Volk* and Racial Supremacy

U.S. Department of State

In 1943, the U.S. Department of State issued a study of the various components of National Socialism in order to explain to the American people the essential characteristics of Nazi ideology. In this excerpt from that study, we discover what proponents of that ideology meant by volk *or "people," and how they saw this concept related to a political unity and a concept of state. More important, we are given an explanation of how they saw the relationship between the concepts of* volk *and "race." This relationship would eventually give rise to a concept of* Herrenvolk *or a master race. As you read about these concepts, consider the ways in which a racial consciousness can lead to false concepts of racial superiority and, eventually, to genocide.*

THE VOLK

Ernst Rudolf Huber, in his basic work *Verfassungsrecht des grossdeutschen Reiches (Constitutional Law of the Greater German Reich)*, published in 1939, states:

> The new constitution of the German Reich . . . is not a constitution in the formal sense such as was typical of the nineteenth century. The new Reich has no written constitutional declaration, but its constitution exists in the unwritten basic political order of the Reich. One recognizes it in the spiritual powers which fill our people, in the real authority in which our political life is grounded, and in the basic laws regarding the structure of the state which have been proclaimed so far. The advantage of such an unwritten constitution over the formal constitution is that the basic principles do not become rigid but remain in a constant, living movement. Not dead institutions but living principles determine the nature of the new constitutional order.

In developing his thesis Huber points out that the National Socialist state rests on three basic concepts, the *Volk* or people, the Führer, and the movement or party. With reference to the first element, the *Volk*, he argues that the democracies develop their concept of the people from the wrong approach: They start with the concept of the state and its functions and consider the people as being made up of all the elements which fall within the borders or under the jurisdiction of the state. National Socialism, on the other hand, starts with the concept of the people, which forms a political unity, and builds the state upon this foundation.

> There is no people without an objective unity, but there is also none without a common consciousness of unity. A people is determined by a number of different factors: by racial derivation and by the character of its land, by language and other forms of life, by religion and history, but also by the common consciousness of its solidarity and by its common will to unity. For the concrete concept of a people, as represented by the various peoples of the earth, it is of decisive significance which of these various factors they regard as determinants for the nature of the people. The new German Reich proceeds from the concept of the political people, determined by the natural characteristics

From *National Socialism* edited by Raymond E. Murphy et al. Washington, D.C.: Government Printing Office, 1943, pp. 23–25, 28–36, 39, 41.

and by the historical idea of a closed community. The political people is formed through the uniformity of its natural characteristics. Race is the natural basis of the people. . . . As a political people the natural community becomes conscious of its solidarity and strives to form itself, to develop itself, to defend itself, to realize itself. "Nationalism" is essentially this striving of a people which has become conscious of itself toward self-direction and self-realization, toward a deepening and renewing of its natural qualities.

This consciousness of self, springing from the consciousness of a historical idea, awakens in a people its will to historical formation: the will to action. The political people is no passive, sluggish mass, no mere object for the efforts of the state at government or protective welfare work. . . . The great misconception of the democracies is that they can see the active participation of the people only in the form of plebiscites according to the principle of majority. In a democracy the people does not act as a unit but as a complex of unrelated individuals who form themselves into parties. . . . The new Reich is based on the principle that real action of a self-determining people is only possible according to the principle of leadership and following.

According to Huber, geographical considerations play a large part in the shaping of a people:

The people stands in a double relation, to its lands; it settles and develops the land, but the land also stamps and determines the people. . . . That a certain territory belongs to a certain people is not justified by state authority alone but it is also determined objectively by its historical, political position. Territory is not merely a field for the exercise of state control but it determines the nature of a people and thereby the historical purpose of the state's activity. England's island position, Italy's Mediterranean position, and Germany's central position between east and west are such historical conditions, which unchangeably form the character of the people.

But the new Germany is based upon a "unity and entirety of the people" which does not stop at geographical boundaries:

The German people forms a closed community which recognizes no national borders. It is evident that a people has not exhausted its possibilities simply in the formation of a national state but that it represents an independent community which reaches beyond such limits.

The state justifies itself only so far as it helps the people to develop itself more fully. In the words of Hitler, quoted by Huber from *Mein Kampf,* " 'It is a basic principle, therefore, that the state represents not an end but a means. It is a condition for advanced human culture, but not the cause of it. . . . Its purpose is in the maintenance and advancement of a community of human beings with common physical and spiritual characteristics.' "

Huber continues:

In the theory of the folk-Reich [*völkisches Reich*], people and state are conceived as an inseparable unity. The people is the prerequisite for the entire political order; the state does not form the people but the people moulds the state out of itself as the form in which it achieves historical permanence. . . .

"The state is a function of the people, but it is not therefore a subordinate, secondary machine which can be used or laid aside at will. It is the form in which the people attains to historical reality. It is the bearer of the historical community of the people, which remains the same in the center of its being in spite of all changes, revolutions, and transformations." . . .

Some of the most striking expressions of the race concept are found in *Die Erziehung im dritten Reich* (*Education in the Third Reich*), by Friedrich Alfred Beck, which was published in 1936. It is worthy of note that the tendency which may be observed in Huber . . .

and Neesse to associate the ideas of *Volk* and race is very marked with Beck. "All life, whether natural or spiritual, all historical progress, all state forms, and all cultivation by education are in the last analysis based upon the racial make-up of the people in question." *Race* finds its expression in human life through the phenomenon of the *people*:

> *Race* and *people* belong together. National Socialism has restored the concept of the people from its modern shallowness and sees in the people something different from and appreciably greater than a chance social community of men, a grouping of men who have the same external interests. By *people* we understand an entire living body which is racially uniform and which is held together by common history, common fate, a common mission, and common tasks. Through such an interpretation the people takes on a significance which is only attributed to it in times of great historical importance and which makes it the center, the content, and the goal of all human work. Only that race still possesses vital energy which can still bring its unity to expression in the totality of the people. The people is the space in which race can develop its strength. Race is the vital law of arrangement which gives the people its distinctive form. In the course of time the people undergoes historical transformations, but race prevents the loss of the people's own nature in the course of these transformations. Without the people the race has no life; without race the people has no permanence. . . . Education, from the standpoint of race and people, is the creation of a form of life in which the racial unity will be preserved through the totality of the people.

Beck describes the politically spiritual National Socialist personality which National Socialist education seeks to develop, in the following terms:

> Socialism is the direction of personal life through dependence on the community, consciousness of the community, feeling for the community, and action in the community; nationalism is the elevation of individual life to a unique (microcosmic) expression of the community in the unity of the personality.

National Socialist education must stress the heroic life and teach German youth the importance of fulfilling their duty to the *Volk*.

> Heroism is that force and that conviction which consecrates its whole life to the service of an idea, a faith, a task, or a duty even when it knows that the destruction of its own life is certain. . . . German life, according to the laws of its ideology, is heroic life. . . . All German life, every person belonging to the community of Germans must bear heroic character within himself. Heroic life fulfils itself in the daily work of the miner, the farmer, the clerk, the statesman, and the serving self-sacrifice of the mother. Wherever a life is devoted with an all-embracing faith and with its full powers to the service of some value, there is true heroism. . . . Education to the heroic life is education fulfilment of duty. . . . One must have experienced it repeatedly that the inner fruition of a work in one's own life has nothing to do with material or economic considerations, that man keeps all of his faculties alive through his obligation to his work and his devotion to his duty, and that he uses them in the service of an idea without any regard for practical considerations, before one recognizes the difference between this world of heroic self-sacrifice and the liberalistic world of barter. Because the younger generation has been brought up in this heroic spirit it is no longer understood by the representatives of the former era who judge the values of life according to material advantage. . . . German life is heroic life. Germany is not a mere community of existence and of interests whose only function is to insure the material and cultural needs of its members, but it also represents an elemental obligation on the part of the members. The eternal Germany cannot be drawn in on the map; it does not consist of the constitution or the laws of the state. This Germany is the com-

munity of those who are solemnly bound together and who experience and realize these eternal national values. This Germany is our eternal mission, our most sacred law. . . . The developing personality must be submerged in the living reality of the people and the nation from earliest youth on, must take an active and a suffering part in it. Furthermore the heroic life demands a recognition and experiencing of the highest value of life which man must serve with all his powers. This value can perhaps be recognized and presented theoretically in the schools but it can only be directly comprehended and personally experienced in the community of the people. Therefore all education must preserve this *direct connection with the community of the people* and school education must derive from it the form and substance of its instruction.

This nationalism, which is based upon the laws of life, has nothing in common with the weak and presumptuous patriotism of the liberalistic world; it is not a gift or a favor, not a possession or a privilege, but it is the form of national life which we have won in hard battle and which suits our Nordic-German racial and spiritual heritage. In the nationalistic personality the powers and values which have been established in the socialistic personality will be purposefully exerted for the perfection of the temporal and eternal idea of life. . . .

Such indeed is the supreme goal of all National Socialist education: to make each individual an expression of "the eternal German":

Whoever wishes fully to realize himself, whoever wishes to experience and embody the eternal German ideal within himself must lift his eyes from everyday life and must listen to the beat of his blood and his conscience. . . . He must be capable of that superhuman greatness which is ready to cast aside all temporal bonds in the battle for German eternity. . . . National Socialist education raises the eternal German character into the light of our consciousness. . . . National Socialism is the eternal law of our German life; the development of the eternal German is the transcendental task of National Socialist education.

RACIAL SUPREMACY

The theory of the racial supremacy of the Nordic, *i.e.* the German, which was developed by Wagner and Stewart Chamberlain reaches its culmination in the writings of Alfred Rosenberg, the high priest of Nazi racial theory and herald of the *Herrenvolk* (master race). Rosenberg developed his ideas in the obscure phraseology of *Der Mythus des 20. Jahrhunderts* (*The Myth of the Twentieth Century*). "The 'meaning of world history,' " he wrote, "has radiated out from the north over the whole world, borne by a blue-eyed blond race which in several great waves determined the spiritual face of the world. . . . These wander-periods were the legendary migration of the Atlantides across north Africa, the migration of the Aryans into India and Persia; the migration of Dorians, Macedonians, Latins; the migration of the Germanic tribes; the colonization of the world by the Germanic occident." He discusses at length Indian, Persian, Greek, Roman, and European cultures; in each case, he concludes, the culture is created by the ruling Nordic element and declines through the racial decay of the Nordics resulting from their intermixture with inferior races.

It has long been accepted, Rosenberg claims, that all the states of the West and their creative values have been generated by Germans; and it follows that if the Germanic blood were to vanish away completely in Europe all Western culture would also fall to ruin.

Rosenberg acclaims the new faith of the blood which is to replace the non-German religion of Christianity. "A *new* faith is arising today: the myth of the blood, the faith to defend with the blood the divine essence of man. The faith, embodied in clearest knowledge, that the Nordic blood represents that *mysterium* which has replaced and overcome the old sacraments."

Rosenberg accepts the classic German view of the *Volk,* which he relates closely to the concept of race.

> The state is nowadays no longer an independent idol, before which everything must bow down; the state is not even an end but is only a means for the preservation of the folk. . . . Forms of the state change, and laws of the state pass away; the folk remains. From this alone follows that the nation is the first and *last,* that to which everything else has to be subordinated. . . . The new thought puts folk and race higher than the state and its forms. It declares protection of the folk more important than protection of a religious denomination, a class, the monarchy, or the republic; it sees in treason against the folk a greater crime than high treason against the state.

The essence of Rosenberg's racial ideas was incorporated in point 4 of the program of the Nazi Party, which reads as follows: "None but members of the nation [*Volk*] may be citizens of the State. None but those of German blood, whatever their creed, may be members of the nation. No Jew, therefore, may be a member of the nation." After the Nazis came to power, this concept was made the basis of the German citizenship law of September 15, 1935.

Commenting upon point 4 of the Nazi program in his pamphlet, *Nature, Principles, and Aims of the NSDAP,* Rosenberg wrote:

> An indispensable differentiation must be made sometime in the German *Volk* consciousness: The right of nationality should not represent something which is received in the cradle as a gift, but should be regarded as a good which must be earned. Although every German is a subject of the state, the rights of nationality should only be received when at the age of twenty or twenty-two he has completed his education or his military service or has finished the labor service which he owes to the state and after having given evidence of honorable conduct. The right to nationality, which must be earned, must become an opportunity for every German to strive for complete humanity and achievement in the service of the *Volk.* This consciousness, which must always be kept alive, will cause him to regard this earned good quite differently from the way it was regarded in the past and today more than ever.
>
> The prevailing concept of state nationality completely ignores the idea of race. According to it, whoever has a German passport is a German, whoever has Czech documents is a Czech, although he may have not a single drop of Czech blood in his veins. . . .
>
> National Socialism also sees in the nature of the structure and leadership of the state an outflowing of a definite character in the *Volk.* If one permits a wholly foreign race—subject to other impulses—to participate therein, the purity of the organic expression is falsified and the existence of the *Volk* is crippled. . . .
>
> This whole concept of the state [parliamentary democracy] is replaced by National Socialism with a basically different concept. National Socialism recognizes that, although the individual racial strains in German-speaking territory differ, they nevertheless belong to closely related races, and that many mixtures among the members of these different branches have produced new and vital strains, among them the complex but still *German* man, but that a mixture with the Jewish enemy race, which in its whole spiritual and physical structure is basically different and antagonistic and has strong resemblances to the peoples of the Near East, can only result in bastardization.

True to the tradition of German imperialism, Rosenberg does not confine his ideas of racial supremacy to the Germans in the Reich alone. He even extends them to the

United States, where he envisages the day when the awakening German element will realize its destiny in this country. In *Der Mythus des 20. Jahrhunderts,* for example, he writes,

> After throwing off the worn-out idea upon which it was founded . . . *i.e.,* after the destruction of the idea represented by New York, the United States of North America has the great task . . . of setting out with youthful energy to put into force the new racial-state idea which a few awakened Americans have already foreseen.

This idea was developed at length by the German geopolitician, Colin Ross. In his book *Unser Amerika* (*Our America*) published in 1936, Ross develops the thesis that the German element in the United States has contributed all that is best in American life and civilization and urges it to become conscious of its racial heritage and to prepare for the day when it may take over complete control of the country.

Reference was made in the preceding section to Beck's *Education in the Third Reich.* On the subject of racial supremacy Beck points out that certain new branches of learning have been introduced into the National Socialist schools and certain old ones have been given a new emphasis. The most important of these are the science of race and the cultivation of race (*Rassenkunde und Rassenpflege*), which teach the pupil to recognize and develop those racial powers which alone make possible the fullest self-realization in the national community. An awakening of a true racial consciousness in the people should lead to a "qualitative and quantitative" racial refinement of the German people by inducing a procreative process of selection which would reduce the strains of foreign blood in the national body.

> German racial consciousness must have pride in the Nordic race as its first condition. It must be a feeling of the highest personal pride to belong to the Nordic race and to have the possibility and the obligation to work within the German community for the advancement of the Nordic race. Beck points out that pupils must be made to realize that the downfall of the Nordic race would mean the collapse of the national tradition, the disintegration of the living community and the destruction of the individual.

Under the influence of war developments, which have given the Nazis a chance to apply their racial theories in occupied territories, their spokesmen have become increasingly open with regard to the political implications of the folk concept. In an article on "The Structure and Order of the Reich," published late in 1941, Ernst Rudolf Huber wrote,

> this folk principle has found its full confirmation for the first time in the events of this war, in which the unity of the folk has been realized to an extent undreamed of through the return to the homeland of territories which had been torn from it and the resettlement of German folk-groups. Thus the awakening of Germandom to become a political folk has had a twofold result: the unity of the folk-community has risen superior to differences of birth or wealth, of class, rank, or denomination; and the unity of Germandom above all state boundaries has been consciously experienced in the European livingspace [*Siedlungsraum*].

Discussion Questions

1. What is multiculturalism and is it possible to have a multicultural identity? Try to answer this question in light of Naomi Zack's discussion of racial and ethnic identity.
2. Why is race a socially constructed, bureaucratic means by which the privileged can oppress others, according to Arendt? How might Arendt suggest we remedy the problem of racial oppression?
3. According to DuBois, why is it difficult for blacks to find an identity in white society? Why do you think he believes knowledge is important for the construction of a sense of *self*?
4. Discuss some of the ways in which immigrants to the United States have been assimilated in light of de Crèvecoeur's essay. Is an identity that is socially constructed an authentic one?
5. In what sense has white culture created Baldwin? According to Baldwin, why is morality dangerous? What does he mean when he says "People are trapped in history and history is trapped in them"?
6. Compare what Paula Gunn Allen says about Native American women to what Baldwin says about blacks in Western civilization. How does each characterize Western culture and civilization and the impact they have on one's identity? In what particular ways have Native American women and African Americans been stereotyped?
7. What is National Socialism and what are some of the ways in which the Nazi ideology gave rise to a false sense of racial superiority?
8. Explain some of the ways in which you have defined yourself and others and have been defined by others, in terms of gender, race, class, or ethnicity.

chapter 5

Class Identity

We begin this chapter with readings that illuminate traditional beliefs in class differences. The first of these is from the Hindu tradition and the second is from the Western tradition as represented by Aristotle. In the Mahabharata, we find the story of the origins of the four castes or classes of human beings. What we are told is that the separation of people into castes came about because of the manner in which individuals acted toward one another. Each caste has its own character, and it is because of this character that they are separated.

Aristotle believed that some people are born with master souls and some people are born with slave souls. Women have a special soul, one that is fulfilled through procreation and household duties. Perhaps Aristotle believed this because he thought that all living things seek to fulfill themselves. Humans in particular seek to fulfill their rational souls. Aristotle thought, however, that one could observe differences in the ways in which humans sought fulfillment. He thought that some humans possessed intellectual and ethical virtues in a capacity that others did not have. Only those who had such capacities were able to achieve the excellence that is required for political interaction and citizenship and, thus, self-fulfillment. Social class, then, according to Aristotle, is a result of natural endowment and not political oppression.

One common complaint about societies is that they regard the interests of only a minority of their members. Some dissent has been raised about considering the interests of the wealthy against the interests of all or the common

Child Laboring in Mill

good. One such voice of dissent is that of Karl Marx. Marx's vision of the good society was one that eliminated exploitation by eradicating class distinctions. He sought a society in which a principle of benevolence would be the only ruling authority. Self-interest would give way to the common social good. His complaint is against the bourgeoisie, those whose only value is monetary, those who increase production for personal profit without regard to the cost to humankind and nature. The degradations caused by the behavior of the bourgeoisie will become its own undoing. Marx saw the revolution of the proletariat as historically inevitable. As you read his criticism of bourgeois society, do not confuse Marx's analysis with the social and political practices of the former Eastern Bloc countries. *Communism* is a word that has been so propagandized that many are acquainted only with the negative stipulations given it by capitalistic societies. Marx was certainly wrong in some of his predictions, but this does not mean there is no truth to be found in his characterizations of capitalistic societies. Remember that a good society provides all its members an equal opportunity for self-actualization. Could it not be that the possibility for self-actualization is severely limited when an individual is compelled to labor continuously in order to survive? When an individual's labor so occupies his or her life that he or she finds little time to relate to others on an intersubjective, human level, has that individual not lost his or her identity? Doesn't such an individual become an object of his or her own labor? Where has the *self as subject* gone?

Donna Langston argues that social class, coupled with race and gender, provides the foundation for inequities in education and the workplace. Further, these inequities are often thought to be "natural," as Aristotle suggested, and are rationalized by academics and other privileged persons to maintain the status of the working poor. Langston argues that the "presumed classless" society of the United States undermines the welfare of the individuals therein. She claims that we must first admit to our privilege in order to recognize the class structure and the dangers it presents to us. For if we continue to deny it, the privileged, too, will perhaps be missing something of value that could make significant contributions to our lives. This requires a deeper understanding of our own attitudes and beliefs. To what extent do we play a role in the marginalization of the others? Don't we all exist in the same reality?

The oppressive values of an industrial society can be viewed through the eyes of Catherine Macleod, who explores her life as a Canadian, having emigrated from Scotland many years ago, and who was raised in a working-class family. Now that she has become a white-collar professional, she wonders why she still sees herself as working class. She eventually learns that she sees herself as others have seen her for so much of her life. How might people define her now? Why do people try to define others, anyway? As we try to answer this latter question, we may find that when we define others, we also define ourselves.

Focusing on the fact that "women have always experienced more poverty than men," Diana Pearce explains that the notion of "the other America," which was described by Michael Harrington in the 1970s, was based on notions of poverty and the poor that are continually changing. One of the more profound changes that has occurred is that the number of women in poverty is increasing by great numbers. Moreover, once poor, women are likely to stay poor. This poverty is further complicated by the marginalization of people based on race and by social attitudes toward women and the family.

As you read this section, examine the ways in which your beliefs and attitudes may have played a role in maintaining poverty and class structures. Have you found yourself stereotyping others who are different from you? In what way(s) do you see yourself as part of the problem of class discrimination and as part of the solution to such a social problem?

On the Origin and Value of the Four Castes

The Mahabharata

In the Western liberal tradition, we are taught to believe that "all humans are created equal." But is this belief universally accepted? In Hinduism, we find a belief in a divinely created caste system. Though each caste is associated with a certain color, it would be a mistake to say that the caste is defined or distinguished by its color. Each caste is in fact distinguished from the others by the inherent virtues and the works of its members. Do we each have by nature inclinations to certain virtues as well as to certain vices?

Brahmā thus formerly created the Brâhmanic Prajāpatis,[a] penetrated by his own energy, and in splendour equalling the sun and fire. The lord then formed truth, righteousness, austere fervour, and the eternal Veda, virtuous practice, and purity for the attainment of heaven. He also formed the gods, demons and men, Brahmins, Kṣatriyas, Vaiśyas, and Śūdras, as well as all other classes of beings. The colour of the Brahmins was white; that of the Kṣatriyas red; that of the Vaiśyas yellow, and that of the Śūdras black.

If the caste of the four classes is distinguished by their colour, then a confusion of all the castes is observable. Desire, anger, fear, cupidity, grief, apprehension, hunger, fatigue, prevail over us all: by what, then, is caste discriminated? Sweat, urine, excrement,

---

[a]Secondary gods, considered as emanating from Brahman.

From *Original Sanskrit Texts,* 2nd ed., J. Muir. London: Trübner and Co., 1872, pp. 141–43.

phlegm, bile, and blood are common to all; the bodies of all decay; by what, then, is caste discriminated? There are innumerable kinds of things moving and stationary; how is the class of these various objects to be determined?

There is no difference of castes: this world, having been at first created by Brahmā entirely Brâhmanic, became afterwards separated into castes in consequence of works. Those Brahmins, who were fond of sensual pleasure, fiery, irascible, prone to violence, who had forsaken their duty, and were red-limbed, fell into the condition of Kṣatriyas. Those Brahmins, who derived their livelihood from kine, who were yellow, who subsisted by agriculture, and who neglected to practise their duties, entered into the state of Vaiśyas. Those Brahmins, who were addicted to mischief and falsehood, who were covetous, who lived by all kinds of work, who were black and had fallen from purity, sank into the condition of Śūdras. Being separated from each other by these works, the Brahmins became divided into different castes. Duty and the rites of sacrifice have not been always forbidden to any of them. Such are the four classes for whom the Brâhmanic Sarasvatī[b] was at first designed by Brahmā, but who thought their cupidity fell into ignorance. Brahmins live agreeably to the prescriptions of the Veda; while they continually hold fast the Veda, and observances, and ceremonies, their austere fervour does not perish. And sacred science was created the highest thing: they who are ignorant of it are no twice-born men. Of these there are various other classes in different places, who have lost all knowledge sacred and profane, and practise whatever observances they please. And different sorts of creatures with the purificatory rites of Brahmins, and discerning their own duties, are created by different Ṛṣis[c] through their own austere fervour. This creation, sprung from the primal god, having its root in *brāhman*, undecaying, imperishable, is called the mind-born creation, and is devoted to the prescriptions of duty.

What is that in virtue of which a man is a Brahmin, a Kṣatriya, a Vaiśya, or a Śūdra; tell me, o most eloquent Ṛṣi.

He who is pure, consecrated by the natal and other ceremonies, who has completely studied the Veda, lives in the practice of the six ceremonies, performs perfectly the rites of purification, who eats the remains of oblations, is attached to his religious teacher, is constant in religious observances, and devoted to truth,—is called a Brahmin. He in whom are seen truth, liberality, inoffensiveness, harmlessness, modesty, compassion, and austere fervour,—is declared to be a Brahmin. He who practises the duty arising out of the kingly office, who is addicted to the study of the Veda, and who delights in giving and receiving,—is called a Kṣatriya. He who readily occupies himself with cattle, who is devoted to agriculture and acquisition, who is pure, and is perfect in the study of the Veda,—is denominated a Vaiśya. He who is habitually addicted to all kinds of food, performs all kinds of work, who is unclean, who has abandoned the Veda, and does not practise pure observances,—is traditionally called a Śūdra. And this which I have stated is the mark of a Śūdra, and it is not found in a Brahmin: such a Śūdra will remain a Śūdra, while the Brahmin who so acts will be no Brahmin.

[a]Secondary gods, considered as emanating from Brahman.

[b]The goddess of speech.

Master and Slave

Aristotle

In the previous article, we learned that some traditions outside Western culture do not necessarily believe that all humans are created equal. But has that belief always been accepted in our own Western tradition? In the opening sections of his work on politics, Aristotle argues that by nature some have the character of masters and some have the character of slaves. Each has its appropriate function in the governance of the household and the state. As you read Aristotle's arguments, ask yourself why he may see a distinction between master and slave as natural and necessary. How would you argue against his position?

BOOK I

1. Every state is a community of some kind, and every community is established with a view to some good; for everyone always acts in order to obtain that which they think good. But, if all communities aim at some good, the state or political community, which is the highest of all, and which embraces all the rest, aims at good in a greater degree than any other, and at the highest good.

Some people think that qualifications of a statesman, king, householder, and master are the same, and that they differ, not in kind, but only in the number of their subjects. For example, the ruler over a few is called a master; over more, the manager of a household; over a still larger number, a statesman or king, as if there were no difference between a great household and a small state. The distinction which is made between the king and the statesman is as follows: When the government is personal, the ruler is a king; when, according to the rules of the political science, the citizens rule and are ruled in turn, then he is called a statesman.

But all this is a mistake, as will be evident to any one who considers the matter according to the method which has hitherto guided us. As in other departments of science, so in politics, the compound should always be resolved into the simple elements or least parts of the whole. We must therefore look at the elements of which the state is composed, in order that we may see in what the different kinds of rule differ from one another, and whether any scientific result can be attained about each one of them.

2. He who thus considers things in their first growth and origin, whether a state or anything else, will obtain the clearest view of them. In the first place there must be a union of those who cannot exist without each other; namely, of male and female, that the race may continue (and this is a union which is formed, not of choice, but because, in common with other animals and with plants, mankind have a natural desire to leave behind them an image of themselves), and of natural ruler and subject, that both may be preserved. For that which can foresee by the exercise of mind is by nature lord and master, and that which can with its body give effect to such foresight is a subject, and by nature a slave; hence master and slave have the same interest. Now nature has distinguished between the female and the slave. For she is not niggardly, like the smith who fashions the Delphian knife for many uses;

she makes each thing for a single use, and every instrument is best made when intended for one and not for many uses. But among barbarians no distinction is made between women and slaves, because there is no natural ruler among them: they are a community of slaves, male and female. That is why the poets say,—

> It is meet that Hellenes should rule over barbarians;

as if they thought that the barbarian and the slave were by nature one.

Out of these two relationships the first thing to arise is the family, and Hesiod is right when he says,—

> First house and wife and an ox for the plough,

for the ox is the poor man's slave. The family is the association established by nature for the supply of men's everyday wants, and the members of it are called by Charondas, "companions of the cupboard," and by Epimenides the Cretan, "companions of the manger." But when several families are united, and the association aims at something more than the supply of daily needs, the first society to be formed is the village. And the most natural form of the village appears to be that of a colony from the family, composed of the children and grandchildren, who are said to be "suckled with the same milk." And this is the reason why Hellenic states were originally governed by kings; because the Hellenes were under royal rule before they came together, as the barbarians still are. Every family is ruled by the eldest, and therefore in the colonies of the family the kingly form of government prevailed because they were of the same blood. As Homer says:

> Each one gives law to his children and to his wives.

For they lived dispersedly, as was the manner in ancient times. That is why men say that the Gods have a king, because they themselves either are or were in ancient times under the rule of a king. For they imagine not only the forms of the Gods but their ways of life to be like their own.

When several villages are united in a single complete community, large enough to be nearly or quite self-sufficing, the state comes into existence, originating in the bare needs of life, and continuing in existence for the sake of a good life. And therefore, if the earlier forms of society are natural, so is the state, for it is the end of them, and the nature of a thing is its end. For what each thing is when fully developed, we call its nature, whether we are speaking of a man, a horse, or a family. Besides, the final cause and end of a thing is the best, and to be self-sufficing is the end and the best.

Hence it is evident that the state is a creation of nature, and that man is by nature a political animal. And he who by nature and not by mere accident is without a state, is either a bad man or above humanity; he is like the

> Tribeless, lawless, hearthless one,

whom Homer denounces—the natural outcast is forthwith a lover of war; he may be compared to an isolated piece at draughts.

Now, that man is more of a political animal than bees or any other gregarious animals is evident. Nature, as we often say, makes nothing in vain, and man is the only animal who has the gift of speech. And whereas mere voice is but an indication of pleasure or pain, and is therefore found in other animals (for their nature attains to the perception of pleasure and pain and the intimation of them to one another, and no further), the power of speech is intended to set forth the expedient and inexpedient, and therefore likewise the just and the unjust. And it is a characteristic of man that he alone has any sense of good and evil, of just and unjust, and the like, and the association of living beings who have this sense makes a family and a state.

Further, the state is by nature clearly prior to the family and to the individual, since the whole is of necessity prior to the part; for example, if the whole body be destroyed, there will be no foot or hand, except homonymously, as we might speak of a stone hand; for when destroyed the hand will be no better than that. But things are defined by their function and power; and we ought not to say that they are the same when they no longer have their proper quality, but only that they are homonymous. The proof that the state is a creation of nature and prior to the individual is that the individual, when isolated, is not self-sufficing; and therefore he is like a part in relation to the whole. But he who is unable to live in society, or who has no need because he is sufficient for himself, must be either a beast or a god: he is no part of a state. A social instinct is implanted in all men by nature, and yet he who first founded the state was the greatest of benefactors. For man, when perfected, is the best of animals, but, when separated from law and justice, he is the worst of all; since armed injustice is the more dangerous, and he is equipped at birth with arms, meant to be used by intelligence and excellence, which he may use for the worst ends. That is why, if he has not excellence, he is the most unholy and the most savage of animals, and the most full of lust and gluttony. But justice is the bond of men in states; for the administration of justice, which is the determination of what is just, is the principle of order in political society.

3. Seeing then that the state is made up of households, before speaking of the state we must speak of the management of the household. The parts of household management correspond to the persons who compose the household, and a complete household consists of slaves and freemen. Now we should begin by examining everything in its fewest possible elements; and the first and fewest possible parts of a family are master and slave, husband and wife, father and children. We have therefore to consider what each of these three relations is and ought to be:—I mean the relation of master and servant, the marriage relation (the conjunction of man and wife has no name of its own), and thirdly, the paternal relation (this also has no proper name). And there is another element of a household, the so-called art of getting wealth, which, according to some, is identical with household management, according to others, a principal part of it; the nature of this art will also have to be considered by us.

Let us first speak of master and slave, looking to the needs of practical life and also seeking to attain some better theory of their relation than exists at present. For some are of the opinion that the rule of a master is a science, and that the management of a household, and the mastership of slaves, and the political and royal rule, as I was saying at the outset, are all the same. Others affirm that the rule of a master over slaves is contrary to nature, and that the distinction between slave and freeman exists by convention only, and not by nature; and being an interference with nature is therefore unjust.

4. Property is a part of the household, and the art of acquiring property is a part of the art of managing the household: for no man can live well, or indeed live at all, unless he is provided with necessaries. And as in the arts which have a definite sphere the workers must have their own proper instruments for the accomplishment of their work, so it is in the management of a household. Now instruments are of various sorts; some are living, others lifeless; in the rudder, the pilot of a ship has a lifeless, in the look-out man, a living instrument; for in the arts the servant is a kind of instrument. Thus, too, a possession is an instrument for maintaining life. And so, in the arrangement of the family, a slave is a living possession, and property a number of such instruments; and the servant is himself an instrument for instruments. For if every instrument could accomplish its own work, obeying or anticipating the will of others, like the statues of Daedalus, or the tripods of Hephaestus, which, says the poet,

> of their own accord entered the assembly of the Gods;

if, in like manner, the shuttle would weave and the plectrum touch the lyre, chief workmen would not want servants, nor masters slaves. Now the instruments commonly so called are instruments of production, whilst a possession is an instrument of action. From a shuttle we get something else besides the use of it, whereas of a garment or of a bed there is only the use. Further, as production and action are different in kind, and both require instruments, the instruments which they employ must likewise differ in kind. But life is action and not production, and therefore the slave is the minister of action. Again, a possession is spoken of as a part is spoken of; for the part is not only a part of something else, but wholly belongs to it; and this is also true of a possession. The master is only the master of the slave; he does not belong to him, whereas the slave is not only the slave of his master, but wholly belongs to him. Hence we see what is the nature and office of a slave; he who is by nature not his own but another's man, is by nature a slave; and he may be said to be another's man who, being a slave, is also a possession. And a possession may be defined as an instrument of action, separable from the possessor.

5. But is there any one thus intended by nature to be a slave, and for whom such a condition is expedient and right, or rather is not all slavery a violation of nature?

There is no difficulty in answering this question, on grounds both of reason and of fact. For that some should rule and others be ruled is a thing not only necessary, but expedient; from the hour of their birth, some are marked out for subjection, others for rule.

And there are many kinds both of rulers and subjects (and that rule is the better which is exercised over better subjects—for example, to rule over men is better than to rule over wild beasts; for the work is better which is executed by better workmen, and where one man rules and another is ruled, they may be said to have a work); for in all things which form a composite whole and which are made up of parts, whether continuous or discrete, a distinction between the ruling and the subject element comes to light. Such a duality exists in living creatures, originating from nature as a whole; even in things which have no life there is a ruling principle, as in a musical mode. But perhaps this is matter for a more popular investigation. A living creature consists in the first place of soul and body, and of these two, the one is by nature the ruler and the other the subject. But then we must look for the intentions of nature in things which retain their nature, and not in things which are corrupted. And therefore we must study the man who is in the most perfect state both of body and soul, for in him we shall see the true relation of the two; although in bad or corrupted natures the body will often appear to rule over the soul, because they are in an evil and unnatural condition. At all events we may firstly observe in living creatures both a despotical and a constitutional rule; for the soul rules the body with a despotical rule, whereas the intellect rules the appetites with a constitutional and royal rule. And it is clear that the rule of the soul over the body, and of the mind and the rational element over the passionate, is natural and expedient; whereas the equality of the two or the rule of the inferior is always hurtful. The same holds good of animals in relation to men; for tame animals have a better nature than wild and all tame animals are better off when they are ruled by man; for then they are preserved. Again, the male is by nature superior, and the female inferior; and the one rules, and the other is ruled; this principle, of necessity, extends to all mankind. Where then there is such a difference as that between soul and body, or between men and animals (as in the case of those whose business is to use their body, and who can do nothing better), the lower sort are by nature slaves, and it is better for them as for all inferiors that they should be under the rule of a master. For he who can be, and therefore is, another's, and he who participates in reason enough to apprehend, but not to have, is a slave by nature. Whereas the lower animals cannot even apprehend reason; they obey their passions. And indeed the use made of slaves and of tame animals is not very different; for both with their bodies minister to the needs of life. Nature would like to distinguish between the bodies of freemen and slaves, making the one strong for servile labour, the other upright, and although useless for such services, useful for political life in the arts both of war and peace. But the opposite often happens—that some have the souls and others have the bodies of freemen. And doubtless if men differed from one another in the mere forms of their bodies as much as the statues of the Gods do from men, all would acknowledge that the inferior class should be slaves of the superior. And if this is true of the body, how much more just that a similar distinction should exist in the soul? But the beauty of the body is seen, whereas the beauty of the soul is not seen. It is clear, then, that some men are by nature free, and others slaves, and that for these latter slavery is both expedient and right.

6. But that those who take the opposite view have in a certain way right on their side, may be easily seen. For the words slavery and slave are used in two senses. There is a slave or slavery by convention as well as by nature. The convention is a sort of agreement—the convention by which whatever is taken in war is supposed to belong to the victors. But this right many jurists impeach, as they would an orator who brought forward an unconstitutional measure; they detest the notion that, because one man has the power of doing violence and is superior in brute strength, another shall be his slave and subject. Even among philosophers there is a difference of opinion. The origin of the dispute, and what makes the views invade each other's territory, is as follows: in some sense excellence, when furnished with means, has actually the greatest power of exercising force: and as superior power is only found where there is superior excellence of some kind, power seems to imply excellence, and the dispute to be simply one about justice (for it is due to one party identifying justice with goodwill, while the other identifies it with the mere rule of the stronger). If these views are thus set out separately, the other views have no force or plausibility against the view that the superior in excellence ought to rule, or be master. Others, clinging, as they think, simply to a principle of justice (for convention is a sort of justice), assume that slavery in accordance with the custom of war is just, but at the same moment they deny this. For what if the cause of the war be unjust? And again, no one would ever say that he is a slave who is unworthy to be a slave. Were this the case, men of the highest rank would be slaves and the children of slaves if they or their parents chanced to have been taken captive and sold. That is why people do not like to call themselves slaves, but confine the term to foreigners. Yet, in using this language, they really mean the natural slave of whom we spoke at first: for it must be admitted that some are slaves everywhere, others nowhere. The same principle applies to nobility. People regard themselves as noble everywhere, and not only in their own country, but they deem foreigners noble only when at home, thereby implying that there are two sorts of nobility and freedom, the one absolute, the other relative. The Helen of Theodectes says:

> Who would presume to call me servant who am on both sides sprung from the stem of the Gods?

What does this mean but that they distinguish freedom and slavery, noble and humble birth, by the two principles of good and evil? They think that as men and animals beget men and animals, so from good men a good man springs. Nature intends to do this often but cannot.

We see then that there is some foundation for this difference of opinion, and that all are not either slaves by nature or freemen by nature, and also that there is in some cases a marked distinction between the two classes, rendering it expedient and right for the one to be slaves and the others to be masters: the one practising obedience, the others exercising the authority and lordship which nature intended them to have. The abuse of this authority is injurious to both; for the interests of part and whole, of body and soul, are the same, and the slave is a part of the master, a living but separated part of his bodily frame. Hence, where the relation of master and slave between them is natural they are friends and have a common interest, but where it rests merely on convention and force the reverse is true.

7. The previous remarks are quite enough to show that the rule of a master is not a constitutional rule, and that all the different kinds of rule are not, as some affirm, the same as each other. For there is one rule exercised over subjects who are by nature free, another over subjects who are by nature slaves. The rule of a household is a monarchy, for every house is under one head: whereas constitutional rule is a government of freemen and equals. The master is not called a master because he has science, but because he is of a certain character, and the same remark applies to the slave and the freeman. Still there may be a science for the master and a science for the slave. The science of the slave would be such as the man of Syracuse taught, who made money by slaves in their ordinary duties. And such a knowledge may be carried further, so as to include cookery and similar menial arts. For some duties are of the more necessary, others of the more honourable sort; as the proverb says, "slave before slave, master before master." But all such branches of knowledge are servile. There is likewise a science of the master, which teaches the use of slaves: for the master as such is concerned, not with the acquisition, but with the use of them. Yet this science is not anything great or wonderful; for the master need only know how to order that which the slave must know how to execute. Hence those who are in a position which places them above toil have stewards who attend to their households while they occupy themselves with philosophy or with politics. But the art of acquiring slaves, I mean of justly acquiring them, differs both from the art of the master and the art of slave, being a species of hunting or war. Enough of the distinction between master and slave.

Bourgeois and Proletarian

Karl Marx

Is the common or social good not more important than any personal profit? According to Marx, the bourgeoisie manipulate the forces of production for personal profit without regard to the cost to humankind and nature. Can there be freedom when individuals are compelled to labor continuously just to survive? Marx contends that such continuous labor leads inevitably to complete alienation. Humans must struggle against this estrangement from self and world.

The history of all hitherto existing society is the history of class struggles.

Freeman and slave, patrician and plebeian, lord and serf, guild-master and journeyman, in a word, oppressor and oppressed, stood in constant opposition to one another, carried on uninterrupted, now hidden, now open fight, a fight that each time ended, either in a revolutionary re-constitution of society at large, or in the common ruin of the contending classes.

In the earlier epochs of history we find almost everywhere a complicated arrangement of society into various orders, a manifold gradation of social rank. In ancient Rome we have patricians, knights, plebeians, slaves; in the middle ages, feudal lords, vassals, guild-masters, journeymen, apprentices, serfs; in almost all of these classes, again, subordinate gradations.

The modern bourgeois society that has sprouted from the ruins of feudal society, has not done away with class antagonisms. It has but established new classes, new conditions of oppression, new forms of struggle in place of the old ones.

Our epoch, the epoch of the bourgeoisie, possesses, however, this distinctive feature; it has simplified the class antagonisms. Society as a whole is more and more splitting up into two great hostile camps, into two great classes directly facing each other: Bourgeoisie and Proletariat.

From the serfs of the middle ages sprang the chartered burghers of the earliest towns. From these burgesses the first elements of the bourgeoisie were developed.

The discovery of America, the rounding of the Cape, opened up fresh ground for the rising bourgeoisie. The East Indian and Chinese markets, the colonization of America, trade with the colonies, the increase in the means of exchange and in commodities generally, gave to commerce, to navigation, to industry, an impulse never before known, and thereby, to the revolutionary element in the tottering feudal society, a rapid development.

The feudal system of industry, under which industrial production was monopolized by closed guilds, now no longer sufficed for the growing wants of the new market. The manufacturing system took its place. The guild-masters were pushed on one side by the manufacturing middle-class: division of labor between the different corporate guilds vanished in the face of division of labor in each single workshop.

Meantime the markets kept ever growing, the demand ever rising. Even manufacture no longer sufficed. Thereupon, steam and machinery revolutionized industrial

From *The Communist Manifesto,* Chapter 1, 1848.

production. The place of manufacture was taken by the giant, Modern Industry, the place of the industrial middle-class, by industrial millionaires, the leaders of whole industrial armies, the modern bourgeois.

Modern industry has established the world market, for which the discovery of America paved the way. This market has given an immense development to commerce, to navigation, to communication by land. This development has, in its turn, reacted on the extension of industry; and in proportion as industry, commerce, navigation, railways extended, in the same proportion the bourgeoisie developed, increased its capital, and pushed into the background every class handed down from the Middle Ages.

We see, therefore, how the modern bourgeoisie is itself the product of a long course of development, of a series of revolutions in the modes of production and of exchange.

Each step in the development of the bourgeoisie was accompanied by a corresponding political advance of that class. An oppressed class under the sway of the feudal nobility, an armed and self-governing association in the mediaeval commune, here independent urban republic (as in Italy and Germany), there taxable "third estate" of the monarchy (as in France), afterwards, in the period of manufacture proper, serving either the semi-feudal or the absolute monarchy as a counterpoise against nobility, and, in fact, corner stone of the great monarchies in general, the bourgeoisie has at last, since the establishment of Modern Industry and of the worldmarket, conquered for itself, in the modern representative State, exclusive political sway. The executive of the modern State is but a committee for managing the common affairs of the whole bourgeoisie.

The bourgeoisie, historically, has played a most revolutionary part.

The bourgeoisie, wherever it has got the upper hand, has put an end to all feudal, patriarchal, idyllic relations. It has pitilessly torn asunder the motley feudal ties that bound man to his "natural superiors," and has left no other nexus between man and man than naked self-interest, than callous "cash payment." It has drowned the most heavenly ecstasies of religious fervor, of chivalrous enthusiasm, of Philistine sentimentalism, in the icy water of egotistical calculation. It has resolved personal worth into exchange value, and in place of the numberless indefeasible chartered freedoms, has set up that single, unconscionable freedom—Free Trade. In one word, for exploitation, veiled by religious and political illusions, it has substituted naked, shameless, direct, brutal exploitation.

The bourgeoisie has stripped of its halo every occupation hitherto honored and looked up to with reverent awe. It has converted the physician, the lawyer, the priest, the poet, the man of science, into its paid wage laborers.

The bourgeoisie has torn away from the family its sentimental veil, and has reduced the family relation to a mere money relation.

The bourgeoisie has disclosed how it came to pass that the brutal display of vigor in the Middle Ages, which reactionists so much admire, found its fitting complement in the most slothful indolence. It has been the first to show what man's activity can bring about. It has accomplished wonders far surpassing Egyptian pyramids, Roman aqueducts and Gothic cathedrals; it has conducted expeditions that put in the shade all former Exoduses of nations and crusades.

The bourgeoisie cannot exist without constantly revolutionizing the instruments of production, and thereby the relations of production, and with them the whole relations of society. Conservation of the old modes of production in unaltered form was, on the contrary, the first condition of existence for all earlier industrial classes. Constant revolutionizing of production, uninterrupted disturbance of all social conditions, everlasting uncertainty and agitation distinguish the bourgeois epoch from all earlier ones. All fixed, fast frozen relations, with their train of ancient and venerable prejudices and opinions, are swept away, all new formed ones become antiquated before they can ossify. All that is solid melts into the air, all that is holy is profaned, and man is at last compelled to face with sober senses, his real conditions of life, and his relations with his kind.

The need of a constantly expanding market for its products chases the bourgeoisie over the whole surface of the globe. It must nestle everywhere, settle everywhere, establish connections everywhere.

The bourgeoisie has through its exploitation of the worldmarket given a cosmopolitan character to production and consumption in every country. To the great chagrin of reactionists, it has drawn from under the feet of industry the national ground on which it stood. All old-established national industries have been destroyed or are daily being destroyed. They are dislodged by new industries, whose introduction becomes a life and death question for all civilized nations, by industries that no longer work up indigenous raw material, but raw material drawn from the remotest zones; industries whose products are consumed, not only at home, but in every quarter of the globe. In place of the old wants, satisfied by the productions of the country, we find new wants, requiring for their satisfaction the products of distant lands and climes. In place of the old local and national seclusion and self-sufficiency, we have intercourse in every direction, universal interdependence of nations. And as in material, so also in intellectual production. The intellectual creations of individual nations become common property. National one-sidedness and narrow-mindedness become more and more impossible, and from the numerous national local literatures there arises a world-literature.

The bourgeoisie, by the rapid improvement of all instruments of production, by the immensely facilitated means of communication draws all, even the most barbarian nations into civilization. The cheap prices of its commodities are the heavy artillery with which it batters down all Chinese walls, with which it forces the barbarians' intensely obstinate hatred of foreigners to capitulate. It compels all nations on pain of extinction, to adopt the bourgeois mode of production; it compels them to introduce what it calls civilization into their midst, *i.e.*, to become bourgeois themselves. In a word, it creates a world after its own image.

The bourgeoisie has subjected the country to the rule of the towns. It has created enormous cities, has greatly increased the urban population as compared with the rural, and has thus rescued a considerable part of the population from the idiocy of rural life. Just as it has made the country dependent on the towns, so it has made barbarian and semi-barbarian countries dependent on civilized ones, nations of peasants on nations of bourgeois, the East on the West.

The bourgeoisie keeps more and more doing away with the scattered state of the population, of the means of production and of property. It has agglomerated population, [has] centralized means of production, and has concentrated property in a few hands. The necessary consequence of this was political centralization. Independent, or but loosely connected provinces, with separate interests, laws, governments, and systems of taxation, became lumped together in one nation, with one government, one code of laws, one national class interest, one frontier and one customs tariff.

The bourgeoisie, during its rule of scarce one hundred years, has created more massive and more colossal productive forces than have all preceding generations together. Subjection of Nature's forces to man, machinery, application of chemistry to industry and agriculture, steam-navigation, railways, electric telegraphs, clearing of whole continents for cultivation, canalization of rivers, whole populations conjured out of the ground—what earlier century had even a presentiment that such productive forces slumbered in the lap of social labor?

We see then: the means of production and of exchange on whose foundation the bourgeoisie built itself up, were generated in feudal society. At a certain stage in the development of these means of production and of exchange, the conditions under which feudal society produced and exchanged, the feudal organization of agriculture and manufacturing industry, in one word, the feudal relations of property became no longer compatible with the already developed productive forces; they became so many fetters. They had to burst asunder; they were burst asunder.

Into their places stepped free competition, accompanied by social and political constitution adapted to it, and by economical and political sway of the bourgeois class.

A similar movement is going on before our own eyes. Modern bourgeois society with its relations of production, of exchange and of property, a society that has conjured up such gigantic means of production and of exchange, is like the sorcerer, who is no longer able to control the powers of the nether world whom he has called up by his spells. For many a decade past, the history of industry and commerce is but the history of the revolt of modern productive forces against modern conditions of production, against the property relations that are the conditions for the existence of the bourgeoisie and of its rule. It is enough to mention the commercial crises that by their periodical return put on its trail, each time more threateningly, the existence of the entire bourgeois society. In these crises a great part not only of the existing products, but also of the previously created productive forces, are periodically destroyed. In these crises there breaks out an epidemic that, in all earlier epochs, would have seemed an absurdity—the epidemic of overproduction. Society suddenly finds itself put back into a state of momentary barbarism; it appears as if a famine, a universal war of devastation, had cut off the supply of every means of subsistence industry and commerce seem to be destroyed; and why? Because there is too much civilization, too much means of subsistence; too much industry, too much commerce. The productive forces at the disposal of society no longer tend to further the development of the conditions of the bourgeois property; on the contrary, they have become too powerful for these conditions by which they are fettered, and as soon as they overcome these fetters they bring disorder into the whole of bourgeois society, endanger the existence of bourgeois property. The conditions of bourgeois society are too narrow to comprise the wealth created by them. And how does the bourgeoisie get over these crises? On the one hand by enforced destruction of a mass of productive forces; on the other, by the conquest of new markets, and by the more thorough exploitation of the old ones. That is to say, by paving the way for more extensive and more destructive crises, and by diminishing the means whereby crises are prevented.

The weapons with which the bourgeoisie felled feudalism to the ground are now turned against the bourgeoisie itself.

But not only has the bourgeoisie forged the weapons that bring death to itself; it has also called into existence the men who are to wield those weapons—the modern working-class—the proletarians.

In proportion as the bourgeoisie, *i.e.*, capital, is developed, in the same proportion as the proletariat, the modern working-class, developed, a class of laborers who live only so long as they find work, and who find work only so long as their labor increases capital. These laborers, who must sell themselves piecemeal, are a commodity, like every other article of commerce, and are consequently exposed to all the vicissitudes of competition, to all the fluctuations of the market.

Owing to the extensive use of machinery and to division of labor, the work of the proletarians has lost all individual character, and, consequently, all charm for the workman. He becomes an appendage of the machine, and it is only the most simple, most monotonous and most easily acquired knack that is required of him. Hence, the cost of production of a workman is restricted almost entirely to the means of subsistence that he requires for his maintenance, and for the propagation of his race. But the price of a commodity, and also of labor, is equal to its cost of production. In proportion, therefore, as the repulsiveness of the work increases the wage decreases. Nay more, in proportion as the use of machinery and division of labor increases, in the same proportion the burden of toil increases, whether by prolongation of the working hours, by increase of the work enacted in a given time, or by increased speed of the machinery, etc.

Modern industry has converted the little workshop of the patriarchal master into the great factory of the industrial capitalist. Masses of laborers, crowded into factories, are organized like soldiers. As privates of the industrial army they are placed under the command of a perfect hierarchy of officers and sergeants. Not only are they the slaves of the bourgeois class and of the bourgeois state, they are daily and hourly enslaved by the machine, by the overlooker, and above all, by the individual bourgeois manufacturer himself. The more openly this despotism proclaims gain to be its end and aim, the more petty, the more hateful and the more embittering it is.

The less the skill and exertion or strength implied in manual labor, in other words, the more modern industry becomes developed, the more is the labor of men superseded by that of women. Differences of age and sex have no longer any distinctive social validity for the working class. All are instruments of labor, more or less expensive to use, according to their age and sex.

No sooner is the exploitation of the laborer by the manufacturer, so far at an end, that he receives his wages in cash, than he is set upon by the other portions of the bourgeoisie, the landlord, the shopkeeper, the pawnbroker, etc.

The lower strata of the middle class—the small tradespeople, shopkeepers and retired tradesmen generally, the handicraftsmen and peasants—all these sink gradually into the proletariat, partly because their diminutive capital does not suffice for the scale on which Modern Industry is carried on, and is swamped in the competition with the large capitalists, partly because their specialized skill is rendered worthless by new methods of production. Thus the proletariat is recruited from all classes of the population.

The proletariat goes through various states of development. With its birth begins its struggle with the bourgeoisie. At first the contest is carried on by individual laborers, then by the workpeople of a factory, then by the operatives of one trade, in one locality, against the individual bourgeois who directly exploits them. They direct their attacks not against the bourgeois conditions of production, but against the instruments of production themselves; they destroy imported wares that compete with their labor, they smash to pieces machinery, they set factories ablaze, they seek to restore by force the vanished status of the workman of the Middle Ages.

At this stage the laborers still form an incoherent mass scattered over the whole country, and broken up by their mutual competition. If anywhere they unite to form more compact bodies, this is not yet the consequence of their own active union, but of the union of the bourgeoisie, which class, in order to attain its own political ends, is compelled to set the whole proletariat in motion, and is moreover yet, for a time, able to do so. At this stage, therefore, the proletarians do not fight their enemies, but the enemies of their enemies, the remnants of absolute monarchy, the landowners, the non-industrial bourgeois, the petty bourgeoisie. Thus the whole historical movement is concentrated in the hands of the bourgeoisie, every victory so obtained is a victory for the bourgeoisie.

But with the development of industry the proletariat not only increases in number; it becomes concentrated in greater masses, its strength grows and it feels that strength more. The various interests and conditions of life within the ranks of the proletariat are more and more equalized, in proportion as machinery obliterates all distinctions of labor, and nearly everywhere reduces wages to the same low level. The growing competition among the bourgeois, and the resulting commercial crises, make the wages of the workers even more fluctuating. The unceasing improvement of machinery, ever more rapidly developing, makes their livelihood more and more precarious; the collisions between individual workmen and individual bourgeois take more and more the character of collisions between two classes. Thereupon the workers begin to form combinations (Trades' Unions) against the bourgeois; they club together in order to keep up the rate of wages; they found permanent associations in order to make provision beforehand for these occasional revolts. Here and there the contest breaks out into riots.

Now and then the workers are victorious, but only for a time. The real fruit of their battle lies not in the immediate result but in the ever-expanding union of workers. This union is helped on by the improved means of communication that are created by modern industry, and that places the workers of different localities in contact with one another. It was just this contact that was needed to centralize the numerous local struggles, all of the same character, into one national struggle between classes. But every class struggle is a political struggle. And that union, to attain which the burghers of the Middle Ages with their miserable highways, required centuries, the modern proletarians, thanks to railways, achieve in a few years.

This organization of the proletarians into a class, and consequently into a political party, is continually being upset again by the competition between the workers themselves. But it ever rises up again, stronger, firmer, mightier. It compels legislative recognition of particular interests of the workers by taking advantage of the divisions among the bourgeoisie itself. Thus the ten hours' bill in England was carried.

Altogether collisions between the classes of the old society further, in many ways, the course of development of the proletariat. The bourgeoisie finds itself involved in a constant battle. At first with the aristocracy; later on, with those portions of the bourgeoisie itself whose interests have become antagonistic to the progress of industry; at all times, with the bourgeoisie of foreign countries. In all these battles it sees itself compelled to appeal to the proletariat, to ask for its help, and thus, to drag it into the political arena. The bourgeoisie itself, therefore, supplies the proletariat with its own elements of political and general education; in other words, it furnishes the proletariat with weapons for fighting the bourgeoisie.

Further, as we have already seen, entire sections of the ruling class are, by the advance of industry, precipitated into the proletariat, or are at least threatened in their conditions of existence. These also supply the proletariat with fresh elements of enlightenment and progress.

Finally, in times when the class-struggle nears the decisive hour, the process of dissolution going on within the ruling class—in fact, within the whole range of an old society—assumes such a violent, glaring character that a small section of the ruling class cuts itself adrift and joins the revolutionary class, the class that holds the future in its hands. Just as, therefore, at an earlier period, a section of the nobility went over to the bourgeoisie, so now a portion of the bourgeoisie goes over to the proletariat, and in particular a portion of the bourgeoisie ideologists, who have raised themselves to the level of comprehending theoretically the historical movements as a whole.

Of all the classes that stand face to face with the bourgeoisie to-day the proletariat alone is a really revolutionary class. The other classes decay and finally disappear in the face of modern industry; the proletariat is its special and essential product.

The lower middle class, the small manufacturer, the shopkeeper, the artisan, the peasant, all these fight against the bourgeoisie, to save from extinction their existence as fractions of the middle class. They are therefore not revolutionary, but conservative. Nay more; they are reactionary, for they try to roll back the wheel of history. If by chance they are revolutionary, they are so only in view of their impending transfer into the proletariat; they thus defend not their present, but their future interests; they desert their own standpoint to place themselves at that of the proletariat.

The "dangerous class," the social scum, that passively rotting mass thrown off by the lowest layers of old society, may, here and there, be swept into the movement by a proletarian revolution; its conditions of life, however, prepare it far more for the part of a bribed tool of reactionary intrigue.

In the conditions of the proletariat, those of the old society at large are already virtually swamped. The proletarian is without property; his relation to his wife and children has no longer anything in common with the bourgeois family relations; modern industrial labor, modern subjection to capital, the same in England as in France, in America as in Germany, has stripped him of every trace of national character. Law, morality, religion, are to him so many bourgeois prejudices, behind which lurk in ambush just as many bourgeois interests.

All the preceding classes that got the upper hand sought to fortify their already acquired status by subjecting society at large to their conditions of appropriation. The proletarians cannot become masters of the productive forces of society, except by abolishing their own previous mode of appropriation, and thereby also every other previous mode of appropriation. They have nothing of their own to secure and to fortify; their mission is to destroy all previous securities for and insurances of individual property.

All previous historical movements were movements of minorities, or in the interest of minorities. The proletarian movement is the self-conscious, independent movement of the immense majority. The proletariat, the lowest stratum of our present society, cannot stir, cannot raise itself up without the whole superincumbent strata of official society being sprung into the air.

Though not in substance, yet in form, the struggle of the proletariat with the bourgeoisie is at first a national struggle. The proletariat of each country must, of course, first of all settle matters with its own bourgeoisie.

In depicting the most general phases of the development of the proletariat, we traced the more or less veiled civil war, raging within existing society, up to the point where that war breaks out into open revolution and where the violent overthrow of the bourgeoisie, lays the foundations for the sway of the proletariat.

Hitherto every form of society has been based, as we have already seen, on the antagonism of oppressing and oppressed classes. But in order to oppress a class, certain conditions must be assured to it under which it can, at least, continue its slavish existence. The serf, in the period of serfdom, raised himself to membership in the commune, just as the petty bourgeois, under the yoke to feudal absolutism, managed to develop into a bourgeois. The modern laborer, on the contrary, instead of rising with the progress of industry, sinks deeper and deeper below the conditions of existence of his own class. He becomes a pauper, and pauperism develops more rapidly than population and wealth. And here it becomes evident that the bourgeoisie is unfit any longer to be the ruling class in society, and to impose its conditions of existence upon society as an over-riding law. It is unfit to rule, because it is incompetent to assure an existence to its slave within his slavery, because it cannot help letting him sink into such a state that it has to feed him, instead of being fed by him. Society can no longer live under this bourgeoisie; in other words, its existence is no longer compatible with society.

The essential condition for the existence, and for the sway of the bourgeois class is the formation and augmentation of capital; the condition for capital is wage labor. Wage labor rests exclusively on competition between the laborers. The advance of industry, whose involuntary promoter is the bourgeoisie, replaces the isolation of the laborers, due to competition, by their involuntary combination, due to association. The development of Modern Industry, therefore, cuts from under its feet the very foundation on which the bourgeoisie produces and appropriates products. What the bourgeoisie therefore produces, above all, are its own grave diggers. Its fall and the victory of the proletariat are equally inevitable.

Tired of Playing Monopoly?

Donna Langston

The fact that as males or females our social and economic class has an impact on our identity is evident by the way we live our lives, the choices we make, and the ways we see ourselves. Despite this, we often choose to ignore the things that most influence the way we live our lives. In this essay, Langston discusses some of the reasons why it is not easy to change the direction of our lives, even though we may try to do so, since the values of our social class cannot (and perhaps should not) be erased. As you read this, reflect upon some of the ways in which the values of your own social class influence your life. To what extent do you think social class is relevant in our society today?

I. Magnin, Nordstrom, The Bon, Sears, Penneys, K mart, Goodwill, Salvation Army. If the order of this list of stores makes any sense to you, then we've begun to deal with the first question which inevitably arises in any discussion of class here in the U.S.—huh? Unlike our European allies, we in the U.S. are reluctant to recognize class differences. This denial of class divisions functions to reinforce ruling class control and domination. America is, after all, the supposed land of equal opportunity where, if you just work hard enough, you can get ahead, pull yourself up by your bootstraps. What the old bootstraps theory overlooks is that some were born with silver shoe horns. Female-headed households, communities of color, the elderly, disabled and children find themselves, disproportionately, living in poverty. If hard work were the sole determinant of your ability to support yourself and your family, surely we'd have a different outcome for many in our society. We also, however, believe in luck and, on closer examination, it certainly is quite a coincidence that the "unlucky" come from certain race, gender and class backgrounds. In order to perpetuate racist, sexist and classist outcomes, we also have to believe that the current economic distribution is unchangeable, has always existed, and probably exists in this form throughout the known universe, i.e., it's "natural." Some people explain or try to account for poverty or class position by focusing on the personal and moral merits of an individual. If people are poor, then it's something they did or didn't do; they were lazy, unlucky, didn't try hard enough, etc. This has the familiar ring of blaming the victims. Alternative explanations focus on the ways in which poverty and class position are due to structural, systematic, institutionalized economic and political power relations. These power relations are based firmly on dynamics such as race, gender, and class.

In the myth of the classless society, ambition and intelligence alone are responsible for success. The myth conceals the existence of a class society, which serves many functions. One of the main ways it keeps the working-class and poor locked into a class-based system in a position of servitude is by cruelly creating false hope. It perpetuates the false hope among the working-class and poor that they can have different opportunities in

From: Jo Whitehorse Cochran, Donna Langston, and Carolyn Woodward (eds.), *Changing Our Power: An Introduction to Women's Studies* (Dubuque, Iowa: Kendall-Hunt, 1988). Reprinted by permission.

life. The hope that they can escape the fate that awaits them due to the class position they were born into. Another way the rags-to-riches myth is perpetuated is by creating enough visible tokens so that oppressed persons believe they, too, can get ahead. The creation of hope through tokenism keeps a hierarchical structure in place and lays the blame for not succeeding on those who don't. This keeps us from resisting and changing the class-based system. Instead, we accept it as inevitable, something we just have to live with. If oppressed people believe in equality of opportunity, then they won't develop class consciousness and will internalize the blame for their economic position. If the working-class and poor do not recognize the way false hope is used to control them, they won't get a chance to control their lives by acknowledging their class position, by claiming that identity and taking action as a group.

The myth also keeps the middle class and upper class entrenched in the privileges awarded in a class-based system. It reinforces middle- and upper-class beliefs in their own superiority. If we believe that anyone in society really can get ahead, then middle- and upper-class status and privileges must be deserved, due to personal merits, and enjoyed—and defended at all costs. According to this viewpoint, poverty is regrettable but acceptable, just the outcome of a fair game: "There have always been poor people, and there always will be."

Class is more than just the amount of money you have; it's also the presence of economic security. For the working class and poor, working and eating are matters of survival, not taste. However, while one's class status can be defined in important ways in terms of monetary income, class is also a whole lot more—specifically, class is also culture. As a result of the class you are born into and raised in, class is your understanding of the world and where you fit in; it's composed of ideas, behavior, attitudes, values, and language; class is how you think, feel, act, look, dress, talk, move, walk; class is what stores you shop at, restaurants you eat in; class is the schools you attend, the education you attain; class is the very jobs you will work at throughout your adult life. Class even determines when we marry and become mothers. Working-class women become mothers long before middle-class women receive their bachelor's degrees. We experience class at every level of our lives; class is who our friends are, where we live and work, even what kind of car we drive, if we own one, and what kind of health care we receive, if any. Have I left anything out? In other words, class is socially constructed and all-encompassing. When we experience classism, it will be because of our lack of money (i.e., choices and power in this society) and because of the way we talk, think, act, move—because of our culture.

Class affects what we perceive as and what we have available to us as choices. Upon graduation from high school, I was awarded a scholarship to attend any college, private or public, in the state of California. Yet it never occurred to me or my family that it made any difference which college you went to. I ended up just going to a small college in my town. It never would have occurred to me to move away from my family for school, because no one ever had and no one would. I was the first person in my family to go to college. I had to figure out from reading college catalogs how to apply—no one in my family could have sat down and said, "Well, you take this test and then you really should think about . . ." Although tests and high school performance had shown I had the ability to pick up white middle-class lingo, I still had quite an adjustment to make—it was lonely and isolating in college. I lost my friends from high school—they were at the community college, vo-tech school, working, or married. I lasted a year and a half in this foreign environment before I quit college, married a factory worker, had a baby and resumed living in a community I knew. One middle-class friend in college had asked if I'd like to travel to Europe with her. Her father was a college professor and people in her family had actually travelled there. My family had seldom been able to take a vacation at all. A couple of times my parents were able—by saving all year—to take the family over to the coast on their annual two-week vacation. I'd seen the time and energy my parents invested in trying to take a family vacation to some place a few hours away; the idea of how anybody ever got to Europe was beyond me.

If class is more than simple economic status but one's cultural background, as well, what happens if you're born and raised middle-class, but spend some of your adult life with earnings below a middle-class income bracket—are you then working-class? Probably not. If your economic position changes, you still have the language, behavior, educational background, etc., of the middle class, which you can bank on. You will always have choices. Men who consciously try to refuse male privilege are still male; whites who want to challenge white privilege are still white. I think those who come from middle-class backgrounds need to recognize that their class privilege does not float out with the rinse water. Middle-class people can exert incredible power just by being nice and polite. The middle-class way of doing things is the standard—they're always right, just by being themselves. Beware of middle-class people who deny their privilege. Many people have times when they struggle to get shoes for the kids, when budgets are tight, etc. This isn't the same as long-term economic conditions without choices. Being working-class is also generational. Examine your family's history of education, work, and standard of living. It may not be a coincidence that you share the same class status as your parents and grandparents. If your grandparents were professionals, or your parents were professionals, it's much more likely you'll be able to grow up to become a yuppie, if your heart so desires, or even if you don't think about it.

How about if you're born and raised poor or working-class, yet through struggle, usually through education, you manage to achieve a different economic level: do you become middle class? Can you pass? I think some working class people may successfully assimilate into the middle class by learning to dress, talk, and act middle-class—to accept and adopt the middle-class way of doing things. It all depends on how far they're able to go. To succeed in the middle-class world means facing great pressures to abandon working-class friends and ways.

Contrary to our stereotype of the working class—white guys in overalls—the working class is not homogeneous in terms of race or gender. If you are a person of color, if you live in a female-headed household, you are much more likely to be working-class or poor. The experience of Black, Latino, American Indian or Asian American working classes will differ significantly from the white working classes, which have traditionally been able to rely on white privilege to provide a more elite position within the working class. Working-class people are often grouped together and stereotyped, but distinctions can be made among the working-class, working-poor and poor. Many working-class families are supported by unionized workers who possess marketable skills. Most working-poor families are supported by non-unionized, unskilled men and women. Many poor families are dependent on welfare for their income.

Attacks on the welfare system and those who live on welfare are a good example of classism in action. We have a "dual welfare" system in this country whereby welfare for the rich in the form of tax-free capital gain, guaranteed loans, oil depletion allowances, etc., is not recognized as welfare. Almost everyone in America is on some type of welfare; but, if you're rich, it's in the form of tax deductions for "business" meals and entertainment, and if you're poor, it's in the form of food stamps. The difference is the stigma and humiliation connected to welfare for the poor, as compared to welfare for the rich, which is called "incentives." Ninety-three percent of AFDC (Aid to Families with Dependent Children, our traditional concept of welfare) recipients are women and children. Eighty percent of food stamp recipients are single mothers, children, the elderly and disabled. Average AFDC payments are $93 per person, per month. Payments are so low nationwide that in only three states do AFDC benefits plus food stamps bring a household *up to* the poverty level. Food stamp benefits average $10 per person, per week (Sar Levitan, *Programs in Aid of the Poor for the 1980s*). A common focal point for complaints about "welfare" is the belief that most welfare recipients are cheaters—goodness knows there are no middle-class income tax cheaters out there. Imagine focusing the same anger and energy on the way corporations and big business cheat on their tax revenues. Now, there would be some dollars worth quibbling about. The "dual welfare" system also assigns a different degree of stigma to programs that benefit women and children, such as AFDC, and programs whose recipients are primarily male, such as veterans' benefits. The implicit assumption is that mothers who raise children do not work and therefore are not deserving of their daily bread crumbs.

Anti-union attitudes are another prime example of classism in action. At best, unions have been a very progressive force for workers, women and people of color. At worst, unions have reflected the same regressive attitudes which are out there in other social structures: classism, racism, and sexism. Classism exists within the working class. The aristocracy of the working class—unionized, skilled workers—have mainly been white and male and have viewed themselves as being better than unskilled workers, the unemployed and poor, who are mostly women and people of color. The white working class must commit itself to a cultural and ideological transformation of racist attitudes. The history of working people, and the ways we've resisted many types of oppressions, are not something we're taught in school. Missing from our education is information about workers and their resistance.

Working-class women's critiques have focused on the following issues:

Education: White middle-class professionals have used academic jargon to rationalize and justify classism. The whole structure of education is a classist system. Schools in every town reflect class divisions: like the store list at the beginning of this article, you can list schools in your town by what classes of kids attend, and in most cities you can also list by race. The classist system is perpetuated in schools with the tracking system, whereby the "dumbs" are tracked into homemaking, shop courses and vocational school futures, while the "smarts" end up in advanced math, science, literature, and college-prep courses. If we examine these groups carefully, the coincidence of poor and working-class backgrounds with "dumbs" is rather alarming. The standard measurement of supposed intelligence is white middle-class English. If you're other than white middle-class, you have to become bilingual to succeed in the educational system. If you're white middle-class, you only need the language and writing skills you were raised with, since they're the standard. To do well in society presupposes middle-class background, experiences and learning for everyone. The tracking system separates those from the working class who can potentially assimilate to the middle class from all our friends, and labels us "college bound."

After high school, you go on to vocational school, community college, or college—public or private—according to your class position. Apart from the few who break into middle-class schools, the classist stereotyping of the working class as being dumb and inarticulate tracks most into vocational and low-skilled jobs. A few of us are allowed to slip through to reinforce the idea that equal opportunity exists. But for most, class position is destiny—determining our educational attainment and employment. Since we must overall abide by middle-class rules to succeed, the assumption is that we go to college in order to "better ourselves"—i.e., become more like them. I suppose it's assumed we have "yuppie envy" and desire nothing more than to be upwardly mobile individuals. It's assumed that we want to fit into their world. But many of us remain connected to our communities and families. Becoming college-educated doesn't mean we have to, or want to, erase our first and natural language and value system. It's important for many of us to remain in and return to our communities to work, live, and stay sane.

Jobs: Middle-class people have the privilege of choosing careers. They can decide which jobs they want to work, according to their moral or political commitments, needs for challenge or creativity. This is a privilege denied the working-class and poor, whose work is a means of survival, not choice (see Hartsock). Working-class women have seldom had the luxury of choosing between work in the home or market. We've generally done both, with little ability to purchase services to help with this double burden. Middle- and upper-class women can often hire other women to clean their houses, take care of their children, and cook their meals. Guess what class and race those "other" women are? Working a double or triple day is common for working-class women. Only middle-class women have an array of choices such as: parents put you through school, then you choose a career, then you choose when and if to have babies, then you choose a support system of working-class women to take care of your kids and house if you choose to resume your career. After the birth of my second child, I was working two part-time jobs—one loading trucks at night—and going to school during the days. While I was quite privileged because I could take my colicky infant with me to classes and the day-time job, I was in a state of continuous semi-consciousness. I had to work to support my family; the only choice I had was between school or sleep: Sleep became a privilege. A white middle-class feminist instructor at the university suggested to me, all sympathetically, that I ought to hire someone to clean my house and watch the baby. Her suggestion was totally out of my reality, both economically and socially. I'd worked for years cleaning other peoples' houses. Hiring a working-class woman to do the shit work is a middle-class woman's solution to any dilemma which her privileges, such as a career, may present her.

Mothering: The feminist critique of families and the oppressive role of mothering has focused on white middle-class nuclear families. This may not be an appropriate model for communities of class and color. Mothering and families may hold a different importance for working-class women. Within this context, the issue of coming out can be a very painful process for working-class lesbians. Due to the homophobia of working-class communities, to be a lesbian is most often to be excommunicated from your family, neighborhood, friends and the people you work with. If you're working-class, you don't have such clearly demarcated concepts of yourself as an individual, but instead see yourself as part of a family and community that forms your survival structure. It is not easy to be faced with the risk of giving up ties which are so central to your identity and survival.

Individualism: Preoccupation with one's self—one's body, looks, relationships—is a luxury working-class women can't afford. Making an occupation out of taking care of yourself through therapy, aerobics, jogging, dressing for success, gourmet meals and proper nutrition, etc., may be responses that are directly rooted in privilege. The middle-class have the leisure time to be preoccupied with their own problems, such as their waistlines, planning their vacations, coordinating their wardrobes, or dealing with what their mother said to them when they were five—my!

The white middle-class women's movement has been patronizing to working-class women. Its supporters think we don't understand sexism. What we don't understand is white middle-class feminism. They act as though they invented the truth, the light, and the way, which they merely need to pass along to us lower-class drudges. What they invented is a distorted form of what working-class women already know—if you're female, life sucks. Only at least we were smart enough to know that it's not just being female, but also being a person of color or class, which makes life a quicksand trap. The class system weakens all women. It censors and eliminates images of female strength. The idea of women as passive, weak creatures totally discounts the strength, self-dependence and inter-dependence necessary to survive as working-class and poor women. My mother and her friends always had a less-than-passive, less-than-enamoured attitude toward their spouses, male bosses, and men in general. I know from listening to their conversations, jokes and what they passed on to us, their daughters, as folklore. When I was five years old, my mother told me about how Aunt Betty had hit Uncle Ernie over the head with a skillet and knocked him out because he was raising his hand to hit her, and how he's never even thought about doing it since. This story was told to me with a good amount of glee and laughter. All the men in the neighborhood were told of the event as an example of what was a very acceptable response in the women's community for that type of male behavior. We kids in the neighborhood grew up with these stories of women giving husbands, bosses, the welfare system, schools, unions and men in general—hell, whenever they deserved it. For me there were many role models of women taking action, control and resisting what was supposed to be their lot. Yet many white middle-class feminists continue to view feminism like math homework, where there's only supposed to be one answer. Never occurs to them that they might be talking algebra while working-class women might be talking metaphysics.

Women with backgrounds other than white middle-class experience compounded, simultaneous oppressions. We can't so easily separate our experiences by categories of gender, or race, or class, i.e., "I remember it well: on Saturday, June 3, I was experiencing class oppression, but by Tuesday, June 6, I was caught up in race oppression, then all day Friday, June 9, I was in the middle of gender oppression. What a week!" Sometimes, for example, gender and class reinforce each other. When I returned to college as a single parent after a few years of having kids and working crummy jobs—I went in for vocational testing. Even before I was tested, the white middle-class male vocational counselor looked at me, a welfare mother in my best selection from the Salvation Army racks, and suggested I quit college, go to vo-tech school and become a grocery clerk. This was probably the highest paying female working-class occupation he could think of. The vocational test results suggested I become an attorney. I did end up quitting college once again, not because of his suggestion, but because I was tired of supporting my children in ungenteel poverty. I entered vo-tech school for training as an electrician and, as one of the first women in a non-traditional field, was able to earn a living wage at a job which had traditionally been reserved for white working-class males. But this is a story for another day. Let's return to our little vocational counselor example. Was he suggesting the occupational choice of grocery clerk to me because of my gender or my class? Probably both. Let's imagine for a moment what this same vocational counselor might have advised, on sight only, to the following people:

1. A white middle-class male: doctor, lawyer, engineer, business executive.
2. A white middle-class female: close to the same suggestions as #1 if the counselor was not sexist, or, if sexist, then: librarian, teacher, nurse, social worker.
3. A middle-class man of color: close to the same suggestions as #1 if the counselor was not racist, or, if racist, then: school principal, sales, management, technician.
4. A middle-class woman of color: close to the same suggestions as #3 if the counselor was not sexist; #2 if not racist; if not racist or sexist, then potentially #1.
5. A white working-class male: carpenter, electrician, plumber, welder.
6. A white working-class female—well, we already know what he told me, although he could have also suggested secretary, waitress and dental hygienist (except I'd already told him I hated these jobs).
7. A working-class man of color: garbage collector, janitor, fieldhand.
8. A working-class woman of color: maid, laundress, garment worker.

Notice anything about this list? As you move down it, a narrowing of choices, status, pay, working conditions, benefits and chances for promotions occurs. To be connected to any one factor, such as gender or class or race, can make life difficult. To be connected to multiple factors can guarantee limited economic status and poverty.

WAYS TO AVOID FACING CLASSISM

Deny Deny Deny: Deny your class position and the privileges connected to it. Deny the existence or experience of the working-class and poor. You can even set yourself up (in your own mind) as judge and jury in deciding who qualifies as working-class by your white middle-class standards. So if someone went to college, or seems intelligent to you, not at all like your stereotypes, they must be middle-class.

Guilt Guilt Guilt: "I feel so bad, I just didn't realize!" is not helpful, but is a way to avoid changing attitudes and behaviors. Passivity—"Well, what can I do about it, anyway?"—and anger—"Well, what do they want!"—aren't too helpful either. Again, with these responses, the focus is on you and absolving the white middle-class from responsibility. A more helpful remedy is to take action. Donate your time and money to local foodbanks. Don't cross picket lines. Better yet, go join a picket line.

HOW TO CHALLENGE CLASSISM

If you're middle-class you can begin to challenge classism with the following:

1. Confront classist behavior in yourself, others and society. Use and share the privileges, like time or money, which you do have.
2. Make demands on working-class and poor communities' issues—anti-racism, poverty, unions, public housing, public transportation, literacy and day care.
3. Learn from the skills and strength of working people—study working and poor people's history; take some Labor Studies, Ethnic Studies, Women Studies classes. Challenge elitism. There are many different types of intelligence: white middle-class, academic, professional intellectualism being one of them (reportedly). Finally, educate yourself, take responsibility and take action.

If you're working-class, just some general suggestions (it's cheaper than therapy—free, less time-consuming and I won't ask you about what your mother said to you when you were five):

1. Face your racism! Educate yourself and others, your family, community, any organizations you belong to; take responsibility and take action. Face your classism, sexism, heterosexism, ageism, able-bodiness, adultism. . . .
2. Claim your identity. Learn all you can about your history and the history and experience of all working and poor peoples. Raise your children to be anti-racist, anti-sexist and anti-classist. Teach them the language and culture of working peoples. Learn to survive with a fair amount of anger and lots of humor, which can be tough when this stuff isn't even funny.
3. Work on issues which will benefit your community. Consider remaining in or returning to your communities. If you live and work in white middle-class environments, look for working-class allies to help you survive with your humor and wits intact. How do working-class people spot each other? We have antennae.

We need not deny or erase the differences of working-class cultures but can embrace their richness, their variety, their moral and intellectual heritage. We're not at the point yet where we can celebrate differences—not having money for a prescription for your child is nothing to celebrate. It's not time yet to party with the white middle-class, because we'd be the entertainment ("Aren't they quaint? Just love their workboots and uniforms and the way they cuss!"). We need to overcome divisions among working people, not by ignoring the multiple oppressions many of us encounter, or by oppressing each other, but by becoming committed allies on all issues which affect working people: racism, sexism, classism, etc. An injury to one is an injury to all. Don't play by ruling-class rules, hoping that maybe you can live on Connecticut Avenue instead of Baltic, or that you as an individual can make it to Park Place and Boardwalk. Tired of Monopoly? Always ending up on Mediterranean Avenue? How about changing the game?

Bob and Cathie's Daughter: Why I Call Myself Working-Class

Catherine Macleod

Catherine Macleod, a Canadian citizen who emigrated from Scotland as a child, has struggled to rise above the socioeconomic limitations of the working class to become educated and attain a professional career. Yet she still considers herself working class. In this essay, Macleod embarks on a reflective journey in an attempt to explain to her friend, as well as herself, why she still considers herself "working class."

A year ago a friend asked me why I called myself working-class. It was a challenge. Nobody had ever asked before.

"I was born in the tenements of Glasgow, Scotland in 1948," I said, feeling a bit like I was grasping at straws. "I had no rich uncles." I added hopefully, under her direct gaze. Well. it's true.

Most, but not all of my uncles, drank too much, sang songs, danced to Glenn Miller and Vera Mills, told (what I learned in 1969 to be sexist and racist) jokes and passed out, pleased with themselves. My aunts' stories, of course, are epic.

My uncles gave their weekly pay packs to their wives, who did all the work at home as well as worked in the shipyards or in shops. The men went to the dog track or soccer matches on Saturdays and owned one suit—for weddings and funerals. They told the same stories over and over again. We actually encouraged them to do this because they told their stories so well.

Surviving the war was their top story. I could see the flames of the bombing of Clydebank in their eyes, as they spoke. Although they read the newspaper every day and listened to the wireless, my uncles rarely read books. Ours was an oral culture.

From *Our Times Magazine,* October/November 1994.

If you couldn't say everything you needed to say in words, and quickly, then you would be considered illiterate among my people. They were magicians with language in all its forms—conversation, patter, the joke, the punch-line, the silence, the wink, the raised eyebrow, the subversive smile, the tear, the raised voice, the lowered eyes, the curse, the fist to the table that shakes the teacup in its saucer.

Oral culture aside, Nanny Gloud, my grandmother, slipped books to me as if she was placing a bet. The first was Louisa May Alcott's *Little Women,* Christmas 1955. The second was *Jane Eyre,* Christmas 1956.

My uncles never read Dr. Spock. They disciplined their children with a belt to the side of the head. Most of my uncles went to school until they were old enough to start their apprenticeship at 14. Most of my uncles worked hard at the shipyards. Most of my uncles were skilled and took pride in their trades.

They liked fried bread and blood pudding, bacon and eggs, porridge oats, fish and chips in newspaper, hot peas in vinegar and Spam sandwiches. Lettuce was for rabbits.

They loved their mothers and feared their fathers' tempers. When they were happy, they got drunk to celebrate. When they were angry, they got drunk to protest.

They respected authority—doctors, teachers, priests or ministers—but not too much. They enjoyed outwitting the police. As a child I'd hear a heavy knock at the door. My grandmother would whisper, "It's the poliss."

My uncles could be violent and angry. Most of them spent at least one or two nights in jail for street fighting. They dreamed of America, of driving Buicks, or winning the Littlewoods Pool. They were sentimental, affectionate, and humble—in a boastful way, if that's possible. I loved them, each and every one.

But my friend was not satisfied with the story of my uncles, and persisted. "That's not you, that was them."

OK, I said. I'll try again. How's this? "I am their niece. Bob and Cathie's daughter. The next generation."

My father and mother immigrated to Canada in 1958. "Canada good country," my father would laugh, imitating a first generation Italian-Canadian accent as he sat in the one-room trailer with no plumbing that we called home that first year in Fruitland, Ontario.

Canadians called us DPs—displaced persons. My mother wasn't as enthusiastic about our dislocation as my father. Neither were my little sister or brother, ruptured as we were from our comfortable state-owned, two-bedroom Glasgow apartment and our large extended family.

As for me, I sided with my father as usual. But I did miss combing my grandmother's long white hair. She used to let me do this on Sunday evenings after the family meal, when the grown ups were playing cards, the coal fire lighting our spirits and keeping us one. I missed combing her hair a lot. It was my job, the thing Nanny Gloud let me do for her. I felt useful and valued. Nanny was Queen Victoria, surveying her kingdom. I stood behind her, a confident five-year-old foot placed firmly on each arm of her big chair.

Every other time I saw Nanny Gloud she was working in the little house with her hair in combs—cooking, cleaning, sorting, carrying, sewing, darning, ironing, washing, comforting, fighting, her fist punching the air in an attempt to bring order to what was often chaos.

I also missed Aunt Ada, who made me pretty frocks, and Aunt Mary, who mothered my mother if she got sick or pregnant. But Canada was the good life, whether I liked it or not. So I made the best of it.

I learned to cook on the two-burner hotplate, took care of my mother (who was, I later realized, severely depressed), looked after my baby sister whose hip was fractured and who wore a body cast for most of a year without medicare. I fought with my younger brother, darned work socks, made beds properly, did laundry, ironed shirts, spoke Canadian, and went to school with people who had no interest in who I was, or where I came from.

All my schoolmates knew of me was that I had a funny accent, wore silly clothes—especially my rubber boots with the orange soles—had a face full of freckles, a severe case of acne, and that I lived in the trailer park with all the poor people. I was easy to scare, eager to please.

Before we owned our own television, my brother and I would slip out on moist Sunday summer nights to perch ourselves on a neighbour's trailer hitch and watch *The Ed Sullivan Show*—or whatever else the Turners were watching—through their window, all to the sound of crickets. If the neighbours knew our faces were pressed against the glass, they never let on.

I wanted out.

I fought my way through school, and eventually into university, taking night classes and working day jobs, qualifying as a mature student. I borrowed money and did without because I wanted so much to be a part of that foreign culture—the "better life"—I thought would make me a better person.

I remember my male professors, filled with Apollo, trying to sharpen my mind and rope me into the traditions of knowledge and culture they knew. I also remember the one exception, Christian Bay, who encouraged me to be myself. That gentle political scientist tried to get me to write what I knew. But the language I spoke could not easily make its way to the pages of the papers I wrote for him.

"Why can't you write the way you speak?" he would ask in exasperation, after marking yet another C– on a paper about class and ideology, or women and liberation. What made Christian exceptional was that he listened to me, one of the few teachers who ever did. Sad but true, I didn't expect to be listened to.

In those days I had no respect for my naive, unstructured ways of thinking and living. I wanted to gain legitimacy in the honoured traditions of the establishment, in my case, the left, male establishment.

By the time I was 25 I had succeeded in shedding my own skin, as painful a process as you can imagine, and left myself with no defense against spiritual, intellectual or cultural conquest. The tools I used to shed my skin were sex, higher education, rock and roll, beer, Andy Warhol, Rochdale College, Ingmar Bergman films with subtitles, and all-nighters on Yorkville Avenue in Toronto.

I had grown up with no desire to preserve or honour myself or my own people. I became a wilful and happy collaborator in the colonization of my mind. I bought the idea that what I was and where I had come from had no value. The only thing I valued was what I could become, if I worked hard enough to hide all vestiges of what, by that time, seemed like my sordid, painful and bewildering past—my badges of shame.

"OK," my friend persisted, still not satisfied. "That was then. This is now."

How can you still call yourself working-class when you have a nice home? she asked. You have your own television set now, a university education, a library of books and music, a new car, a cellular phone, more than one pair of shoes, and you like art. You have been published, produced plays, travelled, organized, and had good-paying jobs. "Surely you are as middle class, in an anti-establishment kind of way, as they get!"

This is what I must say to my friend. If the value of experience and education is freedom then I must, first and foremost, be free to name myself; to not be burdened by the labels my foes—or my friends—may want to tag me with.

See, one of the shrewdest forms of tyranny practised on people who escape from poverty into relative security is the idea that we must abandon our own culture; that we must drop our own values and our own heritage in order to assimilate into the "better" culture. But if we collude in this type of assimilation, we are stripped of any dignity that went with our identity at the very moment the weight of our material restriction lifts. We allow others to name us.

I've learned that if Noam Chomsky's interpreters met me at a book launch they might dismiss me as a member of the "political class." If the enormously compassionate Freddy Engels had studied me in his lifetime, he may have slotted me "bourgeois." Bell Hooks, if she read my poetry, may assume I'm a privileged, cool, feminist white woman who identifies with blacks, lesbians and black lesbians alike. My lesbian friends may speculate that I'm "closeted," happy as I am in a heterosexual marriage at last. My social democratic educators may stamp me a radical, a loose cannon on the deck. My Trotskyist teachers may term me a class traitor. My tutors from the Communist Party may tag me a union bureaucrat, because of the way I have made an itinerant living as an intermittent single mother.

During my work as a staff rep for a labour federation, some in the cultural industry have called me a writer of doggerel, a minion in the porkchop palace.

My mother—my first teacher and critic—used to say I had a head full of magic. "And just who do you think you are?" she'd ask disparagingly. My simple answer to my mother, my friend—and critics—is, as Popeye says, "I yam what I yam." Is that working class?

The struggle of memory against forgetting is at the core of my resistance. I'm not talking here about nostalgia, that longing for something to be as once it was, that useless act. I'm talking about a remembering that illuminates and transforms the here and now of my life.

I know now that I needed the serendipitous combination of street experience and university training to help me see myself and my people as we really were. Being street smart doesn't make me anti-intellectual. On the contrary, I gradually realized it was not only stupid but dangerous to be separated from my cultural roots and history, my power source. I had to go back to the words I knew as a child, and like a child, ask for forgiveness and remembrance from the ghosts of my uncles, my aunts and Nanny Gloud.

My acceptance of who I am, however, happened not a split second before I was brought to my knees in despair of ever escaping my working-class past and being welcomed into a middle class present. I don't learn anything easily. But I have finally learned that I have the power to say to the paralyzing chorus of voices that is as big as St. Michael's Boys' Choir: "One. Two. Three. Let me think. Let me speak. Be gone."

Discovering the strength in my working-class, immigrant, female Scottish heritage has thrown open a new door of spiritual and political possibility for me. What had, for many painful and tortured years, looked like a site of devastation and deprivation, has become, at last, its opposite—a confusing, complicated, amusing and nourishing space of resistance.

This is where I want to be; where I feel most useful.

In the language of some, people like me are creating a "counter-hegemonic discourse," making change by acknowledging our ways of being and the ways we live that are in glorious opposition to the values of the ruling establishments. My Nanny Gloud would have said I'm not putting on airs any more. Be gone.

When Barbara, my new friend and teacher, asked me to explain why I called myself working-class, it was a challenge. I didn't think I had an answer. But now I do; and I'm glad she asked.

The Feminization of Poverty

Diana Pearce

At the beginning of the twenty-first century, as the disparity between rich and poor becomes even greater, it is clear that women and children are quickly becoming a part of the underclass. Unless the hierarchical structure of society is reorganized, and unless the standard of living for women and children increases, how do you think the identity of women and children and their sense of self-worth will be affected? How does Pearce propose we can increase the possibility of positive self-identity and self-worth among women and children?

I'm going to talk about three things today. First, I'm going to give you a description of poverty trends, especially the trend towards the feminization of poverty. Second, I'm going to describe how our welfare system, not AFDC, but unemployment, etc., reinforces women's poverty. Third, I'm going to talk about what the future holds; there will be two topics under this, first, welfare reform, which we already have in the form of the Family Support Act, and secondly, housing reform, which we don't have yet, but desperately need.

The "other America," described two decades ago by Michael Harrington, is a changing neighborhood. Men are moving out, while women, many with children, are moving in. As a result, the War on Poverty, as described by Harrington and many others, was built on images and assumptions about the poor that have become increasingly invalid. I'm going to talk today about the feminization of poverty which has profoundly altered the nature of poverty and therefore the nature of the kinds of solutions that we must propose.

What is the feminization of poverty? Whether it is widows, divorcees, or unmarried mothers, women have always experienced more poverty than men. But in the last two decades, families maintained by women alone have increased from 36 percent to 51.5 percent of all poor families. That is the feminization of poverty.

During the 1970s, there was a net increase each year of about 100,000 poor, woman-maintained families. Between 1979 and 1987, another almost 1 million families headed by women became poor. And of the increase in poor families between 1986 and 1987, the last year for which we have data, ⅔ were headed by women. There are now 3½ million families maintained by women alone with incomes below the poverty level. If one simply extrapolated the present trends and did not take into account any other factors, all of the poor by the year 2000 would be women and children. That is the feminization of poverty.

The relative economic status of families maintained by women alone has also declined, with average income of female-headed families falling from 51 percent to 46 percent of the average male-headed family. Once poor, the female-maintained family is more likely to stay poor—ten times more likely by one estimate. That is the feminization of poverty.

These trends are even greater within the minority community. Particularly in the

From *The Journal for Peace and Justice Studies* Vol. 2. (1990). Reprinted with permission.

1970s, the black community experienced a shift in the burden of poverty from two-parent families to families maintained by the woman alone, so that now, about three out of four poor black families are maintained by women alone. Because of racial discrimination, the statistics for minority women are even more dismal than those for majority women. This shift has increased minority poverty and exacerbated racial inequality. That is the feminization of poverty.

Basically, what has been happening are two opposite trends. First, several groups that have historically experienced disproportionate rates of poverty have been lifted out of poverty by post-war economic growth or by the development of targeted social programs. Many workers who used to be labeled the "working poor" by themselves as well as others, are now economically secure enough to be seen as the "working class" or the "middle class." Older Americans, whose poverty frequently occurred because of a health care crisis or a lack of housing and inadequate Social Security, have been given Medicare—although we've been gutting that—housing chartered specifically for the elderly, and raised and indexed Social Security benefits. As a result, the overall poverty rate for the elderly is actually less than that of the population as a whole.

The opposite trend characterizes families maintained by women alone. Although a decrease in the proportion of these families experienced poverty, about one third of all female-maintained families are poor today, compared to one half in the 1960s. This gain has been overwhelmed by the large increase in the number of women-maintained families, greatly enlarging the pool of those at risk. Most people are aware that the rise in the divorce rate and the increase in the number of children born out of wedlock has increased the number of single-parent families. But this trend is also the result of the fact that, first of all, virtually every woman today is married at some point (about 94 percent of women by the age of sixty-five have tried marriage) and most ever married have children. Only 6 percent remained childless by the age of forty to forty-four in 1980. In 1950, about 20 percent remained childless by the time they got to the end of their child-bearing years. In short, more women are mothers, but fewer do so with a lifelong mate.

But this just begs the question of why women-maintained households have . . . not shared in either the prosperity of the 1950s and 1960s, or . . . the poverty reduction experienced by other high-risk groups. The answer lies in the following two basic phenomena. First, women's poverty is fundamentally different from that experienced by men, and second, poor women are subject to programs designed for poor men. Poor women find that these programs are not only inadequate and inappropriate, but also lock them into a life of poverty.

While many women are poor for some of the same reasons that men are poor—for example, they live in a job-poor area, and/or they lack the necessary skills or education—much of women's poverty can be traced to two causes that are basically unique to women. First, women must provide all or most of the support for their children, and secondly, they are disadvantaged in the labor market as women.

Women bear the economic as well as emotional burden of rearing their children. When a couple with children breaks up, frequently, the man becomes single, while the woman becomes a single parent. Poverty rates for households with children have always been greater than those for households that do not have children and the difference had always been greater for female-headed households. That gap is increasing: 46.1 percent of women-headed households with children under eighteen years of age are in poverty, compared with about 8 percent of households maintained by men with their children living with them. The differential is in part a product of the fact that many families never receive some or all of the support due them from the absent father. For instance, in 1985, only 43 percent of absent fathers paid child support and only about half of those paid the full amount. The amounts paid are small as well, averaging only about $2,200 annually per family, not per child. At a time when the median family income is over $30,000 a year, this is less than 10 percent of average family income. According to one study, a father's child support payment averaged less than his car payment. In other words, fathers pay more to support their cars than to support their kids. What makes matters worse, payments have not kept up with inflation. In the last three years, the real value of the average payment in constant inflation adjusted dollars has fallen 16 percent. I'll talk later about some things that are starting to happen so that the child support picture won't be so dismal in the future.

Public support of dependent children is even more appalling. Using as a standard the amount of money paid a foster mother to take care of children who are not her own, we can see that we have always been more generous to children in two-parent foster homes than to children in their own, single-parent homes. Over the past eight years, however, that ratio has become worse, and now instead of the foster parent getting three times what the AFDC parent gets for food, shelter, and clothes for the child, the foster parent in the average state gets four times as much. In 1982, the average foster child payment was $197 per month while the average payment for an additional child was $49 per month. In some states, the foster parents are paid seven or eight times as much as the child's own mother is to take care of the child.

The other source of women's poverty that is unique to women, is their disadvantage in the labor market, and I think most of you are pretty familiar with that. That is, the average woman only earns about 65 percent of what the average male earns for full-time work and that figure has changed very little—it's gone up and down, and it's going up a little now, but it's still within the range of where it's been since the Korean War.

In 1987, the average woman college graduate working full-time, throughout the year, earned less than the average male high school graduate. We've made some progress—we used to earn less as college graduates than the average male high school dropout.

Equally important, but less well known is another aspect of women's disadvantage in the labor market. More women than men are unable to obtain regular, full-time, year round work. About half the women in the labor force are working part-time or part year, or both, and slightly less than half the women are full-time, year round workers. Many women, especially mothers seeking to support their households on their earnings, encounter serious obstacles with full participation in the labor force, including inadequate, unavailable or unaffordable day care, and discrimination based on full-time work. And, as a result, only about 40 percent of women maintaining households alone are full-time, year round workers, as compared to almost two thirds of male householders. About one third of women heading families alone, compared to 20 percent of the men, are not in the labor force at all. In addition, women are concentrated in a relatively small number of occupations, many of which are underpaid. As women experience occupational segregation and confinement to the pink-collar ghetto, the limitations on opportunities for income growth that accompany such segregation keep women poor. Finally, there are the economic costs of sexual harassment that are almost always borne by the woman alone. Every woman who has lost a promotion, quit to avoid further sexual harassment, or "mysteriously" walked away from an opportunity, has paid an economic as well as a psychic price for being a woman. As far as I know, no one has done a really good job of measuring the "price," the economic costs, of sexual harassment, not sex discrimination, but sexual harassment.

Even working women must work harder to avoid poverty. Eleven percent of minority women single parents who work full-time, all year, are still poor; this is the same percentage of white male householders who are poor, who do not work at all. Because of the higher poverty rates of women associated with each level of participation in the labor market, and because fewer female heads of household participate as full-time workers, having a job is a much less certain route out of poverty for women than for men. Altogether, about 4 percent of families with a working male householder are in poverty, while more than 25 percent of families headed by employed women have incomes below the poverty level. And recent work that I haven't published yet shows that most of the increase in women's labor force participation over the last decade has been as low wage workers, and that's at about $5.85 an hour or less, minimum wage in the 1970s, so that most of our increase in the labor force has been at the very bottom, and it's been particularly bad for single parents. Single parents are working more now and have higher poverty rates than before so that they've now moved from being working poor to being poor.

Now let's look at the welfare system and what it does. It's supposed to provide income support for families when they have inadequate income. Our system was developed to provide income to individuals and families whose earnings are inadequate to meet their needs. But beyond that basic rule, various income support programs differ greatly in every characteristic, such as the amount of benefits, accessibility, and stigma attached to the benefit.

Using such characteristics, these programs can be divided into two broad groups. Programs found in the *primary* sector are for the deserving poor and have been characterized as a right, often but not always, a right which comes from working, from being employed. They have relatively generous benefits and are not means-tested and are not stigmatizing. By contrast, programs in the secondary sector are for the "undeserving poor" and frequently restrict and treat eligibility criteria depending on time and geography. These programs have a strict income limit in order to qualify, and provide benefits that are penurious in amount and stigmatizing. Programs in both sectors are based on male models, primarily a male breadwinner model for the primary sector, and a male pauper model for the secondary sector. An example of a major program in the primary sector is the unemployment compensation program. This program is designed for a limited group of workers. You think of it as something for everybody who's unemployed, but it's not supposed to be. This group of workers is comprised of regular workers, who are presumed also to be the breadwinners in their families, in which the wife had a supporting role but was not herself in paid employment. The original aim was to help these workers, who, through no fault of their own and due to the vagaries of seasonal employment patterns, business cycles, or technological obsolescence, found themselves out of work. The group to be aided by this program was not all the unemployed, since casual workers, or those who worked part time or seasonally, could not prove their attachment to the work force and therefore were not deserving of help. Women and other minority workers were not and are not now statutorily excluded from eligibility for unemployment benefits, but many have been excluded in disproportionate numbers by virtue of their low wages, or their less than full-time status. They are considered "casual" workers, or, because they are part-time, are not eligible for unemployment compensation. This has far-reaching consequences for those who are the sole supporters of their households.

By contrast, the secondary sector is disproportionately composed of women and minorities. In spite of this demographic characteristic, the secondary sector programs are built on the male pauper model, which has its roots in the sixteenth-century poor laws of England, when paupers were ex-soldiers, beggars, and vagabond, landless peasants, and were mostly men. This model offers a simple set of principles: "Most of the poor are poor because they do not work, and most of the poor are able-bodied and could work." Therefore, the solution to poverty, according to the male pauper model, is to "put them to work." Unlike unemployment compensation, there is little concern for the quality of the job, even its monetary return, or in matching workers' skills to jobs with appropriate requirements. Rather, any job will do. When applied to women, such as AFDC mothers, the results are less than positive. First, as we've seen above, having a job is, by itself a less certain route out of poverty for women than it is for men. Second, income from earnings only partially meets the woman's needs and therefore, only partially alleviates her poverty. A woman's responsibility for children and other dependents results in economic and emotional burdens requiring additional income and fringe benefits for child care and health insurance, and flexible or part-time work arrangements, that are not available with most jobs.

The dual welfare system described above is not only inherently discriminatory against women, but also operates to reinforce their disadvantaged status in the labor market. Economists have developed a theory of institutional divisions in the labor market that conceives of the labor market as a dual system, divided into primary and secondary sectors. In the primary sector, workers hold jobs with relatively high pay and good fringe benefits, better working conditions and greater security. If they should lose their jobs, they are likely to be compensated relatively better through unemployment compensation and through other programs such as disability at rates designed to replace 50 percent of lost wages; plus, if they are members of a union, they receive supplementary union benefits. Although theoretically, workers in this sector must return to work as soon as possible, the programs are designed, not only to support the worker and his or her family during unemployment, but also to enable the worker to conduct a job search that will result in reemployment in a job that will maintain his or her skills, occupational status and income. Indeed, many people who receive unemployment do not go through a great income loss over that period of time and return to a job that pays relatively well.

In contrast, workers in the secondary sector find themselves at relatively low wage jobs with little job security and few fringe benefits. If they lose their jobs, which happens relatively more frequently and unpredictably than in the primary sector, these workers often find themselves ineligible for unemployment compensation. Many women in this circumstance turn to AFDC, the "poor woman's unemployment compensation." Studies show that 90 percent of welfare mothers have worked, many of them recently, and many of the women who apply for public assistance do so only after both the labor market and the marriage institution have failed to provide income to adequately support their families. However, they cannot even obtain this help without first impoverishing themselves, by exhausting their resources and savings. Once on welfare, they not only find it penurious in amount and stigmatizing, but they are also pushed to leave it as soon as possible, no matter how poor the new job's pay and long-term prospects, or how inadequate the child care is, or how difficult the transportation. The secondary welfare sector destroys not only one's incentive, but also one's prospects of ever working one's way out of poverty. And, of course, as soon as one's child gets sick, or a crisis happens, or one gets fired, one's back on welfare and the cycle continues and reinforces one's position in the secondary labor market, the secondary welfare system.

Disproportionate numbers of women and minorities are found in the secondary sector. While 87 percent of the recipients of primary benefits are white families headed by men or married couples, only three percent are families maintained by black women alone. Conversely, woman householders account for over two thirds of secondary sector recipients, that is, recipients of welfare and public assistance. As one might expect, there's a great difference in the poverty incidence between the two sectors. While only about 8 percent of those families whose heads have been receiving primary sector benefits, such as unemployment compensation, are poor, almost ¾ of families with heads who receive secondary sector benefits are in poverty. Thus women, particularly minority women, are disproportionately experiencing impoverishing consequences of the dual welfare system.

I'm going to talk now about a new aspect of the problem of women and poverty, the housing crisis and women. Women are disproportionately affected by the housing crisis for all of the reasons I've been describing—their disproportionate low income and poverty incidence and the fact that they tend to be long-term poor as compared to men. One of the consequences of this disproportionate poverty is that women are much more likely to be renters than owners. Two thirds of women-maintained families are renters, as compared to ¾ of all other families who are owners, a tremendous dichotomy in terms of women's positions in the housing market.

The second aspect in the housing market is that women-maintained households have experienced some increase in income, but it hasn't kept up with the increases in rent. So those who are renters are getting the squeeze. Over the decade of 1975–1985, renter women-maintained households' income increased an average of 12 percent, but rents increased an average of 20 percent. As a result of this, the average percent of income that women-maintained households are spending on housing, rent and utilities, rose from 38 percent in 1974 to 58 percent in 1987. They're spending almost 60 percent of their income on housing.

This is worse for black and Hispanic women who have higher poverty rates and higher percentages which go to rent. I think one of the things to keep in mind when we're talking about this particular aspect of poverty is that when you spend money on housing, when you're very poor, you can't cut back on your housing expenditures. If you're very poor, you could skip a meal, not buy new clothes. You can't stop using your living room to cut down on your rent costs. So as we see this increasing squeeze of higher costs and less income, women are really being squeezed by this.

The supply of low-cost housing is disappearing very fast. In 1970, there were 15 million units which were considered "affordable," that is, with an income of $5,000 or less, you could rent them for 30 percent or less of your income. Today, the number of units that are "affordable," adjusting for inflation, is now only 1.8 million. This is about one unit per every two families that are low-income.

We have also seen an increase in discrimination against families with kids, another factor which affects women in the housing market. Families with children are new clients under the Fair Housing Law, but given the effectiveness of the 1968 Fair Housing Act, in terms of race and gender discrimination, I think we shouldn't expect discrimination against families with children to disappear overnight. In fact, we're beginning to hear about new kinds of discrimination against families with children. For example, "we can't rent to families with children because there's lead paint and we don't want to poison the children." Suddenly, I guess they're concerned about children.

What are we doing in terms of public policy in this area? HUD helps about 4.3 million households, not just female headed households but all households. This is about ⅓ of the families in need, that is, families who are eligible either because of low income or inadequate housing.

Since 1981, housing for low income families has been cut more than any other low income budget item, with about 80 percent cut in that area. To give you a specific example illustrating how bad it has gotten, and what's going to happen in the near future, we have had a program called Section 8, which is where you give someone a certificate and they can go and get housing and pay only 30 percent of their income for that housing and the government pays the difference between that and the rent. This year, about 20,000 of those certificates will expire and that means that people will suddenly have to be paying the full rent. Next year, about 200,000 of those certificates will expire and at this point, we have nothing in the budget which will deal with those issues and that's obviously a big part of the battle about housing. And after next year, there will be another several hundred thousand. It will escalate like this: almost all of the housing we built or subsidized for low income families, including Section 8 certificates, had time limits. Somehow, we thought the problem would solve itself, that somehow the local housing authority would start producing housing for low income households, or that we would no longer have poor households. Whichever assumption was made, it was all very unrealistic and it's all coming due. The more recent housing programs have even shorter time frames, so we're going over a cliff in the early nineties in terms of what's going to happen for housing.

One consequence of this squeeze in the housing market and the decline in affordable housing units and the increases in rent, is that families with children, especially women with children, are becoming homeless.

I'd like to talk now, and most of this is drawn from congressional testimony I gave earlier this week, about the problem of the invisibility of homeless families. I think one of the problems we are confronting with public housing policy today, is that women-headed families with children are the most invisible of all of our poverty population. By the way, all of the statistics I gave you on poverty, and the feminization of poverty, don't count the homeless because all those statistics are based on household surveys. If you don't have a house, you're not a household and you're not counted. So all of those official numbers underestimate poverty in the 1980s, because we don't have any count of people even in shelters, we only count people in households when doing the annual survey on income and poverty.

Families with children, most of which are women with children, are the fastest growing segment of the homeless. This is the virtually unanimous conclusion of surveys done by mayors, homeless coalitions, and others. Between 1983 and 1987, the number of women seeking shelter at battered women shelters has increased 100 percent. The proportion of homeless which are families varies widely from city to city from 25 percent to 70 percent of the homeless depending on the city and depending on the person doing the estimate. With the total estimate of up to three million homeless, the number of homeless families could well be in the neighborhood of one million.

But this is truly the proverbial tip of the iceberg. Detailed reports from a number of cities state that the ratio of those turned away to those served is highest for those families with children, with figures of three turnaways for every family served common, as those of you who work in shelters or soup kitchens probably know. For example, in Minneapolis, families with children are 28 percent of the homeless served in shelters and soup kitchens surveyed but are 72 percent of those turned away. The Coalition Against Domestic Violence reports that in 1987, 40 percent of battered women were turned away from domestic violence shelters due to a lack of space and many of the women and their children had to return to the husbands or lovers that were battering them.

Though many have no place to call home, most of these families who are turned away are considered to be "near homeless" or "precariously housed" because they're not in shelters or on the streets. Such terms marginalize these families and keep them invisible when we talk about the "real homeless." Not surprisingly, studies which only count those on the streets and in the shelters (which is, by the way, the predominant method to be used in the 1990 census to count the homeless) estimate not only much smaller numbers of homeless but a much smaller proportion who are families with children. Though they frankly express surprise when they do find women who are homeless, roughly 20–25 percent of homeless population, few if any are homeless mothers with children. And when they do find them, they are characterized as not really homeless. One of the best known studies, done in Chicago by Rossi and others, found no homeless mothers with children in the streets. Of those in the shelters, they noticed there was a "minority of young black women who were typically homeless with their children and apparently in transition from unsatisfactory housing arrangements to establishing new households with those children."

One must ask, "Are not all homeless in some sense, in transition from one housing situation to another?" In short, the more successful homeless families are at hiding their homelessness, the less likely they are to be counted as or seen as homeless, whether by academics, the census bureau, or even by economic service providers, and less likely to have access to the services and housing opportunities which they so desperately need.

It's no accident that families with children are often the invisible homeless. To be counted as homeless, one must become known to someone who is doing the counting: shelter providers, social service officials, or an academic interviewer. Many families with children who are homeless desperately do not want to be known as homeless, for to become known, is to incur the risk of losing their children. That is, if the shelters you go to, or social services you apply to, are not able to provide you with even temporary housing, or they judge your housing situation to be inadequate, officials are empowered by law to make sure the children are not without shelter, and that means putting the children in foster care. Once the children are in foster care, it is extremely difficult to get them back, for the parents are caught in a catch-22. Without their children, they are not eligible for welfare or housing assistance as families; without income and housing, it's very difficult to get the children back.

The threat of foster care is not an idle threat. The number of children in foster care has begun to increase recently, which is highly unusual during a time of economic recovery and relatively low unemployment. While the number of children in foster care each year was about 275,000 in the mid-1980s, it has suddenly increased in the last two years. The House Select Committee on Children, Youth and Families, estimated that the 1988 number will jump as much as 50 percent, from 250,000 to 395,000. In some jurisdictions, homelessness is fast becoming a major reason for children being placed in foster care. While in California, a child cannot be placed in foster care for the sole reason of homelessness, in many other places, families are losing their children to foster care. It is a policy of many jurisdictions, including the District of Columbia—I don't know what is true in Philadelphia—that a baby born to a woman who lives in a women's shelter or on the streets is automatically placed in foster care. The reasoning is that, as a homeless person, she is by definition neglecting her child by not providing food and shelter. In Michigan, families who do not pay their utility bills or rent, can be found guilty of "environmental" neglect, a new kind of neglect, and their children can be put into foster care. All too often, parents in need of counseling, medical care or food must make an awful choice between seeking help and risk losing their kids, or not seeking help and seeing them suffer.

Faced with the threat of foster care and of shelters and welfare hotels, homeless families use five strategies to cope with their situation. These strategies contribute to their not being counted and to their invisibility.

The first strategy, used by many homeless families with children, is to double up with families or friends. This is a particularly common strategy among young, single parents with one or two children. With the cutbacks in welfare payments and public housing, setting up one's own single parent household is precluded. Public housing authorities know that there are large numbers of such families. According to one study, half of the eligible applicants for public housing already live in public housing, just doubled up. According to a recent report in 1986, one third of all children in the District of Columbia, and this isn't one third of the poor children, this is one third of *all* children, now live in doubled up households. It's probably just as high in other cities.

Doubling up forestalls going to shelters or living on the streets, but only for a short time. More than one half of [Washington] DC's homeless families had been doubled up before becoming homeless. The threat of discovery, the fear of reprisals against both families by the landlord, whether public or private, plus the overcrowding, makes such housing strategies inherently short lived. At the same time, fear of discovery prevents these families from seeking access to low-income housing, for which they are eligible, when it is available. For example, applicants from doubled up households who were applying for newly furnished units in a housing development in Brooklyn, New York, if they were not in a shelter, could not give the name of a landlord or even their host as references, because they feared reprisal for themselves or their host family, and thus were effectively excluded from this opportunity. Many people simply stopped filling out their applications when they got to the landlord reference section.

A second strategy used by homeless families with children is to seek hidden housing, such as abandoned cars and empty houses. In the South, some people live in abandoned chicken coops and in the West, on and off freeways. In this and other areas, they live in parks, campgrounds and even in ravines. They are not seen in downtown areas or sleeping in crates. They seek instead the anonymity of more residential suburban and even rural areas. Perhaps the most creative strategy was that of a Montgomery County, Maryland, woman who described her experiences during her years on a waiting list for subsidized housing. This is from a hearing:

> When my husband left and I was with four children, I didn't have a job and I was not able to pay the rent. We were evicted and Community Ministries came and put our furniture in storage, but there were five of us. I went from place to place, but the shelters were full. You know, everybody's sorry. We slept anywhere we could, in basements, in vacant houses. I would find vacant houses during the week, and I'd leave a window open and go in at night. We moved about twelve times throughout the five years while we were waiting. We lived for eight months in a vacant apartment with no heat and no utilities and you don't want too many people to find out, because they'll take my kids away, so we just kept moving. I took midnight shift jobs so the kids could sleep in the building. Finally, I got my certificate, so now I have a house. But when you go to Community Ministries or when you go to the Women's Interfaith Store for your clothes, you hear the same thing: I don't know where I'm going to stay tonight. I've been there for three years and I can't ever forget.

A third strategy used by families who become homeless because of abuse or violence is to go to a shelter for battered women. But because these are not homeless shelters these women are often not thought of as homeless. Although over 300,000 women and children were sheltered last year in over 1100 shelters and safe houses, priorities for housing assistance for victims of domestic violence have not been well publicized. And even when they are, such priorities are not worth much in many communities because waiting lists are years long, or are closed altogether. This is especially a problem, since most battered women's shelters have time limits numbered in days or weeks, not years.

Fourth, homeless families with children who can't find housing together seek out private, informal alternatives to official foster care. In a HUD study done in 1980, and surely the problem is worse now, 20 percent of the families with children ended up splitting up, that is, leaving the children with relatives while they searched for housing. Half of those families remained apart for four months or more. These families also get caught in a catch-22, as when applications for housing assistance, such as Section 8, permit the applicant to list only family members who are currently living with them. Finally, when all else fails, parents force their children to live in a shelter or welfare hotel. Some homeless parents choose to place their children voluntarily into foster care. As I said earlier, in the average state, foster parents receive four times as much per child than the parents or guardians under AFDC. If you had to choose between the kind of housing available and affordable on a welfare grant (or doubling up, or living in a vacant apartment), *versus* your child receiving four times that amount for food and shelter living in a foster home, what would be the best choice to make for your children?

When children enter foster care, homeless families become doubly invisible, for they now appear as two separate statistics, as more children in foster care *and* more homeless adults. Thus, if you go to the shelters for homeless women, you'll find that many of those women have children. In fact, many times, they are in contact with them. They phone them—but they can't get their children back. But as *homeless* families, they become invisible, they disappear. Becoming a whole family again—much less securing housing—is, needless to say, incredibly difficult once your children are in foster care.

I'd like to briefly describe the story of a woman accompanying me when I testified before the U. S. House of Representatives. This is a story from Soberton, Georgia. Her name was Cora Lee Johnson. A woman she knew was the mother of her nephew's child and had three children, including a baby. They were in church one day three weeks ago, and the baby appeared sick, feverish. When they got home and they changed the baby's diaper, they discovered there was blood in the diaper so they took the baby to the hospital. They got a ride to the hospital.

They had to go to another county. (It's in a very poor area and there was no nearby hospital.) They drove thirty miles to the nearest hospital. The mother went with the baby because that is required in most places. They placed the baby in the hospital. When it came time for the baby to leave the hospital, they would not release the baby to the mother and they said that the welfare department, "the Welfare," had come and taken the baby. She called Miss Cora Lee Johnson and asked to have her help, so she came down, but by that time, "the Welfare" had taken the baby and they told the mother, "Forget about this child, you'll never see this child again."

Why did they take the child? Because the woman was living with her three children, doubled up, with another household, and they said her housing was inadequate for her to be able to take care of her children. When she returned home, her other two children had also been taken by welfare and all three children were put in different places.

They took the child out of the hospital without even getting the doctor's permission and the child got sick again and they brought it back to the hospital. The doctors said, "I never released this baby and the baby didn't finish taking the medicine. The baby's very sick and I'm afraid it's going to die. I won't take the baby back under my care because then I'd be responsible for it and I'm not the one who caused the baby to get really sick again and I'm afraid the child will die and I'll be sued."

So they had to take it to yet another hospital. The mother found out where the child was and went to try and see the baby. They posted a policeman at the hospital and refused to let her see the child. She finally was allowed to see it, informally, but was not allowed to take the child. The child did get better, miraculously, given the kind of treatment the child had had. But "the Welfare" placed it in yet another county. That child is still in foster care. The woman who did the testifying, who was a pretty prominent woman and very active and has worked a lot with welfare officials, helped build low-income housing, etc., *she* tried to get the baby placed with her because the baby is actually a relative of hers. They would not place the child with her, even though in Georgia, they do not pay relatives for foster care. She was going to take care of the child, take custody of the child, and they would not place it with her, even though she could do so. They're still fighting it.

As we talked about this incident, she started to tell me other stories about what is happening in terms of housing. There *is* low income housing in Soberton, Georgia, but it is segregated, into black housing projects and white housing projects. She had one woman come to her, who had one child, and she was seven months pregnant with another, and she was living in a car. When she applied for a house, they said her income wasn't high enough because she was on welfare, and these public housing project apartments were for people who were low income and employed. In Georgia, you can be pretty low income and still be employed.

So they were holding them open. There were vacant apartments and she was living in a car. It took two months and they got her in a week before the baby was born. That one ended successfully—we'll see what happens with this other story.

I could leave you there, but that's a particularly down note to leave you on. I think we will solve that particular case—but there are thousands more. Those are just a couple of stories about what's happening out there in terms of children and foster care and homelessness.

I'd like to outline for you what I think we need to do and this is a very broad concept of what we need to do, but I think we need to look at this as a broad issue that needs a broad solution. I think we as a society must begin to take on a share of the risk of children's homelessness in a way we've never done before, except with the risks of aging.

Fifty years ago, when we instituted Social Security, we basically said that the problems of the aging should not be borne by themselves alone or by their families: "It's a risk we all must pass through and we all need to share the risk. We need to share the risk of becoming older." We need to do the same thing with children and not make women who have children and are abandoned by the fathers of those children and now are abandoned by the society as well, bear all the burden and costs of bearing children.

This kind of approach would involve the following things. We need to have universal child care, universally available the way we have public education available. Right now, we ask young parents at a point when they're just starting their careers, when their income is very low, to pay for child care out of relatively low incomes and the result, of course, is that they not only impoverish themselves in trying to work and take care of the children, they impoverish the people taking care of their children so that there's no way you can give people taking care of children decent wages, because they're being paid by people who are young parents themselves. The only way to deal with this is to begin to share the risks among those of us who are at different points in our careers and have higher incomes.

Second, we need some kind of support system for children when they are very young. This would be an annual income support that supplements child support and it should include housing as well. We should have a guarantee that no child will be placed in foster care because the family is homeless. And, in more general terms, we should guarantee that no child shall be punished in terms of poverty by lack of housing, lack of education, because they are in a single-parent as opposed to a typical two-parent family.

Third, we need to give family and medical leave universally, not just to those who are in companies that are large enough and are covered by legislation, or live in states that are covered by legislation. But when people have children, adopt children or they have an ill child or relative that they need to take time off from work, that should be covered so that they are not bearing all the burden for having to take care of that.

Fourth, we need health care for everyone. Obviously, this doesn't need a lot of explanation.

So the first thing we need to do is to create a kind of social security for our children, for our entire age span, not just for over sixty-five. The second thing we really need to do is to look at income and welfare inequality, which is growing very rapidly and has been since the early 1980s. On the income side of it, we've got to do something about minimum wage. We now have a situation where a single parent with one child has to work about fifty hours a week just to make a poverty-level wage and then she has to work about another seven hours to do the Social Security and other automatic reductions. We need to raise taxes to cover things, we need to share socially much more of our burden and not give everybody income tax breaks, because it only increases our inequality.

In the area of wealth inequality, I think we really have to do some imaginative thinking around the issue of housing. We now have a situation where people who rent are becoming poorer and poorer and have no control whatsoever. Housing is the only means of saving. Those of us who own housing are sending our kids to college, are getting wealthy, and we can retire on it; it's everything. It's our catastrophic health insurance, it's our next generation's investment; it's everything. So you cannot get away from house ownership as long as we have these things. Once we start developing policies like national health care, national child care, higher education, then we don't have to have everything, then we don't have to have everyone be a home-owner in order to secure themselves against the future—illness, aging, college educations.

We need to develop a third kind of housing that is in between those two extremes, of private home ownership and public housing, which is shared housing programs such as mutual housing, limited equity co-op, or cooperative housing, where people share some of the benefits of owning housing and share communally some of the benefits, so we get something that's in-between. We really need to do a lot more work on that issue.

Third, we need to renew our commitment to reduce racial inequality and to increase equality of opportunity. We've had a real flagging of those efforts in terms of affirmative action, in terms of access of minority children to higher education all the way across the line. I think we particularly need to pay attention to urban education. We have dropout rates in some schools now of 50 percent, that is, of children entering eighth grade, only about 50 percent of them are finishing high school. Informal reports from people running teaching programs suggest that those who finish high school routinely have reading levels in the range of third, fourth and fifth grade. That's an awful thing to do to people. That means they have no future whatsoever.

Urban education is a euphemism—we're really talking about predominantly minority (students) and what we have not done. We started in the 1960s and early 1970s to really desegregate our school systems. The important thing about desegregation wasn't having black and white school children sitting together, but that we have black and white dollars next to each other. In other words, having an integration of the resources is essential. Until we go back to doing something like that and have real resources and real access and real equality of opportunity, we're going to have racial inequality and I think we really have to renew our efforts in that area.

And finally, we have to attack the root causes of women's poverty. We need to provide adequate support for women raising children, as I described earlier. All the way through women's lives, including earnings-sharing when people retire. At this point, if a young man takes two or three years out of his life when he's eighteen or nineteen or twenty and serves in the Armed Forces, we reward that young man (and sometimes, young woman), with all kinds of veteran's benefits, education benefits, all the way through his/her life, including health benefits all the way through, and even burial benefits.

If a young woman takes two or three years out of her life to raise children, however, she's punished. She's punished in terms of her career, she's punished in terms of Social Security, she's punished in terms of Unemployment Compensation. We do exactly the opposite from those serving in the Armed Forces. I think we have to start looking at raising children as just as much an investment in our society's future and security as having people go into the Armed Forces.

The other side to women's poverty, other than the children, is the employment side and we really need to work in those areas in terms of pay equity, in terms of getting women into non-traditional employment. We need to work on the area of part-time employment, which is a rapidly rising invisible ghetto. Two-thirds of the people in part-time employment are women—they do not get fringe benefits, they do not get any chance to grow in terms of employment, they are pretty much confined to low wages and dead-end jobs and that's a growing area.

None of this is going to happen because it *ought* to happen. It's only going to happen when we work on it so I call upon you as you talk about these issues today and after you leave today to really think about it. These things are wonderful things, but they can only happen if we really work on it. And this means we have to work on it both nationally, on such issues as the minimum wage and locally, on housing, which has to be resolved within the community and within the women's community, sister to sister.

Discussion Questions

1. In the Mahabharata, it is argued that there is a divinely created caste system. What is the rationale for this? How does this compare to views on (in)equality found in other religious belief systems?
2. Why does Aristotle claim that there are some humans born with master souls while others are born with slave souls? How does this distinction predispose some people to success and others to failure?
3. Does Marx's analysis of social ills have any validity and usefulness for us today? Can you use his philosophy to analyze your own set of socioeconomic circumstances?
4. In what sense are we playing Monopoly, according to Langston, and who are the "real" players and who are the pawns? How and why might we not recognize that we are privileged?

5. Based on your reading of Macleod, in what sense do you think that the desire to define others (through stereotypes, etc.) actually represents the attempt to define ourselves?
6. What is the "feminization of poverty"? According to Pearce, what are some of the ways in which the condition of women and children can be improved?
7. Discuss the ways in which poverty and other social diseases foster a personal identity that is different from that of a person with political power.
8. What are some of the ways in which social class determines our future? How might this be changed? Would a classless society remedy the problem? Critically discuss this possibility.

chapter 6

Sexuality and Gender Identity

We relate to others in a variety of ways. Some of the most intimate ways in which we do so are through our sexuality. In this chapter, some traditional ways in which sex and gender have been understood are set forth and critiqued.

One important way in which humans can relate to others is through sex. There is disagreement, however, about its purposefulness. Is sex an animalistic, biological drive to reproduce? Or does it have a value in itself? Must humans be monogamous in their sexual activity? Must it be with the same sex? In the essays that follow, these and other questions are examined in different ways.

Plato suggests that we are "divided selves" who cannot be fulfilled without a "right" person to love us. Love drives us to complete the self by sharing that self with another. The question is whether or not that drive is natural and whether it must be expressed toward another of the same or opposite sex, which raises some controversial issues.

One of the most controversial issues concerning sex is homosexuality. In "Prejudice and Homosexuality," Richard D. Mohr discusses the social dimension of moral claims concerning homosexuality. Mohr argues that homosexuals are often considered perverted and thus are discriminated against. Biased research, and the misguided attempt to argue that because homosexuality appears to be unnatural it is wrong, makes it even more difficult to under-

Gay Rights Protest

stand homosexuality as a viable, moral sex act. Mohr claims that the religious view of homosexuality, which is often set forth as being vehemently against homosexuality, is based on only a limited view of Scripture and that there are many other diverse interpretations of it. Mohr argues that our understanding of gender, and our "choice" of sexual orientation must be reevaluated.

John Stoltenberg claims that humans have a diverse genetic nature. As opposed to simply claiming that there are two sexes, male and female, Stoltenberg argues in "How Men Have (a) Sex" that there are actually many sexes. Like the other authors in this chapter, Stoltenberg believes that we must broaden our views on sexuality in order to truly understand and fulfill our human nature.

In "Intimacy," Sartre tells the story of a woman whose perception of her lovers helps to form her sense of self. Through this, Sartre explores the ways in which one's conception of the self and others is often based upon what one believes to be the way he or she is perceived by others, especially via the body. Can humans know others without knowing themselves? How do one's intimate relationships help to form the *self?* Is it through one's sexuality? In what sense might sex and one's sexuality undermine intimacy? Sartre raises questions about the nature and definition of intimacy and explores what types of activities are required for it. These might be different from what many people imagine.

St. Thomas Aquinas was a man of his time in that he was very much influenced by the view of the Roman Catholic Church that women were created to assist men in reproduction. This presupposed divine purpose, however, still leaves women on the lower level of a hierarchy whereby they are not considered equal to men. Can such a belief coincide with the view that God loves all equally? Does this view help to promote the oppression of women?

Simone de Beauvoir offers a different view of sex and gender in "Women Are Not Our Brothers." De Beauvoir examines the traditional Western view that women are always defined in relation to men. She claims that this is due to the fact that women have not been viewed as equal in the state of nature. Thus, de Beauvoir calls into question the claim that there is, and should be, a hierarchy of male and female in nature and society, and she argues that the oppression resulting from this view is due to nurture and not nature. Surely, the self will find it difficult to develop in a framework of oppression and misguided assumptions.

Rayna Green addresses some of these same issues in light of her Native American view that all things are interrelated. According to Green, the presupposed view that there is a hierarchical order of things in nature must be forfeited in order to give the *self* the opportunity to create itself and develop its natural potential to be virtuous. Without liberating oneself from this view, a framework of oppression will surely continue to exist, even within the *self.*

In summary, as you read these essays, reflect upon the ways in which the problems with society, the self, and identity can be resolved in order to develop an *authentic self.*

Aristophanes' Story of Divided Selves

Plato

In this excerpt from Plato's Symposium, *we encounter Aristophanes' explanation of a divided selfhood. We are told that love drives us to complete our sense of self or person by sharing that selfhood with another. Additionally, we are told that we are not whole as persons or selves, and it is only through love with the right person that we will find wholeness or complete selfhood.*

[Eryximachus:] I dare say that I, too, have omitted much that might be said in praise of Love, but this was not intentional, and you, Aristophanes, may now supply the omission or take some other line of commendation; for I perceive that you are rid of the hiccough.

Yes, said Aristophanes, who followed, the hiccough is gone; not, however, until I applied the sneezing; and I wonder whether the orderly system of the body has a love of such noises and ticklings, for I no sooner applied the sneezing than I was cured.

Eryximachus said: Beware, friend Aristophanes; although you are going to speak, you are making fun of me; and I shall have to watch and see whether I cannot have a laugh at your expense, when you might speak in peace.

You are quite right, said Aristophanes, laughing, and I unsay my words. But do you please not to watch me, as I fear that in the speech which I am about to make, instead of others laughing with me, which is the natural work of our muse and would be satisfactory, I shall only be laughed at by them.

Do you expect to shoot your bolt and escape, Aristophanes? Well, perhaps if you are very careful and bear in mind that you will be called to account, I may be induced to let you off.

Aristophanes professed to open another vein of discourse; he had a mind to praise Love in another way, unlike that of either Pausanias or Eryximachus. Mankind, he said, judging by their neglect of him, have never, as I think, at all understood the power of Love. For if they had understood him they would surely have built noble temples and altars, and offered solemn sacrifices in his honour; but this is not done, and most certainly ought to be done: since of all the gods he is the best friend of men, the helper and the healer of the ills which are the great impediment to the happiness of the race. I will try to describe his power to you, and you shall teach the rest of the world what I am teaching you. In the first place, let me treat of the nature of man and what has happened to it. The original human nature was not like the present, but different. The sexes were not two as they are now, but originally three in number; there was man, woman, and the union of the two, of which the name survives but nothing else. Once it was a distinct kind, with a bodily shape and a name of its own, constituted by the union of the male and the female: but now only the word "androgynous" is preserved, and that as a term of reproach. In the second place, the primeval man was round, his back and sides forming a circle; and he had four hands and the same number of feet, one head with two faces, looking opposite ways, set on a round neck and precisely alike; also four ears, two privy members, and the remainder to correspond. He could walk upright as men now do, backwards or forwards as he pleased, and he could also roll over and over at a great pace, turning on his four hands and four feet, eight in all, like tumblers going over and over with their legs in the air; this was when he wanted to run fast. Now the sexes were three, and such as I have described them; because the sun, moon, and earth are three; and the man was originally the child of the sun, the woman of the earth, and the man-woman of the moon, which is made up of sun and earth, and they were all round and moved round and round because they resembled their parents. Terrible was their might and strength, and the thoughts of their hearts were great, and they made an attack upon the gods; of them is told the tale of Otys and Ephialtes* who, as Homer says, attempted to scale heaven, and would have laid hands upon the gods. Doubt reigned in the celestial councils. Should they kill them and annihilate the race with thunderbolts, as they had done the giants, then there would be an end of the sacrifices and worship which men offered to them; but, on the other hand, the gods could not suffer their insolence to be unrestrained.

At last, after a good deal of reflection, Zeus discovered a way. He said: "Methinks I have a plan which will enfeeble their strength and so extinguish their turbulence; men shall continue to exist, but I will cut them in two and then they will be diminished in strength and increased in numbers; this will have the advantage of making them more profitable to us. They shall walk upright on two legs, and if they continue insolent and will not be quiet, I will split them again and they shall hop about on a single leg." He spoke and cut men in two, like a sorb-apple which is halved for pickling, or as you might divide an egg with a hair; and as he cut them one after another, he bade Apollo give the face and the half of the neck a turn in order that man might contemplate the section of himself: he would thus learn a lesson of humility. Apollo was also bidden to heal their wounds and compose their forms. So he gave a turn to the face and pulled the skin from the sides all over that which in our language is called the belly, like the purses which draw tight, and he made one mouth at the centre, which he fastened in a knot (the same which is called the navel); he also moulded the breast and took out most of the wrinkles, much as a shoemaker might smooth leather upon a last; he left a few, however, in the region of the belly and navel, as a memorial of the primeval state. After the division the two parts of man, each desiring his other half, came together, and throwing their arms about one another, entwined in mutual embraces, longing to

*In Greek mythology, Otys and Ephialtes were the giants who tried to attack the gods on Mount Olympus by stacking mountains on top of each other. They were defeated by the intervention of Artemis (Diana).

grow into one, they began to die from hunger and self-neglect, because they did not like to do anything apart; and when one of the halves died and the other survived, the survivor sought another mate, man or woman as we call them,—being the sections of entire men or women,—and clung to that. Thus they were being destroyed, when Zeus in pity invented a new plan: he turned the parts of generation round to the front, for this had not been always their position, and they sowed the seed no longer as hitherto like grasshoppers in the ground, but in one another; and after the transposition the male generated in the female in order that by the mutual embraces of man and woman they might breed, and the race might continue; or if man came to man they might be satisfied, and rest, and go their ways to the business of life. So ancient is the desire of one another which is implanted in us, reuniting our original nature, seeking to make one of two, and to heal the state of man.

Each of us when separated, having one side only, like a flat fish, is but the tally-half of a man, and he is always looking for his other half. Men who are a section of that double nature which was once called androgynous are lovers of women; adulterers are generally of this breed, and also adulterous women who lust after men. The women who are a section of the woman do not care for men, but have female attachments; the female companions are of this sort. But they who are a section of the male follow the male, and while they are young, being slices of the original man, they have affection for men and embrace them, and these are the best of boys and youths, because they have the most manly nature. Some indeed assert that they are shameless, but this is not true; for they do not act thus from any want of shame, but because they are valiant and manly, and have a manly countenance, and they embrace that which is like them. And these when they grow up become our statesmen, and these only, which is a great proof of the truth of what I am saying. When they reach manhood they are lovers of youth, and are not naturally inclined to marry or beget children,—if at all, they do so only in obedience to custom; but they are satisfied if they may be allowed to live with one another unwedded; and such a nature is prone to love and ready to return love, always embracing that which is akin to him. And when one of them meets with his other half, the actual half of himself, whether he be a lover of youth or a lover of another sort, the pair are lost in an amazement of love and friendship and intimacy, and one will not be out of the other's sight, as I may say, even for a moment: these are the people who pass their whole lives together, and yet they could not explain what they desire of one another. For the intense yearning which each of them has towards the other does not appear to be the desire of lover's intercourse, but of something else which the soul of either evidently desires and cannot tell, and of which she has only a dark and doubtful presentiment. Suppose Hephaestus,* with his instruments, to come to the pair who are lying side by side and to say to them, "What do you mortals want of one another?" they would be unable to explain. And suppose further, that when he saw their perplexity he said: "Do you desire to be wholly one; always day and night in one another's company? for if this is what you desire, I am ready to melt and fuse you together, so that being two you shall become one, and while you live live a common life as if you were a single man, and after your death in the

*Hephaestus (Vulcan) was the son of Zeus and the blacksmith, artisan, and armorer of the Olympian gods.

world below still be one departed soul, instead of two—I ask whether this is what you lovingly desire and whether you are satisfied to attain this?"—there is not a man of them who when he heard the proposal would deny or would not acknowledge that this meeting and melting into one another, this becoming one instead of two, was the very expression of his ancient need. And the reason is that human nature was originally one and we were a whole, and the desire and pursuit of the whole is called love. There was a time, I say, when we were one, but now because of the wickedness of mankind God has dispersed us, as the Arcadians were dispersed into villages by the Lacedaemonians. And if we are not obedient to the gods, there is a danger that we shall be split up again and go about in basso-relievo, like the profile figures showing only one half the nose which are sculptured on monuments, and that we shall be like tallies.

Wherefore let us exhort all men to piety in all things, that we may avoid evil and obtain the good, taking Love for our leader and commander. Let no one oppose him—he is the enemy of the gods who opposes him. For if we are friends of God and at peace with him we shall find our own true loves, which rarely happens in this world at present. I am serious, and therefore I must beg Eryximachus not to make fun or to find any allusion in what I am saying to Pausanias and Agathon, who, as I suspect, are both of the manly nature, and belong to the class which I have been describing. But my words have a wider application—they include men and women everywhere; and I believe that if our loves were perfectly accomplished, and each one returning to his primeval nature had his original true love, then our race would be happy. And if this would be best of all, the best in the next degree must in present circumstances be the nearest approach to such a union; and that will be the attainment of a congenial love. Wherefore, if we would praise him who has given to us the benefit, we must praise the god Love, who is our greatest benefactor, both leading us in this life back to our own nature, and giving us high hopes for the future, for he promises that if we are pious, he will restore us to our original state, and yet heal us and make us happy and blessed. This, Eryximachus, is my discourse of love, which, although different to yours, I must beg you to leave unassailed by the shafts of your ridicule, in order that each may have his turn; each, or rather either, for Agathon and Socrates are the only ones left.

Prejudice and Homosexuality

Richard Mohr

Mohr examines the false generalizations that have been made about gays and the way in which these generalizations reinforce and maintain stereotypes, which in turn create fear, hatred, discrimination, and violence against homosexuals. Mohr argues that nature does not allow for a condemnation of gays, nor would a proper understanding of the Bible allow for such condemnation. By acknowledging the natural rights that homosexuals have, by acknowledging this sexual orientation as an aspect of human diversity, we can culturally enrich ourselves as a society.

Who are gays anyway? A 1993 New York Times–CBS poll found that only one-fifth of Americans suppose that they have a friend or family member who is gay or lesbian. This finding is extraordinary given the number of practicing homosexuals in America. In 1948, Alfred Kinsey published a study of the sex lives of 12,000 white males. Its method was so rigorous that it set the standard for subsequent statistical research across the social sciences, but its results shocked the nation: thirty-seven percent of the men had at least one homosexual experience to orgasm in their adult lives; an additional thirteen percent had homosexual fantasies to orgasm; four percent were exclusively homosexual in their practices; another five percent had virtually no heterosexual experience, and nearly one fifth had at least as many homosexual as heterosexual experiences. Kinsey's 1953 study of the sex lives of 8000 women found the occurrence of homosexual behavior at about half the rates for men.

Every second family in the country has a member who is essentially homosexual and many more people regularly have homosexual experiences. Who are homosexuals? They are your friends, your minister, your teacher, your bankteller, your doctor, your mailcarrier, your officemate, your roommate, your congressional representative, your sibling, parent, and spouse. They are we. We are everywhere, virtually all ordinary, virtually all unknown.

Ignorance about gays, however, has not stopped people from having strong opinions about them. The void which ignorance leaves has been filled with stereotypes. Society holds two oddly contradictory groups of antigay stereotypes. One revolves around an individual's allegedly confused gender identity: lesbians are females who want to be, or at least look and act like, men—bull dykes, diesel dykes; while gay men are males who want to be, or at least look and act like, women—queens, fairies, nances, limpwrists, nellies, sissies, aunties. These stereotypes of mismatches between biological sex and socially defined gender provide the materials through which lesbians and gay men become the butts of ethnic-like jokes. These stereotypes and jokes, though derisive, basically view gays as ridiculous: "How do you identify a bull dyke?" Answer: "She kick-starts her vibrator and rolls her own tampons." Or, "How many fags does it take to change a light bulb?" Answer: "Eight—

From *The Little Book of Gay Rights* by Richard D. Mohr. Copyright © 1994 by Richard D. Mohr. Reprinted by permission of Beacon Press.

one to replace it and seven to scream 'Faaaaaabulous!' "

The other set of stereotypes revolves around gays as a pervasive sinister conspiratorial threat. The core stereotype here is that of the gay person—especially gay man—as child molester, and more generally as sex-crazed maniac. Homosexuality here is viewed as a vampire-like corruptive contagion. These stereotypes carry with them fears of the very destruction of family and civilization itself. Now, that which is essentially ridiculous can hardly have such a staggering effect. Something must be afoot.

Sense can be made of this incoherent amalgam if the nature of stereotypes is clarified. Stereotypes are not simply false generalizations from a skewed sample of cases examined. Admittedly, false generalizing plays some part in the stereotypes society holds about gays and other groups. If, for instance, one takes as one's sample gay men who are in psychiatric hospitals or prisons, as was done in nearly all early investigations, not surprisingly one will probably find them to be of a crazed or criminal cast. Such false generalizations, though, simply confirm beliefs already held on independent grounds, ones that likely led the investigator to the prison and psychiatric ward to begin with. Evelyn Hooker, who in the late 1950s carried out the first rigorous studies of nonclinical gay men, found that psychiatrists, when presented with case files including all the standard diagnostic psychological profiles—but omitting indications of sexual orientation—were unable to distinguish gay files from nongay ones, even though they believed gay men to be crazy and supposed themselves to be experts in detecting craziness. These studies proved a profound embarrassment to the psychiatric establishment, the financial well-being of which has been substantially enhanced by "curing" allegedly insane gays. The studies led the way to the American Psychiatric Association's finally, in 1973, dropping homosexuality from its registry of mental illnesses. Nevertheless, the stereotype of gays as sick continues apace in the mind of America.

False generalizations help maintain stereotypes, they do not form them. As the story of Hooker's discoveries shows, stereotypes have a life beyond facts; their origins lie in a culture's ideology—the general system of beliefs by which it lives—and they are sustained across generations by diverse cultural transmissions, hardly any of which, including slang and jokes, even purport to have a scientific basis. Stereotypes, then, are not the products of bad science, but reflections of society's conception of itself.

On this understanding, it is easy to see that stereotypes about gays as gender-confused reinforce still powerful gender roles in society. If, as these stereotypes presume and condemn, one is free to choose one's social roles independently of one's biological sex, many guiding social divisions, both domestic and commercial, might be threatened. Blurred would be the socially sex-linked distinctions between breadwinner and homemaker, boss and secretary, doctor and nurse, protector and protected, even God and His world. The accusations "fag" and "dyke" serve in significant part to keep women in their place and to prevent men from breaking ranks and ceding away theirs.

The stereotypes of gays as civilization destroyers function to displace (possibly irresolvable) social problems from their actual source to a remote and (society hopes) manageable one. For example, the stereotype of child molester functions to give the traditionally defined family unit a false sheen of innocence. It keeps the unit from being examined too closely for incest, child abuse, wife-battering, and the terrorizing of women and children by a father's constant threats.

The stereotype teaches that the problems of the family are not internal to it, but external.

One can see these cultural forces at work in society's and the media's treatment of current reports of violence, especially domestic violence. When a husband kills his wife or a father rapes his daughter—regular Section B fare even in major urban papers—this is never taken by reporters, columnists, or pundits as evidence that there is something wrong with heterosexuality or with traditional families. These issues are not even raised. But when a homosexual child molestation is reported, it is taken as confirming evidence of the way homosexuals are. One never hears of "heterosexual murders," but one regularly hears of "homosexual" ones.

If this account of stereotypes holds, society has been profoundly immoral. For its treatment of gays is a grand-scale rationalization, a moral sleight-of-hand. The problem is not that society's usual standards of evidence and procedure in decision making have been misapplied to gays, rather when it comes to gays, the standards themselves have simply been ruled out of court and disregarded in favor of mechanisms that encourage unexamined fear and hatred.

Partly because lots of people suppose they don't know any gay people and partly through the maintaining of stereotypes, society at large is unaware of the many ways in which gays are subject to discrimination in consequence of widespread fear and hatred. Contributing to this social ignorance of discrimination is the difficulty for gay people, as an invisible minority, even to complain of discrimination. For if one is gay, to register a complaint would suddenly target oneself as a stigmatized person, and so, especially in the absence of any protection against discrimination, would simply invite additional discrimination. So, discrimination against gays, like rape, goes seriously underreported. Even so, known discrimination is massive.

Annual studies by the National Gay and Lesbian Task Force have consistently found that over ninety percent of gay men and lesbians have been victims of violence or harassment in some form on the basis of their sexual orientation. Greater than one in five gay men and nearly one in ten lesbians have been punched, hit, or kicked; a quarter of all gays have had objects thrown at them; a third have been chased; a third have been sexually harassed; and fourteen percent have been spit on, all just for being perceived to be gay.

The most extreme form of antigay violence is queerbashing—where groups of young men target a person who they suppose is a gay man and beat and kick him unconscious and sometimes to death amid a torrent of taunts and slurs. Few such cases with gay victims reach the courts. Those that do are marked by inequitable procedures and results. Frequently judges will describe queerbashers as "just All-American Boys." A District of Columbia judge handed suspended sentences to queerbashers whose victim had been stalked, beaten, stripped at knife point, slashed, kicked, threatened with castration, and pissed on, because the judge thought the bashers were good boys at heart—they went to a religious prep school. In 1989, a judge in Dallas handed a sentence he acknowledged as light to the eighteen-year-old murderer of two gay men, because the murderer had killed them in a gay cruising zone, where the judge said they might be molesting children. The judge thereby justified a form of vigilantism that bears an eerie resemblance to the lynching of black men on the grounds that they might molest white women. Indeed, queerbashing has the same function that past lynchings of blacks had—to keep a whole stigmatized group in line. As with lynchings, society has routinely averted its eyes, giving its permission or even tacit approval to violence and harassment.

Police and juries will simply discount testimony from gays; they frequently construe assaults on and murders of gays as "justified" self-defense. The killer simply claims his act was an understandably panicked response to a sexual overture. Alternatively, when guilt seems patent, juries will accept highly implausible "diminished capacity" defenses, as in the case of Dan White's 1978 assassination of openly gay San Francisco city councilman Harvey Milk. Hostess Twinkies made him do it, or so the successful defense went. These inequitable procedures collectively show that the life and liberty of gays, like those of blacks, simply count for less than the life and liberty of members of the dominant culture.

The equitable rule of law is the heart of an orderly society. The collapse of the rule of law for gays shows that society is willing to perpetrate the worst possible injustices against them. As the ethnic and religious wars in the former Yugoslavia have made clear, there is only a difference in degree between the collapse of the rule of law and systematic extermination of members of a population simply for having some group status. In the Nazi concentration camps, gays were forced to wear pink triangles as identifying badges, just as Jews were forced to wear yellow stars. In remembrance of that collapse of the rule of law, the pink triangle has become the chief symbol of the gay rights movement.

Gays are also subject to widespread discrimination in employment. Governments are leading offenders here. They do a lot of discriminating themselves, require that others do it, and set precedents favoring discrimination in the private sector. Lesbians and gay men are barred from serving in the armed forces. The federal government has also denied gays employment in the CIA, FBI, National Security Agency, and the state department. The government refuses to give security clearances to gays and so forces the country's considerable private sector military and aerospace contractors to fire employees known to be gay and to avoid hiring those perceived to be gay. State and local governments regularly fire gay teachers, policemen, firemen, social workers, and anyone who has contact with the public. Further, state licensing laws (though frequently honored only in the breech) officially bar gays from a vast array of occupations and professions—everything from doctors, lawyers, accountants, and nurses to hairdressers, morticians, even used car dealers.

Gays are subject to discrimination in a wide variety of other ways, including private-sector employment, public accommodations, housing, insurance of all types, custody, adoption, and zoning regulations that bar "singles" or "nonrelated" couples from living together. A 1988 study by the congressional Office of Technology Assessment found that a third of America's insurance companies openly admit that they discriminate against lesbians and gay men. In nearly half the states, same-sex sexual behavior is illegal, so that the central role of sex to meaningful life is officially denied to lesbians and gay men.

Illegality, discrimination and the absorption by gays of society's hatred of them all interact to impede and, for some, block altogether the ability of gay men and lesbians to create and maintain significant personal relations with loved ones. Every facet of life is affected by discrimination. Only the most compelling reasons could justify it.

Many people think society's treatment of gays is justified because they think gays are extremely immoral. To evaluate this claim, different senses of "moral" must be distinguished. Sometimes by "morality" is meant the values generally held by members of a society—its mores, norms, and customs. On this understanding, gays certainly are not moral: lots of people hate them, and social customs are designed to register widespread disapproval of gays. The problem here is that this sense of morality is merely a descriptive one. On this understanding, every society has a morality—even Nazi society, which had racism and mob rule as central features of its "morality" understood in this sense. What is needed in order to use the notion of morality to praise or condemn behavior is a sense of morality that is prescriptive or normative.

As the Nazi example makes clear, that a belief or claim is descriptively moral does not entail that it is normatively moral. A lot of people in a society saying something is good, even over aeons, does not make it so. The rejection of the long history of socially approved and state-enforced slavery is another good example of this principle at work. Slavery would be wrong even if nearly everyone liked it. So consistency and fairness require that one abandon the belief that gays are immoral simply because most people dislike or disapprove of gays.

Furthermore, recent historical and anthropological research has shown that opinion about gays has been by no means universally negative. It has varied widely even within the larger part of the Christian era and even within the Church itself. There are even societies—current ones—where homosexual behavior is not only tolerated but is a universal compulsory part of male social maturation. Within the last thirty years, American society has undergone a grand turnabout from deeply ingrained, near total condemnation to near total acceptance on two emotionally charged "moral" or "family" issues—contraception and divorce. Society holds its current descriptive morality of gays not because it has to, but because it chooses to.

If popular opinion and custom are not enough to ground moral condemnation of homosexuality, perhaps religion can. Such arguments usually proceed along two lines. One claims that the condemnation is a direct revelation of God, usually through the Bible. The other claims to be able to detect condemnation in God's plan as manifested in nature; homosexuality (it is claimed) is "contrary to nature."

One of the more remarkable discoveries of recent gay research is that the Bible may not be as univocal in its condemnation of homosexuality as many have believed. Christ never mentions homosexuality. Recent interpreters of the Old Testament have pointed out that the story of Lot at Sodom is probably intended to condemn inhospitality rather than homosexuality. Further, some of the Old Testament condemnations of homosexuality seem simply to be ways of tarring those of the Israelites' opponents who happen to accept homosexual practices when the Israelites themselves did not. If so, the condemnation is merely a quirk of history and rhetoric rather than a moral precept.

What does seem clear is that those who regularly cite the Bible to condemn an activity like homosexuality do so by reading it selectively. Do ministers who cite what they take to be condemnations of homosexuality in Leviticus maintain in their lives all the hygienic and dietary laws of Leviticus? If they cite the story of Lot at Sodom to condemn homosexuality, do they also cite the story of Lot in the Cave to praise incestuous rape? It seems then not that the Bible is being used to ground condemnations of homosexuality as much as society's dislike of homosexuality is being used to interpret the Bible.

Even if a consistent portrait of condemnation could be gleaned from the Bible, what social significance should it be given? One of the guiding principles of society, enshrined in the Constitution as a check against the government, is that decisions affecting social policy are not made on religious grounds. The Religious Right has been successful in stymieing sodomy-law reform, in defunding gay safe-sex literature and gay art, and in blocking the introduction of gay materials into school curriculums. If the real ground of the alleged immorality invoked by governments to discriminate against gays is religious (as it seems to be in these cases), then one of the major commitments of our nation is violated. Religious belief is a fine guide around which a person might organize his own life, but an awful instrument around which to organize someone else's life.

People also try to justify society's treatment of gays by saying they are unnatural. Though the accusation of unnaturalness looks whimsical, when applied to homosexuality, it is usually delivered with venom of forethought. It carries a high emotional charge, usually expressing disgust and evincing queasiness. Probably it is nothing but an emotional charge. For people get equally disgusted and queasy at all sorts of things that are perfectly natural, yet that could hardly be fit subjects for moral condemnation. Two typical examples in current American culture are some people's responses to mothers' suckling in public and to women who do not shave body hair. Similarly people fling the term "unnatural" against gays in the same breath and with the same force as when they call gays "sick" and "gross." When people have strong emotional reactions, as they do in these cases, without being able to give good reasons for them, they are thought of not as operating morally, but as being obsessed and manic. So the feelings of disgust that some people have toward gays will hardly ground a charge of immorality.

When "nature" is taken in technical rather than ordinary usages, it also cannot ground a charge of homosexual immorality. When unnatural means "by artifice" or "made by humans," it can be pointed out that virtually everything that is good about life is unnatural in this sense. The chief feature that distinguishes people from other animals is people's very ability to make over the world to meet their needs and desires. Indeed people's well-being depends on these departures from nature. On this understanding of human nature and the natural, homosexuality is perfectly unobjectionable; it is simply a means by which some people adapt nature to fulfill their desires and needs.

Another technical sense of natural is that something is natural and so, good, if it fulfills some function in nature. On this view, homosexuality is unnatural because it violates the function of genitals, which is to produce babies. One problem with this view is that lots of bodily parts have lots of functions and just because some one activity can be fulfilled by only one organ (say, the mouth for eating), this activity does not condemn other functions of the organ to immorality (say, the mouth for talking, licking stamps, blowing bubbles, or having sex). So the possible use of the genitals to produce children does not, without more, condemn the use of the genitals for other purposes, say, achieving ecstasy and intimacy.

The functional view of nature will only provide a morally condemnatory sense to the unnatural if a thing that might have many uses has but one proper function to the exclusion of other possible functions. But whether this is so cannot be established simply by looking at the thing. For what is seen is all its possible functions. The notion of function seemed like it might ground moral authority, but instead it turns out that moral authority is needed to define proper function.

Some people try to fill in this moral authority by appeal to the "design" or "order" of an organ, saying, for instance, that the genitals are designed for the purpose of procreation. But these people cheat intellectually if they do not make explicit who the designer and orderer is. If the "who" is God, we are back to square one—holding others accountable to one's own religious beliefs.

Further, ordinary moral attitudes about child-bearing will not provide the needed supplement which would produce a positive obligation to use the genitals for procreation. Though there are local exceptions, society's general attitude toward a childless couple is that of pity not censure—even if the couple could have children. The pity may be an unsympathetic one, that is, not registering a course one would choose for oneself, but this does not make it a course one would require of others. The couple who discovers they cannot have children are viewed not as having thereby had a debt cancelled, but rather as having to forgo some of the richness of life, just as a quadriplegic is viewed not as absolved from some moral obligation to hop, skip, and jump, but as missing some of the richness of life. Consistency requires then that, at most, gays who do not or cannot have children are to be pitied rather than condemned. What *is* immoral is the willful preventing of people from achieving the richness of life. Immorality in this regard lies with those social customs, regulations, and statutes that prevent lesbians and gay men from establishing blood or adoptive families, not with gays themselves.

Many gays would like to raise or foster children—perhaps those alarming number of gay kids who have been beaten up and thrown out of their "families" for being gay. And indeed many lesbian and gay male couples are now raising robust, happy families where children are the blessings of adoption, artificial insemination, or surrogacy. The country is experiencing something approaching a gay and lesbian babyboom.

Sometimes people attempt to establish authority for a moral obligation to use bodily parts in a certain fashion simply by claiming that moral laws are natural laws and vice versa. On this account, inanimate objects and plants are good in that they follow natural laws by necessity, animals follow them by instinct, and persons follow them by a rational will. People are special in that they must first discover the laws that govern them. Now, even if one believes the view—dubious in the post-Newtonian, post-Darwinian world—that natural laws in the usual sense ($e = mc^2$, for instance) have some moral content, it is not at all clear how one is to discover the laws in nature that apply to people.

On the one hand, if one looks to people themselves for a model—and looks hard enough—one finds amazing variety, including homosexual relations as a social ideal (as in upper-class fifth-century Athens) and even as socially mandatory (as in some Melanesian initiation rites today). When one looks to people, one is simply unable to strip away the layers of social custom, history, and taboo in order to see what's really there to any degree more specific than that people are the creatures that make over their world and are capable of abstract thought. That this is so should raise doubts that neutral principles are to be found in human nature that will condemn homosexuality.

On the other hand, if one looks to nature apart from people for models, the possibilities are staggering. There are fish that change sex over their lifetimes: should we "follow nature" and be operative transsexuals? Orangutans, genetically our next of kin, live completely solitary lives without social organization of any kind among adults: ought we to "follow nature" and be hermits? There are many species where only two members per generation reproduce: shall we be bees? The search in nature for people's purpose far from finding sure models for action is likely to leave one morally rudderless.

But (it might also be asked) aren't gays willfully the way they are? It is generally conceded that if sexual orientation is something over which an individual—for whatever reason—has virtually no control, then discrimination against gays is presumptively wrong, as it is against racial and ethnic classes.

Attempts to answer the question whether or not sexual orientation is something that is reasonably thought to be within one's own control usually appeal simply to various claims of the biological or "mental" sciences. But the ensuing debate over genes, hormones, hypothalamuses, twins, early childhood development, and the like is as unnecessary as it is currently inconclusive. All that is needed to answer the question is to look at the actual experience of lesbians and gay men in current society and it becomes fairly clear that sexual orientation is not likely a matter of choice.

On the one hand, the "choice" of the gender of a sexual partner does not seem to express a trivial desire which might as easily be fulfilled by a simple substitution of the desired object. Picking the gender of a sex partner is decidedly dissimilar, that is, to such activities as picking a flavor of ice cream. If an ice cream parlor is out of one's flavor, one simply picks another. And if people were persecuted, threatened with jail terms, shattered careers, loss of family and housing and the like for eating, say, rocky road ice cream, no one would ever eat it. Everyone would pick another easily available flavor. That gay people abide in being gay even in the face of persecution suggests that being gay is not a matter of easy choice.

On the other hand, even if establishing a sexual orientation is not like making a relatively trivial choice, perhaps it is relevantly like making the central and serious life-choices by which individuals try to establish themselves as being of some type or having some occupation. Again, if one examines gay experience, this seems not to be the general case. For one virtually never sees anyone setting out to become a homosexual, in the way one does see people setting out to become doctors, lawyers, and bricklayers. One does not find gays-to-be picking some end—"At some point in the future, I want to become a homosexual"—and then setting about planning and acquiring the ways and means to that end, in the way one does see people deciding that they want to become lawyers, and then sees them plan what courses to take and what sort of temperaments, habits, and skills to develop in order to become lawyers. Typically gays-to-be simply find themselves having homosexual encounters and yet, at least initially, resisting quite strongly the identification of being homosexual. Such a person even very likely resists having such encounters, but ends up having them anyway. Only with time, luck, and great personal effort, but sometimes never, does the person gradually come to accept her or his orientation, to view it as a given material condition of life, coming as materials do with certain capacities and limitations. The person begins to act in accordance with his or her orientation and its capacities, seeing its actualization as a requisite for an integrated personality and as a central component of personal well-being. As a result, the experience of coming out to oneself has for gays the basic structure of a discovery, not the structure of a choice. And far from signaling immorality, coming out to others affords one of the few remaining opportunities in ever more bureaucratic, technological, and socialistic societies to *manifest* courage.

How would society at large be changed if gays were socially accepted? Suggestions to change social policy with regard to gays are invariably met with claims that to do so would invite the destruction of civilization itself: after all isn't that what did Rome in? Actually, Rome's decay paralleled not the flourishing of homosexuality but its repression under the later Christianized emperors. Predictions of American civilization's imminent demise have been as premature as they have been frequent. Civilization has shown itself to be rather resilient here, in large part because of the country's traditional commitments to respect for privacy, to individual liberties, and especially to people minding their own business. These all give society an open texture and the flexibility to try out things to see what works. And because of this, one now need not speculate about what changes reforms in gay social policy might bring to society at large. For many reforms have already been tried.

Half the states have decriminalized lesbian and gay male sex acts. Can you guess which of the following states still have sodomy laws: Wisconsin, Minnesota; New Mexico, Arizona; Vermont, New Hampshire; Nebraska, Kansas. One from each pair does and one does not have sodomy laws. And yet one would be hard pressed to point out any substantial social differences between the members of each pair. (If you're interested: it is the second of each pair with them.) Empirical studies have shown that there is no increase in other crimes in states that have decriminalized.

Neither has the passage of legislation barring discrimination against gays ushered in the end of civilization. Nearly a hundred counties and municipalities, including some of the country's largest cities (like Chicago and New York City) have passed such statutes, as have eight states: Wisconsin, Connecticut, Massachusetts, Hawaii, New Jersey, Vermont, California, and Minnesota. Again, no more brimstone has fallen in these places than elsewhere. Staunchly antigay cities, like Miami and Houston, have not been spared the AIDS crisis.

Berkeley, California, followed by a couple dozen other cities including New York, has even passed "domestic partner" legislation giving gay couples at least some of the same rights to city benefits as are held by heterosexually married couples, and yet Berkeley has not become more weird than it already was. A number of major universities (like Stanford and the University of Chicago) and respected corporations (like Levi Strauss and Company, the Montefiore Medical Center of New York, and Apple Computer, Inc.) are also following Berkeley's lead.

Seemingly hysterical predictions that the American family would collapse if such reforms would pass proved false, just as the same dire predictions that the availability of divorce would lessen the ideal and desirability of marriage proved unfounded. Indeed if current discrimination, which drives gays into hiding and into anonymous relations, ended, far from seeing gays destroying American families, one would see gays forming them.

Virtually all gays express a desire to have a permanent lover. But currently society and its discriminatory impulse make gay coupling very difficult. It is difficult for people to live together as couples without having their sexual orientation perceived in the public realm and so becoming targets for discrimination. Life in hiding is a pressure-cooker existence not easily shared with another. Members of nongay couples are here asked to imagine what it would take to erase every trace of their own sexual orientation for even just one week.

Even against oppressive odds, gays have shown an amazing tendency to nest. And those gay couples who have survived the odds show that the structure of more usual couplings is not a matter of destiny, but of personal responsibility. The so-called basic unit of society turns out not to be a unique immutable atom, but can adopt different parts, be adapted to different needs, and even be improved. Gays might even have a thing or two to teach others about divisions of labor, the relation of sensuality and intimacy, and the stages of development in such relations.

If discrimination ceased, gay men and lesbians would enter the mainstream of the human community openly and with self-respect. The energies that the typical gay person wastes in the anxiety of leading a day-to-day existence of systematic disguise would be released for use in personal flourishing. From this release would be generated the many spin off benefits that accrue to a society when its individual members thrive.

Society would be richer for acknowledging another aspect of human diversity. Families with gay members would develop relations based on truth and trust rather than lies and fear. And the heterosexual majority would be better off for knowing that they are no longer trampling their gay friends and neighbors.

Finally and perhaps paradoxically, in extending to gays the rights and benefits it has reserved for its dominant culture, America would confirm its deeply held vision of itself as a morally progressing nation, a nation itself advancing and serving as a beacon for others—especially with regard to human rights. The words with which our national pledge ends—"with liberty and justice for all"—are not a description of the present, but a call for the future. America is a nation given to a prophetic political rhetoric that acknowledges that morality is not arbitrary and that justice is not merely the expression of the current collective will. It is this vision that led the black civil rights movement to its successes. Those senators and representatives who opposed that movement and its centerpiece, the 1964 Civil Rights Act, on obscurantist grounds, but who lived long enough and were noble enough came in time to express their heartfelt regret and shame at what they had done. It is to be hoped and someday to be expected that those who now grasp at anything to oppose the extension of that which is best about America to gays will one day feel the same.

How Men Have (a) Sex

John Stoltenberg

In the following essay, Stoltenberg argues that humans are born "with a vast range of genital formations" that contribute to one's individuality. Hence, gender is relative, according to Stoltenberg. As you read this, think about Aristophanes' story of the sexes and about the ways in which you believe the meaning of sex and gender may be relative to our understandings of human nature.

An address to college students

In the human species, how many sexes are there?

Answer A: *There are two sexes.*
Answer B: *There are three sexes.*
Answer C: *There are four sexes.*
Answer D: *There are seven sexes.*
Answer E: *There are as many sexes as there are people.*

I'd like to take you, in an imaginary way, to look at a different world, somewhere else in the universe, a place inhabited by a life form that very much resembles us. But these creatures grow up with a peculiar knowledge. They know that they have been born in an infinite variety. They know, for instance, that in their genetic material they are born with hundreds of different chromosome formations at the point in each cell that we would say determines their "sex." These creatures don't just come in XX or XY; they also come in a XXY and XYY and XXX plus a long list of "mosaic" variations in which some cells in a creature's body have one combination and other cells have another. Some of these creatures are born with chromosomes that aren't even quite X or Y because a little bit of one chromosome goes and gets joined to another. There are hundreds of different combinations, and though all are not fertile, quite a number of them are. The creatures in this world enjoy their individuality; they delight in the fact that they are not divisible into distinct categories. So when another newborn arrives with an esoterically rare chromosomal formation, there is a little celebration: "Aha," they say, "another sign that we are each unique."

These creatures also live with the knowledge that they are born with a vast range of genital formations. Between their legs are tissue structures that vary along a continuum, from clitorises with a vulva through all possible combinations and gradations to penises with a scrotal sac. These creatures live with an understanding that their genitals all developed prenatally from exactly the same little nub of embryonic tissue called a genital tubercle, which grew and developed under the influence of varying amounts of the hormone androgen. These creatures honor and respect everyone's natural-born genitalia—including what we would describe as a microphallus or a clitoris several inches long. What these creatures find amazing and precious is that because everyone's genitals stem from the same embryonic tissue, the nerves inside all their genitals got wired very much alike, so these nerves of touch just go crazy upon contact in a way that resonates completely between them. "My gosh," they think, "you must feel something in your genital tubercle that intensely resembles what I'm feeling in my genital tubercle." Well, they don't exactly *think* that in so many words; they're actually quite heavy into their feelings at that point; but they do feel very connected—throughout all their wondrous variety.

I could go on. I could tell you about the variety of hormones that course through their bodies in countless different patterns and proportions, both before birth and throughout their lives—the hormones that we call "sex hormones" but that they call "individuality inducers." I could tell you how these creatures think about reproduction: For part of their lives, some of them are quite capable of gestation, delivery, and lactation; and for part of their lives, some of them are quite capable of insemination; and for part or all their lives, some of them are not capable of any of those things—so these creatures conclude that it would be silly to lock anyone into a lifelong category based

---

From *Refusing to Be a Man: Essays on Sex and Justice* by John Stoltenberg. Copyright © 1989 by John Stoltenberg.

on a capability variable that may or may not be utilized and that in any case changes over each lifetime in a fairly uncertain and idiosyncratic way. These creatures are not oblivious to reproduction; but nor do they spend their lives constructing a self-definition around their variable reproductive capacities. They don't have to, because what is truly unique about these creatures is that they are capable of having a sense of personal identity without struggling to fit into a group identity based on how they were born. These creatures are quite happy, actually. They don't worry about sorting *other* creatures into categories, so they don't have to worry about whether they are measuring up to some category they themselves are supposed to belong to.

These creatures, of course, have sex. Rolling and rollicking and robust sex, and sweaty and slippery and sticky sex, and trembling and quaking and tumultuous sex, and tender and tingling and transcendent sex. They have sex fingers to fingers. They have sex belly to belly. They have sex genital tubercle to genital tubercle. They *have* sex. They do not have *a* sex. In their erotic lives, they are not required to act out their status in a category system—because there *is* no category system. There are no sexes to belong to, so sex between creatures is free to be between genuine individuals—not representatives of a category. They have sex. They do not have a sex. Imagine life like that.

Perhaps you have guessed the point of this science fiction: Anatomically, each creature in the imaginary world I have been describing could be an identical twin of every human being on earth. These creatures, in fact, are us—in every way except socially and politically. The way they are born is the way we are born. And we are not born belonging to one or the other of two sexes. We are born into a physiological continuum on which there is no discrete and definite point that you can call "male" and no discrete and definite point that you can call "female." If you look at all the variables in nature that are said to determine human "sex," you can't possibly find one that will unequivocally split the species into two. Each of the so-called criteria of sexedness is itself a continuum—including chromosomal variables, genital and gonadal variations, reproductive capacities, endocrinological proportions, and any other criterion you could think of. Any or all of these different variables may line up in any number of ways, and all of the variables may vary independently of one another.

What does all this mean? It means, first of all, a logical dilemma: Either human "male" and human "female" actually exist in nature as fixed and discrete entities and you can credibly base an entire social and political system on those absolute natural categories, or else the variety of human sexedness is infinite. As Andrea Dworkin wrote in 1974:

> The discovery is, of course, that "man" and "woman" are fictions, caricatures, cultural constructs. As models they are reductive, totalitarian, inappropriate to human becoming. As roles they are static, demeaning to the female, dead-ended for male and female both.

The conclusion is inescapable:

> *We are, clearly, a multisexed species which has its sexuality spread along a vast continuum where the elements called male and female are not discrete.*

"*We are . . . a multisexed species.*" I first read those words a little over ten years ago—and that liberating recognition saved my life.

All the time I was growing up, I knew that there was something really problematic in my relationship to manhood. Inside, deep inside, I never believed I was fully male—I never believed I was growing up enough of a man. I believed that someplace out there, in other men, there was something that was genuine authentic all-American manhood—the real stuff—but I didn't have it: not enough of it to convince *me* anyway, even if I managed to be fairly convincing to those around me. I felt like an imposter, like a fake. I agonized a lot about not feeling male enough, and I had no idea then how much I was not alone.

Then I read those words—those words that suggested to me for the first time that the notion of manhood is a cultural delusion, a baseless belief, a false front, a house of cards. It's not true. The category I was trying so desperately to belong to, to be a member of in good standing—it doesn't exist. Poof. Now you see it, now you don't. Now you're terrified you're not really part of it; now you're free, you don't have to worry anymore. However removed you feel inside from "authentic manhood," it doesn't matter. What matters is the center inside yourself—and how you live, and how you treat people, and what you can contribute as you pass through life on this earth, and how honestly you love, and how carefully you make choices. Those are the things that really matter. Not whether you're a real man. There's no such thing.

The idea of the male sex is like the idea of an Aryan race. The Nazis believed in the idea of an Aryan race—they believed that the Aryan race really exists, physically, in nature—and they put a great deal of effort into making it real. The Nazis believed that from the blond hair and blue eyes occurring naturally in the human species, they could construe the existence of a separate *race*—a distinct category of human beings that was unambiguously rooted in the natural order of things. But traits do not a race make; traits only make traits. For the idea to be real that these physical traits comprised a race, the race had to be socially constructed. The Nazis inferiorized and exterminated those they defined as "non-Aryan." With that, the notion of an Aryan race began to seem to come true. That's how there could be a political entity known as an Aryan race, and that's how there could be for some people a personal, subjective sense that they belonged to it. This happened through hate and force, through violence and victimization, through treating millions of people as things, then exterminating them. The belief system shared by people who believed they were all Aryan could not exist apart from that force and violence. The force and violence created a racial class system, *and* it created those people's membership in the race considered "superior." The force and violence served their class interests in large part because it created and maintained the class itself. But the idea of an Aryan race could never become metaphysically true, despite all the violence unleashed to create it, because there simply *is* no Aryan race. There is only the idea of it—and the consequences of trying to make it seem real. The male sex is very like that.

Penises and ejaculate and prostate glands occur in nature, but the notion that these anatomical traits comprise a sex—a discrete class, separate and distinct, metaphysically divisible from some other sex, *the* "other sex"—is simply that: a notion, an idea. The penises exist; the male sex does not. The male sex is socially constructed. It is a political entity that flourishes only through acts of force and sexual terrorism. Apart from the global inferiorization and subordination of those who are defined as "nonmale," the idea of personal membership in the male sex class would have no recognizable meaning. It would make no sense. No one could be a member of it and no one would think they *should* be a member of it. There would be no male sex to belong to. That doesn't mean there wouldn't still be penises and ejaculate and prostate glands and such. It simply means that the center of our selfhood would not be required to reside inside an utterly fictitious category—a category that only seems real to the extent that those outside it are put down.

We live in a world divided absolutely into two sexes, even though nothing about human nature warrants that division. We are sorted into one category or another at birth based solely on a visual inspection of our groins, and the only question that's asked is whether there's enough elongated tissue around your urethra so you can pee standing up. The presence or absence of a long-enough penis is the primary criterion for separating who's to grow up male from who's to grow up female. And among all the ironies in that utterly whimsical and arbitrary selection process is the fact that *anyone* can pee both sitting down and standing up.

Male sexual identity is the conviction or belief, held by most people born with penises, that they are male and not female, that they belong to the male sex. In a society predicated on the notion that there are two "opposite" and "complementary" sexes, this idea not only makes sense, it *becomes* sense; the very idea of a male sexual identity produces sensation, produces the meaning of sensation, becomes the meaning of how one's body feels. The sense and the sensing of a male sexual identity is at once mental and physical, at once public and personal. Most people born with a penis between their legs grow up aspiring to feel and act unambiguously male, longing to belong to the sex that is male and daring not to belong to the sex that is not, and feeling this urgency for a visceral and constant verification of their male sexual identity—for a fleshy connection to manhood—as the driving force of their life. The drive does not originate in the anatomy. The sensations derive from the idea. The idea gives the feelings social meaning; the idea determines which sensations shall be sought.

People born with penises must strive to make the idea of male sexual identity personally real by doing certain deeds, actions that are valued and chosen because they produce the desired feeling of belonging to a sex that is male and not female. Male sexual identity is experienced only in sensation and action, in feeling and doing, in eroticism and ethics. The feeling of belonging to a male sex encompasses both sensations that are explicitly "sexual" and those that are not ordinarily regarded as such. And there is a tacit social value system according to which certain acts are chosen because they make an individual's sexedness feel real and certain other acts are eschewed because they numb it. That value system is the ethics of male sexual identity—and it may well be the social origin of all injustice.

Each person experiences the idea of sexual identity as more or less real, more or less certain, more or less true, depending on two very personal phenomena: one's feelings and one's acts. For many people, for instance, the act of fucking makes their sexual identity feel more real than it does at other times, and they can predict from experience that this feeling of greater certainty will last for at least a while after each time they fuck. Fucking is not the only such act, and not only so-called sex acts can result in feelings of certainty about sexual identity; but the act of fucking happens to be a very good example of the correlation between *doing* a specific act in a specific way and *sensing* the specificity of the sexual identity to which one aspires. A person can decide to do certain acts and not others just because some acts will have the payoff of a feeling of greater certainty about sexual identity and others will give the feedback of a feeling of less. The transient reality of one's sexual identity, a person can know, is always a function of what one does and how one's acts make one feel. The feeling and the act must conjoin for the idea of the sexual identity to come true. We all keep longing for surety of our sexedness that we can feel; we all keep striving through our actions to make the idea real.

In human nature, eroticism is not differentiated between "male" and "female" in any clear-cut way. There is too much of a continuum, too great a resemblance. From all that we know, the penis and the clitoris are identically "wired" to receive and retransmit sensations from throughout the body, and the congestion of blood within the lower torso during sexual excitation makes all bodies sensate in a remarkably similar manner. Simply put, we all share all the nerve and blood-vessel layouts that are associated with sexual arousal. Who can say, for instance, that the penis would not experience sensations the way that a clitoris does if this were not a world in which the penis is supposed to be hell-bent on penetration? By the time most men make it through puberty, they believe that erotic sensation is supposed to *begin* in their penis; that if engorgement has not begun there, then nothing else in their body will heat up either. There is a massive interior dissociation from sensations that do not explicitly remind a man that his penis is still there. And not only there as sensate, but *functional and operational.*

So much of most men's sexuality is tied up with gender-actualizing—with feeling like a real man—that they can scarcely recall an erotic sensation that had no gender-specific cultural meaning. As most men age, they learn to cancel out and deny erotic sensations that are not specifically linked to what they think a real man is supposed to feel. An erotic sensation unintentionally experienced in a receptive, communing mode—instead of in an aggressive and controlling and violative mode, for instance—can shut down sensory systems in an instant. An erotic sensation unintentionally linked to the "wrong" sex of another person can similarly mean sudden numbness. Acculturated male sexuality has built-in fail-safe: Either its political context rectifies manhood or the experience cannot be felt as sensual. Either the act creates his sexedness or it does not compute as a sex act. So he tenses up, pumps up, steels himself against the dread that he be found not male enough. And his dread is not stupid; for he sees what happens to people when they are treated as nonmales.

My point is that sexuality does not *have* a gender; it *creates* a gender. It creates for those who adapt to it in narrow and specified ways the confirmation for the individual belonging to the idea of one sex or the other. So-called male sexuality is a learned connection between specific physical sensations and the idea of a male sexual identity. To achieve this male sexual identity requires that an individual *identify with* the class of males—that is, accept as one's own the values and interests of the class. A fully realized male sexual identity also requires *nonidentification* with that which is perceived to be nonmale, or female. A male must not identify with females; he must not associate with females in feeling, interest, or action. His identity as a member of the sex class men absolutely depends on the extent to which he repudiates the values and interests of the sex class "women."

I think somewhere inside us all, we have always known something about the relativity of gender. Somewhere inside us all, we know that our bodies harbor deep resemblances, that we are wired inside to respond in a profound harmony to the resonance of eroticism inside the body of someone near us. Physiologically, we are far more alike than different. The tissue structures that have become labial and clitoral or scrotal and penile have not forgotten their common ancestry. Their sensations are of the same source. The nerve networks and interlock of capillaries throughout our pelvises electrify and engorge as if plugged in together and pumping as one. That's what we feel when we feel one another's feelings. That's what can happen during sex that is mutual, equal, reciprocal, profoundly communing.

So why is it that some of us with penises think it's sexy to pressure someone into having sex against their will? Some of us actually get harder the harder the person resists. Some of us with penises actually believe that some of us without penises want to be raped. And why is it that some of us with penises think it's sexy to treat other people as objects, as things to be bought and sold, impersonal bodies to be possessed and consumed for our sexual pleasure? Why is it that the some of us with penises are aroused by sex tinged with rape, and sex commoditized by pornography? Why do so many of us with penises want such antisexual sex?

There's a reason, of course. We have to make a lie seem real. It's a very big lie. We each have to do our part. Otherwise the lie will look like the lie that it is. Imagine the enormity of what we each must do to keep the lie alive in each of us. Imagine the awesome challenge we face to make the lie a social fact. It's a lifetime mission for each of us born with a penis: to have sex in such a way that the male sex will seem real—and so that we'll feel like a real part of it.

We all grow up knowing exactly what kind of sex that is. It's the kind of sex you can have when you pressure or bully someone else into it. So it's a kind of sex that makes your will more important than theirs. That kind of sex helps the lie a lot. That kind of sex makes you feel like someone important and it turns the other person into someone unimportant. That kind of sex makes you feel real, not like a fake. It's a kind of sex men have in order to feel like a real man.

There's also the kind of sex you can have when you force someone and hurt someone and cause someone suffering and humiliation. Violence and hostility in sex help the lie a lot too. Real men are aggressive in sex. Real men get cruel in sex. Real men use their penises like weapons in sex. Real men leave bruises. Real men think it's a turn-on to threaten harm. A brutish push can make an erection feel really hard. That kind of sex helps the lie a lot. That kind of sex makes you feel like someone who is powerful and it turns the other person into someone powerless. That kind of sex makes you feel dangerous and in control—like you're fighting a war with an enemy and if you're mean enough you'll win but if you let up you'll lose your manhood. It's a kind of sex men have *in order to have* a manhood.

There's also the kind of sex you can have when you pay your money into a profit system that grows rich displaying and exploiting the bodies and body parts of people without penises for the sexual entertainment of people with. Pay your money and watch. Pay your money and imagine. Pay your money and get real turned on. Pay your money and jerk off. That kind of sex helps the lie a lot. It helps support an industry committed to making people with penises believe that people without are sluts who just want to be ravished and reviled—an industry dedicated to maintaining a sex-class system in which men believe themselves sex machines and men believe women are mindless fuck tubes. That kind of sex helps the lie a lot. It's like buying Krugerrands as a vote of confidence for white supremacy in South Africa.

And there's one more thing: That kind of sex makes the lie indelible—burns it onto your retinas right adjacent to your brain—makes you remember it and makes your body respond to it and so it makes you believe that the lie is in fact true: You really are a real man. That slavish and submissive creature there spreading her legs is really not. You and that creature have nothing in common. That creature is an alien inanimate thing, but your penis is completely real and alive. Now you can come. Thank god almighty—you have a sex at last.

Now, I believe there are many who are sick at heart over what I have been describing. There are many who were born with penises who want to stop collaborating in the sex-class system that needs us to need these kinds of sex. I believe some of you want to stop living out the big lie, and you want to know how. Some of you long to touch truthfully. Some of you want sexual relationships in your life that are about intimacy and joy, ecstasy and equality—not antagonism and alienation. So what I have to say next I have to say to you.

When you use sex to have a sex, the sex you have is likely to make you feel crummy about yourself. But when you have sex in which you are not struggling with your partner in order to act out "real manhood," the sex you have is more likely to bring you close.

This means several specific things:

1. *Consent is absolutely essential.* If both you and your partner have not freely given your informed consent to the sex you are about to have, you can be quite certain that the sex you go ahead and have will make you strangers to each other. How do you know if there's consent? You ask. You ask again if you're sensing any doubt. Consent to do one thing isn't consent to do another. So you keep communicating, in clear words. And you don't take anything for granted.

2. *Mutuality is absolutely essential.* Sex is not something you do *to* someone. Sex is not a one-way transitive verb, with a subject, you, and an object, the body you're with. Sex that is mutual is not about doing and being done to; it's about being-with and feeling-with. You have to really be there to experience what is happening between and within the two of you—between every part of you and within both your whole bodies. It's a matter of paying attention—as if you are paying attention to someone who matters.

3. *Respect is absolutely essential.* In the sex that you have, treat your partner like a real person who, like you, has real feelings—feelings that matter as much as your own. You may or may not love—but you must always respect. You must respect the integrity of your partner's body. It is not yours for the taking. It belongs to someone real. And you do not get ownership of your partner's body just because you are having sex—or just because you have had sex.

For those who are closer to the beginning of your sex lives than to the middle or the end, many things are still changing for you about how you have sex, with whom, why or why not, what you like or dislike, what kind of sex you want to have more of. In the next few years, you are going to discover and decide a lot. I say "discover" because no one can tell you what you're going to find out about yourself in relation to sex—and I say "decide" because virtually without knowing it you are going to be laying down habits and patterns that will probably stay with you for the rest of your life. You're at a point in your sexual history that you will never be at again. You don't know what you don't know yet. And yet you are making choices whose consequences for your particular sexuality will be sealed years from now.

I speak to you as someone who is closer to the middle of my sexual history. As

I look back, I see that I made many choices that I didn't know I was making. And as I look at men who are near my age, I see that what has happened to many of them is that their sex lives are stuck in deep ruts that began as tiny fissures when they were young. So I want to conclude by identifying what I believe are three of the most important decisions about your sexuality that you can make when you are at the beginning of your sexual history. However difficult these choices may seem to you now, I promise you they will only get more difficult as you grow older. I realize that what I'm about to give is some quite unsolicited nuts-and-bolts advice. But perhaps it will spare you, later on in your lives, some of the obsessions and emptiness that have claimed the sexual histories of many men just a generation before you. Perhaps it will not help, I don't know; but I hope very much that it will.

First, you can start choosing now not to let your sexuality be manipulated by the pornography industry. I've heard many unhappy men talk about how they are so hooked on pornography and obsessed with it that they are virtually incapable of a human erotic contact. And I have heard even more men talk about how, when they do have sex with someone, the pornography gets in the way, like a mental obstacle, like a barrier preventing a full experience of what's really happening between them and their partner. The sexuality that the pornography industry needs you to have is not about communicating and caring; it's about "pornographizing" people—objectifying and conquering them, not being with them as a person. You do not have to buy into it.

Second, you can start choosing now not to let drugs and alcohol numb you through your sex life. Too many men, as they age, become incapable of having sex with a clear head. But you need your head clear—to make clear choices, to send clear messages, to read clearly what's coming in on a clear channel between you and your partner. Sex is no time for your awareness to sign off. And another thing: Beware of relying on drugs or alcohol to give you "permission" to have sex, or to trick your body into feeling something that it's not, or so you won't have to take responsibility for what you're feeling or for the sex that you're about to have. If you can't take sober responsibility for your part in a sexual encounter, you probably shouldn't be having it—and you certainly shouldn't be zonked out of your mind in *order* to have it.

Third, you can start choosing now not to fixate on fucking—especially if you'd really rather have sex in other, noncoital ways. Sometimes men have coital sex—penetration and thrusting then ejaculating inside someone—not because they particularly feel like it but because they feel they *should* feel like it: It's expected that if you're the man, you fuck. And if you don't fuck, you're not a man. The corollary of this cultural imperative is that if two people don't have intercourse, they have not had real sex. That's baloney, of course, but the message comes down hard, especially inside men's heads: Fucking is *the* sex act, the act in which you act out what sex is supposed to be—and what sex you're supposed to be.

Like others born with a penis, I was born into a sex-class system that requires my collaboration every day, even in how I have sex. Nobody told me, when I was younger, that I could have noncoital sex and that it would be fine. Actually, much better than fine. Nobody told me about an incredible range of other erotic possibilities for mutual lovemaking—including rubbing body to body, then coming body to body; including multiple, nonejaculatory orgasms; including the feeling you get when even the tiniest place where you and your partner touch becomes like a window through which great tidal storms of passion ebb and flow, back and forth. Nobody told me about the sex you can have when you stop working at having a sex. My body told me, finally. And I began to trust what my body was telling me more than the lie I was supposed to make real.

I invite you too to resist the lie. I invite you too to become an erotic traitor to male supremacy.

Intimacy

Jean-Paul Sartre

In the following story, Sartre explores the extent to which sex plays a role in enhancing, or undermining, intimacy with others. As you read this, examine how Lulu's sense of her self *is determined largely by her body. Is intimacy a result of a physical or a psychological bond with another? What kinds of experiences do you consider "intimate" ones? With whom do you think Lulu is most intimate and why? What relationships do you consider to be the most intimate ones in your own life?*

Lulu slept naked because she liked to feel the sheets caressing her body and also because laundry was expensive.

In the beginning Henri protested: you shouldn't go to bed naked like that, it isn't nice, it's dirty. Anyhow, he finally followed her example, though in this case it was merely laziness; he was stiff as a poker when there was company (he admired the Swiss, particularly the Genevans: he thought them high class because they were so wooden), but he was negligent in small matters, for example, he wasn't very clean, he didn't change his underwear often; when Lulu put it in the dirty laundry bag she couldn't help noticing the bottoms were yellow from rubbing between his legs. Personally, Lulu did not despise uncleanliness: it was more intimate and made such tender shadows; in the crook of the arm, for instance; she couldn't stand the English with their impersonal bodies which smelt of nothing. But she couldn't bear the negligence of her husband, because it was a way of getting himself coddled. In the morning, he was always very tender toward himself, his head full of dreams, and broad daylight, cold water, the coarse bristles of the brush made him suffer brutal injustices.

Lulu was sleeping on her back, she had thrust the great toe of her left foot into a tear in the sheet: it wasn't a tear, it was only the hem coming apart. But it annoyed her; I have to fix that tomorrow, but still she pushed against the threads so as to feel them break. Henri was not sleeping yet, but he was quiet. He often told Lulu that as soon as he closed his eyes he felt bound by tight, resistant

From *The Wall and Other Stories* by Jean-Paul Sartre, trans. by Lloyd Alexander. Copyright © 1948 by New Direction Publishing Corp.

bonds, he could not even move his little finger. A great fly caught in a spider web. Lulu loved to feel this gross, captive body against her. If he could only stay like that, paralysed, I would take care of him, clean him like a child and sometimes I'd turn him over on his stomach and give him a spanking, and other times when his mother came to see him, I'd find some reason to uncover him, I'd pull back the sheet and his mother would see him all naked. I think she'd fall flat on her face, it must be fifteen years since she'd seen him like that. Lulu passed a light hand over her husband's hip and pinched him a little in the groin. Henri muttered but did not move. Reduced to impotence, Lulu smiled; the word "impotence" always made her smile. When she still loved Henri, and when he slept, thus, she liked to imagine he had been patiently tied up by little men like the ones she had seen in a picture when she was a child and reading *Gulliver's Travels*. She often called Henri "Gulliver" and Henri liked that because it was an English name and it made her seem educated, only he would have rather had her pronounce it with the accent. God, how they annoyed me: if he wanted someone educated all he had to do was marry Jeanne Beder, she's got breasts like hunting horns but she knows five languages. When we were still at Sceaux, on Sundays, I got so annoyed with his family I read books, any book; there was always somebody who came and watched what I was reading and his little sister asked me, "Do you understand, Lucie?" The trouble is he doesn't think I'm distinguished enough. The Swiss, yes, they're distinguished all right because his older sister married a Swiss who gave her five children and then they impress him with their mountains. I can't have a child because of my constitution, but I never thought it was distinguished, what he does, when he goes out with me, always going into the *urinoirs* and I have to look at the store windows waiting for him, what does that make me look like? and he comes out pulling at his pants and bending his legs like an old man.

Lulu took her toe out of the slit in the sheet and wiggled her feet for the pleasure of feeling herself alert next to this soft, captive flesh. She heard rumblings: a gurgling stomach, I hate it, I can never tell whether it's his stomach or mine. She closed her eyes; liquids do it, bubbling through packs of soft pipes, everybody has them, Rirette has them, I have them (I don't like to think about it, it makes my stomach hurt). He loves me, he doesn't love my bowels, if they showed him my appendix in a glass, he wouldn't recognize it, he's always feeling me, but if they put the glass in his hands he wouldn't touch it, he wouldn't think "that's hers," you ought to love all of somebody, the esophagus, the liver, the intestines. Maybe we don't love them because we aren't used to them, if we saw the way we saw our hands and arms maybe we'd love them; the starfish must love each other better than we do. They stretch out on the beach when there's sunlight and they poke out their stomachs to get the air and everybody can see them; I wonder where we could stick ours out, through the navel. She had closed her eyes and blue circles began to turn, like a carnival; yesterday I was shooting those circles with rubber arrows and letters lit up, one at every shot and they made the name of a city, he kept me from finishing Dijon with his mania for pressing himself up behind me, I hate people to touch me from behind, I'd rather not have a back, I don't like people to do things to me when I can't see them, they can grab a handful and then you don't see their hands, you can feel them going up and down but you can't tell where they're going, they look at you with all their eyes and you don't see them, he loves that; Henri would never think of it but he, all he thinks about is getting behind me and I know he does it on purpose to touch my behind because he knows I practically die of shame because I have one, when I'm ashamed it excites him but I don't want to think about him (she was afraid) I want to think about Rirette. She thought about Rirette every evening at the same time, just at the moment when Henri began to snuffle and grunt. But there was resistance to the thought and someone else came in her place, she even caught a glimpse of crisp black hair and she thought here it comes and she shuddered because you never know what's coming, if it's the face it's all right, that can still pass, but there were nights she spent without closing her eyes because of those horrible memories coming to the surface, it's terrible when you know all of a man and especially *that.* It isn't the same thing with Henri, I can imagine him from head to foot and it touches me because he's soft with flesh that's all grey except the belly and that's pink, he says when a well built man sits down, his belly makes three folds, but he has six, only he counts by twos and he doesn't want to see the others. She felt annoyed thinking about Rirette: "Lulu, you don't know what the body of a handsome man is like." It's ridiculous, naturally I know, she means a body hard as rock, with muscles, I don't like that, and I felt soft as a caterpillar when he hugged me against him; I married Henri because he was soft, because he looked like a priest. The priests are soft as women with their cassocks and it seems they wear stockings. When I was fifteen I wanted to lift up their skirts quietly and see their men's knees and their drawers, it was so funny they had something between their legs; I would have taken the skirt in one hand and slipped the other up their legs as far as you think, it's not that I like women so much but a man's thing when it's under a skirt is so soft, like a big flower. The trouble is you can never really hold it in your hands, if it would only stay quiet, but it starts moving like an animal, it gets hard, it frightens me when it's hard and sticking up in the air, it's brutal; God, how rotten love is. I loved Henri because his little thing never got hard, never raised its head, I laughed, sometimes I embarrassed him, I wasn't any more afraid of his than of a child's; in the evening I always took his soft little thing between my fingers, he blushed and turned his head away, sighing, but it didn't move, it behaved itself in my hand, I didn't squeeze it, we always stayed like that for a long time and then he went to sleep. Then I stretched out on my back and thought about priests and pure things, about women, and I stroked my stomach first, my beautiful flat stomach, then I slid my hands down and it was pleasure; the pleasure only I know how to give myself.

The crisp hair, the hair of a negro. And anguish in her throat like a ball. But she closed her eyes tightly and finally the ear of Rirette appeared, a small ear, all red and golden, looking like a sugar candy. Lulu had not as much pleasure as usual at the sight of it because she heard Rirette's voice at the same time. It was a sharp, precise voice which Lulu didn't like. "You *should* go away with Pierre, Lulu; it's the only intelligent thing to do." I like Rirette very much, but she annoys me a little when she acts important and gets carried away by what she says. The night before, at the *Coupole,* Rirette was bent over her with a reasonable and somewhat haggard look. "You *can't* stay with Henri, because you don't love him, it would be a crime." She doesn't lose a chance to say something bad about him, I don't think it's very nice, he's always been perfect with her; maybe I don't love him any more, but it isn't up to Rirette to tell me; everything looks so simple and easy to her: you love or you don't love any more: but I'm not simple. First I'm used to it here and then I do like him, he's my husband. I wanted to beat her, I always wanted to hurt her because she's fat. "It would be a crime." She raised her arms, I saw her armpit, I always like her better when she has bare arms. The armpit. It was half-open, you might have thought it was a mouth; Lulu saw purple wrinkled flesh beneath the curly hairs. Pierre calls her "Minerva the Plump," she doesn't like that at all, Lulu smiled because she thought of her little brother Robert who asked her one day when she had on nothing but her slip. "Why do you have hair under your arms?" and she answered, "It's a sickness." She liked to dress in front of her little brother because he made such funny remarks, and you wondered where he picked them up. He always felt her clothes and folded her dresses carefully, his hands were so deft: one day he'll be a great dressmaker. That's a charming business, I'll design the materials for him. It's odd for a little boy to want to be a dressmaker; if I had been a boy I would have wanted to be an explorer or an actor, but not a dressmaker; but he always was a dreamer, he doesn't talk enough, he sticks to his own ideas; I wanted to be a nun and take up collections in beautiful houses. My eyes feel all soft, all soft as flesh, I'm going to sleep. My lovely pale face under the stiff headdress. I would have looked distinguished. I would have seen hundreds of dark hallways. But the maid would have turned the light on right away; then I'd have seen family portraits, bronze statues on the tables. And closets. The woman comes with a little book and a fifty franc note "Here you are, Sister." "Thank you madame, God bless you. Until the next time." But I wouldn't have been a real nun. In the bus, sometimes, I'd have made eyes at some fellow, first he'd be dumbfounded then he'd follow me, telling me a lot of nonsense and I'd have a policeman lock him up. I would have kept the collection money myself. What would I have bought? *Antidote.* It's silly. My eyes are getting softer, I like that, you'd think they were soaked in water and my whole body's comfortable. The beautiful green tiara with emeralds and lapis Iazuli. The tiara turned and it was a horrible bull's head, but Lulu was not afraid, she said, "Birds of Cantal. Attention." A long red river dragged across arid countrysides. Lulu thought of her meat-grinder, then of hair grease.

"It would be a crime." She jumped bolt upright in the blackness, her eyes hard. They're torturing me. "You'll come to my house, I want you all for good intentions," but she who's so reasonable for other people, she ought to know I need to think it over. He said "You'll come!" making fiery eyes at me. "You'll come into my house, I want you all for myself!" His eyes terrify me when he wants to hypnotize; he kneaded my arms; when I see him with eyes like that I always think of the hair he has on his chest. You will come, I want you all for myself; how can he say things like that? I'm not a dog.

When I sat down, I smiled at him. I had changed my powder for him and I made up my eyes because he likes that, but he didn't see a thing, he doesn't look at my face, he looks at my breasts and I wish they'd dry up, just to annoy him, even though I don't have too much, they're so small. You will come to my villa in Nice. He said it was white with a marble staircase, that it looked out on the sea, and we'd live naked all day, it must be funny to go up a stairway when you're naked; I'd make him go up ahead of me so that he wouldn't look at me; or else I wouldn't be able to move a foot, I'd stay motionless, wishing with all my heart he'd go blind; anyhow, that would hardly change anything; when he's there I always think I'm naked. He took me by the arm, he looked wicked, he told me "You've got me under your skin!" and I was afraid and said, "Yes"; I want to make you happy, we'll go riding in the car, in the boat, we'll go to Italy and I'll give you everything you want. But his villa is almost unfurnished and we'd have to sleep on a mattress on the floor. He wants me to sleep in his arms and I'll smell his odor; I'd like his chest because it's brown and wide, but there's a pile of hair on it, I wish men didn't have hair, his is black and soft as moss, sometimes I stroke it and sometimes I'm horrified by it, I pull back as far as possible but he hugs me against him. He'll want me to sleep in his arms, he'll hug me in his arms and I'll smell his odor; and when it's dark we'll hear the noise of the sea and he may wake me up in the middle of the night if he wants to do it: I'll never be able to sleep peacefully except when I have my sickness because, then, he'll shut up but even so it seems there are men who do it with women then and afterwards they have blood on them, blood that isn't theirs, and there must be some on the sheets, everywhere, it's disgusting, why must we have bodies?

Lulu opened her eyes, the curtains were colored red by a light coming from the street, there was a red reflection in the mirror: Lulu loved this red light and there was an armchair which made funny shadows against the window. Henri had put his pants on the arm of the chair, and his suspenders were hanging in emptiness. I have to buy him new suspenders. Oh I don't want to, I don't want to leave. He'll kiss me all day and I'll be *his,* I'll be his pleasure, he'll look at me, he'll think, "this is my pleasure, I touched her there and there and I can do it again if it pleases me." At Port-Royal. Lulu kicked her feet in the sheets, she hated Pierre when she remembered what happened at Port-Royal. She was behind the hedge, she thought he had stayed in the car, looking at the map, and suddenly she saw him, running up behind her, he looked at her. Lulu kicked Henri. He's going to wake up. But Henri said "Humph," and didn't waken. I'd like to know a handsome young man, pure as a girl, and we wouldn't touch each other, we'd walk along the seashore and we'd hold hands, and at night we'd sleep in twin beds, we'd stay like brother and sister and talk till morning. I'd like to live with Rirette, it's so charming, women living together; she has fat, smooth shoulders; I was miserable when she was in love with Fresnel, and it worried me to think he petted her, that he passed his hands slowly over her shoulders and thighs and she sighed. I wonder what her face must look like when she's stretched out like that, all naked, under a man, feeling hands on her flesh. I wouldn't touch her for all the money in the world, I wouldn't know what to do with her, even if she wanted, even if she said, "I want it!" I wouldn't know how, but if I were invisible I'd like to be there when somebody was doing it to her and watch her face (I'd be surprised if she still looked like Minerva) and stroke her spread knees gently, her pink knees and hear her groan. Dry throated, Lulu gave a short laugh: sometimes you think about things like that. Once she pretended Pierre wanted to rape Rirette. And I helped him, I held Rirette in my arms. Yesterday. She had fire in her cheeks, we were sitting on her sofa, one against the other, her legs were pressed together, but we didn't say anything, we'll never say anything. Henri began to snore and Lulu hissed. I'm here, I can't sleep, I'm upset and he snores, the fool. If he were to take me in his arms, beg me, if he told me, "You are all mine, Lulu, I love you, don't go!" I'd make the sacrifice for him, I'd stay, yes, I'd stay with him all my life to give him pleasure.

On the Production of Woman

Thomas Aquinas

St. Thomas Aquinas lived during a time when the state was subordinate to the church. In this excerpt from his Summa Theologica, *Aquinas inquires as to why God created woman, since woman is "defective" and there must be a reason why God would create something defective. Aquinas reasons that the purpose must be to assist the male in procreation, a purpose that Aquinas views as important but one that is less noble than the "intellectual" purpose that men have. He thus establishes the foundation for a legitimation of an imbalance of power between men and women in all other contexts. As you read this, think of some of the ways in which Aquinas's argument is problematic and also some of the ways in which his argument continues to be reaffirmed in our contemporary society.*

FIRST PART

Question 92

Article 1

Whether the woman should have been made in the first production of things?

Objection 1. It would seem that the woman should not have been made in the first production of things. For the Philosopher says (De Gener. ii, 3), that "the female is a misbegotten male." But nothing misbegotten or defective should have been in the first production of things. Therefore woman should not have been made at that first production.

Objection 2. Further, subjection and limitation were a result of sin, for to the woman was it said after sin (Gn. 3:16): "Thou shalt be under the man's power"; and Gregory says that, "Where there is no sin, there is no inequality." But woman is naturally of less strength and dignity than man; "for the agent is always more honorable than the patient," as Augustine says (Gen. ad lit. xii, 16). Therefore woman should not have been made in the first production of things before sin.

Objection 3. Further, occasions of sin should be cut off. But God foresaw that the woman would be an occasion of sin to man. Therefore He should not have made woman.

On the contrary, It is written (Gn. 2:18): "It is not good for man to be alone; let us make him a helper like to himself."

I answer that, It was necessary for woman to be made, as the Scripture says, as a "helper" to man; not, indeed, as a helpmate in other works, as some say, since man can be more efficiently helped by another man in other works; but as a helper in the work of generation. This can be made clear if we observe the mode of generation carried out in various living things. Some living things do not possess in themselves the power of generation, but are generated by some other specific agent, such as some plants and animals by the influence of the heavenly bodies, from some fitting matter and not from seed: others possess the active

---

From *Summa Theologica* by Thomas Aquinas. Translated by the Fathers of the English Dominican Province. Copyright © 1947 Benzinger Brothers Inc., Hypertext Version Copyright © 1995, 1996 New Advent Inc.

and passive generative power together; as we see in plants which are generated from seed; for the noblest vital function in plants is generation. Wherefore we observe that in these the active power of generation invariably accompanies the passive power. Among perfect animals the active power of generation belongs to the male sex, and the passive power to the female. And as among animals there is a vital operation nobler than generation, to which their life is principally directed; therefore the male sex is not found in continual union with the female in perfect animals, but only at the time of coition; so that we may consider that by this means the male and female are one, as in plants they are always united; although in some cases one of them preponderates, and in some the other. But man is yet further ordered to a still nobler vital action, and that is intellectual operation. Therefore there was greater reason for the distinction of these two forces in man; so that the female should be produced separately from the male; although they are carnally united for generation. Therefore directly after the formation of woman, it was said: "And they shall be two in one flesh" (Gn. 2:24).

Reply to Objection 1. As regards the individual nature, woman is defective and misbegotten, for the active force in the male seed tends to the production of a perfect likeness in the masculine sex; while the production of woman comes from defect in the active force or from some material indisposition, or even from some external influence; such as that of a south wind, which is moist, as the Philosopher observes (De Gener. Animal. iv, 2). On the other hand, as regards human nature in general, woman is not misbegotten, but is included in nature's intention as directed to the work of generation. Now the general intention of nature depends on God, Who is the universal Author of nature. Therefore, in producing nature, God formed not only the male but also the female.

Reply to Objection 2. Subjection is twofold. One is servile, by virtue of which a superior makes use of a subject for his own benefit; and this kind of subjection began after sin. There is another kind of subjection which is called economic or civil, whereby the superior makes use of his subjects for their own benefit and good; and this kind of subjection existed even before sin. For good order would have been wanting in the human family if some were not governed by others wiser than themselves. So by such a kind of subjection woman is naturally subject to man, because in man the discretion of reason predominates. Nor is inequality among men excluded by the state of innocence, as we shall prove (96, 3).

Reply to Objection 3. If God had deprived the world of all those things which proved an occasion of sin, the universe would have been imperfect. Nor was it fitting for the common good to be destroyed in order that individual evil might be avoided; especially as God is so powerful that He can direct any evil to a good end.

Whether woman should have been made from man?

Objection 1. It would seem that woman should not have been made from man. For sex belongs both to man and animals. But in the other animals the female was not made from the male. Therefore neither should it have been so with man.

Objection 2. Further, things of the same species are of the same matter. But male and female are of the same species. Therefore, as man was made of the slime of the earth, so woman should have been made of the same, and not from man.

Objection 3. Further, woman was made to be a helpmate to man in the work of generation. But close relationship makes a person unfit for that office; hence near relations are debarred from intermarriage, as is written (Lev. 18:6). Therefore woman should not have been made from man. On the contrary, It is written (Ecclus. 17:5): "He created of him," that is, out of man, "a helpmate like to himself," that is, woman. I answer that, When all things were first formed, it was more suitable for the woman to be made from man that (for the female to be from the male) in other animals.

First, in order thus to give the first man a certain dignity consisting in this, that as God is the principle of the whole universe, so the first man, in likeness to God, was the principle of the whole human race. Wherefore Paul says that "God made the whole human race from one" (Acts 17:26).

Secondly, that man might love woman all the more, and cleave to her more closely, knowing her to be fashioned from himself. Hence it is written (Gn. 2:23, 24): "She was taken out of man, wherefore a man shall leave father and mother, and shall cleave to his wife." This was most necessary as regards the human race, in which the male and female live together for life; which is not the case with other animals.

Thirdly, because, as the Philosopher says (Ethic. viii, 12), the human male and female are united, not only for generation, as with other animals, but also for the purpose of domestic life, in which each has his or her particular duty, and in which the man is the head of the woman. Wherefore it was suitable for the woman to be made out of man, as out of her principle.

Fourthly, there is a sacramental reason for this. For by this is signified that the Church takes her origin from Christ. Wherefore the Apostle says (Eph. 5:32): "This is a great sacrament; but I speak in Christ and in the Church."

Reply to Objection 1 is clear from the foregoing.

Reply to Objection 2. Matter is that from which something is made. Now created nature has a determinate principle; and since it is determined to one thing, it has also a determinate mode of proceeding. Wherefore from determinate matter it produces something in a determinate species. On the other hand, the Divine Power, being infinite, can produce things of the same species out of any matter, such as a man from the slime of the earth, and a woman from out of man.

Reply to Objection 3. A certain affinity arises from natural generation, and this is an impediment to matrimony. Woman, however, was not produced from man by natural generation, but by the Divine Power alone. Wherefore Eve is not called the daughter of Adam; and so this argument does not prove.

Whether the woman was fittingly made from the rib of man?

Objection 1. It would seem that the woman should not have been formed from the rib of man. For the rib was much smaller than the woman's body. Now from a smaller thing a larger thing can be made only—either by addition (and then the woman ought to have been described as made out of that which was added, rather than out of the rib itself)—or by rarefaction, because, as Augustine says (Gen. ad lit. x): "A body cannot increase in bulk except by rarefaction." But the woman's body is not more rarefied than man's—at least, not in the proportion of a rib to Eve's body. Therefore Eve was not formed from a rib of Adam.

Objection 2. Further, in those things which were first created there was nothing superfluous. Therefore a rib of Adam belonged to the integrity of his body. So, if a rib was removed, his body remained imperfect; which is unreasonable to suppose.

Objection 3. Further, a rib cannot be removed from man without pain. But there was no pain before sin. Therefore it was not right for a rib to be taken from the man, that Eve might be made from it.

On the contrary, It is written (Gn. 2:22): "God built the rib, which He took from Adam, into a woman."

I answer that, It was right for the woman to be made from a rib of man.

First, to signify the social union of man and woman, for the woman should neither "use authority over man," and so she was not made from his head; nor was it right for her to be subject to man's contempt as his slave, and so she was not made from his feet.

Secondly, for the sacramental signification; for from the side of Christ sleeping on the Cross the Sacraments flowed—namely, blood and water—on which the Church was established.

Reply to Objection 1. Some say that the woman's body was formed by a material increase, without anything being added; in the same way as our Lord multiplied the five loaves. But this is quite impossible. For such an increase of matter would either be by a change of the very substance of the matter itself, or by a change of its dimensions. Not by change of the substance of the matter, both because matter, considered in itself, is quite unchangeable, since it has a potential existence, and has nothing but the nature of a subject, and because quantity and size are extraneous to the essence of matter itself. Wherefore multiplication of matter is quite unintelligible, as long as the matter itself remains the same without anything added to it; unless it receives greater dimensions. This implies rarefaction, which is for the same matter to receive greater dimensions, as the Philosopher says (Phys. iv). To say, therefore, that the same matter is enlarged, without being rarefied, is to combine contradictories—viz. the definition with the absence of the thing defined.

Wherefore, as no rarefaction is apparent in such multiplication of matter, we must admit an addition of matter: either by creation, or which is more probable, by conversion. Hence Augustine says (Tract. xxiv in Joan.) that "Christ filled five thousand men with five loaves, in the same way as from a few seeds He produces the harvest of corn"—that is, by transformation of the nourishment. Nevertheless, we say that the crowds were fed with five loaves, or that woman was made from the rib, because an addition was made to the already existing matter of the loaves and of the rib.

Reply to Objection 2. The rib belonged to the integral perfection of Adam, not as an individual, but as the principle of the human race; just as the semen belongs to the perfection of the begetter, and is released by a natural and pleasurable operation. Much more, therefore, was it possible that by the Divine power the body of the woman should be produced from the man's rib.

From this it is clear how to answer the third objection.

Women Are Not Our Brothers

Simone de Beauvoir

The identity of woman has been viewed in relation to the identity of man. In many societies, women have not been identified as individuals who have social standing. Some people have argued that this is because women and men are not equals by nature, and thus they have a hierarchical relationship naturally. In this essay, Beauvoir explores this hierarchical dichotomy between woman and man and questions whether or not there is a necessary relationship between them. Is this hierarchy due to nature or nurture? As you read this, reflect upon some of the ways in which your own identity is related to that of other women or men. Is it possible to have a self identity without the other?

CONCLUSION

No, woman is not our brother; through indolence and depravity we have made of her a being apart, unknown, having no weapon other than her sex, which not only means constant strife but is moreover an unfair weapon of the eternal little slave's mistrust—adoring or hating, but never our frank companion, a being set apart as if in *esprit de corps* and freemasonry.

Many men would still subscribe to these words of Laforgue; many think that there will always be "strife and dispute," as Montaigne put it, and that fraternity will never be possible. The fact is that today neither men nor women are satisfied with each other. But the question is to know whether there is an original curse that condemns them to rend each other or whether the conflicts in which they are opposed merely mark a transitional moment in human history.

We have seen that in spite of legends no physiological destiny imposes an eternal hostility upon Male and Female as such; even the famous praying mantis devours her male only for want of other food and for the good of the species: it is to this, the species, that all individuals are subordinated, from the top to the bottom of the scale of animal life. Moreover, humanity is something more than a mere species: it is a historical development; it is to be defined by the manner in which it deals with its natural, fixed characteristics, its *facticité*. Indeed, even with the most extreme bad faith in the world, it is impossible to demonstrate the existence of a rivalry between the human male and female of a truly physiological nature. Further, their hostility may be allocated rather to that intermediate terrain between biology and psychology: psychoanalysis. Woman, we are told, envies man his penis and wishes to castrate him; but the childish desire for the penis is important in the life of the adult woman only if she feels her femininity as a mutilation; and then it is as a symbol of all the privileges of manhood that she wishes to appropriate the male organ. We may readily agree that her dream of castration has this symbolic significance: she wishes, it is thought, to deprive the male of his transcendence.

From *The Second Sex* by Simone de Beauvoir, trans. by H. M. Parshley. Copyright 1952, renewed 1980 by Alfred A. Knopf, Inc. Reprinted by permission of Alfred A. Knopf, a Division of Random House, Inc.

But her desire, as we have seen, is much more ambiguous: she wishes, in a contradictory fashion, *to have* this transcendence, which is to suppose that she at once respects it and denies it, that she intends at once to throw herself into it and keep it within herself. This is to say that the drama does not unfold on a sexual level; further, sexuality has never seemed to us to define a destiny, to furnish in itself the key to human behavior, but to express the totality of a situation that it only helps to define. The battle of the sexes is not immediately implied in the anatomy of man and woman. The truth is that when one evokes it, one takes for granted that in the timeless realm of Ideas a battle is being waged between those vague essences the Eternal Feminine and the Eternal Masculine; and one neglects the fact that this titanic combat assumes on earth two totally different forms, corresponding with two different moments of history.

The woman who is shut up in immanence endeavors to hold man in that prison also; thus the prison will be confused with the world, and woman will no longer suffer from being confined there: mother, wife, sweetheart are the jailers. Society, being codified by man, decrees that woman is inferior: she can do away with this inferiority only by destroying the male's superiority. She sets about mutilating, dominating man, she contradicts him, she denies his truth and his values. But in doing this she is only defending herself; it was neither a changeless essence nor a mistaken choice that doomed her to immanence, to inferiority. They were imposed upon her. All oppression creates a state of war. And this is no exception. The existent who is regarded as inessential cannot fail to demand the re-establishment of her sovereignty.

Today the combat takes a different shape; instead of wishing to put man in a prison, woman endeavors to escape from one; she no longer seeks to drag him into the realms of immanence but to emerge, herself, into the light of transcendence. Now the attitude of the males creates a new conflict: it is with a bad grace that the man lets her go. He is very well pleased to remain the sovereign subject, the absolute superior, the essential being; he refuses to accept his companion as an equal in any concrete way. She replies to his lack of confidence in her by assuming an aggressive attitude. It is no longer a question of a war between individuals each shut up in his or her sphere: a caste claiming its rights goes over the top and it is resisted by the privileged caste. Here two transcendences are face to face; instead of displaying mutual recognition, each free being wishes to dominate the other.

This difference of attitude is manifest on the sexual plane as on the spiritual plane. The "feminine" woman in making herself prey tries to reduce man, also, to her carnal passivity; she occupies herself in catching him in her trap, in enchaining him by means of the desire she arouses in him in submissively making herself a thing. The emancipated woman, on the contrary, wants to be active, a taker, and refuses the passivity man means to impose on her. Thus Elise and her emulators deny the values of the activities of virile type; they put the flesh above the spirit, contingence above liberty, their routine wisdom above creative audacity. But the "modern" woman accepts masculine values: she prides herself on thinking, taking action, working, creating, on the same terms as men; instead of seeking to disparage them, she declares herself their equal.

In so far as she expresses herself in definite action, this claim is legitimate, and male insolence must then bear the blame. But in men's defense it must be said that women are wont to confuse the issue. A Mabel Dodge Luhan intended to subjugate D. H. Lawrence by her feminine charms so as to dominate him spiritually thereafter; many women, in order to show by their successes their equivalence to men, try to secure male support by sexual means; they play on both sides, demanding old-fashioned respect and modern esteem, banking on their old magic and their new rights. It is understandable that a man becomes irritated and puts himself on the defensive; but he is also double-dealing when he requires woman to play the game fairly while he denies them the indispensable trump cards through distrust and hostility. Indeed, the struggle cannot be clearly drawn between them, since woman is opaque in her very being; she stands before man not as a subject but as an object paradoxically endued with subjectivity; she takes herself simultaneously as *self* and as *other*, a contradiction that entails baffling consequences. When she makes weapons at once of her weakness and of her strength, it is not a matter of designing calculation: she seeks salvation spontaneously in the way that has been imposed on her, that of passivity, at the same time when she is actively demanding her sovereignty; and no doubt this procedure is unfair tactics, but it is dictated to her by the ambiguous situation assigned her. Man, however, becomes indignant when he treats her as a free and independent being and then realizes that she is still a trap for him; if he gratifies and satisfies her in her posture as prey, he finds her claims to autonomy irritating; whatever he does, he feels tricked and she feels wronged.

The quarrel will go on as long as men and women fail to recognize each other as peers; that is to say, as long as femininity is perpetuated as such. Which sex is the more eager to maintain it? Woman, who is being emancipated from it, wishes none the less to retain its privileges; and man, in that case, wants her to assume its limitations. "It is easier to accuse one sex than to excuse the other," says Montaigne. It is vain to apportion praise and blame. The truth is that if the vicious circle is so hard to break, it is because the two sexes are each the victim at once of the other and of itself. Between two adversaries confronting each other in their pure liberty, an agreement could be easily reached: the more so as the war profits neither. But the complexity of the whole affair derives from the fact that each camp is giving aid and comfort to the enemy; woman is pursuing a dream of submission, man a dream of identification. Want of authenticity does not pay: each blames the other for the unhappiness he or she has incurred in yielding to the temptations of the easy way; what man and woman loathe in each other is the shattering frustration of each one's own bad faith and baseness.

We have seen why men enslaved women in the first place; the devaluation of femininity has been a necessary step in human evolution, but it might have led to collaboration between the two sexes; oppression is to be explained by the tendency of the existent to flee from himself by means of identification with the other, whom he oppresses to that end. In each individual man that tendency exists today; and the vast majority yield to it. The husband wants to find himself in his wife, the lover in his mistress, in the form of a stone image; he is seeking in her the myth of his virility, of his sovereignty, of his immediate reality. "My husband never goes to the movies," says his wife, and the dubious masculine opinion is graved in the marble of eternity. But he is himself the slave of his double: what an effort to build up an image in which he is always in danger! In spite of everything his success in this depends upon the capricious freedom of women: he must constantly try to keep this propitious to him. Man is concerned with the effort to appear male, important, superior; he pretends so as to get pretense in return; he, too, is aggressive, uneasy; he feels hostility for women because he is afraid of them, he is afraid of them because he is afraid of the personage, the image, with which he identifies himself. What time and strength he squanders in liquidating, sublimating, transferring complexes, in talking about women, in seducing them, in fearing them! He would be liberated himself in their liberation. But this is precisely what he dreads. And so he obstinately persists in the mystifications intended to keep woman in her chains.

That she is being tricked, many men have realized. "What a misfortune to be a woman! And yet the misfortune, when one is a woman, is at bottom not to comprehend that it is one," says Kirkegaard.[1] For a long time there have been efforts to disguise this misfortune. For example, guardianship has been done away with: this women have been given "protectors," and if they are invested with the rights of the old-time guardians, it is in woman's own interest. To forbid her working, to keep her at home, is to defend her against herself and to assure her happiness. We have seen what poetic veils are thrown over her monotonous burdens of housekeeping and maternity: in exchange for her liberty she has received the false treasures of her "femininity." Balzac illustrates this maneuver very well in counseling man to treat her as a slave while persuading her that she is a queen. Less cynical, many men try to convince themselves that she is really privileged. There are American sociologists who seriously teach today the theory of "low-class gain." In France, also, it has often been proclaimed—although in a less scientific manner—that the workers are very fortunate in not being obliged to "keep up appearances" and still more so the bums who can dress in rags and sleep on the sidewalks, pleasures forbidden to the Count de Beaumont and the Wendels. Like the carefree wretches gaily scratching at their vermin, like the merry Negroes laughing under the lash and those joyous Tunisian Arabs burying their starved children with a smile, woman enjoys that incomparable privilege: irresponsibility. Free from troublesome burdens and cares, she obviously has "the better part." But it is disturbing that with an obstinate perversity—connected no doubt with original sin—down through the centuries and in all countries, the people who have the better part are always crying to their benefactors: "It is too much! I will be satisfied with yours!" But the munificent capitalists, the generous colonists, the superb males, stick to their guns: "Keep the better part, hold on to it!"

It must be admitted that the males find in woman more complicity than the oppressor usually finds in the oppressed. And in bad faith they take authorization from this to declare that she has *desired* the destiny they have imposed on her. We have seen that all the main features of her training combine to bar her from the roads of revolt and adventure. Society in general—beginning with her respected parents—lies to her by praising the lofty values of love, devotion, the gift of herself, and then concealing from her the fact that neither lover nor husband nor yet her children will be inclined to accept the burdensome charge of all that. She cheerfully believes these lies because they invite her to follow the easy slope: in this others commit their worst crime against her; throughout her life from childhood on, they damage and corrupt her by designating as her true vocation this submission, which is the temptation of every existent in the anxiety of liberty. If a child is taught idleness by being amused all

[1] *In Vino Veritas.* He says further: "Politeness is pleasing—essentially—to woman, and the fact that she accepts it without hesitation is explained by nature's care for the weaker, for the unfavored being, and for one to whom an illusion means more than a material compensation. But this illusion, precisely, is fatal to her. . . . To feel oneself freed from distress thanks to something imaginary, to be the dupe of something imaginary, is that not a still deeper mockery? . . . Woman is very far from being *verwahrlost* (neglected), but in another sense she is, since she can never free herself from the illusion that nature has used to console her."

day long and never being led to study, or shown its usefulness, it will hardly be said, when he grows up, that he chose to be incapable and ignorant; yet this is how woman is brought up, without ever being impressed with the necessity of taking charge of her own existence. So she readily lets herself come to count on the protection, love, assistance, and supervision of others, she lets herself be fascinated with the hope of self-realization without *doing* anything. She does wrong in yielding to the temptation; but man is in no position to blame her, since he has led her into the temptation. When conflict arises between them, each will hold the other responsible for the situation; she will reproach him with having made her what she is: "No one taught me to reason or to earn my own living"; he will reproach her with having accepted the consequences: "You don't know anything, you are an incompetent," and so on. Each sex thinks it can justify itself by taking the offensive; but the wrongs done by one do not make the other innocent.

The innumerable conflicts that set men and women against one another come from the fact that neither is prepared to assume all the consequences of this situation which the one has offered and the other accepted. The doubtful concept of "equality in inequality," which the one uses to mask his despotism and the other to mask her cowardice, does not stand the test of experience: in their exchanges, woman appeals to the theoretical equality she has been guaranteed, and man the concrete inequality that exists. The result is that in every association an endless debate goes on concerning the ambiguous meaning of the words *give* and *take:* she complains of giving her all, he protests that she takes his all. Woman has to learn that exchanges—it is a fundamental law of political economy—are based on the value the merchandise offered has for the buyer, and not for the seller: she has been deceived in being persuaded that her worth is priceless. The truth is that for man she is an amusement, a pleasure, company, an inessential boon; he is for her the meaning, the justification of her existence. The exchange, therefore, is not of two items of equal value.

This inequality will be especially brought out in the fact that the time they spend together—which fallaciously seems to be the same time—does not have the same value for both partners. During the evening the lover spends with his mistress he could be doing something of advantage to his career, seeing friends, cultivating business relationships, seeking recreation; for a man normally integrated in society, time is a positive value: money, reputation, pleasure. For the idle, bored woman, on the contrary, it is a burden she wishes to get rid of; when she succeeds in killing time, it is a benefit to her: the man's presence is pure profit. In a liaison what most clearly interests the man, in many cases, is the sexual benefit he gets from it: if need be, he can be content to spend no more time with his mistress than is required for the sexual act; but—with exceptions—what she, on her part, wants is to kill all the excess time she has on her hands; and—like the storekeeper who will not sell potatoes unless the customer will take turnips also—she will not yield her body unless her lover will take hours of conversation and "going out" into the bargain. A balance is reached if, on the whole, the cost does not seem too high to the man, and this depends, of course, on the strength of his desire and the importance he gives to what is to be sacrificed. But if the woman demands—offers—too much time, she becomes wholly intrusive, like the river overflowing its banks, and the man will prefer to have nothing rather than too much. Then she reduces her demands; but very often the balance is reached at the cost of a double tension: she feels that the man has "had" her at a bargain, and he thinks her price is too high. This analysis, of course, is put in somewhat humorous terms; but—except for those affairs of jealous and exclusive passion in which the man wants total possession of the woman—this conflict constantly appears in cases of affection, desire, and even love. He always has "other things to do" with his time; whereas she has time to burn; and he considers much of the time she gives him not as a gift but as a burden.

As a rule he consents to assume the burden because he knows very well that he is on the privileged side, he has a bad conscience; and if he is of reasonable good will he tries to compensate for the inequality by being generous. He prides himself on his compassion, however, and at the first clash he treats the woman as ungrateful and thinks, with some irritation: "I'm too good to her." She feels she is behaving like a beggar when she is convinced of the high value of her gifts, and that humiliates her.

Here we find the explanation of the cruelty that woman often shows she is capable of practicing; she has a good conscience because she is on the unprivileged side; she feels she is under no obligation to deal gently with the favored caste, and her only thought is to defend herself. She will even be very happy if she has occasion to show her resentment to a lover who has not been able to satisfy all her demands: since he does not give her enough, she takes savage delight in taking back everything from him. At this point the wounded lover suddenly discovers the value *in toto* of a liaison each moment of which he held more or less in contempt: he is ready to promise her everything, even though he will feel exploited again when he has to make good. He accuses his mistress of blackmailing him: she calls him stingy; both feel wronged.

Once again it is useless to apportion blame and excuses: justice can never be done in the midst of injustice. A colonial administrator has no possibility of acting rightly toward the natives, nor a general toward his soldiers; the only solution is to be neither colonist nor military chief; but a man could not prevent himself from being a man. So there he is, culpable in spite of himself and laboring under the effects of a fault he did not himself commit; and here she is, victim and shrew in spite of herself. Sometimes he rebels and becomes cruel, but then he makes himself an accomplice of the injustice, and the fault becomes really his. Sometimes he lets himself be annihilated, devoured, by his demanding victim; but in that case he feels duped. Often he stops at a compromise that at once belittles him and leaves him ill at ease. A well-disposed man will be more tortured by the situation than the woman herself: in a sense it is always better to be on the side of the vanquished; but if she is well-disposed also, incapable of self-sufficiency, reluctant to crush the man with the weight of her destiny, she struggles in hopeless confusion.

In daily life we meet with an abundance of these cases which are incapable of satisfactory solution because they are determined by unsatisfactory conditions. A man who is compelled to go on materially and morally supporting a woman whom he no longer loves feels he is victimized; but if he abandons without resources the woman who has pledged her whole life to him, she will be quite as unjustly victimized. The evil originates not in the perversity of individuals—and bad faith first appears when each blames the other—it originates rather in a situation against which all individual action is powerless. Women are "clinging," they are a dead weight, and they suffer for it; the point is that their situation is like that of a parasite sucking out the living strength of another organism. Let them be provided with living strength of their own, let them have the means to attack the world and wrest from it their own subsistence, and their dependence will be abolished—that of man also. There is no doubt that both men and women will profit greatly from the new situation.

A world where men and women would be equal is easy to visualize, for that precisely is what the Soviet Revolution *promised:* women raised and trained exactly like men were to work under the same conditions[2] and for the same wages. Erotic liberty was to be recognized by custom, but the sexual act was not to be considered a "service" to be paid for; woman was to be *obliged* to provide herself with other ways of earning a living; marriage was to be based on a free agreement that the spouses could break at will; maternity was to be voluntary, which meant that contraception and abortion were to be authorized and that, on the other hand, all mothers and their children were to have exactly the same rights, in or out of marriage; pregnancy leaves were to be paid for by the State, which would assume charge of the children, signifying not that they would be *taken away* from their parents, but that they would not be *abandoned* to them.

But is it enough to change laws, institutions, customs, public opinion, and the whole social context, for men and women to become truly equal? "Women will always be women," say the skeptics. Other seers prophesy that in casting off their femininity they will not succeed in changing themselves into men and they will become monsters. This would be to admit that the woman of today is a creation of nature; it must be repeated once more that in human society nothing is natural and that woman, like much else, is a product elaborated by civilization. The intervention of others in her destiny is fundamental: if this action took a different direction, it would produce a quite different result. Woman is determined not by her hormones or by mysterious instincts, but by the manner in which her body and her relation to the world are modified through the action of others than herself. The abyss that separates the adolescent boy and girl has been deliberately opened out between them since earliest childhood; later on, woman could not be other than what she *was made,* and that past was bound to shadow her for life. If we appreciate its influence, we see clearly that her destiny is not predetermined for all eternity.

We must not believe, certainly, that a change in woman's economic condition alone is enough to transform her, though this factor has been and remains the basic factor in her evolution; but until it has brought about the moral, social, cultural, and other consequences that it promises and requires, the new woman cannot appear. At this moment they have been realized nowhere, in Russia no more than in France or the United States; and this explains why the woman of today is torn between the past and the future. She appears most often as a "true woman" disguised as a man, and she feels herself as ill at ease in her flesh as in her masculine garb. She must shed her old skin and cut her own new clothes. This she could do only through a social evolution. No single educator could fashion a *female human being* today who would be the exact homologue of the *male human being;* if she is raised like a boy, the young girl feels she is an oddity and thereby she is given a new kind of sex specification. Stendhal understood this when he said: "The forest must be planted all at once." But if we imagine, on the contrary, a society in which the equality of the sexes would be concretely realized, this equality would find new expression in each individual.

[2]That certain too laborious occupations were to be closed to women is not in contradiction to this project. Even among men there is an increasing effort to obtain adaptation to profession; their varying physical and mental capacities limit their possibilities of choice; what is asked is that, in any case, no line of sex or caste be drawn.

If the little girl were brought up from the first with the same demands and rewards, the same severity and the same freedom, as her brothers, taking part in the same studies, the same games, promised the same future, surrounded with women and men who seemed to her undoubted equals, the meanings of the castration complex and of the Œdipus complex would be profoundly modified. Assuming on the same basis as the father the material and moral responsibility of the couple, the mother would enjoy the same lasting prestige; the child would perceive around her an androgynous world and not a masculine world. Were she emotionally more attracted to her father—which is not even sure—her love for him would be tinged with a will to emulation and not a feeling of powerlessness; she would not be oriented toward passivity. Authorized to test her powers in work and sports, competing actively with the boys, she would not find the absence of the penis—compensated by the promise of a child—enough to give rise to an inferiority complex; correlatively, the boy would not have a superiority complex if it were not instilled into him and if he looked up to women with as much respect as to men.[3] The little girl would not seek sterile compensation in narcissism and dreaming, she would not take her fate for granted; she would be interested in what she was *doing*, she would throw herself without reserve into undertakings.

I have already pointed out how much easier the transformation of puberty would be if she looked beyond it, like the boys, toward a free adult future: menstruation horrifies her only because it is an abrupt descent into femininity. She would also take her young eroticism in much more tranquil fashion if she did not feel a frightened disgust for her destiny as a whole; coherent sexual information would do much to help her over this crisis. And thanks to coeducational schooling, the august mystery of Man would have no occasion to enter her mind: it would be eliminated by everyday familiarity and open rivalry.

Objections raised against this system always imply respect for sexual taboos; but the effort to inhibit all sex curiosity and pleasure in the child is quite useless; one succeeds only in creating repressions, obsessions, neuroses. The excessive sentimentality, homosexual fervors, and platonic crushes of adolescent girls, with all their train of silliness and frivolity, are much more injurious than a little childish sex play and a few definite sex experiences. It would be beneficial above all for the young girl not to be influenced against taking charge herself of her own existence, for then she would not seek a demigod in the male—merely a comrade, a friend, a partner. Eroticism and love would take on the nature of free transcendence and not that of resignation; she could experience them as a relation between equals. There is no intention, of course, to remove by a stroke of the pen all the difficulties that the child has to overcome in changing into an adult; the most intelligent, the most tolerant education could not relieve the child of experiencing things for herself; what could be asked is that obstacles should not be piled gratuitously in her path. Progress is already shown by the fact that "vicious" little girls are no longer cauterized with a red-hot iron. Psychoanalysis has given parents some instruction, but the conditions under which, at the present time, the sexual training and initiation of woman are accomplished are so deplorable that none of the objections

[3]I knew a little boy of eight who lived with his mother, aunt, and grandmother, all independent and active women, and his weak old half-crippled grandfather. He had a crushing inferiority complex in regard to the feminine sex, although he made efforts to combat it. At school he scorned comrades and teachers because they were miserable males.

advanced against the idea of a radical change could be considered valid. It is not a question of abolishing in woman the contingencies and miseries of the human condition, but of giving her the means for transcending them.

Woman is the victim of no mysterious fatality; the peculiarities that identify her as specifically a woman get their importance from the significance placed upon them. They can be surmounted, in the future, when they are regarded in new perspectives. Thus, as we have seen, through her erotic experience woman feels—and often detests—the domination of the male; but this is no reason to conclude that her ovaries condemn her to live forever on her knees. Virile aggressiveness seems like a lordly privilege only within a system that in its entirety conspires to affirm masculine sovereignty; and woman *feels* herself profoundly passive in the sexual act only because she already *thinks* of herself as such. Many modern women who lay claim to their dignity as human beings still envisage their erotic life from the standpoint of a tradition of slavery: since it seems to them humiliating to lie beneath the man, to be penetrated by him, they grow tense in frigidity. But if the reality were different, the meaning expressed symbolically in amorous gestures and postures would be different, too: a woman who pays and dominates her lover can, for example, take pride in her superb idleness and consider that she is enslaving the male who is actively exerting himself. And here and now there are many sexually well-balanced couples whose notions of victory and defeat are giving place to the idea of an exchange.

As a matter of fact, man, like woman, is flesh, therefore passive, the plaything of his hormones and of the species, the restless prey of his desires. And she, like him, in the midst of the carnal fever, is a consenting, a voluntary gift, an activity; they live out in their several fashions the strange ambiguity of existence made body. In those combats where they think they confront one another, it is really against the self that each one struggles, projecting into the partner that part of the self which is repudiated; instead of living out the ambiguities of their situation, each tries to make the other bear the abjection and tries to reserve the honor for the self. If, however, both should assume the ambiguity with a clear-sighted modesty, correlative of an authentic pride, they would see each other as equals and would live out their erotic drama in amity. The fact that we are human beings is infinitely more important than all the peculiarities that distinguish human beings from one another; it is never the given that confers superiorities: "virtue," as the ancients called it, is defined at the level of "that which depends on us." In both sexes is played out the same drama of the flesh and the spirit, of finitude and transcendence; both are gnawed away by time and laid in wait for by death, they have the same essential need for one another; and they can gain from their liberty the same glory. If they were to taste it, they would no longer be tempted to dispute fallacious privileges, and fraternity between them could then come into existence.

I shall be told that all this is utopian fancy, because woman cannot be "made over" unless society has first made her really the equal of man. Conservatives have never failed in such circumstances to refer to that vicious circle; history, however, does not revolve. If a caste is kept in a state of inferiority, no doubt it remains inferior; but liberty can break the circle. Let the Negroes vote and they become worthy of having the vote; let woman be given responsibilities and she is able to assume them. The fact is that oppressors cannot be expected to make a move of gratuitous generosity; but at one time the revolt of the oppressed, at another time even the very evolution of the privileged caste itself, creates new situations; thus men have been led, in their own interest, to give partial emancipation to women: it remains only for women to continue their ascent, and the successes they are obtaining are an encouragement for them to do so. It seems almost certain that sooner or later they will arrive at complete economic and social equality, which will bring about an inner metamorphosis.

However this may be, there will be some to object that if such a world is possible it is not desirable. When woman is "the same" as her male, life will lose its salt and spice. This argument, also, has lost its novelty: those interested in perpetuating present conditions are always in tears about the marvelous past that is about to disappear, without having so much as a smile for the young future. It is quite true that doing away with the slave trade meant death to the great plantations, magnificent with azaleas and camellias, it meant ruin to the whole refined Southern civilization. The attics of time have received its rare old laces along with the clear pure voices of the Sistine *castrati*,[4] and there is a certain "feminine charm" that is also on the way to the same dusty repository. I agree that he would be a barbarian indeed who failed to appreciate exquisite flowers, rare lace, the crystal-clear voice of the eunuch, and feminine charm.

When the "charming woman" shows herself in all her splendor, she is a much more exalting object than the "idiotic paintings, overdoors, scenery, showman's garish signs, popular chromos," that excited Rimbaud; adorned with the most modern artifices, beautified according to the newest techniques, she comes down from the remoteness of the ages, from Thebes, from Crete, from Chichén-Itzá; and she is also the totem set up deep in the African jungle; she is a helicopter and she is a bird; and there is this, the greatest wonder of all: under her tinted hair the forest murmur becomes a thought, and words issue from her breasts. Men stretch forth avid hands toward the marvel, but when they grasp it it is gone; the wife, the mistress, speak like everybody else through their mouths: their words are worth just what they are worth; their breasts also. Does such a fugitive miracle—and one so rare—justify us in perpetuating a situation that is baneful for both sexes? One can appreciate the beauty of flowers, the charm of women, and appreciate them at their true value; if these treasures cost blood or misery, they must be sacrificed.

But in truth this sacrifice seems to men a peculiarly heavy one; few of them really wish in their hearts for woman to succeed in making it; those among them who hold woman in contempt see in the sacrifice nothing for them to gain, those who cherish her see too much that they would lose. And it is true that the evolution now in progress threatens more than feminine charm alone: in beginning to exist for herself, woman will relinquish the function as double and mediator to which she owes her privileged place in the masculine universe; to man, caught between the silence of nature and the demanding presence of other free beings, a creature who is at once his like and a passive thing seems a great treasure. The guise in which he conceives his companion may be mythical, but the experiences for which she is the source or the pretext are none the less real: there are hardly any more precious, more intimate, more ardent. There is no denying that feminine dependence, inferiority, woe, give women

[4]Eunuchs were long used in the male choirs of the Sistine Chapel in Rome, until the practice was forbidden by Pope Leo XIII in 1880. The operation of castration caused the boy's soprano voice to be retained into adulthood, and it was performed for this purpose.—Tr.

their special character; assuredly woman's autonomy, if it spares men many troubles, will also deny them many conveniences; assuredly there are certain forms of the sexual adventure which will be lost in the world of tomorrow. But this does not mean that love, happiness, poetry, dream, will be banished from it.

Let us not forget that our lack of imagination always depopulates the future; for us it is only an abstraction; each one of us secretly deplores the absence there of the one who was himself. But the humanity of tomorrow will be living in its flesh and in its conscious liberty; that time will be its present and it will in turn prefer it. New relations of flesh and sentiment of which we have no conception will arise between the sexes; already, indeed, there have appeared between men and women friendships, rivalries, complicities, comradeships—chaste or sensual—which past centuries could not have conceived. To mention one point, nothing could seem to me more debatable than the opinion that dooms the new world to uniformity and hence to boredom. I fail to see that this present world is free from boredom or that liberty ever creates uniformity.

To begin with, there will always be certain differences between man and woman; her eroticism, and therefore her sexual world, have a special form of their own and therefore cannot fail to engender a sensuality, a sensitivity, of a special nature. This means that her relations to her own body, to that of the male, to the child, will never be identical with those the male bears to his own body, to that of the female, and to the child; those who make much of "equality in difference" could not with good grace refuse to grant me the possible existence of differences in equality. Then again, it is institutions that create uniformity. Young and pretty, the slaves of the harem are always the same in the sultan's embrace; Christianity gave eroticism its savor of sin and legend when it endowed the human female with a soul; if society restores her sovereign individuality to woman, it will not thereby destroy the power of love's embrace to move the heart.

It is nonsense to assert that revelry, vice, ecstasy, passion, would become impossible if man and woman were equal in concrete matters; the contradictions that put the flesh in opposition to the spirit, the instant to time, the swoon of immanence to the challenge of transcendence, the absolute of pleasure to the nothingness of forgetting, will never be resolved; in sexuality will always be materialized the tension, the anguish, the joy, the frustration, and the triumph of existence. To emancipate woman is to refuse to confine her to the relations she bears to man, not to deny them to her; let her have her independent existence and she will continue none the less to exist for him *also:* mutually recognizing each other as subject, each will yet remain for the other an *other.* The reciprocity of their relations will not do away with the miracles—desire, possession, love, dream, adventure—worked by the division of human beings into two separate categories; and the words that move us—giving, conquering, uniting—will not lose their meaning. On the contrary, when we abolish the slavery of half of humanity, together with the whole system of hypocrisy that it implies, then the "division" of humanity will reveal its genuine significance and the human couple will find its true form. "The direct, natural, necessary relation of human creatures is the *relation of man to woman,*" Marx has said.[5] "The nature of this relation determines to what point man himself is to be considered as a *generic being,* as mankind; the relation of man to

[5]*Philosophical Works,* Vol. VI (Marx's italics).

woman is the most natural relation of human being to human being. By it is shown, therefore, to what point the *natural* behavior of man has become *human* or to what point the *human* being has become his *natural* being, to what point his *human nature* has become his *nature*."

The case could not be better stated. It is for man to establish the reign of liberty in the midst of the world of the given. To gain the supreme victory, it is necessary, for one thing, that by and through their natural differentiation men and women unequivocally affirm their brotherhood.

Culture and Gender in Indian America

Rayna Green

The stories that Green relays to us are an expression of her identity as a Native American woman. She explains her belief in the interrelatedness of all things in nature, and she stresses the importance of family and other relations in her life. Through the use of metaphor and symbolism, she explains why virtue is important in her community and how she as a woman is considered to be powerful. As you read this, reflect upon some of the differences in the ways in which women are viewed in her community as opposed to how they have been viewed in American and European communities. How do our worldviews have an impact on our identity and the ways in which we create ourselves?

I don't have a theory or line of argument this morning. I want to go through a series of vignettes, all of which cast a different light, cast a different slant, and give a slightly different ear to each other.

My first story is about two friends of mine, both Sioux women who were up at the Capitol one day. Up on top of the Capitol there's a statue. It's a marvelous statue. If you get very close to that statue, you'll see that it's clearly a female figure, and it might look something like Miss Liberty standing out in New York Harbor. Nobody knows much about her. These two young Sioux women I know went up to the guard and they said, "What's the statue? What's it about?" He said, "Well, you know, that statue, a lot of people seem to think it's an Indian. Her name is Freedom. But Freedom isn't an Indian. She's a woman." And my two friends laughed to think that in this country freedom could be either. But the truth is, in this country freedom is both. And that's what I want to talk about today. And I want to talk about justice and liberty, and about America. I want to talk about home, family, and about women. I want to talk about changing our names, and

From *Sojourner: The Women's Forum* 15 (September 1989): 20–22. Reprinted by permission.

taking hold of our names. And I want to talk about coming home.

Freedom is an Indian and a woman. She's also Black and a woman. She's also Jewish, Vietnamese, and Salvadoran, and a woman. She is all of those things. But her iconography is clear. She comes from the fifteenth century, when the first images of the New World went back to Europe. Freedom, in the early days of America, was pictured as this large, bare-breasted Indian woman. She was a queen. She was our kind of girl. She was pictured with her foot on the head of an alligator, her spear in her hands. Pineapples, corn, all these wonderful bounteous crops spilling out of her arms. Her warriors stood behind her. She was in control; she was the New World, the promise of everything that everyone wanted.

And they took her away from us. As the two centuries moved forward and things happened here that we now must pay for, dearly, she changed. They took away her flesh. They covered her breasts. She couldn't be naked, the symbol of innocence in the fifteenth, sixteenth century; the symbol of virtue. They had to cover her and make her less savage, less pagan. They took away her alligator. I mean, can you imagine taking a girl's alligator away? She must have been angry. They took away all of the fruits of her fields. And she became a Renaissance little wonder woman icon, like Minerva, draped in little tasteful white garments with her breasts covered. And they wouldn't even let her be like Minerva; they robbed her of her power. Thin and powerless, with a tiny little diadem on her head. She never needed a crown to know she was a queen. But now, she's changed. And that's who stands in the New York harbor. Someone who changed. And that's who stands on top of the Capitol. But we need to know her name. Her name is Freedom, and she is who I have described. And we need to go back to her to begin to look to the future.

That future is vague and muddy, though. That future is opaque. We all have difficulties now knowing who we are, and what our names are. We try to put on different names, give ourselves a kind of identity. We struggle through various ways of looking at an identity. Indian people have been forced to confront lots of different faces in the mirror, and those faces are confusing for all of us. At one level, Indians are totally insignificant. They exist in no number to matter—to the economy, to the judicial system, to anything else. There are fewer Indians in America than Vietnamese. And so why do Indians matter? I'll tell you why they matter: simply because of the history I've spoken of.

But Indians cannot simply be functions of the historic past. They can't simply be reminders of an America that once was, bad or good. They can't simply function as vague, ghostly reminders of poverty index levels, of hunger and homelessness in America; that's irrelevant. What is relevant is that there is a metaphor here that stands for all of us in some ways and doesn't encompass the experience of others in another. What is relevant is that as my friend Roberta Hill Whiteman says, "Indians know how to wait." And it is the waiting that will dignify us all. The waiting for freedom and justice to come in the form of an Indian woman, once again, to reclaim us all. In Roberta's words:

> Look west long enough, the moon will grow
> inside you.
> Coyote hears her song, he'll
> teach you now.
> Mirrors follow trails of blood and lightning.
> Mother needs the strength of one like you.
> Let blood
> dry, but seize the lightning. Hold it like your
> mother

rocks the trees. In your fear, watch the road,
breathe deeply.
Indians know how to wait.
(from "Lines for Marking Time")

What are we waiting for? Are we waiting for a moment like that which happened at the National Women's Studies Association Conference in Minneapolis last year? The planning group invited a young Indian girl to dance for the opening event. Typically, and profoundly, she came with her uncle, and a group of young men who drummed for her. In Indian culture, an uncle is like your father. An uncle raises you. An aunt raises you. Your own father and mother are perhaps even less significant in some ways. Her uncle came with her because her father had just died. And her uncle, to honor her, and to honor the women who had come to see her, spoke for her.

In our world, people speak for you when you're honored. It's a gift to speak for someone. And when that man, who was honoring everyone there by his presence, rose to speak for her, he was booed. Because in an environment where we've gotten our signals crossed, we don't know the faces of other people, we don't know how they live, and we cannot speak to them directly. He gave them even a further gift, he explained to them why she was not wearing her jingle dress. (A jingle dress is a wonderful buckskin or cloth dress filled with little tin coins that make a marvelous noise when a young lady dances.) She was in her menstrual period, and a girl does not wear a jingle dress when she's menstruating, because the noise of those coins, you see, is a prayer, and it's a prayer for power. Music goes up, music calls down the spirits to look at you, and asks for power. Because a menstruating woman is already so powerful, to wear the jingle dress is to really risk a problem; to call down uncontrolled power, perhaps. He gave them the gift of telling them this. He was explaining something rather arcane, something that people don't just discuss in public. It was a women's event. He wanted to reach out. And they booed him for that, because they thought he was talking about pollution.

I'm not here, as I said, to accuse. This is not accusatory. That is not what Indian women and Indian men are about. This is about knowing our own names and knowing our faces. A gift was refused because no one knew it was a gift. We have got to come forward and know the gifts that different people give us. And that's why a meeting like this is essential—to look in the face of different gifts and to learn to honor each other, by accepting the terms on which those gifts are given.

Sometimes, because things get so confused in moments like that, we're forced to change our names. Sometimes we have to change our shape. Shape shifters are important for all of us; all of our worlds have shape shifters. Sometimes we have to shift shape because guns are aimed at us, and we must escape. Sometimes the old shape has become too uncomfortable. Sometimes, like the queen in the early days, our original form is taken—we're sent to the diet center, forced on cultural aerobics until we change. And I say it's time to change our shape because we want to, to change our names because we want to.

Sometimes when we're forced to change those shapes it's painful; sometimes it's a joy. In Indian cultures, there is a tradition of name-changing and shape-shifting, and it's an important tradition to look to for all of us because it enables us to be empowered; it enables us to be in control. We are all women, certainly; we are all men; we are all gay; we are all straight; we are all old; we are all young. And in Indian cultures I go back to my families and there is no division. There are distinctions, certainly, about the way people are treated, and the authority they have, but I want to reclaim the power to move through categories, so that I do not have to stay fixed in any one place. Jesse [Jackson] said a couple of years ago, in the presidential elections, "God ain't finished with me yet, she never will be finished." We can all move and grow.

Some of the categories become so restrictive, we have to be able to move out of them. One category that Indian people suffer from is that of "half-breed." It's staggering to think about that kind of marginality; to suggest that someone is a quart low of whatever it is that makes them real is to take their life and breath and squeeze it until it stops. We're all half-breeds, if you come right down to it. As my mom used to say, "Heinz 57." We locate our internal space, perhaps, in one place that gives us a name to call ourselves that we're proud of, but we are all out there on the margins (and there are no people on the margin like women, because we have to shift into so many shapes). But the category of "half-breed" is tragic, damaging in so many ways, we've got to give it up. It is like Freedom. We've got to put a name to it that enables us to stand up again.

I am a German Jew. I feel comfortable with that. I've lived my life as a German Jew. One of my grandmothers was a German Jew who became a profound Texan. I will not deny her. I will not look at my mother, with her blue eyes, her white skin, and deny her. My father is only one part of me. He must be claimed, too. And I gravitate toward that part of him, and his world, and my other grandmother, who gave me a name and space. But I will not deny any one part of that world to force Indian people, native people, any people to live on a margin, where they cannot define their own existence as a whole, whatever parts may be there, just to rob them of a future, and to force them to die somewhere in a past.

My German grandmother was a remarkable person. She is my mother, the primary character in my life. She shaped and formed me; she gave me stories, language, and songs. In many ways, she gave me more than my Indian grandmother, who was afraid because of all the things that had happened to her; afraid to sing, to breathe, to leave town. Her pain transferred over, so I took joy from the maternal grandmother, and I took the name from the other one. We take what we can from each one of our relatives and honor them.

My German grandmother was an extraordinary woman who loved to dance, loved to sing, loved to tell dirty stories. She was the mistress of them all. She wanted to be a dancer on the Palace stage. Dressed to kill, she'd play whorehouse songs on the piano, or sad ones that would make us cry and beg for more. On that summer porch, we believed she could have been anything, living in her ruby pleasures. Oh, she glittered then, dancing across that summer porch, dancing the stories that made me dream over her shattered breath. She is mine, and she is yours, too. Never walk away from all the faces you've known in your life, who gave you birth. That's the Indian way, certainly. But it's all of our way. If we only can have the courage to look back for them.

Some of the shape-shifting sometimes makes it important to walk away from being female. Being female is painful. Being male is painful, never more than lately, as we look into the faces of our young men on the streets of urban cities. We see death in their faces, and it pains us. If only they had the freedom we have, to walk into a female body, into a female metaphor, and say, "That's not my world. Those guns, that dope, those drugs are not my world. That world that lures me only because my name is man, that world that pains me because I have to live trapped in a metaphor, that will not work for me."

We have an option that makes us live, an option women have always had, an extraordinary option. Some women take it in different ways. Some women call themselves mothers, some sisters, some lovers. Some women call themselves men, and walk into Coyote's terrible dream, which enables us to move through the changes. We can take any of those options at any one time. But to take those options means we have to teach our baby boys to grow up and be all those things, too. We don't have to claim the men in us by being tough. We only have to look in our children's and our brothers' faces, and bring them up to live with us.

There's a gift that moves in Indian country, and that gift is an extraordinary gift. It is the gift of giving itself. All of us have it in our worlds. At dances, various ceremonial occasions, you'll see women walk over and put shawls on other people's backs—men's backs, too. In ceremonial occasions these shawls get piled so high, you never know how anybody stands up under them. (I want to eartag a shawl during a powwow season sometime like biologists do animals, see how it migrates across the room.) Those gifts are extraordinary.

I want to take the metaphor of that shawl, and I want to wrap it around your shoulders now, and say you are my sister, you are my mother, you are my friend, you are my brother, you are my husband, you are my uncle, you are my aunt, come into that dance circle. It is the gift that keeps on moving, because it brings us into the circle. The richest person in Indian country is the person who gives the most away, not the person who keeps the most for themselves. And this is a gift that America needs. We would not have homeless people on our streets, if we truly believed we lived in Indian country. If freedom was really the Indian woman we know she is, we would not have people living out on the margin, children selling themselves for one shot, for a pint of Thunderbird. We have got to wrap that shawl around the rest of us, and women can do that.

To talk about culture in this country, to talk about gender, is to talk about giving. And it is in the heart and face of our own cultures, and our own passions that we can look and see the gift that we have to wrap again, and keep moving, and keep giving. But in order to do that, we have to know what real wealth is. Real wealth lies in our own hearts, and not in something that is a commodity beyond it. Indian country knows that. The gift that moves will carry us to that place. I think of the warrior women who reputedly used to carry their husbands' and brothers' and friends' bodies off the field and take up the bow or the gun or the spear themselves. And I say, this is not militance, this is not warrior behavior (although at one level it is: it is what is required to survive). All of us in our communities now are carrying those boys' bodies off the field. What will we do when there are no more of them? Will we become the warriors? Are we willing to take that battle on? Perhaps the gift is not to keep thinking of it as a battle, but to think of it as a role for us all, in the survival of our people, in the raising of our children. What is a real warrior woman—in Indian terms, even? Certainly, it is not to take up a spear. If you have to, you do, to defend your life or that of your children. But I don't want to talk about defensiveness; I want to talk about survival. And there are keys to survival.

In 1642, a group of British got off a boat in Virginia somewhere and migrated to what we call North Carolina; and there they met a delegation of Cherokees, led by a man who had been a warrior. His name was Outacitty, which means man-killer. He was a great warrior, a red chief, sent by the Beloved Woman and the clan-mothers to make war. But this time they had asked him not to make war. The Beloved Woman of the

Nation, Ghigau had asked him to become a white chief, a peace chief, and to go and make peace with these people. And so Outacitty rode up to meet them. The first thing he said to them was, "Where are your women?" These men had come to do serious business, and they had no women with them. Peace is a very serious business. No act of war, no act of peace in my country is made without the women there. And Outacitty was shocked: the British dared to come without their women. "Where are your women?" he said. And he went back and reported that there was a problem here. "We cannot do business with these men," he said. They were clearly missing half of the people needed to do business with.

And in 1987, a young woman named Wilma Mankiller was elected principal chief of the Cherokee nation, and I say to you she is him, come back, and she knows it. And the old people knew it. When we'd go out to campaign with her, the old ladies would say, "Good name, good name." And they didn't mean war. They didn't mean hunting; they didn't mean power. They meant she's back. She has returned; the Beloved has returned. You see, she is all of those converged together. Like all of us can be. Warrior, peacemaker, mother, father, Beloved woman, Beloved man, the white and the red merged together, to take our own story back.

And that's an interesting story. It's a story about family. Everybody in Indian country talks about the family as the center of their lives, just as in Black culture, in Irish-American communities. Because to talk about family is to talk about community, about survival, about the future.

The central figure in this next story about family is a woman called Buffalo Birdwoman who could not give up the old way. She was a great farmer. When the time came to make her change, they brought in the tractors, they brought in the freight wagons, and she said, "I don't want to do that. I'll stick to my digging stick. Because I grow corn better than your corn. I know how to grow corn, and I will not give up on corn songs. I will not forget the corn songs. The corn is my family, my mother, my grandmother, the corn gave me birth. And to give up my corn songs is to give up my family." Tradition is not a yoke around our neck, if we know its name. Tradition is not the chains that bind us, if we know how to use it. Tradition is not the deadly past wrapped around us like a coffin. Tradition, for the Indian family, for the Indian woman, is simply remembering who you are, and it is that story we must reclaim once more. Hear Linda Hogan, Chickasaw:

calling myself home

There were old women
who lived on amber.
Their dark hands
laced the shells of turtles
together, pebbles inside
and they danced
with rattles strong on their legs.

There is a dry river
between them and us.
Its banks divide up our land.
Its bed was the road
I walked to return.

We are plodding creatures like the turtle
born of an old people.
We are nearly stone
turning slow as the earth.
Our mountains are underground
they are so old.

This land is the house
we have always lived in.
The women,
their bones are holding up the earth.

The red tail of a hawk
cuts open the sky
and the sun

brings their faces back
with the new grass.

Dust from yarrow
is in the air,
the yellow sun.
Insects are clicking again.

I came back to say good-bye
to the turtle
to those bones
to the shells locked together
on his back
gold atoms dancing underground.

The turtle in the stories of some Indian people is our mother. On her back the earth grew. We were born in the mud of her back. It doesn't matter which story you claim. Whether you think it was Corn or the Turtle Mother or the Spider Woman that gave you birth. Coyote came from all these. His tricking lies give us the ability to change our shapes. He is necessary to us. But the earth and where we were born is that woman's back and that woman's breast; she cuts it open to feed us and make us whole again.

Sun over the horizon, a sweating yellow force, our continuance. The uncountable distance that sweeps through our hands, the first prayers in the morning. It is this that I believe in. The galloping sun. In my whole life, a rider. It is that round earth—I call it Indian country, you call it the name you need to call it—the moon, the stars, and that sweating sun, that enables me to be the writer I am. If I choose not to climb on that galloping horse, that galloping sun, it is my own choice. But it is a choice I cannot make. I need to come home. I need my family. I need you, my brothers and sisters, my father, my uncle, and I need my aunties. The metaphor of family is simply one that works in Indian country because it brings that circle round. We all join in the dance that brings us to a place called America, where Freedom may be lots of things. And you can put the shape and face to her you wish.

The bottom line is very simple; it is morning once more. And that galloping sun races across the horizon. For me to come home to Indian country means I must climb on that sun and race across the horizon, with other people. I don't want to leave any of you behind. America has a way of leaving some of us out on the edge. I say it's time for the women of America, all of us—we're not separate, we belong with each other—to reclaim our families. To climb on that sun with me in that eternal morning. Once again, your whole life, a rider.

Ed. note: The poems quoted in this article are from *That's What She Said* edited by Rayna Green (Indiana University Press, 1984).

Discussion Questions

1. What is the importance of Plato's discussion of Aristophanes' "Story of 'Divided Selves' "? How can the self be "whole" or complete? Does it make sense to talk about an incomplete or divided self if the self is dynamic and constantly changing?
2. What are some of the ways in which biased research has contributed to prejudice against homosexuals? How may religion have contributed to a bias against homosexuality?
3. How do you think that Stoltenberg would answer the question "How many sexes are there?" How would you answer the same question? Why do you think you answered the way you did?
4. What do you think Sartre considers to be "intimacy," and how might bonds of intimacy be fostered or undermined? In what sense does our conception of the body have an impact on the conception of the self?
5. Why does Aquinas claim that woman had to be created separately from man? Why does he believe women are defective and misbegotten? In what way, do you believe, may Aquinas's views have been shaped by his religious beliefs?
6. According to de Beauvoir, women have always been defined in relation to men. How might she reject a relational theory of identity? In what sense might she reaffirm it?
7. Discuss the different views of women that appear in traditional Western culture and in the culture of Native America. How does Rayna Green's personal story enable us to reflect upon the importance of family influence on the beliefs in our lives?
8. Critically discuss the viability of the view that our identity is, at least in part, formed through our social and sexual relations.

chapter 7

The Self in Context: Marriage and Parenthood

While some cultures, particularly Judeo-Christian ones, hold the view that it is important to make a commitment to only one person in our lives, it is also clear that this view is challenged by many other cultures. Indeed, in light of the essays in the preceding chapters, one can call into question the imbalance that has occurred in traditional marriages in which the male and female are not considered equal partners.

Many philosophers and social scientists have argued that one reason marriages fail is that society encourages males and females to adopt specific gender roles. They argue that such gender-role orientation can be supported by a long tradition and by various ancient scriptures. One example can be found in the Rig-Veda and Manusmirti. Here, as in Judeo-Christian tradition, the role that women are to undertake is that of child bearer and wife. These qualities are considered to make women virtuous. Moreover, women in marriage are expected to remain monogamous. Does this seem to be a double standard that may be inconsistent with virtue? Do you think that there might be the possibility that ancient scriptures have been interpreted relative to the social and political contexts in which they have emerged?

Immanuel Kant may serve as a good example of this. Kant lived in the eighteenth century, during a time when women (and men?) were expected to be monogamous. Kant claims that it is out of a moral duty to herself that a

Immanuel Kant

woman not treat herself as a means to an end. Indeed, for Kant, this would apply to men, too. As people cannot be used as means to ends, Kant argues that sexual activity must be based on mutual desire and that marriage must be monogamous. Do you think that this refutes the notion of sex for its own sake? Suppose there is mutual desire between a woman and her spouse, but suppose the woman or man also has desires for others who also desire them? Do you think that this is possible? Perhaps this raises similar questions as to whether or not we can love more than one person at a time. Could loving someone other than one's spouse enhance a marriage?

John McMurtry's critique of monogamy may give us more compelling reasons to reconsider its value. He evaluates monogamy in light of the limitations that it places on individuals in marriages. He claims that our potential to express our affection may actually be undermined by focusing on a single person. Such focus may prompt the other to take advantage of us, disempower us, and oppress us. Perhaps monogamy increases the tendency to socialize males and females into gender-specific roles. Thus, we must consider the importance of seeing ourselves as social beings who need others (and not just another) for fulfillment. You may well ask yourself, does monogamy foster commitment or hinder it? Does it enhance or divide our affections?

Another important way in which we relate to others is as parents and children. As parents in the modern age, women and men have been dictated different roles by society. Although the history of child rearing is interesting in that women, from time to time, have been considered incapable of rearing children, at all times they have been the bearers of children. The capacity to bear children has left them subject to a variety of sex-specific roles in society—being a mother means something different from being a father. In light of this, women have been denied access to the positions to which men have had access in society and, thus, have been disempowered. Such disempowerment has given women little social and political recourse in the world.

In her examination of the traditional concept of motherhood, Carolynne Timko argues that motherhood is a sociopolitical concept that has been used to intentionally disempower women. Timko argues that women have not been disempowered simply because of their physical capacity to bear children. Rather, society wants us to believe that it is that physical capacity that has led women to the roles that they have "chosen." To be a woman and choose not to bear children is considered a violation of one's nature by many people. Yet Timko gives us good reason to believe that there is much more to motherhood than nature.

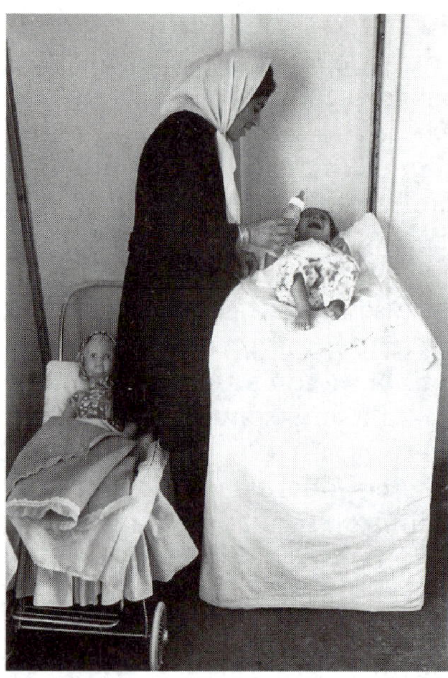
A Woman as Viewed in a Traditional Role

Bonnie Steinbock examines the role women have played as parents by examining the notion of surrogate motherhood. Steinbock argues that women are used as means to ends, as receptacles, to fulfill the desires of men in a patriarchal society. She examines the claim that surrogate motherhood increases the freedom of women to bear children and argues that it actually undermines the freedom of women. Perhaps the notion of surrogate motherhood itself is as paradoxical as biological motherhood, even in surrogacy, is a fact. How does our culture define motherhood? Does surrogate motherhood enhance the likelihood that race, class, and gender will become greater issues of concern than ever before? Through surrogate parenting, are we simply trying to devise a more perfect human race? How does this enhance, or undermine, the self?

From a different perspective, Thomas W. Laqueur explains "The Facts of Fatherhood." Laqueur argues that men have been limited in their roles as fathers just as women have been limited in their roles as mothers. As breadwinners, men have been denied the opportunity to raise their children. They have been denied the kinds of intimate relationships that women have had with their children; and although society is slowly changing, being a househusband or primary caregiver is not what men are considered to be capable of doing.

Looking at the roles that both men and women have played as stepparents, Joan Whitman Hoff argues that while stepmothers particularly have been subjected to disparate treatment in society, so have stepfathers. Even though stepparenting is not a new phenomenon, as the divorce rate soars so do stepfamilies increase in number. Hoff argues that society needs to rethink its laws—if not for the sake of women and men, definitely for the sake of the children in those families. As you read this, reflect upon your own notion of stepfamilies and speculate upon how stepfamilies, and members therein, are identified in our society.

In closing, whether or not we can resolve the dilemmas that arise in our intimate relationships with others, perhaps reflecting on these issues will bring us to a new understanding of ourselves as partners, parents, or children. Whether or not we reject monogamy or adopt the view that marriage of some sort is a moral necessity, it seems clear we must re-evaluate our own identity in light of the relationships we form and the ideals that we have. Do you think that marriage will help define you? How do you think your identity might be influenced by a partner in a marriage? Should marriage be abolished? How does the current notion and institution of marriage in the United States and

Canada enhance or detract from our ability to make commitments to others in society? How does it help to enhance or detract from our sense of self? These are just some of the questions upon which we must reflect.

Marriage and the Role of Women

The Rig-Veda and the Manusmirti

Earlier in this text you may have read about the caste system in the Hindu tradition. In these two short entries, we learn more about personal and social relationships in Hindu culture. First, we encounter a religious hymn about the wedding ritual in which the bride is compared to the goddess Surya. Here the emphasis is on the new bride's role in procreation and in caring for her husband. In the second passage, which constitutes part of the legal codes of Hindu society, we gain insight into what role the woman must play in the performance of household duties. Ask yourself whether, in Western society, we expect women as wives to fill a similar role and exercise similar "virtues."

MARRIAGE

Mount the world of immortality, O Surya, that is adorned with red flowers and made of fragrant wood, carved with many forms and painted with gold, rolling smoothly on its fine wheels. Prepare an exquisite wedding voyage for your husband. "Go away from here! For this woman has a husband." Thus I implore Visvavasu[1] with words of praise as I bow to him. "Look for another girl who is ripe and still lives in her father's house." That is your birthright; find it. "Go away from here, Visvavasu, we implore you as we bow. Look for another girl, willing and ready. Leave the wife to unite with her husband." May the roads be straight and thornless on which our friends go courting. May Aryaman and Bhaga united lead us together. O Gods, may the united household be easy to manage. I free you from Varuna's snare, with which the gentle Savitr bound you. In the seat of the Law, in the world of good action, I place you unharmed with your husband. [25] I free her from here, but not from there.[2] I have bound her firmly there, so that through the grace of Indra she will have fine sons and be fortunate in her husband's love. Let Pusan lead you from here, taking you by the hand; let the Asvins carry you in their chariot. Go home to be mistress of the house with the right to speak commands to the gathered people. May

[1]*Visvavasu:* a demigod who possesses virgins.

Rig-Veda 10.85.20–47.

[2]*here:* her father's house; *there:* her new house with her husband.

happiness be fated for you here through your progeny. Watch over this house as mistress of the house.

Mingle your body with that of your husband, and even when you are grey with age you will have the right to speak to the gathered people. The purple and red appears, a magic spirit; the stain is imprinted.[3] Her family prospers, and her husband is bound in the bonds. Throw away the gown, and distribute wealth to the priests. It becomes a magic spirit walking on feet, and like the wife it draws near the husband. [30] The body becomes ugly and sinisterly pale, if the husband with evil desire covers his sexual limb with his wife's robe. The diseases that come from her own people and follow the glorious bridal procession, may the gods who receive sacrifices lead them back whence they have come. Let no highwaymen, lying in ambush, fall upon the wedding couple. Let the two of them on good paths avoid the dangerous path. Let all demonic powers run away. This bride has auspicious signs; come and look at her. Wish her the good fortune of her husband's love, and depart, each to your own house. It burns, it bites, it has claws, it is as dangerous as poison to eat.[4] Only the priest who knows the Surya hymn is able to receive the bridal gown. [35] Cutting, carving, and chopping into pieces—see the colors of Surya, which the priest alone purifies.

I [the husband] take your hand for good fortune, so that with me as your husband you will attain a ripe old age. Bhaga, Asyaman, Savitr, Purandhi—the gods have given you to me to be mistress of the house. Pusan, rouse her to be most eager to please, the woman in whom men sow their seed, so that she will spread her thighs in her desire for us and we,[5] in our desire, will plant our penis in her. To you first of all they led Surya, circling with the bridal procession. Give her back to her husbands, Agni, now as a wife with progeny. Agni has given the wife back again, together with long life and beauty. Let her have a long lifespan, and let her husband live for a hundred autumns. [40] Soma first possessed her, and the Gandharva possessed her second. Agni was your third husband, and the fourth was the son of a man. Soma gave her to the Gandharva, and the Gandharva gave her to Agni. Agni gave me wealth and sons—and her.

Stay here and do not separate. Enjoy your whole lifespan playing with sons and grandsons and rejoicing in your own home. Let Prajapati create progeny for us; let Aryaman anoint us into old age. Free from evil signs, enter the world of your husband. Be good luck for our two-legged creatures and good luck for our four-legged creatures. Have no evil eye; do not be a husband-killer.[6] Be friendly to animals, good-tempered and glowing with beauty. Bringing forth strong sons, prosper as one beloved of the gods and eager to please. Be good luck for our two-legged creatures and good luck for our four-legged creatures. [45] Generous Indra, give this woman fine sons and the good fortune of her husband's love. Place ten sons in her and make her husband the eleventh.[7] Be an empress over your husband's father, an empress over your husband's mother; be an empress over your husband's sister and an empress over your husband's brothers. Let all the gods and the waters together

[3]*The purple and red appears . . . imprinted:* In the consummation of the marriage, the bride bleeds on her wedding robe as her hymen is ruptured. The resulting stain becomes a magic spirit with power to curse and destroy the marriage. The procedure for dealing with the robe is given at the end of this paragraph.

[4]*it:* the spirit arising from the stained robe.

[5]*us, we:* the husband, and the gods who are said to have spiritually possessed the wife before her marriage.

[6]*Have no evil eye . . . husband-killer:* a charm against any evil possibly residing in the wife that may threaten her husband.

[7]*her husband the eleventh:* a common Hindu idea is that the husband is the last son of the wife, perhaps signifying the care given to the husband by his wife.

anoint our two hearts together. Let Matarisvan[8] together with the Creator and together with her who shows the way join the two of us together.

DUTIES OF WOMEN

By a girl, by a young woman, or even by an aged one, nothing must be done independently, even in her own house.

In childhood a female must be subject to her father, in youth to her husband; when her lord is dead, to her sons; a woman must never be independent.

She must not seek to separate herself from her father, husband, or sons; by leaving them she would make both her own and her husband's families contemptible.

She must always be cheerful, clever in the management of her household affairs, careful her utensils, and economical in expenditure.

Him to whom her father may give her, or her brother with the father's permission, she shall obey as long as he lives, and when he is dead, she must not insult his memory.

For the sake of procuring good fortune to brides, the recitation of benedictory texts, and the sacrifice to the Lord of creatures are used at weddings; but the betrothal by the father or guardian is the cause of the husband's dominion over his wife.

The husband who wedded her with sacred texts, always gives happiness to his wife, both in season and out of season, in this world and in the next.

[8]*Matarisvan:* an assistant of Agni.

From *The Laws of Manu* by G. Bühler. Oxford, Clarendon Press, 1886.

Though destitute of virtue, or seeking pleasure elsewhere, or devoid of good qualities, yet a husband must be constantly worshipped as a god by a faithful wife.

No sacrifice, no vow, no fast must be performed by women apart from their husbands; if a wife obeys her husband, she will for that reason alone be exalted in heaven.

A faithful wife, who desires to dwell after death with her husband, must never do anything that might displease him who took her hand, whether he be alive or dead.

At her pleasure let her emaciate her body by living on pure flowers, roots, and fruit; but she must never mention the name of another man after her husband has died.

Until death let her be patient of hardships, self-controlled, and chaste, and strive to fulfill that most excellent duty which is prescribed for wives who have one husband only.

By violating her duty towards her husband, a wife is disgraced in this world; after death she enters the womb of a jackal, and is tormented by diseases, the punishment of her sin.

She who, controlling her thoughts, words, and deeds, never slights her lord, resides after death with her husband in heaven, and is called a virtuous wife.

A twice-born man, versed in the sacred law, shall burn a wife of equal caste who conducts herself thus and dies before him, with the sacred fires used for the Agnihotra, and with the sacrificial implements.

Having thus, at the funeral, given the sacred fires to his wife who dies before him, he may marry again, and again kindle the fires.

(*Ibid.*, 5.147–158, 164, 165, 167, 168)

On Marriage

Immanuel Kant

In this brief excerpt, we find Kant's moral reflections on marriage. Consistent with his belief that humans are ends in themselves, Kant argues that one's body is part of one's moral personhood and therefore any sexual activity must be bound by the rules of morality. He concludes that marriage is the only possible condition in which human sexuality may be expressed as a moral activity. Notice his emphasis on reciprocal *relations,* mutual *desire, and* equality. *Also, note that he argues that marriage must, of moral necessity, be monogamous.*

THE NATURAL BASIS OF MARRIAGE.

The domestic relations are founded on marriage, and marriage is founded upon the natural reciprocity or intercommunity (*commercium*) of the sexes.* This natural union of the sexes proceeds according to the mere animal nature (*vaga libido, venus vulgivaga, fornicatio*), or according to the law. The latter is marriage (*matrimonium*), which is the union of two persons of different sex for life-long reciprocal possession of their sexual faculties. The end of producing and educating children may be regarded as always the end of nature in implanting mutual desire and inclination in the sexes; but it is not necessary for the rightfulness of marriage that those who marry should set this before themselves as the end of their union, otherwise the marriage would be dissolved of itself when the production of children ceased.

And even assuming that enjoyment in the reciprocal use of the sexual endowments is an end of marriage, yet the contract of marriage is not on that account a matter of arbitrary will, but is a contract necessary in its nature by the law of humanity. In other words, if a man and a woman have the will to enter on reciprocal enjoyment in accordance with their sexual nature, they must necessarily marry each other; and this necessity is in accordance with the juridical laws of pure reason.

THE RATIONAL RIGHT OF MARRIAGE.

For, this natural *commercium*—as a *usus membrorum sexualium alterius*—is an enjoyment for which the one person is given up to the other. In this relation the human individual makes himself a res, which is contrary to the right of humanity in his own person. This, however, is only possible under the one condition, that as the one person is acquired by the other as a res, that same person also equally acquires the other reciprocally, and thus regains and reestablishes the rational personality. The acquisition of a part of the

**Commercium sexuale est usus membrorum et facultatum sexualium alterius.* This "*usus*" is either natural, by which human beings may reproduce their own kind, or unnatural, which, again, refers either to a person of the same sex or to an animal of another species than man. These transgressions of all law, as *crimina carnis contra naturam,* are even "not to be named"; and, as wrongs against all humanity in the person, they cannot be saved, by any limitation or exception whatever, from entire reprobation.

From *The Philosophy of Law* by Immanuel Kant. Trans. W. Hastie, 1887.

human organism being, on account of its unity, at the same time the acquisition of the whole person, it follows that the surrender and acceptation of, or by, one sex in relation to the other, is not only permissible under the condition of marriage, but is further only really possible under that condition. But the personal right thus acquired is, at the same time, real in kind; and this characteristic of it is established by the fact that if one of the married persons run away or enter into the possession of another, the other is entitled, at any time, and incontestably, to bring such a one back to the former relation, as if that person were a thing.

MONOGAMY AND EQUALITY IN MARRIAGE.

For the same reasons, the relation of the married persons to each other is a relation of equality as regards the mutual possession of their persons, as well as of their goods. Consequently marriage is only truly realized in monogamy; for in the relation of polygamy the person who is given away on the one side, gains only a part of the one to whom that person is given up, and therefore becomes a mere *res.* But in respect of their goods, they have severally the right to renounce the use of any part of them, although only by a special contract.

From the principle thus stated, it also follows that concubinage is as little capable of being brought under a contract of right as the hiring of a person on any one occasion, in the way of a *pactum fornicationis.* For, as regards such a contract as this latter relation would imply, it must be admitted by all that any one who might enter into it could not be legally held to the fulfillment of their promise if they wished to *resile* from it. And as regards the former, a contract of concubinage would also fall as a *pactum turpe;* because as a contract of the hire (*locatio, conductio*), of a part for the use of another, on account of the inseparable unity of the members of a person, any one entering into such a contract would be actually surrendering as a res to the arbitrary will of another. Hence any party may annul a contract like this if entered into with any other, at any time and at pleasure; and that other would have no ground, in the circumstances, to complain of a lesion of his right. The same holds likewise of a morganatic or "left-hand" marriage, contracted in order to turn the inequality in the social status of the two parties to advantage in the way of establishing the social supremacy of the one over the other; for, in fact, such a relation is not really different from concubinage, according to the principles of natural right, and therefore does not constitute a real marriage. Hence the question may be raised as to whether it is not contrary to the equality of married persons when the law says in any way of the husband in relation to the wife, "he shall be thy master," so that he is represented as the one who commands, and she is the one who obeys. This, however, cannot be regarded as contrary to the natural equality of a human pair, if such legal supremacy is based only upon the natural superiority of the faculties of the husband compared with the wife, in the effectuation of the common interest of the household, and if the right to command is based merely upon this fact. For this right may thus be deduced from the very duty of unity and equality in relation to the end involved.

FULFILLMENT OF THE CONTRACT OF MARRIAGE.

The contract of marriage is completed only by conjugal cohabitation. A contract of two persons of different sex, with the secret understanding either to abstain from conjugal cohabitation or with the consciousness on either side of incapacity for it, is a simulated contract; it does not constitute a marriage, and it may be dissolved by either of the parties at will. But if the incapacity only arises after marriage, the right of the contract is not annulled or diminished by a contingency that cannot be legally blamed.

The acquisition of a spouse, either as a husband or as a wife, is therefore not constituted facto—that is, by cohabitation—without a preceding contract; nor even *pacto*—by a mere contract of marriage, without subsequent cohabitation; but only *lege*, that is, as a juridical consequence of the obligation that is formed by two persons entering into a sexual union solely on the basis of a reciprocal possession of each other, which possession at the same time is only effected in reality by the reciprocal *usus facultatum sexualium alterius.*

Monogamy: A Critique

John McMurtry

It may be an assumption of our culture and our religious and moral traditions that monogamous marriage relationships have some intrinsic value. John McMurtry asks us to challenge such an assumption. He lists a number of disadvantages of monogamous marriage, arguing that it may promote jealousy, powerlessness, alienation, and overconsumption and may limit the amount of affection available to both adult partners and the children of such relationships. All this may occur, he argues, because monogamy may be nothing more than a tool of an oppressive capitalist socioeconomic system.

"Remove away that black'ning church
Remove away that marriage hearse
Remove away that man of blood
You'll quite remove the ancient curse."
William Blake

—I—

Almost all of us have entered or will one day enter a specifically standardized form of monogamous marriage. This cultural requirement is so very basic to our existence that we accept it for most part as a kind of intractable given: dictated by the laws of God, Nature, Government and Good Sense all at once. Though it is perhaps unusual for a social practice to be so promiscuously underwritten, we generally find comfort rather than curiosity in this fact and seldom wonder how something could be divinely inspired, biologically determined, coerced and reasoned out all at the same time. We simply take it for granted.

Those in society who are officially charged with the thinking function with

Copyright © 1972, *The Monist,* La Salle, Illinois 61301. Reprinted by permission.

regard to such matters are no less responsible for this uncritical acceptance than the man on the street. The psychoanalyst traditionally regards our form of marriage as a necessary restraint on the anarchic id and no more to be queried than civilization itself. The lawyer is as undisposed to questioning the practice as he is to criticizing the principle of private property (this is appropriate, as I shall later point out). The churchman formally perceives the relationship between man and wife to be as inviolable and insusceptible to question as the relationship between the institution he works for and the Christ. The sociologist standardly accepts the formalized bonding of heterosexual pairs as the indispensable basis of social order and perhaps a societal universal. The politician is as incapable of challenging it as he is the virtue of his own continued holding of office. And the philosopher (at least the English-speaking philosopher) as with most issues of socially controversial or sexual dimensions, ignores the question almost together.

Even those irreverent adulterers and unmarried couples who would seem to be challenging the institution in the most basic possible way, in practice, tend merely to mimic its basic structure in unofficial form. The coverings of sanctity, taboo and cultural habit continue to hold them with the grip of public clothes.

■ —II—

"Monogamy" means, literally, "one marriage." But it would be wrong to suppose that this phrase tells us much about our particular species of official wedlock. The greatest obstacle to the adequate understanding of our monogamy institution has been the failure to identify clearly and systematically the full complex of principles it involves. There are four such principles, each carrying enormous restrictive force and together constituting a massive social control mechanism that has never, so far as I know, been fully schematized.

To come straight to the point, the four principles in question are as follows:

1. *The partners are required to enter a formal contractual relation:* (*a*) whose establishment demands a specific official participant, certain conditions of the contractors (legal age, no blood ties, etc.) and a standard set of procedures; (*b*) whose governing terms are uniform for all and exactly prescribed by law; and (*c*) whose dissolution may only be legally effected by the decision of state representatives.

The ways in which this elaborate principle of contractual requirement are importantly restrictive are obvious. One may not enter into a marriage union without entering into a contract presided over by a state-investured official.[1] One may not set any of the terms of the contractual relationship by which one is bound for life. And one cannot dissolve the contract without legal action and costs, court proceedings and in many places actual legislation. (The one and only contract in all English-speaking law that is not dissoluble by the consent of the contracting parties.) The extent of control here—over the most intimate and putatively "loving" relationships in all social intercourse—is so great as to be difficult to catalogue without exciting in oneself a sense of disbelief.

Lest it be thought there is always the real option of entering a common law relationship free of such encumbrances, it should be noted that: (*a*) these relationships themselves are subject to state regulation, though of a less imposing sort; and (much more important) (*b*) there are very formidable selective pressures against common law partnerships such as employment and job discrimination, exclusion from housing and lodging facilities, special legal disablements,[2] loss of social and moral status (consider such phrases as "living in sin," "make her an honest woman," etc.), family shame and embarrassment, and so on.

2. *The number of partners involved in the marriage must be two and only two* (as opposed to three, four, five or any of the almost countless other possibilities of intimate union).

This second principle of our specific form of monogamy (the concept of "one marriage," it should be pointed out, is consistent with any number of participating partners) is perhaps the most important and restrictive of the four principles we are considering. Not only does it confine us to just *one* possibility out of an enormous range, but it confines us to that single possibility which involves the *least* number of people, two. It is difficult to conceive of a more thoroughgoing mechanism for limiting extended social union and intimacy. The fact that this monolithic restriction seems so "natural" to us (if it were truly "natural" of course, there would be no need for its rigorous cultural prescription by everything from severe criminal law[3] to ubiquitous housing regulations) simply indicates the extent to which its hold is implanted in our social structure. It is the institutional basis of what I will call the "binary frame of sexual consciousness," a frame through which all our heterosexual relationships are typically viewed ("two's company, three's a crowd") and in light of which all larger circles of intimacy seem almost inconceivable.[4]

3. *No person may participate in more than one marriage at a time or during a lifetime* (unless the previous marriage has been officially dissolved by, normally, one partner's death or successful divorce).

Violation of this principle is, of course, a criminal offence (bigamy) which is punishable by a considerable term in prison. Of various general regulations of our marriage institution it has experienced the most significant modification: not indeed in principle, but in the extent of flexibility of its "escape hatch" of divorce. The case with which this escape hatch is opened has increased considerably in the past few years (the grounds for divorce being more permissive than previously) and it is in this regard most of all that the principles of our marriage institution have undergone formal alteration. That is, in plumbing rather than substance.

4. *No married person may engage in any sexual relationship with any person whatever other than the marriage partner.*

Although a consummated sexual act with another person alone constitutes an act of adultery, lesser forms of sexual and erotic relationships[5] may also constitute grounds for divorce (i.e., cruelty) and are generally prescribed as well by informal social convention and taboo. In other words, the fourth and final principle of our marriage institution involves not only a prohibition of sexual intercourse per se outside one's wedlock (this term deserves pause) but a prohibition of all one's erotic relations whatever outside this bond. The penalties for violation here are as various as they are severe, ranging from permanent loss of spouse, children, chattel, and income to job dismissal and social ostracism. In this way, possibly the most compelling natural force towards expanded intimate relations with others[6] is strictly confined within the narrowest possible circle for (barring delinquency) the whole of adult life. The sheer weight and totality of this restriction is surely one of the great wonders of all historical institutional control.

— III —

With all established institutions, apologetics for perpetuation are never wanting. Thus it is with our form of monogamous marriage.

Perhaps the most celebrated justification over the years has proceeded from a belief in a Supreme Deity who secretly utters sexual and other commands to privileged human representatives. Almost as well known a line of defence has issued from a conviction, similarly confident, that the need for some social regulation of sexuality demonstrates the need for our specific type of two-person wedlock. Although these have been important justifications in the sense of being very widely supported, they are not—having other grounds than reasons—susceptible to treatment here.

If we put aside such arguments, we are left I think with two major claims. The first is that our form of monogamous marriage promotes a profound affection between the partners which is not only of great worth in itself but, invaluable as a sanctuary from the pressures of outside society. Since, however, there are no secure grounds whatever for supposing that such "profound affection" is not at least as easily achievable by any number of *other* marriage forms (i.e., forms which differ in one or more of the four principles), this justification conspicuously fails to perform the task required of it.

The second major claim for the defence is that monogamy provides a specially loving context for child upbringing. However here again there are no grounds at all for concluding that it does so as, or any more, effectively than other possible forms of marriage (the only alternative type of upbringing to which it has apparently been shown to be superior is nonfamily institutional upbringing, which of course is not relevant to the present discussion). Furthermore, the fact that at least half the span of a normal monogamous marriage *involves no child-upbringing at all* is disastrously overlooked here, as is the reinforcing fact that there is no reference to or mention of the quality of child-upbringing in any of the prescriptions connected with it.

In brief, the second major justification of our particular type of wedlock scents somewhat too strongly of red herring to pursue further.

There is, it seems, little to recommend the view that monogamy specially promotes "profound affection" between the partners or a "loving context" for child-upbringing. Such claims are simply without force. On the other hand, there are several aspects to the logic and operation of the four principles of this institution which suggest that it actually *inhibits* the achievement of these desiderata. Far from uniquely abetting the latter, it militates against them. In these ways:

(1) Centralized official control of marriage (which the Church gradually achieved through the mechanism of Canon Law after the Fall of the Roman Empire[7] in one of the greatest seizures of social power in history) necessarily alienates the partners from full responsibility for and freedom in their relationship. "Profound closeness" between the partners—or least an area of it—is thereby expropriated rather than promoted, and "sanctuary" from the pressures of outside society prohibited rather than fostered.

(2) Limitation of the marriage bond to two people necessarily restricts, in perhaps the most unilateral way consistent with offspring survival, the number of adult sources of affection, interest, material support and instruction for the young. The "loving context for child-upbringing" is thereby desiccated rather than nourished: providing the structural conditions for such notorious and far-reaching problems as (*a*) sibling rivalry for scarce adult attention,[8] and (*b*) parental oppression through exclusive monopoly of the child's means of life.[9]

(3) Formal exclusion of all others from erotic contact with the marriage partner systematically promotes conjugal insecurity, jealousy and alienation by:

(a) Officially underwriting a literally totalitarian expectation of sexual confinement on the part of one's husband or wife: which expectation is, *ceteris paribus*, inevitably more subject to anxiety and disappointment than one less extreme in its demand and/or cultural-juridical backing;[10]

(b) Requiring so complete a sexual isolation of the marriage partners that should one violate the fidelity code the other is left alone and susceptible to a sense of fundamental deprivation and resentment;

(c) Stipulating such a strict restraint of sexual energies that there are habitual violations of the regulation: which violations *qua* violations are frequently if not always attended by (I) wilful deception and reciprocal suspicion about the occurrence or quality of the extramarital relationship, (ii) anxiety and fear on both sides of permanent estrangement from partner and family, and/or (iii) overt and covert antagonism over the prohibited act in both offender (who feels "trapped") and offended (who feels "betrayed").

The disadvantages of the four principles of monogamous marriage do not, however, end with inhibiting the very effects they are said to promote. There are further shortcomings:

(1) The restriction of marriage union to two partners necessarily prevents the strengths of larger groupings. Such advantages as the following are thereby usually ruled out.

(a) The security, range and power of larger socioeconomic units;

(b) The epistemological and emotional substance, variety and scope of more pluralist interactions;

(c) The possibility of extra-domestic freedom founded on more adult providers and upbringers as well as more broadly based circles of intimacy.

(2) The sexual containment and isolation which the four principles together require variously stimulates such social malaises as:

(a) Destructive aggression (which notoriously results from sexual frustration);

(b) Apathy, frustration and dependence within the marriage bond;

(c) Lack of spontaneity, bad faith and distance in relationships without the marriage bond;

(d) Sexual phantasizing, perversion, fetishism, prostitution and pornography in the adult population as a whole.[11]

Taking such things into consideration, it seems difficult to lend credence to the view that the four principles of our form of monogamous marriage constitute a structure beneficial either to the marriage partners themselves or to their offspring (or indeed to anyone else). One is moved to seek for some other ground of the institution, some ground that lurks beneath the reach of our conventional apprehensions.

— IV —

The ground of our marriage institution, the essential principle that underwrites all four restrictions, is this: *the maintenance by one man or woman of the effective right to exclude indef-*

initely all others from erotic access to the conjugal partner.

The first restriction creates, elaborates on, and provides for the enforcement of this right to exclude. And the second, third and fourth restrictions together ensure that the said right to exclude is—respectively—not cooperative, not simultaneously or sequentially distributed, and not permissive of even casual exception.

In other words, the four restrictions of our form of monogamous marriage together constitute a state-regulated, indefinite and exclusive ownership by two individuals of one another's sexual powers. Marriage is simply a form of private property.[12]

That our form of monogamous marriage is when the confusing layers of sanctity, apologetic and taboo are cleared away another species of private property should not surprise us.[13] The history of the institution is so full of suggestive indicators—dowries, inheritance, property alliances, daughter sales (of which women's wedding rings are a carry-over), bride exchanges, legitimacy and illegitimacy—that it is difficult not to see some intimate connections between marital and ownership ties. We are better able still to apprehend the ownership essence of our marriage institution, when in addition we consider:

(a) That until recently almost the only way to secure official dissolution of consummated marriage was to be able to demonstrate violation of one or both partner's sexual ownership (i.e., adultery);

(b) That the imperative of premarital chastity is tantamount to a demand for retrospective sexual ownership by the eventual marriage partner;

(c) That successful sexual involvement with a married person is prosecutable as an expropriation of ownership—"alienation of affections"—which is restituted by cash payment;

(d) That the incest taboo is an iron mechanism which protects the conjugal ownership of sexual properties: both the husband's and wife's from the access of affectionate offspring and the offsprings (who themselves are future marriage partners) from access of siblings and parents;[14]

(e) That the language of the marriage ceremony is the language of exclusive possession ("take," "to have and to hold," "forsaking all others and keeping you only unto him/her," etc.), not to mention the proprietary locutions associated with the marital relationship (e.g., "he's mine," "she belongs to him," "keep to your own husband," "wife stealer," "possessive husband," etc.).

— V —

Of course, it would be remarkable if marriage in our society was not a relationship akin to private property. In our socioeconomic system we relate to virtually everything of value by individual ownership: by, that is, the effective right to exclude others from the thing concerned.[15] That we do so as well with perhaps the most highly valued thing of all—the sexual partners' sexuality—is only to be expected. Indeed it would probably be an intolerable strain on our entire social structure if we did otherwise.

This line of thought deserves pursuit. The real secret of our form of monogamous marriage is not that it functionally provides for the needs of adults who love one another or the children they give birth to, but that it serves the maintenance of our present social system. It is an institution which is indispensable to the persistence of the capitalist order,[16] in the following ways:

(1) A basic principle of current social relations is that some people legally acquire the use of other people's personal powers from which they may exclude other members of society. This system operates in the workplace (owners and hirers of all types contractually acquire for their exclusive use workers' regular labor powers) and in the family (husbands and wives contractually acquire for their exclusive use their partner's sexual properties). A conflict between the structures of these primary relations—as would obtain were there a suspension of the restrictions governing our form of monogamous marriage—might well undermine the systemic coherence of present social intercourse.

(2) The fundamental relation between individuals and things which satisfy their needs is, in our present society, that each individual has or does not have the effective right to exclude other people from the thing in question.[17] A rudimentary need is that for sexual relationship(s). Therefore the object of this need must be related to the one who needs it as owner or not owner (i.e., via marriage or not-marriage, or approximations thereto) if people's present relationship to what they need is to retain—again—systemic coherence.

(3) A necessary condition for the continued existence of the present social formation is that its members feel powerful motivation to gain favorable positions in it. But such social ambition is heavily dependent on the preservation of exclusive monogamy in that:

(a) The latter confines the discharge of primordial sexual energies to a single unalterable partner and thus typically compels the said energies to seek alternative outlet, such as business or professional success;[18]

(b) The exclusive marriage necessarily reduces the sexual relationships available to any one person to absolute (nonzero) minimum, a unilateral promotion of sexual shortage which in practice renders hierarchical achievement essential as an economic and "display" means for securing scarce partners.[19]

(4) Because the exclusive marriage necessarily and dramatically reduces the possibilities of sexual-love relationships, it thereby promotes the existing economic system by:

(a) Rendering extreme economic self-interest—the motivational basis of the capitalistic process—less vulnerable to altruistic subversion;

(b) Disciplining society's members into the habitual repression of natural impulse required for long-term performance of repetitive and arduous work tasks;

(c) Developing a complex of suppressed sexual desires to which sales techniques may effectively apply in creating those new consumer wants which provide indispensable outlets for ever-increasing capital funds.

(5) The present form of marriage is of fundamental importance to:

(a) The continued relative powerlessness of the individual family: which, with larger numbers would constitute a correspondingly increased command of social power;

(b) The continued high demand for homes, commodities and services: which, with the considerable economies of scale that extended unions would permit, would otherwise falter;

(c) The continued strict necessity for adult males to sell their labour power and adult women to remain at home (or vice versa): which strict necessity would diminish as the economic base of the family unit extended;

(d) The continued immense pool of unsatisfied sexual desires and energies in the population at large: without which powerful interests and institutions would lose much of their conventional appeal and force;[20]

(e) The continued profitable involvement of lawyers, priests and state officials in the jurisdictions of marriage and divorce and the myriad official practices and proceedings connected thereto.[21]

— VI —

If our marriage institution is a linchpin of our present social structure, then a breakdown in this institution would seem to indicate a breakdown in our social structure. On the face of it, the marriage institution is breaking down—enormously increased divorce rates, nonmarital sexual relationships, wife-swapping, the Playboy philosophy, and communes. Therefore one might be led by the appearance of things to anticipate a profound alteration in the social system.

But it would be a mistake to underestimate the tenacity of an established order or to overestimate the extent of change in our marriage institution. Increased divorce rates merely indicate the widening of a traditional escape hatch. Nonmarital relationships imitate and culminate in the marital mold. Wife-swapping presupposes ownership, as the phrase suggests. The Playboy philosophy is merely the view that if one has the money one has the right to be titillated, the commercial call to more fully exploit a dynamic sector of capital investment. And communes—the most hopeful phenomenon—almost nowhere offer a *praxis* challenge to private property in sexuality. It may be changing. But history, as the old man puts it, weighs like a nightmare on the brains of the living.

Notes

1. Any person who presides over a marriage and is not authorized by law to do so is guilty of a criminal offense and is subject to several years' imprisonment (e.g., Canadian Criminal Code, Sec. 258).

2. For example, offspring are illegitimate, neither wife nor children are legal heirs, and husband has no right of access or custody should separation occur.

3. "Any kind of conjugal union with more than one person at the same time, whether or not it is by law recognized as a binding form of marriage—is guilty of an indictable offence and is liable to imprisonment for five years" (Canadian Criminal Code, Sec. 257, [I][al[ii]). Part 2 of the same section adds: "Where an accused is charged with an offence under this section, no averment or proof of the method by which the alleged relationship was entered into, agreed to or consented to is necessary in the indictment or upon the trial of the accused, nor is it necessary upon the trial to prove that the persons who are alleged to have entered into the relationship had or intended to have sexual intercourse."

(Here and elsewhere, I draw examples from Canadian criminal law. There is no reason to suspect the Canadian code is eccentric in these instances.)

4. Even the sexual revolutionary Wilhelm Reich seems constrained within the limits of this "binary frame." Thus he says (my emphasis): "Nobody has the right to prohibit his or her partner from entering a temporary or lasting sexual relationship with someone else. He has only the right *either to withdraw or to win the partner back.*" (Wilhelm Reich, *The Sexual Revolution*, trans. by T. P. Wolfe [New York: Farrar, Strauss & Giroux, 1970], p. 28.) The possibility of sexual partners extending their union to include the other loved party as opposed to one partner having either to "win" against this third party or to "withdraw" altogether, does not seem even to occur to Reich.

5. I will be using "sexual" and "erotic" interchangeably throughout the paper.

6. It is worth noting here that: (*a*) man has by nature the most "open" sexual instinct—year-round operativeness and variety of stimuli—of all the species (except perhaps the dolphin); and (*b*) it is a principle of human needs in general that maximum satisfaction involves regular variation in the form of the need-object.

7. "Roman Law had no power of intervening in the formation of marriages and there was no legal form of marriage. . . . Marriage was a matter of simple private agreement and divorce was a private transaction" (Havelock Ellis, *Studies in the Psychology of Sex* [New York: Random House, 1963], Vol. II, Part 3, p. 429).

8. The dramatic reduction of sibling rivalry through an increased number of adults in the house is a phenomenon which is well known in contemporary domestic communes.

9. One of the few other historical social relationships I can think of in which persons hold thoroughly exclusive monopoly over other persons' means of life is slavery. Thus, as with another's slave, it is a criminal offence "to receive" or "harbour" another's child without "right of possession" (Canadian Criminal Code, Sec. 250).

10. Certain cultures, for example, permit extramarital sexuality by married persons with friends, guests, or in-laws with no reported consequences of

jealousy. From such evidence, one is led to speculate that the intensity and extent of jealousy at a partner's extramarital sexual involvement is in direct proportion to the severity of the accepted cultural regulations against such involvements. In short such regulations do not prevent jealousy so much as effectively engender it.

11. It should not be forgotten that at the same time marriage excludes marital partners from sexual contact with others, it necessarily excludes those others from sexual contact with marital partners. Walls face two ways.

12. Those aspects of marriage law which seem to fall outside the pale of sexual property holding—for example, provisions for divorce if the husband fails to provide or is convicted of a felony or is an alcoholic—may themselves be seen as simply prescriptive characterizations of the sort of sexual property which the marriage partner must remain to retain satisfactory conjugal status: a kind of permanent warranty of the "good working order" of the sexual possession.

What constitutes the "good working order" of the conjugal possession is, of course, different in the case of the husband and in the case of the wife: an *asymmetry* within the marriage institution which, I gather, women's liberation movements are anxious to eradicate.

13. I think it is instructive to think of even the nonlegal aspects of marriage, for example, its sentiments as essentially private property structured. Thus the preoccupation of those experiencing conjugal sentiments with expressing how much "my very own," "my precious," the other is: with expressing that is, how valuable and inviolable the ownership is and will remain.

14. I think the secret to the long mysterious incest taboo may well be the fact that in all its forms it protects sexual property: not only conjugal (as indicated above) but paternal and tribal as well. This crucial line of thought, however, requires extended separate treatment.

15. Sometimes—as with political patronage, criminal possession, *de facto* privileges and so forth—a *power* to exclude others exists with no corresponding "right" (just as sometimes a right to exclude exists with no corresponding power). Properly speaking, thus, I should here use the phrase "power to exclude," which covers "effective right to exclude" as well as all non-juridical enablements of this sort.

16. It is no doubt indispensable as well—in some form or other—to any private property order. Probably (if we take the history of Western society as our data base) the more thoroughgoing and developed the private property formation is, the more total the sexual ownership prescribed by the marriage institution.

17. Things in unlimited supply—like, presently, oxygen—are not of course related to people in this way.

18. This is, of course, a Freudian or quasi-Freudian claim. "Observation of daily life shows us," says Freud, "that most persons direct a very tangible part of their sexual motive powers to their professional or business activities" (Sigmund Freud, *Dictionary of Psychoanalysis*, ed. by Nandor Fodor and Frank Gaynor [New York: Fawcett Publications, Premier Paperback, 1966], p. 139).

19. It might be argued that exclusive marriage also protects those physically less attractive persons who—in an "open" situation—might be unable to secure any sexual partnership at all. The force of this claim depends, I think, on improperly continuing to posit the very principle of exclusiveness which the "open" situation rules out (e.g., in the latter situation, x might be less attractive to y than z is and yet z not be rejected, any more than at present an intimate friend is rejected who is less talented than another intimate friend).

20. The sexual undercurrents of corporate advertisements, religious systems, racial propaganda and so on are too familiar to dwell on here.

21. It is also possible that exclusive marriage protects the adult-youth power structure.

Motherhood: A Sociopolitical Concept

Carolynne Timko

Is motherhood simply a natural, biological phenomenon, or is it more accurately a role defined by the social, political, and economic interests of males? Carolynne Timko examines some of the "traditional" expressions and beliefs about motherhood and concludes that it exists as a form of the oppression of women. Whether you initially agree or disagree with her position, examine closely the claims she makes about how patriarchical societies have conceived the role of motherhood and the effects this may have had on personal identity.

> Motherhood: Men's appropriation of women's bodies as a resource to reproduce patriarchy.
> (Allen 92)

Though most women have the physical capability to bear children, some women remain childless. The decision to forego childbearing and motherhood is not easy for many because women have been prepared for the role of motherhood from their earliest childhood. Society expects women to bear children. "More sacred than religion, more binding than the law, more habitual than methods of eating, we are each and all born into the accepted idea of motherhood and trained in it; and in maturity we hand it down unquestioningly" (Delger 174).

Motherhood has always been a social obligation and it is only in recent history that the possibility of choice, frequency, and number of pregnancies has become available. Many people still do not consider motherhood a matter of choice, in fact the political and social institutions of power are structured to create a climate where women do not realize that they may choose to become a mother or not. Motherhood remains an obligation imposed by the social custom due to male dominance in both social and political culture.

Girls are socialized from earliest childhood to believe that their future lies in marriage and childbearing. While boys are given toys of construction (blocks, etc.), destruction (guns, etc.), and action (trucks, etc.), girls are given doll houses and baby dolls. They call themselves mommy to the doll and play at being a good mother through lavish attention and care of baby. This sex role behavior is encouraged by families, outside child care givers, and the business community which manufactures a sex role stereotype through advertisements directed toward children and adult groups. It is very difficult for women to escape the subtle and overt demands and restrictions placed on them by private and public sectors of society. Shulamith Firestone writes that "the heart of women's oppression is her childbearing and childrearing roles. Women's reproductive function . . . is the critical distinction upon which all inequities toward women are grounded" (72).

Women are oppressed in most societies. Historically, women's existence was acknowledged only through their fathers or husbands. A woman was the property of the dominant male in the family; he could marry her off to any man he wished or even the Church. Many marriages were arranged

From *Voiceprint* Vol. II, No. 1, Winter/Spring 1993, c/o MALS Program DePaul University.

without the woman's consent. Women could not own property; even an inheritance would become the property of a woman's husband or closest male relative if she were unmarried.

Women have traditionally been discouraged and even barred from participation in the institutions of society such as politics, business, and enfranchisement. The more women were oppressed by the male power structure, the more easily the women adopted those oppressive attitudes so they, in fact, contributed to their own oppression (Dally 11). Some women were so indoctrinated with the belief of their inferiority that they supported the male power structure's opposition to their own freedom, i.e., enfranchisement, ownership of property, and reproduction rights. Many women still believe that they are the weaker sex, the gentle and fair sex who need men to protect and care for them and voice opposition to social and reproductive freedom.

The idealization of motherhood was strengthened during Victorian times and has continued into the mid and late twentieth century. By idealizing women's roles, men could keep women under control, forcing them by law and social custom to adhere to certain behavioral patterns. Since motherhood was considered to be the true fulfillment of womanhood this ideal was fostered in all strata of society. Government studies during and after World War II "proved" that children needed their mothers' full time attention for normal development (Daily 98, 152). These studies actually followed the progress of British orphans who were permanently separated from their mothers, through death or desertion during the war, but the analysis of the data was applied to children of working mothers who lived with their children. These studies were then used to prove that mothers needed to be with their children constantly in an attempt to force women back into their pre-war roles of homemaker and mother and make them believe that this was their rightful place. Television images of women like those in "Father Knows Best" and "Leave It to Beaver" showed that those women who stayed home, cared for their children, and deferred to their husbands were happy and fulfilled.

Prior to the industrial revolution and the rise of cities as the focal point for commerce, women traditionally worked on the farms in the fields along with the men and older children. Since the decline of the rural economy women suddenly became weak and the role expectation for women became more restrictive. Marriage, childbearing and work in the home became the only sphere suitable for the "fairer" sex. Women who did work in shops or as teachers or nurses were expected to retire to the home upon marriage. Societal pressures made women feel guilty and out of the mainstream if they did not have children. As economic and business needs lured women back to work in the paid labor market, the pressures to have children did not diminish but the problems surrounding children and child care increased. Child care has always been viewed as women's work, so it comes as no surprise that it continued as women moved out of the home and into the paid labor market. The pressures on women to continue to have children did not decrease as women's presence in the work force increased.

The women's movement in the sixties and seventies made more women aware of reproductive choices, but the pressure grew for women to have a career and be successful wives and mothers. Even the early modern feminists were unsympathetic to the dilemma of women regarding motherhood. It was trivialized by the ideas expressed in their writings or totally neglected as a feminist concern. Germaine Greer wrote that

"[B]ringing up children is not a real occupation, because children come up just the same, brought or not" (278). Feminist writers cautioned women that if they must reproduce, women should return to their "real work" in the paid labor force as soon as possible. They supported and encouraged the devaluation of motherhood. In fact, according to O'Brien, feminists like De Beauvoir regarded "childbirth as an inferior animal activity and the biological curse of femininity" (104).

Though the intent of early modern feminists was to liberate women from their traditionally female roles, they continued the social oppression by creating a new set of ideals while offering no solution to the dilemma of motherhood nor the tools needed to fight oppression.

Since the rise of the second wave of feminism in mid-century, women have been encouraged to work outside the home. Housework is considered menial and demeaning, but women are expected to be mother, worker, wife, and independent, self-sufficient person all at once. Even the feminists send mixed messages to women . . . childbearing is a demeaning task but you must have children and paid employment to prove you can do "it all." As long as sex roles are culturally defined and femininity is defined as the greatest adherence to traditional and cultural characteristics, women will remain oppressed, dependent and unable to control their own bodies.

It is very difficult to fight the weight of tradition and culture. Women are indoctrinated with the belief that they must have children through the myth of Maternal Instinct. Women are bombarded with the myth that says they must innately want children simply because they are female. Because women are biologically designed to reproduce, their minds are programmed by all elements of society, even by their mothers, to comply with their physiology. According to the myth, women have a natural need to nurture and love, and this can only be fulfilled through childbearing. Despite the pervasive socialization of this myth in our culture, and the fact that nature endowed women with the capability to reproduce, there is no innate desire to do so. This is a need learned through the constant bombardment of socializing factors.

Inherent in the myth of maternal instinct is the idea that childbearing gives a woman's sexuality a spiritual purpose. Procreation justifies women's powerful sexuality and gives it a sense of spirituality to purify and decrease its potency. Women are inundated with socio-cultural pressures through advertising, different expectations in education due to gender, etc., that make motherhood appear to be a normal corollary for their femininity (Silverman 7–8, 10, 14) and encourage women to deny their sexuality. Knowing and understanding the power of their sexual nature helps empower women to fight oppression and classification.

In the last few decades the rise of fundamentalist religions has encouraged the return to "traditional values and ways of life," i.e., mother at home with children while father works. This is not only seen in Christian fundamentalism but in non-Christian religions as well. This return to religious fundamentalism fosters the oppression of women. In Islam, Judaism, and Christianity women are considered inferior to men and therefore required to be obedient and submissive to men. The Christian churches propagate the submissiveness of women as the correct way of Christian life. The Bible tells women to be "submissive to their husbands as if to the Lord" (Ephesians 5:22), thus raising the rule of the husband in the home to the equivalent of the Lord over the universe. In Islam women are veiled and hidden from public, and every morning Jewish men offer prayers of thanks for not being born a woman. These attitudes keep women in inferior and submissive roles with no control over their lives, bodies, or futures.

In the last twenty years the government has successfully dismantled significant health and social programs geared toward the health and welfare of women and children. In 1971 President Nixon vetoed a comprehensive Child Development Act saying it would 'sovietize' American families and further stigmatize child care. Throughout that decade child care relief continued to be ignored until President Ford signed an important supplemental appropriations bill to aid child care in 1976. Since this was signed on the eve of the election, one can only see it as an attempt to ensure votes rather than a legitimate attempt to restore child- and family-oriented legislation. President Reagan cut federal day care assistance by twenty-five percent. Since 1967 no major legislation has been passed which provides directly for or expands programs of publicly funded day care (Hoffnung 183). Politicians now chant the rhetoric of "family values" which can be interpreted as women in their place with no options and men at the head of the family with all the power. Family is again defined in male terminology which demands submission of women and erosion of their rights.

While the male dominated Congress continues to destroy or ignore the needs of women and children, the 1973 affirmation of the right of autonomy and privacy is continually under attack from what I think are antidemocratic, anti-choice forces who believe that a woman has no right to control her own reproductive functions. The movement to gut Roe v. Wade continues and reflects the belief in this country that women are not truly suited for anything more than motherhood and menial work. Though it claims to have its basis in the return to Christian morality, the anti-choice movement really intends to return women to the status of chattel without legal or social rights, without identity and self control, an invisible class. These anti-choice radicals put the contents of the womb, a potential life, ahead of the actual life of the woman, again sending a clear signal to women that their sole purpose is to be vessels for procreation rather than whole beings.

Luker states that the abortion debate is really about the meaning of women's lives, not about the life of an embryo (194). Her 1984 report indicated that ninety-four percent of the pro-choice women worked in the paid labor market, over half had incomes in the top ten percent of women's incomes in the country and ten percent had personal incomes of over $30,000 per year. The anti-choice women were least likely to work in paid labor markets, but those who did were usually not married. Only fourteen percent of the anti-choice married women had personal incomes, but not usually from formal jobs. They most likely earned their money at casual labor like selling cosmetics, etc. Fifty percent of the anti-choice women who did work were at the lowest pay scale and were usually married to skilled workers or owners of small businesses (194, 195).

These statistics show the opinions among women of different educational and occupational goals and support Luker's position that the anti-choice women tend to be housewives or workers in inferior jobs who may perhaps take the anti-choice position to validate themselves in the face of their own lack of power and choice. Luker continues that when "pregnancy is discretionary . . . motherhood has been demoted from a sacred calling to a job. Abortion strips the veil of sanctity from motherhood" (204, 205). Thus the anti-choice advocates need to oppose abortion to maintain the myth of motherhood and the concomitant control of women. Women who unite to fight this myth and its practical ramifications find a sisterhood and a sense of comfort, but preservation of the right to abortion will not change the attitude of men and women who believe that women's role is to reproduce.

Though it seems to be a trend among modern working women to delay pregnancies until they are established in the business world and can afford to risk the time off work to tend to pregnancy and newborn baby, hire nannies or babysitters, and then return to their jobs, the majority of women do not have the opportunity to determine when they will have babies. Many more women live near or below the poverty line than ever before in modern history, and they usually do not have the luxury of choosing when it is convenient to bear children. Family planning clinics which receive federal funding are not allowed to discuss all aspects of family planning because they may not discuss abortion as an alternative to motherhood. (Only a physician may discuss abortion but many clinics do not have physicians present at all times to make this counseling readily available to all women.) Family planning clinics are frequently blockaded by the anti-choice radicals who intend to physically prevent women from receiving safe and legal abortions. According to recent television reports, safe and legal abortions are now unavailable in eighty-three percent of the country.

Many women in lower socioeconomic groups have several children because safe abortion is unavailable for them. Many women in this situation cannot work to get off welfare because safe and affordable child and health care is not available and if they do work then benefits, especially health care, will be cut. They cannot earn enough to support their families, but with the benefits provided with welfare, they can. Social and government agencies are not structured to encourage women to be independent and assist them in getting jobs and off welfare. They are structured to keep women dependent and powerless.

The question remains then: Why has the myth of motherhood lasted so long? Silverman offered several suggestions which I think are valid. Despite the fact that many women are moving into the business community and the number of female-owned and -operated businesses grows each year, business has a vested interest in making women believe that the best and only truly feminine "choice" in life is motherhood and work in the home. The ideal of large families was promoted in order to increase population, the number of actual and potential workers, and therefore increase profits. This, of course, has failed as the population continues to soar causing planetary problems, not the least of which is unemployment, rapid use of natural resources, decreasing room, increasing racism and intolerance.

Legislators continue to vote against abortion whenever possible, and though women are slowly moving into the government power structure, male dominance and government intrusion into the control of women's bodies continue. It is not an issue of morality but the maintenance of power and dominance over a social group.

Social pressures continue to foster the myth of motherhood in order to immortalize the culture of a society. This has the opposite effect because overpopulation will destroy the culture as the society is destroyed. Women themselves continue to profess the myth of motherhood as if to validate themselves and avoid depersonalization and disempowerment. For many women, having children gives them an identity with individual prestige and perceived power in the home (Silverman 29–33).

Many women live in male-dominated situations where there is little opportunity to challenge their established role, and express independence in reproductive choices. Children come from male-dominated and male-defined social intercourse (Allen 94) and many women do not have the resources (personal, social, or political) to defy or challenge that dominance. Women are traditionally socialized to believe that their true worth, despite education, career, and economic success, lies in their ability to reproduce. Women are told that having children gives them power, as demonstrated by the cliche "the hand that rocks the cradle rules the world." Women have allowed themselves to believe that this is true, perhaps to ease the pain of their perceived inferior status and their role as reproductive machines.

Women who try to work at "having it all," i.e., career, children and marriage, remain the primary providers of child care. If a child is ill, it is generally presumed that the mother will take time off work to care for that child. A woman who goes to work while her child is ill is often ridiculed by coworkers as a terrible mother for not being there when her child needs her. The assumption that a woman is the only parent who can provide nurturing and gentle care for an ill child persists and demonstrates the attitude generally held in society that raising children is woman's work and any woman who shirks that work or willingly gives it over to another, e.g., nanny, sitter or father, is less than a good mother and, therefore, less than a real woman.

It is the responsibility of women to recognize this tyrannical social norm and teach not only our daughters, but also our sons that this concept of women solely as machines of reproduction is incorrect and dangerous to the formation of healthy and respectful interpersonal relationships and a healthy society. All people must come to realize that motherhood is a choice that must be freely made without the intrusion of government, religion, or general society.

Motherhood continues to be the most successful tool used to oppress and subvert women. This is one form of tyranny and oppression that is difficult to fight because of the enormous social, political, and economic structures that continually reinforce the myth of motherhood and keep women subjugated. Motherhood under these circumstances is the most dangerous road a woman can take, for she risks the total annihilation of herself and her continued subservience to others.

Works Consulted

Allen, Jeffner. "Motherhood: The Annihilation of Women." *Women and Values, Readings in Recent Feminist Philosophy.* Ed. Marilyn Pearsall. Belmont: Wadsworth, 1986. 91–101.

Dally, Ann. *Inventing Motherhood.* New York: Schocken, 1983.

Firestone, Shulamith. *The Dialectic of Sex.* New York: Bantam, 1971.

Gilman, Charlotte Perkins. *Women and Economics.* Ed. Carl Delger. New York: Harper Torchbooks, 1966.

Greer, Germaine. *The Female Eunuch.* London: Paladin, 1971.

Hoffnung, Michele. "Motherhood: Contemporary Conflict for Women." *Women's Issues and Social Work Practice.* Elaine Norman and Arlene Mancuso, eds. Itasca, IL: F. E. Peacock, 1986.

Luker, Kristin. *Abortion and the Politics of Motherhood.* Berkeley: U of California P, 1982.

O'Brien, Mary. "Feminist Theory and Dialectic Logic." *Feminist Theory: A Critique of Ideology.* Nannerl O. Keohane, Michelle Z. Rosaldo, and Barbara C. Gelpi, eds. Chicago: U of Chicago P, 1982.

Ranke-Heinemann, Uta. *Eunuchs for the Kingdom of Heaven.* Trans. Peter Heinegg. New York: Doubleday, 1990.

Silverman, Anna and Arnold. *The Case Against Having Children.* New York: David McKay, 1971.

Surrogate Motherhood

Bonnie Steinbock

The technology that allows for the possibility of surrogate motherhood has created a heated controversy. On one side, we hear arguments about the further biological oppression of women, and on the other, praises for the possibility of increasing freedom to have children when otherwise impossible. Steinbock examines the issues of paternalism, exploitation, human dignity, privacy, and harm, favoring a cautious approach to the use of surrogate mothers. How does surrogacy affect a woman's sense of self?

The recent case of "Baby M" has brought surrogate motherhood to the forefront of American attention. Ultimately, whether we permit or prohibit surrogacy depends on what we take to be good reasons for preventing people from acting as they wish. A growing number of people want to be, or hire, surrogates; are there legitimate reasons to prevent them? Apart from its intrinsic interest, the issue of surrogate motherhood provides us with an opportunity to examine different justifications for limiting individual freedom.

In the first section, I examine the Baby M case, and the lessons it offers. In the second section, I examine claims that surrogacy is ethically unacceptable because exploitive, inconsistent with human dignity, or harmful to the children born of such arrangements. I conclude that these reasons justify restrictions on surrogate contracts, rather than an outright ban.

I. BABY M

Mary Beth Whitehead, a married mother of two, agreed to be inseminated with the sperm of William Stern, and to give up the child to him for a fee of $10,000. The baby (whom Mrs. Whitehead named Sara, and the Sterns named Melissa) was born on March 27, 1986. Three days later, Mrs. Whitehead took her home from the hospital, and turned her over to the Sterns.

Then Mrs. Whitehead changed her mind. She went to the Sterns' home, distraught, and pleaded to have the baby temporarily. Afraid that she would kill herself, the Sterns agreed. The next week, Mrs. Whitehead informed the Sterns that she had decided to keep the child, and threatened to leave the country if court action was taken.

At that point, the situation deteriorated into a cross between the Keystone Kops and Nazi storm troopers. Accompanied by five policemen, the Sterns went to the Whitehead residence armed with a court order giving them temporary custody of the child. Mrs. Whitehead managed to slip the baby out of a window to her husband, and the following morning the Whiteheads fled with the child to Florida, where Mrs. Whitehead's parents lived. During the next three months, the Whiteheads lived in roughly twenty different hotels, motels, and homes to avoid apprehension. From time to time, Mrs. Whitehead telephoned Mr. Stern to discuss the matter: He taped these conversations on the advice of his counsel. Mrs. Whitehead

"Surrogate Motherhood as Prenatal Adoption," by Bonnie Steinbock, *Law, Medicine & Health Care* 16, no. 1 (Spring/Summer 1988): 44–50. Reprinted with the permission of the American Society of Law, Medicine & Ethics.

threatened to kill herself, to kill the child, and falsely to accuse Mr. Stern of sexually molesting her older daughter.

At the end of July 1986, while Mrs. Whitehead was hospitalized with a kidney infection, Florida police raided her mother's home, knocking her down, and seized the child. Baby M was placed in the custody of Mr. Stern, and the Whiteheads returned to New Jersey, where they attempted to regain custody. After a long and emotional court battle, Judge Harvey R. Sorkow ruled on March 31, 1987, that the surrogacy contract was valid, and that specific performance was justified in the best interests of the child. Immediately after reading his decision, he called the Sterns into his chambers so that Mr. Stern's wife, Dr. Elizabeth Stern, could legally adopt the child.

This outcome was unexpected and unprecedented. Most commentators had thought that a court would be unlikely to order a reluctant surrogate to give up an infant merely on the basis of a contract. Indeed, if Mrs. Whitehead had never surrendered the child to the Sterns, but had simply taken her home and kept her there, the outcome undoubtedly would have been different. It is also likely that Mrs. Whitehead's failure to obey the initial custody order angered Judge Sorkow, and affected his decision.

The decision was appealed to the New Jersey Supreme Court, which issued its decision on February 3, 1988. Writing for a unanimous court, Chief Justice Wilentz reversed the lower court's ruling that the surrogacy contract was valid. The court held that a surrogacy contract which provides money for the surrogate mother, and which includes her irrevocable agreement to surrender her child at birth, is invalid and unenforceable. Since the contract was invalid, Mrs. Whitehead did not relinquish, nor were there any other grounds for terminating, her parental rights. Therefore, the adoption of Baby M by Mrs. Stern was improperly granted, and Mrs. Whitehead remains the child's legal mother.

The Court further held that the issue of custody is determined solely by the child's best interests, and it agreed with the lower court that it was in Melissa's best interests to remain with the Sterns. However, Mrs. Whitehead, as Baby M's legal as well as natural mother, is entitled to have her own interest in visitation considered. The determination of what kind of visitation rights should be granted to her, and under what conditions, was remanded to the trial court.

The distressing details of this case have led many people to reject surrogacy altogether. Do we really want police officers wrenching infants from their mothers' arms, and prolonged custody battles when surrogates find they are unable to surrender their children, as agreed? Advocates of surrogacy say that to reject the practice wholesale, because of one unfortunate instance, is an example of a "hard case" making bad policy. Opponents reply that it is entirely reasonable to focus on the worst potential outcomes when deciding public policy. Everyone can agree on at least one thing: This particular case seems to have been mismanaged from start to finish, and could serve as a manual of how not to arrange a surrogate birth.

First, it is now clear that Mary Beth Whitehead was not a suitable candidate for surrogate motherhood. Her ambivalence about giving up the child was recognized early on, although this information was not passed on to the Sterns.[1] Second, she had contact with the baby after birth, which is usually avoided in "successful" cases. Typically, the adoptive mother is actively involved in the pregnancy, often serving as the pregnant woman's coach in labor. At birth, the baby is given to the adoptive, not the biological, mother. The joy of the adoptive parents in holding their child serves both to promote their bonding, and to lessen the pain of separation of the biological mother.

At Mrs. Whitehead's request, no one at the hospital was aware of the surrogacy arrangement. She and her husband appeared as the proud parents of "Sara Elizabeth Whitehead," the name on her birth certificate. Mrs. Whitehead held her baby, nursed her, and took her home from the hospital—just as she would have done in a normal pregnancy and birth. Not surprisingly, she thought of Sara as her child, and she fought with every weapon at her disposal, honorable and dishonorable, to prevent her being taken away. She can hardly be blamed for doing so.[2]

Why did Dr. Stern, who supposedly had a very good relationship with Mrs. Whitehead before the birth, not act as her labor coach? One possibility is that Mrs. Whitehead, ambivalent about giving up her baby, did not want Dr. Stern involved. At her request, the Sterns' visits to the hospital to see the newborn baby were unobtrusive. It is also possible that Dr. Stern was ambivalent about having a child. The original idea of hiring a surrogate was not hers, but her husband's. It was Mr. Stern who felt a "compelling" need to have a child related to him by blood, having lost all his relatives to the Nazis.

Furthermore, Dr. Stern was not infertile, as was stated in the surrogacy agreement. Rather, in 1979 she was diagnosed by two eye specialists as suffering from optic neuritis, which meant that she "probably" had multiple sclerosis. (This was confirmed by all four experts who testified.) Normal conception was ruled out by the Sterns in late 1982, when a medical colleague told Dr. Stern that his wife, a victim of multiple sclerosis, had suffered a temporary paralysis during pregnancy. "We decided the risk wasn't worth it," Mr. Stern said.[3]

Mrs. Whitehead's lawyer, Harold J. Cassidy, dismissed the suggestion that Dr. Stern's "mildest case" of multiple sclerosis determined their decision to seek a surrogate. He noted that she was not even treated for multiple sclerosis until after the Baby M dispute had started. "It's almost as though it's an afterthought," he said.[4]

Judge Sorkow deemed the decision to avoid conception "medically reasonable and understandable." The Supreme Court did not go so far, noting that "her anxiety appears to have exceeded the actual risk, which current medical authorities assess as minimal."[5] Nonetheless the court acknowledged that her anxiety, including fears that pregnancy might precipitate blindness and paraplegia, was "quite real." Certainly, even a woman who wants a child very much may reasonably wish to avoid becoming blind and paralyzed as a result of pregnancy. Yet is it believable that a woman who really wanted a child would decide against pregnancy *solely* on the basis of *someone else's* medical experience? Would she not consult at least one specialist on her *own* medical condition before deciding it wasn't worth the risk? The conclusion that she was at best ambivalent about bearing a child seems irresistible.

This possibility conjures up many people's worst fears about surrogacy: That prosperous women, who do not want to interrupt their careers, will use poor and educationally disadvantaged women to bear their children. I will return shortly to the question of whether this is exploitive. The issue here is psychological: What kind of mother is Dr. Stern likely to be? If she is unwilling to undergo pregnancy, with its discomforts, inconveniences, and risks, will she be willing to make the considerable sacrifices which good parenting requires? Mrs. Whitehead's ability to be a good mother was repeatedly questioned during the trial. She was portrayed as immature, untruthful, hysterical, overly identified with her children, and prone to smothering their independence. Even if all this description is true—and I think that Mrs. Whitehead's inadequacies were exaggerated—Dr. Stern may not be such a prize either. The choice for Baby M may have been between a highly strung, emotional, over-involved mother, and a remote, detached, even cold one.

The assessment of Mrs. Whitehead's ability to be a good mother was biased by the middle-class prejudices of the judge and the mental health officials who testified. Mrs. Whitehead left school at 15, and is not conversant with the latest theories on child rearing: She made the egregious error of giving Sara teddy bears to play with, instead of the more "age-appropriate," expert-approved pans and spoons. She proved to be a total failure at patty-cake. If this is evidence of parental inadequacy, we're all in danger of losing our children.

The Supreme Court felt that Mrs. Whitehead was "rather harshly judged" and acknowledged the possibility that the trial court was wrong in its initial award of custody. Nevertheless, it affirmed Judge Sorkow's decision to allow the Sterns to retain custody, as being in Melissa's best interests. George Annas disagrees with the "best interests" approach. He points out that Judge Sorkow awarded temporary custody of Baby M to the Sterns in May 1986 without giving the Whiteheads notice or an opportunity to obtain legal representation. That was a serious wrong and injustice to the Whiteheads. To allow the Sterns to keep the child compounds the original unfairness: ". . . justice requires that reasonable consideration be given to returning Baby M to the permanent custody of the Whiteheads."[6]

But a child is not a possession, to be returned to the rightful owner. It is not fairness to all parties that should determine a child's fate, but what is best for her. As Chief Justice Wilentz rightly stated, "The child's interests come first: We will not punish it for judicial errors, assuming any were made."[7]

Subsequent events have substantiated the claim that giving custody to the Sterns was in Melissa's best interests. After losing custody of Melissa, Mrs. Whitehead, whose husband had undergone a vasectomy, became pregnant by another man. She divorced her husband and married Dean R. Gould last November. These developments indicate that the Whiteheads were not able to offer a stable home, although the argument can be made that their marriage might have survived, but for the strains introduced by the court battle, and the loss of Baby M. But even if Judge Sorkow had no reason to prefer the Sterns to the Whiteheads back in May 1986, he was still right to give the Sterns custody in March 1987. To take her away then, at nearly eighteen months of age, from the only parents she had ever known, would have been disruptive, cruel, and unfair to her.

Annas's preference for a just solution is premised partly on his belief that there *is* no "best interest" solution to this "tragic custody case." I take it that he means that however custody is resolved, Baby M is the loser. Either way, she will be deprived of one parent. However, a best interests solution is not a perfect solution. It is simply the solution which is on balance best for the child, given the realities of the situation. Applying this standard, Judge Sorkow was right to give the Sterns custody, and the Supreme Court was right to uphold the decision.

The best interests argument is based on the assumption that Mr. Stern has at least a *prima facie* claim to Baby M. We certainly would not consider allowing a stranger who kidnapped a baby, and managed to elude the police for a year, to retain custody on the grounds that he was providing a good home to a child who had known no other parent. However, the Baby M case is not analogous. First, Mr. Stern is Baby M's biological father and, as such, has at least some claim to raise her, which no non-parental kidnapper has. Second, Mary Beth Whitehead agreed to give him their baby at birth. Unlike the miller's daughter in *Rumpelstiltskin,* the fairy tale to which the Baby M case is sometimes compared, she was not forced into this agreement. Because both Mary Beth Whitehead and Mr. Stern have *prima facie* claims to Baby M, the decision as to who should raise her should be based on her present best interests. Therefore we must, regretfully, tolerate the injustice to Mrs. Whitehead, and try to avoid such problems in the future.

It is unfortunate that the Court did not decide the issue of visitation on the same basis as custody. By declaring Mrs. Whitehead Gould the legal mother, and maintaining that she is entitled to visitation, the Court has prolonged the fight over Baby M. It is hard to see how this can be in her best interests. This is no ordinary divorce case, where the child has a relation with both parents which is desirable to maintain. As Mr. Stern said at the start of the court hearing to determine visitation, "Melissa has a right to grow and be happy and not be torn between two parents."[8]

The court's decision was well-meaning but internally inconsistent. Out of concern for the best interests of the child, it granted the Sterns custody. At the same time, by holding Mrs. Whitehead Gould to be the legal mother, with visitation rights, it precluded precisely what is most in Melissa's interest, a resolution of the situation. Further, the decision leaves open the distressing possibility that a Baby M situation could happen again. Legislative efforts should be directed toward ensuring that this worst-case scenario never occurs.

II. SHOULD SURROGACY BE PROHIBITED?

On June 27, 1988, Michigan became the first state to outlaw commercial contracts for women to bear children for others. Yet making a practice illegal does not necessarily make it go away: Witness black market adoption. The legitimate concerns which support a ban on surrogacy might be better served by careful regulation. However, some practices, such as slavery, are ethically unacceptable, regardless of how carefully regulated they are. Let us consider the arguments that surrogacy is intrinsically unacceptable.

A. Paternalistic Arguments

These arguments against surrogacy take the form of protecting a potential surrogate from a choice she may later regret. As an argument for banning surrogacy, as opposed to providing safeguards to ensure that contracts are freely and knowledgeably undertaken, this is a form of paternalism.

At one time, the characterization of a prohibition as paternalistic was a sufficient reason to reject it. The pendulum has swung back, and many people are willing to accept at least some paternalistic restrictions on freedom. Gerald Dworkin points out that even Mill made one exception to his otherwise absolute rejection of paternalism: He thought that no one should be allowed to sell himself into slavery, because to do so would be to destroy his future autonomy.

This provides a narrow principle to justify some paternalistic interventions. To preserve freedom in the long run, we give up the freedom to make certain choices, those which have results which are "far-reaching, potentially dangerous and irreversible."[9] An example would be a ban on the sale of crack. Virtually everyone who uses crack becomes addicted and, once addicted, a slave to its use. We reasonably and willingly give up our freedom to buy the drug, to protect our ability to make free decisions in the future.

Can a Dworkinian argument be made to rule out surrogacy agreements? Admittedly, the decision to give up a child is permanent, and may have disastrous effects on the surrogate mother. However, many decisions may have long-term, disastrous effects (e.g., postponing childbirth for a career, having an abortion, giving a child up for adoption). Clearly we do not want the state to make decisions for us in all these matters. Dworkin's argument is rightly restricted to paternalistic interferences which protect the individual's autonomy or ability to make decisions in the future. Surrogacy does not involve giving up one's autonomy, which distinguishes it from both the crack and selling-oneself-into-slavery examples. Respect for individual freedom requires us to permit people to make choices which they may later regret.

B. Moral Objections

Four main moral objections to surrogacy were outlined in the Warnock Report.[10]

1. It is inconsistent with human dignity that a woman should use her uterus for financial profit.
2. To deliberately become pregnant with the intention of giving up the child distorts the relationship between mother and child.
3. Surrogacy is degrading because it amounts to child-selling.
4. Since there are some risks attached to pregnancy, no woman ought to be asked to undertake pregnancy for another in order to earn money.

We must all agree that a practice which exploits people or violates human dignity is immoral. However, it is not clear that surrogacy is guilty on either count.

1. Exploitation The mere fact that pregnancy is *risky* does not make surrogate agreements exploitive, and therefore morally wrong. People often do risky things for money; why should the line be drawn at undergoing pregnancy? The usual response is to compare surrogacy and kidney-selling. The selling of organs is prohibited because of the potential for coercion and exploitation. But why should kidney-selling be viewed as intrinsically coercive? A possible explanation is that no one would do it, unless driven by poverty. The choice is both forced and dangerous, and hence coercive.

The situation is quite different in the case of the race car driver or stunt performer. We do not think that they are *forced* to perform risky activities for money: They freely choose to do so. Unlike selling one's kidneys, these are activities which we can understand (intellectually, anyway) someone choosing to do. Movie stuntmen and women, for example, often enjoy their work, and derive satisfaction from doing it well. Of course they "do it for the money," in the sense that they would not do it without compensation; few people are willing to work "for free." The element of coercion is missing, however, because they enjoy the job, despite the risks, and could do something else if they chose.

The same is apparently true of most surrogates. "They choose the surrogate role primarily because the fee provides a better economic opportunity than alternative occupations, but also because they enjoy being pregnant and the respect and attention that it draws."[11] Some may derive a feeling of self-worth from an act they regard as highly altruistic: providing a couple with a child they could not otherwise have. If these motives are present, it is far from clear that the surrogate is being exploited. Indeed, it seems objectionably paternalistic to insist that she is.

2. Human Dignity It may be argued that even if womb-leasing is not necessarily exploitive, it should still be rejected as inconsistent with human dignity. But why? As John Harris points out, hair, blood, and other tissue is often donated or sold; what is so special about the uterus?[12]

Human dignity is more plausibly invoked in the strongest argument against surrogacy, namely, that it is the sale of a child. Children are not property, nor can they be bought or sold. It could be argued that surrogacy is wrong because it is analogous to slavery, and so is inconsistent with human dignity.

However, there are clearly important differences between slavery and a surrogate agreement. The child born of a surrogate is not treated cruelly or deprived of freedom or resold; none of the things which make slavery so awful are part of surrogacy. Still, it may be thought that simply putting a market value on a child is wrong. Human life has its own intrinsic value; it is literally priceless. Arrangements which ignore this belief violate our deepest notions of the value of human life. It is profoundly disturbing to hear the boyfriend of a surrogate say, quite candidly in a television documentary on surrogacy, "We're in it for the money."

Judge Sorkow accepted the premise that producing a child for money denigrates human dignity, but he denied that this happens in a surrogate agreement. Mrs. Whitehead was not paid for the surrender of the child to the father: She was paid for her willingness to be impregnated and carry Mr. Stern's child to term. The child, once born, is his biological child. "He cannot purchase what is already his."

This is misleading, and not merely because Baby M is as much Mrs. Whitehead's child as Mr. Stern's. It is misleading because it glosses over the fact that the surrender of the child was part—indeed, the whole point—of the agreement. If the surrogate were paid merely for being willing to be impregnated and carrying the child to term, then she would fulfill the contract upon giving birth. She could take the money *and* the child. Mr. Stern did not agree to pay Mrs. Whitehead merely to *have* his child, but to provide him with a child. The New Jersey Supreme Court held that this violated New Jersey's laws prohibiting the payment or acceptance of money in connection with adoption.

One way to remove the taint of baby-selling would be to limit payment to medical expenses associated with the birth or incurred by the surrogate during pregnancy (as is allowed in many jurisdictions, including New Jersey, in ordinary adoptions). Surrogacy could be seen not as baby-selling, but as a form of adoption. Nowhere did the Supreme Court find any legal prohibition against surrogacy when there is no payment, and when the surrogate has the right to change her mind and keep the child. However, this solution effectively prohibits surrogacy, since few women would become surrogates solely for self-fulfillment or reasons of altruism.

The question, then, is whether we can reconcile paying the surrogate, beyond her medical expenses, with the idea of surrogacy as prenatal adoption. We can do this by separating the terms of the agreement, which include surrendering the infant at birth to the biological father, from the justification for payment. The payment should be seen as compensation for the risks, sacrifice, and discomfort the surrogate undergoes during pregnancy. This means that if, through no fault on the part of the surrogate, the baby is stillborn, she should still be paid in full, since she has kept her part of the bargain. (By contrast, in the Stern-Whitehead agreement, Mrs. Whitehead was to receive only $1,000 for a stillbirth.) If, on the other hand, the surrogate changes her mind and decides to keep the child, she would break the agreement, and would not be entitled to any fee, or compensation for expenses incurred during pregnancy.

C. The Right of Privacy

Most commentators who invoke the right of privacy do so in support of surrogacy. However, George Annas makes the novel argument that the right to rear a child you have borne is also a privacy right, which cannot be prospectively waived. He says:

> [Judge Sorkow] grudgingly concedes that [Mrs. Whitehead] could not prospectively give up her right to have an abortion during pregnancy. . . . This would be an intolerable restriction on her liberty and under *Roe v. Wade*, the state has no constitutional authority to enforce a contract that prohibits her from terminating her pregnancy.
>
> But why isn't the same logic applicable to the right to rear a child you have given birth to? Her constitutional rights to rear the child she has given birth to are even stronger since they involve even more intimately, and over a lifetime, her privacy rights to reproduce and rear a child in a family setting.[13]

Absent a compelling state interest (such as protecting a child from unfit parents), it certainly would be an intolerable invasion of privacy for the state to take children from their parents. But Baby M has two parents, both of whom now want her. It is not clear why only people who can give birth (i.e., women) should enjoy the right to rear their children.

Moreover, we do allow women to give their children up for adoption after birth. The state enforces those agreements, even if the natural mother, after the prescribed waiting period, changes her mind. Why should the right to rear a child be unwaivable before, but not after, birth? Why should the state have the constitutional authority to uphold postnatal, but not prenatal, adoption agreements? It is not clear why birth should affect the waivability of this right, of have the constitutional significance which Annas attributes to it.

Nevertheless, there are sound moral and policy, if not constitutional, reasons to provide a postnatal waiting period in surrogate agreements. As the Baby M case makes painfully clear, the surrogate may underestimate the bond created by gestation, and the emotional trauma caused by relinquishing the baby. Compassion requires that we acknowledge these feelings, and not deprive a woman of the baby she has carried because, before conception, she underestimated the strength of her feelings for it. Providing a waiting period, as in ordinary postnatal adoptions, will help protect women from making irrevocable mistakes, without banning the practice.

Some may object that this gives too little protection to the prospective adoptive parents. They cannot be sure that the baby is theirs until the waiting period is over. While this is hard on them, a similar burden is placed on other adoptive parents. If the absence of a guarantee serves to discourage people from entering surrogacy agreements, that is not necessarily a bad thing, given all the risks inherent in such contracts. In addition, this requirement would make stricter screening and counseling of surrogates essential, a desirable side effect.

D. Harm to Others

Paternalistic and moral objections to surrogacy do not seem to justify an outright ban.

What about the effect on the offspring of such contracts? We do not yet have solid data on the effects of being a "surrogate child." Any claim that surrogacy creates psychological problems in the children is purely speculative. But what if we did discover that such children have deep feelings of worthlessness from learning that their natural mothers deliberately created them with the intention of giving them away? Might we ban surrogacy as posing an unacceptable risk of psychological harm to the resulting children?

Feelings of worthlessness are harmful. They can prevent people from living happy, fulfilling lives. However, a surrogate child, even one whose life is miserable because of these feelings, cannot claim to have been harmed by the surrogate agreement. Without the agreement, the child would never have existed. Unless she is willing to say that her life is not worth living because of these feelings, that she would be better-off never having been born, she cannot claim to have been harmed by being born of a surrogate mother.

Children can be *wronged* by being brought into existence, even if they are not, strictly speaking, *harmed*. They are wronged if they are deprived of the minimally decent existence to which all citizens are entitled. We owe it to our children to see that they are not born with such serious impairments that their most basic interests will be doomed in advance. If being born to a surrogate is a handicap of this magnitude, comparable to being born blind or deaf or severely mentally retarded, then surrogacy can be seen as wronging the offspring. This would be a strong reason against permitting such contracts. However, it does not seem likely. Probably the problems arising from surrogacy will be like those faced by adopted children and children whose parents divorce. Such problems are not trivial, but neither are they so serious that the child's very existence can be seen as wrongful.

If surrogate children are neither harmed nor wronged by surrogacy, it may seem that the argument for banning surrogacy on grounds of its harmfulness to the offspring evaporates. After all, if the children themselves have no cause for complaint, how can anyone else claim to reject it on their behalf? Yet it seems extremely counterintuitive to suggest that the risk of emotional damage to the children born of such arrangements is not even relevant to our deliberations. It seems quite reasonable and proper—even morally obligatory—for policymakers to think about the possible detrimental effects of new reproductive technologies, and to reject those likely to create physically or emotionally damaged people. The explanation for this must involve the idea that it is wrong to bring people into the world in a harmful condition, even if they are not, strictly speaking, harmed by having been brought into existence. Should evidence emerge that surrogacy produces children with serious psychological problems, that would be a strong reason for banning the practice.

There is some evidence on the effect of surrogacy on the other children of the surrogate mother. One woman reported that her daughter, now 17, who was 11 at the time of the surrogate birth, "is still having problems with what I did, and as a result she is still angry with me." She explains, "Nobody told me that a child could bond with a baby while you're still pregnant. I didn't realize then that all the times she listened to his heartbeat and felt his legs kick that she was becoming attached to him."[14]

A less sentimental explanation is possible. It seems likely that her daughter, seeing one child given away, was fearful that the same might be done to her. We can expect anxiety and resentment on the part of children whose mothers give away a brother or sister. The psychological harm to these children is clearly relevant to a determination of whether surrogacy is contrary to public policy. At the same time, it should be remembered that many things, including divorce, remarriage, and even moving to a new neighborhood, create anxiety and resentment in children. We should not use the effect on children as an excuse for banning a practice we find bizarre or offensive.

Conclusion

There are many reasons to be extremely cautious of surrogacy. I cannot imagine becoming a surrogate, nor would I advise anyone else to enter into a contract so fraught with peril. But the fact that a practice is risky, foolish, or even morally distasteful is not sufficient reason to outlaw it. It would be better for the state to regulate the practice, and minimize the potential for harm, without infringing on the liberty of citizens.

Notes

1. Had the Sterns been informed of the psychologist's concerns as to Mrs. Whitehead's suitability to be a surrogate, they might have ended the arrangement, costing the Infertility Center its fee. As Chief Justice Wilentz said, "It is apparent that the profit motive got the better of the Infertility Center." In the matter of Baby M, Supreme Court of New Jersey, A-39, at 45.

2. "[We] think it is expecting something well beyond normal human capabilities to suggest that this mother should have parted with her newly born infant without a struggle. . . . We . . . cannot conceive of any other case where a perfectly fit mother was expected to surrender her newly born infant, perhaps forever, and was then told she was a bad mother because she did not." *Id at* 79.

3. Father recalls surrogate was "perfect." *New York Times*, January 6,1987, B2.

4. *Id.*

5. In the matter of Baby M, *supra* note 1, at 8.

6. Annas GJ: Baby M: babies (and justice) for sale. *Hastings Center Report* 17 (3): 15, June 1987.

7. In the matter of Baby M, *supra* note 1, at 75.

8. Anger and anguish at Baby M visitation hearing. *New York Times,* March 29, 1988, 17.

9. Dworkin G: Paternalism. In Wasserstrom RA, ed., *Morality and the Law.* Belmont, Cal: Wadsworth, 1971; reprinted in Feinberg J, Gross H, eds., *Philosophy of Law,* 3rd ed. Wadsworth, 1986, p. 265.

10. Warnock M, chair: *Report of the committee of inquiry into human fertilisation and embryology.* London: Her Majesty's Stationery Office, 1984.

11. Robertson, JA: Surrogate mothers: not so novel after all. *Report* 13 (5): 29, 1983. Citing Parker P: Surrogate mother's motivations: initial findings. *American Journal of Psychiatry* (140): 1, 1983.

12. Harris J: *The Value of Life.* London: Routledge & Kegan Paul, 1985, p. 144.

13. Annas, *supra* note 6.

14. Baby M case stirs feelings of surrogate mothers. *New York Times,* March 2,1987, B1.

The Facts of Fatherhood

Thomas W. Laqueur

Laqueur explores parenthood through the eyes of a father. Arguing that we lack a "history of fatherhood," Laqueur examines what it means to be a father through various stories about people and their biological and cultural assumptions about fatherhood. What do you think it means to be a father? How does your view of fatherhood compare to your view of motherhood?

This essay puts forward a labor theory of parenthood in which emotional work counts. I want to say at the onset, however, that it is not intended as a nuanced, balanced academic account of fatherhood or its vicissitudes. I write it in a glum, polemical mood.

In the first place I am annoyed that we lack a history of fatherhood, a silence which I regard as a sign of a more systemic pathology in our understanding of what being a man and being a father entail. There has unfortunately been no movement comparable to modern feminism to spur the study of men. Or conversely, history has been written almost exclusively as the history of men and therefore man-as-father has been subsumed under the history of a pervasive patriarchy—the history of inheritance and legitimate descent, the history of public authority and its transmission over generations. Fatherhood, insofar as it has been thought about at all, has been regarded as a backwater of the dominant history of public power. The sources, of course, support this view. Fathers before the eighteenth century appear in prescriptive texts about the family largely in their public roles, as heads of families or clans, as governors of the "little commonwealth," of the state within the state.

The rule of the patriarchy waned, but historians have not studied the cultural consequences for fathers of its recession. Instead, they have largely adopted the perspective of nineteenth-century ideologues: men belong to the public sphere of the marketplace and women to the private sphere of the family. A vast prescriptive literature explains how to be a good mother: essentially how to exercise proper moral influence and display appropriate affections in the home, duties that in earlier centuries would have fallen to the father. But there is little in the era of "separate spheres" on how to be the new public man in private. A rich and poignant source material on the affective relationship between fathers and children in the nineteenth century—Gladstone's account of watching for days by the bedside of his dying daughter, for example—speaks to the power of emotional bonds, but historians have largely ignored it. They have instead taken some Victorians at their word and written the father out of the family except as a parody of the domestic autocrat or as the representative of all those forces which stood in the way of the equality of the sexes.

Second, I write in the wake of Baby M and am annoyed with the neo-essentialism it has spawned. Baby M was the case of the decade in my circles, a "representative anecdote" for ancient but ageless questions in the late twentieth century. Like most people, I saw some right on both sides and had little sympathy for the marketplace in babies that brought them together. On the one hand Mary Beth Whitehead this . . .; on the other William Stern that. . . . The baby broker who arranged the deal was manifestly an unsavory character, the twentieth-century avatar of the sweatshop owners who in ages past profited unconscionably from the flesh of women. It was difficult not to subscribe to the doctrine that the baby's best interests must come first and it was by no means consistently clear where these lay. Each day brought new emotional tugs as the narrative unfolded on the front pages of every paper.

I was surprised that, for so many people, this transaction between a working-class woman and a professional man (a biochemist) became an epic prism through which the evils of capitalism and class society were refracted. It did not seem newsworthy to me that the poor sold their bodies or that the rich exploited their willingness to do so. What else would they sell? Malthus had pointed out almost two centuries ago that those who labored physically gave of their flesh and in the long run earned just enough to maintain and replenish it. So had

Marx, who also identified women as the agents of social re-production.

Admittedly, the contract entered into by Whitehead and Stern was stripped of all shreds of decency and aesthetic mystification, flatfootedly revealing the deal for what it was—not a womb rental but a baby sale. This is why the New Jersey Supreme Court ruled it unenforceable. Every account that one reads of the surrogate baby broker's operations, with its well-dressed couples sitting in little cubicles interviewing long lines of less well-dressed but hopeful, spiffed-up women seeking work as surrogates, conjures up distasteful reminders of depression labor exchanges, starlet casting couches, or academic hiring fairs. But there surely are no new horrors in this case. Basically the Baby M narratives are modern versions of the industrial novel and allied genres in which factory labor is portrayed as wage slavery; in which children's tiny thin fingers are metamorphosed into the pin wire they hour after hour produce; in which paupers, whose labor is worthless on the open market, are depicted pounding bones into meal so that they might remain just this side of starvation. In short, I remain cynical when some commentators discover Mary Beth Whitehead as the anti-capitalist Everywoman. If "surrogate" mothers were as well organized as the doctors who perform the much more expensive *in vitro* fertilization or as unionized baseball players they would earn a decent wage—say $100,000 instead of the ludicrously low $10,000—and opposition to surrogacy as emblematic of the evils of a free market in labor might be considered muted. (Though of course then the story might shift to emphasize the power of money to dissolve the very fabric of social decency, another nineteenth-century trope.)

I am, however, primarily interested in this case as the occasion for a return to naturalism. Feminism has been the most powerful de-naturalizing theoretical force in my intellectual firmament and, more generally, a major influence in the academic and cultural affairs that concern me. I regard it as both true and liberating that "the idea that men and women are two mutually exclusive categories must arise out of something other than a nonexistent 'natural' opposition," and that "gender is a socially imposed division of the sexes." A major strand of commentary on Baby M, however, rejects this tradition and instead insists that the category "mother" is natural, a given of the world outside culture. Phyllis Chesler, for example, in the major article of a special "Mothers" issue of *Ms.* (May, 1988) argues that motherhood is a "fact," an ontologically different category than "fatherhood," which is an "idea." Thus, "in order for the *idea* [my emphasis] of fatherhood to triumph over the *fact* of motherhood," she says, "we had to see Bill as the 'birth father' and Mary Beth as the 'surrogate uterus.' " (Actually Chesler misstates the claims. Mary Beth has been, rightly or wrongly, called the "surrogate mother," not the "surrogate uterus." But since the point of the article seems to be that mother and uterus are more or less the same thing this may be an intentional prevarication.)

I resist this view for obvious emotional reasons: it assumes that being the "factual" parent entails a stronger connection to the child than being the "ideational" parent. (This assumption is widespread. During my daughter Hannah's five-week stay in the preemie nursery her caretakers, in the "social comments" column of her chart, routinely recorded my wife's visits to her incubator as "mother in to bond," whereas my appearances were usually noted with the affectively neutral "father visited.") While I do not want to argue against the primacy of material connection directly I do want to point out that it is not irrational to hold the opposite view and that, "in fact," the incorporeal quality of fatherhood has been the foundation of patriarchy's ideological edifice since the Greeks. In other words, simply stating that mothers have a greater material connection with the child is not to make an argument but to state a premise which historically has worked against Chesler's would-be conclusion. The Western philosophical tradition has generally valued idea over matter; manual labor for millennia was the great horizontal social divide. In other words, precisely because the mother's claim was "only" corporeal, because it was a matter of "fact," it was valued less.

I will recount some of the history of this discourse, but I also want to argue against its basic operating assumption: the unproblematic nature of fact especially in relation to such deeply cultural designations as mother or father and to the rights, emotions, or duties that are associated with them. The "facts" of motherhood—and of fatherhood for that matter—are not "given" but come into being as science progresses and as the adversaries in political struggles select what they need from the vast, ever-growing storehouses of knowledge. The idea that a child is of one's flesh and blood is very old while its biological correlatives and their cultural importance depend on the available supplies of fact and on their interpretation.

But the reason that the facts of motherhood and fatherhood are not "given" has less to do with what is known or not known than with the fundamental gap, recognized by David Hume, between facts and their meaning. *Is* does not imply *ought*, and more generally no fact or set of facts taken together entails or excludes a moral right or commitment. Laws, customs, and precepts, sentiments, emotion, and the power of the imagination make biological facts assume cultural significance. An Algonquin chief, confronted by a Jesuit in the seventeenth century with the standard European argument against women's promiscuity (how else would you know that a child is yours?), replied that he found it puzzling that whites could apparently only love "their" children, i.e., that only individual ownership entailed caring and affection.

Before proceeding I want to again warn my readers that some of my evidence and most of my passion arise from personal circumstance. I write as the father of a daughter to whom I am bound by the "facts" of a visceral love, not the molecular biology of reproduction. The fact of the matter is that from the instant the five-minute-old Hannah—a premature baby of 1430 grams who was born by Caesarean section—grasped my finger (I know this was due to reflex and not affection) I felt immensely powerful, and before the event, inconceivably strong bonds with her. Perhaps if practitioners of the various sub-specialties of endocrinology had been present they might have measured surges of neuro-transmitters and other hormones as strong as those that accompany parturition. But then what difference would that make—with what is one to feel if not with the body?

I also write as the would-be father, some sixteen months before Hannah came along, of a boy weighing something less than 800 grams who was aborted late one night—an induced stillbirth really—after twenty-four weeks of gestation because of a burst amniotic sac and the ensuing infection. I can recapture my sadness at his demise vividly and still regard the whole episode as one of the gloomiest of my life. Gail, my wife, was ambivalent about having the child—she was, she says, unprepared at age 40 for becoming pregnant the very first month at risk—and regards the abortion as a painful but not especially fraught episode which cleared the emotional ground to allow her to welcome Hannah's birth unequivocally.

Finally I write as the male member of a family in which gender roles are topsy turvy: Hannah early on announced that she would prefer being a daddy to being a mommy because mommies had to go to work— hers is a lawyer—while daddies only had to go to their study. (As she has grown older and observed my not silent suffering as I finished a book begun the year she was born her views have been somewhat revised.) I am far guiltier of the stereotypical vices of motherhood—neurotic worry about Hannah's physical and mental well being, unfounded premonitions of danger, excessive emotional demands, and general nudginess—than is Gail. In short, my experiences—ignoring for the moment a vast ethnographic and somewhat smaller historical literature make me suspect of the naturalness of "mother" or "father" in any culturally meaningful sense.

The association of fatherhood with ideas and motherhood with facts is ancient; only its moral valences have been recently reversed by some feminists. The Marquis de Sade suggests that the "idea" of fatherhood—the notion that a child is "born of the father's blood" and only incidentally of a mother's body—means that it "owes filial tenderness to him alone, an assertion not without its appealing qualities. . . ." Sade is the most rabid of anti-maternalists and his argument is made to induce a girl to sexually defile and humiliate her mother; but his relative valuation of fact and idea is standard. The "idea" of fatherhood gave, and displayed, the power of patriarchy for much of Western history since the Greeks.

Bolingbrooke in *Richard II* (1, 3, 69) addresses his father as

> Oh thou, the earthly author of my blood,
> Whose youthful spirit, in me regenerate.

He is author and authority because, like the poet who has in his mind the design for the verses that subsequently appear, he has the conceit for the child in him. The physical act of writing, or of producing the child, matters little. Conceiving a child in this model is a man's sparking of an idea in the uterus which contains, like a block of marble, a form waiting to be liberated. It is like writing on a piece of paper awaiting inscription. The "generation of things in Nature and the generation of things in Art take place in the same way," argued the great seventeenth-century physician William Harvey, who discovered circulation of the blood. "Now the brain is the instrument of conception of the one . . . and of the other the uterus or egg." And being the instrument is less elevated than being the author: "He," speaking of God, "was the author, thou the instrument," says King Henry in offering pardon to Warwick (*3 Henry VI*, 4, 6,18).

But the idea of "father" as bound to his child in the way a poet is to verse, i.e., its genitor, is much older than Shakespeare. It is, argues Freud, one of the cornerstones of culture; believing in fathers, like believing in the Hebrew God, reflects the power of abstract thought and hence of civilization itself.

The "Moses religion's" insistence that God cannot be seen—the graven image proscription—"means that a sensory perception was given second place to what may be called an abstract idea." This God represents "a triumph of intellectuality over sensuality [*Triumph der Geistigkeit uber de Sinnlichkeit*], or strictly speaking, an instinctual renunciation . . ." Freud briefs precisely the same case for fathers as for God in his analysis of Aeschylus' *Eumenides,* which follows immediately his discussion of the Second Commandment. Orestes denies that he has killed his mother by denying that being born of her entails special bonds or obligation. Apollo makes the defense's case: appearances notwithstanding, no man has a mother. "The mother is no parent of that which is called her child, but only nurse of the new-planted seed that grows." She is but "a stranger." The only true parent is "he who mounts."

Here is the founding myth of the Father. "Paternity" [*Vaterschaft*], Freud concludes, "is a supposition" and like belief in the Jewish God it is "based on an inference, a premise," while "maternity" [*Mutterschaft*], like the old gods, is based on evidence of the senses alone. The invention of paternity, like that of a transcendent God, was thus also "a momentous step"; it likewise—Freud repeats the phrase but with a more decisive military emphasis—was "a conquest [*einen Sieg*] of intellectuality over sensuality." It too represented a victory of the more elevated, the more refined, the more spiritual over the less refined, the sensory, the material. It too is a world-historical *"Kulturfortschritt,"* a great cultural stride forward.

Similarly, the great medieval encyclopedist Isidore of Seville could, without embarrassment, make three different claims about the nature of seed—that only men had *sperma*, that only women had *sperma*, and that both had *sperma*—which would be mutually contradictory if they were about the body but perfectly compatible if they were instead corporeal illustrations of cultural truths purer and more fundamental than biological "fact." Isidore's entire work is predicated on the belief that the origin of words informs one about the pristine, uncorrupted, essential nature of their referents, of a reality beyond the corrupt senses, beyond facts.

In the first case Isidore is explaining consanguinity and, as one would expect in a society in which inheritance and legitimacy pass through the father, he is at pains to emphasize the exclusive origins of the seed in the father's blood, in the purest, frothiest, white part of that blood shaken from the body as the foam is beaten from the sea as it crashes on the rocks. For a child to have a father *means* that it is "from one blood," the father's; and conversely to be a father is to produce the substance, semen, through which blood is passed on to one's successors. Generation seems to happen without woman at all and there is no hint that blood—"that by which man is animated, and is sustained, and lives," as Isidore tells us elsewhere—could in any fashion be transmitted other than through the male. Now case two, illegitimate descent. This presents a quite different biology: the child under these circumstances is from the *body* of the mother alone; it is "spurious," he explains, because "the ancients called the female genitalia the *spurium*" (9, 5, 24). So, while the legitimate child is from the froth of the father, the illegitimate child seems to come solely from factual flesh, from the seed of the mother's genitals, as if the father did not exist. And finally, when Isidore is explaining why children resemble their progenitors and is not interested in motherhood or fatherhood he remarks pragmatically that "newborns resemble fathers, if the semen of the father is potent, and resemble mothers if the mothers' semen is potent." Both parents, in this account, have seeds which engage in repeated combat for domination every time, and in each generation, a child is conceived (Isidore, 11, 1,145).

These three distinct and mutually exclusive arguments are a dramatic illustration that much of the debate about the nature of the seed and of the bodies that produce it was in fact not about bodies at all but rather about power, legitimacy, and the politics of fatherhood. They are in principle not resolvable by recourse to the senses. One might of course argue that "just so" stories like Isidore's or Aeschylus' are simply no longer tenable given what has been known since the nineteenth century about conception. Modern biology makes perfectly clear what "mother" and "father" are. But science is relevant only if these stories are understood as reductionistic, as claiming to be true because of biology which is, rightly, not the sort of claim Isidore and Aeschylus are making. The facts they adduce to illustrate essentially cultural claims may no longer be acceptable and we may persist in reading their cultural claims as based in a false biology. But the "fact" of women bearing children has never been in dispute and has nonetheless counted for relatively little historically in establishing their claims to recognition or authority over children or property.

Facts, as I suggested earlier, are but shifting sands for the construction of motherhood or fatherhood. They come and go and are ludicrously open to interpretation. Regnier de Graaf's discovery of the ovum in 1672 seemed to relegate the male/father to an unaccustomed and distinctly secondary role in reproduction. (Actually de Graaf discovered the follicle that bears his name but which he and others mistakenly took to be the egg. Karl Ernst von Baer in 1827 was the first to observe a mammalian egg and an unfertilized human egg was not seen until 1930.) The female after de Graaf could be imagined to provide the matter for the fetus in a pre-formed if not immediately recognized form while the male "only serv'd to Actuate it." This, one contemporary observed, "derogates much from the dignity of the Male-Sex," which he thought was restored when "Mons. Leeuwenhoek by the Help of his Exquisite Microscope . . . detected Innumerable small *Animals* in the Masculine sperm, and by his Noble Discovery, at once removed that Difficulty. . . ."

I hope by this egregious example to suggest that the form of the argument, and not just its factual premises, are flawed; both conclusions are silly. And, the discovery, still accepted, that neither egg nor sperm contains a pre-formed human but that the fetus develops epigenetically according to plans acquired from both parents does not settle the question of the comparative claims of mother or father, just as the mistaken notions of the past did not entail judgements of their comparative dignities.

Interpretations, not facts, are at issue. The Archbishop of Hartford announced in the *New York Times* on August 26, 1988, that he had quit the Democratic party because it supported abortion: "it is officially in favor of executing unborn babies whose only crime is that they temporarily occupy their mother's womb." No one would dispute that the "thing" in the mother's womb is, under some construction, an unborn baby. "Baby" is a common term for fetus as well as for a very young child and the phrase "the baby is kicking again" to refer to an intrauterine action is generally acceptable; baby-as-fetus is indisputably only a temporary occupant. The Archbishop's interpretation is objectionable because he elides the difference between "baby-in-the-womb" and "baby-in-the-world," between the womb and any other space an infant might occupy, and therefore between abortion and execution. At issue here is meaning, not nature.

David Hume makes manifest the chasm between the two. A beautiful fish, a wild animal, a spectacular landscape, or indeed "anything that neither belongs, nor is related to us," he says, inspires in us no pride or vanity or sense of obligation. We might with perfect reason fear a minor injury to ourselves and care almost nothing about the deaths of millions of distant strangers. The fault is not with the objects themselves but with their relationship to us. They are too detached and distant to arouse passion. Only, Hume argues, when these "external objects acquire any particular relation to ourselves, and are associated or connected with us," do they engage the emotions. Owing the "external object" seems for Hume to be the most obvious way for this to happen, although ownership itself is, of course, an immensely elastic notion. A biological parent, uncle, clan, "family" can "own" a child in such a fashion as to love and cherish it. But more generally Hume is suggesting that moral concern and action are engendered not by the logic of the relationship between human beings but by the degree to which the emotional and imaginative connections which entail love or obligation have been forged.

The "fact" of motherhood is precisely the psychic labor that goes into making these connections, into appropriating the fetus and then child into a mother's moral and emotional economy. The "fact" of fatherhood is of a like order. If a labor theory of value gives parents rights to a child, that labor is of the heart, not the hand. (The heart, of course, does its work through the hand; we feel through the body. But I will let the point stand in its polemical nakedness.)

While I was working as a volunteer in an old people's home I was attracted to, and ultimately became rather good friends with, a gay woman who was its director of activities. At lunch one day—she had alerted me that she wanted to discuss "something" and not just, as we usually did, schmooz—she asked whether I would consider donating sperm should she and her long-time lover decide, as they were on the verge of doing, to have a child. I was for her a generally appropriate donor—Jewish, fit, with no history of genetic disorders in my family. She was asking me also, she said, because she liked me. It was the first, and remains the only, time I had been asked by anyone, much less someone I liked, and so I was flattered and pleased.

I was also hesitant. My wife the lawyer raised serious legal difficulties with donating "owned" sperm, i.e., sperm that is not given or sold for anonymous distribution. I would remain legally liable for child-support for at least twenty-one years, not to speak of being generally entangled with the lives of a couple I liked but did not know well. (Anonymous sperm is alienated from its producer and loses its connection with him as if it were the jetsam and flotsam of the sea or an artisan's product in the marketplace. Semen, in other words, counts as one of these products of the body that can be alienated, like plasma and blood cells, and not like kidneys or eyes, whose marketing is forbidden.)

Legal issues, however, did not weigh heavily with me. The attractive part of the proposition—that I was being asked because of who I was and therefore that I was to be a father and not just a donor—also weighed mightily against it. A thought experiment with unpleasant results presented itself. I immediately imagined this would-be child as a version of Hannah, imagined that I could see her only occasionally and for short periods of time, imagined that her parents would take her back to their native Israel and that I would never see her again. Potential conflicts with my friend about this baby were almost palpable on the beautiful sunny afternoon of our lunch. In short, I was much too cathexed with this imaginary child to ever give up the sperm to produce her.

I recognize now, and did at the time, that my response was excessive. My reveries of fatherhood sprang from a fetishistic attachment to one among millions of rapidly replenished microscopic organisms—men make on the order of 400 billion sperm in a lifetime—swimming in an abundant, nondescript saline fluid. All that I was really being asked to do was "to produce" some semen—a not unpleasant process—and to give it to my friend so that a very, very tiny sperm—actually only its 4–5 micrometers long and 2.5 to 3.5 micrometers wide (c. 1/10,000 to 1/20,000 of an inch) head—

might contribute the strands of DNA wafting about in it to her egg. Since we humans apparently share 95% of our genetic material with chimpanzees, the sperm in question must share a still higher percentage of base pairs with those of my fellow humans. In short, my unique contribution to the proposed engagement, that which I did not share with billions of other men and monkeys, was infinitesimally small. I was making a mountain out of much, much, much less than a molehill and not very much more than a molecule.

But this is as it should be. For much of history the problem has been to make men take responsibility for their children. Prince and pauper as circumstances required could easily deny the paternity that nature did so little to make evident. The double standard or sexual morality served to insure that however widely they sowed their wild oats the fruits of their wives' wombs would be unambiguously theirs. In fact, until very recently paternity was impossible to prove and much effort went into developing histo-immunological assays that could establish the biological link between a specific man and child. The state, of course, has an interest in making some male, generally the "biological father," responsible for supporting "his" children. In short, a great deal of cultural work has gone into giving meaning to a small bit of matter. Ironically, now that tests make it possible to identify the father with about 100% accuracy, women—those who want children *without* a father—have considerable difficulty obtaining sperm free of filiation. History, social policy, imagination, and culture continue to encumber this cell with its haploid of chromosomes.

In 1978, Mary K., a gay woman living in Sonoma County, California, decided that she wanted to have a child which she would "co-parent" with a close gay woman friend living nearby. Mary wanted to find a sperm donor herself rather than use anonymous sperm for several reasons which she later more or less clearly articulated. She did not want to make the repeated trips to Berkeley, the location of the nearest sperm bank; she did not want to use a physician in her community who might be able to acquire sperm anonymously because she felt that as a nurse she could not be assured confidentiality; and—this would come to haunt her—she wanted some vestige of an individual human being to be associated with the sperm and with the hoped-for baby. She wanted a "father" of some ill-defined sort, and after a month or so of looking around and after interviewing three potential donors, she was introduced one January evening to a young gay man, Jhordan C., who seemed to fit her needs. He would become "father" of her child, despite the fact that he did not have the red hair that she had originally sought in a donor.

Neither Jhordan or Mary thought very rigorously about what they expected from their relationship or just what his paternal rights and obligations would be. Neither sought legal counsel; they signed no contract or other written understanding and resolved only the most basic practical details of the matter: Jhordan, upon being notified that Mary was ovulating, would journey to her house, and "produce" sperm, which she would introduce into herself. It took six months before Mary conceived and each of his visits was apparently attended by commonplace social intercourse—some chit chat, tea, and other pleasantries.

After Mary conceived she and Jhordan saw each other occasionally. She accepted his invitation to a small New Year's party at the home of one of his close friends. She testifies that he "reiterated" to her that "he wanted to be known as the father—and I told him I would let the child know who the biological father was—and that he wanted to travel with the child when the child was older." In all other respects she believed that they had an implicit understanding that she would be the child's guardian and primary parent; that Victoria T., Mary's friend, would be co-parent; and that Jhordan would play effectively no role in the life of *her* child.

On the basis of Jhordan's own testimony, he did not know precisely what he meant by wanted "to be known as the father." The court-appointed psychologist described him as a young man of unsettled plans and interests. But Jhordan knew that he wanted somehow to be acknowledged. He was upset when Mary informed him, some months before the birth, that his name would not be on the birth certificate and he became increasingly uneasy as he came to realize that he was being increasingly written out of the family drama that he had helped launch.

Mary admits that she too had been vague about what Jhordan's being her child's father meant to her and that he did have some grounds for his expectation that he would play some sort of paternal role. Language failed her when she tried to describe it:

> I had thought about and I was considering whether or not I would tell Sean [not his real name] who the father was, but I didn't know if I would tell him as a father. Like he would know that Jhordan helped donate the sperm, but I did not know if he would ever know Jhordan—How do I say this? I didn't plan on Sean relating as a father. No.

The confusion of names and collapse of grammar here suggests precisely the underlying ambiguities of this case.

When Sean was born Mary felt increasingly threatened by Jhordan's insistence on seeing him, on displaying him to his family, on taking pictures to show to friends and relatives, and in general in acting like a parent, a role that Mary had thought was reserved for herself and Victoria. Jhordan, on the other hand, told the psychologist who interviewed him to determine his fitness as a parent that when "he looked into Sean's eyes, he saw his whole family there." Whatever uncertainties he might have felt before vanished in the face of his imagined flesh and blood.

Mary finally refused to allow Jhordan to see the baby at all and he eventually gave up trying. There matters might have rested had not, a year later, Mary applied for welfare. The state sued Jhordan for child support (it was after all his sperm) and he, of course, eagerly agreed to pay. Two years and two lawyers later he won visiting rights with Sean at the home of Mary's friend and co-parent, Victoria. These privileges were subsequently expanded. From here on the story is like that of countless divorced couples: quarrels about visitation hours and pick-up times, about where Sean would spend his holidays and birthdays, about whether Jhordan allowed him to eat too much sugar, and about other of the many controversial niceties of child-raising that divide parents in even the tightest of families. A court promulgated guidelines and issued orders; an uneasy peace settled over all the parties.

The trial judge in this case was a rather old-fashioned sort who did not seem terribly interested in the subtleties of the law regarding the rights of sperm donors but believed that "blood is thicker than water" and that Sean both needed, and had "a right to," a father. Jhordan was the father and therefore ought, in the judge's view, to be given commensurate visitation rights.

Mary appealed (*Jhordan C. v Mary K.* [1986] 179 CA3d 386, 224 CR 530). The central question before the high court was how to interpret sections 7005(a) and (b) of the California Civil Code. These provide that if, under the supervision of a doctor, a married woman is inseminated by semen from a man who is not her husband, that man under certain circumstances is treated as if he were not the natural father while the husband is treated as if he were. Mary's lawyers argued that while their client's case did not quite fit under this statute it was close enough and that the only possible distinction was one of sexual orientation, which ought not to matter. Other California statutes provide that the law must not discriminate against unconventional parenting arrangements in adoption and other reproductive rights issues. If Mary had been married to someone and had acquired Jhordan's sperm in precisely the same circumstances—admittedly not meeting all the conditions of the statute—it would be ludicrous to suppose that the State would give him rights that infringed upon those of the husband. (A German court has held that a man has no claims on a child of a married woman even if he is acknowledged to be the "biological father." Today, as has been generally true for centuries, children born in wedlock are presumed to belong to the husband of the woman who bore them.)

Moreover, Mary's lawyers argued, section 7005a's reference to semen given "to a licensed physician" was not intended to limit the law's application only to such cases but reflected simply a legislative directive to insure proper health standards by recourse to a physician. Mary, because of her training as a nurse, was able to comply with the standard on her own. Her lawyers also cited another court case which held—admittedly in different circumstances—that

> A child conceived through heterologous artificial insemination [i.e. with semen from a man other than the woman's husband] does not have a "natural father." . . . The anonymous donor of sperm can not be considered the "natural father," as he is no more responsible for the use made of his sperm than is a donor of blood or a kidney.

Echoes of Isidore of Seville. Jhordan might not have been anonymous but he was certainly a stranger to Mary.

His lawyers naturally argued for a stricter construal of section 7005a-b and the appeals court sided with them. By not employing a physician, the court agreed, Mary had excluded herself from the law's protection. Moreover, the court viewed the case before it as being more like those in which artificial insemination occurred within the context of an established relationship and in which the sperm donor retained paternal rights than it was like cases of anonymous donation. Jhordan's lawyer cited a New Jersey Supreme Court case for example, in which a man and a woman were dating and intended to marry. She wanted to bear his child but didn't want to have premarital intercourse so they resorted to artificial insemination. Three months into the pregnancy they broke up and she declared that she wanted nothing more to do with him and that she certainly would not allow him to visit their child. He sued for a paternity and won.

Mary and Jhordan were obviously not as intimately involved as this couple but, the court felt, neither were they the anonymous strangers envisaged by statute. Enough humanity remained in Jhordan's transaction with Mary to allow him to believe that his sperm, however introduced into Mary's body, retained some of him.

As this case and others like it suggest, the legal status of a sperm donor remains deeply problematic and, advises a National Lawyers Guild Handbook, those "consulted by a lesbian considering artificial insemination must be extremely careful to explain the ramifications of the various choices available to their clients." Using a medically supervised sperm bank where the identity of the donor is unknown to the recipient is the most certain way to guarantee that the donor will not at some time in the future be construed as the father. Other possibilities include having a friend secure semen but keeping the source secret; using semen from multiple donors (not recommended because of possible immune reactions); using a known donor but having a physician as an intermediary. Some lawyers recommend having the recipient pay the donor for his sperm and describing the transaction in an ordinary commercial contract of the sort with which the courts are familiar. And even if agreements between sperm donors and recipients are not predictably enforceable, lawyers suggest that the parties set down their understanding of their relationship as clearly as possible.

Any or all of these strategies might have stripped Jhordan's sperm of paternity, not just in the eyes of the law but more importantly in his heart, and might thus have saved Mary and her co-parent their struggles with the parental claims of a near stranger. Mary was wrong to eschew a doctor's mediation or at least underestimated the hold that a very small bit of matter can, in the right circumstances, have on a man's imagination.

In designating a physician as middleman the legislature did not blindly medicalize an essentially social transaction but sought rather to appropriate one of modern medicine's least attractive features—its lack of humanity—for a socially useful end. Everyone knows, even politicians, that artificial insemination does not require a physician. Depaternalizing sperm might. A strange doctor in a lab coat working amidst white formica furniture, high tech instruments, officious nurses, and harried receptionists in a boxy office in a nondescript glass and steel building set in a parking lot may offer cold comfort to the sick and needy; he or she might, however, be perfect at taking the sparkle off sperm.

Had Jhordan donated sperm not at Mary's house, where he was offered tea and conversation, but at a clinic; had he never spoken to her after the inseminations began but only to the doctor's nurse, who would have whisked away the vial of fresh semen; had he never seen Mary pregnant or celebrated New Year's Eve with her, the fetish of the sperm might have been broken. The doctor as broker would have performed his or her priestly function, de-blessed the sperm, and gotten rid of its "paternity." (This I imagine as the inversion of normal priestly work, providing extra emotional glue between the participants in weddings, funerals, and the like.) Similarly, selling sperm at a price fixed by contract—the lawyer or sperm bank owner as deblessing agent—would take off some of its paternal blush. Without such rites, a father's material claim in his child is small but his imaginative claims can be as endless as a mother's. Great care must be taken to protect and not to squash them.

Because fatherhood is an "idea," it is not limited to men. In a recent case litigated in Alameda County, California (Lofton v. Flouroy), a woman was, rightly in my view, declared to be a child's father, if not its male parent. Ms. Lofton and Ms. Flouroy lived together and decided to have a child. Lofton's brother Larry donated the required sperm but expressed no interest in having any further role in the matter. Ms. Lofton introduced her brother's semen into Flouroy with a turkey baster, Flouroy became pregnant, and in due course a baby was born. The "birth mother" was listed on its birth certificate as "mother," and L. Lofton—Linda, not Larry, but who was to know?—was listed as "father."

Everything went well and the women treated the child as theirs until, two years later, they split up. The mother kept the child and there matters might have rested had not, as in the case of Mary and Jhordan, the State intervened. Flouroy applied for welfare benefits, i.e., aid to dependent children, and when asked by the Family Support Bureau to identify the father she produced, in a moment of unabashed concreteness, the turkey baster. The Bureau, not amused, did what it was meant to do and went after the "father" on the birth certificate—Linda, it was surprised to learn, not Larry. Like Jhordan she welcomed the opportunity to claim paternity, did not dispute the claim and eagerly paid the judgment entered against her: child support, current and retroactive. She also demanded paternal visitation rights, which Ms. Flouroy resisted. Lofton then asked the court to compel mediation. It held that she was indeed a "psychological parent" and thus, had standing to have her rights mediated. The other L. Lofton, Larry, makes no appearance in this drama.

Linda's claim is manifestly not biological nor even material. That she borrowed her brother's sperm or owned the turkey baster is irrelevant. What matters is that, in the emotional economy of her relationship with her lover and their child, she was the father, whatever that means, and enjoyed the rights and bore the obligations of that status. She invested the required emotional and imaginitive capital in the impregnation, gestation, and subsequent life to make the child in some measure hers.

I hasten to add that I do not regard biology in all circumstances as counting for nothing. Women have claims with respect to the baby within them simply by virtue of spatial relations and rights to bodily integrity. These are not the right to be or not to be a mother as against the right to be or not to be a father, nor the claims of a person as against those of a non-person—the terms in which the abortion debate is usually put—but the right shared by all mentally competent adults to control and monitor corporeal boundaries, to maintain a body as theirs. Thus I would regard a court compelling a woman to bear a child against her will as a form of involuntary servitude however much its would-be father might wish for the child. And I would regard an enforced abortion as an even more egregious assault on her body. But this is not to acknowledge the "fact" of motherhood as much as the "fact" of flesh. History bears witness to the evils that ensue when the state abrogates a person's rights in her body.

The flesh does not make a mother's body an ahistorical font of motherhood and maternity. A writer who wants, but cannot herself have, a child and who finds surrogate motherhood morally unacceptable "can not imagine" that "there are plenty of women now, the huge majority of surrogates who have, to hear them tell it, not suffered such a loss [as Mary Beth Whitehead's]." While her empathic instincts extend easily to Whitehead she cannot, despite testimony to the contrary, conceive of a mother *not* feeling an instant and apparently unmediated bond to her child. Ms. Fleming cannot accept that feelings do not follow from flesh so that "surrogate mothers" who feel otherwise than they supposedly should must suffer, like un-class-conscious workers, from false consciousness.

Ms.'s special "Mothers Issue," quite apart from Chesler's article, is striking by its very cover—an air-brushed, soft-toned picture of a 1950's young Ivory Soap woman, with straight blonde hair of the sort that waves in shampoo commercials, holding a blue-eyed baby to her bare bosom and looking dreamily out of the frame of the picture—which would have been denounced by feminists as perpetuating an unacceptable stereotype of women had it appeared in *Family Circle* a decade ago. In 1988 it unashamedly represents the Mother in America's largest selling feminist magazine.

What exactly are the facts of motherhood and what of significance ought to follow from them? For advocates of Mrs. Whitehead's, like Phyllis Chesler, her egg and its genetic contents are not especially relevant. She shares with Bill, a.k.a. Dr. Stern, the provision of chromosomes. The critical fact is therefore her nine months of incubation, which would remain a fact even if the fertilized egg she was bringing to term were not hers. Her claim, it appears, rests on labor, on her physical intimacy with the child within her, and would be just as strong if a second woman sought a stake in the child on the basis of her contribution to half its chromosomes.

I am immensely sympathetic to this view but not because of a fact of nature. Capitalist societies, as I suggested earlier, are not usually friendly to the notion that putting labor into a product entitles one to ownership or even to much credit. It is the rare company that gives its workers shares of stock. We associate a new production of *The Magic Flute* with David Hockney and not with those who sawed, hammered, and painted the sets; everyone knows that Walt Disney produced *Bambi* but only the "cognoscenti" could name even one of the artists who actually made the pictures. Having the idea or the plan is what counts, which is why Judge Sokoloff told Dr. Stern that in getting Melissa he was only getting what was already his. (The Judge should, of course, have said, "half his.")

I became so exercised by Baby M because Dr. Stern's claims have been reduced in some circles to his ownership of his sperm which, as I said earlier, amounts to owning very little. This puts him—all fathers—at a distinct material disadvantage to Mrs. Whitehead—all women—who contribute so much more matter. But, this essay has suggested, his claims, like hers, arise from the intense and profound bonding with a child, unborn and born, that its biological kinship might spark in the moral and affective imagination but which it does not entail.

The problem, of course, is that emotional capital does not accumulate steadily, visibly, and predictably as in a psychic payroll deduction plan. That is why, for example, it is unreasonable to demand of a woman specific performance on a surrogate mothering contract as if the baby were a piece of land or a work of art whose attributes would be well known to their vendor. A "surrogate mother," like a mother who offers to give up her baby for adoption to a stranger, must be allowed a reasonable time to change her mind and if she does, in the case of a surrogacy arrangement, be prepared to argue for her rights against those of the father.

Each parent would bring to such a battle claims to have made another person emotionally part of themselves. "Facts" like bearing the child would obviously be significant evidence but would not be unimpeachable, would not be nature speaking unproblematically to culture. While we can continue to look forward to continuing conflict over the competing claims of parents I suggest that we abandon the notion that biology—facts—will somehow provide the resolution. Neither, of course, will ideas alone in a world in which persons exist corporeally. The way out of the fact/idea dichotomy is to recognize its irrelevance in these matters. The "facts" of such socially powerful and significant categories as mother and father come into being only as culture imbues things, actions, and flesh with meaning. This is the process that demands our continued attention.

The Other Woman

Joan Whitman Hoff

In this essay, Hoff explores briefly the role that women are presumed to play in stepfamilies. Although stepfamilies are not a new phenomenon, in our contemporary society they are often seen as contributing to immorality. Women, in particular, no matter what their history, are seen as "the other woman." What do you think about stepfamilies? Think about some of the ways in which the myth of the "wicked stepmother" prevails in our world.

As we approach the twenty-first century, it is estimated that one out of two families in the United States is a stepfamily. This statistic is often viewed as frightening evidence that society is falling apart, and the recent discussion concerning the decline of the traditional family by politicians such as Dan Quayle and Newt Gingrich is an example of how alternative families—indeed stepfamilies—are viewed as aberrations. In reality, however, stepfamilies have existed for thousands of years. For example, Aristotle discussed his experience as a member of a stepfamily and noted the importance of respecting one's stepparent as one's biological parent.

Stepfamilies, however, have been marginalized historically. Negative stereotypes concerning stepfamilies and stepparents and children have been perpetuated by myths found in fairy tales and the media; these stereotypes have often led to adverse consequences for stepparents. Moreover, women seem to have been harmed particularly by these myths as societies, cross-culturally, have marginalized women, and motherhood has been devalued despite the political rhetoric that is used seemingly to stress its importance. Even in professional literature on parenting, stepparents (and stepmothers particularly) have been marginalized. As Rhona and Robert N. Rapoport and Ziona Strelitz state, "The stepparent relationship is ill-defined . . . [and] very little professional attention has been paid to it even though it has 'fascinated story-tellers, gossips and dramatists since antiquity' " (1980, 109–10). When it *is* discussed, it is done so ambiguously. For example, in discussing the negative images of stepmothers in fairy tales, Shari L. Thurer states,

> Feminists love to hate fairy tales for their sexist values. . . . But there are real facts of life at work in these stories too. Stepmothers may very well have been wicked in early modern Europe. In an age of high death rates, few children lived out childhood with both parents alive. Fathers often remarried. Since father's new wife, the child's stepmother, was dependent on her husband for security and status, it is only natural that she would strive on behalf of her own children against her predecessor's offspring—even to the point of murdering them. Sadly, the wicked stepmother may not have been a fairy tale. (1994, 152)

Later, Thurer states,

> Neither, perhaps, was the cruel mother. Mom also remarried after the spouse's death [and when she] rewed, it was customary . . . to leave *with* her dowry but *without* her children. . . . Objectively speaking, these mothers may have been more sinned against than sinning. They were pawns in a social structure that presented them with a choice as bitter as Sophie's: their children or a mate. (1994, 152)

Thurer' s views are representative of the assumptions that are made about stepmothers and the difficult position that society has enforced upon women. There still seems to be little empathy for the real role that stepmothers play, however, and it appears that even scholars have been left to draw conclusions with no rational foundation. Or they have been made invisible by a lack of discussion and understanding. As Rapoport and Strelitz note, the law, psychiatry, and social etiquette "pretend that there is no such thing," and thus the stepfamily becomes invisible (1980).

Brenda Maddox and Helen Thompson attempt to explain some of the reasons that stepparenting has not received serious attention in professional literature. They note that writers of fiction and fairy tales have painted the stepparent as cruel, and this is particularly true of the way in which stepmothers have been stereotyped. Examples of evil stepmothers can be found in well-respected and influential works such as *Hamlet* and *Anna Karenina,* and we all know about the wicked stepmother of *Cinderella.* These stereotypes, according to Maddox, have made stepparents themselves feel unsure about their own feelings and role in the family. Laws and social etiquette were often put into place with these stereotypes in mind. For example, as Rapoport and Strelitz note, for centuries stepmothers in China were not allowed to punish their stepchildren, and even today their ambiguity in the family is further complicated by a lack of legal rights, despite enormous obligations such as child care.

In essence, then, both the law and social etiquette have attempted to make the stepfamily invisible and/or extraneous. As Rapoport and Strelitz note in their discussion of Maddox's work, "The word 'stepparent' is never used in ecclesiastical or civil law, both of which refer instead to the 'mother's husband' or 'father's wife.' " (1980, 111). Thus, they are considered "other" by society at large, and this has a significant impact on how the children view the relationship and the family. Because there is no biological bond between a stepmother and child, it is also assumed that there can be no spiritual bond between them; when there is a bond, it is viewed as misplaced and unnatural.

This relationship is further complicated by natural or socially contrived conflict between the natural parents and stepparents. The "new wife" is believed to be particularly better off than the first wife due to her husband. For example, in *Second Chances,* Judith Wallerstein and Sandra Blakeslee (1990) claim that men who remarry find themselves in much better financial situations than women who remarry, and they also claim that the second wife is therefore better off than the first. While studies indicate that women who are divorced are indeed worse off financially than men who divorce, it is most often due to the fact that women do not remarry, and when they do, they are either not employed, do not have the skills to obtain employment with a significant salary, or are subject to discrimination in the workplace (which is significant and of various types). Moreover, men often remarry women who have careers and have an income independently of their husbands. This coincides with the fact (unlike the myth) that men remarry women who are similar in age. Indeed, even current literature (such as that by Wallerstein and Blakeslee) illustrates the fact that women (stepmothers and second wives) are being held accountable for the problems that other women (natural mothers and first wives) have while the systems (social, political, legal, and cultural) that have marginalized women in general and stepmothers in particular remain problematic and ambiguous.

Another but no less significant problem in light of this concerns the children of remarriage, who often are called "half-brothers and half-sisters" or "stepbrothers and stepsisters." The use of the words "step" and "half" further illustrates the way in which stepchildren are considered "other" and marginalized in society and in the family. As in the case of surrogate parenting, these children have no legal or social rights to form relationships with one another in the event that the stepfamily "splits."

A number of other significant problems emerge as a result of this exclusion; perhaps the most controversial one is that family values may indeed suffer but not because of the breakdown of the traditional family. Rather, it is difficult to maintain family integrity when that family is, from the beginning, viewed as fragmented and not whole. As long as nature and not nurture is deemed to be the prevailing force in the grounding of family values, the stepfamily will continue to struggle for recognition as "family" without the omnipresent shadow of the "step."

In closing, it seems clear that we need to be more inclusive in our understanding of families. Furthermore, we must also understand that, as Mary Midgley suggests, culture can not only serve to help us achieve an identity, but it can also oppress us (1993). In positioning the stepmother as cruel, unnatural, and "other," societies and their "step" family language oppresses the "step" mother in her attempt to help nurture positive values in the family. What we need is a change of attitude. Let's drop the "step." Let's drop the "other."

Commercium sexuale est usus membrorum et facultatum sexualium alterius. This "*usus*" is either natural, by which human beings may reproduce their own kind, or unnatural, which, again, refers either to a person of the same sex or to an animal of another species than man. These transgressions of all law, as *crimina carnis contra naturam,* are even "not to be named"; and, as wrongs against all humanity in the person, they cannot be saved, by any limitation or exception whatever, from entire reprobation.

Author's Note:

This essay is an overview of a book in progress on stepparenting. I focus on issues regarding women and stepmothers because that is clearly the focus in both fiction and professional literature.

References

Brenda Maddox. 1975. *The Half Parent* (London: Andre Deutsch); cf Rapoport and Strelitz.

Mary Midgley. 1993. *Can't We Make Moral Judgments?* (New York: St. Martin's Press).

Rhona and Robert N. Rapoport and Ziona Strelitz. 1980. *Fathers, Mothers and Society* (New York: Vintage Books).

H. Thompson. 1966. *The Successful Stepparent* (London: W. H. Allen); cf Rapoport and Strelitz.

Shari L. Thurer. 1994. *The Myths of Motherhood, How Culture Reinvents the Good Mother* (New York: Penguin Books).

Judith S. Wallerstein and Sandra Blakeslee. 1990. *Second Chances* (New York: Ticknor & Fields).

Discussion Questions

1. What is the bride's role and purpose, according to Hindu doctrine? How is this view similar to that of other religious traditions? How does it call into question the nature of a divine universe?
2. Why does Kant claim that monogamy is a moral necessity? Why does he claim that human sexuality is a moral activity?
3. McMurtry claims there are a number of disadvantages to monogamy. Can you think of any advantages it may have? What may be the advantages or disadvantages of polygamy? Of group marriage?
4. What does Timko mean when she says that motherhood has been used to disempower women? Can you cite some examples from your own experience that might support this view?
5. In what sense does surrogate motherhood undermine the integrity of women, according to Steinbock? Could surrogacy be approached in a way that would preserve respect for the moral personhood of women?
6. What does Laqueur mean when he claims that men have been denied the opportunity for intimate relationships with their children? How could such relationships contribute to a stronger sense of identity and self-worth in males?
7. In what sense have stepparents, especially stepmothers, been marginalized, according to Hoff? In your opinion, how can such marginalization contribute to a sense of alienation in stepparents?
8. In what sense can sexual relations and monogamous marriage help or hinder intimacy in our world today? How can an understanding of our intimate relationships help us to understand ourselves?

chapter 8

The Self and Religious Experience

One of the most fundamental yet most disturbing and controversial issues that we address as human beings is the issue of God's existence. Is there a higher reality? If so, is that higher reality God? What is God's nature? Or is there no God? If there is a God, can God have a sex? Should I have faith even if I have no proof of God? Is it natural to seek the answers to these questions? Can the answers come from anywhere but within our own selves?

In the essays that follow, several philosophers attempt to answer some of these questions. They explore the nature of faith and belief in God through a variety of perspectives. We begin our journey through religious experience with a passage from the Bhagavad Gita. Here we encounter the metaphysical experience of Oneness, a mystical vision of the Absolute. The vision is about inner knowledge and spiritual discipline, about freeing oneself from all material attachments, about giving oneself in love.

Religious faith and the construction of a self that follows from that faith may occur because of a crisis in one's life. Sometimes that crisis may be the result of an illness or intense suffering. Sometimes it comes simply as the result of encountering the fact that something is missing in one's life. In "Faith and the Meaning of Life," Leo Tolstoy takes us on the painful journey of a man whose friends have tried to convince him to believe in God, but to no avail. What he finds is that faith comes only from within.

Brahma

Cynthia Ozick also discusses our search for God in "The Riddle of the Ordinary." Ozick claims that we think of God as extraordinary (not simple or commonplace) and thus never think of God in the realm of the ordinary; but this is our mistake. For Ozick, the ordinary *is* extraordinary. Thus, our search for an understanding of God largely depends on our attitude toward our day-to-day lives and the people with whom we interact. We may be closer to God than we think.

How should we relate to a reality that remains beyond the capabilities of sense experience, especially if that relationship may be necessary to bring goodness into our lives? William James reminds us that religious experiences are not about empty abstractions as much as they are about the liveliness of faith, that is, an experience of a presence in our lives. Such an experience may not be *sensible,* but it is nevertheless *real.* Must religious belief be rational? We may have to continually remind ourselves that not everything that we find meaningful will have a logical or scientific explanation.

Should religion enable us to approach those different from us with a sense of justice, fairness, and respect? Should the test of the value of a religious belief be its ability to see people of different backgrounds, of different races, as individuals with dignity? Should religion foster brotherhood among peoples and not the domination of one people by another? Can one religion assert its authority or sovereignty over another without robbing a people of a sense of *self*? See if you can find answers to these questions in Chief Red Jacket's responses to the Reverend Mr. Cram.

Kwasi Wiredu reminds us of the varieties of religious experiences and how religious attitudes can differ from culture to culture. In examining Akan culture, he demonstrates how Akans approach the ideas of a supreme being, human destiny, and moral practice. Noting differences in belief with regard to how a supreme being relates to the world between Akans and Christians, he says that the most important difference may be in how each approaches the questions of the spiritual and the meaning of life. For the Akan people, what is important for life are self, family, community, and the belief that nothing that transcends life in a human society can be constitutive of life's meaning. His essay reminds us that we may need to broaden our understanding of "religion" and accept that human communities may practice religion differently from one another. Ask yourself, if religion helps us understand who we are, can that religion be alien to our daily lives and our social practices?

Can it be possible for a person to grow up with and be deeply committed to a set of religious beliefs, and at some point in his or her life authentically set aside or reject those beliefs? Lin Yutang had such an experience; he rejected one set of religious beliefs for what he believed to be a more satisfying belief system. He found Christianity too complex, somewhat arrogant, and capable of creating a psychological dependency on its beliefs. In contrast, he found Chinese paganism more conducive to the development of personal independence and virtue. Keep in mind that what he rejects is what Christianity appears to have become, namely, a series of theological doctrines and philosophical intricacies. Also, keep in mind that he believes religion to be a personal experience and therefore refuses to make generalized or universal claims about its application.

In this section, we examine the nature of religious faith (and the absence of such faith), and what power or value it may have in shaping our lives. Ask yourself why we do not consciously consider that our religious beliefs and attitudes (or the absence of such beliefs and attitudes) contribute to the formation of our identities. Even Freud, who would argue vociferously against religious worldviews, was well aware of how religious beliefs could shape our lives and determine our view of reality. Though he would prefer that humankind adopt a scientific view of the world, he knew too well the power religious conviction would have in shaping individuals, and indeed in shaping civilizations.

Cosmic Law and Spiritual Life

Bhagavad Gita

In the eleventh chapter of the Bhagavad Gita, *we encounter Arjuna's vision of the unity, terror, and beauty of the divine Absolute, which is revealed as Krishna. We discover that the vision is not for the faint of heart, and that it comes not from the performance of rituals, not from the study of philosophy or sacred scripture, or even from personal sacrifice. It can come only through the innermost power of the self, which is the power of the soul to love.*

CHAPTER 11: THE LORDS TRANSFIGURATION

Arjuna Wishes to See the Universal Form of God

Arjuna said:

1. The supreme mystery, the discourse concerning the Self which thou hast given out of grace for me—by this my bewilderment is gone from me.

2. The birth and passing away of things have been heard by me in detail from Thee, O Lotus-eyed (Krsna), as also Thy imperishable majesty.

3. As Thou hast declared Thyself to be, O Supreme Lord, even so it is. (But) I desire to see Thy divine form, O Supreme Person.

4. If Thou, O Lord, thinkest that by me, It can be seen, then reveal to me, Thy Imperishable Self, O Lord of *yoga* (Krsna).

The Revelation of the Lord

The Blessed Lord said:

5. Behold, O Partha (Arjuna), My forms, a hundredfold, a thousandfold, various in kind, divine, of various colours and shapes.

6. Behold, the Adityas, the Vasus, the Rudras, the two Asvins and also the Maruts. Behold, O Bharata (Arjuna), many wonders never seen before.

7. Here today, behold the whole universe, moving and unmoving and whatever else thou desirest to see, O Gudakesa (Arjuna), all unified in My body.

8. But thou canst not behold Me with this [human] eye of yours; I will bestow on thee the supernatural eye. Behold My divine power.

Samjaya Describes the Form

Samjaya said:

9. Having thus spoken, O King, Hari, the great lord of *yoga*, then revealed to Partha (Arjuna), His Supreme and Divine Form.

10. Of many mouths and eyes, of many visions of marvel, of many divine ornaments, of many divine uplifted weapons.

11. Wearing divine garlands and raiments, with divine perfumes and ointments, made up of all wonders, resplendent, boundless, with face turned everywhere.

From *Bhagavad-Gita,* trans. by Juan Mascaro Bolle. Copyright © 1979 by Princeton University Press.

12. If the light of a thousand suns were to blaze forth all at once in the sky, that might resemble the splendour of that exalted Being.

13. There the Pandava (Arjuna) beheld the whole universe, with its manifold divisions gathered together in one, in the body of the God of gods.

Arjuna Addresses the Lord

14. Then he, the Winner of wealth (Arjuna), struck with amazement, his hair standing on end, bowed down his head to the Lord, with hands folded [in salutation], said:

15. In Thy body, O God, I see all the gods and the varied hosts of beings as well, Brahma, the Lord seated on the lotus throne and all the sages and heavenly *nagas.*

16. I behold Thee, infinite in form on all sides, with numberless arms, bellies, faces and eyes, but I see not Thy end or Thy middle or Thy beginning, O Lord of the universe, O Form Universal.

17. I behold Thee with Thy crown, mace and discus, glowing everywhere as a mass of light, hard to discern, [dazzling] on all sides with the radiance of the flaming fire and sun, incomparable.

18. Thou art the Imperishable, the Supreme to be realized. Thou art the ultimate resting-place of the universe; Thou art the undying guardian of the eternal law. Thou art the Primal Person, I think.

19. I behold Thee as one without beginning, middle or end, of infinite power, of numberless arms, with the moon and the sun as Thine eyes, with Thy face as a flaming fire, whose radiance burns up this universe.

20. This space between heaven and earth is pervaded by Thee alone, also all the quarters [directions of the sky]. O Exalted One, when this wondrous, terrible form of Thine is seen, the three worlds tremble.

21. Yonder hosts of gods enter Thee and some, in fear, extol Thee, with folded hands, and bands of great seers and perfected ones cry "hail" and adore Thee with hymns of abounding praise.

22. The Rudras, the Adityas, the Vasus, the Sadhyas; the Visvas, the two Asvins, the Maruts and the manes and the hosts of Gandharvas, Yaksas, Asuras and Siddhas, all gaze at Thee and are quite amazed.

23. Seeing Thy great form, of many mouths and eyes, O Mighty-armed, of many arms, thighs and feet, of many bellies, terrible with many tusks, the worlds tremble and so do I.

24. When I see Thee touching the sky, blazing with many hues, with the mouth opened wide, and large glowing eyes, my inmost soul trembles in fear and I find neither steadiness nor peace, O Visnu!

25. When I see Thy mouths terrible with their tusks, like Time's devouring flames, I lose sense of the directions and find no peace. Be gracious, O Lord of gods, Refuge of the worlds!

26. All yonder sons of Dhrtarastra together with the hosts of kings and also Bhisma, Drona and Karna along with the chief warriors on our side too,—

27. Are rushing into Thy fearful mouths set with terrible tusks. Some caught between the teeth are seen with their heads crushed to powder.

28. As the many rushing torrents to rivers race towards the ocean, so do these heroes of the world of men rush into Thy flaming mouths.

29. As moths rush swiftly into a blazing fire to perish there, so do these men rush into Thy mouths with great speed to their own destruction.

30. Devouring all the worlds on every side with Thy flaming mouths, thou lickest them up. Thy fiery rays fill this whole universe and scorch it with their fierce radiance, O Visnu!

31. Tell me who Thou art with form so terrible. Salutation to Thee, O Thou Great Godhead, have mercy. I wish to know Thee [who art] the Primal One, for I know not Thy working.

God as the Judge

The Blessed Lord said:

32. Time am I, world-destroying, grown mature, engaged here in subduing the world. Even without thee [thy action], all the warriors standing arrayed in the opposing armies shall cease to be.

33. Therefore arise thou and gain glory. Conquering thy foes, enjoy a prosperous kingdom. By Me alone are they slain already. Be thou merely the occasion, O Savyasacin (Arjuna).

34. Slay, Drona, Bhisma, Jayadratha, Karna and other great warriors as well, who are already doomed by Me, Be not afraid. Fight, thou shalt conquer the enemies in battle.

Samjaya said:

35. Having heard this utterance of Kesava (Krsna), Kiritin (Arjuna), with folded hands and trembling, saluted again and prostrating himself with great fear, spoke in a faltering voice to Krsna.

Arjuna's Hymn of Praise

Arjuna said:

36. O Hrsikesa (Krsna), rightly does the world rejoice and delight in Thy magnificence. The Raksasas are fleeing in terror in all directions and all the hosts of perfected ones are bowing down before Thee (in adoration).

37. And why should they not do Thee homage, O Exalted One, who art greater than Brahma, the original creator? O Infinite Being, Lord of the gods, Refuge of the universe, Thou art the Imperishable, the being and the non-being and what is beyond that.

38. Thou art the First of gods, the Primal Person, the Supreme Resting Place of the world. Thou art the knower and that which is to be known and the supreme goal. And by Thee is this universe pervaded, O Thou of infinite form!

39. Thou art Vayu [the wind], Yama [the destroyer], Agni [the fire], Varuna [the sea-god] and Sasanka [the moon], and Prajapati, the grandsire [of all]. Hail, hail to Thee, a thousand times. Hail, hail to Thee again and yet again.

40. Hail to Thee in front, [hail] to Thee behind and hail to Thee on every side, O All; boundless in power and immeasurable in might, Thou dost penetrate all and therefore Thou art All.

41. For whatsoever I have spoken in rashness to Thee, thinking that Thou art my companion and unaware of this [fact of] Thy greatness, "O Krsna, O Yadava, O Comrade"; out of my negligence or may be through fondness,

42. And for whatsoever disrespect was shown to Thee in jest, while at play or on the bed or seated or at meals, either alone or in the presence of others, I pray, O Unshaken One, forgiveness from Thee, the Immeasurable.

43. Thou art the father of the world of the moving and the unmoving. Thou art the object of its worship and its venerable teacher. None is equal to Thee; how then could there be one greater than Thee in the three worlds, O Thou of incomparable greatness?

44. Therefore bowing down and prostrating my body before Thee, Adorable Lord, I seek Thy grace. Thou, O God, shouldst bear with me as a father to his son, as a friend to his friend, as a lover to his beloved.

45. I have seen what was never seen before and I rejoice but my heart is shaken with fear. Show me that other [previous] form of Thine, O God, and be gracious, O Lord of the gods and Refuge of the Universe!

46. I wish to see Thee even as before with They crown, mace, and disc in Thy hand. Assume Thy four-armed shape, O Thou of a thousand arms and of universal form.

The Lord's Grace and Assurance

The Blessed Lord said:

47. By My grace, through My divine power, O Arjuna, was shown to thee this supreme form, luminous, universal, infinite and primal which none but thee has seen before.

48. Neither by the Vedas, [nor by] sacrifices nor by study nor by gifts nor by ceremonial rites nor by severe austerities can I with this form be seen in the world of men by one else but thee, O hero of the Kurus (Arjuna).

49. May you not be afraid, may you not be bewildered seeing this terrific form of Mine. Free from fear and glad at heart, behold again this other [former] form of Mine.

Samjaya said:

50. Having thus spoken to Arjuna, Vasudeva (Krsna) revealed to him again His own form. The Exalted One, having assumed again the form of grace, comforted the terrified Arjuna.

Arjuna said:

51. Beholding again this Thy gracious human form, O Janardana (Krsna), I have now become collected in mind and am restored to my normal nature.

The Blessed Lord said:

52. This form of Mine which is indeed very hard to see, thou hast seen. Even the gods are ever eager to see this form.

53. In the form in which thou has seen Me now, I cannot be seen either by the Vedas or by austerities or by gifts or by sacrifices.

54. But by unswerving devotion to Me, O Arjuna, I can be thus known, truly seen and entered into, O Oppressor of the foe (Arjuna).

55. He who does work for Me, he who looks upon Me as his goal, he who worships Me, free from attachment, who is free from enmity to all creatures, he goes to Me, O Pandava (Arjuna).

This is the eleventh chapter, entitled "The Vision of the Cosmic Form."

CHAPTER 12: WORSHIP OF THE PERSONAL LORD IS BETTER THAN MEDITATION OF THE ABSOLUTE

Devotion and Contemplation

Arjuna said:

1. Those devotees who, thus ever harmonized, worship Thee and those, again, who worship the Imperishable and the Unmanifested—which of these have the greater knowledge of *yoga*?

The Blessed Lord said:

2. Those who fixing their minds on Me worship Me, ever harmonized and possessed of supreme faith—them do I consider most perfect in *yoga*.

3. But those who worship the Imperishable, the Undefinable, the Unmanifested, the Omnipresent, the Unthinkable, the Unchanging and the Immobile, the Constant,

4. By restraining all the senses, being even-minded in all conditions, rejoicing in the welfare of all creatures—they come to Me indeed [just like the others].

5. The difficulty of those whose thoughts are set on the Unmanifested is greater, for the goal of the Unmanifested is hard to reach by the embodied beings.

Different Approaches

6. But those who, laying all their actions on Me, intent on Me, worship, meditating on Me, with unswerving devotion,

7. These whose thoughts are set on Me, I straightway deliver from the ocean of death-bound existence, O Partha (Arjuna).

8. On Me alone fix thy mind, let thy understanding dwell in Me; In Me alone shalt thou live thereafter. Of this there is no doubt.

9. If, however, thou art not able to fix thy thought steadily on Me, then seek to reach Me by the practice of concentration, O winner of wealth (Arjuna).

10. If thou art unable even to seek by practice, then be as one whose supreme aim is My service; even performing actions for My sake, thou shalt attain perfection.

11. If thou art not able to do even this, then, taking refuge in My disciplined activity, renounce the fruit of all action, with the self subdued.

12. Better indeed is knowledge than the practice of concentration; better than knowledge is meditation; better than meditation is the renunciation of the fruit of action; on renunciation follows immediately peace.

The True Devotee

13. He who has no ill will to any being, who is friendly and compassionate, free from egoism and self-sense, even-minded in pain and pleasure, and patient,

14. The *yogi* who is ever content, self-controlled, unshakable in determination, with mind and understanding given up to Me—he, My devotee, is dear to Me.

15. He from whom the world does not shrink and who does not shrink from the world and who is free from joy and anger, fear and agitation—he too is dear to Me.

16. He who has no expectation, is pure, skilful in action, unconcerned, and untroubled, who has given up all initiative in action—he, My devotee, is dear to Me.

17. He who neither rejoices nor hates, neither grieves nor desires, and who has renounced good and evil—he who is thus devoted is dear to Me.

18. He who [behaves] alike to foe and friend, also to good and evil repute, and who is alike in cold and heat, pleasure and pain, and who is free from attachment,

19. He who holds equal blame and praise, who is silent [restrained in speech], content with anything that comes, who has no fixed abode and is firm in mind—that man who is devoted is dear to Me.

20. But those who with faith, holding Me as their supreme aim, follow this immortal wisdom—those devotees are exceedingly dear to Me.

This is the twelfth chapter entitled "The *Yoga* of Devotion."

Faith and the Meaning of Life

Leo Tolstoy

In this story, we journey through the struggle of a man in his search for meaning and purpose in life. His friends have tried to convince him, time and time again, that he ought to have faith in God, but to no avail. One fateful day, however, he falls victim to an accident from which he never recovers—one that changes his life in many ways. What he finally discovers is that faith comes from within, not outside, oneself. Do you agree? How often have you tried to convince others of your belief or nonbelief, and how often have others tried to convince you of theirs?

Thus I lived; but, five years ago, a strange state of mind began to grow upon me: I had moments of perplexity, of a stoppage, as it were, of life, as if I did not know how I was to live, what I was to do, and I began to wander, and was a victim to low spirits. But this passed, and I continued to live as before. Later, these periods of perplexity began to return more and more frequently, and invariably took the same form. These stoppages of

From *My Confession in Tolstoís Works* by Leo Tolstoy, trans. Nathan H. Dole. New York: T. Y. Crowell Co., 1899, pp. 12–57 (with omissions).

life always presented themselves to me with the same questions: "Why?" and "What after?"

At first it seemed to me that these were aimless unmeaning questions; it seemed to me that all they asked about was well known, and that if at any time when I wished to find answers to them I could do so without much trouble—that just at that time I could not be bothered with this, but whenever I should stop to think them over I should find an answer. But these questions presented themselves to my mind with ever-increasing frequency, demanding an answer with still greater and greater persistence, and like dots grouped themselves into one black spot.

It was with me as it happens in the case of every mortal internal ailment—at first appear the insignificant symptoms of indisposition, disregarded by the patient; then these symptoms are repeated more and more frequently, till they merge in uninterrupted suffering. The sufferings increase, and the patient is confronted with the fact that what he took for a mere indisposition has become more important to him than anything else on earth, that it is death!

This is exactly what happened to me. I became aware that this was not a chance indisposition, but something very serious, and that if all these questions continued to recur, I should have to find an answer to them. And I tried to answer them. The questions seemed so foolish, so simple, so childish; but no sooner had I taken hold of them than I was convinced, first, that they were neither childish nor silly, but were concerned with the deepest problems of life; and, in the second place, that I could not decide them—could not decide them, however I put my mind upon them.

Before occupying myself with my Samara estate, with the education of my son, with the writing of books, I was bound to know why I did these things. As long as I do not know the reason "why" I cannot do anything. I cannot live. While thinking about the management of my household and estate, which in these days occupied much of my time, suddenly this question came into my head:

"Well and good, I have now six thousand desyatins in the government of Samara, and three hundred horses—what then?"

I was perfectly disconcerted, and knew not what to think. Another time, dwelling on the thought of how I should educate my children, I ask myself "*Why*"? Again, when considering by what means the well-being of the people might best be promoted, I suddenly exclaimed, "But what concern have I with it?" When I thought of the fame which my works were gaining me, I said to myself:

"Well, what if I should be more famous than Gogol, Pushkin, Shakespeare, Molière—than all the writers of the world—well, and what then?" . . .

I could find no reply. Such questions will not wait: they demand an immediate answer; without one it is impossible to live; but answer there was none.

I felt that the ground on which I stood was crumbling, that there was nothing for me to stand on, that what I had been living for was nothing, that I had no reason for living. . . .

My life had come to a stop. I was able to breathe, to eat, to drink, to sleep, and I could not help breathing, eating, drinking, sleeping; but there was no real life in me because I had not a single desire, the fulfillment of which I could feel to be reasonable. If I wished for anything, I knew beforehand that, were I to satisfy the wish, or were I not to satisfy it, nothing would come of it. Had a fairy appeared and offered me all I desired, I should not have known what to say. If I had, in moments of excitement, I will not say wishes, but the habits of former wishes, at calmer moments I knew that it was a delusion, that I really wished for nothing I could not even wish to know the truth, because I guessed in what it consisted.

The truth was, that life was meaningless. Every day of life, every step in it, brought me, as it were, nearer the precipice, and I saw clearly that before me there was nothing but ruin. And to stop was impossible; and it was impossible to shut my eyes so as not to see that there was nothing before me but suffering and actual death, absolute annihilation.

Thus, I, a healthy and a happy man, was brought to feel that I could live no longer,—some irresistible force was dragging me onward to escape from life. I do not mean that I wanted to kill myself.

The force that drew me away from life was stronger, fuller, and more universal than any wish; it was a force like that of my previous attachment to life, only in a contrary direction. With all my force I struggled away from life. The idea of suicide came as naturally to me as formerly that of bettering my life. This thought was so attractive to me that I was compelled to practise upon myself a species of self-deception in order to avoid carrying it out too hastily. I was unwilling to act hastily, only because I wanted to employ all my powers in clearing away the confusion of my thoughts; if I should not clear them away, I could at any time kill myself. And here was I, a man fortunately situated, hiding away a cord, to avoid being tempted to hang myself by it to the transom between the closets of my room, where I undressed alone every evening; and I ceased to go hunting with a gun because it offered too easy a way of getting rid of life. I knew not what I wanted; I was afraid of life; I struggled to get away from it, and yet there was something I hoped for from it.

Such was the condition I had to come to, at a time when all the circumstances of my life were preeminently happy ones, and when I had not reached my fiftieth year. I had a good, loving, and beloved wife, good children, and a large estate, which, without much trouble on my part, was growing and increasing; I was more than ever respected by my friends and acquaintances; I was praised by strangers, and could lay claim to having made my name famous without much self-deception. Moreover, I was not mad or in an unhealthy mental state; on the contrary, I enjoyed a mental and physical strength which I have seldom found in men of my class and pursuits; I could keep up with a peasant in mowing, and could continue mental labor for eight or ten hours at a stretch, without any evil consequences. And in this state of things it came to this,—that I could not live, and as I feared death I was obliged to employ ruses against myself so as not to put an end to my life.

The mental state in which I then was seemed to me summed up in the following: My life was a foolish and wicked joke played on me by some one. Notwithstanding the fact that I did not recognize a "Some one," who may have created me, this conclusion that some one had wickedly and foolishly made a joke of me in bringing me into the world seemed to me the most natural of all conclusions.

It was this that was terrible! And to get free from this horror of what awaited me; I knew that this horror was more horrible than the position itself, but I could not patiently await the end. However persuasive the argument might be that all the same a blood-vessel in the heart would be ruptured or something would burst and all be over, still I could not patiently await the end. The horror of the darkness was too great to bear, and I longed to free myself from it as speedily as possible by a rope or a pistol ball. This was the feeling that, above all, drew me to think of suicide. . . .

"But is it possible that I have overlooked something, that I have failed to understand something," I asked myself; "may it not be that this state of despair is common among men?"

And in every branch of human knowledge I sought an explanation of the questions that tormented me; I sought that explanation painfully and long, not out of mere curiosity; I did not seek it indolently, but painfully, obstinately, day and night; I sought it as a perishing man seeks safety, and I found nothing.

I sought it in all branches of knowledge, and not only did I fail, but, moreover, I convinced myself that all those who had searched like myself had likewise found nothing; and not only had found nothing, but had come, as I had, to the despairing conviction, that the only absolute knowledge man can possess is this,—that life is without meaning.

I sought in all directions, and thanks to a life spent in study, and also to my connections with the learned world, the most accomplished scholars in all the various branches of knowledge were accessible to me, and they did not refuse to open to me all the sources of knowledge both in books and through personal intercourse. I knew all that learning could answer to the question, "What is life?" . . .

I had lost my way in the forest of human knowledge, in the light of the mathematical and experimental sciences which opened out for me clear horizons where there could be no house, and in the darkness of philosophy, plunging me into a greater gloom with every step I took, until I was at last persuaded that there was, and could be, no issue.

When I followed what seemed the bright light of learning, I saw that I had only turned aside from the real question. However alluring and clear were the horizons unfolded before me, however alluring it was to plunge into the infinity of these kinds of knowledge, I saw that the clearer they were the less did I need them, the less did they give me an answer to my question.

Thus my wanderings over the fields of knowledge not only failed to cure me of my despair, but increased it. One branch of knowledge gave no answer at all to the problem of life; another gave a direct answer which confirmed my despair, and showed that the state to which I had come was not the result of my going astray, of any mental disorder, but, on the contrary, it assured me that I was thinking rightly, that I was in agreement with the conclusions of the most powerful intellects among mankind.

I could not be deceived. All is vanity. A misfortune to be born. Death is better than life; life's burden must be got rid of.

My position was terrible. I knew that from the knowledge which reason has given man, I could get nothing but the denial of life, and from faith nothing but the denial of reason, which last was even more impossible than the denial of life. By the knowledge founded on reason it was proved that life is an evil and that men know it to be so, that men may cease to live if they will, but that they have lived and they go on living—I myself lived on, though I had long known that life was meaningless and evil. If I went by faith it resulted that, in order to understand the meaning of life, I should have to abandon reason, the very part of me that required a meaning in life! . . .

When I had come to this conclusion, I understood that it was useless to seek an answer to my question from knowledge founded on reason, and that the answer given by this form of knowledge is only an indication that no answer can be obtained till the question is put differently—till the question be made to include the relation between the finite and the infinite. I also understand that, however unreasonable and monstrous the answers given by faith, they have the advantage of bringing into every question the relation of the finite to the infinite, without which there can be no answer.

However I may put the question, How am I to live? the answer is, "By the law of God."

Will anything real and positive come of my life, and what?

Eternal torment, or eternal bliss.

What meaning is there not to be destroyed by death?

Union with an infinite God, paradise.

In this way I was compelled to admit that, besides the reasoning knowledge, which I once thought the only true knowledge, there was in every living man another kind of knowledge, an unreasoning one,—faith,—which gives a possibility of living. . . .

I was now ready to accept any faith that did not require of me a direct denial of reason, for that would be to act a lie; and I studied Buddhism and Mohammedanism in their books, and especially also Christianity, both in its writings and in the lives of its professors around me.

I naturally turned my attention at first to the believers in my own immediate circle, to learned men, to orthodox divines, to the older monks, to the orthodox divines of a new shade of doctrine, the so-called New Christians, who preach salvation through faith in a Redeemer. I seized upon these believers, and asked them what they believed in, and what for them gave a meaning to life.

No arguments were able to convince me of the sincerity of the faith of these men. Only actions, proving their conception of life to have destroyed the fear of poverty, illness, and death, so strong in myself, could have convinced me, and such actions I could not see among the various believers of our class. Such actions I saw, indeed, among the open infidels of my own class in life, but never among the so-called believers of our class.

I understood, then, that the faith of these men was not the faith which I sought; that it was no faith at all, but only one of the Epicurean consolations of life. I understood that this faith, if it could not really console, could at least soothe the repentant mind of a Solomon on his deathbed; but that it could not serve the enormous majority of mankind, who are born, not to be comforted by the labors of others, but to create a life for themselves. For mankind to live, for it to continue to live and be conscious of the meaning of its life, all these milliards must have another and a true conception of faith. It was not, then, the fact that Solomon, Schopenhauer, and I had not killed ourselves, which convinced me that faith existed, but the fact that these milliards have lived and are now living, carrying along with them on the impulse of their life both Solomon and ourselves.

I began to draw nearer to the believers among the poor, the simple, and the ignorant, the pilgrims, the monks, the raskolniks, and the peasants. The doctrines of these men of the people, like those of the pretended believers of my own class, were Christian. Here also much that was superstitious was mingled with the truths of Christianity, but with this difference, that the superstition of the believers of our class was entirely unnecessary to them, and never influenced their lives beyond serving as a kind of Epicurean distraction; while the superstition of the believing laboring class was so interwoven with their lives that it was impossible to conceive them without it—it was a necessary condition of their living at all. The whole life of the believers of our class was in flat contradiction with their faith, and the whole life of the believers of the people was a confirmation of the meaning of life which their faith gave them.

Thus I began to study the lives and the doctrines of the people, and the more I studied the more I became convinced that a true faith was among them, that their faith was for them a necessary thing, and alone gave them a meaning in life and a possibility of living. In direct opposition to what I saw in our circle—where life without faith was possible, and where not one in a thousand professed himself a believer—amongst the people there was not a single unbeliever in a thousand. In direct opposition to what I saw in our circle—where a whole life is spent in idleness, amusement, and dissatisfaction with life—I saw among the people whole lives passed in heavy labor and unrepining content. In direct opposition to what I saw in our circle—men resisting and indignant with the privations and sufferings of their lot—the people unhesitatingly and unresistingly accepting illness and sorrow, in the quiet and firm conviction that all these must be and could not be otherwise, and that all was for the best. In contradiction to the theory that the less learned we are the less we understand the meaning of life, and see in our sufferings and death but an evil joke, these men of the people live, suffer, and draw near to death, in quiet confidence and oftenest with joy. In contradiction to the fact that an easy death, without terror or despair, is a rare exception in our class, a death which is uneasy, rebellious, and sorrowful is among the people the rarest exception of all.

These people, deprived of all that for us and for Solomon makes the only good in life, and experiencing at the same time the highest happiness, form the great majority of mankind. I looked more widely around me, I studied the lives of the past and contemporary masses of humanity, and I saw that, not two or three, or ten, but hundreds, thousands, millions had so understood the meaning of life that they were able both to live and to die. All these men infinitely divided by manners, powers of mind, education, and position, all alike in opposition to my ignorance, were well acquainted with the meaning of life and of death, quietly labored, endured privation and suffering, lived and died, and saw in all this, not a vain, but a good thing.

I began to grow attached to these men. The more I learned of their lives, the lives of the living and of the dead of whom I read and heard, the more I liked them, and the easier I felt it so to live. I lived in this way during two years, and then there came a change which had long been preparing in me, and the symptoms of which I had always dimly felt: the life of our circle of rich and learned men, not only became repulsive, but lost all meaning. All our actions, our reasoning, our science and art, all appeared to me in a new light. I understood that it was all child's play, that it was useless to seek a meaning in it. The life of the working classes, of the whole of mankind, of those that create life, appeared to me in its true significance. I understood that this was life itself, and that the meaning given to this life was true, and I accepted it. . . .

When I remembered how these very doctrines had repelled me, how senseless they had seemed when professed by men whose lives were spent in opposition to them, and how these same doctrines had attracted me and seemed reasonable when I saw men living in accordance with them, I understood why I had once rejected them and thought them unmeaning, why I now adopted them and thought them full of meaning. I understood that I had erred, and how I had erred. I had erred, not so much through having thought incorrectly, as through having lived ill. I understood that the truth had been hidden from me, not so much because I had erred in my reasoning, as because I had led the exceptional life of an epicure bent on satisfying the lusts of the flesh. I understood that my question, "What is my life," and the answer, "An evil," were in accordance with the truth of things. The mistake lay in my having applied to life in general an answer which only concerned myself. I had asked what my own life was, and the answer was "An evil and absurdity." Exactly so, my life—a life of indulgence, of sensuality—was an absurdity and an evil, and the answer, "Life is meaningless and evil," therefore, referred only to my own life, and not to human life in general.

I understood the truth which I afterwards found in the Gospel: "That men loved darkness rather than light because their deeds were evil. For every man that doeth evil hateth the light, neither cometh to the light, lest his deeds should be reproved."

I understood that, for the meaning of life to be understood, it was necessary first that life should be something more than evil and meaningless, and afterwards that there should be the light of reason to understand it. I understood why I had so long been circling round this self-evident truth without apprehending it, and that if we would think and speak of the life of mankind, we must think and speak of that life as a whole, and not merely of the life of certain parasites on it.

This truth was always a truth, as 2 + 2 = 4, but I had not accepted it, because, besides acknowledging 2 + 2 = 4, I should have been obliged to acknowledge that I was evil. It was of more importance to me to feel that I was good, more binding on me, than to believe 2 + 2 = 4. I loved good men, I hated myself, and I accepted truth. Now it was all clear to me. . . .

My conviction of the error into which all knowledge based on reason must fall assisted me in freeing myself from the seductions of idle reasoning. The conviction that a knowledge of truth can be gained only by living, led me to doubt the justness of my own life; but I had only to get out of my own particular groove, and look around me, to observe the simple life of the real working class, to understand that such a life was the only real one. I understand that, if I wished to understand life and its meaning, I must live, not the life of a parasite, but a real life; and, accepting the meaning given to it by the combined lives of those that really form the great human whole, submit it to a close examination.

At the time I am speaking of, the following was my position:

During the whole of that year, when I was asking myself almost every minute whether I should or should not put an end to it all with a cord or a pistol, during the time my mind was occupied with the thoughts which I have described, my heart was oppressed by a tormenting feeling. This feeling I cannot describe otherwise than as a searching after God.

This search after God was not an act of my reason, but a feeling, and I say this advisedly, because it was opposed to my way of thinking; it came from the heart. It was a feeling of dread, of orphanhood, of isolation amid things all apart from me, and of hope in a help I knew not from whom.

I remember one day in the early springtime I was alone in the forest listening to the woodland sounds, and thinking only of one thing, the same of which I had constantly thought for two years—I was again seeking for a God.

I said to myself:

"Very good, there is no God, there is none with a reality apart from my own imaginings, none as real as my own life—there is none such. Nothing, no miracles can prove there is, for miracles only exist in my own unreasonable imagination."

And then I asked myself:

"But my idea of the God whom I seek, whence comes it?"

And again at this thought arose the joyous billows of life. All around me seemed to revive, to have a new meaning. My joy, though, did not last long. Reason continued its work:

"The idea of a God is not God. The idea is what goes on within myself; the idea of God is an idea which I am able to rouse in my mind or not as I choose; it is not what I seek, something without which life could not be."

Then again all seemed to die around and within me, and again I wished to kill myself.

After this I began to retrace the process which had gone on within myself, the hundred times repeated discouragement and revival. I remembered that I had lived only when I believed in a God. As it was before, so it was now; I had only to know God, and I lived; I had only to forget Him, not to believe in Him, and I died.

What was this discouragement and revival? I do not live when I lose faith in the existence of a God; I should long ago have killed myself, if I had not had a dim hope of finding Him. I really live only when I am conscious of Him and seek Him. "What more, then, do I seek?" A voice seemed to cry within me, "This is He, He without whom there is no life. To know God and to live are one. God is life."

Live to seek God, and life will not be without God. And stronger than ever rose up life within and around me, and the light that then shone never left me again.

The Riddle of the Ordinary

Cynthia Ozick

Ozick claims that people look at the day-to-day routine of life as ordinary, but, in fact, she claims it is extraordinary. Our attitude has an impact on the meaning and purpose we find in life. She claims that we look for God in extraordinary events that occur in our lives, but we seldom see God as part of the ordinary. Essentially, we look for God in all the wrong places. Do you agree?

Though we all claim to be monotheists, there is one rather ordinary way in which we are all also dualists: we all divide the world into the Ordinary and the Extraordinary. This is undoubtedly the most natural division the mind is subject to—plain and fancy, simple and recondite, commonplace and awesome, usual and unusual, credible and incredible, quotidian and intrusive, natural and unnatural, regular and irregular, boring and rhapsodic, secular and sacred, profane and holy: however the distinction is characterized, there is no human being who does not, in his own everydayness, feel

From *Art and Ardor* by Cynthia Ozick. Copyright © 1983 by Cynthia Ozick. Reprinted by permission of Alfred A. Knopf, Inc.

the difference between the Ordinary and the Extraordinary.

The Extraordinary is easy. And the more extraordinary the Extraordinary is, the easier it is: "easy" in the sense that we can almost always recognize it. There is no one who does not know when something special is happening: the high, terrifying, tragic, and ecstatic moments are unmistakable in any life. Of course the Extraordinary can sometimes be a changeling, and can make its appearance in the cradle of the Ordinary; and then it is not until long afterward that we become aware of how the visitation was not, after all, an ordinary one. But by and large the difference between special times and ordinary moments is perfectly clear, and we are never in any doubt about which are the extraordinary ones.

How do we respond to the Extraordinary? This too is easy: by paying attention to it. The Extraordinary is so powerful that it commands from us a redundancy, a repetition of itself: it seizes us so undividedly, it declares itself so dazzlingly or killingly, it is so deafening with its LOOK! SEE! NOTICE! PAY ATTENTION! that the only answer we can give is to look, see, notice, and pay attention. The Extraordinary sets its own terms for its reception, and its terms are inescapable. The Extraordinary does not let you shrug your shoulders and walk away.

But the Ordinary is a much harder case. In the first place, by making itself so noticeable—it is around us all the time—the Ordinary has got itself in a bad fix with us: we hardly ever notice it. The Ordinary, simply by *being* so ordinary, tends to make us ignorant or neglectful; when something does not insist on being noticed, when we aren't grabbed by the collar or struck on the skull by a presence or an event, we take for granted the very things that most deserve our gratitude.

And this is the chief vein and deepest point concerning the Ordinary: that it *does* deserve our gratitude. The Ordinary lets us live out our humanity; it doesn't scare us, it doesn't excite us, it doesn't distract us—it brings us the safe return of the school bus every day, it lets us eat one meal after another, put one foot in front of the other. In short, it is equal to the earth's provisions; it grants us life, continuity, the leisure to recognize who and what we are, and who and what our fellows are, these creatures who live out their everydayness side by side with us in their own unextraordinary ways. Ordinariness can be defined as a breathing-space: the breathing-space between getting born and dying, perhaps; or else the breathing-space between rapture and rapture; or, more usually, the breathing-space between one disaster and the next. Ordinariness is sometimes the *status quo,* sometimes the slow, unseen movement of a subtle but ineluctable cycle, like a ride on the hour hand of the clock; in any case the Ordinary is above all *what is expected.*

And what is expected is not often thought of as a gift.

The second thing that ought to be said about the Ordinary is that it is sometimes extraordinarily dangerous to notice it. And this is strange, because I have just spoken of the gratitude we owe to the unnoticed foundations of our lives, and how careless we always are about this gratitude, how unthinking we are to take for granted the humdrum dailiness that is all the luxury we are ever likely to know on this planet. There are ways to try to apprehend the nature of this luxury, but they are psychological tricks, and do no good. It is pointless to contemplate, only for the sake of feeling gratitude, the bitter, vicious, crippled, drugged, diseased, deformed, despoiled, or corrupted lives that burst against their own mortality in hospitals, madhouses, prisons, all those horrendous lives chained to poverty and its variegated spawn in the long, bleak wastes on the outer margins of Ordinariness, mired in the dread of a ferocious Extraordinariness that slouches in insatiably every morning and never departs even in sleep—contemplating this, who would deny gratitude to our own Ordinariness, though it does not come easily, and has its demeaning price? Still, comparison confers relief more often than gratitude, and the gratitude that rises out of reflection on the extraordinary misfortune of others is misbegotten.—You remember how in one of the Old English poets we are told how the rejoicing hosts of heaven look down at the tortures of the damned, feeling the special pleasure of their own exemption. The consciousness of Ordinariness *is* the consciousness of exemption.

That is one way it is dangerous to take special notice of the Ordinary.

The second danger, I think, is even more terrible. But before I am ready to speak of this new, nevertheless very ancient, danger, I want to ask this question: If we are willing to see the Ordinary as a treasure and a gift, what are we to *do* about it? Or, to put it another way, what is to be gained from noticing the Ordinary? Morally and metaphysically, what are our obligations to the Ordinary? Here art and philosophy meet with a quizzical harmony unusual between contenders. "Be one of those upon whom nothing is lost," Henry James advised; and that is one answer, the answer of what would appear to be the supreme aesthetician. For the sake of the honing of consciousness, for the sake of becoming sensitive, at every moment, *to* every moment, for the sake of making life as superlatively polished as the most sublime work of art, we ought to notice the Ordinary.

No one since the Greek sculptors and artisans has expressed this sense more powerfully than Walter Pater, that eloquent Victorian whose obsession with attaining the intensest sensations possible casts a familiar light out toward the century that followed him. Pater, like Coleridge before him and James after him, like the metaphysicians of what has come to be known as the Counterculture, was after all the highs he could accumulate in a lifetime. "We are all under sentence of death," he writes, ". . . we have an interval, and then our place knows us no more. Some spend this interval in listlessness, some in high passions, the wisest . . . in art and song. For our only chance lies in expanding that interval, in getting as many pulsations as possible into the given time. Great passions may give us this quickened sense of life. . . . Only be sure it is passion—that it does yield you this fruit of a quickened, multiplied consciousness. . . . Of this wisdom, the poetic passion, the desire for beauty, the love of art for art's sake, has most; for art comes to you professing frankly to give nothing but the highest quality to your moments as they pass, and simply for those moments' sake." And like a Zen master who seizes on the data of life only to transcend them, he announces: "Not the fruit of experience, but experience itself, is the end."

What—in this view, which once more has the allegiance of the *Zeitgeist*—what is Art? It is first noticing, and then sanctifying, the Ordinary. It is making the Ordinary into the Extraordinary. It is the impairment of the distinction between the Ordinary and the Extraordinary.

The aestheticians—the great Experiencers—can be refuted. I bring you a Hebrew melody to refute them with. It is called "The Choice"; the poet is Yeats; and since the poem is only eight lines long I would like to give over the whole of it. It begins by discriminating between essence and possession: life interpreted as *doing* beautiful things or *having* beautiful things:

> The intellect of man is forced to choose
> Perfection of the life, or of the work,

And if it take the second must refuse
A heavenly mansion, raging in the dark.
When all that story's finished, what's the
  news?
In luck or out the toil has left its mark:
That old perplexity an empty purse,
Or the day's vanity, the night's remorse.

Our choice, according to Yeats, is the choice between pursuing the life of Deed, where acts have consequences, where the fruit of experience is more gratifying than the experience itself, and pursuing the life of Art, which signifies the celebration of shape and mood. Art, he tells us, turns away from the divine preference, and finishes out a life in empty remorse; in the end the sum of the life of Art is nothing. The ironies here are multitudinous, for no one ever belonged more to the mansion of Art than Yeats himself, and it might be said that in this handful of remarkable lines Yeats condemned his own passions and his own will.

But there is a way in which the Yeats poem, though it praises Deed over Image, though it sees the human being as a creature to be judged by his acts rather than by how well he has made something—there is a way in which this poem is after all *not* a Hebrew melody. The Jewish perception of how the world is constituted also tells us that we are to go in the way of Commandment rather than symbol, goodness rather than sensation: but it will never declare that the price of Art, Beauty, Experience, Pleasure, Exaltation is a "raging in the dark" or a loss of the "heavenly mansion."

The Jewish understanding of the Ordinary is in some ways very close to Pater, and again very far from Yeats, who would punish the "perfection of the work" with an empty destiny.

With David the King we say, "All that is in the heaven and the earth is thine," meaning that it is all there for our wonder and our praise. "Be one of those upon whom nothing is lost"—James's words, but the impulse that drives them is the same as the one enjoining the observant Jew (the word "observant" is exact) to bless the moments of this world at least one hundred times a day. One hundred times: but Ordinariness is more frequent than that, Ordinariness crowds the day, we swim in the sense of our dailiness; and yet there is a blessing for every separate experience of the Ordinary.

Jewish life is crammed with such blessings—blessings that take note of every sight, sound, and smell, every rising-up and lying-down, every morsel brought to the mouth, every act of cleansing. Before he sits down to his meal, the Jew will speak the following: "Blessed are You, O Lord our God, Ruler of the Universe, whose Commandments hallow us and who commands us to wash our hands." When he breaks his bread, he will bless God for having "brought forth bread from the earth." Each kind of food is similarly praised in turn, and every fruit in its season is praised for having renewed itself in the cycle of the seasons. And when the meal is done, a thanksgiving is said for the whole of it, and table songs are sung with exultation.

The world and its provisions, in short, are *observed*—in the two meanings of "observe." Creation is both noticed and felt to be sanctified. Everything is minutely paid attention to, and then ceremoniously praised. Here is a Talmudic saying: "Whoever makes a profane use of God's gifts"—which means partaking of any worldly joy without thanking God for it—"commits a theft against God." And a Talmudic dispute is recorded concerning which is the more important Scriptural utterance: loving your neighbor as yourself, or the idea that we are all the children of Adam. The sage who has the final word chooses the children-of-Adam thesis, because, he explains, our common creatureliness includes the necessity of love.

But these celebrations through noticing are not self-centered and do not stop at humanity, but encompass every form of life and non-life. So there are blessings to rejoice in on smelling sweet woods or barks, fragrant plants, fruits, spices, or oils. There is a blessing on witnessing lightning, falling stars, great mountains and deserts: "Blessed are You . . . who fashioned Creation." The sound of thunder has its praise, and the sight of the sea, and a rainbow; beautiful animals are praised, and trees in their first blossoming of the year or for their beauty alone, and the new moon, and new clothing, and sexual delight. The sight of a sage brings a blessing for the creation of human wisdom, the sight of a disfigured person praises a Creator who varies the form of his creatures. From the stone to the human being, creatureliness is extolled.

This huge and unending shower of blessings on our scenes and habitations, on all the life that occupies the planet, on every plant and animal, and on every natural manifestation, serves us doubly: in the first place, what you are taught to praise you will not maim or exploit or destroy. In the second place, the categories and impulses of Art become the property of the simplest soul: because it is all the handiwork of the Creator, everything Ordinary is seen to be Extraordinary. The world, and every moment in it, is seen to be sublime, and not merely "seen to be," but brought home to the intensest part of consciousness.

Come back with me now to Pater: "The service of philosophy," he writes, "of speculative culture, toward the human spirit is to rouse, to startle it into sharp and eager observation. Every moment some form grows perfect in hand or face; some tone on the hills or the sea is choicer than the rest; some mood of passion or insight or intellectual excitement is irresistibly real and attractive to us—for that moment only." And now here at last is Pater's most celebrated phrase, so famous that it has often been burlesqued: "To burn always with this hard, gemlike flame, to maintain this ecstasy, is success in life."

But all this is astonishing. An idolator singing a Hebrew melody? I call Pater an idolator because he is one; and so is every aesthetician who sees the work of art as an end in itself. Saying "Experience itself is the end" is the very opposite of blessing the Creator as the source of all experience.

And just here is the danger I spoke of before, the danger Yeats darkly apprehended—the deepest danger our human brains are subject to. The Jew has this in common with the artist: he means nothing to be lost on him, he brings all his mind and senses to bear on noticing the Ordinary, he is equally alert to Image and Experience, nothing that passes before him is taken for granted, everything is exalted. If we are enjoined to live in the condition of noticing all things—or, to put it more extremely but more exactly, in the condition of awe—*how can we keep ourselves from sliding off from awe at God's Creation to worship of God's Creation?* And does it matter if we do?

The difference, the reason it matters, is a single and shattering one: the difference is what keeps us from being idolators.

What is an idol? Anything that is allowed to come between ourselves and God. Anything that is *instead* of God. Anything that we call an end in itself, and yet is not God Himself.

The Mosaic vision concerning all this is uncompromisingly pure and impatient with self-deception, and this is the point on which Jews are famously stiff-necked—nothing but the Creator, no substitute and no mediator. The Creator is not contained in his own Creation; the Creator is incarnate in nothing, and is free of any image or imagining. God is not any part of Nature, or in any part of Nature; God is not any man, or in any man. When we praise Nature or man or any experience or work of man, we are worshipping the Creator, and the Creator alone.

But there is another way of thinking which is easier, and sweeter, and does not require human beings to be so tirelessly uncompromising, or to be so cautious about holding on to the distinction between delight in the world and worship of the world.

Here is a story. A Buddhist sage once rebuked a person who excoriated an idolator: "Do you think it makes any difference to God," he asked, "whether this old woman gives reverence to a block of wood? Do you think God is incapable of taking the block of wood into Himself? Do you think God will ignore anyone's desire to find Him, no matter where, and through whatever means? All worship goes up to God, who is the source of worship."

These are important words; they offer the most significant challenge to purist monotheism that has ever been stated. They tell us that the Ordinary is not merely, when contemplated with intensity, the Extraordinary, but more, much more than that—that the Ordinary is also the divine. Now there are similar comments in Jewish sources, especially in Hasidism, which dwell compassionately on the nobility of the striving for God, no matter through what means. But the striving is always toward the Creator Himself, the struggle is always toward the winnowing-out of every mediating surrogate. The Kotzker Rebbe went so far in his own striving that he even dared to interpret the command against idols as a warning not to make an idol out of a command of God.—So, in general, Jewish thought balks at taking the metaphor for the essence, at taking the block of wood as symbol or representation or mediator for God, despite the fact that the wood and its worshiper stand for everything worthy of celebration: the tree grew in its loveliness, the carver came and fashioned it into a pleasing form, the woman is alert to holiness; the tree, the carver, the woman who is alert to holiness are, all together, a loveliness and a reason to rejoice in the world. But still the wood does not mean God. It is instead of God.

It is not true, as we so often hear, that Judaism is a developmental religion, that there is a progression upward from Moses to the Prophets. The Prophets enjoined backsliders to renew themselves through the Mosaic idea, and the Mosaic idea is from then to now, and has survived unmodified: "Take heed to yourselves, that your heart be not deceived, and ye turn aside, and serve other gods, and worship them." (Deut. 11:16.) This perception has never been superseded. To seem to supersede it is to transgress it.

So it is dangerous to notice and to praise the Ordinariness of the world, its inhabitants and its events. We want to do it, we rejoice to do it, above all we are commanded to do it—but there is always the easy, the sweet, the beckoning, the lenient, the *interesting* lure of the *Instead Of:* the wood of the tree instead of God, the rapture-bringing horizon instead of God, the work of art instead of God, the passion for history instead of God, philosophy and the history of philosophy instead of God, the state instead of God, the shrine instead of God, the sage instead of God, the order of the universe instead of God, the prophet instead of God.

There is no Instead Of. There is only the Creator. God is alone. That is what we mean when we utter the ultimate Idea which is the pinnacle of the Mosaic revolution in human perception: God is One.

The child of a friend of mine was taken to the Egyptian galleries of the Museum. In a glass case stood the figure of a cat resplendent in the perfection of its artfulness—long-necked, gracile, cryptic, authoritative, beautiful, spiritual, autonomous, complete in itself. "I understand," said the child, "how they wanted to bow down to this cat. I feel the same." And then she said a Hebrew word: *asur*—forbidden—the great hallowed No that tumbles down the centuries from Sinai, the No that can be said only after the world is no longer taken for granted, the No that can rise up only out of the abundant celebrations and blessings of Yes, Yes, Yes, the shower of Yeses that praise fragrant oils, and wine, and sex, and scholars, and thunder, and new clothes, and falling stars, and washing your hands before eating.

The Unseen Order

William James

Must a religious experience be bound to any particular creed or religious doctrine? What may be the nature and content of authentic religious experiences? In the reading that follows, William James examines some answers to these questions. What he finds is that a religious experience may have elements of the irrational in it; a religious experience may come with a feeling of unreality or a sense of a "quasi-sensible" reality. Whatever else, it seems to be an experience of a presence.

Were one asked to characterize the life of religion in the broadest and most general terms possible, one might say that it consists of the belief that there is an unseen order, and that our supreme good lies in harmoniously adjusting ourselves thereto. This belief and this adjustment are the religious attitude in the soul. I wish during this hour to call your attention to some of the psychological peculiarities of such an attitude as this, or belief in an object which we cannot see. All our attitudes, moral, practical, or emotional, as well as religious, are due to the "objects" of our consciousness, the things which we believe to exist, whether really or ideally, along with ourselves. Such objects may be present to our senses, or they may be present only to our thought. In either case they elicit from us a *reaction;* and the reaction due to things of thought is notoriously in many cases as strong as that due to sensible presences. It may be even stronger. The memory of an insult may make us angrier than the insult did when we received it. We are frequently more ashamed of our blunders afterwards than we were at the moment of making them; and in general our whole higher prudential and moral life is based on the fact that material sensations actually present may have a weaker influence on our action than ideas of remoter facts.

The more concrete objects of most men's religion, the deities whom they worship, are known to them only in idea. It has

From *The Varieties of Religious Experience* by William James. New York: Macmillan, 1961, pp. 59–60, 61–63, 66–72, 73–77.

been vouchsafed, for example, to very few Christian believers to have had a sensible vision of their Saviour; though enough appearances of this sort are on record, by way of miraculous exception, to merit our attention later. The whole force of the Christian religion, therefore, so far as belief in the divine personages determines the prevalent attitude of the believer, is in general exerted by the instrumentality of pure ideas, of which nothing in the individual's past experience directly serves as a model.

But in addition to these ideas of the more concrete religious objects, religion is full of abstract objects which prove to have equal power. God's attributes as such, his holiness, his justice, his mercy, his absoluteness, his infinity, his omniscience, his triunity, the various mysteries of the redemptive process, the operation of the sacraments, etc., have proved fertile wells of inspiring meditation for Christian believers.[1] We shall see later that the absence of definite sensible images is positively insisted on by the mystical authorities in all religions as the *sine qua non* of a successful orison, or contemplation of the higher divine truths. Such contemplations are expected (and abundantly verify the expectation, as we shall also see) to influence the believer's subsequent attitude very powerfully for good. . . .

This absolute determinability of our mind by abstractions is one of the cardinal facts in our human constitution. Polarizing and magnetizing us as they do, we turn towards them and from them, we seek them, hold them, hate them, bless them, just as if they were so many concrete beings. And beings they are, beings as real in the realm which they inhabit as the changing things of sense are in the realm of space.

Plato gave so brilliant and impressive a defense of this common human feeling, that the doctrine of the reality of abstract objects has been known as the platonic theory of ideas ever since. Abstract Beauty, for example, is for Plato a perfectly definite individual being, of which the intellect is aware as of something additional to all the perishing beauties of the earth. "The true order of going," he says, in the often quoted passage in his "Banquet," "is to use the beauties of earth as steps along which one amounts upwards for the sake of that other Beauty, going from one to two, and from two to all fair forms, and from fair forms to fair actions, and from fair actions to fair notions, until from fair notions, he arrives at the notion of absolute Beauty, and at last knows what the essence of Beauty is."[2] In our last lecture we had a glimpse of the way in which a platonizing writer like Emerson may treat the abstract divineness of things, the moral structure of the universe, as a fact worthy of worship. In those various churches without a God which to-day are spreading through the world under the name of ethical societies, we have a similar worship of the abstract divine, the moral law believed in as an ultimate object. "Science" in many minds is genuinely taking the place of a religion. Where this is so, the scientist treats the "Laws of Nature" as objective facts to be revered. A brilliant school of interpretation of Greek mythology would have it that in their origin the Greek gods were only half-metaphoric personifications of those great spheres of abstract law and order into which

[1]Example: "I have had much comfort lately in meditating on the passages which show the personality of the Holy Ghost, and his distinctness from the Father and Son. It is a subject that requires searching into to find out, but, when realized, gives one so much more true and lively a sense of the fullness of the Godhead, and its works in us, than when only thinking of the Spirit in its effect on us." Augustus Hare: Memorials, i, 224, Maria Hare to Lucy H. Hare.

[2]Symposium, Jowett, 1871, i. 527.

the natural world falls apart—the sky-sphere, the ocean-sphere, the earth-sphere, and the like; just as even now we may speak of the smile of the morning, the kiss of the breeze, or the bite of the cold, without really meaning that these phenomena of nature actually wear a human face.[3]

As regards the origin of the Greek gods, we need not at present seek an opinion. But the whole array of our instances leads to a conclusion something like this: It is as if there were in the human consciousness a *sense of reality, a feeling of objective presence, a perception* of what we may call "something there," more deep and more general than any of the special and particular "senses" by which the current psychology supposes existent realities to be originally revealed. If this were so, we might suppose the senses to waken our attitudes and conduct as they so habitually do, by first exciting this sense of reality; but anything else, any idea, for example, that might similarly excite it, would have that same prerogative of appearing real which objects of sense normally possess. So far as religious conceptions were able to touch this reality-feeling, they would be believed in spite of criticism, even though they might be so vague and remote as to be almost unimaginable, even though they might be such non-entities in point of *whatness*, as Kant makes the objects of his moral theology to be. . . .

In an earlier book of mine I have cited at full length a curious case of presence felt by a blind man. The presence was that of the figure of a gray-bearded man dressed in a pepper and salt suit, squeezing himself under the crack of the door and moving across the floor of the room towards a sofa. The blind subject of this quasi-hallucination is an exceptionally intelligent reporter. He is entirely without internal visual imagery and cannot represent light or colors to himself, and is positive that his other senses, hearing, etc., were not involved in this false perception. It seems to have been an abstract conception rather, with the feelings of reality and spatial outwardness directly attached to it—in other words, a fully objectified and exteriorized *idea*.

Such cases, taken along with others which would be too tedious for quotation, seem sufficiently to prove the existence in our mental machinery of a sense of present reality more diffused and general than that which our special senses yield. For the psychologists the tracing of the organic seat of such a feeling would form a pretty problem—nothing could be more natural than to connect it with the muscular sense, with the feeling that our muscles were innervating themselves for action. Whatsoever thus innervated our activity, or "made our flesh creep"—our senses are what do so oftenest—might then appear real and present, even though it were but an abstract idea. But with such vague conjectures we have no concern at present, for our interest lies with the faculty rather than with its organic seat.

Like all positive affections of consciousness, the sense of reality has its negative counterpart in the shape of a feeling of unreality by which persons may be haunted, and of which one sometimes hears complaint:—

> "When I reflect on the fact that I have made my appearance by accident upon a globe itself whirled through space as the sport of the catastrophes of the heavens," says Madame Ackermann; "when I see myself surrounded by beings as ephemeral and incomprehensible as I am myself, and all excitedly pursuing pure

[3]Example: "Nature is always so interesting, under whatever aspect she shows herself, that when it rains, I seem to see a beautiful woman weeping. She appears the more beautiful, the more afflicted she is." B. de St. Pierre.

> chimeras, I experience a strange feeling of being in a dream. It seems to me as if I have loved and suffered and that erelong I shall die, in a dream. My last word will be, 'I have been dreaming.' "[4]

In another lecture we shall see how in morbid melancholy this sense of the unreality of things may become a carking pain, and even lead to suicide.

We may now lay it down as certain that in the distinctively religious sphere of experience, many persons (how many we cannot tell) possess the objects of their belief, not in the form of mere conceptions which their intellect accepts as true, but rather in the form of quasi-sensible realities directly apprehended. As his sense of the real presence of these objects fluctuates, so the believer alternates between warmth and coldness in his faith. Other examples will bring this home to one better than abstract description, so I proceed immediately to cite some. The first example is a negative one, deploring the loss of the sense in question. I have extracted it from an account given me by a scientific man of my acquaintance, of his religious life. It seems to me to show clearly that the feeling of reality may be something more like a sensation than an intellectual operation properly so-called.

> "Between twenty and thirty I gradually became more and more agnostic and irreligious, yet I cannot say that I ever lost that 'indefinite consciousness' which Herbert Spencer describes so well, of an Absolute Reality behind phenomena. For me this Reality was not the pure Unknowable of Spencer's philosophy, for although I had ceased my childish prayers to God, and never prayed to *It* in a formal manner, yet my more recent experience shows me to have been in a relation to *It* which practically was the same thing as prayer. Whenever I had any trouble, especially when I had conflict with other people, either domestically or in the way of business, or when I was depressed in spirits or anxious about affairs, I now recognize that I used to fall back for support upon this curious relation I felt myself to be in to this fundamental cosmical *It*. It was on my side, or I was on Its side, however you please to term it, in the particular trouble, and it always strengthened me and seemed to give me endless vitality to feel its underlying and supporting presence. In fact, it was an unfailing fountain of living justice, truth, and strength, to which I instinctively turned at times of weakness, and it always brought me out. I know now that it was a personal relation I was in to it, because of late years the power of communicating with it has left me, and I am conscious of a perfectly definite loss. I used never to fail to find it when I turned to it. Then came a set of years when sometimes I found it, and then again I would be wholly unable to make connection with it. I remember many occasions on which at night in bed, I would be unable to get to sleep on account of worry. I turned this way and that in the darkness, and groped mentally for the familiar sense of that higher mind of my mind which had always seemed to be close at hand as it were, closing the passage, and yielding support, but there was no electric current. A blank was there instead of *It:* I couldn't find anything. Now, at the age of nearly fifty, my power of getting into connection with it has entirely left me; and I have to confess that a great help has gone out of my life. Life has become curiously dead and indifferent; and I can now see that my old experience was probably exactly the same thing as the prayers of the orthodox, only I did not call them by that name. What I have spoken of as 'It' was practically not Spencer's Unknowable, but just my own instinctive and individual God, whom I relied upon for higher sympathy, but whom somehow I have lost."

Nothing is more common in the pages of religious biography than the way in which seasons of lively and of difficult faith are

---

[4]Pensées d'un Solitaire, p. 66.

described as alternating. Probably every religious person has the recollection of particular crisis in which a director vision of the truth, a direct perception, perhaps, of a living God's existence, swept in and overwhelmed the languor of the more ordinary belief. In James Russell Lowell's correspondence there is a brief memorandum of an experience of this kind:—

> "I had a revelation last Friday evening. I was at Mary's, and happening to say something of the presence of spirits (of whom, I said, I was often dimly aware), Mr. Putnam entered into an argument with me on spiritual matters. As I was speaking, the whole system rose up before me like a vague destiny looming from the Abyss. I never before so clearly felt the Spirit of God in me and around me. The whole room seemed to me full of God. The air seemed to waver to and fro with the presence of Something I knew not what. I spoke with the calmness and clearness of a prophet. I cannot tell you what this revelation was. I have not yet studied it enough. But I shall perfect it one day, and then you shall hear it and acknowledge its grandeur."[5]

Here is a longer and more developed experience from a manuscript communication by a clergyman—I take it from Starbuck's manuscript collection:—

> "I remember the night, and almost the very spot on the hilltop, where my soul opened out, as it were, into the Infinite, and there was a rushing together of the two worlds, the inner and the outer. It was deep calling unto deep—the deep that my own struggle had opened up within being answered by the unfathomable deep without, reaching beyond the stars. I stood alone with Him who had made me, and all the beauty of the world, and love, and sorrow, and even temptation. I did not seek Him, but felt the perfect unison of my spirit with His. The ordinary sense of things around me faded. For the moment nothing but an ineffable joy and exultation remained. It is impossible fully to describe the experience. It was like the effect of some great orchestra when all the separate notes have melted into one swelling harmony that leaves the listener conscious of nothing save that his soul is being wafted upwards, and almost bursting with its own emotion. The perfect stillness of the night was thrilled by a more solemn silence. The darkness held a presence that was all the more felt because it was not seen. I could not any more have doubted that *He* was there than that I was. Indeed, I felt myself to be, if possible, the less real of the two.
>
> "My highest faith in God and truest idea of him were then born in me. I have stood upon the Mount of Vision since, and felt the Eternal round about me. But never since has there come quite the same stirring of the heart. Then, if ever, I believe, I stood face to face with God, and was born anew of his spirit. There was, as I recall it, no sudden change of thought or of belief, except that my early crude conception, had, as it were, burst into flower. There was no destruction of the old, but a rapid, wonderful unfolding. Since that time no discussion that I have heard of the proofs of God's existence has been able to shake my faith. Having once felt the presence of God's spirit, I have never lost it again for long. My most assuring evidence of his existence is deeply rooted in that hour of vision, in the memory of that supreme experience, and in the conviction, gained from reading and reflection, that something the same has come to all who have found God. I am aware that it may justly be called mystical. I am not enough acquainted with philosophy to defend it from that or any other charge. I feel that in writing of it I have overlaid it with words rather than put it clearly to your thought. But, such as it is, I have described it as carefully as I now am able to do."

Here is another document, even more definite in character, which, the writer

[5]Letters of Lowell, i, 75.

being a Swiss, I translate from the French original.[6]

"I was in perfect health: we were on our sixth day of tramping, and in good training. We had come the day before from Sixt to Trient by Buet. I felt neither fatigue, hunger, nor thirst, and my state of mind was equally healthy. I had had at Forlaz good news from home; I was subject to no anxiety, either near or remote, for we had a good guide, and there was not a shadow of uncertainty about the road we should follow. I can best describe the condition in which I was by calling it a state of equilibrium. When all at once I experienced a feeling of being raised above myself, I felt the presence of God—I tell of the thing just as I was conscious of it—as if his goodness and his power were penetrating me altogether. The throb of emotion was so violent that I could barely tell the boys to pass on and not wait for me. I then sat down on a stone, unable to stand any longer, and my eyes overflowed with tears. I thanked God that in the course of my life he had taught me to know him, that he sustained my life and took pity both on the insignificant creature and on the sinner that I was. I begged him ardently that my life might be consecrated to the doing of his will. I felt his reply, which was that I should do his will from day to day, in humility and poverty, leaving him, the Almighty God, to be judge of whether I should some time be called to bear witness more conspicuously. Then, slowly, the ecstasy left my heart; that is, I felt that God had withdrawn the communion which he had granted, and I was able to walk on, but very slowly, so strongly was I still possessed by the interior emotion. Besides, I had wept uninterruptedly for several minutes, my eyes were swollen, and I did not wish my companions to see me. The state of ecstasy may have lasted for four or five minutes, although it seemed at the time to last much longer. My comrades waited for me ten minutes at the cross of Barine, but I took about twenty-five or thirty minutes to join them, for as well as I can remember, they said that I had kept them back for about half an hour. The impression had been so profound that in climbing slowly the slope I asked myself if it were possible that Moses on Sinai could have had a more intimate communication with God. I think it well to add that in this ecstasy of mine God had neither form, color, odor, nor taste; moreover, that the feeling of his presence was accompanied with no determinate localization. It was rather as if my personality had been transformed by the presence of a *spiritual spirit*. But the more I seek words to express this intimate intercourse, the more I feel the impossibility of describing the thing by any of our usual images. At bottom the expression most apt to render what I felt is this: God was present, though invisible; he fell under no one of my senses, yet my consciousness perceived him."

The adjective "mystical" is technically applied, most often, to states that are of brief duration. Of course such hours of rapture as the last two persons describe are mystical experiences, of which in a later lecture I shall have much to say. Meanwhile here is the abridged record of another mystical or semi-mystical experience, in a mind evidently framed by nature for ardent piety. I owe it to Starbuck's collection. The lady who gives the account is the daughter of a man well known in his time as a writer against Christianity. The suddenness of her conversion shows well how native the sense of God's presence must be to certain minds. She relates that she was brought up in entire ignorance of Christian doctrine, but, when in Germany, after being talked to by Christian friends, she read the Bible and prayed, and finally the plan of salvation flashed upon her like a stream of light.

"To this day," she writes, "I cannot understand dallying with religion and the commands of God. The very instant I heard my Father's cry calling unto me, my heart bounded in recog-

[6]I borrow it, with Professor Flournoy's permission, from his rich collection of psychological documents.

nition. I ran, I stretched forth my arms, I cried aloud, 'Here, here I am, my Father.' Oh, happy child, what should I do? 'Love me,' answered my God. 'I do, I do,' I cried passionately. 'Come unto me,' called my Father. 'I will,' my heart panted. Did I stop to ask a single question? Not one. It never occurred to me to ask whether I was good enough, or to hesitate over my unfitness, or to find out what I thought of his church, or . . . to wait until I should be satisfied. Satisfied! I was satisfied. Had I not found my God and my Father? Did he not love me? Had he not called me? Was there not a Church into which I might enter? . . . Since then I have had direct answers to prayer—so significant as to be almost like talking with God and hearing his answer. The idea of God's reality has never left me for one moment."

Here is still another case, the writer being a man aged twenty-seven, in which the experience, probably almost as characteristic, is less vividly described:—

"I have on a number of occasions felt that I had enjoyed a period of intimate communion with the divine. These meetings came unasked and unexpected, and seemed to consist merely in the temporary obliteration of the conventionalities which usually surround and cover my life. . . . Once it was when from the summit of a high mountain I looked over a gashed and corrugated landscape extending to a long convex of ocean that ascended to the horizon, and again from the same point when I could see nothing beneath me but a boundless expanse of white cloud, on the blown surface of which a few high peaks, including the one I was on, seemed plunging about as if they were dragging their anchors. What I felt on these occasions was a temporary loss of my identity, accompanied by an illumination which revealed to me a deeper significance than I had been wont to attach to life. It is in this that I find my justification for saying that I have enjoyed communication with God. Of course the absence of such a being as this would be chaos. I cannot conceive of life without its presence."

Of the more habitual and so to speak chronic sense of God's presence the following sample from Professor Starbuck's manuscript collection may serve to give an idea. It is from a man aged forty-nine—probably thousands of unpretending Christians would write an almost identical account.

"God is more real to me than any thought or thing or person. I feel his presence positively, and the more as I live in closer harmony with his laws as written in my body and mind. I feel him in the sunshine or rain; and awe mingled with a delicious restfulness most nearly describes my feelings. I talk to him as to a companion in prayer and praise, and our communion is delightful. He answers me again and again, often in words so clearly spoken that it seems my outer ear must have carried the tone, but generally in strong mental impressions. Usually a text of Scripture, unfolding some new view of him and his love for me, and care for my safety. I could give hundreds of instances, in school matters, social problems, financial difficulties, etc. That he is mine and I am his never leaves me, it is an abiding joy. Without it life would be a blank, a desert, a shoreless, trackless waste."

. . . I spoke of the convincingness of these feelings of reality, and I must dwell a moment longer on that point. They are as convincing to those who have them as any direct sensible experience can be, and they are, as a rule, much more convincing than results established by mere logic ever are. One may indeed be entirely without them; probably more than one of you here present is without them in any marked degree; but if you do have them, and have them at all strongly, the probability is that you cannot help regarding them as genuine perceptions of truth, as revelations of a kind of reality which no adverse argument, however unanswerable by you in words, can expel from your belief. The opinion opposed to mysticism in philosophy is sometimes spoken of as *rationalism.* Rationalism insists that all our beliefs ought ultimately to find for themselves articulate grounds. Such grounds, for rationalism, must consist of four things: (1) definitely statable abstract principles; (2) definite facts of sensation; (3) definite hypotheses based on such facts; and (4) definite inferences logically drawn. Vague impressions of something indefinable have no place in the rationalistic system, which on its positive side is surely a splendid intellectual tendency, for not only are all our philosophies fruits of it, but physical science (amongst other good things) is its result.

Nevertheless, if we look on man's whole mental life as it exists, on the life of men that lies in them apart from their learning and science, and that they inwardly and privately follow, we have to confess that the part of it of which rationalism can give an account is relatively superficial. It is the part that has the *prestige* undoubtedly, for it has the loquacity, it can challenge you for proofs, and chop logic, and put you down with words. But it will fail to convince or convert you all the same, if your dumb intuitions are opposed to its conclusions. If you have intuitions at all, they come from a deeper level of your nature than the loquacious level which rationalism inhabits. Your whole subconscious life, your impulses, your faiths, your needs, your divinations, have prepared the premises, of which your consciousness now feels the weight of the result; and something in you absolutely *knows* that that result must be truer than any logic-chopping rationalistic talk, however clever, that may contradict it. This inferiority of the rationalistic level in founding belief is just as manifest when rationalism argues for religion as when it argues against it. That vast literature of the proofs of God's existence drawn from the order of nature, which a century ago seemed so overwhelmingly convincing, today does little more than gather dust in libraries, for the simple reason that our generation has ceased to believe in the kind of God it argued for. Whatever sort of a being God may be, we *know* to-day that he is nevermore that mere external inventor of "contrivances" intended to make manifest his "glory" in which our great-grandfathers took such satisfaction, though just how we know this we cannot possibly make clear by words either to others or to ourselves. I defy any of you here fully to account for your persuasion that if a God exist he must be a more cosmic and tragic personage than that Being.

The truth is that in the metaphysical or religious sphere, articulate reasons are cogent for us only when our inarticulate feelings of reality have already been impressed in favor of the same conclusion. Then, indeed, our intuitions and our reason work together, and great world-ruling systems, like that of the Buddhist or of the Catholic philosophy, may grow up. Our impulsive belief is here always what sets up the original body of truth, and our articulately verbalized philosophy is but its showy translation into formulas. The unreasoned and immediate assurance is the deep thing in us, the reasoned argument is but a surface exhibition. Instinct leads, intelligence does but follow. If a person feels the presence of a living God after the fashion shown by my quotations, your critical arguments, be they never so superior, will vainly set themselves to change his faith.

Please observe, however, that I do not yet say that it is *better* that the subconscious and non-rational should thus hold primacy in the religious realm. I confine myself to simply pointing out that they do so hold it as a matter of fact.

So much for our sense of the reality of the religious objects. Let me now say a brief word more about the attitudes they characteristically awaken.

We have already agreed that they are *solemn;* and we have seen reason to think that the most distinctive of them is the sort of joy which may result in extreme cases from absolute self-surrender. The sense of the kind of object to which the surrender is made has much to do with determining the precise complexion of the joy; and the whole phenomenon is more complex than any simple formula allows. In the literature of the subject, sadness and gladness have each been emphasized in turn. The ancient saying that the first maker of the Gods was fear receives voluminous corroboration from every age of religious history; but none the less does religious history show the part which joy has evermore tended to play. Sometimes the joy has been primary; sometimes secondary, being the gladness of deliverance from the fear. This latter state of things, being the more complex, is also the more complete; and as we proceed, I think we shall have abundant reason for refusing to leave out either the sadness or the gladness, if we look at religion with the breadth of view which it demands. Stated in the completest possible terms, a man's religion involves both moods of contraction and moods of expansion of his being. But the quantitative mixture and order of these moods vary so much from one age of the world, from one system of thought, and from one individual to another, that you may insist either on the dread and the submission, or on the peace and the freedom as the essence of the matter, and still remain materially within the limits of the truth. The constitutionally sombre and the constitutionally sanguine onlooker are bound to emphasize opposite aspects of what lies before their eyes.

The constitutionally sombre religious person makes even of his religious peace a very sober thing. Danger still hovers in the air about it. Flexion and contraction are not wholly checked. It were sparrowlike and childish after our deliverance to explode into twittering laughter and caper-cutting, and utterly to forget the imminent hawk on bough. Lie low, rather, lie low; for you are in the hands of a living God. In the Book of Job, for example, the impotence of man and the omnipotence of God is the exclusive burden of its author's mind. "It is as high as heaven; what canst thou do?—deeper than hell; what canst thou know?" There is an astringent relish about the truth of this conviction which some men can feel, and which for them is as near an approach as can be made to the feeling of religious joy.

> "In Job," says that coldly truthful writer, the author of Mark Rutherford, "God reminds us that man is not the measure of his creation. The world is immense, constructed on no plan or theory which the intellect of man can grasp. It is *transcendent* everywhere. This is the burden of every verse, and is the secret, if there be one, of the poem. Sufficient or insufficient, there is nothing more. . . . God is great, we know not his ways. He takes from us all we have, but yet if we possess our souls in patience, we *may* pass the valley of the shadow, and come out in sunlight again. We may or we may not! . . . What more have we to say now than God said from the whirlwind over two thousand five hundred years ago?"[7]

If we turn to the sanguine onlooker, on the other hand, we find that deliverance is felt as incomplete unless the burden be altogether overcome and the danger forgotten. Such onlookers give us definitions that seem to the sombre minds of whom we have just been speaking to leave out all the solemnity that makes religious peace so different from merely animal joys. In the opinion of some writers an attitude might be called religious, though no touch were left in it of sacrifice or submission, no tendency to flexion, no bowing of the head. Any "habitual and regulated admiration," says Professor J. R. Seeley,[8] "is worthy to be called a religion"; and accordingly he thinks that our Music, our Science,

---

[7]Mark Rutherford's Deliverance, London, 1885, pp. 196, 198.

[8]In his book (too little read, I fear), Natural Religion, 3d edition, Boston, 1886, pp. 91, 122.

and our so-called "Civilization," as these things are now organized and admiringly believed in, form the more genuine religions of our time. Certainly the unhesitating and unreasoning way in which we feel that we must inflict our civilization upon "lower" races, by means of Hotchkiss guns, etc., reminds one of nothing so much as the early spirit of Islam spreading its religion by the sword.

A Dialogue

Chief Red Jacket and the Missionary

Must it be necessary that we all experience God in the same way? Should people of a particular religious persuasion attempt to take away the religious beliefs of others? More important, should not those who have come to a new land to escape persecution and to practice their religion freely allow the native people the same freedom? As you read this dialogue between Chief Red Jacket and the missionary, ask yourself what may be the relation between religion and social justice.

[In the summer of 1805, a number of the principal Chiefs and Warriors of the Six Nations, principally Senecas, assembled at Buffalo Creek, in the state of New York, at the particular request of Rev. Mr. Cram, a Missionary from the state of Massachusetts. The Missionary being furnished with an Interpreter, and accompanied by the Agent of the United States for Indian affairs, met the Indians in Council, when the following talk took place.]

FIRST, BY THE AGENT. "*Brothers of the Six Nations;* I rejoice to meet you at this time, and thank the Great Spirit, that he has preserved you in health, and given me another opportunity of taking you by the hand.

"*Brothers;* The person who sits by me, is a friend who has come a great distance to hold a talk with you. He will inform you what his business is, and it is my request that you would listen with attention to his words."

MISSIONARY. "*My Friends;* I am thankful for the opportunity afforded us of uniting together at this time. I had a great desire to see you, and inquire into your state and welfare; for this purpose I have travelled a great distance, being sent by your old friends, the Boston Missionary Society. You will recollect they formerly sent missionaries among you, to instruct you in religion, and labor for your good. Although they have not heard from you for a long time, yet they have not forgotten their brothers the Six Nations, and are still anxious to do you good.

"*Brothers;* I have not come to get your lands or your money, but to enlighten your minds, and to instruct you how to worship the Great Spirit agreeably to his mind and will, and to preach to you the gospel of his

From *Indian Speeches; Delivered by Farmer's Brother and Red Jacket, Two Seneca Chiefs* (1809).

son Jesus Christ. There is but one religion, and but one way to serve God, and if you do not embrace the right way, you cannot be happy hereafter. You have never worshipped the Great Spirit in a manner acceptable to him; but have, all your lives, been in great errors and darkness. To endeavor to remove these errors, and open your eyes, so that you might see clearly, is my business with you.

"*Brothers;* I wish to talk with you as one friend talks with another and, if you have any objections to receive the religion which I preach, I wish you to state them; and I will endeavor to satisfy your minds, and remove the objections.

"*Brothers;* I want you to speak your minds freely; for I wish to reason with you on the subject, and, if possible, remove all doubts, if there be any on your minds. The subject is an important one, and it is of consequence that you give it an early attention while the offer is made you. Your friends, the Boston Missionary Society, will continue to send you good and faithful ministers, to instruct and strengthen you in religion, if, on your part, you are willing to receive them.

"*Brothers;* Since I have been in this part of the country, I have visited some of your small villages, and talked with your people. They appear willing to receive instruction, but, as they look up to you as their older brothers in council, they want first to know your opinion on the subject.

"You have now heard what I have to propose at present. I hope you will take it into consideration, and give me an answer before we part."

[After about two hours consultation among themselves, the Chief, commonly called by the white people, Red Jacket (whose Indian name is Sagu-yu-what-hah, which interpreted is *Keeper awake*) rose and spoke as follows:]

"*Friend and Brother;* It was the will of the Great Spirit that we should meet together this day. HE orders all things, and has given us a fine day for our Council. HE has taken his garment from before the sun, and caused it to shine with brightness upon us. Our eyes are opened, that we see clearly; our ears are unstopped, that we have been able to hear distinctly the words you have spoken. For all these favors we thank the Great Spirit; and HIM *only.*

"*Brother;* This council fire was kindled by you. It was at your request that we came together at this time. We have listened with attention to what you have said. You requested us to speak our minds freely. This gives us great joy; for we now consider that we stand upright before you, and can speak what we think. All have heard your voice, and all speak to you now as one man. Our minds are agreed.

"*Brother;* You say you want an answer to your talk before you leave this place. It is right you should have one, as you are a great distance from home, and we do not wish to detain you. But we will first look back a little, and tell you what our fathers have told us, and what we have heard from the white people.

"*Brother;* Listen to what we say.

"There was a time when our forefathers owned this great island. Their seats extended from the rising to the setting sun. The Great Spirit had made it for the use of Indians. HE had created the buffalo, the deer, and other animals for food. HE had made the bear and the beaver. Their skins served us for clothing. HE had scattered them over the country, and taught us how to take them. HE had caused the earth to produce corn for bread. All this HE had done for his red children, because HE loved them. If we had some disputes about our hunting ground, they were generally settled without the shedding of much blood. But an evil day came upon us. Your forefathers crossed the great water, and landed on this island. Their numbers were small. They found friends and not enemies. They told us they had fled from their country for fear of wicked men, and had come here to enjoy their religion. They asked for a small seat. We took pity on them, granted their request; and they sat down amongst us. We gave them corn and meat, they gave us poison [alluding, it is supposed, to ardent spirits] in return.

"The white people had now found our country. Tidings were carried back, and more came amongst us. Yet we did not fear them. We took them to be friends. They called us brothers. We believed them, and gave them a larger seat. At length their numbers had greatly increased. They wanted more land; they wanted our country. Our eyes were opened and our minds became uneasy. Wars took place. Indians were hired to fight against Indians, and many of our people were destroyed. They also brought strong liquor amongst us. It was strong and powerful, and has slain thousands.

"*Brother;* Our seats were once large and yours were small. You have now become a great people, and we have scarcely a place left to spread our blankets. You have got our country, but are not satisfied; you want to force your religion upon us.

"*Brother;* Continue to listen.

"You say that you are sent to instruct us how to worship the Great Spirit agreeably to his mind, and, if we do not take hold of the religion which you white people teach, we shall be unhappy hereafter. You say that you are right and we are lost. How do we know this to be true? We understand that your religion is written in a book. If it was intended for us as well as you, why has not the Great Spirit given to us, and not only to us, but why did he not give to our forefathers, the knowledge of that book, with the means of understanding it rightly? We only know what you tell us about it. How shall we know when to believe, being so often deceived by the white people?

"*Brother;* You say there is but one way to worship and serve the Great Spirit. If there is but one religion; why do you white people differ so much about it? Why not all agreed, as you can all read the book?

"*Brother;* We do not understand these things.

"We are told that your religion was given to your forefathers, and has been handed down from father to son. We also have a religion, which was given to our forefathers, and has been handed down to us their children. We worship in that way. It teaches us to be thankful for all the favors we receive; to love each other, and to be united. We never quarrel about religion.

"*Brother;* The Great Spirit has made us all, but he has made a great difference between his white and red children. HE has given us different complexions and different customs. To you HE has given the arts. To these HE has not opened our eyes. We know these things to be true. Since HE has made so great a difference between us in other things; why may we not conclude that HE has given us a different religion according to our understanding? The Great Spirit does right. HE knows what is best for his children; we are satisfied.

"*Brother;* We do not wish to destroy your religion, or take it from you. We only want to enjoy our own.

"*Brother;* We are told that you have been preaching to the white people in this place. These people are our neighbors. We are acquainted with them. We will wait a little while, and see what effect your preaching has upon them. If we find it does them good, makes them honest and less disposed to cheat Indians; we will then consider again of what you have said.

"*Brother;* You have now heard our answer to your talk, and this is all we have to say at present.

"As we are going to part, we will come and take you by the hand, and hope the

Great Spirit will protect you on your journey, and return you safe to your friends."

[As the Indians began to approach the missionary, he rose hastily from his seat and replied, that he could not take them by the hand; that there was no fellowship between the religion of God and the works of the devil.

This being interpreted to the Indians, they smiled, and retired in a peaceable manner.

It being afterwards suggested to the missionary that his reply to the Indians was rather indiscreet; he observed, that he supposed the ceremony of shaking hands would be received by them as a token that he assented to what they had said. Being otherwise informed, he said he was sorry for the expressions.]

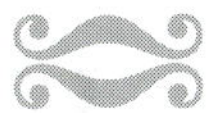

Religion from an African Perspective

Kwasi Wiredu

Perhaps we need to reflect on the possibility that religious attitudes and religious experiences differ from culture to culture. Kwasi Wiredu explains how the Akan people may express their belief in a supreme being and supernatural reality differently from the Europeans who sent Christian missionaries to his African culture. As he explains how the Akan language expresses concepts of God and spirituality, Wiredu also reflects on the ways in which religious beliefs express an ethic of responsibility and a sense of personhood.

Two assumptions that may safely be made about the human species are one, that the entire race shares some fundamental categories and criteria of thought in common and two, that, nevertheless, there are some very deep disparities among the different tribes of humankind in regard to their modes of conceptualization in some sensitive areas of thought. The first accounts for the possibility of communication among different peoples, the second for the difficulties and complications that not infrequently beset that interaction.

Is religion a field of convergence or divergence of thought among the peoples and cultures of the world? The obvious answer, in alignment with our opening reflection, is that religion is both. There is also an obvious sequel: What are the specifics? But here an obvious answer is unavailable, at least, as concerns Africa vis-à-vis, for instance, the West. In fact, it is not at all obvious in what sense the English word "religion" is applicable to any aspect of African life and thought.

This last remark, of course, amounts to discounting the frequent affirmations, in the literature of African studies, of the immanent religiosity of the African mind. What exactly are the features of life and thought that are appealed to in that characterization? In

From Kwasi Wiredu, "Universalism and Particularism in Religion from an African Perspective," *Journal of Humanism and Ethical Religion* 3(1): Fall 1990. Reprinted by permission of the publisher. Footnotes deleted.

investigating this issue I am going to have to be rather particularistic. I am going to have particular, though not exclusive, recourse to the Akans of West Africa, for the considerations to be adduced presuppose a level of cultural and linguistic insight to which I cannot pretend in regard to any African peoples except that particular ethnic group which I know through birth, upbringing, reading and deliberate reflective observation. This particularism has, at least, the logical potential of all counterexamples against universal claims.

Let us return to the word "religion." It has been suggested, even by some authors by whose reckoning African life is full of religion, that there is no word in many African languages which translates this word. Whether this is true of all African languages or not I do not know, but it is certainly true of Akan, in the traditional use of that language, that is. Not only is there no single word for religion but there is also no periphrastic equivalent. There is, indeed, the word "Anyamesom" which many translators might be tempted to proffer. But the temptation ought to be resisted. The word is a Christian invention by which the missionaries distinguished, in Akan speech, between their own religion and what they perceived to be the religion of the indigenous "pagans." Thus, it means, not religion, pure and simple, but Christianity. Ironically, in this usage the Christian missionaries were constrained by linguistic exigencies to adapt a word which the Akans use for the Supreme Being. "Onyame" is one among several names for the Supreme Being in Akan. Another very frequent one is "Onyankopon" which literally means The Being That Is Alone Great, in other words, That Than Which a Greater Cannot Be Conceived (with apologies to Saint Anselm). The remaining component of the word "Anyamesom" is "som" which means "to serve," so that the whole word means, literally, "the service of the Supreme Being" or, if you follow Christian methods of translation, "the service of God." In turn, this was taken to mean the *worship* of God.

By way of a designation for what they saw as indigenous religion, the Christians used the word "Abosomsom." This is a combination of two words "Obosom" and "Som." Etymologically, "obosom" means the service of stones. Thus, literally, the barbarism means the service of stone service! Still, it served its Christian purpose. But why stones? That is an allusion to the fact that the Akans traditionally believe that various objects, such as certain special rocks, trees and rivers, are the abode of extra-human forces and beings of assorted grades.

Having gathered from the foregoing remarks that the Akans, in fact, believe in the existence of a supreme being and a variety of extra-human forces and beings, the reader might be disposed to wonder why I make any issue of the sense in which "religion" might be applied to any aspect of Akan culture. If so, let him or her attend to the following considerations. To begin with, religion, however it is defined, involves a certain kind of attitude. If a given religion postulates a supra-human supreme being, that belief must, on any common showing, necessarily be joined to an attitude not only of unconditional reverence but also of worship. Some will go as far as to insist that this worshipful attitude will have to be given practical expression through definite rituals, especially if the being in question is supposed to be the determiner or controller of human destiny. There is a further condition of the utmost importance; it is one which introduces an ethical dimension into the definition. Essential to any religion in the primary sense is a conception of moral uprightness. If it involves supra-human beliefs, the relevant ethic will be based logically or psychologically on the "supra" being or beings concerned. Typically, but by no means invariably, a religion will have a social framework. In that case, it will have organized hortatory and other procedures for instilling or revivifying the commitment to moral virtue.

Consider, now, the character of the Akan belief in the Supreme Being. There is, indeed, generally among the Akans a confirmed attitude of unconditional reverence for *Onyankopon*, the Supreme Being. However, there is, most assuredly, no attitude or ritual of worship directed to that being either at a social or an individual level. They regard Him as good, wise and powerful in the highest. He is the determiner of human destiny as of everything else. But in all this they see no rationale for worship. Neither is the Akan conception or practice of morality based logically or even psychologically on the belief in the Supreme Being. Being good in the highest, He disapproves of evil; but, to the Akan mind, the reason why people should not do evil is not because he disapproves of it but rather because it is contrary to human well-being, which is why He disapproves of it, in the first place.

The early European visitors to Africa, especially the missionaries, were quick to notice the absence of any worship of God among the Akans and various other African peoples. They were hardly less struck by the fact that God was not the foundation of Akan morals. On both grounds they deduced a spiritual and intellectual immaturity in the African. Notice the workings here of a facile universalism. It seems to have been assumed that belief in God must move every sound mind to worship. Perhaps, even now, such an assumption might sound plausible to many Western ears. It is, of course, not likely in this day and age that many can be found to suppose that any person of a sound mind must necessarily embrace belief in God. But given the prevailing tendencies in Western and even some non-Western cultures, it might be tempting to think that if people believe in God, then the *natural* thing for them to do is to worship Him. Yet, consider the notion of a perfect being. Why would he (she, it) need to be worshipped? What would be the point of it? It is well-known that the Judeo-Christian God *jealously* demands to be worshipped—witness The Ten Commandments—but, from an Akan point of view, such clamoring for attention must be paradoxical in the extreme in a perfect being, and I confess to being an unreconstructed Akan in this regard.

There is, in their resort to the word "Abosomsom" (the worship of stones) to name what they took to be Akan religion, an odd manifestation of the special importance that the Christian missionaries attached to worship. Having seen that the Akans did not worship God, they were keen to find out what it was that they worshipped, for surely a whole people must worship something. They quickly settled on the class of what I have called extra-human forces and beings, which, as I have already hinted, is a feature of the Akan worldview. There is, indeed, a great variety of such entities postulated in the Akan ontology (as in any other African ontology that I know of). Some are relatively person-like; others somewhat automatic in their operation. The former can, it is believed, be communicated with through some special procedures, and are credited with a moral sense. Commonly, a being of this sort would be believed to be localized at a household "shrine" from where it would protect the given group from evil forces. More person-like still are the ancestors who are thought to live in a realm closely linked with the world of the living.

Actually, the ancestors are conceived of as persons who continue to be members of their premortem families, watching over their affairs and generally helping them. They are regarded as persons, but not as mortal persons; for they have tasted death and transcended it. Accordingly, they are not thought to be constrained by all the physical laws which circumscribe the activities of persons with fully physical bodies. For this reason, they are supposed to be more powerful than mortals. Additionally, they are considered to be more irreversibly moral than any living mortal. All these attributes are taken to entitle the ancestors to genuine reverence. Not quite the same deference is accorded to the first group of beings, but in view of their presumed power to promote human well-being, they are approached with considerable respect.

More types of extra-human forces and beings are spoken of in the Akan ontology than we have mentioned, but these are among the most relevant, and they will suffice for the impending point; which is this: The Akan attitude to the beings in question bears closer analogy to secular esteem than religious worship. The reverence given to the ancestors is only a higher degree of the respect that in Akan society is considered to be due to the earthly elders. For all their post-mortem ontologic transformation, the ancestors are, let it be repeated, regarded as members of their families. The libations that are poured to them on ceremonial and other important occasions are simply invitations to them to come and participate in family events. Moreover, everybody hopes eventually to become an ancestor, but this is not seen as a craving for self-apotheosis. Ancestorship is simply the crowning phase of human existence.

The non-religious character of the Akan attitude to the non-ancestral forces is even more clear. Real religious devotion to a being must be unconditional. But that is the one thing that the Akan approach to those beings is not; it is purely utilitarian: if they bring help, praise be to them, and other things besides. On the other hand, if they fail, particularly if that happens consistently, they can fall into disrepute or worse. K. A. Busia and J. B. Danquah, the two most celebrated expositors of Akan thought, have borne unambiguous and, as it seems to me, reliable testimony to this fact. Busia says, "The gods are treated with respect if they deliver the goods, and with contempt if they fail. . . . Attitudes to [the gods] depend on their success, and vary from healthy respect to sneering contempt." Danquah goes somewhat further: ". . . the general tendency is to sneer at and ridicule the fetish and its priest." There is an even more radical consideration. According to popular belief, these "gods" are capable of dying. Of a "god" who is finished the Akans say *nano atro,* that is, its powers have become totally blunted. This may happen through unknown causes, but it may also happen through human design. People can cause the demise of a "god" simply by permanently depriving it of attention. Or, for more rapid results, apply an antithetical substance to its "shrine." Such antidotes are known for at least some of these "gods," according to popular belief. It ought, perhaps, to be emphasized that in this matter the thought is not that a "god" has betaken itself elsewhere, but rather that it has ceased to be a force to be reckoned with at all. In light of all this, it is somewhat of a hyperbole to call the procedures designed for establishing satisfactory relations with the beings in question religious worship.

The considerations rehearsed so far should be enough, I think, to suggest the need for a review of the enthusiastic, not to say indiscriminate, attributions of religiosity to African peoples. But there are deeper reasons of the same significance. And in studying them we will see the role which the hasty universalization of certain Western categories of thought have played in the formation of the misapprehensions under scrutiny. Take, then, the Akan belief in the Supreme Being. In English discourse about Akan thought the word "God" is routinely used to refer to this being. This has led, or has been due, to the supposition that both the Akans and the Christians are talking of the same being when they speak of the Supreme Being, notwithstanding any divergences of cultural perception. This supposed identity of reference has come in handy to Christianized Africans wishing to demonstrate that they can profess Christianity and still remain basically true to their indigenous religions: There is, after all, only one God, and we are all trying to reach Him.

Yet, in spite of any apparent similarities, such as the postulation of That Than Which a Greater Cannot Be Conceived in both traditions of thought, the Akan supreme being is profoundly different from the Christian one. The Christian God is a creator of the world out of nothing. In further philosophical characterization, He is said to be transcendent, supernatural and spiritual in the sense of immaterial, non-physical. In radical contrast, the Akan supreme being is a kind of cosmic architect, a fashioner of the world order, who occupies the apex of the same hierarchy of being which accommodates, in its intermediate ranges, the ancestors and living mortals and, in its lower reaches, animals, plants and inanimate objects. This universe of being is ontologically homogenous. In other words, everything that exists exists in exactly the same sense as everything else. And this sense is empirical, broadly speaking. In the Akan language to exist is to "wo ho" which, in literal translation, means to be at some place. There is no equivalent, in Akan, of the existential "to be" or "is" of English, and there is no way of pretending in that medium to be speaking of the existence of something which is not in space. This locative connotation of the Akan concept of existence is irreducible except metaphorically. Thus you might speak of there existing an explanation for something (*ne nkyerease wo ho*) without incurring any obligation of spatial specification, because an explanation is not an object in any but a metaphorical sense; and to a metaphorical object corresponds only a metaphorical kind of space. The same applies to the existence of all so-called abstract entities. In the Akan conceptual framework, then, existence is spatial. Now, since, whatever transcendence means in this context, it implies existence beyond space, it follows that talk of any transcendent being is not just false, but unintelligible, from an Akan point of view.

But not only transcendence goes by the board. Neither the notion of the supernatural nor that of the spiritual can convey any coherent meaning to an Akan understanding in its traditional condition. No line is drawn in the Akan worldview demarcating one area of being corresponding to nature from another corresponding to supernature. Whatever is real belongs to one or another of the echelons of being postulated in that worldview. In that context it has all the explanation that is appropriate to it. An important axiom of Akan thought is that everything has its explanation, *biribiara wo nenkyerease*—a kind of principle of sufficient reason; and a clear presupposition of Akan explanations of phenomena is that there are interactions among all the orders of existents in the world. Accordingly, if an event in human affairs, for instance, does not appear explicable in human terms, there is no hesitation in invoking extra-human causality emanating from the higher or even the lower rungs of the hierarchy of beings. In doing this there is no sense of crossing an ontological chasm; for the idea is that there is only one universe of many strata wherein God, the ancestors, humans, animals, plants and all the rest of the furniture of the world have their being.

In this last connection, it might, perhaps, enhance understanding to regiment our terminology a little. Suppose we use the term "the world" to designate the totality of ordered existents fashioned out by God in the process of "creation," then, of course, God, being the author of the world, is not a part of it, in the Akan scheme of things. But we might, then, reserve the term "universe" for the totality of absolutely all existents. In this sense God would be part of the universe. Apart from regimenting our terminology, this gives us the opportunity to reinforce the point regarding the Akan sense of the inherent law-likeness of reality. And the crucial consideration is that God's relationship with the rest of the universe, that is, the world, is also conceived to be inherently law-like. This is the implication of the Akan saying that "The Creator created Death and Death killed the Creator," *Odomankoma boo Owuo na Owuo kum Odomankoma,* which, in my opinion, is one of the profoundest in the Akan corpus of metaphysical aphorisms.

But though God's relation with the world is conceived to be law-like, He is not made the basis of the explanation of any specific phenomenon, for since everything is ultimately traceable to Him, *Biribiara ne Nyame,* references to Him are incapable of helping to explain why any particular thing is what it is and not another thing. Divine law-likeness only ensures that there will be no arbitrary interferences in the course of the world-process. Thus the reason why Akan explanations of specific things do not invoke God is not because He is thought to be transcendent or supernatural or anything like that, but rather because He is too immanently implicated in the nature and happening of things to have any explanatory value.

Still, however, in facing the cognitive problems of this world all the mundane theaters of being, human and extra-human, are regarded as *equally* legitimate sources of explanation. Thus, if an Akan explains a mysterious malady in terms of, say, the wrath of the ancestors, it makes little sense to ascribe to him or her a belief in the supernatural. That characterization is intelligible only in a conceptual framework in which the natural/supernatural dichotomy has a place. But the point is that it has no place in the Akan system of thought. We may be sure, then, that the widespread notion that Africans are given to supernatural explanations is the result of the superimposition of alien categories of thought on African thought-structures, in the Akan instance, at least. There is nothing particularly insidious in the fact that Western writers on African thought have generally engaged in this practice; for, after all, one thinks most naturally in terms of the conceptual framework of one's intellectual upbringing, and the natural/supernatural distinction is very endemic, indeed, in Western thought. I do not mean by this, of course, that there is a universal belief in the supernatural in the West. The suggestion is only that this concept together with its logical complement is a customary feature of Western conceptualizations; so much so, that even the Western philosophical naturalist, in denying the existence of anything supernatural, does not necessarily dispute the coherence of that concept. It is a more striking fact that many contemporary African expositors of their own traditional systems of thought yield no ground to their Western colleagues in stressing the role of belief in the supernatural in African thinking. It is hard not to see this as evidence of the fact that in some ways Christian proselytization and Western education have been over-successful in Africa.

But an interesting and important question arises. Suppose it granted that, as I have been arguing, the natural/supernatural dichotomy has no place in Akan and, perhaps, African thought generally. Does that not still leave the question of its objective validity intact? And, if it should turn out to be objectively valid, would it not be reasonable to think that it would be a good thing for Africans to learn to think along that line? My answer to both questions is affirmative; which implies a rejection of relativism. This disavowal is fully premeditated and is foreshadowed in the opening paragraph of this essay. However, for reasons of the division of preoccupation, I cannot try to substantiate my anti-relativism here.

Stated baldly, my thesis is that there is such a thing as the objective validity of an idea. Were it not for the recent resurgence of relativism in Philosophy, this would have been too platitudinous for any words. Furthermore, and rather less obviously, if an idea is objectively valid (or invalid or even incoherent) in any given language or conceptual framework, both the idea and its status can, in principle, be *represented* in, if not necessarily translated into, any other language or conceptual framework.

A corollary of the foregoing contention is that, however natural it may be to think in one's native framework of concepts, it is possible for human beings to think astride conceptual frameworks. In the absence of extended argumentation for this general claim, I will content myself with an illustration with respect to the idea of the supernatural. A relevant question, then, is: "Do the Akans need to incorporate the natural/supernatural distinction into their modes of thought?" I think not; for not only is Akan thought inhospitable to this distinction but also the distinction is, in my opinion, objectively incoherent. If this is so, it follows from our principle that it ought to be demonstrable (to the extent that such speculative matters are susceptible of demonstration) in any language and, in particular, in English. In fact, a simple argument suffices for this purpose.

In the sense pertinent to our discussion, the supernatural is that which surpasses the order of nature. In other words, a supernatural event is one whose occurrence is contrary to the laws of nature. But if the event actually happens, then any law that fails to reckon with its possibility is inaccurate and is in need of some modification, at least. However, if the law is suitably amended, even if only by means of an exceptive rider, the event is no longer contrary to natural law. Hence no event can be consistently described as supernatural.

What of the notion of the spiritual? Again, I begin with a disclaimer on behalf of Akan ontological thinking. As can be expected from the spatial character of the Akan concept of existence, the radical dualism of the material and the spiritual can find no home in the Akan scheme of reality. All the extra-human beings and powers, even including God, are spoken of in language irreducibly charged with spatial imagery. It is generally recognized by students of African eschatology that the *place* of the dead, the *abode* of the ancestors, is almost completely modelled on the world of living mortals. If the replication is not complete, it is only because the ancestors are not thought of as having *fully* material bodies. Some analogue of material bodies they surely must be supposed to have, given the sorts of things that are said about them. For example, a postulated component of a person that is supposed to survive death and eventually become an ancestor, all things being equal, is believed soon after death to travel *by land and by river* before arriving at the abode of the ancestors. For this reason in traditional times coffins were stuffed with travel needs such as clothing and money for the payment of ferrying charges. I have never heard it suggested in traditional circles that this practice was purely symbolic. If it were a purely symbolic gesture, that, certainly, would have been carrying symbolism rather far. But, in any case, the practice was of a piece with the conception, and the conception is decidedly quasi-material.

I use the term "quasi-material" to refer to any being or entity conceived as spatial but lacking some of the properties of material objects. The ancestors, for instance, although they are thought of as occupying space, are believed to be invisible to the naked eye and inaudible to the normal ear, except rarely when they choose to *manifest* themselves to particular persons for special reasons. On such occasions they can, according to very widely received conceptions among the Akans, appear and disappear at will unconstrained by those limitations of speed and impenetrability to which the gross bodies of the familiar world are subject. This is held to be generally true of all the relatively personalized forms of extra-human phenomena.

It is apparent from what has just been said that if the extra-human beings of the Akan worldview are not fully material, they are not fully immaterial either. Further to confirm this last point, we might note that, although the beings in question are not supposed to be generally visible to the *naked* eye, they are widely believed to be perceivable to the superior eyes of certain persons of special gift or training. People reputed to be of this class will sometimes tell you, "If you had but eyes to see, you would be amazed at what is going on right here around where you are standing." And here imagery tends to be so lustily spatial that, but for their selective invisibility, one would be hard put to distinguish between the quasi-material apparitions and the garden variety objects of the material world. Descriptions of human-like creatures gyrating on their heads are not unknown in such contexts. Whatever one may think of such claims, the conceptual point itself is clear, namely, that the extra-human existents of the Akan ontology do not belong to the category of the spiritual in the Cartesian sense of non-spatial, unextended. The category itself is conceptually inadmissible in this system of thought. Should the reader be curious at this stage as to whether mind too is quasi-material in the Akan way of thinking, the short answer is that mind is not thought of as an entity at all but rather simply as the *capacity*, supervenient upon brain states and processes, to do various things. Hence the question whether mind is a spiritual or material or quasi-material entity does not arise.

The Akan worldview, then, involves no sharp ontological cleavages such as the Cartesian dichotomy of the material and the spiritual; what difference in nature there is between ordinary material things and those extra-human beings and forces so often called "spirits" in the literature is the difference between the fully material and the partially material. I ought, by the way, to stress that the absence of the spiritual, in the metaphysical sense, from the Akan conceptual framework does not imply the absence of spirituality, in the popular sense, from Akan life. In the latter sense spirituality is sensitivity to the less gross aspects of human experience.

But let us return to the class of quasi-material entities. A legitimate question is whether there is adequate evidence that such entities exist. Actually, this is not a question which faces Akan thought alone. All cultures, East, West and Central, abound in stories of quasi-material goings-on. In the West investigating the veridity and theoretical explicability of such stories is one of the main concerns of Parapsychology. In Africa there are any number of people who would be willing to bet their lives on the reality of such things, on the basis, reputedly, of first hand experience. Basically, the issue is an empirical one, though probably not completely; for if such phenomena were to be definitively confirmed, their explanation would be likely to have conceptual reverberations. Speaking for myself, I would say that neither in Africa nor elsewhere have I seen compelling evidence of such things; though dogmatism would be ill-advised. At all events, it is worth noting that the plausibility of specific quasi-material claims tends to dwindle in the face of advancing scientific knowledge, a consideration which any contemporary African would need to take to heart.

It is, however, interesting to note that the waning, in Africa, of belief in extra-material entities and forces would leave the indigenous orientation thoroughly empirical; for the African worldview, at any rate, the Akan one, makes room for only material and quasi-material existents. The contrary seems to be the case in the West. Here any reduction in quasi-material beliefs has not automatically resulted in gains for empirical thinking in the minds of a large mass of people; for in addition to the categories of material and quasi-material, there is that of the spiritual, i.e. the immaterial, which exercises the profoundest influence in philosophic and quasi-philosophic speculation. Not only is actual belief in immaterial entities widespread in the West but also the intelligibility of the material/immaterial contrast seems to be taken for granted even more widely. Moreover, in spite of the fact that, to say the least, quasi-material beliefs are not at all rare in the West, the tendency is for thinking to be governed by an exclusive disjunction of the material with the immaterial. Thus, for many, though, of course, not everybody, in the West, if a thing is not supposed to be material, it is necessarily immaterial. The Europeans who imposed on themselves the "burden" of bringing "salvation" to the souls of the peoples of Africa certainly had this particular either-or fixation. Consequently, those of them who made sympathetic, though not necessarily empathetic, studies of African thought could not but formulate their results in terms of that and cognate schemes of thought. A visible outcome of their assiduous evangelism is the great *flock* of faithful African converts who think in the same language, proudly attributing to their own peoples belief in sundry things spiritual and supernatural.

Yet, not only is the notion of the spiritual unintelligible within a thought system such as that of the Akans, but also it is objectively a very problematic one. One searches in vain for a useful definition of the spiritual. The sum total of the information available from Cartesian and many other spiritually dedicated sources is that the spiritual is that which is non-material. But, definition by pure negation, such as this, brings little enlightenment. The word "that" in the definition suggests that one is envisaging some *sort* of a referent, but this possibility of reference is given absolutely no grounding. How are we to differentiate between the spiritual and the void, for instance? Some negative definitions can be legitimate, but only if their context provides suitable information. In the present case the context seems to be a veritable void!

An even more unfortunate definition of the spiritual than the foregoing is sometimes encountered. It is explained that the spiritual is the unperceivable, the invisible, or, to adapt a phrase of Saint Paul's, the unseen. The problem with this definition is not its apparent negativeness, for the conditions of unperceivability are concrete enough; the problem is that it is so broad as to make gravity, for example, spiritual. It is, of course, not going to help to protest that although gravity is unseen, its effects are seen and felt; for exactly the same is what is claimed for the spiritual. Nor would it be of greater avail to add the condition of non-spatiality to that of invisibility, for something like the square root of four is neither spatial nor visible, and yet one wonders how spiritual it is.

Of the material/spiritual (immaterial) dichotomy, then, we can say the following. It is not a universal feature of human thinking, since the Akans, at least, do not use it. And, in any case, its coherence is questionable. It is not to be assumed, though, that if a mode of conceptualization is universal among humankind, then it is, for that reason, objectively valid. Belief in quasi-material entities, for example, seems to be universal among cultures (though not among all individuals) but the chances are that the concepts involved denote nothing.

After all the foregoing the reader is unlikely to be surprised to learn that the idea of creation out of nothing too does not make sense in the Akan framework of thinking. Avenues to that concept are blocked in Akanland from the side both of the concept of creation and that of nothingness. To take the latter first: Nothingness in the Akan language is relative to location. The idea is expressed as the absence of anything at a given location, *se whee nni ho,* literally, the circumstance of there not being something there. Note here the reappearance of the locative conception of existence. If you subtract the locative connotation from this construal of nothingness, you have exactly nothing left, that is, nothing of the conception remains in your understanding.

The concept of creation in the Akan language is similarly non-transcendent. To create is to *bo,* and the most self-explanatory word in Akan for the creator is *Obooade. Ade* means thing, and bo means to make in the sense of to fashion out, which implies the use of raw materials. Any claim to *bo* and *ade* without the use of absolutely any raw material would sound decidedly self-contradictory in the language. Thus the Akan Supreme Being is a maker of things, but not out of nothing; so that if the word "Creator" is used for him, it should be clearly understood that the concept of creation involved is fundamentally different from that involved in, say, orthodox Christian talk of creation. The Akan creator is the architect of the world order, but not the *ex nihilo* inventor of its stuff.

Interestingly, even within Western philosophy the concept of *ex nihilo* creation was not in the conceptual vocabulary of some of the greatest thinkers. It is well known, for example, that neither Plato nor Aristotle made use of any such concept. Of course, whether it is intelligible is a separate question. On the face of it, at least, there are tremendous paradoxes in that concept, and unless its exponents can offer profound clarifications, its absence from a conceptual framework can hardly be taken as a mark of insufficiency. Be that as it may, it is clear that the word "creation" should not be used in the context of Akan cosmology without due caution. It should be apparent also that considerable semantical circumspection is called for in using the word "God" for the Akan Supreme Being. Any transcendental inferences from that usage are misplaced.

So, then, we have the following picture of the outlook of the Akans. They believe in a supreme being, but they do not worship Him. Moreover, for conceptual reasons, this being cannot be said to be a spiritual or supernatural being. Nor is He a creator out of nothing. Furthermore, the foundations of Akan ethical life and thought have no necessary reference to Him. It will be recalled also that although the Akans believe in the existence of a whole host of extra-human beings and forces, they view these as regular resources of the world order which can be exploited for good or, sometimes for ill, given appropriate knowledge and the right approach. To all this we might add the fact that the customary procedures in Akan society pertaining to important stages in life, such as naming, marriage and death, which are well-structured, elaborate and highly cherished as providing concrete occasions for the manifestation of communal caring and solidarity, have no necessary involvement with the belief in the Supreme Being. These considerations, by the way, explain why some early European students of African cosmology called the African God an absentee God. In my opinion those visitors to Africa had their finger on something real, but the pejorative tenor of the observation can only be put down to a universalistic conceit. As for the ancestors, they are called upon to come and participate in all these ceremonies, but as revered members of the family, not as gods.

If we now renew the question of the applicability of the concept of religion to any aspect of Akan culture, we must be struck by the substantial disanalogies between the Akan setup of cosmological and moral ideas viewed in relation to practical life, on the one hand, and Western conceptions of reality and the good life viewed in the same relation. For the purpose of this discussion the most important disparity revolves round the slicing up of human experience into the categories of the religious and the secular. To start from the Western end of the comparison: whether we interpret the concept of the religious in a supernatural or non-supernatural sense, it is not a simple matter to discover an analogue of it in the traditional Akan context.

It might be thought that there is substantial common ground between Akan life and thought and that of, say, the Christian religion, since, even if the Akan Nyame is not thought of as supernatural, he is still regarded as in some sense the author of the world and determiner of its destiny. But conceptions or beliefs that do not dovetail into the fabric of practical life can hardly constitute a religion in the primary sense.

That the belief in Nyame has no essential role in the conduct of Akan life can be seen from a little exercise of the imagination. Imagine the belief in Nyame to be altogether removed from the Akan consciousness. What losses will be incurred in terms of sustenance for any institutions or procedures of practical life? The answer is, "Exactly zero." Customs and moral rules relating to the critical (or even non-critical) stages and circumstances in the lives of individuals do not have their basis in the belief in Nyame. The same is true of the institutions of traditional Akan public life. Thus neither the pursuit of moral virtue and noble ideals by individuals nor the cooperative endeavors of the community towards the common good can be said to stand or fall with the belief in Nyame; they all have a solid enough basis in considerations of human well-being, considerations, in other words, which are completely "this-worldly."

To elaborate a little on this last point: to the traditional Akan what gives meaning to life is usefulness to self, family, community and the species. Nothing transcending life in human society and its empirical conditions enters into the constitution of the meaning of life. In particular, there is not, in Akan belief, in contrast, for instance, to Christian belief, any notion of an afterlife of possible salvation and eternal bliss; what afterlife there is thought to be is envisaged very much on the model of this life, as previously hinted. More importantly, that afterlife is not pictured as a life of eternal fun for the immortals but rather as one of eternal vigilance—vigilance over the affairs of the living with the sole purpose of promoting their well-being within the general constraints of Akan ethics. Indeed, this is what is taken to give meaning to their survival. From everything said (to my knowledge) about the ancestors, they are generally believed never to relent in this objective;

which is one reason why they are held in such high esteem. The inhabitants of the world of the dead, then, are themselves thoroughly "this-worldly" in their orientation, according to Akan traditional conceptions.

Basically the same considerations would seem to discourage attributing to the Akans any sort of non-supernaturalistic religiosity. One great difficulty would be how to articulate such a notion within the Akan conceptual framework. Suppose we construe religion as life and thought impregnated by a sense of the sacred. Then, since the primary meaning of the word "sacred" presupposes some conception of deity, we would be in duty bound to give some notification of a broadening of meaning. Accordingly, the sacred might be understood as that in ethical life most worthy of respect, reverence and commitment. But this, in turn, would presuppose a system of values and ideals, and, in the case of the Akans, would bring us back to their irreducibly "this-worldly" ethic. Now, the remarkable thing is that in this ethic a demonstrated basic commitment to the values and ideals of the society is a component of the very concept of a person. An individual is not a person in the fullest sense unless he or she has shown a responsiveness to those ideals in confirmed habits of life. Not, of course, that an individual failing this test is denuded of human rights; for every individual, simply on the grounds of being human, is regarded as a center of quite extensive rights. On the other hand, there is a prestige attached to the status of personhood, or more strictly, superlative personhood—for indeed the status is susceptible of degrees—to which all Akans of sound mind aspire. But this is simply the aspiration to become a responsible individual in society, an individual who, through intelligent thinking, judicious planning and hard work, is able to carve out an adequate livelihood for himself and family and make significant contributions to the well-being of the community. The problem, now, is that if this is what, in the specific context of Akan culture, living a life informed by a sense of the sacred means, then applying the concept of religion to it would scarcely pick out anything in the culture corresponding to what in, say, Western culture might be called a non-supernaturalistic religion. In Western society there are historical as well as conceptual reasons why one might want to organize one's life on the lines of what might be called a nonsupernaturalist religion. In Akan society there are really none. In the West, loss of the belief in God, for example, usually results in disengagement from certain well-known institutions and practices. The consequent psychological or social void might be filled for some by a "non-theistic" religion. In the Akan situation, on the other hand, no such void is to be anticipated from a comparable belief mutation. Speaking from my own experience, failure to retain the belief in *Nyame*—I make no mention here of the Christian God, the conception of whom registers no coherent meaning upon my understanding—has caused me not the slightest alienation from any of the institutions or practices of Akan culture.

Not unexpectedly, what has cost me some dissonance with the culture is my skepticism regarding the continued existence of our ancestors. The pouring of libation, for example, is a practice in which, as previously hinted, the Akans call upon the ancestors to come and participate in important functions and lend their good auspices to any enterprise launched. This is a significant and not infrequent ceremony in Akan life. But obviously, if one does not believe that the ancestors are actually there, one cannot pretend to call them, or, what is the same thing, one can only pretend to do so. I cannot personally, therefore, participate in a custom like this with any total inwardness. In this, by the way, I do not stand alone. Any

Akan Christian—and there are great numbers of them—is logically precluded from believing such things as the Akan doctrine of ancestors, for it does not cohere with Christian eschatology. As far as I am concerned, however, there is a saving consideration. This custom of libation, and many other customs of a like quasi-material basis, can be retained by simply reinterpreting the reference to the ancestors as commemoration rather than invocation. That, of course, would entail obvious verbal reformulations, but it should present no problem. What of customs that prove not to be susceptible to such revisions in the face of advancing skepticism? One hopes that they would eventually be abandoned. The culture is rich enough not to suffer any real existential deficit from such a riddance. Nor is the atrophy of custom under the pressure of changing times at all rare in the history of culture.

Be that as it may, the fact remains that as already argued, the Akan belief in the existence and power of such beings as the ancestors, and the procedures associated with that belief do not constitute a religion in any reliable sense. We are now, therefore, brought to the following conclusion: The concept of religion is not unproblematically applicable within all cultures, and Akan culture is a case in point. Nevertheless, there may be some justification for speaking of Akan religion in a broadened sense of the word "religion." In this sense the word would refer simply to the fact that the Akans believe in Nyame, a being regarded as the architect of the world order. Certainly, this is an extremely attenuated concept of religion. As pointed out already, religion in the fullest sense, whether it be supernaturalistic or not, is not just a set of beliefs and conceptions but also a way of life based on those ideas. What we have seen, however, is that the Akan way of life is not based on the belief in Nyame. Hence, if we do use the word "religion" in the Akan context on the grounds of the belief in Nyame, we should evince some consciousness of the fact that we have made a considerable extension of meaning; otherwise we propagate a subtle misunderstanding of Akan and cognate cultures under the apparently widespread illusion that religion is a cultural universal.

Yet, surely, something must be universal. Consider the ease with which Christian missionaries have been able to convert large masses of Africans to Christianity by relaying to them "tidings" which are in some important parts most likely conceptually incoherent or, at any rate, incongruous with categories deeply embedded in indigenous ways of thinking. To be sure, it cannot be assumed that in the large majority of cases conversion has been total in terms of moral and cosmological outlook. Still there are impressive enough numbers of African converts, some in the high reaches of ecclesiastical authority, whose understanding of and dedication to the Christian religion challenges the severest comparisons among the most exalted practitioners of the same faith in the West. I take this as testimony to the malleability of the human mind which enables the various peoples of the world to share not only their insights but also their incoherences. This characteristic of the mind, being fundamental to the human status, makes our common humanity the one universal which potentially transcends all cultural particularities.

Chinese Paganism

Lin Yutang

This essay begins with a brief but provocative statement, namely, that religion is personal. Lin Yutang argues that religious experiences are born from personal struggle. He tells his personal story, one of a struggle between a Christian upbringing and an attraction to Chinese paganism. He characterizes the struggle as one of both emotional pride and intellectual humility. Ultimately, it was an appeal to the intrinsic dignity of human life that led him to paganism, which he believes rescues "religion from theology" and restores "simplicity of belief and dignity of feeling" to religion.

Religion is always an individual, personal thing. Every person must work out his own views of religion, and if he is sincere, God will not blame him, however it turns out. Every man's religious experience is valid for himself, for . . . it is not something that can be argued about. But the story of an honest soul struggling with religious problems, told in a sincere manner, will always be of benefit to other people. That is why, in speaking about religion, I must get away from generalities and tell my personal story.

I am a pagan. The statement may be taken to imply a revolt against Christianity; and yet "revolt" seems a harsh word and does not correctly describe the state of mind of a man who has passed through a very gradual evolution, step by step, away from Christianity, during which he clung desperately, with love and piety, to a series of tenets which, against his will, were slipping away from him. Because there was never any hatred, therefore it is impossible to speak of a rebellion.

As I was born in a pastor's family and at one time prepared for the Christian ministry, my natural emotions were on the side of religion during the entire struggle rather than against it. In this conflict of emotions and understanding, I gradually arrived at a position where I had, for instance, definitely renounced the doctrine of redemption, a position which could most simply be described as that of a pagan. It was, and still is, a condition of belief concerning life and the universe in which I feel natural and at ease, without having to be at war with myself. The process came as naturally as the weaning of a child or the dropping of a ripe apple on the ground; and when the time came for the apple to drop, I would not interfere with its dropping. In Taoistic phraseology, this is but to live in the Tao, and in Western phraseology it is but being sincere with oneself and with the universe, according to one's lights. I believe no one can be natural and happy unless he is intellectually sincere with himself, and to be natural is to be in heaven. To me, being a pagan is just being natural.

"To be a pagan" is no more than a phrase, like "to be a Christian." It is no more than a negative statement, for, to the average reader, to be a pagan means only that one is not a Christian; and since "being a Christian" is a very broad and ambiguous term, the meaning of "not being a Christian" is equally ill-defined. It is all the worse when

---

From *The Importance of Living*. Copyright © 1937, The John Day Company. Reprinted by permission of Taiyi Lin Lai and Hsiang Ju Lin.

one defines a pagan as one who does not believe in religion or in God, for we have yet to define what is meant by "God" or by the "religious attitude toward life." Great pagans have always had a deeply reverent attitude toward nature. We shall therefore have to take the word in its conventional sense and mean by it simply a man who does not go to church (except for an aesthetic inspiration, of which I am still capable), does not belong to the Christian fold, and does not accept its usual, orthodox tenets.

On the positive side, a Chinese pagan, the only kind of which I can speak with any feeling of intimacy, is one who starts out with this earthly life as all we can or need to bother about, wishes to live intently and happily as long as his life lasts, often has a sense of the poignant sadness of this life and faces it cheerily, has a keen appreciation of the beautiful and the good in human life wherever he finds them, and regards doing good as its own satisfactory reward. I admit, however, he feels a slight pity or contempt for the "religious" man, who does good in order to get to heaven and who, by implication, would not do good if he were not lured by heaven or threatened with hell. If this statement is correct, I believe there are a great many more pagans in this country than are themselves aware of it. The modern liberal Christian and the pagan are really close, differing only when they start out to *talk* about God.

I think I know the depths of religious experience, for I believe one can have this experience without being a great theologian like Cardinal Newman—otherwise Christianity would not be worth having or must already have been horribly misinterpreted. As I look at it at present, the difference in spiritual life between a Christian believer and a pagan is simply this: the Christian believer lives in a world governed and watched over by God, to whom he has a constant personal relationship, and therefore in a world presided over by a kindly father; his conduct is also often uplifted to a level consonant with this consciousness of being a child of God, no doubt a level which is difficult for a human mortal to maintain consistently at all periods of his life or of the week or even of the day; his actual life varies between living on the human and the truly religious levels.

On the other hand, the pagan lives in this world like an orphan, without the benefit of that consoling feeling that there is always someone in heaven who cares and who will, when that spiritual relationship called prayer is established, attend to his private personal welfare. It is no doubt a less cheery world; but there is the benefit and dignity of being an orphan who by necessity has learned to be independent, to take care of himself, and to be more mature, as all orphans are. It was this feeling rather than any intellectual belief—this feeling of dropping into a world without the love of God—that really scared me till the very last moment of my conversion to paganism; I felt, like many born Christians, that if a personal God did not exist the bottom would be knocked out of this universe.

And yet a pagan can come to the point where he looks on that perhaps warmer and cheerier world as at the same time a more childish, I am tempted to say a more adolescent, world; useful and workable, if one keep the illusion unspoiled, but no more and no less justifiable than a truly Buddhist way of life; also a more beautifully coloured world but consequently less solidly true and therefore of less worth. For me personally, the suspicion that anything is coloured or not solidly true is fatal. There is a price one must be willing to pay for truth; whatever the consequences, let us have it. This position is comparable to and psychologically the same as that of a murderer: if one has committed a murder, the best thing he can do next is to confess it. That is why I say it takes a little courage to become a pagan. But, after one has accepted the worst, one is also without fear. Peace of mind is that mental condition in which you have accepted the worst. (Here I see for myself the influence of Buddhist or Taoist thought.)

Or I might put the difference between a Christian and a pagan world like this: the pagan in me renounced Christianity out of both pride and humility, emotional pride and intellectual humility, but perhaps on the whole less out of pride than of humility. Out of emotional pride because I hated the idea that there should be any other reason for our behaving as nice, decent men and women than the simple fact that we are human beings; theoretically, and if you want to go in for classifications, classify this as a typically humanist thought. But more out of humility, of intellectual humility, simply because I can no longer, with our astronomical knowledge, believe that an individual human being is so terribly important in the eyes of that Great Creator, living as the individual does, an infinitesimal speck on their earth, which is an infinitesimal speck of the solar system, which is again an infinitesimal speck of the universe of solar systems. The audacity of man and his presumptuous arrogance are what stagger me. What right have we to conceive of the character of a Supreme Being, of whose work we can see only a millionth part, and to postulate about His attributes?

The importance of the human individual is undoubtedly one of the basic tenets of Christianity. But let us see what ridiculous arrogance that leads to in the usual practice of Christian daily life.

Four days before my mother's funeral there was a pouring rain, and if it continued, as was usual in July in Changchow, the city would be flooded, and there could be no funeral. As most of us came from Shanghai, the delay would have meant some inconvenience. One of my relatives—a rather extreme but not an unusual example of a Christian believer in China—told me that she had faith in God, Who would always provide for His children. She prayed, and the rain stopped, apparently in order that a tiny family of Christians might have their funeral without delay. But the implied idea that, but for us, God would willingly subject the tens of thousands of Changchow inhabitants to a devastating flood, as was often the case, or that He did not stop the rain because of them but because of us who wanted to have a conveniently dry funeral, struck me as an unbelievable type of selfishness. I cannot imagine God providing for such selfish children.

There was also a Christian pastor who wrote the story of his life, attesting to many evidences of the hand of God in his life, for the purpose of glorifying God. One of the evidences adduced was that, when he had got together 600 silver dollars to buy his passage to America, God lowered the rate of exchange on the day this so very important individual was to buy his passage. The difference in the rate of exchange for 600 silver dollars could have been at most ten or twenty dollars, and God was willing to rock the bourses in Paris, London, and New York in order that this curious child of His might save ten or twenty dollars. Let us remind ourselves that this way of glorifying God is not at all unusual in any part of Christendom.

Oh, the impudence and conceit of man, whose span of life is but three-score and ten! Mankind as an aggregate may have a significant history, but man as an individual, in the words of Su Tungp'o, is no more than a grain of millet in an ocean or an insect *fuyu* born in the morning and dying at eve, as compared with the universe. The Christian will not be humble. He will not be satisfied with the aggregate immortality of his great stream of life, of which he is already a part, flowing on to eternity, like a mighty stream which empties into the great sea and changes and yet does not change. The clay vessel will ask of the potter, "Why hast thou cast me into this shape and why hast thou made me so brittle?" The clay vessel is not satisfied that it can leave little vessels of its own kind when it cracks up. Man is not satisfied that he has received this marvellous body, this almost divine body. He wants to live for ever! And he will not let God alone. He must say his prayers and he must pray daily for small personal gifts from the Source of All Things. Why can't he let God alone?

There was once a Chinese scholar who did not believe in Buddhism, and his mother who did. She was devout and would acquire merit for herself by mumbling, "*Namu omitabha*!" a thousand times day and night. But every time she started to call Buddha's name, her son would call, "Mamma!" The mother became annoyed. "Well," said the son, "don't you think Buddha would be equally annoyed, if he could hear you?"

My father and mother were devout Christians. To hear my father conduct the evening family prayers was enough. And I was a sensitively religious child. As a pastor's son I received the facilities of missionary education, profited from its benefits, and suffered from its weaknesses. For its benefits I was always grateful and its weaknesses I turned into my strength. For according to Chinese philosophy there are no such things in life as good and bad luck.

I was forbidden to attend Chinese theatres, never allowed to listen to Chinese minstrel singers, and entirely cut apart from the great Chinese folk tradition and mythology. When I entered a missionary college, the little foundation in classical Chinese given me by my father was completely neglected. Perhaps it was just as well—so that later, after a completely Westernized education, I could go back to it with the freshness and vigorous delight of a child of the West in an Eastern wonderland. The complete substitution of the fountain pen for the writing brush during my college and adolescent period was the greatest luck I ever had and preserved for me the freshness of the Oriental mental world unspoiled, until I should become ready for it. If Vesuvius had not covered up Pompeii, Pompeii would not be so well preserved, and the imprints of carriage-wheels on her stone pavements would not be so clearly marked to-day. The missionary college education was my Vesuvius.

Thinking was always dangerous. More than that, thinking was always allied with the devil. The conflict during the collegiate-adolescent period, which, as usual, was my most religious period, between a heart which felt the beauty of the Christian life and a head which had a tendency to reason everything away, was taking place. Curiously enough, I can remember no moments of torment or despair, of the kind that drove Tolstoy almost to suicide. At every stage I felt myself a unified Christian, harmonious in my belief, only a little more liberal than the last, and accepting some fewer Christian doctrines. Anyway, I could always go back to the Sermon on the Mount. The poetry of a saying like "Consider the lilies of the field" was too good to be untrue. It was that and the consciousness of the inner Christian life that gave me strength.

But the doctrines were slipping away terribly. Superficial things first began to annoy me. The "resurrection of the flesh," long disproved when the expected second coming of Christ in the first century did not come off and the Apostles did not rise bodily from their graves, was still there in the Apostles' Creed. This was one of those things.

Then, enrolling in a theological class and initiated into the holy of holies, I learned that another article in the creed, the virgin birth, was open to question, different deans in American theological seminaries holding different views. It enraged me that Chinese believers should be required to believe categorically in this article before they could be baptized, while the theologians of the same church regarded it as an open question. It did not seem sincere and somehow it did not seem right.

Further schooling in meaningless commentary scholarship as to the whereabouts of the "water gate" and such minutiae completely relieved me of responsibility to take such theological studies seriously, and I made a poor showing in my grades. My professors considered that I was not cut out for the Christian ministry, and the bishop thought I might as well leave. They would not waste their instruction on me. Again this seems to me now a blessing in disguise. I doubt, if I had gone on with it and put on the clerical garb, whether it would have been so easy for me to be honest with myself later on. But this feeling of rebellion against the discrepancy of the beliefs required of the theologian and of the average convert was the nearest kind of feeling to what I may call a "revolt."

By this time I had already arrived at the position that the Christian theologians were the greatest enemies of the Christian religion. I could never get over two great contradictions. The first was that the theologians had made the entire structure of the Christian belief hang upon the existence of an apple. If Adam had not eaten an apple, there would be no original sin, and if there were no original sin, there would be no need of redemption. That was plain to me, whatever the symbolic value of the apple might be. This seemed to be preposterously unfair to the teachings of Christ, who never said a word about the original sin or the redemption. Anyway, from pursuing literary studies, I feel, like all modern Americans, no consciousness of sin and simply do not believe in it. All I know is that if God loves me only half as much as my mother does, He will not send me to Hell. That is a final fact of my inner consciousness, and for no religion could I deny its truth.

Still more preposterous another proposition seemed to me. This was the argument that, when Adam and Eve ate an apple during their honeymoon, God was so angry that He condemned their posterity to suffer from generation to generation for that little offence but that, when the same posterity murdered the same God's only Son, God was so delighted that He forgave them all. No matter how people explain and argue, I cannot get over this simple untruth. This was the last of the things that troubled me.

Still, even after my graduation, I was a zealous Christian and voluntarily conducted a Sunday school at Tsing Hua, a non-Christian college at Peking, to the dismay of many faculty members. The Christmas meeting of the Sunday school was a torture to me, for here I was passing on to the Chinese children the tale of herald angels singing upon a midnight clear when I did not believe it myself. Everything had been reasoned away, and only love and fear remained: a kind of clinging love for an all-wise God which made me feel happy and peaceful and suspect that I should not have been so happy and peaceful without that reassuring love—and fear of entering into a world of orphans.

Finally my salvation came. "Why," I reasoned with a colleague, "if there were no God, people would not do good and the world would go topsy-turvy."

"Why?" replied my Confucian colleague. "We should lead a decent human life simply because we are decent human beings," he said.

This appeal to the dignity of human life cut off my last tie to Christianity, and from then on I was a pagan.

It is all so clear to me now. The world of pagan belief is a simpler belief. It postulates nothing, and is obliged to postulate nothing. It seems to make the good life more immediately appealing by appealing to the good life alone. It better justifies doing good by making it unnecessary for doing good to justify itself. It does not encourage men to do, for instance, a simple act of charity by dragging in a series of hypothetical postulates—sin, redemption, the cross, laying up treasure in heaven, mutual obligation among men on account of a third-party relationship in heaven—all so unnecessarily complicated and roundabout, and none capable of direct proof. If one accepts the statement that doing good is its own justification, one cannot help regarding all theological baits to right living as redundant and tending to cloud the lustre of a moral truth. Love among men should be a final, absolute fact. We should be able just to look at each other and love each other without being reminded of a third party in heaven. Christianity seems to me to make morality appear unnecessarily difficult and complicated and sin appear tempting, natural, and desirable. Paganism, on the other hand, seems alone to be able to rescue religion from theology and restore it to its beautiful simplicity of belief and dignity of feeling.

In fact, I seem to be able to see how many theological complications arose in the first, second, and third centuries and turned the simple truths of the Sermon on the Mount into a rigid, self-contained structure to support a priestcraft as an endowed institution. The reason was contained in the word *revelation*—the revelation of a special mystery or divine scheme given to a prophet and kept by all apostolic succession, which was found necessary in all religions, from Mohammedanism and Mormonism to the Living Buddha's Lamaism and Mrs. Eddy's Christian Science, in order for each of them to handle exclusively a special, patented monopoly of salvation. All priestcraft lives on the common staple food of revelation. The simple truths of Christ's teaching on the Mount must be adorned, and the lily He so marvelled at must be gilded. Hence we have the "first Adam" and the "second Adam," and so on and so forth.

But Pauline logic, which seemed so convincing and unanswerable in the early days of the Christian era, seems weak and unconvincing to the more subtle modern critical consciousness; and in this discrepancy between the rigorous Asiatic deductive logic and the more pliable, more subtle appreciation of truth of the modern man, lies the weakness of the appeal to the Christian revelation or any revelation for the modern man. Therefore, only by a return to paganism and renouncing the revelation can one return to primitive (and for me more satisfying) Christianity.

It is wrong, therefore, to speak of a pagan as an irreligious man: irreligious he is only as one who refuses to believe in any special variety of revelation. A pagan always believes in God but would not like to say so, for fear of being misunderstood. All Chinese pagans believe in God, the most commonly met with designation in Chinese literature being the term *chaowu*, or the Creator of Things. The only difference is that the Chinese pagan is honest enough to leave the Creator of Things in a halo of mystery, toward whom he feels a kind of awed piety and reverence. What is more, that feeling suffices for him. Of the beauty of this universe, the clever artistry of the myriad things of this creation, the mystery of the stars, the grandeur of heaven, and the dignity of the human soul he is equally aware. But that again suffices for him. He accepts death as he accepts pain and suffering and weighs them against the gift of life and the fresh country breeze and the clear mountain moon and he does not complain. He regards bending to the will of Heaven as the truly religious and pious attitude and calls it "living in the Tao." If the Creator of Things wants him to die at seventy, he gladly dies at seventy. He also believes that "heaven's way always goes round" and that there is no permanent injustice in this world. He does not ask for more.

Discussion Questions

1. Referring to the Bhagavad Gita, explain why commitment to the notion of a greater reality, especially a divine one, is not for "the faint of heart."
2. If one is to have faith in God, why must that faith come from within oneself and not be imposed by others?
3. Can you explain the distinction that Ozick draws between the ordinary and the extraordinary? Why would it be wrong to worship God's creation or even God's law *instead of* God, according to Ozick?
4. According to James, why might religious experience be broader than that which is often experienced within the context of organized religion? Why must we be more open to its meaning and the experience itself?
5. Chief Red Jacket explains some of the problems with religious persecution. Cannot belief come only from within? How might proselytizing be antithetical to religious experience?
6. According to Wiredu, how might religious expressions differ from culture to culture? Discuss the Akan philosophy concerning God and spirituality.
7. What is Chinese paganism? How does Lin Yutang characterize it as a religion, nonetheless, and one that emphasizes the importance of the dignity of humanity?
8. In your opinion, why is it difficult for people to discuss God's existence or nonexistence, God's nature, and their religious beliefs? Do we feel threatened in our identity when our religious beliefs are questioned by others?

chapter 9

Taking Risks/ Acting Philosophically

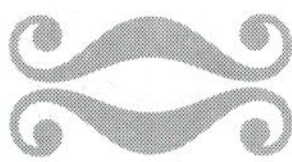

The Good Life has been defined by some to be a life of self-actualization, a balancing of self-interest with other interest. Can this be achieved? To answer this question, we begin by listening to the words of *Socrates' Apology,* a defense of his life and the choices he made. Socrates tells us that the actualization of the self begins with self-examination, continues through self-understanding, and culminates in the attainment of self-respect. But such an examination does not occur in isolating ourselves from others. Rather it arises out of an active engagement with others. Many pretend to have knowledge of truth, justice, and goodness, but how many actually possess it? Socrates cautions us not to accept unquestioningly the opinions and beliefs of others. He encouraged the youth of Athens to ask questions, to demand explanations. But he also reminded them not to criticize others until they first examined their own motives and intentions. He was charged with corrupting the youth of Athens. You need to ask yourself what it means to corrupt someone or something. If corruption is a change, can this change under certain conditions not be seen in other than a negative light? Of what was Socrates truly guilty? Of arrogance? Of living life fully? Make your judgment as did the men of Athens, but remember you must support that judgment since others will question it.

What is the highest good that each of us can attain? What makes for our happiness? Epicurus suggests that happiness and the good life can be found in seeking our pleasure, in embracing life. Longevity is not as valuable as leading

Confucius

a pleasant life, or what could be called a life of blessedness. Avoid pain or disturbance to the health of the body, and choose the pleasures of "sober reasoning." Ultimately it is in the exercise of three virtues—prudence, honor, and justice—that we discover the good life.

In his Analects, Confucius tells us that how we live our lives matters. He claims that it is not enough to believe that one is living a virtuous life but that one *does live* a virtuous life. We must examine ourselves daily and nurture our roots. This will enable us better to grow in virtue. Confucius tells us that speaking well of others, being trustworthy, being friendly, and treating others kindly—and wanting to do all these things—will bring forth in us the greatest authentic and virtuous self. Here, then, we can see the importance of our social relations in helping to determine the self and how the self lives. Our actions help or hinder the potential for others to achieve the virtuous self, too. But to what extent do they do so? What are the limits of other-responsibility and self-responsibility?

Epicurus told us that motive, sound judgment, and act are all necessary conditions of the good life. The words of the Sermon on the Mount are not inconsistent with such a philosophy. As Saint Matthew recounts the sermon, we are reminded that the intent formed in our hearts conditions the rightness of our act. More important, goodness and rightness are found in not only refraining from wrongful deeds but in acting positively and beneficently toward others. I am not virtuous by the fact that I do no injustice to my neighbor, but I am virtuous by the fact that I make friends with my neighbor and seek his or her welfare as actively as I seek my own. Here we see the distinction between acts that are merely not wrong by virtue of their consistency with a moral principle and acts that are truly praiseworthy. Virtue is found not merely in refraining from doing harm, but in preventing the possibility of harm by actively doing good for others. To think of doing harm is to have acted wrongfully, but to think of doing good is not sufficient for being good.

The good society is a progressive society in that it fosters self-actualization, and self-actualization, in turn, requires an adequate amount of liberty to think, to speak, and to act. A truly moral individual, a mature citizen, is not one who acts or chooses on the compulsion of a despotic authority, even though this authority may be very beneficent in its intent and act. The morally responsible individual is one who chooses in light of maximizing the good for the self and the good for others. Can a good society survive without the moral conscience the authors within this chapter have given us? Without a moral conscience would the good society lapse into indifference and tyranny?

UN Peacekeepers in Bosnia

Perhaps two of the more pressing moral issues confronting the global village are violence and political tyranny. Sara Ruddick discusses these issues, arguing for "A Women's Politics of Resistance." Ruddick specifically calls for a resistance that will take into consideration the problems that women face due to actions that undermine their possibilities as women (for example, the responsibility for their children's health). To be responsible in this light means to resist rather than serve the state, and thus the nature of this resistance will be culturally determined. Even though the particulars of the resistance are culturally determined, on a universal level such resistance will incorporate a "sentimental" politics that Ruddick claims men will have difficulty in accepting, let alone practicing.

From a different perspective, Eagle Man sees himself as a part of a whole system through which the virtues of truth, honesty, and courage are believed to bring forth harmony in the universe. Focusing on the importance of human relationships, Eagle Man challenges us to reflect upon the wisdom of the "old ways" of Native Americans in order to develop the respect necessary for survival, and fulfillment, in society. We must view Mother Earth as holy and not simply as a tool to be used as a means to an end. We must abandon the bad activities that bring forth bad things and embrace the good through good actions that are respectful toward all things. But is this easy to do? How do we get caught up in the bad? Why do you think that it might be important to stop and reflect upon our relationship to all things and not just other humans? Why is it not enough to simply look within ourselves for the answers to what is good?

It may be that leading a good life requires that we educate ourselves in a way that ensures the full development of our human personality. It can be argued that social, political, and moral progress would be impossible without such an education. Just what might be the nature of that education? It could be an education for freedom, an education for critical consciousness. Paulo Freire suggests that society move toward what he calls a "transitive consciousness." It is a consciousness that is antithetical to "assistencialism," that is, a welfare policy that does little to engage self-respect, let alone self-realization. The latter requires that we develop the critical self-consciousness necessary to being human. Transitive consciousness engages each man and woman in the world. It is a consciousness of a fully examined self, that of an authentic human being.

In the final analysis, perhaps it can be claimed that no one can live a meaningful life in isolation from others or from an involvement in community. We are in the world and with others, a situation we cannot avoid. To what extent are my actions and choices for defining myself determined by what others say and do? Must I conform to cultural and societal norms if I am to survive to continue my journey through life? What is it I must do in terms of self-respect and other-respect in order to live what is called "the good life"? If I must sacrifice some choices for the sake of others, to what extent can I hold on to pleasure and a sense of self-gratification? Each of these questions pushes us to examine carefully the dynamics of everyday living and the choices we cannot avoid.

The ultimate question, then, involves what can be done and what must be done by individuals to protect the sense of *self* that is necessary for all. An examined life may inevitably lead to an active life, a life of critical consciousness and simple human dignity.

Socrates' Apology

Plato

Written by Plato, Socrates' Apology *is a dramatic defense of a way of life. In his oral arguments before an Athenian jury, Socrates gives us an unparalleled picture of moral character and virtue. Socrates insists it is the proper function of a good person to examine beliefs, to question oneself and others, to communicate constantly with others in order to uncover the truth. To live the good life, one must not calculate consequences or material interests. If one lives such a good life, one need not fear death.*

How you, O Athenians, have been affected by my accusers, I cannot tell; but I know that they almost made me forget who I was—so persuasively did they speak; and yet they have hardly uttered a word of truth. But of the many falsehoods told by them, there was one which quite amazed me;—I mean when they said that you should be upon your guard and not allow yourselves to be deceived by the force of my eloquence. To say this, when they were certain to be detected as soon as I opened my lips and proved myself to be anything but a great speaker, did indeed appear to me most shameless—unless by the force of eloquence they mean the force of truth; for if such is their meaning, I admit that I am eloquent. But in how different a way from theirs! Well, as I was saying, they have scarcely spoken the truth at all; but from me you shall hear the whole truth: not, however, delivered after their manner in a set oration duly ornamented with words and phrases. No, by heaven! but I shall use the words and arguments which occur to me at the moment, for I am confident in the justice of my cause[1]: at my time of life I ought not to be appearing before you, O men of Athens, in the character of a juvenile orator—let no one expect it of me. And I must beg of you to grant me a favour:—If I defend myself in my accustomed manner, and you hear me using the words which I have been in the habit of

---

From Plato, "The Apology," in *The Dialogues of Plato,* translated by Benjamin Jowett.

using in the agora, at the tables of the money-changers, or anywhere else, I would ask you not to be surprised, and not to interrupt me on this account. For I am more than seventy years of age, and appearing now for the first time in a court of law, I am quite a stranger to the language of the place; and therefore I would have you regard me as if I were really a stranger, whom you would excuse if he spoke in his native tongue, and after the fashion of his country:—Am I making an unfair request of you? Never mind the manner, which may or may not be good; but think only of the truth of my words, and give heed to that: let the speaker speak truly and the judge decide justly.

And first, I have to reply to the older charges and to my first accusers, and then I will go on to the later ones. For of old I have had many accusers, who have accused me falsely to you during many years; and I am more afraid of them than of Anytus and his associates, who are dangerous, too, in their own way. But far more dangerous are the others, who began when you were children, and took possession of your minds with their falsehoods, telling of one Socrates, a wise man, who speculated about the heaven above, and searched into the earth beneath, and made the worse appear the better cause. The disseminators of this tale are the accusers whom I dread; for their hearers are apt to fancy that such enquirers do not believe in the existence of the gods. And they are many, and their charges against me are of ancient date, and they were made by them in the days when you were more impressible than you are now—in childhood, or it may have been in youth—and the cause when heard went by default, for there was none to answer. And hardest of all, I do not know and cannot tell the names of my accusers; unless in the chance case of a Comic poet. All who from envy and malice have persuaded you— some of them having first convinced themselves—all this class of men are most difficult to deal with; for I cannot have them up here, and cross-examine them, and therefore I must simply fight with shadows in my own defence, and argue when there is no one who answers. I will ask you then to assume with me, as I was saying, that my opponents are of two kinds; one recent, the other ancient: and I hope that you will see the propriety of my answering the latter first, for these accusations you heard long before the others, and much oftener.

Well, then, I must make my defence, and endeavor to clear away in a short time, a slander which has lasted a long time. May I succeed, if to succeed be for my good and yours, or likely to avail me in my cause! The task is not an easy one; I quite understand the nature of it. And so leaving the event with God, in obedience to the law I will now make my defence.

I will begin at the beginning, and ask what is the accusation which has given rise to the slander of me, and in fact has encouraged Meletus to prefer this charge against me. Well, what do the slanderers say? They shall be my prosecutors, and I will sum up their words in an affidavit: "Socrates is an evildoer, and a curious person, who searches into things under the earth and in heaven, and he makes the worse appear the better cause; and he teaches the aforesaid doctrines to others." Such is the nature of the accusation: it is just what you have yourselves seen in the comedy of Aristophanes[2] who has introduced a man whom he calls Socrates, going about and saying that he walks in air, and talking a deal of nonsense concerning matters of which I do not pretend to know either much or little—not that I mean to speak disparagingly of any one who is a student of natural philosophy. I should be very sorry if Meletus could bring so grave a charge against me. But the simple truth is, O Athenians, that I have nothing to do with physical speculations.

Very many of those here present are witnesses to the truth of this, and to them I appeal. Speak then, you who have heard me, and tell your neighbours whether any of you have ever known me hold forth in few words or in many upon such matters. . . . You hear their answer. And from what they say of this part of the charge you will be able to judge of the truth of the rest.

As little foundation is there for the report that I am a teacher, and take money; this accusation has no more truth in it than the other. Although, if a man were really able to instruct mankind, to receive money for giving instruction would, in my opinion, be an honour to him. There is Gorgias of Leontium, and Prodicus of Ceos, and Hippias of Elis, who go the round of the cities, and are able to persuade the young men to leave their own citizens by whom they might be taught for nothing, and come to them whom they not only pay, but are thankful if they may be allowed to pay them. There is at this time a Parian philosopher residing in Athens, of whom I have heard; and I came to hear of him in this way:—I came across a man who has spent a world of money on the Sophists, Callias, the son of Hipponicus, and knowing that he had sons, I asked him: "Callias," I said, "if your two sons were foals or calves, there would be no difficulty in finding some one to put over them; we should hire a trainer of horses, or a farmer probably, who would improve and perfect them in their own proper virtue and excellence; but as they are human beings, whom are you thinking of placing over them? Is there any one who understands human and political virtue? You must have thought about the matter, for you have sons; is there any one?" "There is," he said. "Who is he?" said I; "and of what country? and what does he charge?" "Evenus the Parian," he replied; "he is the man, and his charge is five minae." Happy is Evenus, I said to myself, if he really has this wisdom, and teaches at such a moderate charge. Had I the same, I should have been very proud and conceited; but the truth is that I have no knowledge of the kind.

I dare say, Athenians, that some one among you will reply, "Yes, Socrates, but what is the origin of these accusations which are brought against you; there must have been something strange which you have been doing? All these rumours and this talk about you would never have arisen if you had been like other men: tell us, then, what is the cause of them, for we should be sorry to judge hastily of you." Now I regard this as a fair challenge, and I will endeavour to explain to you the reason why I am called wise and have such an evil fame. Please to attend then. And although some of you may think that I am joking, I declare that I will tell you the entire truth. Men of Athens, this reputation of mine has come of a certain sort of wisdom which I possess. If you ask me what kind of wisdom, I reply, wisdom such as may perhaps be attained by man, for to that extent I am inclined to believe that I am wise; whereas the persons of whom I was speaking have a superhuman wisdom, which I may fail to describe, because I have it not myself; and he who says that I have, speaks falsely, and is taking away my character. And here, O men of Athens, I must beg you not to interrupt me, even if I seem to say something extravagant. For the word which I will speak is not mine. I will refer you to a witness who is worthy of credit; that witness shall be the God of Delphi—he will tell you about my wisdom, if I have any, and of what sort it is. You must have known Chaerephon; he was early a friend of mine, and also a friend of yours, for he shared in the recent exile of the people, and returned with you. Well, Chaerephon, as you know, was very impetuous in all his doings, and he went to Delphi and boldly asked the oracle to tell him whether—as I was saying, I must beg you not to interrupt—he asked the oracle to tell him whether any one was wiser than I was, and the Pythian prophetess answered, that there was no man wiser. Chaerephon is dead himself; but his brother, who is in court, will confirm the truth of what I am saying.

Why do I mention this? Because I am going to explain to you why I have such an evil name. When I heard the answer, I said to myself, What can the god mean? and what is the interpretation of his riddle? for I know that I have no wisdom, small or great. What then can he mean when he says that I am the wisest of men? And yet he is a god, and cannot lie; that would be against his nature. After long consideration, I thought of a method of trying the question. I reflected that if I could only find a man wiser than myself, then I might go to the god with a refutation in my hand. I should say to him, "Here is a man who is wiser than I am; but you said that I was the wisest." Accordingly I went to one who had the reputation of wisdom, and observed him—his name I need not mention; he was a politician whom I selected for examination—and the result was as follows: When I began to talk with him, I could not help thinking that he was not really wise, although he was thought wise by many, and still wiser by himself, and thereupon I tried to explain to him that he thought himself wise, but was not really wise; and the consequence was that he hated me, and his enmity was shared by several who were present and heard me. So I left him, saying to myself, as I went away: Well, although I do not suppose that either of us knows anything really beautiful and good, I am better off than he is,—for he knows nothing, and thinks that he knows; I neither know nor think that I know. In this latter particular, then, I seem to have slightly the advantage of him. Then I went to another who had still higher pretensions to wisdom, and my conclusion was exactly the same. Whereupon I made another enemy of him, and of many others besides him.

Then I went to one man after another, being not unconscious of the enmity which I provoked, and I lamented and feared this: But necessity was laid upon me,—the word of God, I thought, ought to be considered first. And I said to myself, Go I must to all who appear to know, and find out the meaning of the oracle. And I swear to you, Athenians, by the dog I swear!—for I must tell you the truth—the result of my mission was just this: I found that the men most in repute were all but the most foolish; and that others less esteemed were really wiser and better. I will tell you the tale of my wanderings and of the "Herculean" labours, as I may call them, which I endured only to find at last the oracle irrefutable. After the politicians, I went to the poets; tragic, dithyrambic, and all sorts. And there, I said to myself, you will be instantly detected; now you will find out that you are more ignorant than they are. Accordingly, I took them some of the most elaborate passages in their own writings, and asked what was the meaning of them—thinking that they would teach me something. Will you believe me? I am almost ashamed to confess the truth, but I must say that there is hardly a person present who would not have talked better about their poetry than they did themselves. Then I knew that not by wisdom do poets write poetry, but by a sort of genius and inspiration; they are like diviners or soothsayers who also say many fine things, but do not understand the meaning of them. The poets appeared to me to be much in the same case; and I further observed that upon the strength of their poetry they believed themselves to be the wisest of men in other things in which they were not wise. So I departed, conceiving myself to be superior to them for the same reason that I was superior to the politicians.

At last I went to the artisans, for I was conscious that I knew nothing at all, as I may say, and I was sure that they knew many fine things; and here I was not mistaken, for they did know many things of which I was ignorant, and in this they certainly were wiser than I was. But I observed that even the good artisans fell into the same error as the poets;—because they were good workmen they thought that they also knew all sorts of high matters, and this defect in them overshadowed their wisdom; and therefore I asked myself on behalf of the oracle, whether I would like to be as I was, neither having their knowledge nor their ignorance, or like them in both; and I made answer to myself and to the oracle that I was better off as I was.

This inquisition has led to my having many enemies of the worst and most dangerous kind, and has given occasion also to many calumnies. And I am called wise, for my hearers always imagine that I myself possess the wisdom which I find wanting in others: but the truth is, O men of Athens, that God only is wise; and by his answer he intends to show that the wisdom of men is worth little or nothing; he is not speaking of Socrates, he is only using my name by way of illustration, as if he said, He, O men, is the wisest, who, like Socrates, knows that his wisdom is in truth worth nothing. And so I go about the world, obedient to the god, and search and make enquiry into the wisdom of any one, whether citizen or stranger, who appears to be wise; and if he is not wise, then in vindication of the oracle I show him that he is not wise; and my occupation quite absorbs me, and I have no time to give either to any public matter of interest or to any concern of my own, but I am in utter poverty by reason of my devotion to the god.

There is another thing:—young men of the richer classes, who have not much to do, come about me of their own accord; they like to hear the pretenders examined, and they often imitate me, and proceed to examine others; there are plenty of persons, as they quickly discover, who think that they know something, but really know little or nothing; and then those who are examined by them instead of being angry with themselves are angry with me: This confounded Socrates, they say; this villainous misleader of youth!—and then if somebody asks them, Why, what evil does he practise or teach? they do not know, and cannot tell; but in order that they may not appear to be at a loss, they repeat the ready-made charges which are used against all philosophers about teaching things up in the clouds and under the earth, and having no gods, and making the worse appear the better cause; for they do not like to confess that their pretense of knowledge has been detected—which is the truth; and as they are numerous and ambitious and energetic, and are drawn up in battle array and have persuasive tongues, they have filled your ears with their loud and inveterate calumnies. And this is the reason why my three accusers, Meletus and Anytus and Lycon, have set upon me; Meletus, who has a quarrel with me on behalf of the poets; Anytus, on behalf of the craftsmen and politicians; Lycon, on behalf of the rhetoricians: and as I said at the beginning, I cannot expect to get rid of such a mass of calumny all in a moment. And this, O men of Athens, is the truth and the whole truth; I have concealed nothing, I have dissembled nothing. And yet, I know that my plainness of speech makes them hate me, and what is their hatred but a proof that I am speaking the truth?—Hence has arisen the prejudice against me; and this is the reason of it, as you will find out either in this or in any future enquiry.

I have said enough in my defence against the first class of my accusers; I turn to the second class. They are headed by Meletus, that good man and true lover of his country, as he calls himself. Against these, too, I must try to make a defence:—Let their affidavit be read: it contains something of this kind: It says that Socrates is a doer of evil, who corrupts the youth; and who does not believe in the gods of the state, but has other new divinities of his own. Such is the charge; and now let us examine the particular counts. He says that I am a doer of evil, and corrupt the youth; but I say, O men of Athens that Meletus is a doer of evil, in that he pretends to be in earnest when he is only in jest, and is so eager to bring men to trial from a pretended zeal and interest about matters in which he really never had the smallest interest. And the truth of this I will endeavour to prove to you.

Come hither, Meletus, and let me ask a question of you. You think a great deal about the improvement of youth?

Yes, I do.

Tell the judges, then, who is their improver; for you must know, as you have taken the pains to discover their corrupter, and are citing and accusing me before them. Speak, then, and tell the judges who their improver is.—Observe, Meletus, that you are silent, and have nothing to say. But is not this rather disgraceful, and a very considerable proof of what I was saying, that you have no interest in the matter? Speak up, friend, and tell us who their improver is.

The laws.

But that, my good sir, is not my meaning. I want to know who the person is, who, in the first place, knows the laws.

The judges, Socrates, who are present in court.

What, do you mean to say, Meletus, that they are able to instruct and improve youth?

Certainly they are.

What, all of them, or some only and not others?

All of them.

By the goddess Herè, that is good news! There are plenty of improvers, then. And what do you say of the audience,—do they improve them?

Yes, they do.

And the senators?

Yes, the senators improve them.

But perhaps the members of the assembly corrupt them?—or do they too improve them?

They improve them.

Then every Athenian improves and elevates them; all with the exception of myself; and I alone am their corrupter? Is that what you affirm?

That is what I stoutly affirm.

I am very unfortunate if you are right. But suppose I ask you a question: How about horses? Does one man do them harm and all the world good? Is not the exact opposite the truth? One man is able to do them good, or at least not many;—the trainer of horses, that is to say, does them good, and others who have to do with them rather injure them? Is not that true, Meletus, of horses, or of any other animals? Most assuredly it is; whether you and Anytus say yes or no. Happy indeed would be the condition of youth if they had one corrupter only, and all the rest of the world were their improvers. But you, Meletus, have sufficiently shown that you never had a thought about the young: your carelessness is seen in your not caring about the very things which you bring against me.

And now, Meletus, I will ask you another question—by Zeus I will: Which is better, to live among bad citizens, or among good ones? Answer, friend, I say; the question is one which may be easily answered. Do not the good do their neighbours good, and the bad do them evil?

Certainly.

And is there any one who would rather be injured than benefited by those who live with him? Answer, my good friend, the law requires you to answer—does any one like to be injured?

Certainly not.

And when you accuse me of corrupting and deteriorating the youth, do you allege that I corrupt them intentionally or unintentionally?

Intentionally, I say.

But you have just admitted that the good do their neighbours good, and evil do them evil. Now, is that a truth which your superior wisdom has recognized thus early in life, and am I, at my age, in such darkness and ignorance as not to know that if a man with whom I have to live is corrupted by me, I am very likely to be harmed by him; and yet I corrupt him, and intentionally, too—so you say, although neither I nor any other human being is ever likely to be convinced by you. But either I do not corrupt them, or I corrupt them unintentionally; and on either view of the case you lie. If my offence is unintentional, the law has no cognizance of unintentional offences: you ought to have taken me privately, and warned and admonished me; for if I had been better advised, I should have left off doing what I only did unintentionally—no doubt I should; but you would have nothing to say to me and refused to teach me. And now you bring me up in this court, which is a place not of instruction, but of punishment.

It will be very clear to you, Athenians, as I was saying, that Meletus has no care at all, great or small, about the matter. But still I should like to know, Meletus, in what I am affirmed to corrupt the young, I suppose you mean, as I infer from your indictment, that I teach them not to acknowledge the gods which the state acknowledges, but some other new divinities or spiritual agencies in their stead. These are the lessons by which I corrupt the youth, as you say.

Yes, that I say emphatically.

Then, by the gods, Meletus, of whom we are speaking, tell me and the court, in somewhat plainer terms, what you mean! for I do not as yet understand whether you affirm that I teach other men to acknowledge some gods, and therefore that I do believe in gods, and am not an entire atheist—this you do not lay to my charge,—but only you say that they are not the same gods which the city recognizes—the charge is that they are different gods. Or, do you mean that I am an atheist simply, and a teacher of atheism?

I mean the latter—that you are a complete atheist.

What an extraordinary statement! Why do you think so, Meletus? Do you mean that I do not believe in the godhead of the sun or moon, like other men?

I assure you, judges, that he does not: for he says that the sun is stone, and the moon earth.

Friend Meletus, you think that you are accusing Anaxagoras: and you have but a bad opinion of the judges, if you fancy them illiterate to such a degree as not to know that these doctrines are found in the books of Anaxagoras the Clazomenian, which are full of them. And so, forsooth, the youth are said to be taught them by Socrates, when there are not unfrequently exhibitions of them at the theatre (price of admission one drachma at the most); and they might pay their money, and laugh at Socrates if he pretends to father these extraordinary views. And so, Meletus, you really think that I do not believe in any god?

I swear by Zeus that you believe absolutely in none at all.

Nobody will believe you, Meletus, and I am pretty sure that you do not believe yourself. I cannot help thinking, men of Athens, that Meletus is reckless and impudent, and that he has written this indictment in a spirit of mere wantonness and youthful bravado. Has he not compounded a riddle, thinking to try me? He said to himself:—I shall see whether the wise Socrates will discover my facetious contradiction, or whether I shall be able to deceive him and the rest of them. For he certainly does appear to me to contradict himself in the indictment as much as if he said that Socrates is guilty of not believing in the gods, and yet of believing in them—but this is not like a person who is in earnest.

I should like you, O men of Athens, to join me in examining what I conceive to be his inconsistency; and do you, Meletus, answer. And I must remind the audience of my request that they would not make a disturbance if I speak in my accustomed manner:

Did ever man, Meletus, believe in the existence of human things, and not of human beings? . . . I wish, men of Athens, that he would answer, and not be always trying to get up an interruption. Did ever any man believe in horsemanship, and not in horses? or in flute-playing, and not in flute-players? No, my friend; I will answer to you and to the court, as you refuse to answer for yourself. There is no man who ever did. But now please to answer the next question: Can a man believe in spiritual and divine agencies, and not in spirits or demigods?

He cannot.

How lucky I am to have extracted that answer, by the assistance of the court! But then you swear in the indictment that I teach and believe in divine or spiritual agencies (new or old, no matter for that); at any rate, I believe in spiritual agencies,—so you say and swear in the affidavit; and yet if I believe in divine beings, how can I help believing in spirits or demigods;—must I not? To be sure I must; and therefore I may assume that your silence gives consent. Now what are spirits or demigods? are they not either gods or the sons of gods?

Certainly they are.

But this is what I call the facetious riddle invented by you: the demigods or spirits are gods, and you say first that I do not believe in gods, and then again that I do believe in gods; that is, if I believe in demigods. For if the demigods are the illegitimate sons of gods, whether by the nymphs or by any other mothers, of whom they are said to be the sons—what human being will ever believe that there are no gods if they are the sons of gods? You might as well affirm the existence of mules, and deny that of horses and asses. Such nonsense, Meletus, could only have been intended by you to make trial of me. You have put this into the indictment because you had nothing real of which to accuse me. But no one who has a particle of understanding will ever be convinced by you that the same men can believe in divine and superhuman things, and yet not believe that there are gods and demigods and heroes.

I have said enough in answer to the charge of Meletus: any elaborate defence is unnecessary; but I know only too well how many are the enmities which I have incurred, and this is what will be my destruction if I am destroyed;—not Meletus, nor yet Anytus, but the envy and detraction of the world, which has been the death of many good men, and will probably be the death of many more; there is no danger of my being the last of them.

Some one will say: And are you not ashamed, Socrates, of a course of life which is likely to bring you to an untimely end? To him I may fairly answer: There you are mistaken: a man who is good for anything ought not to calculate the chance of living or dying; he ought only to consider whether in doing anything he is doing right or wrong—acting the part of a good man or of a bad. Whereas, upon your view, the heroes who fell at Troy were not good for much, and the son of Thetis above all, who altogether despised danger in comparison with disgrace; and when he was so eager to slay Hector, his goddess mother said to him, that if he avenged his companion Patroclus, and slew Hector, he would die himself—"Fate," she said, in these or the like words, "waits for you next after Hector;" he, receiving this warning, utterly despised danger and death, and instead of fearing them, feared rather to live in dishonour, and not to avenge his friend. "Let me die forthwith," he replies, "and be avenged of my enemy, rather than abide here by the beaked ships, a laughing-stock and a burden of the earth." Had Achilles any thought of death and danger? For wherever a man's place is, whether the place which he has chosen or that in which he has been placed by a commander, there he ought to remain in the hour of danger; he should not think of death or of anything but of disgrace. And this, O men of Athens, is a true saying.

Strange, indeed, would be my conduct, O men of Athens, if I who, when I was ordered by the generals whom you chose to command me at Potidaea and Amphipolis and Delium, remained where they placed me, like any other man, facing death—if now, when, as I conceive and imagine, God orders me to fulfil the philosopher's mission of searching into myself and other men, I were to desert my post through fear of death, or any other fear; that would indeed be strange, and I might justly be arraigned in court for denying the existence of the gods, if I disobeyed the oracle because I was afraid of death, fancying that I was wise when I was not wise. For the fear of death is indeed the pretense of wisdom, and not real wisdom, being a pretense of knowing the unknown; and no one knows whether death, which men in their fear apprehend to be the greatest evil, may not be the greatest good. Is not this ignorance of a disgraceful sort, the ignorance which is the conceit that man knows what he does not know? And in this respect only I believe myself to differ from men in general, and may perhaps claim to be wiser than they are:—that whereas I know but little of the world below, I do not suppose that I know: but I do know that injustice and disobedience to a better, whether God or man, is evil and dishonourable, and I will never fear or avoid a possible good rather than a certain evil. And therefore if you let me go now, and are not convinced by Anytus, who said that since I had been prosecuted I must be put to death (or if not that I ought never to have been prosecuted at all); and that if I escape now, your sons will all be utterly ruined by listening to my words—if you say to me, Socrates, this time we will not mind Anytus, and you shall be let off, but upon one condition, that you are not to enquire and speculate in this way any more, and that if you are caught doing so again you shall die;—if this was the condition on which you let me go, I should reply: Men of Athens, I honour and love you; but I shall obey God rather than you, and while I have life and strength I shall never cease from the practice and teaching of philosophy, exhorting any one whom I meet and saying to him after my manner; You, my friend,—a citizen of the great and mighty and wise city of Athens,—are you not ashamed of heaping up the greatest amount of money and honour and reputation, and caring so little about wisdom and truth and the greatest improvement of the soul, which you never regard or heed at all? And if the person with whom I am arguing, says: Yes, but I do care; then I do not leave him or let him go at once; but I proceed to interrogate and examine and cross-examine him, and if I think that he has no virtue in him, but only says that he has, I reproach him with undervaluing the greater, and overvaluing the less. And I shall repeat the same words to every one whom I meet, young and old, citizen and alien, but especially to the citizens, inasmuch as they are my brethren. For know that this is the command of God; and I believe that no greater good has ever happened in the state than my service to the God. For I do nothing but go about persuading you all, old and young alike, not to take thought for your persons or your properties, but first and chiefly to care about the greatest improvement of the soul. I tell you that virtue is not given by money, but that from virtue comes money and every other good of man, public as well as private. This is my teaching, and if this is the doctrine which corrupts the youth, I am a mischievous person. But if any one says that this is not my teaching, he is speaking an untruth. Wherefore, O men of Athens, I say to you, do as Anytus bids or not as Anytus bids, and either acquit me or not; but whichever you do, understand that I shall never alter my ways, not even if I have to die many times.

Men of Athens, do not interrupt, but hear me; there was an understanding between us that you should hear me to the end: I have something more to say, at which you may be inclined to cry out; but I believe that to hear me will be good for you, and therefore I beg that you will not cry out. I would have you know, that if you kill such an one as I am, you will injure yourselves more than you will injure me. Nothing will injure me, not Meletus nor yet Anytus—they cannot, for a bad man is not permitted to injure a better than himself. I do not deny that Anytus may, perhaps, kill him, or drive him into exile, or deprive him of civil rights; and he may imagine, and others may imagine, that he is inflicting a great injury upon him: but there I do not agree. For the evil of doing as he is doing—the evil of unjustly taking away the life of another—is greater far.

And now, Athenians, I am not going to argue for my own sake, as you may think, but for yours, that you may not sin against the God by condemning me, who am his gift to you. For if you kill me you will not easily find a successor to me, who, if I may use such a ludicrous figure of speech, am a sort of gadfly, given to the state by God; and the state is a great and noble steed who is tardy in his motions owing to his very size, and requires to be stirred into life. I am that gadfly which God has attached to the state, and all day long and in all places am always fastening upon you, arousing and persuading and reproaching you. You will not easily find another like me, and therefore I would advise you to spare me. I dare say that you may feel out of temper (like a person who is suddenly awakened from sleep), and you think that you might easily strike me dead as Anytus advises, and then you would sleep on for the remainder of your lives, unless God in his care of you sent you another gadfly. When I say that I am given to you by God, the proof of my mission is this:—if I had been like other men, I should not have neglected all my own concerns or patiently seen the neglect of them during all these years, and have been doing yours, coming to you individually like a father or elder brother, exhorting you to regard virtue; such conduct, I say, would be unlike human nature. If I had gained anything, or if my exhortations had been paid, there would have been some sense in my doing so; but now, as you will perceive, not even the impudence of my accusers dares to say that I have ever exacted or sought pay of any one; of that they have no witness. And have a sufficient witness to the truth of what I say—my poverty.

Some one may wonder why I go about in private giving advice and busying myself with the concerns of others, but do not venture to come forward in public and advise the state. I will tell you why. You have heard me speak at sundry times and in diverse places of an oracle or sign which comes to me, and is the divinity which Meletus ridicules in the indictment. This sign, which is a kind of voice, first began to come to me when I was a child; it always forbids but never commands me to do anything which I am going to do. This is what deters me from being a politician. And rightly, as I think. For I am certain, O men of Athens, that if I had engaged in politics, I should have perished long ago, and done no good either to you or to myself. And do not be offended at my telling you the truth: for the truth is, that no man who goes to war with you or any other multitude, honestly striving against the many lawless and unrighteous deeds which are done in a state, will save his life; he who will fight for the right, if he would live even for a brief space, must have a private station and not a public one.

I can give you convincing evidence of what I say, not words only, but what you value far more—actions. Let me relate to you a passage of my own life which will prove to you that I should never have yielded to injustice from any fear of death, and that "as I should have refused to yield" I must have died at once. I will tell you a tale of the courts, not very interesting perhaps, but nevertheless true. The only office of state which I ever held, O men of Athens, was that of senator: the tribe Antiochis, which is my tribe, had the presidency at the trial of the generals who had not taken up the bodies of the slain after the battle of Arginusae; and you proposed to try them in a body, contrary to law, as you all thought afterwards; but at the time I was the only one of the Prytanes who was opposed to the illegality, and I gave my vote against you; and when the orators threatened to impeach and arrest me, and you called and shouted, I made up my mind that I would run the risk, having law and justice with me, rather than take part in your injustice because I feared imprisonment and death. This happened in the days of the democracy. But when the oligarchy of the Thirty was in power, they sent for me and four others into the rotunda, and bade us bring Leon the Salaminian from Salamis, as they wanted to put him to death. This was a specimen of the sort of commands which they were always giving with the view of implicating as many as possible in their crimes; and then I showed, not in word only but in deed, that, if I may be allowed to use such an expression, I cared not a straw for death, and that my great and only care was lest I should do an unrighteous or unholy thing. For the strong arm of that oppressive power did not frighten me into doing wrong; and when we came out of the rotunda the other four went to Salamis and fetched Leon, but I went quietly home. For which I might have lost my life, and not the power of the Thirty shortly afterwards come to an end. And many will witness to my words.

Now do you really imagine that I could have survived all these years, if I had led a public life, supposing that like a good man I had always maintained the right and had made justice, as I ought, the first thing? No indeed, men of Athens, neither I nor any other man. But I have been always the same in all my actions, public as well as private, and never have I yielded any base compliance to those who are slanderously termed my disciples, or to any other. Not that I have any regular disciples. But if any one likes to come and hear me while I am pursuing my mission, whether he be young or old, he is not excluded. Nor do I converse only with those who pay; but any one, whether he be rich or poor, may ask and answer me and listen to my words; and whether he turns out to be a bad man or a good one, neither result can be justly imputed to me; for I never taught or professed to teach him anything. And if any one says that he has ever learned or heard anything from me in private which all the world has not heard, let me tell you that he is lying.

But I shall be asked, Why do people delight in continually conversing with you? I have told you already, Athenians, the whole truth about this matter: they like to hear the cross-examination of the pretenders to wisdom; there is amusement in it. Now this duty of cross-examining other men has been imposed upon me by God; and has been signified to me by oracles, visions, and in every way in which the will of divine power was ever intimated to any one. This is true, O Athenians; or, if not true, would be soon refuted. If I am or have been corrupting the youth, those of them who are now grown up and become sensible that I gave them bad advice in the days of their youth should come forward as accusers, and take their revenge; or if they do not like to come themselves, some of their relatives, fathers, brothers, or other kinsmen, should say what evil their families have suffered at my hands. Now is their time. Many of them I see in the court. There is Crito, who is of the same age and of the same deme with myself, and there is Critobulus his son, whom I also see. Then again there is Lysanias of Sphettus, who is the father of Aeschines—he is present; and also there is Antiphon of Cephisus, who is the father of Epigenes; and there are the brothers of several who have associated with me. There is Nicostratus the son of Theosdotides, and the brother of Theodotus (now Theodotus himself is dead, and therefore he, at any rate, will not seek to stop him); and there is Paralus the son of Demodocus, who had a brother Theages; and Adeimantus the son of Ariston, whose brother Plato is present; and Aeantodorus, who is the brother of Apollodorus, whom I also see. I might mention a great many others, some of whom Meletus should have produced as witnesses in the course of his speech; and let him still produce them, if he has forgotten—I will make way for him. And let him say, if he has any testimony of the sort which he can produce. Nay, Athenians, the very opposite is the truth. For all these are ready to witness on behalf of the corrupter, of the injurer of their kindred, as Meletus and Anytus call me; not the corrupted youth only—there might have been a motive for that—but their uncorrupted elder relatives. Why should they too support me with their testimony? Why, indeed, except for the sake of truth and justice, and because they know that I am speaking the truth, and that Meletus is a liar.

Well, Athenians, this and the like of this is all the defence which I have to offer. Yet a word more. Perhaps there may be some one who is offended at me, when he calls to mind how he himself on a similar, or even a less serious occasion, prayed and entreated the judges with many tears, and how he produced his children in court, which was a moving spectacle, together with a host of relations and friends; whereas I, who am probably in danger of my life, will do none of these things. The contrast may occur to his mind, and he may be set against me, and vote in anger because he is displeased at me on this account. Now if there be such a person among you,—mind, I do not say that there is,—to him I may fairly reply: My friend, I am a man, and like other men, a creature of flesh and blood, and not "of wood or stone," as Homer says; and I have a family, yes, and sons, O Athenians, three in number, one almost a man, and two others who are still young; and yet I will not bring any of them hither in order to petition you for an acquittal. And why not? Not from any self-assertion or want of respect for you. Whether I am or am not afraid of death is another question, of which I will not now speak. But, having regard to public opinion, I feel that such conduct would be discreditable to myself, and to you, and to the whole state. One who has reached my years, and who has a name for wisdom, ought not to demean himself. Whether this opinion of me be deserved or not, at any rate the world has decided that Socrates is in some way superior to other men. And if those among you who are said to be superior in wisdom and courage, and any other virtue, demean themselves in this way, how shameful is their conduct! I have seen men of reputation, when they have been condemned, behaving in the strangest manner: they seemed to fancy that they were going to suffer something dreadful if they died, and that they could be immortal if you only allowed them to live; and I think that such are a dishonour to the state, and that any stranger coming in would have said of them that the most eminent men of Athens, to whom the Athenians themselves give honour and command, are no better than women. And I say that these things ought not to be done by those who have a reputation; and if they are done, you ought not to permit them; you ought rather to show that you are far more disposed to condemn the man who gets up a doleful scene and makes the city ridiculous, than him who holds his peace.

But, setting aside the question of public opinion, there seems to be something wrong in asking a favour of a judge, and thus procuring an acquittal, instead of informing and convincing him. For his duty is, not to make a present of justice, but to give judgment; and he has sworn that he will judge according to the laws, and not according to his own good pleasure; and we ought not to encourage you, nor should you allow yourself to be encouraged, in this habit of perjury—there can be no piety in that. Do not then require me to do what I consider dishonourable and impious and wrong, especially now, when I am being tried for impiety on the indictment of Meletus. For if, O men of Athens, by force of persuasion and entreaty I could overpower your oaths, then I should be teaching you to believe that there are no gods, and in defending should simply convict myself of the charge of not believing in them. But that is not so—far otherwise. For I do believe that there are gods, and in a sense higher than that in which any of my accusers believe in them. And to you and to God I commit my cause, to be determined by you as is best for you and me.

There are many reasons why I am not grieved, O men of Athens, at the vote of condemnation. I expected it, and am only surprised that the votes are so nearly equal; for I had thought that the majority against me would have been far larger; but now, had thirty votes gone over to the other side, I should have been acquitted. And I may say, I think, that I have escaped Meletus. I may say more; for without the assistance of Anytus and Lycon, any one may see that he would not have had a fifth part of the votes, as the law requires, in which case he would have incurred a fine of a thousand drachmae.

And so he proposes death as the penalty. And what shall I propose on my part, O men of Athens? Clearly that which is my due. And what is my due? What return shall be made to the man who has never had the wit to be idle during his whole life; but has been careless of what the many care for—wealth, and family interests, and military offices, and speaking in the assembly, and magistracies, and plots, and parties. Reflecting that I was really too honest a man to be a politician and live, I did not go where I could do no good to you or to myself; but where I could do the greatest good privately to every one of you, thither I went, and sought to persuade every man among you that he must look to himself, and seek virtue and wisdom before he looks to his private interests, and look to the state before he looks to the interests of the state; and that this should be the order which he observes in all his actions. What shall be done to such [a] one? Doubtless some good thing, O men of

Athens, if he has his reward; and the good should be of a kind suitable to him. What would be a reward suitable to a poor man who is your benefactor, and who desires leisure that he may instruct you? There can be no reward so fitting as maintenance in the Prytaneum, O men of Athens, a reward which he deserves far more than the citizen who has won the prize at Olympia in the horse or chariot race, whether the chariots were drawn by two horses or by many. For I am in want, and he has enough; and he only gives you the appearance of happiness, and I give you the reality. And if I am to estimate the penalty fairly, I should say that maintenance in the Prytaneum is the just return.

Perhaps you think that I am braving you in what I am saying now, as in what I said before about the tears and prayers. But this is not so. I speak rather because I am convinced that I never intentionally wronged any one, although I cannot convince you—the time has been too short; if there were a law at Athens, as there is in other cities, that a capital cause should not be decided in one day, then I believe that I should have convinced you. But I cannot in a moment refute great slanders; and, as I am convinced that I never wronged another, I will assuredly not wrong myself. I will not say of myself that I deserve any evil, or propose any penalty. Why should I? Because I am afraid of the penalty of death which Meletus proposes? When I do not know whether death is a good or an evil, why should I propose a penalty which would certainly be an evil? Shall I say imprisonment? And why should I live in prison, and be the slave of the magistrates of the year—of the Eleven? Or shall the penalty be a fine, and imprisonment until the fine is paid? There is the same objection. I should have to lie in prison, for money I have none, and cannot pay. And if I say exile (and this may possibly be the penalty which you will affix), I must indeed be blinded by the love of life, if I am so irrational as to expect that when you, who are my own citizens, cannot endure my discourses and words, and have found them so grievous and odious that you will have no more of them, others are likely to endure me. No indeed, men of Athens, that is not very likely. And what a life should I lead, at my age, wandering from city to city, ever changing my place of exile, and always being driven out! For I am quite sure that wherever I go, there, as here, the young men will flock to me; and if I drive them away, their elders will drive me out at their request; and if I let them come, their fathers and friends will drive me out for their sakes.

Some one will say: Yes, Socrates, but cannot you hold your tongue, and then you may go into a foreign city, and no one will interfere with you? Now I have great difficulty in making you understand my answer to this. For if I tell you that to do as you say would be a disobedience to the God, and therefore that I cannot hold my tongue, you will not believe that I am serious; and if I say again that daily to discourse about virtue, and of those other things about which you hear me examining myself and others, is the greatest good of man, and that the unexamined life is not worth living, you are still less likely to believe me. Yet I say what is true, although a thing of which it is hard for me to persuade you. Also, I have never been accustomed to think that I deserve to suffer any harm. Had I money I might have estimated the offence at what I was able to pay, and not have been much the worse. But I have none, and therefore I must ask you to proportion the fine to my means. Well, perhaps I could afford a mina, and therefore I propose that penalty: Plato, Crito, Critobulus, and Apollodorus, my friends here, bid me say thirty minae, and they will be the sureties. Let thirty minae be the penalty; for which sum they will be ample security to you.

Not much time will be gained, O Athenians, in return for the evil name which you will get from the detractors of the city, who will say that you killed Socrates, a wise man; for they will call me wise, even although I am not wise, when they want to reproach you. If you had waited a little while, your desire would have been fulfilled in the course of nature. For I am far advanced in years, as you may perceive, and not far from death. I am speaking now not to all of you, but only to those who have condemned me to death. And I have another thing to say to them: You think that I was convicted because I had no words of the sort which would have procured my acquittal—I mean, if I had thought fit to leave nothing undone or unsaid. Not so; the deficiency which led to my conviction was not of words—certainly not. But I had not the boldness or impudence or inclination to address you as you would have liked me to do, weeping and wailing and lamenting, and saying and doing many things which you have been accustomed to hear from others, and which, as I maintain, are unworthy of me. I thought at the time that I ought not to do anything common or mean when in danger: nor do I now repent of the style of my defence; I would rather die having spoken after my manner, than speak in your manner and live. For neither in war nor yet at law ought I or any man to use every way of escaping death. Often in battle there can be no doubt that if a man will throw away his arms, and fall on his knees before his pursuers, he may escape death; and in other dangers there are other ways of escaping death, if a man is willing to say and do anything. The difficulty, my friends, is not to avoid death, but to avoid unrighteousness; for that runs faster than death. I am old and move slowly, and the slower runner has overtaken me, and my accusers are keen and quick, and the faster runner, who is unrighteousness, has overtaken them. And now I depart hence condemned by you to suffer the penalty of death,—they too go their ways condemned by the truth to suffer the penalty of villainy and wrong; and I must abide by my award—let them abide by theirs. I suppose that these things may be regarded as fated,—and I think that they are well.

And now, O men who have condemned me, I would fain prophesy to you; for I am about to die, and in the hour of death men are gifted with prophetic power. And I prophesy to you who are my murderers, that immediately after my departure punishment far heavier than you have inflicted on me will surely await you. Me you have killed because you wanted to escape the accuser, and not to give an account of your lives. But that will not be as you suppose: far otherwise. For I say that there will be more accusers of you than there are now; accusers whom hitherto I have restrained: and as they are younger they will be more inconsiderate with you, and you will be more offended at them. If you think that by killing men you can prevent some one from censuring your evil lives, you are mistaken; that is not a way of escape which is either possible or honourable; the easiest and the noblest way is not to be disabling others, but to be improving yourselves. This is the prophecy which I utter before my departure to the judges who have condemned me.

Friends, who would have acquitted me, I would like also to talk with you about the thing which has come to pass, while the magistrates are busy, and before I go to the place at which I must die. Stay then a little, for we may as well talk with one another while there is time. You are my friends, and I should like to show you the meaning of this event which has happened to me. O my judges—for you I may truly call judges—I should like to tell you of a wonderful circumstance. Hitherto the divine faculty of which the internal oracle is the source has constantly been in the habit of opposing me even about trifles, if I was going to make a slip or error in any matter; and now as you see there has come upon me that which may be thought, and is generally believed to be, the last and worst evil. But the oracle made no sign of opposition, either when I was leaving my house in the morning, or when I was on my way to the court, or while I was speaking, at anything which I was going to say; and yet I have often been stopped in the middle of a speech, but now in nothing I either said or did touching the matter in hand has the oracle opposed me. What do I take to be the explanation of this silence? I will tell you. It is an intimation that what has happened to me is a good, and that those of us who think that death is an evil are in error. For the customary sign would surely have opposed me had I been going to evil and not to good.

Let us reflect in another way, and we shall see that there is great reason to hope that death is a good; for one of two things—either death is a state of nothingness and utter unconsciousness, or, as men say, there is a change and migration of the soul from this world to another. Now if you suppose that there is no consciousness, but a sleep like the sleep of him who is undisturbed even by dreams, death will be an unspeakable gain. For if a person were to select the night in which his sleep was undisturbed even by dreams, and were to compare with this the other days and nights of his life, and then were to tell us how many days and nights he had passed in the course of his life better and more pleasantly than this one, I think that any man, I will not say a private man, but even the great king will not find many such days or nights, when compared with the others. Now if death be of such a nature, I say that to die is gain; for eternity is then only a single night. But if death is the journey to another place, and there, as men say, all the dead abide, what good, O my friends and judges, can be greater than this? If indeed when the pilgrim arrives in the world below, he is delivered from the professors of justice in this world, and finds the true judges who are said to give judgment there, Minos and Rhadamanthus and Aeacus and Triptolemus, and other sons of God who were righteous in their own life, that pilgrimage will be worth making. What would not a man give if he might converse with Orpheus and Musaeus and Hesiod and Homer? Nay, if this be true, let me die again and again. I myself, too, shall have a wonderful interest in there meeting and conversing with Palamedes, and Ajax the son of Telamon, and any other ancient hero who has suffered death through an unjust judgment; and there will be no small pleasure, as I think, in comparing my own sufferings with theirs. Above all, I shall then be able to continue my search into true and false knowledge; as in this world, so also in the next; and I shall find out who is wise, and who pretends to be wise, and is not. What would not a man give, O judges, to be able to examine the leader of the great Trojan expedition; or Odysseus or Sisyphus, or numberless others, men and women too! What infinite delight would there be in conversing with them and asking them questions! In another world they do not put a man to death for asking questions: assuredly not. For besides being happier than we are, they will be immortal, if what is said is true.

Wherefore, O judges, be of good cheer about death, and know of a certainty, that no evil can happen to a good man, either in life or after death. He and his are not neglected by the gods; nor has my own approaching end happened by mere chance. But I see clearly that the time had arrived when it was better for me to die and be released from trouble; wherefore the oracle gave no sign. For which reason, also, I am not angry with my condemners, or with my accusers; they have done me no harm, although they did not mean to do me any good; and for this I may gently blame them.

Still I have a favour to ask of them. When my sons are grown up, I would ask you, O my friends, to punish them; and I would have you trouble them, as I have troubled you, if they seem to care about riches, or anything, more than about virtue; or if they pretend to be something when they are really nothing,—then reprove them, as I have reproved you, for not caring about that for which they ought to care, and thinking that they are something when they are really nothing. And if you do this, both I and my sons will have received justice at your hands.

The hour of departure has arrived, and we go our ways—I to die, and you to live. Which is better God only knows.

Notes

1. Or, I am certain that I am right in taking this course.
2. Aristoph., Clouds, 225 ff.
3. Probably in allusion to Aristophanes who caricatured, and to Euripides who borrowed the notions of Anaxagoras, as well as to other dramatic poets.

Letter to Menoeceus

Epicurus

It should not be surprising that a philosopher would urge us to seek our pleasure in order to lead a proper and philosophical life. What will be surprising is how someone such as Epicurus defines pleasure. Certainly, he urges us to avoid pain, but pleasure is to be found in achieving the simple life and, most important, in "quietude of the soul." Here we find again that spiritual goods are believed more valuable than the satisfaction of physical desires.

Let no one when young delay to study philosophy, nor when he is old grow weary of his study. For no one can come too early or too late to secure the health of his soul. And the man who says that the age for philosophy has either not yet come or has gone by is like the man who says that the age for happiness is not yet come to him, or has passed away. Wherefore both when young and old a man must study philosophy, that as he grows old he may be young in blessings through the grateful recollection of what has been, and that in youth he may be old as well, since he will know no fear of what is to come. We must then meditate on the things that make our happiness, seeing that when that is with us we have all, but when it is absent we do all to win it.

The things which I used unceasingly to commend to you, these do and practise, considering them to be the first principles of the good life. First of all believe that god is a being immortal and blessed, even as the common idea of a god is engraved on men's minds, and do not assign to him anything

Epicurus lived from 351 to 270 B.C.

alien to his immortality or ill-suited to his blessedness: but believe about him everything that can uphold his blessedness and immortality. For gods there are, since the knowledge of them is by clear vision. But they are not such as the many believe them to be: for indeed they do not consistently represent them as they believe them to be. And the impious man is not he who denies the gods of the many, but he who attaches to the gods the beliefs of the many. For the statements of the many about the gods are not conceptions derived from sensation, but false suppositions, according to which the greatest misfortunes befall the wicked and the greatest blessings the good by the gift of the gods. For men being accustomed always to their own virtues welcome those like themselves, but regard all that is not of their nature as alien.

Become accustomed to the belief that death is nothing to us. For all good and evil consists in sensation, but death is deprivation of sensation. And therefore a right understanding that death is nothing to us makes the mortality of life enjoyable, not because it adds to it an infinite span of time, but because it takes away the craving for immortality. For there is nothing terrible in life for the man who has truly comprehended that there is nothing terrible in not living. So that the man speaks but idly who says that he fears death not because it will be painful when it comes, but because it is painful in anticipation. For that which gives no trouble when it comes, is but an empty pain in anticipation. So death, the most terrifying of ills, is nothing to us, since so long as we exist death is not with us; but when death comes, then we do not exist. It does not then concern either the living or the dead, since for the former it is not, and the latter are no more.

But the many at one moment shun death as the greatest of evils, at another yearn for it as a respite from the evils in life. But the wise man neither seeks to escape life nor fears the cessation of life, for neither does life offend him nor does the absence of life seem to be any evil. And just as with food he does not seek simply the larger share and nothing else, but rather the most pleasant, so he seeks to enjoy not the longest period of time, but the most pleasant.

And he who counsels the young man to live well, but the old man to make a good end, is foolish, not merely because of the desirability of life, but also because it is the same training which teaches to live well and to die well. Yet much worse still is the man who says it is good not to be born, but

> once born make haste to pass the gates of Death. (Theognis, 427)

For if he says this from conviction why does he not pass away out of life? For it is open to him to do so, if he had firmly made up his mind to this. But if he speaks in jest, his words are idle among men who cannot receive them.

We must then bear in mind that the future is neither ours, nor yet wholly not ours, so that we may not altogether expect it as sure to come, nor abandon hope of it, as if it will certainly not come.

We must consider that of desires some are natural, others vain, and of the natural some are necessary and others merely natural; and of the necessary some are necessary for happiness, others for the repose of the body, and others for very life. The right understanding of these facts enables us to refer all choice and avoidance to the health of the body and the soul's freedom from disturbance, since this is the aim of the life of blessedness. For it is to obtain this end that we always act, namely, to avoid pain and fear. And when this is once secured for us, all the tempest of the soul is dispersed, since the living creature has not to wander as though in search of something that is missing, and to look for some other thing by which he can fulfill the good of the soul and the good of the body. For it is then that we have need of pleasure, when we feel pain owing to the absence of pleasure; but when we do not feel pain, we no longer need pleasure. And for this cause we call pleasure the beginning and end of the blessed life. For we recognize pleasure as the first good innate in us, and from pleasure we begin every act of choice and avoidance, and to pleasure we return again, using the feeling as the standard by which we judge every good.

And since pleasure is the first good and natural to us, for this very reason we do not choose every pleasure, but sometimes we pass over many pleasures, when greater discomfort accrues to us as the result of them: and similarly we think many pains better than pleasures, since a greater pleasure comes to us when we have endured pains for a long time. Every pleasure then because of its natural kinship to us is good, yet not every pleasure is to be chosen: even as every pain also is an evil, yet not all are always of a nature to be avoided. Yet by a scale of comparison and by the consideration of advantages and disadvantages we must form our judgment on all these matters. For the good on certain occasions we treat as bad, and conversely the bad as good.

And again independence of desire we think a great good—not that we may at all times enjoy but a few things, but that, if we do not possess many, we may enjoy the few in the genuine persuasion that those have the sweetest pleasure in luxury who least need it, and that all that is natural is easy to be obtained, but that which is superfluous is hard. And so plain savours bring us a pleasure equal to a luxurious diet, when all the pain due to want is removed; and bread and water produce the highest pleasure, when one who needs them puts them to his lips. To grow accustomed therefore to simple and not luxurious diet gives us health to the full, and makes a man alert for the needful employments of life, and when after long intervals we approach luxuries, disposes us better towards them, and fits us to be fearless of fortune.

When, therefore, we maintain that pleasure is the end, we do not mean the pleasures of profligates and those that consist in sensuality, as is supposed by some who are either ignorant or disagree with us or do not understand, but freedom from pain in the body and from trouble in the mind. For it is not continuous drinkings and revellings, nor the satisfaction of lusts, nor the enjoyment of fish and other luxuries of the wealthy table, which produce a pleasant life, but sober reasoning, searching out the motives for all choice and avoidance, and banishing mere opinions, to which are due the greatest disturbance of the spirit.

Of all this the beginning and the greatest good is prudence. Wherefore prudence is a more precious thing even than philosophy: for from prudence are sprung all the other virtues, and it teaches us that it is not possible to live pleasantly without living prudently and honourably and justly, nor again, to live a life of prudence, honour, and justice without living pleasantly. For the virtues are by nature bound up with the pleasant life, and the pleasant life is inseparable from them. For indeed who, think you, is a better man than he who holds reverent opinions concerning the gods, and is at all times free from fear of death, and has reasoned out the end ordained by nature? He understands that the limit of good things is easy to fulfill and easy to attain, whereas the course of ills is either short in time or slight in pain: he laughs at destiny, whom some have introduced as the mistress of all things.

He thinks that with us lies the chief power in determining events, some of which happen by necessity and some by chance, and some are within our control; for while necessity cannot be called to account, he sees that chance is inconstant, but that which is in our control is subject to no master, and to it are naturally attached praise and blame. For, indeed, it were better to follow the myths about the gods than to become a slave to the destiny of the natural philosophers: for the former suggests a hope of placating the gods by worship, whereas the latter involves a necessity which knows no placation. As to chance, he does not regard it as a god as most men do (for in god's acts there is no disorder), nor as an uncertain cause of all things: for he does not believe that good and evil are given by chance to man for the framing of a blessed life, but that opportunities for great good and great evil are afforded by it. He therefore thinks it better to be unfortunate in reasonable action than to prosper in unreason. For it is better in a man's actions that what is well chosen should fail, rather than that what is ill chosen should be successful owing to chance.

Meditate therefore on these things and things akin to them night and day by yourself, and with a companion like to yourself, and never shall you be disturbed waking or asleep, but you shall live like a god among men. For a man who lives among immortal blessings is not like to a mortal being.

Analects

Confucius

Confucius was an ancient Chinese philosopher whose beliefs had a lasting impact on the people of China. Emphasizing the importance of virtue and family, Confucius tells us that the ways in which we interact with others are important to our identity. Our outward appearance and actions represent who we are and what we believe. As you read this essay, examine your own actions and think about what these actions reflect about your own beliefs. What do they tell others, and yourself, about your identity? Do you think that it is important to be virtuous?

BOOK I

1.1 The Master said, "Is it not pleasant to learn with a constant perseverance and application? Is it not delightful to have friends coming from distant quarters? Is he not a man of complete virtue, who feels no discomposure though men may take no note of him?"

1.2 The philosopher Yu said, "They are few who, being filial and fraternal, are fond of offending against their superiors. There have been none, who, not liking to offend

"Analects of Confucius," trans. by James Legge, from *The Chinese Classics*, Oxford: Oxford University Press, 1893.

against their superiors, have been fond of stirring up confusion. The superior man bends his attention to what is radical. That being established, all practical courses naturally grow up. Filial piety and fraternal submission—are they not the root of all benevolent actions?"

1.3 The Master said, "Fine words and an insinuating appearance are seldom associated with true virtue."

1.4 The philosopher Tsang said, "I daily examine myself on three points: whether, in transacting business for others, I may have been not faithful; whether, in intercourse with friends, I may have been not sincere; whether I may have not mastered and practiced the instructions of my teacher."

1.6 The Master said, "A youth, when at home, should be filial, and, abroad, respectful to his elders. He should be earnest and truthful. He should overflow in love to all, and cultivate the friendship of the good. When he has time and opportunity, after the performance of these things, he should employ them in polite studies."

1.7 Tsze-hsia said, "If a man withdraws his mind from the love of beauty, and applies it as sincerely to the love of the virtuous; if, in serving his parents, he can exert his utmost strength; if, in serving his prince, he can devote his life; if, in his intercourse with his friends, his words are sincere: although men say that he has not learned, I will certainly say that he has."

1.8 The Master said, "If the scholar be not grave, he will not call forth any veneration, and his learning will not be solid. Hold faithfulness and sincerity as first principles. Have no friends not equal to yourself. When you have faults, do not fear to abandon them."

1.14 The Master said, "He who aims to be a man of complete virtue in his food does not seek to gratify his appetite, nor in his dwelling place does he seek the appliances of ease; he is earnest in what he is doing, and careful in his speech; he frequents the company of men of principle that he may be rectified: such a person may be said indeed to love to learn."

1.16 The Master said, "I will not be afflicted at men's not knowing me; I will be afflicted that I do not know men."

BOOK II

2.5 Mang I asked what filial piety was. The Master said, "It is not being disobedient." Soon after, as Fan Ch'ih was driving him, the Master told him, saying, "Mang-sun asked me what filial piety was, and I answered him, 'not being disobedient.' " Fan Ch'ih said, "What did you mean?" The Master replied, "That parents, when alive, be served according to propriety; that, when dead, they should be buried according to propriety; and that they should be sacrificed to according to propriety."

2.7 Tsze-yu asked what filial piety was. The Master said, "The filial piety nowadays means the support of one's parents. But dogs and horses likewise are able to do something in the way of support; without reverence, what is there to distinguish the one support given from the other?"

2.13 Tsze-kung asked what constituted the superior man. The Master said, "He acts before he speaks, and afterwards speaks according to his actions."

2.15 The Master said, "Learning without thought is labor lost; thought without learning is perilous."

2.17 The Master said, "Yu, shall I teach you what knowledge is? When you know a thing, to hold that you know it; and when you do not know a thing, to allow that you do not know it—this is knowledge."

BOOK III

3.3 The Master said, "If a man be without the virtues proper to humanity, what has he to do with the rites of propriety? If a man be without the virtues proper to humanity, what has he to do with music?"

BOOK IV

4.2 The Master said, "Those who are without virtue cannot abide long either in a condition of poverty and hardship, or in a condition of enjoyment. The virtuous rest in virtue; the wise desire virtue."

4.3 The Master said, "It is only the truly virtuous man, who can love, or who can hate, others."

4.4 The Master said, "If the will be set on virtue, there will be no practice of wickedness."

4.5 The Master said, "Riches and honors are what men desire. If they cannot be obtained in the proper way, they should not be held. Poverty and meanness are what men dislike. If they cannot be avoided in the proper way, they should not be avoided. If a superior man abandon virtue, how can he fulfill the requirements of that name? The superior man does not, even for the space of a single meal, act contrary to virtue. In moments of haste, he cleaves to it. In seasons of danger, he cleaves to it."

4.6 The Master said, "I have not seen a person who loved virtue, or one who hated what was not virtuous. He who loved virtue, would esteem nothing above it. He who hated what is not virtuous, would practice virtue in such a way that he would not allow anything that is not virtuous to approach his person. Is any one able for one day to apply his strength to virtue? I have not seen the case in which his strength would be insufficient. Should there possibly be any such case, I have not seen it."

4.10 The Master said, "The superior man, in the world, does not set his mind either for anything, or against anything; what is right he will follow."

4.11 The Master said, "The superior man thinks of virtue; the small man thinks of comfort. The superior man thinks of the sanctions of law; the small man thinks of favors which he may receive."

4.16 The Master said, "The mind of the superior man is conversant with righteousness; the mind of the mean man is conversant with gain."

4.17 The Master said, "When we see men of worth, we should think of equaling them; when we see men of a contrary character, we should turn inwards and examine ourselves."

4.24 The Master said, "The superior man wishes to be slow in his speech and earnest in his conduct."

BOOK VI

6.20 Fan Ch'ih asked what constituted wisdom. The Master said, "To give one's self earnestly to the duties due to men, and, while respecting spiritual beings, to keep aloof from them, may be called wisdom." He asked about perfect virtue. The Master said,

"The man of virtue makes the difficulty to be overcome his first business, and success only a subsequent consideration;—this may be called perfect virtue."

6.28 Tsze-kung said, "Suppose the case of a man extensively conferring benefits on the people, and able to assist all, what would you say of him? Might he be called perfectly virtuous?" The Master said, "Why speak only of virtue in connection with him? Must he not have the qualities of a sage? Even Yao and Shun were still solicitous about this. Now the man of perfect virtue, wishing to be established himself, seeks also to establish others; wishing to be enlarged himself, he seeks also to enlarge others. To be able to judge of others by what is nigh in ourselves—this may be called the art of virtue."

BOOK XII

12.1 Yen Yuan asked about perfect virtue. The Master said, "To subdue one's self and return to propriety, is perfect virtue. If a man can for one day subdue himself and return to propriety, an under heaven will ascribe perfect virtue to him. Is the practice of perfect virtue from a man himself, or is it from others?" Yen Yuan said, "I beg to ask the steps of that process." The Master replied, "Look not at what is contrary to propriety; listen not to what is contrary to propriety; speak not what is contrary to propriety; make no movement which is contrary to propriety." Yen Yuan then said, "Though I am deficient in intelligence and vigor, I will make it my business to practice this lesson."

12.2 Chung-kung asked about perfect virtue. The Master said, "It is, when you go abroad, to behave to every one as if you were receiving a great guest; to employ the people as if you were assisting at a great sacrifice; not to do to others as you would not wish done to yourself; to have no murmuring against you in the country, and none in the family." Chung-kung said, "Though I am deficient in intelligence and vigor, I will make it my business to practice this lesson."

12.16 The Master said, "The superior man seeks to perfect the admirable qualities of men, and does not seek to perfect their bad qualities. The mean man does the opposite of this."

12.22 Fan Ch'ih asked about benevolence. The Master said, "It is to love all men." He asked about knowledge. The Master said, "It is to know all men."

BOOK XIII

13.26 The Master said, "The superior man has a dignified ease without pride. The mean man has pride without a dignified ease."

13.27 The Master said, "The firm, the enduring, the simple, and the modest are near to virtue."

BOOK XIV

14.29 The Master said, "The superior man is modest in his speech, but exceeds in his actions."

14.30 The Master said, "The way of the superior man is threefold, but I am not equal to it. Virtuous, he is free from anxieties; wise, he is free from perplexities; bold, he is free from fear."

14.36 Some one said, "What do you say concerning the principle that injury should be recompensed with kindness?" The Master said, "With what then will you recompense kindness? Recompense injury with justice, and recompense kindness with kindness."

14.45 Tsze-lu asked what constituted the superior man. The Master said, "The cultivation of himself in reverential carefulness." "And is this all?" said Tsze-lu. "He cultivates himself so as to give rest to others," was the reply. "And is this all?" again asked Tsze-lu. The Master said, "He cultivates himself so as to give rest to all the people. He cultivates himself so as to give rest to all the people—even Yao and Shun were still solicitous about this."

BOOK XV

15.8 The Master said, "The determined scholar and the man of virtue will not seek to live at the expense of injuring their virtue. They will even sacrifice their lives to preserve their virtue complete."

15.17 The Master said, "The superior man in everything considers righteousness to be essential. He performs it according to the rules of propriety. He brings it forth in humility. He completes it with sincerity. This is indeed a superior man."

15.31 The Master said, "The object of the superior man is truth. Food is not his object. There is plowing; even in that there is sometimes want. So with learning; emolument may be found in it. The superior man is anxious lest he should not get truth; he is not anxious lest poverty should come upon him."

15.32 The Master said, "When a man's knowledge is sufficient to attain, and his virtue is not sufficient to enable him to hold, whatever he may have gained, he will lose again. When his knowledge is sufficient to attain, and he has virtue enough to hold fast, if he cannot govern with dignity, the people will not respect him. When his knowledge is sufficient to attain, and he has virtue enough to hold fast; when he governs also with dignity, yet if he try to move the people contrary to the rules of propriety:—full excellence is not reached."

BOOK XVI

16.4 Confucius said, "There are three friendships which are advantageous, and three which are injurious. Friendship with the upright; friendship with the sincere; and friendship with the man of much observation: these are advantageous. Friendship with the man of specious airs; friendship with the insinuatingly soft; and friendship with the glib-tongued: these are injurious."

16.10 Confucius said, "The superior man has nine things which are subjects with him of thoughtful consideration. In regard to the use of his eyes, he is anxious to see clearly. In regard to the use of his ears, he is anxious to hear distinctly. In regard to his countenance, he is anxious that it should be benign. In regard to his demeanor, he is anxious that it should be respectful. In regard to his speech, he is anxious that it should be sincere. In regard to his doing of business, he is anxious that it should be reverently careful. In regard to what he doubts about, he is anxious to question others. When he is angry, he thinks of the difficulties his anger may involve him in. When he sees gain to be got, he thinks of righteousness."

BOOK XVII

17.6 Tsze-chang asked Confucius about perfect virtue. Confucius said, "To be able to practice five things everywhere under heaven constitutes perfect virtue." He begged to ask what they were, and was told, "Gravity, generosity of soul, sincerity, earnestness, and kindness. If you are grave, you will not be treated with disrespect. If you are generous, you will win all. If you are sincere, people will repose trust in you. If you are earnest, you will accomplish much. If you are kind, this will enable you to employ the services of others."

17.8 The Master said, "Yu, have you heard the six words to which are attached six becloudings?" Yu replied, "I have not." "Sit down, and I will tell them to you. There is the love of being benevolent without the love of learning; the beclouding here leads to a foolish simplicity. There is the love of knowing without the love of learning; the beclouding here leads to dissipation of mind. There is the love of being sincere without the love of learning; the beclouding here leads to an injurious disregard of consequences. There is the love of straightforwardness without the love of learning; the beclouding here leads to rudeness. There is the love of boldness without the love of learning; the beclouding here leads to insubordination. There is the love of firmness without the love of learning; the beclouding here leads to extravagant conduct."

Jesus' Sermon on the Mount

St. Matthew

Leading the good life may not consist in simply refraining from bad or harmful actions; it may require that we go beyond this to do good to others. It may also require that we make every effort to do this good. Further, not only must we do what is good for others, we must form the right intention to do good and refrain from forming bad intentions in our soul.

• CHAPTER 5

And seeing the multitudes, he went up into a mountain: and when he was set, his disciples came unto him:

2 And he opened his mouth, and taught them, saying,

3 Blessed *are* the poor in spirit: for theirs is the kingdom of heaven.

4 Blessed *are* they that mourn: for they shall be comforted.

From Matthew 5–7 in the New Testament of the King James Version of the Bible, first published in 1611.

5 Blessed *are* the meek: for they shall inherit the earth.

6 Blessed *are* they which do hunger and thirst after righteousness: for they shall be filled.

7 Blessed *are* the merciful: for they shall obtain mercy.

8 Blessed *are* the pure in heart: for they shall see God.

9 Blessed *are* the peacemakers: for they shall be called the children of God.

10 Blessed *are* they which are persecuted for righteousness' sake: for theirs is the kingdom of heaven.

11 Blessed are ye, when *men* shall revile you, and persecute *you*, and shall say all manner of evil against you falsely, for my sake.

12 Rejoice, and be exceeding glad: for great *is* your reward in heaven: for so persecuted they the prophets which were before you.

13 Ye are the salt of the earth: but if the salt have lost his savour, wherewith shall it be salted? it is thenceforth good for nothing, but to be cast out, and to be trodden under foot of men.

14 Ye are the light of the world. A city that is set on an hill cannot be hid.

15 Neither do men light a candle, and put it under a bushel, but on a candlestick; and it giveth light unto all that are in the house.

16 Let your light so shine before men, that they may see your good works, and glorify your Father which is in heaven.

17 Think not that I am come to destroy the law, or the prophets: I am not come to destroy, but to fulfil.

18 For verily I say unto you, Till heaven and earth pass, one jot or one tittle shall in no wise pass from the law, till all be fulfilled.

19 Whosoever therefore shall break one of these least commandments, and shall teach men so, he shall be called the least in the kingdom of heaven: but whosoever shall do and teach *them* the same shall be called great in the kingdom of heaven.

20 For I say unto you, That except your righteousness shall exceed *the righteousness* of the scribes and Pharisees, ye shall in no case enter into the kingdom of heaven.

21 Ye have heard that it was said by them of old time, Thou shalt not kill; and whosoever shall kill shall be in danger of the judgment:

22 But I say unto you, That whosoever is angry with his brother without a cause shall be in danger of the judgment: and whosoever shall say to his brother, Raca, shall be in danger of the council: but whosoever shall say, Thou fool, shall be in danger of hell fire.

23 Therefore if thou bring thy gift to the altar, and there rememberest that thy brother hath ought against thee;

24 Leave there thy gift before the altar, and go thy way; first be reconciled to thy brother, and then come and offer thy gift.

25 Agree with thine adversary quickly, whiles thou art in the way with him; lest at any time the adversary deliver thee to the judge, and the judge deliver thee to the officer, and thou be cast into prison.

26 Verily I say unto thee, Thou shalt by no means come out thence, till thou hast paid the uttermost farthing.

27 Ye have heard that it was said by them of old time, Thou shalt not commit adultery:

28 But I say unto you, That whosoever looketh on a woman to lust after her hath committed adultery with her already in his heart.

29 And if thy right eye offend thee, pluck it out, and cast *it* from thee: for it is profitable for thee that one of thy members should perish, and not *that* thy whole body should be cast into hell.

30 And if thy right hand offend thee, cut it off, and cast *it* from thee: for it is profitable for thee that one of thy members should perish, and not *that* thy whole body should be cast into hell.

31 It hath been said, Whosoever shall put away his wife, let him give her a writing of divorcement:

32 But I say unto you, That whosoever shall put away his wife, saving for the cause of fornication, causeth her to commit adultery: and whosoever shall marry her that is divorced committeth adultery.

33 Again, ye have heard that it hath been said by them of old time, Thou shalt not forswear thyself, but shalt perform unto the Lord thine oaths:

34 But I say unto you, Swear not at all; neither by heaven; for it is God's throne:

35 Nor by the earth; for it is his footstool: neither by Jerusalem; for it is the city of the great King.

36 Neither shalt thou swear by thy head, because thou canst not make one hair white or black.

37 But let your communication be, Yea, yea; Nay, nay: for whatsoever is more than these cometh of evil.

38 Ye have heard that it hath been said, An eye for an eye, and a tooth for a tooth:

39 But I say unto you, That ye resist not evil: but whosoever shall smite thee on thy right cheek, turn to him the other also.

40 And if any man will sue thee at the law, and take away thy coat, let him have *thy* cloak also.

41 And whosoever shall compel thee to go a mile, go with him twain.

42 Give to him that asketh thee, and from him that would borrow of thee turn not thou away.

43 Ye have heard that it hath been said, Thou shalt love thy neighbour, and hate thine enemy.

44 But I say unto you, Love your enemies, bless them that curse you, do good to them that hate you, and pray for them which despitefully use you, and persecute you;

45 That ye may be the children of your Father which is in heaven: for he maketh his sun to rise on the evil and on the good, and sendeth rain on the just and on the unjust.

46 For if ye love them which love you, what reward have ye? do not even the publicans the same?

47 And if ye salute your brethren only, what do ye more *than others?* do not even the publicans so?

48 Be ye therefore perfect, even as your Father which is in heaven is perfect.

• CHAPTER 6

Take heed that ye do not your alms before men, to be seen of them: otherwise ye have no reward of your Father which is in heaven.

2 Therefore when thou doest *thine* alms, do not sound a trumpet before thee, as the hypocrites do in the synagogues and in the streets, that they may have glory of men. Verily I say unto you, They have their reward.

3 But when thou doest alms, let not thy left hand know what thy right hand doeth:

4 That thine alms may be in secret: and thy Father which seeth in secret himself shall reward thee openly.

5 And when thou prayest, thou shalt not be as the hypocrites *are,* for they love to pray standing in the synagogues and in the corners of the streets, that they may be seen of men. Verily I say unto you, They have their reward.

6 But thou, when thou prayest, enter into thy closet, and when thou hast shut thy door, pray to thy Father which is in secret; and thy Father which seeth in secret shall reward thee openly.

7 But when ye pray, use not vain repetitions, as the heathen *do*: for they think that they shall be heard for their much speaking.

8 Be not ye therefore like unto them: for your Father knoweth what things ye have need of, before ye ask him.

9 After this manner therefore pray ye: Our Father which art in heaven, Hallowed be thy name.

10 Thy kingdom come. Thy will be done in earth, as *it is* in heaven.

11 Give us this day our daily bread.

12 And forgive us our debts, as we forgive our debtors.

13 And lead us not into temptation, but deliver us from evil: For thine is the kingdom, and the power, and the glory, for ever. Amen.

14 For if ye forgive men their trespasses, your heavenly Father will also forgive you:

15 But if ye forgive not men their trespasses, neither will your Father forgive your trespasses.

16 Moreover when ye fast, be not, as the hypocrites, of a sad countenance: for they disfigure their faces, that they may appear unto men to fast. Verily I say unto you, They have their reward.

17 But thou, when thou fastest, anoint thine head, and wash thy face;

18 That thou appear not unto men to fast, but unto thy Father which is in secret:

and thy Father, which seeth in secret, shall reward thee openly.

19 Lay not up for yourselves treasures upon earth, where moth and rust doth corrupt, and where thieves break through and steal:

20 But lay up for yourselves treasures in heaven, where neither moth nor rust doth corrupt, and where thieves do not break through nor steal:

21 For where your treasure is, there will your heart be also.

22 The light of the body is the eye: if therefore thine eye be single, thy whole body shall be full of light.

23 But if thine eye be evil, thy whole body shall be full of darkness. If therefore the light that is in thee be darkness, how great *is* that darkness!

24 No man can serve two masters: for either he will hate the one, and love the other; or else he will hold to the one, and despise the other. Ye cannot serve God and mammon.

25 Therefore I say unto you, Take no thought for your life, what ye shall eat, or what ye shall drink; nor yet for your body, what ye shall put on. Is not the life more than meat, and the body than raiment?

26 Behold the fowls of the air: for they sow not, neither do they reap, nor gather into barns; yet your heavenly Father feedeth them. Are ye not much better than they?

27 Which of you by taking thought can add one cubit unto his stature?

28 And why take ye thought for raiment? Consider the lilies of the field, how they grow; they toil not, neither do they spin:

29 And yet I say unto you, That even Solomon in all his glory was not arrayed like one of these.

30 Wherefore, if God so clothe the grass of the field, which to day is, and to morrow is cast into the oven, *shall he* not much more *clothe* you, O ye of little faith?

31 Therefore take no thought, saying, What shall we eat? or, What shall we drink? or, Wherewithal shall we be clothed?

32 (For after all these things do the Gentiles seek:) for your heavenly Father knoweth that ye have need of all these things.

33 But seek ye first the kingdom of God, and his righteousness; and all these things shall be added unto you.

34 Take therefore no thought for the morrow: for the morrow shall take thought for the things of itself. Sufficient unto the day *is* the evil thereof.

• CHAPTER 7

Judge not, that ye be not judged.

2 For with what judgment ye judge, ye shall be judged: and with what measure ye mete, it shall be measured to you again.

3 And why beholdest thou the mote that is in thy brother's eye, but considerest not the beam that is in thine own eye?

4 Or how wilt thou say to thy brother, Let me pull out the mote out of thine eye; and, behold, a beam *is* in thine own eye?

5 Thou hypocrite, first cast out the beam out of thine own eye; and then shalt thou see clearly to cast out the mote out of thy brother's eye.

6 Give not that which is holy unto the dogs, neither cast ye your pearls before swine, lest they trample them under their feet, and turn again and rend you.

7 Ask, and it shall be given you; seek, and ye shall find; knock, and it shall be opened unto you:

8 For every one that asketh receiveth; and he that seeketh findeth; and to him that knocketh it shall be opened.

9 Or what man is there of you, whom if his son ask bread, will he give him a stone?

10 Or if he ask a fish, will he give him a serpent?

11 If ye then, being evil, know how to give good gifts unto your children, how much more shall your Father which is in heaven give good things to them that ask him?

12 Therefore all things whatsoever ye would that men should do to you, do ye even so to them: for this is the law and the prophets.

13 Enter ye in at the strait gate: for wide *is* the gate, and broad *is* the way, that leadeth to destruction, and many there be which go in thereat:

14 Because strait *is* the gate, and narrow *is* the way, which leadeth unto life, and few there be that find it.

15 Beware of false prophets, which come to you in sheep's clothing, but inwardly they are ravening wolves.

16 Ye shall know them by their fruits. Do men gather grapes of thorns, or figs of thistles?

17 Even so every good tree bringeth forth good fruit; but a corrupt tree bringeth forth evil fruit.

18 A good tree cannot bring forth evil fruit, neither *can* a corrupt tree bring forth good fruit.

19 Every tree that bringeth not forth good fruit is hewn down, and cast into the fire.

20 Wherefore by their fruits ye shall know them.

21 Not every one that saith unto me, Lord, Lord, shall enter into the kingdom of heaven; but he that doeth the will of my Father which is in heaven.

22 Many will say to me in that day, Lord, Lord, have we not prophesied in thy name? and in thy name have cast out devils? and in thy name done many wonderful works?

23 And then will I profess unto them, I never knew you: depart from me, ye that work iniquity.

24 Therefore whosoever heareth these sayings of mine, and doeth them, I will liken him unto a wise man, which built his house upon a rock:

25 And the rain descended, and the floods came, and the winds blew, and beat upon that house; and it fell not: for it was founded upon a rock.

26 And every one that heareth these sayings of mine, and doeth them not, shall be likened unto a foolish man, which built his house upon the sand:

27 And the rain descended, and the floods came, and the winds blew, and beat upon that house; and it fell: and great was the fall of it.

28 And it came to pass, when Jesus had ended these sayings, the people were astonished at his doctrine:

29 For he taught them as *one* having authority, and not as the scribes.

A Women's Politics of Resistance

Sara Ruddick

Do women have both a specific role and a specific power in resisting tyranny and oppression? Ruddick claims that a women's politics of resistance is culturally relative, and that whatever else it may be, a women's politics of resistance arises from maternal practice. This practice is itself essentially pacifistic and a reflection of the culture in which it is found.

A women's politics of resistance is identified by three characteristics: its participants are women, they explicitly invoke their culture's symbols of femininity, and their purpose is to resist certain practices or policies of their governors.

Women, like men, typically act out of social locations and political allegiances unconnected to their sex; women are socialists or capitalists, patriots or dissidents, colonialists or nationalists. Unlike other politics, a women's politics is organized and acted out by women. Women "riot" for bread, picket against alcohol, form peace camps outside missile bases, protect their schools from government interference, or sit in against nuclear testing. A women's politics often includes men: women call on men's physical strength or welcome the protection that powerful male allies offer. Nonetheless it is women who organize themselves self-consciously as women. The reasons women give for organizing range from an appreciation of the protection afforded by "womanliness" to men's unwillingness to participate in "sentimental" politics to the difficulty in speaking, much less being taken seriously, with men around. Typically, the point of women's politics is not to claim independence from men but, positively, to organize as

From *Material Thinking* by Sara Ruddick. Copyright © 1989, 1995 by Sara Ruddick. Reprinted by permission of Beacon Press, Boston.

women. Whatever the reasons for their separatism, the fact that women organize, direct, and enact a politics enables them to exploit their culture's symbols of femininity.

Women can also organize together without evoking common understandings of femininity. Feminist actions, for example, are often organized by women who explicitly repudiate the roles, behavior, and attitudes expected of "women." What I am calling a women's politics of resistance affirms obligations traditionally assigned to women and calls on the community to respect them. Women are responsible for their children's health; in the name of their maternal duty they call on the government to halt nuclear testing, which epitomizing a general unhealthiness, leaves strontium-90 in nursing mothers' milk. If women are to be able to feed their families then the community must produce sufficient food and sell it at prices homemakers can afford. If women are responsible for educating young children, then they resist government efforts to interfere with local schools.

Not all women's politics are politics of resistance. There are politics organized by women that celebrate women's roles and attitudes but that serve rather than resist the state. In almost every war, mothers of heroes and martyrs join together in support of military sons, knitting, writing, and then mourning, in the service of the military state. The best-known instance of women's politics is the organization of Nazi women in praise of *Kinder, Küche, Kirche.*[1] Today in Chile, a women's organization under the direction of the dictator Pinochet's wife celebrates "feminine power" (*el poder femenino*), which expresses itself through loyalty to family and fatherland.

A women's politics of *resistance* is composed of women who take responsibility for the tasks of caring labor and then find themselves confronted with policies or actions that interfere with their right or capacity to do their work. In the name of womanly duties that they have assumed and that their communities expect of them, they resist. This feminine resistance has made some philosophers and feminists uneasy. Much like organized violence, women's resistance is difficult to predict or control. Women in South Boston resist racial integration; mothers resist the conscription of their children in just wars.

Even where women aim to resist tyranny, their "feminine" protest seems too acceptable to be effective. As Dorothy Dinnerstein eloquently laments, women are *meant* to weep while men rule and fight:

> Women's resigned, implicitly collusive, ventilation of everybody's intuition that the world men rule is murderously crazy is a central theme in folklore, literature, drama [and women's politics of resistance].
>
> Think, for instance, of the proverb that groups woman with wine and song as a necessary counterpoint to battle, a counterpoint that makes it possible for men to draw back from their will to kill just long and far enough so that they can then take it up again with new vigor. Or think of the saying "Men must work and women must weep." Woman's tears over what is lethal in man's work, this saying implies, are part of the world's eternal, unalterable way. . . . [Her] tears serve not to deter man but to help him go on, for she is doing his weeping for him and he is doing what she weeps about for her.[2]

Christa Wolf expresses a related fear that women's resistance is as fragile as their dependence on individual men, loyalty to kin, and privileges of class:

> I was slow on the uptake. My privileges intruded between me and the most necessary insights; so did my attachment to my own family, which did not depend upon the privileges I enjoyed.[3]

For whatever reasons, feminists are apt to be disappointed in the sturdiness and extent of women's resistance. Dorothy Dinnerstein expresses this feminist disappointment:

> The absurd self-importance of his striving has been matched by the abject servility of her derision, which has on the whole been expressed only with his consent and within boundaries set by him, and which has on the whole worked to support the stability of the realm he rules.[4]

While some people fear that "feminine" resistance is inevitably limited—and their fears seem to me not groundless—I place my hope in its unique potential effectiveness, namely, women's social position makes them inherently "disloyal to the civilization"[5] that depends on them. Thus Hegel worries, and I hope, that ostensibly compliant women are on the edge of dissidence. The state, whose most powerful governors depend on women's work and whose stability rests on the authority of the Fathers, "creates for itself in what it suppresses and what it depends upon an internal enemy—womankind in general.[6] Underlining as Hegel does women's exclusion from power, Julia Kristeva celebrates a woman who is "an eternal dissident in relation to social and political consensus, in exile from power, and therefore always singular, fragmentary, demonic, a witch."[7] Yet like Kristeva, I find that the dissident mother, perhaps unlike other witches, is not only a potential critic of the order that excludes her but also and equally a conserver and legitimator of the order it is her duty to instill in her children. Kristeva expects from this dissident mother an "attentiveness to ethics" rooted in a collective experience and tradition of mothering. And I would expect from her the ambivalence that Jane Lazarre believes keeps the heart alive, even as it slows the trigger finger. This attentiveness to ethics can become effectively militant in a women's politics of resistance. Its ambivalence, while a spur to compassion, does not slow action if women are governed by principles of nonviolence that allow them to hate and frustrate oppressors they neither mutilate nor murder.

Women's politics of resistance are as various as the cultures from which they arise. Of the many examples I could choose, I select one, the resistance of Argentinian and Chilean women to military dictatorship, specifically to the policy of kidnapping, imprisonment, torture, and murder of the "disappeared." The resistance of the Madres (mothers) of Argentina to its military regime and the similar, ongoing resistance of Chilean women to the Pinochet dictatorship politically exemplify central maternal concepts such as the primacy of bodily life and the connectedness of self and other. At the same time, these movements politically transform certain tendencies of maternal militarism such as cheery denial and parochialism.

Although women's work is always threatened by violence and although women in war always suffer the hunger, illness, mutilation, and loss of their loved ones, the crime of "disappearance" is especially haunting. Kidnapping and rumors of torture and murder destroy lives and families. Yet because the fate of the disappeared person is unclear, because no one in power acknowledges her or his existence, let alone disappearance, even mourning is impossible:

> To *disappear* means to be snatched off a street corner, or dragged from one's bed, or taken from a movie theater or cafe, either by police, or soldiers, or men in civilian clothes, and from that moment on to disappear from the face of the earth leaving not a single trace. It means that all knowledge of the *disappeared* is totally

> lost. Absolutely nothing is known about them. What was their fate? If they are alive, where are they? What are they enduring? If they are dead, where are their bones?[8]

Nathan Laks describes the Argentinian protest that began in Buenos Aires in 1976:

> Once in power [in Argentina in 1976], the military systematized and accelerated the campaign of terror, quickly annihilating the armed organizations of the Left and the unarmed ones, as well as many individuals with little or no connection to either. The indiscriminate nature of the kidnapping campaign and the impunity with which it was carried out spread terror—as intended. Relationships among friends and relatives were shattered by unprecedented fear. Perfectly decent individuals suddenly became afraid even to visit the parents of a kidnap victim, for any such gesture of compassion might condemn the visitor to a terrible fate. In this terrorized society, a small organization of women, mother's and other relatives of kidnapped Argentines staged a stunning act of defiance. One Thursday afternoon they gathered in the Plaza de Mayo, the main square in Buenos Aires and the site of countless historic incidents beginning in 1810 with the events that led to Argentina's separation from the Spanish Empire. In the center of the Plaza de Mayo, within clear sight of the presidential palace, the national cathedral, and several headquarters of ministries and corporations, the Mothers paraded in a closed circle.[9]

The Madres met each other outside hospitals or prisons, where they took food and other provisions and looked for traces of the disappeared, or outside government offices, where they tried, almost invariably without success, to get some accounting of their loved ones' whereabouts. When they marched, the Madres wore white kerchiefs with the names of the disappeared embroidered on them. Often they carried lighted candles and almost always they wore or carried photographs of the disappeared. In Chile, women chained themselves to the steps of the capitol, formed a human chain to a mine, Lonquen, where a mass grave was discovered, and took over a stadium where disappeared people had been rounded up, later to be tortured and killed.

The Latin American women's movements are clearly politics of resistance. The women who engage in them court imprisonment and torture and in some cases have become "disappeared" themselves. Knowing what fearful things could happen to them, women in Chile trained themselves to name and deal with what they feared:

> If they were afraid of facing police, they were told simply to find a policeman and stare at him until they could see him as a man and not as a representative of the state. [They] circled police vans on foot, until these symbols of the regime appeared as just another kind of motor vehicle. The women also instructed one another how to deal with the tear gas . . . to stop eating two hours before demonstrations, to dress in casual clothing, to take off makeup but to put salt on their cheekbones to keep teargas powder from entering their eyes, . . . to carry lemon to avoid teargas sting and to get a jar with homemade smelling salts made up of salt and ammonia.[10]

The women talked among themselves about their terrors, found others who shared their fears, and marched with them in affinity groups. And thus they brought their bodies to bear against the state.

As in many women's politics of resistance, the Argentinian and Chilean women emphasize mothering among women's many relations. They are Madres, whether or not they are biological or adoptive mothers of individual disappeared; a later group is made up of Abuelas (grandmothers). Their presence and the character of their action, as well as the interviews they have given, invariably evoke an experience of mothering that is central to their lives, whatever other home work or wage labor they engage in. Repeatedly they remember and allude to ordinary tasks—clothing, feeding, sheltering, and most of all tending to extensive kin work. All these works, ordinarily taken for granted, are dramatically present just because they are interrupted; they are made starkly visible through the eerie "disappearance," the shattering mockery of a maternal and childlike "unchanging expectation of good in the heart."[11]

As these women honor mothering, they honor themselves. The destruction of the lives of their children, often just on the verge of adulthood, destroys years of their work; their loss and the impossibility of mourning it constitutes a violent outrage against them. Yet there is something misleading about this way of talking. The women do not speak of their work but of their children; they carry children's photographs; not their own. The distinctive structuring of the relation between self and other, symbolized in birth and enacted in mothering, is now politicized. The children, the absent ones, are *not* their mothers, who have decidedly *not* disappeared but are bodily present. The singular, irreplaceable children are lost. Yet as the pictures the Madres carry suggest, the children are not, even in disappearance, apart from their mothers but, in their absence, are still inseparable from them.

For these Argentinian and Chilean women, as for women in most cultures, mothering is intuitively or "naturally" connected to giving birth. The Abuelas, especially, have made a political point of the emotional significance of genetic continuity. Since the fall of the military regime, one of their projects has been to form a genetic bank to trace the biological parentage of children adopted by people close to the ruling class at the time the military was in power. The insistence on genetic connection is one aspect of a general affirmation of the body. Indeed, the vulnerability, promise, and power of human bodies is central to this women's politics of resistance, as it is to maternal practice:

> Together with the affirmation of life, the human body is a very important reference for these women. They often speak of physical pain, the wounds caused by the disappearance. It seems that wearing a photograph of the missing one attached to the clothing or in a locket around the neck is a way of feeling closer to them.[12]

Because they have suffered military violence—have been stripped naked, sexually humiliated, and tortured—children's bodies become a locus of pain. Because the violation of bodies is meant to terrify the body itself becomes a place where terror is wrought. In resistance to this violation mothers' bodies become instruments of nonviolent power. Adorned with representations of bodies loved and violated, they express the necessity of love even amid terror, "in the teeth of all experience of crimes committed, suffered and witnessed."[13]

In their protests, these women fulfill traditional expectations of femininity and at the same time violate them. These are women who may well have expected to live out an ideology of "separate spheres" in which men and women had distinct but complementary tasks. Whatever ideology of the sexual division of labor they may have espoused, their political circumstances, as well as the apparently greater vulnerability and the apparently greater timidity and conventionality of the men they lived among, required that they act publicly as women. Women who bring to the public plazas of a police state pictures of their loved ones, like women who put pillowcases, toys, and other artifacts of attachment against the barbed wire fences of missile bases, translate the symbols of mothering into political speech. Preservative love, singularity in connection, the promise of birth and the resilience of hope, the irreplaceable treasure of vulnerable bodily being—these clichés of maternal work are enacted in public, by women insisting that their governors name and take responsibility for their crimes. They speak a "women's language" of loyalty, love, and outrage; but they speak with a public anger in a public place in ways they were never meant to do.

Although not a "peace politics" in a conventional sense, the Latin American protest undermines tendencies of maternal practice and thinking that are identifiably militarist. To some extent, this is a matter of shifting a balance between tendencies in mothering that support militarism toward tendencies that subvert it. In this case, the balance shifts from denial to truthfulness, from parochialism to solidarity, and from inauthenticity to active responsibility. Writing about André Trocme and his parishioners in the French village of Le Chambon during World War II, Phillip Hallie identified three characteristics that enabled them to penetrate the confusion and misinformation with which Nazis covered their policy and then to act on their knowledge. "*Lucid knowledge, awareness of the pain of others*, and *stubborn decision* dissipated for the Chambonnais the Night and Fog that inhabited the minds of so many people in Europe, and the world at large, in 1942."[14] In the transformed maternal practice of the Argentinian and Chilean women, these same virtues of nonviolent resistance are at work.

Cheery denial is an endemic maternal temptation. A similar "willingness to be self-deceived," as the resistance leader André Trocme called it, also sustains many decent citizens' support of war policy. It is notorious that few people can bear, except very briefly, to acknowledge the dangers of nuclear weapons and the damage they have done and could still do. Similarly, few citizens really look at the political aims and material-emotional lives of people affected by their own country's interventionist war policies. By contrast, the Argentinian and Chilean women insist on, and then disseminate, "lucid knowledge" of military crimes. "What is so profoundly moving about them is their determination to find out the truth."[15] They insist that others, too, hear the truth. They are "ready to talk immediately; they need to talk, to make sure their story, so tragic and so common, . . . be told, be known."[16] In addition to talking, they make tapestries, "arpilleras," that tell stories of daily life including workers' organizing, police brutality, kidnapping, and resistance. The protests, tales, and arpilleras extend the maternal task of storytelling, maintaining ordinary maternal values of realism in the face of temptation to deny or distort. In this context, their ordinary extraordinary work becomes a politics of remembering.

After fighting in World War II the philosopher J. Glenn Gray wrote:

> The great god Mars tries to blind us when we enter his realm, and when we leave he gives us a generous cup of the waters of Lethe to drink. . . . When I consider how easily we forget the millions who suffered unbearably, either permanently maimed in body or mind, or who gave up their lives before they realized their purpose, I rebel at the whole insane spectacle of human existence.[17]

After the junta fell, Argentinian women insisted that violated bodies be remembered, which required that crimes be named, the men who committed them be brought to trial, and the bodies themselves, alive or dead, be accounted for and, where possible, returned.

"Awareness of the pain of others." The Argentinian and Chilean Madres spoke first of their own pain and the pain of relatives and friends of others disappeared. Similarly, maternal nonviolence is rooted, and typically limited by, a commitment to one's "own" children and the people they live among. . . . I spoke of this limitation as a principal source of maternal militarism; the parochialism of maternal practice can become the racialism that fuels organized violence. This tribal parochialism was also broken down in the Argentinian and Chilean protests.

As in mothering generally, women found it easiest to extend their concern for their own children to other mothers "like them"; only in this political context likeness had to do not with race or ethnicity but with common suffering. In Argentina, where protests are marked by the "singularity" of photographs, the women came to wear identical masks to mark their commonality. In Chile one woman said:

> Because of all this suffering we are united. I do not ask for justice for my child alone, or the other women just for their children. We are asking for justice for all. All of us are equal. If we find one disappeared one I will rejoice as much as if they had found mine.[18]

Concern for all victims then sometimes extended to collective concern for all the people of the nation:

> We are the women and mothers of this land, of the workers, of the professionals, of the students and of future generations.[19]

This is still "nationalism," though of a noble sort. Many of the women went further as they explicitly identified with all victims of military or economic violence:

> In the beginning we only wanted to rescue our children. But as time passed we acquired a different comprehension. We understood better what is going on in the world. We know that when babies do not have enough to eat that, too, is a violation of human rights.[20]
>
> We should commit ourselves to make Lonquen [the mine where a mass grave was discovered] a blessed spot. May it be a revered spot, so that never again will a hostile hand be raised against any other person that lives on the earth.[21]

It would be foolish to believe that every woman in the Argentinian and Chilean protest movements extended concern from her own children to all the disappeared then to all of the nation, and finally to all victims everywhere. Why should women whose children and loved ones have been singularly persecuted extend sympathetic protection to all victims, an extension that is extraordinary even among women and men who do not suffer singular assault? Yet many of these women did so extend themselves—intellectually, politically, emotionally. They did not "transcend" their particular loss and love; particularity was the emotional root and source of their protest. It is through acting on that particularity that they extended mothering to include sustaining and protecting any people whose lives are blighted by violence.

"Stubborn decision." As children remind us, stubborn decision is a hallmark of maternity. And mothers reply: what looks like stubborn decision may well be a compound of timidity, vacillation, and desperation. Women in resistance are (almost certainly) not free from ordinary mothers' temptations to inauthenticity, to letting others—teachers, employers, generals, fathers, grandparents—establish standards of acceptability and delegating to them responsibility for children's lives. And like ordinary mothers, women in resistance probably include in their ranks *individuals* who in ordinary times could speak back to the teacher or organize opposition to the local corporate polluter. But

"stubborn decision" takes on a new and collective political meaning when women acting together walk out of their homes to appropriate spaces they never were meant to occupy.

Like their counterparts in resistance elsewhere, these stubbornly decisive Argentinian and Chilean women, whatever their personal timidities, publicly announce that they take responsibility for protecting the world in which they and their children must live. These women are the daughters, the heirs, of Kollwitz's *mater dolorosa.* As in Kollwitz's representations, a mother is victimized through the victimization of her children. These women are themselves victims; moreover, they bear witness to victimization first of loved ones, then of strangers; they stand against those in power, in solidarity with those who are hurt. Yet there is also a sense in which, by their active courage, they refuse victimization. More accurately, they mock dichotomies that still riddle political thought. There is no contradiction between "playing the role of victim" and taking responsibility for public policies. It is possible to act powerfully while standing with those who are hurt. It is neither weak nor passive to reveal one's own suffering while refusing to damage or mutilate in return. The Latin American *mater dolorosa* has learned how to fight as a victim for victims, not by joining the strong, but by resisting them.

A women's politics of resistance is not inherently a peace politics. Women can organize to sabotage peace treaties or to celebrate the heroes and martyrs of organized violence. During the Malvinas-Falklands war, Argentinian and English women sought each other out at a women's meeting in New York to denounce together their countries' militarism and imperialism. Yet during that same war, the Argentinian Madres were reported to use patriotic rhetoric to reinforce their own aims: "The Malvinas belong to us and so do our sons."

Nonetheless, in their own contexts, the Argentinian protest had and the Chilean protest still has antimilitarist implications. The regimes against which the women protest were and are militarist; the omnipresence of the soldier as oppressor and the general as the torturers' commander was—and in Chile still is—sufficient to symbolize a contrast between women and war. Moreover, the generals' actions have not been accidentally related to militarism. As Plato saw, when he rejected militarist rule in his totalitarian state, torture, kidnapping and other physical terrorism infect the rule of fearful tyrants, just as atrocities infect the best organized war. In their deliberately and increasingly brutal strategies to ensure absolute control, the generals exemplify the excesses inherent in militarized tyranny. Hence in the women's protests, not only a particular government but military rule is brought to trial.

Whatever their militarist sentiments or rhetoric, the Argentinian and Chilean protests express to the world the ideals of nonviolence. Although effective protest inevitably hurts its opponents and those associated with them, the protesters did not set out to injure but to end injuring. None of their actions even risked serious, lasting physical damage. Their aim was steadfastly one of reconnection and restoration of a just community, even though and because those responsible for violence were held accountable and were punished. By providing an example of persistent, stubborn action, the Argentinian and Chilean women have offered a model of nonviolent resistance to other Latin American countries and to the world. They have therefore contributed to collective efforts to invent peace, whatever their degree of effectiveness within their own countries. Like the maternal practice from which it grows, a women's politics of resistance may remain racial, tribal, or chauvinist; we cannot expect of women in resistance the rare human ability to stand in solidarity with all victims of violence. Yet if these Latin American protests are at all emblematic, they suggest that the peacefulness latent in maternal practice tends to be realized as participants act against, and therefore reflect on, violence itself.

Notes

1. For a discussion of women's participation in (and occasional resistance to) the Nazi German government, see Claudia Koontz, *Mothers in the Fatherland: Women, the Family, and Nazi Politics* (New York: St. Martin's, 1987). Among the many virtues of this fascinating book is its tracing of the complex interconnections between women's separate spheres, the Nazi and feminist use of women's difference, and women's participation in but also disappointment in the Nazi state.

2. Dorothy Dinnerstein, *The Mermaid and the Minotaur* (New York: Harper & Row, 1976), p. 226.

3. Christa Wolf, *Cassandra* (New York: Farrar Straus & Giroux, 1984), p. 53.

4. Dorothy Dinnerstein, "The Mobilization of Eros," in *Face to Face* (Greenwood Press, 1982). Manuscript courtesy of the author. For an intellectually sophisticated and high-spirited account of an American women's politics of resistance, see Amy Swerdlow's work on Women's Strike for Peace, forthcoming from the University of Chicago Press. For an example of her work, see "Pure Milk, Not Poison: Women's Strike for Peace and the Test Ban Treaty of 1963," in *Rocking the Ship of State: Toward a Feminist Peace Politics*, ed. Adrienne Harris and Ynestra King (Westview Press, 1989).

5. The title of a well-known essay by Adrienne Rich in *Lies, Secrets and Silence* (New York: Norton, 1979), pp. 275–310.

6. Hegel, *The Phenomenology of Mind*, part VI, A, b, "Ethical Action: Knowledge Human and Divine: Guilt and Destiny" (New York: Harper, 1967), p. 496.

7. Julia Kristeva, "Talking about *Polygoue*" (an interview with Francoise van Rossum-Guyon), in *French Feminist Thought*, ed. Toril Moi (Oxford: Basil Blackwell, 1987), p. 113.

8. Marjorie Agosin, "Emerging from the Shadows: Women in Chile," *Barnard Occasional Papers on Women's Issues*, vol. 2, no. 3, Fall 1987, p. 12. I am very grateful to Temma Kaplan, historian and director of the Barnard College Women's Center, whose interest in "motherist" and grass-roots womens' resistance movements inspired this section. Temma Kaplan provided me with the material on the Madres and discussed an earlier draft of the chapter.

9. Nathan Laks, cited in Nora Amalia Femenia, "Argentina's Mothers of Plaza de Mayo: The Mourning Process from Junta to Democracy," *Feminist Studies*, vol. 13, no. 1, p. 10. The Argentinian Madres protested until the fall of the military regime and still exist today, though they are now divided in their political aims.

10. Marjorie Agosin, Temma Kaplan, Teresa Valduz, "The Politics of Spectacle in Chile," *Barnard Occasional Papers on Women's Issues*, vol. 2, no. 3, Fall 1987, p. 6.

11. Simone Weil, "Human Personality," in *Simone Weil Reader*, p. 315.

12. Agosin, "Emerging," p. 18.

13. Simone Weil, "Human Personality," in *Simone Weil Reader*, p. 315.

14. Philip Hallie, *Lest Innocent Blood Be Shed* (New York: Harper & Row, 1979), p. 104. (Italics added.)

15. Agosin, "Emerging," p. 16.

16. Agosin, "Emerging," p. 14.

17. J. Glenn Gray, *The Warriors* (New York: Harper & Row, 1970), pp. 21, 23.

18. Agosin, "Emerging," p. 21.

19. Patricia M. Chuchryk, "Subversive Mothers: The Women's Opposition to the Military Regime in Chile," paper presented at the International Congress of the Latin American Studies Association, Boston, 1986, p. 9.

20. Rene Epelbaum, member of the Argentinian protest, in an interview with Jean Bethke Elshtain, personal communication.

21. Agosin, "Emerging," p. 18.

We Are All Related

Eagle Man

According to most indigenous peoples' philosophies, all things flow from Mother Earth. Our attitudes and actions towards one another have an impact on all things and may enhance or undermine our well-being. Our identity is thus dependent on the whole, and it is cyclical as is life itself. In this essay, Eagle Man tells us how we might achieve peace and well-being, and he also explains why we have not yet achieved this. In what ways do you think that your own attitudes and actions have influenced the attainment of peace in the world? What kinds of changes do you think must take place in order to achieve this?

The plight of the non-Indian world is that it has lost respect for Mother Earth, from where we all come.

We all start out in this world as tiny seeds—no different from our animal brothers and sisters, the deer, the bear, the buffalo, or the trees, the flowers, the winged people. Every particle of our bodies comes from the good things Mother Earth has put forth. Mother Earth is our real mother, because every bit of us truly comes from her, and daily she takes care of us.

The tiny seed takes on the minerals and the waters of Mother Earth. It is fueled by *Wiyo*, the sun, and given spirit by *Wakan Tanka*.

This morning at breakfast we took from Mother Earth to live, as we have done every day of our lives. But did we thank her for giving us the means to live? The old Indian did. When he drove his horse in close to a buffalo running at full speed across the prairie, he drew his bowstring back and said as he did so, "Forgive me, brother, but my people must live." After he butchered the buffalo, he took the skull and faced it toward the setting sun as a thanksgiving and an acknowledgment that all things come from Mother Earth. He brought the meat back to camp and gave it first to the old, the widowed, and the weak. For thousands of years great herds thrived across the continent because the Indian never took more than he needed. Today, the buffalo is gone.

You say *ecology*. We think the words *Mother Earth* have a deeper meaning. If we wish to survive, we must respect her. It is very late, but there is still time to revive and discover the old American Indian value of respect for Mother Earth. She is very beautiful, and already she is showing us signs that she may punish us for not respecting her. Also, we must remember she has been placed in this universe by the one who is the All Powerful, the Great Spirit Above, or *Wakan Tanka*—God. But a few years ago, there lived on the North American continent people, the American Indians, who knew a respect and value system that enabled them to live on their native grounds without having to migrate, in contrast to the white brothers and sisters who migrated by the thousands from their homelands because they had developed a value system different from that of the American Indian. There is no place now to which we can migrate, which means we can no longer ignore the red man's value system.

From *Mother Earth Spirituality* by Ed McGaa. Copyright © 1990 by Ed McGaa. Reprinted by permission of HarperCollins Publishers, Inc.

Carbon-dating techniques say that the American Indian has lived on the North American continent for thousands upon thousands of years. If we did migrate, it was because of a natural phenomenon—a glacier. We did not migrate because of a social system, value system, and spiritual system that neglected its responsibility to the land and all living things. We Indian people say we were always here.

We, the American Indian, had a way of living that enabled us to live within the great, complete beauty that only the natural environment can provide. The Indian tribes had a common value system and a commonality of religion, without religious animosity, that preserved that great beauty that the two-leggeds definitely need. Our four commandments from the Great Spirit are: (1) respect for Mother Earth, (2) respect for the Great Spirit, (3) respect for our fellow man and woman, and (4) respect for individual freedom (provided that individual freedom does not threaten the tribe or the people or Mother Earth).

We who respect the great vision of Black Elk see the four sacred colors as red, yellow, black, and white. They stand for the four directions— red for the east, yellow for the south, black for the west, and white for the north.

From the east comes the rising sun and new knowledge from a new day.

From the south will come the warming south winds that will cause our Mother to bring forth the good foods and grasses so that we may live.

To the west where the sun goes down, the day will end, and we will sleep; and we will hold our spirit ceremonies at night, from where we will communicate with the spirit world beyond. The sacred color of the west is black; it stands for the deep intellect that we will receive from the spirit ceremonies. From the west come the lifegiving rains.

From the north will come the white winter snow that will cleanse Mother Earth and put her to sleep, so that she may rest and store up energy to provide the beauty and bounty of springtime. We will prepare for aging by learning to create, through our arts and crafts, during the long winter season. Truth, honesty, strength, endurance, and courage also are represented by the white of the north. Truth and honesty in our relationships bring forth harmony.

All good things come from these sacred directions. These sacred directions, or four sacred colors, also stand for the four races of humanity: red, yellow, black, and white. We cannot be a prejudiced people, because all men and women are brothers and sisters and because we all have the same mother—Mother Earth. One who is prejudiced, who hates another because of that person's color, hates what the Great Spirit has put here. Such a one hates that which is holy and will be punished, even during this lifetime, as humanity will be punished for violating Mother Earth. Worse, one's conscience will follow into the spirit world, where it will be discovered that all beings are equal. This is what we Indian people believe.

We, the Indian people, also believe that the Great Spirit placed many people throughout this planet: red, yellow, black, and white. What about the brown people? The brown people evolved from the sacred colors coming together. Look at our Mother Earth. She, too, is brown because the four directions have come together. After the Great Spirit, *Wakan Tanka,* placed them in their respective areas, the *Wakan Tanka* appeared to each people in a different manner and taught them ways so that they might live in harmony and true beauty. Some men, some tribes, some nations have still retained the teachings of the Great Spirit. Others have not. Unfortunately, many good and peaceful religions have been assailed by narrow-minded zealots. Our religious beliefs and our traditional Indian people have suffered the stereotype that we are pagans, savages, or heathens; but we do not believe that only one religion controls the way to the spirit world that lies beyond. We believe that *Wakan Tanka* loves all of its children equally, although the Great Spirit must be disturbed at times with those children who have destroyed proven value systems that practiced sharing and generosity and kept Mother Earth viable down through time. We kept Mother Earth viable because we did not sell her or our spirituality!

Brothers and sisters, we must go back to some of the old ways if we are going to truly save our Mother Earth and bring back the natural beauty that every person seriously needs, especially in this day of vanishing species, vanishing rain forests, overpopulation, poisoned waters, acid rain, a thinning ozone layer, drought, rising temperatures, and weapons of complete annihilation.

Weapons of complete annihilation? Yes, that is how far the obsession with war has taken us. These weapons are not only hydraheaded; they are hydroheaded as well, meaning that they are the ultimate in hydrogen bomb destruction. We will have to divert our obsession with defense and wasteful, all-life-ending weapons of war to reviving our environment. . . .

The quest for peace can be more efficiently pursued through communication and knowledge than by stealth and unending superior weaponry. If the nations of the world scale back their budgets for weaponry, we will have wealth to spend to solve our serious environmental problems. Our home planet is under attack. It is not an imagined problem. This calamity is upon us now. We are in a real war with the polluting, violating blue man of Black Elk's vision.

Chief Sitting Bull advised us to take the best of the white man's ways and to take the best of the old Indian ways. He also said, "When you find something that is bad, or turns out bad, drop it and leave it alone."[1]

The fomenting of fear and hatred is something that has turned out very badly. This can continue no longer; it is a governmental luxury maintained in order to support pork-barrel appropriations to the Department of Defense, with its admirals and generals who have substituted their patriotism for a defense contractor paycheck after retirement. War has become a business for profit. In the last two wars, we frontline warriors—mostly poor whites and minorities—were never allowed to win our wars, which were endlessly prolonged by the politicians and profiteers, who had their warrior-aged sons hidden safely away or who used their powers, bordering on treason, to keep their offspring out of danger. The wrong was that the patriotic American or the poor had to be the replacement. The way to end wars in this day and age is to do like the Indian: put the chiefs and their sons on the front lines.

Sitting Bull answered a relative, "Go ahead and follow the white man's road and do whatever the [Indian] agent tells you. But I cannot so easily give up my old ways and Indian habits; they are too deeply ingrained in me."[2]

My friends, I will never cease to be an Indian. I will never cease respecting the old Indian values, especially our four cardinal commandments and our values of generosity and sharing. It is true that many who came to our shores brought a great amount of good to this world. Modern medicine, transportation, communication, and food production are but a few of the great achievements that we should all appreciate. But it is also true that too many of those who migrated to North America became so greedy and excessively materialistic that great harm has been caused. We have seen good ways and bad ways. The good way of the non-Indian way I am going to keep. The very fact that we can hold peaceseeking communication and that world leaders meet and communicate for peace shows the wisdom of the brothers and sisters of this time. By all means, good technology should not be curtailed, but care must be taken lest our water, air, and earth become irreparably harmed. The good ways I will always respect and support. But, my brothers and sisters, I say we must give up this obsession with excess consumption and materialism, especially when it causes the harming of the skies surrounding our Mother and the pollution of the waters upon her. *She is beginning to warn us*!

Keep those material goods that you need to exist, but be a more sharing and generous person. You will find that you can do with less. Replace this empty lifestyle of hollow impressing of the shallow ones with active participation for your Mother Earth. At least then, when you depart into the spirit world, you can look back with pride and fulfillment. Other spirit beings will gather around you, other spirits of your own higher consciousness will gather around you and share your satisfaction with you. The eternal satisfaction of knowing you did not overuse your Mother Earth and that you were here to protect her will be a powerful satisfaction when you reach the spirit world.

Indian people do not like to say that the Great Mystery is exactly this or exactly that, but we do know there is a spirit world that lies beyond. We are allowed to know that through our ceremonies. We know nothing of hell-fire and eternal damnation from some kind of unloving power that placed us here as little children. None of that has ever been shown to us in our powerful ceremonies, conducted by kind, considerate, proven, and very nonmaterialistic leaders. We do know that everything the Great Mystery makes is in the form of a circle. Our Mother Earth is a very large, powerful circle.

Therefore, we conclude that our life does not end. A part of it is within that great circle. If there is a hell, then our concept of hell would be an eternal knowing that one violated or took and robbed from Mother Earth and caused this suffering that is being bestowed upon the generations unborn. This then, if it were to be imprinted upon one's eternal conscience, this would surely be a terrible, spiritual, mental hell. Worse, to have harmed and hurt one's innocent fellow beings, and be unable to alter (or conceal) the harmful actions would also be a great hell. Truth in the spirit world will not be concealed, nor will it be for sale. Lastly, we must realize that the generations unborn will also come into the spirit world. Let us be the ones that they wish to thank and congratulate, rather than eternally scorn.

While we are shedding our overabundant possessions, and linking up with those of like minds, and advancing spiritual and environmental appreciations, we should develop a respect for the aged and for family-centered traditions, even those who are single warriors, fighting for the revitalization of our Mother on a lone, solitary, but vital front. We should have more respect for an extended family, which extends beyond a son or daughter, goes beyond to grandparents and aunts and uncles, goes beyond to brothers, sisters, aunts, and uncles that we have adopted or made as relatives—and further beyond, to the animal or plant world as our brothers and sisters, to Mother Earth and Father Sky and then above to *Wakan Tanka*, the *Unci/Tankashilah*, the Grandparent of us all. When we pray directly to the Great Spirit, we say *Unci* (Grandmother) or *Tankashilah* (Grandfather) because we are so family-minded that we think of the Great Power above as a grandparent, and we are the grandchildren. Of course, this is so because every particle of our being is from Mother Earth, and our energy and life force are fueled by Father Sky. This is a vital part of the great, deep feeling and spiritual psychology that we have as Indian people. It is why we preserved and respected our ecological environment for such a long period. *Mitakuye oyasin!* We are all related!

In conclusion, our survival is dependent on the realization that Mother Earth is a truly holy being, that all things in this world are holy and must not be violated, and that we must share and be generous with one another. You may call this thought by whatever fancy words you wish—psychology, theology, sociology, or philosophy—but you must think of Mother Earth as a living being. Think of your fellow men and women as holy people who were put here by the Great Spirit. Think of being related to all things! With this philosophy in mind as we go on with our environmental ecology efforts, our search for spirituality, and our quest for peace, we will be far more successful when we truly understand the Indians' respect for Mother Earth.

Notes

1. John F. McBride, *Modern Indian Psychology* (Vermillion, SD: University of South Dakota, Indian Studies Department, 1971), p. 1.
2. David Humphreys Miller, *Ghost Dance* (Lincoln, NE: University of Nebraska Press, 1959), p. 65.

Education for a Critical Consciousness

Paulo Freire

Notice Freire's opening statement about what it means to be human. He argues that humans must become integrated if they are to be subjects of their own actions. This means they must be able critically to transform reality. Integrated subjects are not sectarian in their interests but are true radical transformers, taking responsibility as authentic human beings and forsaking assistance that encourages continued passive response.

To be human is to engage in relationships with others and with the world. It is to experience that world as an objective reality, independent of oneself, capable of being known. Animals, submerged within reality, cannot relate to it; they are creatures of mere *contacts*. But man's separateness from and openness to the world distinguishes him as a being of *relationships*. Men, unlike animals, are not only *in* the world but with the world.

Human relationships with the world are plural in nature. Whether facing widely different challenges of the environment or the same challenge, men are not limited to a single reaction pattern. They organize themselves, choose the best response, test themselves, act, and change in the very act of

Education for Critical Consciousness by Paulo Freire, Copyright © 1973 by Paulo Freire. Reprinted by permission of The Continuum Publishing Company.

responding. They do all this consciously, as one uses a tool to deal with a problem.

Men relate to their world in a critical way. They apprehend the objective data of their reality (as well as the ties that link one datum to another) through reflection—not by reflex, as do animals. And in the act of critical perception, men discover their own temporality. Transcending a single dimension, they reach back to yesterday, recognize today, and come upon tomorrow. The dimensionality of time is one of the fundamental discoveries in the history of human culture. In illiterate cultures, the "weight" of apparently limitless time hindered people from reaching that consciousness of temporality, and thereby achieving a sense of their historical nature. A cat has no historicity; his inability to emerge from time submerges him in a totally one-dimensional "today" of which he has no consciousness. Men exist[1] in time. They are inside. They are outside. They inherit. They incorporate. They modify. Men are not imprisoned within a permanent "today"; they emerge, and become temporalized.

As men emerge from time, discover temporality, and free themselves from "today," their relations with the world become impregnated with consequence. The normal role of human beings in and with the world is not a passive one. Because they are not limited to the natural (biological) sphere but participate in the creative dimension as well, men can intervene in reality in order to change it. Inheriting acquired experience, creating and re-creating, integrating themselves into their context, responding to its challenges, objectifying themselves, discerning, transcending, men enter into the domain which is theirs exclusively—that of History and of Culture.[2]

Integration with one's context, as distinguished from *adaptation*, is a distinctively human activity. Integration results from the capacity to adapt oneself to reality *plus* the critical capacity to make choices and to transform that reality. To the extent that man loses his ability to make choices and is subjected to the choices of others, to the extent that his decisions are no longer his own because they result from external prescriptions, he is no longer integrated. Rather, he has adapted. He has "adjusted." Unpliant men, with a revolutionary spirit, are often termed "maladjusted."

The integrated person is person as *Subject*. In contrast, the adaptive person is person as *object*, adaptation representing at most a weak form of self-defense. If man is incapable of changing reality, he adjusts himself instead. Adaptation is behavior characteristic of the animal sphere; exhibited by man, it is symptomatic of his dehumanization. Through history men have attempted to overcome the factors which make them accommodate or adjust, in a struggle—constantly threatened by oppression—to attain their full humanity.

As men relate to the world by responding to the challenges of the environment, they begin to dynamize, to master, and to humanize reality. They add to it something of their own making, by giving temporal meaning to geographic space, by creating culture. This interplay of men's relations with the world and with their fellows does not (except in cases of repressive power) permit social or cultural immobility. As men create, re-create, and decide, historical epochs begin to take shape.[3] And it is by creating, re-creating, and deciding *that men should participate* in these epochs.

An historical epoch is characterized by a series of aspirations, concerns, and values in search of fulfillment; by ways of being and behaving; by more or less generalized attitudes. The concrete representations of many of these aspirations, concerns, and values, as well as the obstacles to their fulfillment, constitute the themes of that epoch, which in turn indicate tasks to be carried out.[4] The epochs are fulfilled to the degree that their themes are grasped and their tasks solved; and they are superseded when their themes and tasks no longer correspond to newly emerging concerns.

Men play a crucial role in the fulfillment and in the superseding of the epochs. Whether or not men can perceive the epochal themes and above all, how they act upon the reality within which these themes are generated will largely determine their humanization or dehumanization, their affirmation as Subjects or their reduction as objects. For only as men grasp the themes can they intervene in reality instead of remaining mere onlookers. And only by developing a permanently critical attitude can men overcome a posture of adjustment in order to become integrated with the spirit of the time. To the extent that an epoch dynamically generates its own themes, men will have to make "more and more use of intellectual, and less and less of emotional and instinctive functions. . . ."[5]

But unfortunately, what happens to a greater or lesser degree in the various "worlds" into which the world is divided is that the ordinary person is crushed, diminished, converted into a spectator, maneuvered by myths which powerful social forces have created. These myths turn against him; they destroy and annihilate him. Tragically frightened, men fear authentic relationships and even doubt the possibility of their existence. On the other hand, fearing solitude, they gather in groups lacking in any critical and loving ties which might transform them into a cooperating unit, into a true community. "Gregariousness is always the refuge of mediocrities," said Nikolai Nikolaievich Vedeniapin in *Dr. Zhivago*. It is also an imprisoning armor which prevents men from loving.

Perhaps the greatest tragedy of modern man is his domination by the force of these myths and his manipulation by organized advertising, ideological or otherwise. Gradually, without even realizing the loss, he relinquishes his capacity for choice; he is expelled from the orbit of decisions. Ordinary men do not perceive the tasks of the time; the latter are interpreted by an "elite" and presented in the form of recipes, of prescriptions. And when men try to save themselves by following the prescriptions, they drown in leveling anonymity, without hope and without faith, domesticated and adjusted.

As Erich Fromm said in *Escape from Freedom:*[6]

> [Man] has become free from the external bonds that would prevent him from doing and thinking as he sees fit. He would be free to act according to his own will, if he knew what he wanted, thought, and felt. But he does not know. He conforms to anonymous authorities and adopts a self which is not his. The more he does this, the more powerless he feels, the more is he forced to conform. In spite of a veneer of optimism and initiative, modern man is overcome by a profound feeling of powerlessness which makes him gaze toward approaching catastrophes as though he were paralyzed.

If men are unable to perceive critically the themes of their time, and thus to intervene actively in reality, they are carried along in the wake of change. They see that the times are changing, but they are submerged in that change and so cannot discern its dramatic significance. And a society beginning to move from one epoch to another requires the development of an especially flexible, critical spirit. Lacking such a spirit, men cannot perceive the marked contradictions which occur in society as emerging values in search of affirmation and fulfillment clash with earlier values seeking self-preservation. The time of epochal transition constitutes an historical-cultural "tidal wave." Contradictions increase between the ways of being, understanding, behaving, and valuing which belong to yesterday and other ways of perceiving and valuing which announce the future. As the contradictions deepen, the "tidal wave" becomes stronger and its climate increasingly emotional. This shock between a *yesterday* which is losing relevance but still seeking to survive, and a *tomorrow* which is gaining substance, characterizes the phase of transition as a time of announcement and a time of decision. Only, however, to the degree that the choices result from a critical perception of the contradictions are they real and capable of being transformed in action. Choice is illusory to the degree it represents the expectations of others.

While all transition involves change, not all change results in transition. Changes can occur within a single historical epoch that do not profoundly affect it in any way. There is a normal interplay of social readjustments resulting from the search for fulfillment of the themes. However, when these themes begin to lose their substance and significance and new themes emerge, it is a sign that society is beginning to move into a new epoch. The time of transition involves a rapid movement in search of new themes and new tasks. In such a phase man needs more than ever to be integrated with his reality. If he lacks the capacity to perceive the "mystery" of the changes, he will be a mere pawn at their mercy.

Brazil, in the 1950s and early 1960s, was precisely in this position of moving from one epoch to another. Which were the themes and the tasks which had lost and were losing their substance in Brazilian society? All those characteristic of a "closed society."[7] For instance, Brazil's non-autonomous status had generated the theme of cultural alienation. Elite and masses alike lacked integration with Brazilian reality. The elite lived "superimposed" upon that reality; the people, submerged within it. To the elite fell the task of importing alien cultural models; to the people, the task of following, of being *under*, of being ruled by the elite, of having no task of their own.

With the split in Brazilian society, the entire complex of themes and tasks assumed a new aspect. The particular meaning and emphasis given by a closed society to themes like democracy, popular participation, freedom, property, authority, and education were no longer adequate for a society in transition. (Similarly, the military *coup* of 1964 required a new perception of the themes and tasks characteristic of the transitional phase.) If Brazil was to move surely toward becoming a homogeneously open society, the correct perception of new aspirations and a new perception of old themes were essential. Should a distortion of this perception occur, however, a corresponding distortion in the transition would lead not to an open society but toward a "massified" society[8] of adjusted and domesticated men.

Thus, in that transitional phase, education became a highly important task. Its potential force would depend above all upon our capacity to participate in the dynamism of the transitional epoch. It would depend upon our distinguishing clearly which elements truly belonged to the transition and which were simply present in it. As the link between one epoch in exhaustion and another gaining substance, the transition had aspects of prolonging and conserving the old society at the same time that it extended forward into the new society. The new perceptions did not prevail easily or without sacrifice; the old themes had to exhaust their validity before they could give way to the new. Thus the dynamic of transition involved the confusion of flux and reflux, advances and retreats. And those who lacked the ability to perceive the mystery of the times responded to each retreat with tragic hopelessness and generalized fear.

In the last analysis, retreats do not deter the transition. They do not constitute backward movement, although they can retard movement or distort it. The new themes (or new perceptions of old themes) which are repressed during the retreats will persist in their advance until such time as the validity of the old themes is exhausted and the new ones reach fulfillment. At that point, society will once more find itself in its normal rhythm of changes, awaiting a new moment of transition. Thus the moment of transition belongs much more to "tomorrow," to the new time it announces, than it does to the old.

The starting point for the Brazilian transition was that closed society to which I have already referred, one whose raw material export economy was determined by an external market, whose very center of economic decision was located abroad—a "reflex," "object" society, lacking a sense of nationhood. Backward. Illiterate. Antidialogical. Elitist.

That society split apart with the rupture of the forces which had kept it in equilibrium. The economic changes which began in the last century with industrialization, and which increased in this century, were instrumental in this cleavage. Brazil was a society no longer totally closed but not yet truly open: a society in the *process* of opening. The urban centers had become predominantly open, while the rural areas remained predominantly closed. Meanwhile the society ran the risk (due to the continual possibility of retreats, *viz.*, the present military regime) of a catastrophic return to closure.

The democratic salvation of Brazil would lie in making our society homogeneously open. The challenge of achieving that openness was taken up by various contradictory forces, both external and internal. Some groups truly believed that the increasing political participation of the people during the transitional epoch would make it possible to achieve an open, autonomous society without violence. Other, reactionary, forces sought at all costs to obstruct any advance and to maintain the status quo indefinitely—or worse still, to bring about a retreat. While it would be impossible to return the emerging masses to their previous state of submersion, it might be possible to lead them to immobility and silence in the name of their own freedom. Men and institutions began to divide into two general categories—reactionaries and progressives; into those men and institutions which were *in* the process *of* transition and those which were not only in but of transition. The deepening of the clash between old and new encouraged a tendency to choose one side or the other; and the emotional climate of the time encouraged the tendency to become radical about that choice.

Radicalization involves increased commitment to the position one has chosen. It is predominantly critical, loving, humble, and communicative, and therefore a positive stance. The man who has made a radical option does not deny another man's right to choose, nor does he try to impose his own choice. He can discuss their respective positions. He is convinced he is right, but respects another man's prerogative to judge himself correct. He tries to convince and convert, not to crush his opponent. The radical does, however, have the duty, imposed by love itself, to react against the violence of those who try to silence him—of those who, in the name of freedom, kill his freedom and their own.[9] To be radical does not imply self-flagellation. Radicals cannot passively accept a situation in which the excessive power of a few leads to the dehumanization of all.

Unfortunately, the Brazilian people, elite and masses alike, were generally unprepared to evaluate the transition critically; and so, tossed about by the force of the contending contradictions, they began to fall into sectarian positions instead of opting for radical solutions. Sectarianism is predominantly emotional and uncritical. It is arrogant, antidialogical and thus anticommunicative. It is a reactionary stance, whether on the part of a rightist (whom I consider a "born" sectarian) *or* a leftist. The sectarian creates nothing because he cannot love. Disrespecting the choices of others, he tries to impose his own choice on everyone else. Herein lies the inclination of the sectarian to activism: action without the vigilance of reflection; herein his taste for sloganizing, which generally remains at the level of myth and half-truths and attributes absolute value to the purely relative.[10] The radical, in contrast, rejects activism and submits his actions to reflection.

The sectarian, whether rightist or leftist, sets himself up as the proprietor of history, as its sole creator, and the one entitled to set the pace of its movement. Rightist and leftist sectarians do differ in that one desires to stop the course of history, the other to anticipate it. On the other hand, they are similar in imposing their own convictions on the people, whom they thereby reduce to mere masses. For the sectarian, the people matter only as a support for his own goals. The sectarian wishes the people to be present at the historical process as activists, maneuvered by intoxicating propaganda. They are not supposed to think. Someone else will think for them; and it is as protégés, as children, that the sectarian sees them. Sectarians can never carry out a truly liberating revolution, because they are themselves unfree.

The radical is a Subject to the degree that he perceives historical contradictions in increasingly critical fashion; however, he does not consider himself the proprietor of history. And while he recognizes that it is impossible to stop or to anticipate history without penalty, he is no mere spectator of the historical process. On the contrary, he knows that as a Subject he can and ought, together with other Subjects, to participate creatively in that process by discerning transformations in order to aid and accelerate them.[11]

In the Brazilian transition, it was the sectarians, especially those of the right, who predominated, rather than the radicals.[12] And fanaticism flourished, fanned by the irrational climate arising as the contradictions in society deepened. This fanaticism, which separated and brutalized men, created hatred, thus threatening the essential promises of the transition—the humanization of the Brazilian people and their extraordinary sense of hope, hope rooted in the passage of Brazilian society from its previous colonial, reflex status to that of a Subject.

In alienated societies, men oscillate between ingenuous optimism and hopelessness. Incapable of autonomous projects, they seek to transplant from other cultures solutions to their problems. But since these borrowed solutions are neither generated by a critical analysis of the context itself, nor adequately adapted to the context,[13] they prove inoperative and unfruitful. Finally the older generations give in to disheartenment and feelings of inferiority. But at some point in the historical process of these societies, new facts occur which provoke the first attempts at self-awareness, whereupon a new cultural climate begins to form. Some previously alienated intellectual groups begin to integrate themselves with their cultural reality. Entering the world, they perceive the old themes anew and grasp the tasks of their time. Bit by bit, these groups begin to see themselves and their society from their own perspective; they become aware of their own potentialities. This is the point at which hopelessness begins to be replaced by hope. Thus, nascent hope coincides with an increasingly critical perception of the concrete conditions of reality. Society now reveals itself as something unfinished, not as something inexorably given; it has become a challenge rather than a hopeless limitation. This new, critical optimism requires a strong sense of social responsibility and of engagement in the task of transforming society; it cannot mean simply letting things run on.

But the climate of hope is adversely affected by the impact of sectarianism, which arises as the split in the closed society leads to the phenomenon Mannheim has called "fundamental democratization." This democratization, opening like a fan into interdependent dimensions (economic, social, political, and cultural), characterized the unprecedented participating presence of the Brazilian people in the phase of transition. During the phase of the closed society, the people are *submerged* in reality. As that society breaks open, they *emerge.* No longer *mere spectators,* they uncross their arms, renounce expectancy, and demand intervention. No longer satisfied to watch, they want to participate. This participation disturbs the privileged elite, who band together in self-defense.

At first, the elite react spontaneously. Later, perceiving more clearly the threat involved in the awakening of popular consciousness, they organize. They bring forth a group of "crisis theoreticians" (the new cultural climate is usually labeled a crisis); they create social assistance institutions and armies of social workers; and—in the name of a supposedly threatened freedom—they repel the participation of the people.

The elite defend a *sui generis* democracy, in which the people are "unwell" and require "medicine"—whereas in fact their "ailment" is the wish to speak up and participate. Each time the people try to express themselves freely and to act, it is a sign they continue to be ill and thus need more medicine. In this strange interpretation of democracy, health is synonymous with popular silence and inaction. The defenders of this "democracy" speak often of the need to protect the people from what they call "foreign ideologies"—i.e., anything that could contribute to the active presence of the people in their own historical process. Similarly, they label as "subversives" all those who enter into the dynamics of the transition and become its representatives. "These people are subversive" (we are told) "because they threaten order." Actually, the elite have no alternative. As the dominant social class, they must preserve at all costs the social "order" in which they are dominant. They cannot permit any basic changes which would affect their control over decision-making. So from their point of view, every effort to supersede such an order means to subvert it criminally.

During the Brazilian transition, as the popular classes renounced a position of accommodation and claimed their right to participate actively in the historical process, reactionary groups saw clearly the resulting threat to their interests. To end this uncomfortable quandary, they needed—in addition to the power they already possessed—the government, which at least in part they did not possess. Eventually, a *coup d' e'tat* was to solve that problem.

In such an historical-cultural climate, it is virtually impossible for intensely emotional forces not to be unleashed. This irrational climate bred and nourished sectarian positions on the part of those who wished to stop history in order to maintain their own privileges, and of those who hoped to anticipate history in order to "end" privileges. Both positions contributed to the massification and the relegation of the Brazilian people, who had only just begun to become a true "people." Misunderstood and caught in the middle (though they were not centrists) were the radicals, who wanted solutions to be found *with* the people, not *for* them or *superimposed upon* them. Radicals rejected the palliatives of "assistencialism,"[14] the force of decrees, and the irrational fanaticism of "crusades," instead defending basic transformations in society which would treat men as persons and thus as Subjects. Internal reactionary forces centered around latifundiary[15] interests were joined and given support by external forces that wished to prevent Brazil's transformation from an object to a Subject society. These external forces attempted their own pressures and their own assistencial solutions.

Assistencialism is an especially pernicious method of trying to vitiate popular participation in the historical process. In the first place, it contradicts man's natural vocation as Subject in that it treats the recipient as a passive object, incapable of participating in the process of his own recuperation; in the second place, it contradicts the process of "fundamental democratization." The greatest danger of assistencialism is the violence of its anti-dialogue, which by imposing silence and passivity denies men conditions likely to develop or to "open" their consciousness. For without an increasingly critical consciousness men are not able to integrate themselves into a transitional society, marked by intense change and contradictions. Assistencialism is thus both an effect and a cause of massification.

The important thing is to help men (and nations) help themselves,[16] to place them in consciously critical confrontation with their problems, to make them the agents of their own recuperation. In contrast, assistencialism robs men of a fundamental human necessity—responsibility, of which Simone Weil says:

> For this need to be satisfied it is necessary that a man should often have to take decisions in matters great or small affecting interests that are distinct from his own, but in regard to which he feels a personal concern.[17]

Responsibility cannot be acquired intellectually, but only through experience. Assistencialism offers no responsibility, no opportunity to make decisions, but only gestures and attitudes which encourage passivity. Whether the assistance is of foreign or national origin, this method cannot lead a country to a democratic destination.

Brazil in transition needed urgently to find rapid and sure solutions to its distressing problems—but *solutions with the people and never for them or imposed upon them.* What was needed was to go to the people and help them to enter the historical process critically. The prerequisite for this task was a form of education enabling the people to reflect on themselves, their responsibilities, and their role in the new cultural climate—indeed to reflect on their very *power* of reflection. The resulting development of this power would mean an increased capacity for choice. Such an education would take into the most serious account the various levels at which the Brazilian people perceived their reality, as being of the greatest importance for the process of their humanization. Therein lay my own concern to analyze these historically and culturally conditioned levels of understanding.

Men submerged in the historical process are characterized by a state I have described as "semi-intransitivity of consciousness."[18] It is the consciousness of men belonging to what Fernando de Azevedo has called "circumscribed" and "introverted" communities,[19] the consciousness which prevailed in the closed Brazilian society and which predominates even today in the most backward regions of Brazil. Men of semi-intransitive consciousness cannot apprehend problems situated outside their sphere of biological necessity. Their interests center almost totally around survival, and they lack a sense of life on a more historic plane. The concept of semi-intransitivity does not signify the closure of a person within himself, crushed by an all-powerful time and space. Whatever his state, man is an open being. Rather, semi-intransitive consciousness means that his sphere of perception is limited, that he is impermeable to challenges situated outside the sphere of biological necessity. In this sense only, semi-intransitivity represents a near disengagement between men and their existence. In this state, discernment is difficult. Men confuse their perceptions of the objects and challenges of the environment, and fall prey to magical explanations because they cannot apprehend true causality.

As men amplify their power to perceive and respond to suggestions and questions arising in their context, and increase their capacity to enter into dialogue not only with other men but with their world, they become "transitive." Their interests and concerns now extend beyond the simple vital sphere. Transitivity of consciousness makes man "permeable." It leads him to replace his disengagement from existence with almost total engagement. Existence is a dynamic concept, implying eternal dialogue between man and man, between man and the world, between man and his Creator. It is this dialogue which makes of man an historical being.

There is, however, an initial, predominantly naïve, stage of transitive consciousness. *Naïve transitivity,* the state of consciousness which predominated in Brazilian urban centers during the transitional period, is characterized by an over-simplification of problems; by a nostalgia for the past; by underestimation of the common man; by a strong tendency to gregariousness; by a lack of interest in investigation, accompanied by an accentuated taste for fanciful explanations; by fragility of arguments; by a strongly emotional style; by the practice of polemics rather than dialogue; by magical explanations. (The magical aspect typical of intransitivity is partially present here also. Although men's horizons have expanded and they respond more openly to stimuli, these responses still have a magical quality.) Naïve transitivity is the consciousness of men who are still almost part of a mass, in whom the developing capacity for dialogue is still fragile and capable of distortion. If this consciousness does not progress to the stage of *critical transitivity,* it may be deflected by sectarian irrationality into fanaticism.

The critically transitive consciousness is characterized by depth in the interpretation of problems; by the substitution of causal principles for magical explanations; by the testing of one's "findings" and by openness to revision; by the attempt to avoid distortion when perceiving problems and to avoid preconceived notions when analyzing them; by refusing to transfer responsibility; by rejecting passive positions; by soundness of argumentation; by the practice of dialogue rather than polemics; by receptivity to the new for reasons beyond mere novelty and by the good sense not to reject the old just because it is old—by accepting what is valid in both old and new. Critical transitivity is characteristic of authentically democratic regimes and corresponds to highly permeable, interrogative, restless and dialogical forms of life—in contrast to silence and inaction, in contrast to the rigid, militarily authoritarian state presently prevailing in Brazil, an historical retreat which the usurpers of power try to present as a reencounter with democracy.

There are certain positions, attitudes, and gestures associated with the awakening of critical awareness, which occur naturally due to economic progress. These should not be confused with an authentically critical position, which a person must make his own by intervention in and integration with his own context. *Conscientização* represents the *development* of the awakening of critical awareness. It will not appear as a natural byproduct of even major economic changes, but must grow out of a critical educational effort based on favorable historical conditions.

In Brazil, the passage from a predominantly intransitive consciousness to a predominantly naïve transitivity paralleled the transformation of economic patterns. As the process of urbanization intensified, men were thrust into more complex forms of life. As men entered a larger sphere of relationships and received a greater number of suggestions and challenges to their circumstances, their consciousness automatically became more transitive. However, the further, crucial step from naïve transitivity to critical transitivity would *not* occur automatically. Achieving this step would thus require an active, dialogical educational program concerned with social and political responsibility, and prepared to avoid the danger of massification.

There is a close potential relationship between naïve transitivity and massification. If a person does not move from naïve transitivity to a critical consciousness but instead falls into a *fanaticized consciousness*,[20] he will become even more disengaged from reality than in the semi-intransitive state. To the extent that a person acts more on the basis of emotionality than of reason,[21] his behavior occurs adaptively and cannot result in commitment, for committed behavior has its roots in critical consciousness and capacity for genuine choice. The adaptation and lack of engagement typical of semi-intransitivity are thus more prevalent still in a state of massification. The power to perceive authentic causality is obliterated in the semi-intransitive state; hence the latter's *magical* quality. In massification this power is distorted, producing a *mythical* quality. In the semi-intransitive state, men are predominantly *illogical;* in fanaticized consciousness the distortion of reason makes men *irrational*. The possibility of dialogue diminishes markedly. Men are defeated and dominated, though they do not know it; they fear freedom, though they believe themselves to be free. They follow general formulas and prescriptions as if by their own choice. They are directed; they do not direct themselves. Their creative power is impaired. They are objects, not Subjects. For men to overcome their state of massification, they must be enabled to reflect about that very condition. But since authentic reflection cannot exist apart from action, men must also act to transform the concrete reality which has determined their massification.

In short, naïve transitive consciousness can evolve toward critical transitivity, characteristic of a legitimately democratic mentality, or it can be deflected toward the debased, clearly dehumanized, fanaticized consciousness characteristic of massification. During the Brazilian transition, as the emotional climate became more intense and sectarian irrationality (especially of the right) grew stronger, there was increasing resistance to an educational program capable of helping the people move from ingenuity to criticism. Indeed, if the people were to become critical, enter reality, increase their capacity to make choices (and therefore their capacity to reject the prescriptions of others), the threat to privilege would increase as well. To irrational sectarians, the humanization of the Brazilian people loomed as the specter of their own dehumanization, and any effort toward this end as subversive action. But such an effort was imperative, for those who believed that the destiny of men is to become authentic human beings.

Notes

1. In the English language, the terms "live" and "exist" have assumed implications opposite to their etymological origins. As used here, to exist is more than to live, because it is more than being in the world; it is to be with the world as well. And this capacity for communication between the being which exists and the objective world gives to "existing" a quality of critical capacity not present in mere "living." Transcending, discerning, entering into dialogue (communicating and participating) are exclusively attributes of existence. One can only exist in relation to others who also exist and in communication with them. In this regard, see Karl Jaspers, *The Origin and Goal of History* (New Haven, 1953), and *Reason and Anti-reason in Our Time* (New Haven, 1952).

2. See Erich Kahler, *Historia Universal del Hombre*.

3. See Hans Freyer, *Teoría de la época atual* (Mexico).

4. See Paulo Freire, *Pedagogy of the Oppressed* (New York, 1970), pp. 91–92. (Translator's note.)

5. Zevedei Barbu, *Democracy and Dictatorship, Their Psychology and Patterns of Life* (New York, 1956), p. 4.

6. (New York, 1960), pp. 255–256.

7. See Karl Popper, *The Open Society and Its Enemies* (Princeton, 1966).

8. A "massified" society is one in which the people, after entering the historical process, have been manipulated by the elite into an unthinking, manageable agglomeration. This process is termed "massification." It stands in contrast to conscientização, which is the process of achieving a critical consciousness. (Translator's note.)

9. Every relationship of domination, of exploitation, of oppression, is by definition violent, whether or not the violence is expressed by drastic means. In such a relationship, dominator and dominated alike are reduced to things—the former dehumanized by an excess of power, the latter by lack of it. And things cannot love. When the oppressed legitimately rise up against their oppressor, however, it is they who are usually labelled "violent," "barbaric," "inhuman," and "cold." (Among the innumerable rights claimed by the dominating consciousness is the right to define violence, and to locate it. Oppressors never see themselves as violent.)

10. See Tristão de Ataíde, *O Existencialismo e Outros Mitos do Nosso Tempo* (Rio de Janeiro, 1956).

11. For a further discussion of radicalization and sectarianism, see *Pedagogy of the Oppressed*, pp. 21–24. (Translator's note.)

12. At that time, radical positions in the sense I have described them were being taken principally, although not exclusively, by groups of Christians who believed with Mounier that "History," both the history of the world and the history of human beings, has meaning. (This is the first of Mounier's four fundamental ideas regarding the idea of progress as a modem theme. The second is that progress proceeds continuously, although diverse vicissitudes may complicate its course, and that its movement is the movement of man's liberation. The third idea is that the development of science and technique which characterizes the modern Western age and is spreading over the entire world constitutes a decisive aspect of this liberation. The last is that in this ascent man is charged with being the author of his own liberation. See Emanuel Mounier, "Le christianisme et la notion de Progrès," *La Petit Peur du xxe Siecle* [Paris, 1948] pp. 97–152.) Irrational sectarians, including some Christians, either did not understand or did not want to understand the radicals' search for integration with Brazilian problems. They did not understand the radicals' concern with progress, leading toward human liberation. And so they accused these radicals of attempting to dehumanize the Brazilian people.

13. See Alberto Guerreiro Ramos, *A Redução Sociológica* (Rio de Janeiro, 1958).

14. Assistencialism: a term used in Latin America to describe policies of financial or social assistance which attack symptoms, but not causes, of social ills.

15. *Latifundium*: a noun of Latin origin which, in Spanish and Portuguese, means a large privately owned landholding. (Translator's note.)

16. Speaking of the relations between rich and poor nations, developed and developing nations, Pope John XXIII urged the rich not to aid the poor by means of what he termed "disguised forms of colonial domination." Rather he said, aid should be given without self-interest, with the sole intention of making it possible for nations to develop themselves economically and socially. Assistencialism cannot do this, for it is precisely one of those forms of colonial domination. See "Christianity and Social Progress," from the Encyclical Letter *Mater et Magistra*, articles 171 and 172.

17. *The Need for Roots* (New York, 1952), p. 15.

18. This theme is treated in greater detail in my *Cultural Action for Freedom*, Monograph Series No. 7, 1970, Harvard Educational Review, Center for the Study of Development and Social Change.

19. *Educaçao entre Dois Mundos* (São Paulo), p. 34.

20. See Gabriel Marcel, *Man Against Mass Society* (Chicago, 1962).

21. Barbu sees reason as "the individual capacity to grasp the order in change, and the unity in variety." *Op cit.*, p. 4.

Discussion Questions

1. According to Socrates, why are questioning, dialogue, and knowledge important in the formation of "the good life"? Why should we pay less attention to material values and more attention to spiritual values if we are to discover the good life?
2. According to Epicurus, why should we not fear the gods or death? Can you compare what Epicurus says about "the good life" to what Socrates says?
3. Confucius emphasizes the importance of virtue and the family. How does respect for, and obedience to, one's family members enhance one's virtue?
4. What role do motive or intent, character, and habit play in the moral philosophy of the Sermon on the Mount? Take any two principles of the sermon and show first, how they address a contemporary moral or social issue, and second, what they specifically require in motive and act.
5. From what universal practice does a women's resistance arise and why? Why might a women's resistance be culturally relative?
6. Eagle Man tells us that in order to achieve peace we must be aware of our natural relationship with all things in nature. Why does he make this claim, and in what sense is he correct in his assumption?
7. Explain the importance of the differences that Freire sees between adaptation and integration. Why is a reflective or critical consciousness necessary for the development of a free society? What are the dangers of assistencialism? Of sectarianism? Of a fanaticized consciousness?
8. Re-examine what you believe "the good life" to be in light of the essays in this chapter. Explain some of the ways in which you think people can achieve a good life.

Afterword

From "Song of Myself"

Walt Whitman

16

I am of old and young, of the foolish as much as the wise,
Regardless of others, ever regardful of others,
Maternal as well as paternal, a child as well as a man,
Stuff'd with the stuff that is coarse and stuff'd with the stuff that is fine,
One of the Nation of many nations, the smallest the same and the largest the same,

From "Song of Myself" in *Leaves of Grass* by Walt Whitman, Philadelphia, 1883.

A Southerner soon as a Northerner, a planter nonchalant and hospitable down by the Oconee I live,
A Yankee bound my own way ready for trade, my joints the limberest joints on earth and the sternest joints on earth,
A Kentuckian walking the vale of the Elkhorn in my deer-skin leggings, a Louisianian or Georgian,
A boatman over lakes or bays or along coasts, a Hoosier, Badger, Buckeye:
At home on Kanadian snow-shoes or up in the bush, or with fisherman off Newfoundland,
At home in the fleet of ice-boats, sailing with the rest and tacking,

At home on the hills of Vermont or in the woods of Maine, or the Texan ranch,
Comrade of Californians, comrade of free North Westerners, (loving their big proportions,)
Comrade of raftsmen and coalmen, comrade of all who shake hands and welcome to drink and meat,
A learner with the simplest, a teacher of the thoughtfullest,
A novice beginning yet experient of myriads of seasons,
Of every hue and caste am I, of every rank and religion,
A farmer, mechanic, artist, gentleman, sailor, quaker,
Prisoner, fancy-man, rowdy, lawyer, physician, priest.

I resist any thing better than my own diversity,
Breathe the air but leave plenty after me,
And am not stuck up, and am in my place.

(The moth and the fish-eggs are in their place,
The bright suns I see and the dark suns I cannot see are in their place.
The palpable is in its place and the impalpable is in its place.)

17

These are really the thoughts of all men in all ages and lands, they are not original with me,
If they are not yours as much as mine they are nothing, or next to nothing,
If they are not the riddle and the untying of the riddle they are nothing,
If they are not just as close as they are distant they are nothing.

This is the grass that grows wherever the land is and the water is,
This the common air that bathes the globe.

Author Index

Title Index

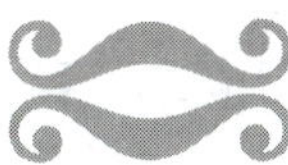

W

Photo Credits

Page 2: Reprinted by permission of Ms. Magazine, © 1972.
Page 38: Courtesy of the Library of Congress.
Page 95: © Bettmann/CORBIS.
Page 148: American Museum of Natural History.
Page 149: Hulton Getty/Archive Photos.
Page 204: Courtesy of the Library of Congress.
Page 249: Laima Druskis/Pearson Education/PH College.
Page 301: Courtesy of the Library of Congress.
Page 302: Stock Boston.
Page 351: © Bettman/CORBIS
Page 404: EMG Education Management Group.
Page 405: Kevin Weaver/Hulton Getty/Archive Photos.